GT02

HERMANNUS SCHOTTENNIUS HESSUS

CONFABULATIONES TIRONUM LITTERARIORUM

(COLOGNE, 1525)

Published by Manchester University Press
Oxford Road, Manchester M13 9NR, UK
and Room 400, 175 Fifth Avenue, New York, NY 10010, USA
www.manchesteruniversitypress.co.uk

Distributed exclusively in the USA by
Palgrave, 175 Fifth Avenue, New York NY 10010, USA

Distributed exclusively in Canada by
UBC Press, University of British Columbia, 2029 West Mall,
Vancouver, BC, Canada V6T 1Z2

British Library Cataloguing-in-Publication Data
A catalogue record for this book is available from the British Library

Library of Congress Cataloging-in-Publication Data
A catalog record for this book is available from the Library of Congress

ISBN 13: 978 0 7190 8185 9

First published 2007
First digital paperback edition published 2010

Printed by Lightning Source

Hermannus Schottennius Hessus

Confabulationes tironum litterariorum (Cologne, 1525)

Edited by

Peter Macardle

Durham Modern Languages Series 2007

Contents

List of Illustrations

Non-Bibliographic Abbreviations

adj.: adjective.
BA: Baccalaureus Artium.
BFTh: Baccalaureus Formatus Theologiae.
BJurCiv: Baccalaureus Jurium Ciuilium.
BM: Bibliothèque Municipale.
BN: Bibliothèque Nationale.
BSB: Bayerische Staatsbibliothek.
BTh: Baccalaureus Theologiae.
CGk: Classical Greek.
CL: Classical Latin.
conj.: conjunction.
dim.: diminutive.
esp.: especially.
HAStK: Cologne, Historisches Archiv der Stadt Köln.
JCivB: Jurium Civilium Baccalaureus.
LB: Landesbibliothek.
LicA: Licentia Artium.
LL: Late Latin.
MA: Magister Artium.
ML: Medieval Latin.
NL: Neo-Latin.
ÖNB: Österreichische Nationalbibliothek.
StBPK: Staatsbibliothek Preußischer Kulturbesitz.
s.v.: *sub verbo.* (dictionaries) the word under discussion.
UB: Universitätsbibliothek.
UL: University Library.

Non-Bibliographic Abbreviations

Acknowledgements

Many years ago, looking for background information on Hermann Schotten, I came across the *Confabulationes* in the British Library. I was immediately charmed by the colloquies, and their vivid depiction of early modern Cologne, and determined there and then that they should be made properly known to modern scholarship. If, after a long time, I have succeeded in doing this, it is only thanks to a very great number of people.

Many colleagues in Durham and elsewhere, by no means all in the early modern field, have offered encouragement, information and expert criticism: especially Jenny and Richard Britnell, Anna Carrdus, David Cowling, Ian Doyle, Gabriele Fischer, John Flood, Margaret Harvey, Tim Jackson, Jonathan Long, Ann Moss, Nigel Palmer, Nicholas Saul and Michael Straeter.

A great deal of help has come from the various libraries and archives where my research has been done; above all the magnificent Historisches Archiv der Stadt Köln. I am grateful to the Director, Dr Joachim Deeters, to Dr Manfred Huiskes, and to Dr Manfred Groten, now Professor of History at the University of Bonn, for a great deal of specialist information and advice. Thanks too to all the helpful staff who brought me (quite literally) trolley-loads of fascinating material, much of which has been directly used in this study, and answered queries of the most diverse kinds. Other Cologne collections, too, have been extremely helpful, notably the Universitäts- und Stadtbibliothek Köln, especially the Historic Collection, the Erzbischöfliche Diözesan- und Dombibliothek, and the Historisches Archiv des Erzbistums Köln.

It has always seemed a good omen that Wilhelm Levison, once Professor of History at the University of Bonn, spent his last years (1939–1947) in exile from the Nazi regime at Durham, and that many obscure, but to me extremely relevant works were in the collection he bequeathed to Durham University Library. To that library, especially the helpful and accommodating staff of Archives and Special Collections, Palace Green, go sincere thanks; as also to the Chapter Library and the Meissen Library of Durham Cathedral, and the library of Ushaw College. Beyond Durham, I must thank particularly the British Library, the library of the Warburg Institute, the Herzog August Bibliothek, Wolfenbüttel, and the Stadtbibliothek Trier.

It is a pleasure to acknowledge the support of the British Academy, whose award of a Small Research Grant made possible an intensive two months of archival research in Cologne, which allowed me to make out at least the outlines of the career of a strangely elusive humanist. I am also profoundly grateful for generous financial support, towards both research visits and publication costs, from the Durham University School of Modern Languages and Cultures.

Everyone connected with the Durham University Modern Languages Series has my sincere gratitude: Mike Thompson, the General Editor, for some very careful and helpful reading; Leah Tether, for helping to design such an attractive book cover. Very special thanks must go to the Assistant Editor Janet Starkey, who has been efficiency and good humour incarnate as she has coped with every aspect of taking this study through the press with remarkable dispatch.

Best thanks of all must go to my wife Fiona, for companionship, support and encouragement at every stage of a long and sometimes arduous project.

This edition is dedicated in gratitude to Nesta McIlwaine and John Wilson, who first taught me Latin; Eileen Scott, who taught me German; and Charles Burrowes, who taught me French, and gave me a first insight into what it is to be a scholar.

Introduction

Some time in the earlier part of 1525 there appeared a collection of Latin colloquies, dialogues designed to teach Latin to schoolboys. The *Confabulationes tironum litterariorum* contained one hundred and twenty-three short dialogues covering a wide range of topics and conversational situations. It was composed in a humanist Classical Latin, modelled mainly on the racy but elegant colloquial language of Terence. Its author, Hermannus Schottennius Hessus or Hermann Schotten, was still unknown to the literary world: he was perhaps about twenty-two, and at the time was a schoolmaster at a 'trivial' school, a grammar school, somewhere in the city of Cologne.

This new colloquy collection was entirely in the spirit of the humanist pedagogy which was establishing itself at the leading schools in Germany and the Netherlands. It took its place amongst a number of extant prestigious collections such as those of Erasmus, Petrus Mosellanus, Christoph Hegendorff and Hadrianus Barlandus. But Schotten had a distinctive voice, and his *Confabulationes* were refreshingly different from what had gone before and what would come after. They were an instant success. The edition which has up till now been regarded as the princeps (Augsburg: S. Ruff, 1525) was in fact very likely a pirated version of a now lost Cologne first edition (see section Ic). An expanded Cologne second edition which appeared in 1526 was enthusiastically reprinted in Germany and farther afield. By the end of the sixteenth century, fifty-seven editions are recorded; no doubt there were even more, some of which have not survived.

All the more surprising, then, that this book, not only a milestone of Latin pedagogy and humanist culture but also a singularly pleasurable read, has never had a modern edition, and that Schotten's person, career and other work have gone almost uninvestigated. Schotten may not have been a 'major humanist', yet the *Confabulationes*, his first substantial work, made a major contribution to humanist pedagogy, and deserve a modern critical appraisal. It is this aim which this critical edition of the *Confabulationes*, and the companion monograph, *Confabulations*, attempt to serve.[1]

Ia. Hermannus Schottennius Hessus: Life and Work

The life of Hermannus Schottennius Hessus, or Hermann Schotten, is not adequately recorded in any biographical reference work: the only detailed account is in an article of my own of 1994.[2] His biography and career are known almost solely from official records of the University of Cologne, particularly the Matricula, the record of students matriculated at the University, and the Arts *Dekanatsbuch*, the official minutes of the Arts Faculty proceedings.[3] Piecing together the brief and often cryptic information in these and other sources is far from simple, and in many cases there is the danger of constructing narratives which are gratifying but which may be largely mistaken. Schotten's biography is the subject of a detailed

---

1 Peter Macardle, *Confabulations. Cologne Life and Humanism in Hermann Schotten's* Confabulationes tironum litterariorum *(Cologne, 1525)* (Durham: Durham Modern Languages Series, 2007).

2 Macardle, 'Cologne Life and Cologne University Humanism', esp. pp. 142–57. Inadequate accounts in *ADB*, XXXII, p. 412; *DBE*, IX, p. 123.

3 Matricula: HAStK, 150, A 39; edited as *Matrikel*. *Dekanatsbuch*: HAStK, 150, A 481.

appraisal in Macardle, *Confabulations*, Chapter 1. What follows here is a brief summary.

Hermann Schotten's date of birth is unknown: it was probably no later than 1503 or 1504, but might have been a few years earlier. His family name seems to have been Ortmann, and 'Schottennius' is almost certainly a toponymic from the town of Schotten in the Vogelsberg region of Hessia from which he probably hailed. It is also a distinctively humanist name, which Schotten consistently used.

In December 1517 he matriculated (as 'Schottennius') in the Arts Faculty of the University of Cologne; he was a member of the Bursa Laurentiana, one of the leading *bursae*, student halls or colleges, of that university.[4] His student career was at first entirely normal. He took the degree of BA in 1519, and the MA in 1520.[5] He was obviously aiming at an academic career, for he stayed on after his MA, putting in the two years' further study and teaching required to become a full member of the Arts Faculty *consilium* or board. In this period, too, he probably began the study of Theology. In 1522 he was duly 'receptus ad consilium facultatis'.[6]

The normal next step would have been to become an established teacher in the Arts Faculty, to fulfil examining and administrative duties, and to continue with study in one of the higher faculties of Law, Medicine or Theology. For Schotten, however, this did not immediately materialize: indeed, he had to wait eight years before he was officially appointed as an Arts Faculty lecturer and could begin a proper university career. There seem to have been two reasons for this delay.

---

4 Matriculation: HAStK, 150, A 39, fol. 91^{r}; *Matrikel*, 516,100. Bursa: HAStK, 150, A 481, fol. 126^{r}.

5 HAStK, 150, A 481, fols 125^{v}, 126^{r} (BA); fol. 131^{r-v} (MA).

6 HAStK, 150, A 481, fol. 143^{v}.

The first was that in the 1520s Cologne, once the largest of the German universities, was going through a period of drastic reduction in student numbers, caused by a combination of factors, including the effects of the Reformation.[7] There was naturally ever less demand for Arts Faculty teachers, and almost no need to engage new ones. This combined with the fact that, since the later fifteenth century, the *bursae*, which had originally been student residences offering some additional Arts tuition, had developed a complete monopoly on Arts Faculty teaching. The only way of becoming a faculty lecturer was to be appointed as a salaried *lector* in a *bursa*.[8] Between 1516 and 1530 the Laurentiana engaged only five *lectores*; and Schotten succeeded in being appointed only in 1530.[9]

Favouritism and nepotism may have played a part here, though this is not certain.[10] But there may have been another reason. In 1523, Schotten was planning to speak at the *Disputatio* quodlibetica, a disputation on topics outside the normal curriculum held every year in December. He was prevented from taking part by the senior academic Johannes Jacobi de Campis, the principal of the Bursa Laurentiana, who invoked ecclesiastical censures on account of some debts of Schotten's, probably money which he owed to the Laurentiana.[11] De Campis's motives are not certain, but it is likely that disapproval of Schotten's humanism played a part. Schotten had planned to speak on 'De institutione puerorum in patria', which was

---

7 Meuthen, *Universität*, pp. 77–79; Eulenberg, *Die Frequenz der deutschen Universitäten*, pp. 285–89; Macardle, *Confabulations*, pp. 33, 48–49.

8 Meuthen, 'Artesfakultät', pp. 367–85; Tewes, *Bursen*, pp. 121–219; Macardle, *Confabulations*, pp. 22–23, 152–54.

9 HAStK, 150, A 760, fols 10^{r}–11^{r}.

10 Schwinges, 'Sozialgeschichtliche Aspekte', p. 533; Macardle, *Confabulations*, esp. pp. 48–51.

11 HAStK, 150, A 481, fol. 152A^{r}.

almost certainly a plea for humanist education to be available in the city of Cologne, and perhaps even in the curriculum of the Arts Faculty. For the 1523 Quodlibet, like that of 1522, took place in the context of attempts by humanists at the university to change the heavily scholastic and Aristotelian Arts curriculum, attempts which had been resisted by the more conservative dons. Humanists used the 1522 and 1523 disputations as a platform for their campaign, and the atmosphere in both years was confrontational and tense.[12] De Campis was almost certainly one of the senior academics who had opposed the reforms, and it is entirely possible that debarring Schotten was a vindictive measure against someone from his own *bursa* whom he saw as a dangerous opponent of tradition.

Whether Schotten's debarment from the 1523 Quodlibet was the beginning of a period of 'exile' from the university, however, is not entirely clear. He may well already have left the university and gone into school-teaching as a deliberate strategy: this was a common career move amongst young academics of the period, and would certainly have made sense in the context of the depletion of the Arts Faculty at the time.[13] At any rate, Schotten spent several years, from 1522 or 1523, teaching boys at a 'trivial' (grammar) school somewhere in Cologne. As to which school this was, there is no clear evidence. One or two topographical references in the *Confabulationes* and in one of Schotten's dedicatory letters suggest that it could have been the parish school of St Aposteln, in the west of the city, but this is by no means certain.[14] A number of details strongly suggest that it was

---

12 HAStK, 150, A 481, fols 146^{v}–47^{r}, 152A^{r}; Tewes, 'Die Universität Köln im Umbruch'; Macardle, *Confabulations*, pp. 29–37.

13 See Macardle, *Confabulations*, esp. pp. 43–46.

14 Schotten's dedication of the *Ludus martius* to Georg Lauer: see Macardle, *Confabulations*, pp. 191–95, and notes to colloquies 26, 69 and 87.

a school completely separate from the university, and not a pre-university stream in the Bursa Laurentiana itself, though the *bursae* certainly offered such tuition to students, many of them under-age, who had come up under-prepared for the Arts curriculum.[15] Dating evidence from the *Confabulationes* shows that some of the dialogues were composed in late 1524 and early 1525, but cannot establish when Schotten began his teaching career.[16]

Around 1528 there is evidence that Schotten was making a return to the university. In that year he was giving lectures or talks of some kind on the Psalms (whether these were official Theology Faculty classes is unclear, and must be very doubtful).[17] In 1530 he was appointed as a *lector* at the Laurentiana.[18] The circumstances are slightly obscure, and the documentation scanty. Schotten may have been engaged only after the death of Johannes de Campis, the same principal who had debarred him from the Quodlibet seven years previously, suggesting that he had been excluded from the university as a consequence of the Quodlibet incident, and that Schotten the humanist had been victimized by a reactionary scholastic don. But equally, the scenario may have been much less dramatic, and Schotten may simply have been an obvious candidate to fill a vacant post.[19]

After his appointment at the Laurentiana, Schotten was a legitimate university lecturer, and began to fill the usual Faculty positions: as examiner for the BA and MA;[20]

---

15 See notes to colloquy 60, and Macardle, *Confabulations*, pp. 189–91.

16 See notes to colloquies 33, 36, 40, 83 and 91, and Macardle, *Confabulations*, pp. 80–86.

17 Kluppel, *Chronik*, ed. by Jürges, pp. 154–55; Macardle, *Confabulations*, pp. 28–29.

18 HAStK, 150, A 760, fol. 11r.

19 See Macardle, *Confabulations*, pp. 51–52.

20 Examiner: numerous mentions in HAStK, 150, A 481, between fols 182r and 222r.

in various administrative offices, eventually as dean of the Arts Faculty.[21] He also continued his studies in Theology, gaining the *Baccalaureus Theologiae* in 1532 and the higher *Baccalaureus Formatus Theologiae* in 1536.[22] It is unknown whether he was ever ordained to the priesthood, as many academics were. It is also unknown whether he worked towards the Licentiate, the highest examined theological degree, and the mark of the senior Cologne don; but he certainly did not attain it. In the university's own terms, then, Schotten's was a somewhat mediocre career, seen most clearly in the number of students whom he 'promoted' to degrees, one of the hallmarks of the leading teachers in the university. His most successful colleagues promoted hundreds of students; he himself managed only six.[23]

After February 1542 Schotten disappears from the Faculty minutes; since he died only in 1546, it is likely that he was ill for the last few years of his life, and thus inactive in the Faculty.[24] If he was indeed born in about 1503, he had lived only into his early forties, by no means an advanced age even for that time.

Schotten's works

Schotten's work is entirely given over to humanist pedagogy and ethical writing in a humanist vein. Some works

21 Quodlibetar: HAStK, 150, A 481, fol. 183^{r}. Arts Faculty receptor (treasurer): ibid., fol. 208^{r}; HAStK, 150, A 516, fols 84^{r}–85^{v}. Arts intrans: HAStK, 150, A 39, fols 144^{r}, 151^{r}. Dean: HAStK, 150, A 481, fol. 187^{v}.

22 BTh: HAStK, 150, A 230 (Theological *Dekanatsbuch*), fol. 9^{r}; HAStK, 150, A 481, fol. 184^{r}. BFTh: HAStK, 150, A 481, fol. 203^{v}. See Macardle, *Confabulations*, p. 23.

23 Tewes, *Bursen*, pp. 116–17; Macardle, *Confabulations*, p. 25.

24 Last mentioned: HAStK, 150, A 481, fol. 222^{r}. Death: HAStK, 150, A 516, fol. 105^{r}. See Macardle, *Confabulations*, pp. 25–26.

survive only in very small numbers. With the exception of one of his plays, the *Ludus martius*, none of them has been the object of modern critical study, though there is much that would reward scholarly attention.

In the same year as the *Confabulationes* Schotten authored two short works on Latin and on the study of *bonae litterae*, the *Ludus grammaticus* and the *Meta studii literarii*.[25] In the next two years he wrote his two plays: the *Ludus martius* (1526), an extremely original and interesting treatment of the German Peasants' War of the previous year, and the *Ludus imperatorius* (1527), a lengthy, and frankly somewhat tedious, allegorical celebration of the reign and achievements of Emperor Charles V.[26] More works on humanist education followed: the *Instructio prima puerorum* (1527) and the *Elementale Dialectices* (1528).[27] 1527 also saw the *Vita honesta*, a treatise on personal and civic ethics, forgotten today, but at the time by far the most popular of Schotten's writings, going through a very large number of editions in several European countries; this work and its reception deserve a scholarly appraisal.[28]

The hypothesis that Schotten was attempting to return from the trivial school to the university about 1528

---

25 *Ludus grammaticus latinae Linguae tramitem ostendens* (Coloniae: S. Kruffter, 1525); *Meta Studii literarii [e]t quomodo in eam sint ducenda omnium scientiarum genera [...]* (Cologne: S. Kruffter, [possibly 1525, but this is not certain]). For these and all Schotten's works, see the detailed listings in the bibliography.

26 *Ludus martius sive bellicus [...]* (Cologne: P. Quentel, 1526); see Macardle, 'Our Reading of an Early "Documentary Drama"'. *Ludus imperatorius sive caesareus [...]* (Cologne: P. Quentel, 1527).

27 *Instructio prima puerorum [...] per colloquia mutua* (Cologne: P. Quentel, 1527); *Elementale Dialectices [...]* (Cologne: [P. Quentel], 1528).

28 *Vita honesta sive virtutis [...]* (Cologne: P. Quentel, 1527).

is supported by the way in which his stream of humanist pedagogical writings dries up with the *Centuria epistolarum proverbialium* of 1529,[29] after which Schotten writes nothing till his last two works, the *Colloquia philosophica* and *Colloquia moralia* of 1535.[30] This would certainly fit the scenario of a change from 'trivial' schoolteaching, which left time for literary composition and for dramatic writing and performance, to university teaching, examining and administration, with the attendant need to continue study in Theology, when Schotten would have had little time or energy to spare for writing and publishing.[31]

Ib. The editions of the Confabulationes

That the *Confabulationes* are amongst the most fascinating and entertaining of the colloquy collections of the sixteenth century is reflected in the large number of editions which they went through. The first edition which survives is one printed by the Augsburg printer Simpert or Simprecht Ruff in July 1525.[32] Yet there is no reason to believe that Schotten ever left Cologne; all his writings were first published in that city, most by the leading printer Peter Quentel; and he had no known connections with Augsburg. There is the strong suspicion that the

29 *Centuria epistolarum proverbialium [...]* (Cologne: [P. Quentel], 1529).

30 *Colloquia philosophica, & consolatoria, ac exhortatoria [...]* (Cologne: P. Quentel, 1535); *Colloquia moralia ex variis philosophorum dictis condita [...]* (Cologne: P. Quentel, 1535).

31 See Macardle, *Confabulations*, pp. 46–47.

32 *Confabulationes tironum literariorum, ad amussim Colloquiorum Erasmi Roterodami, Authore Hermanno Schotten. Hesso. M.D.XXV* (*VD 16*, S 4005). Copies in Munich, UB, 8° Misc. 604a; Stuttgart, Evangelischer Oberkirchenrat, 443.

Augsburg edition was in fact a swiftly pirated version of a true Cologne princeps. The evidence for this is fully discussed in section Ic.

In 1526 a revised version of the text was published in Cologne: it contained the 123 short colloquies of the first edition, with some minor additions, but also a section of thirty *conuiuia* or 'banquets', longer dialogues probably inspired by the *conuiuia* which Erasmus had begun to add to editions of his *Colloquia*. This Cologne edition became the basis for a very large number of reprints. The first surviving one was produced in Augsburg in 1529 by Alexander Weißenhorn (also discussed in section Ic). It was followed by fifty-six more, which are listed below.

The list of editions, though fuller and more accurate than anything else in print, is still provisional. It is probably not complete. Many editions have come to light only as the result of the digitization of library catalogues, and it is likely that the next few years will see the opening up of ever smaller and more obscure collections in this way. It will contain some inaccuracies: questions such as whether two apparently identical editions held in widely separated libraries actually are identical in all respects are as yet unresolved in most cases, since it has not been possible to make a personal inspection of all known copies of the book. However, since the last edition with which Schotten had anything personally to do was that of Cologne 1526, the subsequent history of the editions does not affect the *Confabulationes* as he composed them.

The printed and online sources cited here in abbreviated form are:

CCFr: *Catalogue Collectif de France.*
KVK: *Karlsruher Virtueller Katalog.*
N&K: Nijhoff and Kronenberg, *Nederlandsche Bibliographie van 1500 tot 1540.*
NUC: *The National Union Catalog*
VD 16: *Verzeichnis der im deutschen Sprachbereich erschienenen Drucke des XVI. Jahrhunderts.*

Full details of all these are found in the bibliography.

Where the readily accessible major printed sources (*VD 16*, N&K) give adequate information on library holdings, this has not been included here. Where editions are known from individual library catalogues, or from electronic catalogues such as *VD 16 online*, *KVK* or *CCFr*, details of library holdings have been added.

First edition: 123 colloquies only:

Augsburg: S. Ruff, July 1525. *VD 16*, S 4005; Munich, UB, 8° Misc. 604a; *KVK*: Stuttgart, Evangelischer Oberkirchenrat, 443.

Editions including the *conuiuia*:

Cologne: P. Quentel, 1526. *VD 16 online*, ZV 14151; Trier, Stadtbibliothek, 2 an: G 59 8°; *KVK*: Besançon, BM, 246809.

Augsburg: A. Weißenhorn, 1529. *VD 16*, S 4006; *NUC*, 529, 615.

Antwerp: M. de Keyser, September 1530. N&K, 3861.

[Antwerp]: M. [Hillen van Hoochstraten], n.d. [1531?]. N&K, 3865.

Vienna: J. Singriener, 1531. *NUC*: Cornell UL, Rare PA 8577 S27C7 1531.

Zwickau: W. Meyerpeck, 1531. *VD 16*, S 4007; Berlin, StBPK, Prf 2996.

Augsburg: A. Weißenhorn, 1532. Vienna, ÖNB, 74.Y.99*

Leipzig: N. Schmidt, March 1532. *VD 16*, S 4008.

Nuremberg: J. Petreius, 1532. *VD 16*, S 4009.

Antwerp: M. de Keyser, 1533. N&K, 3862.

Augsburg: A. Weißenhorn, 1533. *VD 16*, S 4010.

Augsburg: A. Weißenhorn, 1534. *KVK*: Florence, Biblioteca Nazionale Centrale, MAGL.11.9.142/b.

Augsburg: A. Weißenhorn, 1535. *VD 16*, S 4011; *KVK*.

[Leipzig]: [N. Schmidt], 1535. *VD 16*, S 4012.

Leipzig: N. Schmidt, 1535. *VD 16 online*, ZV 14149.

Augsburg: A. Weißenhorn, 1536. *VD 16*, S 4013; *KVK*.

Nuremberg: J. Petreius, 1536. *VD 16*, S 4014; *CCFr*.

Antwerp: M. Hillen van Hoochstraten, 1536. N&K, 3863.

Antwerp: M. [Hillen van Hoochstraten], [*ca.* 1537?]. N&K, 3865.

Antwerp: Widow of M. de Keyser for J. Cock, 1537. N&K, 3864.

Augsburg: A. Weißenhorn, 1537. *VD 16*, S 4015.

Leipzig: N. Schmidt, 1537. *VD 16 online*, ZV 22363: Dresden, Sächsische LB, 3.A.10384, angeb. 2.

Leipzig: N. Schmidt, 1538. *VD 16*, S 4016.

Augsburg: A. Weißenhorn, 1540. *VD 16*, S 4017.

[Leipzig]: [N. Wolrab], [*ca.* 1540?]. *VD 16*, S 4018.

Leipzig: N. Schmidt, 1540. *VD 16 online*, ZV 14150.

Leipzig: N. Schmidt, [*ca.* 1540?]. *VD 16*, S 4019.

Nuremberg: n.pr., *ca.* 1540. Oxford, Bodleian Library, Vet. D1 f. 97.

Augsburg: H. Steiner, 1541. *VD 16*, S 4020.

Ingolstadt: A. Weißenhorn, 1542. *NUC*: Chicago, Newberry Library, Case Y 682 .s3832.

Lyon: J. & F. Frellon, 1543. *KVK*: Mannheim, UB, Sch 072/265 an 1; Florence, Biblioteca Nazionale Centrale, MAGL.5.9. 232/a.

Nuremberg: J. Petreius, 1543. *VD 16 online*, ZV 20803: Munich, BSB, L.lat. 1014v; *KVK*: Vienna, ÖNB, 73.Y.60;

Augsburg: V. Otmar, 1544. *VD 16*, S 4021.

Venice: F. Bindoni and M. Pasini, 1544. *KVK*: Jesi, Biblioteca Comunale Planettiana.

Lyon: J. & F. Frellon, 1545. *CCFr*: Paris, BN, RES P–X–411 1.

Lyon: T. Payen, 1545. *CCFr*: Marseille, BM, 81771/2.

Lyon: A. Vincent, 1545. *CCFr*: Grenoble, BM, F 3711 CGA.

Lyon: T. Payen, 1547. *CCFr*: Toulouse, Bibliothèque d'Etude et du Patrimoine, Fa D 8879, Fonds ancien 2.

Leipzig: n.pr., 1548. *KVK*: Dresden, Sächsische LB, 39.8.5780.

Frankfurt an der Oder: J. Eichorn [*ca.* 1550]. *KVK*: Berlin, StBPK, 2 an: @Wp 1232.

Ingolstadt: A. and S. Weißenhorn, 1550. *VD 16 online*, ZV 22001: Munich, BSB, L.lat. 1014y.

[Leipzig]: [N. Wolrab?], [*ca.* 1550?]. *KVK*: Wolfenbüttel, Herzog August Bibliothek, QuH 160.1 3.

Augsburg: V. Otmar, 1551. *VD 16*, S 4022. (The colophon carries the date 1546).

N.p., n.pr., 1551. *NUC*: Washington: Folger Shakespeare Library, Folger PA 8577 S25 C5 cage; *KVK*: Bamberg, Staatsbibliothek, 22/L.r.r.o.267–a; Basel, UB, DB IX 28:2.

Lyon: J. Frellon, 1552. *KVK*: Universitat de Barcelona, UL, no shelfmark.

Augsburg: H. Zimmermann, 1553. *VD 16*, S 4023.

Lyon: T. Payen, 1556. *CCFr*: Le Mans, Médiathèque Aragon, 2e st BL 8* 270 Fonds anciens; Lyon, BM, B 510183 CGA.

[Strasbourg?]: n.pr., 1556. *KVK*: Augsburg, Staats- und Stadtbibliothek, Th B V 49.

N.p., n.pr., 1556. *VD 16*, S 4024; Oxford, Bodleian Library, Vet. D1 f. 136.

N.p., n.pr., 1559. *KVK*: Stuttgart, Württembergische LB, Phil. oct. 2306; Augsburg, UB, 221/FX 105001 C25.559.

Nuremberg: U. or V. Neuber, 1561. *KVK*: Regensburg, Staatliche Bibliothek, 999/Lat. rec. 638.

Strasbourg: [C. Mylius], [*ca.* 1565]. *VD 16*, S 4025.

Lyon: A. Gryphius, 1566. *KVK*: Rome, Biblioteca Universitaria Alessandrina, M.g.39.

Copenhagen: n.pr., 1576. *KVK*: Copenhagen, Royal Library, 52, –14 8°.

Lyon: A. Vincent, 1621. *KVK*: Milan, Biblioteca Nazionale Braidense, 25.15.K.0005/01.

Undatable editions:

Frankfurt am Main: n.pr., n.d. *KVK* : Greifswald, UB, 542/Ch 722.

Frankfurt an der Oder: n.pr., n.d. *KVK*: Copenhagen, Royal Library, 166, 1031 051 26.

What is most remarkable is the sheer number of printings: fifty-eight editions in total, nearly all produced within forty years, a very large number for an early-sixteenth-century book. Mosellanus's *Paedologia* went through about seventy editions before 1570; not many more than the *Confabulationes*, though its reputation is now much higher.[33]

At least one edition of the *Confabulationes* appeared in practically every year till the mid-1550s, and another four between then and the mid-1560s, when the work's popularity seems at an end. Amazing too is the frequency with which the *Confabulationes* were printed by leading presses in major German and Dutch printing centres, notably Antwerp, Augsburg, Leipzig and Nuremberg (though Frankfurt am Main, the leading German centre of the book trade, seems not to have developed an interest in the book). This suggests that printers saw in them a text which would sell well over a wide geographical area. It also suggests that printers in these places, far from Cologne and in many cases in Protestant cities and regions, did not imagine that their intended readership would have any problem with the many references to Cologne reality in the *Confabulationes*, or with Schotten's occasional expressions of relatively orthodox Catholic attitudes.[34]

The *Confabulationes* remained a mainly German phenomenon (the 1544 Venice printing seems not to have had any Italian progeny); though they enjoyed a notable success in the vastly important French printing town of Lyon in the 1540s, where five surviving editions were produced in quick succession by three different printers, again suggesting that publishers in this Mecca of the book trade recognized a good seller when then they saw one. The presence of Lyon editions in libraries in Grenoble, Marseille and Toulouse suggests that the work was dif-

33 Barth, 'Mosellanus, *Paedologia*', cols 427–28.

34 See the discussion of these aspects in Macardle, *Confabulations*, Chapter 2.

fused from Lyon into the south and south-east of France, and perhaps even into Switzerland.

The extreme popularity of the *Confabulationes* in their day is hardly surprising. They offered models of an elegant, Terentian colloquial Latin. Schotten's Latinity, though classical and humanist, was not pedantically Ciceronian; in many ways it imitated Erasmus's usage, but it had its own integrity. If it showed many traces of Late Latin, and even certain Medieval Latin features, there were no more than were typical of humanist usage of the time.[35]

The *Confabulationes* took up many of the themes of the leading colloquy collections, notably Erasmus's *Colloquia familiaria* and Petrus Mosellanus's *Paedologia*, but what Schotten engaged in was not slavish imitation but a very independent adaptation. Specifically, whilst being clearly and avowedly Erasmian in style, he avoided Erasmus's tendency to introduce theological themes which were both too advanced for a schoolboy readership, and suspect to orthodox theologians.[36]

Then too, the *Confabulationes* were firmly rooted in reality. Though they were read and used by far more boys in other German and European regions than by those in Cologne itself, their appeal to a Cologne schoolboy of the time must have been immense. For a reading of the *Confabulationes* shows that Schotten was again and again alluding with considerable specificity and accuracy of detail to places, institutions, traditions and cultural practices of Cologne. These local allusions are recorded in the notes to

35 See the detailed discussion of Schotten's Latinity in Macardle, *Confabulations*, Chapter 4. See also the list of non-classical vocabulary, section IIIc.

36 The relationship of the *Confabulationes* to other important colloquy collections is discussed in detail in Macardle, *Confabulations*, Chapter 3.

this edition, and they are discussed in detail in Macardle, *Confabulations*, Chapter 2.

Ic. The Earliest Printings of the Confabulationes

There is no systematic bibliographical study of the *Confabulationes*. The only relevant sources, Bömer's monograph on the humanist schoolboy colloquies and the printed edition of *VD 16*, record the first two editions as having been printed in Augsburg: the first in July 1525 by Simprecht Ruff; the second in October 1529 by Alexander Weißenhorn.[37] These editions are here given the sigla 'A' and 'C' respectively.

The past few years, however, have seen the digitization and collation of German library catalogues, not least in connection with the online supplement to *VD 16*, a process which has revealed many previously unknown editions of texts. One important find was the true second edition of the *Confabulationes* (here called edition B), printed in Cologne by Peter Quentel in 1526, month unspecified.[38] At present only two copies are known, held by

---

37 *Confabulationes tironum literariorum, ad amussim Colloquiorum Erasmi Roterodami, Authore Hermanno Schotten. Hesso. M.D.XXV.* (titlepage). Colophon: 'Augustae Vindelicorum, per Simpertum Ruff. Anno a nato Iesu. M.D.XXV. mense Iulio.' (sig. H8^v). *VD 16*, S 4005. *CONFA | BVLATIONES TYRONVM | literariorum, ad amußim | Colloquioru[m] | Erasmi Roterodami, Autho= | re Hermanno | Schotten= | nio Hesso. | Ab authore recognitæ & auctæ, / triginta Conuiuijs lepidißimis. | M. D. XXIX.* (titlepage). Colophon: 'Augustæ Vindelicorum in officina Ale= | xandri Weyssenhorn. Anno repa= | ratæ salutis M. D. XXIX. | Mense Octobri.' (sig. L8^r). *VD 16*, S 4006; Bömer, *Die lateinischen Schülergespräche*, p. 46.

38 *CONFA | BVLATIONES TI | ronum literarioru[m] adamussim*

the Stadtbibliothek in Trier and the Bibliothèque Municipale in Besançon.[39]

Edition B was revised by Schotten. He made minor changes to the 1525 text, and to the 123 short colloquies of the first edition he added thirty *conuiuia*, or 'banquets', longer discussions set at meals of various kinds; these were probably inspired by the *conuiuia* in Erasmus's *Colloquia*. B, the last known edition to have enjoyed authorial revision, is the obvious base text for the present critical edition. But the comparative investigation of edition A raises intriguing questions about its production and status.

Edition A, Augsburg: Simprecht Ruff, July 1525

Simprecht or Simpert Ruff was the master printer of the important Augsburg publishing partnership of Sigmund Grimm and Marx Wirsung. Wirsung died in 1521, and from 1523 on editions appeared with Ruff's rather than Grimm's name as publisher.[40] Why would Schotten, all of whose other first editions were published in Cologne, nearly all by Peter Quentel (see pp. 9–10 above), have taken the *Confabulationes* to this printer in such a faraway city?[41] One of the still slightly obscure episodes in

| *Colloquiorum Erasmi Rote=* | *rodami, Autore Hermanno* | *Schottennio Hesso.* | *Et ab autore Anno. M. D.* / *XXVI. recognitæ &* / *auctæ.* / *Triginta conuiuijs lepidissimis.* (titlepage). Colophon: 'Coloniæ in officina honesti ciuis Petri | Quentell. Anno. M. D. XXVI.' (sig. M8[r]). *VD 16 online*, ZV 14151.

39 Trier, Stadtbibliothek, shelfmark 2 an: G 59 8°. Besançon, BM, shelfmark 246809. The Stadtbibliothek Trier kindly provided me with a digital copy of this edition.

40 *VD 16*, III. Abteilung (= vol. XXV), p. 17 (Ruff).

41 For the same reason the 1527 Erfurt edition of the *Formulae* of the Nuremberg humanist Sebald Heyden is probably not the actual princeps: Heyden, *Nomenclatura rerum domesti-*

Schotten's career is in December 1523, when he was debarred from speaking at the *Disputatio quodlibetica* on account of debts by Johannes Jacobi de Campis, the principal of the Bursa Laurentiana, of which Schotten was or had been a member. This may have been related to humanist–scholastic antagonisms at a time when the Cologne Arts Faculty was going through a period of debate about curricular reform.[42] It is not unthinkable that Schotten had been marginalized by de Campis to the extent that Cologne presses would not touch him; for close links had existed between Cologne printers and the *bursae* since the fifteenth century.[43] But Schotten printed the brief *Ludus grammaticus*, and possibly also the *Meta studii literarii*, with Servas Kruffter in Cologne in 1525, suggesting he was not a pariah in Cologne at the time.[44] In any case, Quentel's connections were not with the Laurentiana but with the Bursa Kuyck, whose principal, the humanist Ortwin Gratius, was Quentel's reader and adviser.[45]

Religious considerations might lead a Cologne writer to publish in Augsburg. Whereas Cologne printers were on the whole conservatively Catholic, those in Augsburg were not. Ruff was one of many who favoured the Reformation, and many of his publications were Lutheran.[46]

---

carum, ed. by Müller and van der Elst, p. 7*; Riecke, 'Sebald Heydens "Formulae puerilium colloquiorum"', p. 101.

42 The incident is discussed in Macardle, *Confabulations*, pp. 29–42.

43 Corsten, 'Universität und Buchdruck', passim (fifteenth century); Rautenberg, *Überlieferung und Druck*, p. 219 (sixteenth century).

44 See the bibliography of Schotten's works, p. 579. The 1525 dating of the *Meta studii literarii* is not certain.

45 *CoE*, II, p. 124; Meuthen, *Universität*, pp. 251–52; Rautenberg, *Überlieferung und Druck*, pp. 220–21.

46 Götze, *Die hochdeutschen Drucker der Reformationszeit*, p. 7: 'Lebhaft reformatorisch'.

But this can hardly have been Schotten's reason: his gentle persiflage of clerics and occasional moderate Erasmian critique of religious practice (e.g. colloquies 57, 89, 90, 91, 95) could not have been too much for a Cologne publisher, nor strong enough to seem even implicitly pro-Reform – especially since Schotten included heartfelt deplorations of the effects of Lutheranism (e.g. colloquies 88, 107), and since in general the *Confabulationes* often seem like a consciously orthodox collection, avoiding, even implicitly countering, Erasmus's more radical critical sallies against the church.[47]

There is then no discernible reason why Schotten would have been interested in Grimm and Ruff as publishers. But there is a very good commercial reason why Grimm and Ruff would have been interested in Schotten as an author. When Wirsung, a wealthy Lutheran merchant, died in 1521, and his heirs withdrew their capital from the business in 1522, Grimm was in serious financial difficulties: in 1527 he was declared bankrupt.[48] In the intervening years he engaged in a rather desperate survival strategy, which had two major prongs. The first was a series of démarches to stave off formal bankruptcy. The appearance of books naming Ruff as publisher, which was once thought to mean that Ruff had actually taken over the firm,[49] was probably a legal ruse to prevent creditors from seizing Grimm's equipment. The fact that Grimm's bankruptcy in 1527 closed the printshop suggests it was still under his control, not that of Ruff, who did not indeed have the means to own a business of this size.[50]

47 Discussed in detail in Macardle, *Confabulations*, pp. 93–106.

48 Künast, *'Getruckt zu Augspurg'*, pp. 66–70.

49 E.g. Götze, *Die hochdeutschen Drucker der Reformationszeit*, p. 7.

50 Künast, *'Getruckt zu Augspurg'*, pp. 43–44, 51, 53–54, 66–70; cf. Benzing, *Die Buchdrucker des 16. und 17. Jahrhunderts*, p. 16.

The second prong was a drastically changed publications profile. The Grimm and Wirsung list had been remarkable in size and range. The more than 120 titles produced between 1518 and 1522 included few publisher's standbys such as liturgical books or medieval works of devotion. Instead there was a rich mixture of classical literature, Arabic and Hebrew, patristic and medieval philosophy and theology, humanist writings, and Catholic and Lutheran controversialists.[51] Once Wirsung had gone, however, and with him the money that had financed this probably loss-making business, the profile changed considerably, as Ruff and Grimm rationalized production to titles that would sell well and recoup costs quickly. Perhaps reflecting Ruff's own Protestantism, there was a higher proportion of Lutheran writing, from Luther and Melanchthon down to lesser figures like Theobald Gerlacher or Heinrich of Zütphen. But there were also Catholic controversialists, major ones like Eck and Schatzgeyer, and more obscure ones like Matthias Kretz and Leopold Dick.[52] There were sensational books like the astrological prognostications of Paul of Middelburg and the esoterica of Paul Ricius, the humanist and kabbalist.[53] A lively and accessible humanist school text like the *Confabulationes* would have made an ideal addition to Grimm and Ruff's list; no doubt this was why in

---

51 *VD 16*, III. Abteilung (= vol. XXV), pp. 6–7 (Grimm); pp. 7–8 (Grimm and Wirsung).

52 *VD 16*, III. Abteilung (= vol. XXV), p. 17 (Ruff); p. 7 (Grimm 1523–1525; Grimm and Ruff). Gerlacher: Jöcher, II, cols 955–56. Heinrich of Zütphen: *NDB*, VIII, p. 431. Kretz (*ca.* 1480–1543): *CoE*, II, pp. 274–75. Dick: Jöcher, II, cols 109–10.

53 *Prognosticum [...] ostendens Anno. M.D.XXIIII. nullum [...] diluuium futurum [...]* (1524): *VD 16*, P 1063; *Ain fast nutzlich büchlin [...] Von dem Sindtfluß [...]* (1524): *VD 16*, P 1064. Paul (1445–1553): *CoE*, III, pp. 57–58. *Pauli Ricii Apologetica [...] in allegorizantium dogma [...]* (1525): *VD 16*, R 2309. Ricius (d. 1541): *CoE*, III, pp. 158–60.

1523 they had printed Erasmus's *Colloquia* (twice), and the first Augsburg edition of Mosellanus's *Paedologia*.[54]

But if Grimm and Ruff wished to printed the *Confabulationes*, yet Schotten probably did not offer them the manuscript, what text did they work from? Might Ruff's have been not the actual first edition of the *Confabulationes* but a pirated reprint of a now lost Cologne princeps? This is by no means unlikely. The existence of the 1526 Cologne second edition (B) has become generally known only recently: previously Alexander Weißenhorn's 1529 Augsburg edition (C) was assumed to be the second edition. The production of what seemed to be the first two editions of the *Confabulationes* in Augsburg could suggest that Schotten had some connection with the printers of that city. This impression was strengthened by the fact that Weißenhorn printed the *Confabulationes* seven more times in Augsburg, and twice more in Ingolstadt,[55] and that another four editions were produced in Augsburg.[56]

Now that B can be collated with C, however, it is evident that Weißenhorn simply reprinted B, or possibly even a now lost post-1526 printing, perhaps on the basis of Augsburg inside knowledge that Grimm and Ruff's 1525 edition had sold well: it is unlikely that Schotten

54 Erasmus, *Colloquiorum familiarium formulae* (August and November 1523): *VD 16*, E 2342, 2343; another edition in July 1524: *VD 16*, E 2348. *Paedologia Petri Mosellani [...] Dialogi pueriles Christophori Hegendorphini [...]* (August 1523): *VD 16*, S 2153.

55 Augsburg: 1532, 1533, 1534, 1535, 1536, 1537, 1540 (Vienna, ÖNB, 74.Y.99*; *VD 16*, S 4010; Florence, Biblioteca Nazionale Centrale, MAGL.11.9.142/b; *VD 16*, S 4011, S 4013, S 4015, S 4017). Ingolstadt: 1542, 1550 (Chicago, Newberry Library, Case Y 682 .s3832; Munich, BSB, L.lat. 1014y).

56 H. Steiner, 1541 (*VD 16*, S 4020); V. Otmar, 1544 and 1546 (*VD 16*, S 4021, S 4022); H. Zimmermann, 1553 (*VD 16*, S 4023).

was involved in any way. Yet this does not appear from the 1529 edition: Weißenhorn – understandably – never hints that he is reprinting a Cologne original, and the same could in principle have been true for the 1525 Ruff edition A. Timing not only permits this scenario, it may even suggest it. Schotten's dedicatory epistle to the *Confabulationes* is dated mid-February 1525; Ruff's edition was printed in July 1525, up to five and a half months later, ample time for a Cologne first edition to have appeared and been pirated by Grimm and Ruff.[57] Too few of Schotten's works carry a printing date detailed enough to show how long they typically took from dedication to publication; but the *Ludus imperatorius* of 1527 was out in two months at most and the *Colloquia philosophica* of 1535 in an absolute maximum of four.[58] Five months between dedication and printing seems almost suspiciously long for a genuine first edition.

Nothing in edition A conclusively shows whether it is original or not. Nevertheless, a number of mistakes taken together suggest that the edition could well have been a copy rather than an original printing.

In colloquy 111, the name Quirinus found in B and subsequent editions is given in A as 'Quintinus' (B, sig. G1ᵛ–2ʳ; A, sig. G7ᵛ–8ʳ). This is surely more than a simple misreading. Quirinus is a distinctively Cologne name: St Quirinus of Neuß was a first-century Roman martyr whose relics were preserved in a specially built

57 Dedicatory epistle: 'Coloniae ex aedibus meis decimoquinto Kalendas Martias. Anno millesimo quingentesimo uigesimo quinto' (15 February 1525) (A, sig. A2ᵛ); but see below for a critical look at this dating. Colophon: 'Augustae Vindelicorum, per Simpertum Ruff. Anno a nato Iesu. M.D.XXV. mense Iulio.' (A, sig. H8ᵛ).

58 *Ludus imperatorius*: ep. ded. 22 October 1527; printed by end of 1527. *Colloquia philosophica*: ep. ded. 23 August 1535; printed by end of 1535.

church in Neuß, and Cologne was one of the centres of his cult (*ÖH*). The name was not, however, well known in Augsburg, which would explain why an Augsburg compositor faced with 'Quirinus' misread it, or even assumed it was a mistake, and set 'Quintinus' instead.[59] In the same way the specifically Cologne saint's name Evergis(i)lus was misprinted in C as 'Evergissus' by Weißenhorn (see colloquy 56, apparatus). This, however, shows only that Ruff was an Augsburg printer working with Cologne material; it does not prove that he was pirating a Cologne edition.

Three further errors in A, however, seem more clearly to indicate that this edition was a copy rather than an original. In colloquy 95, ll. 35–36, Theophilus quotes from Galatians 1.10. In B and subsequent editions this reads 'At contra Diui Pauli uerbum est, "Si hominibus placerem, Christi seruus non essem"' (B, sig. F3[v]; C, sig. F1[r]). The reading in A (sig. F8[v]) is 'At contra diu isti seruus non essem'. B is undoubtedly correct and must represent Schotten's authorial intention: Theophilus counters a reference to Plato with one to St Paul. The version in A, by contrast, is self-evidently wrong: it is grammatically shaky ('istius' would be preferable to 'isti'), and makes no sense in context. It is clear, in fact, that the A reading is a simple truncation of the correct version, leaving out everything from the final 'i' of 'Diui' to the initial 'Chr' of 'Christi'. This missing string of text must have been in Schotten's original manuscript, and the omission can only have been made by a copyist. Four cases could explain the error:

1. A was the true first edition of the *Confabulationes*; the compositor worked from a copy of Schotten's original

59 Quirinus is not found in the Augsburg liturgical calendars collated by Grotefend (online). Quintin or Quentin was a late-third-century martyr in Picardy (*ÖH*).

manuscript which had a scribal error here, and followed it exactly.

2. A was the true first edition; the compositor worked from Schotten's original manuscript or a faithful copy, but copied it incorrectly.
3. A was itself a copy of a now lost (Cologne?) first edition; the compositor worked from the true first edition, which was itself defective here, and copied it exactly.
4. A was itself a copy of the first edition; the compositor worked from the true first edition, which was here correct, and copied it incorrectly.

One detail makes the fourth situation the most probable. In the rather large typeface used in B, the text string omitted is the almost exact equivalent of one line of print: if the abbreviations (on 'uerbum', 'hominibus' and 'placerem') were written out in full, it would equate to a full line. If there was a Cologne first edition, it would presumably also have been printed by Quentel, probably set in a similar fount, and the text string could have filled a single line of type. If Grimm and Ruff's compositor was working from such an original, his eye could easily have leapt over the line (haplography). Situation 3 is possible: that Grimm and Ruff were working from an extant first edition which had itself introduced the error. But this would still make A a copy, not the authentic princeps. The second possibility, that Grimm and Ruff miscopied a manuscript of Schotten's, cannot be absolutely excluded, but it seems unlikely both that Schotten would have sent them his manuscript, and that the omitted text would have occupied exactly one line of writing.

Alineation could explain another telling mistake in A. In colloquy 33, Iaspar asks Melchior who he intends to vote for as the school 'boy bishop': he uses the phrase 'Cui tuam dabis uocem?' which Melchior condemns as uncouth, suggesting several alternatives. In B, and the editions, from C on, based on it, part of the exchange reads:

> IASPAR. Poterisne et alio pacto eloqui?
> MELCHIOR. Possum. 'In cuius personam eligendam tu consenties?'
> IASPAR. Memoriae istas recondam orationes. Ego suffragabor tibi. (B, sig. B8[r], ll. 24–27).

This makes entire sense in context: Melchior is the good scholar who criticizes Iaspar's formulations and is able to offer alternatives. In A, however, the speakers get reversed:

> IASPAR. Poteris ne & alio pacto eloqui?
> MELCHIOR. Possum.
> IASPAR. In cuius personam eligendam tu consenties?
> MELCHIOR. Memoriae istas recondam orationes.
> IASPAR. Ego sufragabor tibi. (A, sig. C2[r])

Schotten would certainly not have written this version. Like the text omission discussed above it must have been produced by a compositor either misreading a manuscript or an extant edition, or accurately reproducing an erroneous manuscript copy or print version. The alineation of the text in A suggests how the mistake could have been made:

> IAS. Poteris ne & alio pacto eloqui? MEL. Possum.
> IASPAR. In cuius personam eligendam tu consenties?
> MEL. Memoriae istas recondam orationes. IAS. Ego sufragabor tibi. (A, sig. C2[r], ll. 13–16).

The compositor has fitted Iaspar's question and the first word of Melchior's reply, 'Possum', into a single line. He has however mistaken 'Possum' for the whole reply, and has set Melchior's second sentence as Iaspar's line, adding 'IASPAR' in full, so taking up another complete line. The question mark at the end of this line signals a change of speaker, and the compositor has duly, though incorrectly, switched to Melchior. The full stop after 'orationes' signals another change of speaker, and he has switched – correctly now – to Iaspar and is back on track.

In the first instance, of course, this tells us only about A and not about the copy from which it may have worked. But if the A compositor was working from the actual princeps, and if this was a Quentel edition, it may have had a fount, layout and line-length similar to B. And in B, the corresponding lines are arranged quite similarly, thus:

> IAS. Poteris ne et alio pacto eloq[ui]? MEL.Possum,
> In cuius persona[m] eligendam tu consenties? IAS.
> Memoriae istas reconda[m] orationes. Ego suffraga-
> bor tibi. (B, sig. B8r, ll. 24–27)

If the A compositor had in front of him a printed edition alineated like this, the 'Possum' at the line end could trigger the chain of misreadings, which preserve the dialogue but confuse the speakers. And a Quentel princeps would very probably have had this alineation. Again this is not absolutely conclusive, but points suggestively in the same direction as the other evidence.

There is a further intriguing detail of dating. In A, Schotten's dedicatory epistle is dated 15 February 1525, 'decimoquinto Kalendas Martias'; in B, however, it is dated 11 February, '19. Kal. Martias'.[60] The normal presumption would be that B, the edition revised by Schotten, would have the correct date. In A the date is written out: 'decimoquinto Kalendas Martias'; in B it is in numerals: '19. Kal. Martias'. There seem to be only three situations which could explain these data:

---

60 'Coloniae ex aedibus meis decimoquinto Kalendas Martias. Anno millesimo quingentesimo uigesimo quinto' (A, sig. A2v). 'Colonię ex aedib[us] meis .19. Kal. Martias. Anno. M. D. XXV' (B, sig. A2r); copied as 'Coloniae ex aedib. meis 19. Kal. Mar. 1525' (C, sig. A2r).

1. Edition A was the true princeps with the correct date, and B wrongly copied it. This seems highly improbable, however, for two reasons. First, B was supervised by Schotten, who would have been less likely than an outsider to misdate his own dedication. Secondly, it is unlikely that a printer reading 'decimoquinto' would set it as '19'. Other possible mistakes, however would be much easier to explain, and this suggests two other scenarios:

2. There was a true (probably Cologne) princeps with the correct date '19' in numerals, which the A compositor misread as '15'. This is entirely plausible: a smudged, damaged or unevenly impressed '9', particularly if its top right section was missing, could readily be confused with a '5'. The A printer then set this misread numeral in full. B, however, overseen by Schotten, reproduced the correct date.

3. There was a true princeps which read '15' in numerals: A read it correctly, though expressing it as a word ('decimoquinto'), and B misread it as '19'. This is perhaps slightly less likely, since B was supervised by Schotten, whom one might not expect to make mistakes in dating his own dedication. Yet even an author could make an error in a date of this kind. In this way A could have preserved the correct, original date whilst still being a copy.

None of these interesting details is decisive in itself, but taken together they make it a very definite possibility that A was a copy rather than an original. Add the fact that Schotten had no demonstrable connection with printers in Augsburg, or indeed with printers anywhere other than Cologne, and there almost exclusively with Peter Quentel; remember that he had no discernible reason for seeking such a connection; but that Grimm and Ruff had every reason to look out for promising texts to pirate. In the light of all this it is entirely possible, even probable, that A was copied by Grimm and Ruff from a no longer extant princeps, printed almost certainly in Cologne, and very probably by Schotten's regular publisher Peter Quentel.

Edition B, Cologne: Peter Quentel, 1526

The appearance, or reappearance, of the true second edition of the *Confabulationes* was an important, though completely unmarked, bibliographical event. Not often does a previously unknown and unsuspected early edition of an early modern literary work, incorporating changes and important additions, and overseen by the author, suddenly turn up. As has already been discussed, the collation of the undoubtedly genuine B with A strongly supports the suspicion that A was not in fact the true princeps of the *Confabulationes*.

To the 123 colloquies in A, B adds a block of thirty *conuiuia*, 'banquets', almost certainly inspired by the *conuiuia* which had started to appear in editions of Erasmus's *Colloquia*. B however makes no additions to the colloquies in A, and the order and naming remains the same as in A.

The most significant textual changes to A are the brief additions which Schotten makes to many colloquies in the very last line or two. Time and again, the ending of a colloquy in A is extended slightly. This can be by as little as a few words, as in colloquy 33, where l. 37, 'Mirum quod audio' (A), becomes 'Mirum quod audio, sed haud et aegre credibile est' in B. It can also be as much as a line or two of dialogue, as in colloquy 10, where Valterus explains that his parents are afraid of going out on the streets at night: 'Timent noctu plateas emetiri' (l. 26). In A the colloquy ends here; B adds a further exchange:

PETRVS. Vane timent.

> VALTERVS. Nequaquam, nescis noctem nihil boni, sed saepe pugnos afferre. (B, ll. 27–28)

These minor extensions are made to thirty-six out of 123 colloquies, 30% of the total. In only three (22, 95, 119) are extra words inserted anywhere but at the end; and one of these three (22) has an addition at the end too.[61] It might seem that Schotten had an almost compulsive need to make these brief additions; yet the few added words nearly always do make the ending of the colloquy clearer, more convincing or more final. They say much for Schotten's formal sensitivity and finely tuned ear for dialogue.

The other changes which B made to the text of the original 123 colloquies, though numerous, are relatively minor. B attempts to correct or slightly improve A in the following categories.

Typographical errors. The most major is the string of text omitted from colloquy 95, ll. 35–36, discussed in detail in the consideration of edition A above. The others are minor and usually obvious, like 'memorantur' for 'me morantur' (colloquy 62, l. 36) or 'iudicat' for 'indicat' (colloquy 113, l. 11).

Grammatical forms. Some of these could have been typos, like 'commodat' corrected to 'commodet' (colloquy 4, l. 33) or 'consequi potest' corrected to or 'consequi potes' (colloquy 91, l. 18). Some are clearly morphological or syntactic mistakes, like 'cibum abhorreo', corrected to 'a cibo abhorreo' (colloquy 28, l. 35); or 'furiunt', corrected to 'furunt' (colloquy 36, l. 19).

Some Latin idiom. A uses medieval or simply incorrect forms such as the deponent 'diuinor', corrected to 'diuino' (colloquy 22, ll. 13, 14); or 'tui *se* miserabuntur', corrected

---

[61] Colloquies 22, ll. 32, 38–39; 95, ll. 25–26; 119, ll. 19–20.

to 'tui miserebuntur' (colloquy 111, l. 26). B also improves on A's word-choices in such cases as 'contueri', changed to 'conspici' (colloquy 96, l. 29) and 'nostra gratia', changed to 'nostra causa' (colloquy 77, l. 17). Occasionally, slightly coarse expressions are replaced, as in 'lectum concacaui', changed to 'lectum oleto foedaui' (colloquy 69, ll. 18–19). B also picks up miscellaneous other mistakes, such as 'Poetarum semper uanae sunt fabulae', corrected to 'Poetarum *non* semper uanae sunt fabulae' (colloquy 37, l. 3), or 'nisi aliqua me *non* morarentur', corrected to 'nisi aliqua me morarentur' (colloquy 55, ll. 17–18).

* * *

Some of the alterations to A made in B are debatable. In colloquy 10, l. 20, the word 'culina', 'kitchen', in A is changed in B to 'popina'. Yet 'popina' properly means 'cook-shop' or 'restaurant'; the sense 'kitchen' is Medieval Latin (see note to colloquy 10, l. 20). Schotten's attempt to improve on his first version was ill-advised. And B perpetrates its own quota of typos and similar mistakes.

Most gravely, on three occasions B leaves out necessary lines of text which are found in A. The first is in colloquy 14, ll. 23–29. A reads correctly:

> PE. Actutum cras decima postquam sonuerit uenias.
> GE. In tempore adero.
> PE. Domi nostrae nil plus dicas quam parentes saluta.
> GE. Essem adeo inciuilis?
> PE. Te a me inuitatum loquitor.
> GE. Faciam, tum audacior ero, ingrediendo domum et ad mensam edendo et bibendo. (A, sig. A8^{v})

B, however, leaves out a line (the second line above) and so wrongly attributes the next line:

> PETRVS. Actutum cras decima postquam sonuerit uenias.
> GEORGIVS. Domi nostrae nil plus dicas quam parentes saluta.

> GEORGIVS. Essem adeo inciuilis?
> PETRVS. Te a me inuitatum loquitor. (B, sig. A7^{v})

This mistake seems to have been simple inadvertence, possibly helped along by the way A (sig. A8^{v}) abbreviates the boys' names to the easily confused forms 'GE.' and 'PE.'.

The second such omission is in colloquy 48. In A, ll. 8–11 read:

> VDALRICVS. Torquebimus globum per annulum ferreum.
> VINANDVS. Si tibi lubet, ipse recusabo nihil.
> VDALRICVS. In me nihil erit morae.
> VINANDVS. Age, propere eamus. (A, sig. D1^{v})

The second and third lines above (ll. 9–10) are absent from B (sig. C6^{v}–7^{r}), and this is undoubtedly a mistake, for without them the exchange is much less coherent. It is perhaps explained by the fact that in B, Vinandus's 'Age, propere eamus.' begins a new page (sig. C7^{r}): the break involved in setting a new forme could have distracted the compositor.

Finally, in colloquy 123, ll. 52–55, A reads:

> HOSPES. Abluite singuli manus et discumbite, in tempore incipiamus quo hilaritati sat restet spatii.
> CONVIVAE. Vt tibi fuerit uisum.
> HOSPES. Heus puer, ades dum, consecra cenam.
> (A, sig. H6^{r-v})

B, however, omits the proper 'Conuiuae' line (l. 54), and makes the guests tell the serving-boy to say grace (l. 55: B, sig. G8^{r}). Again this is probably a mistake, since this line is more proper for the host than for his guests.

Edition C, Augsburg: Alexander Weißenhorn, 1529

Alexander Weißenhorn, unlike most Augsburg printers, remained steadfastly Catholic. As the Reformation tightened its grip on Augsburg, his work came increasingly from the Catholic bastion of Ingolstadt, and in 1539 he moved there permanently.[62]

The discovery of B has made it clear that C, Weißenhorn's Augsburg edition of 1529, is not the true second edition of the *Confabulationes* but a (probably unauthorized) reprint of B, or possibly of a now lost post-1526 reprint. This of course means that it cannot now be treated as a primary textual witness. However, C still has its editorial uses. Collation shows that it is by no means a slavish copy of B, but the result of a generally attentive critical reading, which manages to correct several mistakes in that edition. Given that B introduces its own errors, that there is no further known edition of the *Confabulationes* overseen by Schotten, and that C is the first surviving edition after B, Weißenhorn is extremely helpful in drawing the modern editor's attention to textual problems in B, and in helping to resolve difficult cases. For this reason the critical apparatus, though it does not include all the variants of C, notes some which shed light on textual problems.

The best example of Weißenhorn's careful reading of B is in colloquy 101, where Iulius and Morus are disagreeing about the relative merit of knowledge and virtue:

> IVLIVS. Pluris tamen constat scientia quam uirtus.
> MORVS. Nonnunquam scientia facilius adipiscitur, sed sine moribus probis scientia nihil habet laudis.
> IVLIVS. Nescius sum istius. (ll. 8–11: C, sig. F3^{r})

---

[62] Benzing, *Die Buchdrucker des 16. und 17. Jahrhunderts*, pp. 17–18; Künast, *'Getruckt zu Augspurg'*, esp. pp. 81–82; *VD 16*, III. Abteilung (= vol. XXV), pp. 27–28 (Augsburg, 1528–40); pp. 141–42 (Ingolstadt, 1539–50); pp. 142–44 (Weißenhorn's descendants in Ingolstadt).

This is Weißenhorn's version. In A and B, however, the lines are divided thus:

> IVLIVS. Pluris tamen constat scientia quam uirtus.
> MORVS. Nonnunquam scientia facilius adipiscitur.
> IVLIVS. Sed sine moribus probis scientia nihil habet laudis.
> MORVS. Nescius sum istius.
> (A, sig. G3[r], ll. 12–16; B, sig. F5[v], l. 30–sig. F6[r], l. 2)

Thereafter, the speakers are reversed by comparison with C. Though this is the version in the edition revised by Schotten, it cannot be correct. At the start of the dialogue, Morus is the militant spokesman for virtue and 'ingenui mores', Iulius the boy who thinks them unimportant: this pattern is firmly established in ll. 3–8. The sudden role-reversal in A and B is a serious internal inconsistency, and it is a testimony to Weißenhorn's generally careful and critical use of B that he spotted and corrected it. There are numerous other less dramatic examples.

Weißenhorn was not infallible, however, and managed to introduce his own mistakes, though their number is small. Only one suggests an Augsburg printer struggling with Cologne material: in colloquy 56, the distinctively Cologne bishop's name 'Evergislus', unknown in Augsburg, becomes 'Evergissus'.

What is clear, however, is that Weißenhorn did not consult Ruff's edition A, or the putative genuine princeps. In the three cases discussed above where B mistakenly leaves out entire lines in A (colloquies 14, 48 and 123), C follows B. Had the C compositor seen the self-evidently correct A readings in these cases he would certainly have reproduced them.

The score of C readings which differ from B but are the same as A are cases where the C editor has seen the B readings as mistaken or substandard, and substituted others which happen to be those of A. Most are overt errors, such as B's incorrect preposition in 'auscultantis in eos' (colloquy 20, l. 1) corrected to 'auscultantis eos'; or 'si licet' (colloquy 62, l. 4) corrected to 'si liceret'; in these and many other cases the A reading is simply the obviously right version. Others are words wrong in context, such as B's 'Fuge, aut te tactu petam' (colloquy 46, l. 32) corrected to '[...] te iactu petam', and stylistic improvements such as 'Praedico, mi conuiuae' (B, colloquy 78, l. 24) altered in C to 'Praedico uobis, mi conuiuae'; both of these are also the A readings. The cases where C agrees with A have been noted in the apparatus.

Where A differs from B, but where B is not clearly wrong, however, C follows B, showing itself unaware of variants in A, some of which are superior. A good example is in colloquy 32: Paulus's teacher singles out some boys for harsh punishment; Thomas suggests that he does this to boys he particularly likes. B reads 'Quos seuius tractat, illos prae aliis diligit.' (l. 29; sig. B8r). C (sig. B6v) follows B, presumably understanding 'seuius' as 'saeuius'. However in B, simple 'e' for 'ae', though not unknown, is unusual: normally 'ae' or 'ę' ('e caudata') are used. The A reading, 'Quos seuerius tractat' (sig. C1v), is highly suggestive: B's 'seuius' could have been a wrongly copied 'seuerius', which indeed is arguably the more appropriate word in this context.

The bare dozen cases where the C reading differs from both A and B are nearly all ones where C corrects obvious mistakes in B which are also made in A. Most are morphological, like 'conferretur' (A and B, colloquy 40, l. 24) corrected to 'conferetur', or 'inuiset' (A and B, colloquy 39, l. 31) corrected to 'inuisat'. A very few are typos, like 'onere' (A and B, colloquy 74, l. 33) corrected to 'onera'. Only rarely does C venture to improve Schotten's Latinity. The phrase 'bibliothecae litteratae' (A and B, colloquy 51, l. 37) becomes 'bibliothecae litterariae'; a clear improvement, since 'litteratus' means 'educated, cultured', and applies to persons, not institutions. 'Praeceptor [...] instruit' (A and B, colloquy 103, l. 13) is changed to

'Praeceptor [...] instituit', again a slightly better choice of word.[63] All these cases, too, are noted in the apparatus.

One day, perhaps, further bibliographical finds will shed more light on the earliest editions of the *Confabulationes.* In our present state of knowledge the facts noted here, and the hypothesis concerning the true princeps of the work, are as far as one can go.

63 *OLD*, 'instruo', 8; 'instituo', 6.

II. *Confabulationes*: the text edition

IIa. Editorial principles and conventions

What follows is a critical edition of edition B (Cologne: Peter Quentel, 1526). This is the first edition of the *Confabulationes* to contain the thirty *conuiuia* added to the first edition, and so to represent the complete form in which the work was reprinted throughout the sixteenth century. It is also both the first and last edition definitely supervised by Schotten.

The critical apparatus records all variants of edition A (Augsburg: S. Ruff, 1525), the first known edition of the *Confabulationes*, though probably not the actual princeps. It also records those variants of edition C (Augsburg: A. Weißenhorn, 1529) which are of editorial interest: see the detailed discussion in Section Ic. Since C is not a primary textual witness, however, not all its readings are listed.

The text of B has been corrected in two cases: where B omits or wrongly arranges material; and where a B reading is clearly wrong. In the first case, full details are noted in the apparatus, and there is full discussion in the notes and/or in Section Ic. Instances where B readings are wrong are not, however, always self-evident. The *Confabulationes* are an important historical document, not least a document of the development of humanist Latin. Some of Schotten's usages which would have appalled a nineteenth-century schoolmaster are by no means uncommon amongst humanists of the early sixteenth century (see Macardle, *Confabulations*, Chapter 4). In general I have taken as tolerant a view as possible of 'correctness'.

Obvious typographical errors have been silently corrected; but if they allow confusion with other forms or words, they have been corrected and noted in the apparatus. Morphological and syntactical forms which are indisputably wrong (some may be typographical mistakes) have also been corrected and noted. However, vocabulary and usages which reflect Medieval rather than Classical Latin, or which seem to be part of Schotten's own (sometimes questionable) Latin idiolect, have been allowed to stand, but are discussed in the notes. The boundaries between these situations are not always easy to decide; but in all these cases the apparatus allows the reconstruction of the actual B reading, and the notes discuss unconventional lexis and usage, so readers are always in a position to reach their own conclusions. Readings in A are sometimes arguably better than those of B, but they have not been substituted for those of B in the main text unless those of B are intrinsically wrong.

Orthography follows modern standards for Classical Latin, as used in the *Oxford Latin Dictionary* and most modern editions of classical texts: that of A, B and C is close to this standard. The apparatus includes a small number of variants which are typical of Medieval Latin orthography, or in some other way significant. Abbreviations have been silently resolved. The long *ſ* is represented by *s*, and the character *ß* by *ss*.

The punctuation of B has been silently conformed to modern standards, to which it is in any case close. In a very few places where punctuation affects the meaning of the text, variants have been included in the apparatus.

The text, which is set continuously in A, B and C (and in all the sixteenth-century printings of the *Confabulationes*), has been laid out in lines, following modern conventions for printing plays and dialogues. The names of speakers, often heavily abbreviated in the original, are given in full. The numbering of the colloquies, and the line-numbering, are editorial. The foliation of B is indicated in square brackets in the text.

A note on the translation

The facing English translation is not a word-for-word version of the original, and cannot be used as a consistently reliable crib to the Latin. Readers for whom the Latin poses no problems will not need the English; and those who cannot cope with the Latin easily, or perhaps at all, need above all to be given some idea in English of the stylistic verve of Schotten's Latin, which was what made these dialogues so refreshingly distinctive and attractive in the first place. This I have tried to do, as far as is practicable, and as far as my own skill permits. This has been harder to achieve in the *conuiuia*, where Schotten cultivates a longer-winded and more ponderous style. In cases where Latin idiomatic phrases have had to be rendered in a quite different way in English, the notes will usually indicate the literal meaning of the Latin.

DIFFICILE ESSE LATINVM DI
scere sermonē,& unde dicat̄ sermo latinus.
¶Albertus, & Antonius.

Vid tu hic terrarū geris? AN. Hic
lris incumbo. AL. Qñ uenisti huc?
AN. Añ paucos dies AL. Quis te
cū? AN. Pr̄ meus AL. Penit ipse
deinde solus in patriā. AN. Nō, sed
habuit comitē unū aut alterū. AL.
Qui isti fuerunt? AN. Nr̄i cōciues fuerūt. AL. Mili
tas in schola sermonis latini uł germanici? AN. La
tinę linguę. AL D. Difficile est latinum addiscere
sermonem. AN. Cōsentio. AL. nisi qs sp loquat̄ la
tine ęgre addiscet. AN. nō dissentio. AL. Sed scis,
ne, quare dicat̄ lingua latina? AN. Credo qđ ab Ita
lia quae quondā latiū est dicta. AL. Venit tūc ab Ita
lia ligua latina ad nos Germanos? AN. Ita, ignoras
illud? AL. Optime credo, qa sermo Italorū est medi
us latinus. AN. nō aberras. AL. Sed cur Italia olim
dicta ē latiū? AN. Quia poetę scribūt dū Saturnus
a suo filio Ioue e cœlo esset expulsus, tū latuit in Ita
lia inde a latendo dr̄ latiū. Et a latio latinus, a um.
AL. Vbi in Italia latina lingua ē orta? AN. Dicunt
in urbe Romana quae Italiae caput est.

¶De salutatione Matutina
Vilhelmus & Volfgangus.

BOnū mane. VOL. Semp sane. VIL. Sic
ipse nō respōderē. VOL. Cur nō? VIL.
Quia barbarum est & doctis displicet.
VOL. Tamē multos sacerdotes ita fa
ri audiui, uerū dic tu, si nosti elegantius
VIL. Et tibi quoqȝ dicere. VOL. Et ita posthac re
sponsum salutāti dabo. VIL. Bonus uł bona dies.

First page of the *Confabulationes* (Cologne: Quentel, 1526), sig. A2v.

HERMANNUS SCHOTTENNIUS HESSUS

CONFABULATIONES TIRONUM LITTERARIORUM

(COLOGNE, 1525)

Colloquies

[A1v]

HERMANNVS SCHOTTENNIVS HESSVS candido lectori

Cum nuper hasce conderem nugas pueriles, candide lector, in eorum usum qui sub mea agunt ferula, illico exoriebantur nonnulli (nescio an amore uel odio ducti) qui dicerent se satis admirari non posse, edendi colloquia prouinciam me uelle subire post Erasmum illum Germaniae decus et litterarum uerarum uindicem nostra aetate, cuius colloquia omnium iuuenum palatis satisfacerent. Horum stomacho paucis respondere lubet. Admiror ego rursus ipsos qui credant nihil me audere debere in confabulationibus nouis componendis, ob Erasmi auctoritatem. Nonne in litterariorum munere multos in eandem harenam descendisse legimus, neque absterritos ob id, quod alii albis (ut aiunt) equis precesserint? Nam ut inquit Cicero in Oratore ad Brutum, quod in poetis Graecis non soli Homero est locus, aut Artilocho, aut Sophocli, aut Pindaro, sed horum uel secundis uel etiam infra secundos. Neque uero in philosophia Aristotelem a scribendo deterruit amplitudo Platonis. Nec ipse Aristoteles admirabili scientia et copia ceterorum studia restinxit. Demosthenes quamuis Graecorum oratorum excellentior esset, multi tamen alii eo tempore uiguerunt, neque postea defecerunt. Quare et ego semipaganus, ac in litteris camelus saltans, ausus sum post Erasmum colloquia tironum litterariorum conscribere, quae si non optima reddidi, contentus saltem ipsa uel optimis proxima censeri. Solum enim haec in meorum discipulorum usum composui, et illorum, quorum ingenia humi repunt, ac Latinum sermonem nondum neque a limine salutarunt, neque primoribus labiis attigerunt.

[A2r]

HERMANNVS SCHOTTENNIVS HESSVS

to the esteemed reader

Dear reader, when I recently composed these boyish trifles for the use of those who are my pupils, there suddenly appeared some people (whether guided by love or hate, I am not sure) who said that they were really amazed that I had wanted to take on the task of writing colloquies after Erasmus, that glory of Germany and champion of true literature in our age, whose colloquies satisfied the tastes of all boys. I would like to make a brief reply to their expression of annoyance. I in my turn am amazed at such people as think that I ought not to dare to compose new colloquies in view of the authoritative stature of Erasmus. For in the literary sphere have we not read that many have entered the fray, undeterred by the fact that others have gone before them, 'riding on white horses', as the saying goes? For as Cicero says in the *Orator*, amongst the Greek poets there is room not only for Homer, or Artilochus, or Sophocles, or Pindar, but for those of the second rank, or even below. In philosophy, Aristotle was not deterred from writing by the greatness of Plato, nor did Aristotle's amazing learning and gifts of expression stifle the activity of others. Though Demosthenes was the leading Greek orator, many others flourished at the same time; nor was there any lack of them afterwards. And so I, an unworthy, clumsy practitioner in the field of literature, have dared to write colloquies for schoolboys after Erasmus. If I have not produced the very best, I am happy if they are judged to be close to the best. For I have composed them solely for my pupils' use, and for those who are intellectually in their infancy, and who have not yet made a beginning on Latin, or gained the slightest acquaintance with it.

ET GENERE ET MORIBVS ADOLESCENTI INGENVO

Gisberto Sterckenberg Hermannus Schottennius Hessus S.P.D.

Platonem quondam discipuli rogitarunt, ut ea quae ipsis lectionibus uariis tradidisset in unum redigeret uolumen, quorum precibus philosophiae praeceptor ille diuinus facile consensit, conscribens libros complures in philosophiae consecutionem. Huius ego excitatus exemplo, ut fidus aestimarer ingeniorum saginator, Latinas locutiones, quas hactenus satis abunde tibi tuisque commilitonibus litterariis dictaui, in unum hunc confabulationum libellum congessi, quo tuam Mineruam Latine loquendi copia irrigarem, ut quandoque elimatior reddita, patris tui, uiri prudentissimi, mihi amicissimi, expectationi de te tuisque aliis duobus fratribus Ioanne et Matthia, respondeat. A cuius uestigiis te degenerare turpissimum certe esset, huius ut uotis auscultes (feruide scilicet amplectendo litteras) aequissimum erit, tibique multo magis quam ipsi conducet. Et ut facilius emergas tu, ceterique tui fratres et sorores, neque unquam egestate obruamini, ipse pater uester uirtutum uerum domicilium, huius inclytae urbis Agrippinae de albo senatorum prudentia nulli secundus, omni conatu, omne mouendo saxum, etiam et caelibem ducendo uitam, id unicum agit, quo te tuosque fratres et sorores ditet, locupletet, uobis ut congerat reliquae uitae commeatum. Suis igitur Gisberte, discipule dilectissime, expectationibus rogo respondeas, tunc autem respondebis, si scientia et uirtute te pulchre ornaueris.

Vale, Gisberte carissime, ac cum tuis commilitonibus, aliis mihi discipulis, strenue studeas. Animus mihi est in litteratos uos euehere uiros, uobis animus sit uelle proficere. Faxit Deus ut utrumque utrique bene succedat.

Iterum uale.

Coloniae ex aedibus meis, 19. Kalendas Martias, Anno M.D.XXV.

---

13 mihi] mihique A | 19 neque unquam] neque ut unquam A | 19–20 pater uester] pater ille uester A | 33 19.] decimoquinto A

TO GISBERT STARCKENBERG, A BOY DISTINGUISHED BY BIRTH AND BY BEHAVIOUR,

Hermannus Schottennius Hessus sends his fondest greetings.

Plato's pupils once asked him to collect in a single volume everything which he had handed on to them in a number of lectures. The divine teacher of philosophy was pleased to consent to their requests, and wrote many books investigating philosophy. I was stimulated by his example, and wanted to be thought of as a faithful nourisher of intellects; so I have taken the Latin dialogues which up till now I have written in considerable quantity for you and your classmates, and combined them into this single book of colloquies. My purpose is to give you a command of speaking in Latin, nourishing your intellect so that eventually, when it has been given a greater polish, it will fulfil the expectations which your father, a most provident man, and a great friend of mine, has of you and your two brothers, Iohannes and Matthias. It would indeed be shameful for you to depart from his footsteps, so it will be very fitting for you to listen to his wishes (that is, by eagerly embracing the study of letters), and it will be much more to your advantage than to his. And so that you, and the rest of your brothers and sisters, should advance in life more easily, and never be overtaken by poverty, your father, that true dwelling of virtues, a councillor of this renowned city of Cologne second to none in providence, has made it his sole aim to enrich you and your brothers and sisters, so as to build up financial provision for you for the rest of your lives. He has spurned no effort to do this, left no stone unturned, even to the extent of living without a wife. And so Gisbert, my dearest pupil, I ask you to fulfil his expectations; and this you will do if you equip yourself thoroughly with knowledge and virtue.

Farewell, my dearest Gisbert: study hard along with your classmates, my other pupils. My intention is to turn you into learned men; let your intention be to try to make progress. May God grant that each of us is successful in our aim.

Farewell once again.
Cologne, from my house, 11 February 1525.

[A2v]

1. DIFFICILE ESSE LATINVM DISCERE SERMONEM, ET VNDE DICATVR SERMO LATINVS

Albertus et Antonius

ALBERTVS. Quid tu hic terrarum geris?
ANTONIVS. Hic litteris incumbo.
ALBERTVS. Quando uenisti huc?
ANTONIVS. Ante paucos dies.
ALBERTVS. Quis tecum?
ANTONIVS. Pater meus.
ALBERTVS. Rediit ipse deinde solus in patriam?
ANTONIVS. Non, sed habuit comitem unum aut alterum.
ALBERTVS. Qui isti fuerunt?
ANTONIVS. Nostri conciues fuerunt.
ALBERTVS. Militas in schola sermonis Latini uel Germanici?
ANTONIVS. Latinae linguae.
ALBERTVS. Difficile est Latinum addiscere sermonem.
ANTONIVS. Consentio.
ALBERTVS. Nisi quis semper loquatur Latine, aegre addiscet.
ANTONIVS. Non dissentio.
ALBERTVS. Sed scisne quare dicatur lingua Latina?
ANTONIVS. Credo quod ab Italia, quae quondam Latium est dicta.
ALBERTVS. Venit tunc ab Italia lingua Latina ad nos Germanos?
ANTONIVS. Ita, ignoras illud?
ALBERTVS. Optime credo, quia sermo Italorum est medius Latinus.
ANTONIVS. Non aberras.
ALBERTVS. Sed cur Italia olim dicta est Latium?
ANTONIVS. Quia poetae scribunt, dum Saturnus a suo filio Ioue e caelo esset expulsus, tum latuit in Italia; inde a latendo dicitur Latium, et a Latio Latinus, -a, -um.
ALBERTVS. Vbi in Italia Latina lingua est orta?
ANTONIVS. Dicunt in urbe Romana, quae Italiae caput est.

32–34 dicitur Latium … caput est.] dicitur Latium. A

1. LEARNING LATIN IS HARD; AND WHY THE LANGUAGE IS CALLED LATIN

Albertus and Antonius

ALBERTUS. What are you doing in this part of the world?
ANTONIUS. I'm applying myself to learning here.
ALBERTUS. When did you come here?
ANTONIUS. A few days ago.
ALBERTUS. Who came with you?
ANTONIUS. My father.
ALBERTUS. And then did he go back to your own region alone?
ANTONIUS. No, he had one or two companions.
ALBERTUS. Who were they?
ANTONIUS. Other people from our town.
ALBERTUS. Are you at a Latin or a German school?
ANTONIUS. A Latin one.
ALBERTUS. Latin is hard to learn.
ANTONIUS. I agree.
ALBERTUS. You'll hardly learn Latin unless you speak it all the time.
ANTONIUS. I can't disagree.
ALBERTUS. But do you know why the language is called Latin?
ANTONIUS. From Italy, I believe, which used to be called Latium.
ALBERTUS. And then did Latin come from Italy to us Germans?
ANTONIUS. Yes, don't you know that?
ALBERTUS. I can well believe it, because Italian is half Latin.
ANTONIUS. You're not wrong.
ALBERTUS. But why was Italy called Latium in the olden days?
ANTONIUS. Because the poets write that when Saturn was thrown out of heaven by his son Jupiter, he hid in Italy; then from the Latin word for 'hide', 'latere', it's called Latium; and that gives the adjective 'Latinus, -a, -um'.
ALBERTUS. Where in Italy did the Latin language begin?
ANTONIUS. In the city of Rome, they say, the capital of Italy.

2. DE SALVTATIONE MATVTINA

Vilhelmus et Volfgangus

VILHELMVS. Bonum mane.
VOLFGANGVS. Semper sane.
VILHELMVS. Sic ipse non responderem.
VOLFGANGVS. Cur non?
VILHELMVS. Quia barbarum est, et doctis displicet.
VOLFGANGVS. Tamen multos sacerdotes ita fari audiui; uerum dic tu, si nosti elegantius.
VILHELMVS. Et tibi quoque dicerem.
VOLFGANGVS. Et ita posthac responsum salutanti dabo.
VILHELMVS. Bonus uel bona dies. [A3r]
VOLFGANGVS. Et tibi.
VILHELMVS. Precor tibi hunc diem candidum.
VOLFGANGVS. Tibi quoque et talem rursus precor.
VILHELMVS. Felix sit tibi huius diei exordium.
VOLFGANGVS. Et tibi quoque.
VILHELMVS. Opto tibi diem felicem.
VOLFGANGVS. Eiusmodi et tibi opto uicissim.
VILHELMVS. Candidus sit tibi hic dies.
VOLFGANGVS. Tibi etiam.
VILHELMVS. Precor ut hoc die tibi prospere succedant omnia.
VOLFGANGVS. Rursus et tibi fiat istud.
VILHELMVS. Opto ut hodie nihil tibi accidat mali.
VOLFGANGVS. Non aliud et ego opto tibi.
VILHELMVS. Auspicatum tibi diem precor.
VOLFGANGVS. Non inauspicatum tibi per uices precor.
VILHELMVS. Faxit Deus ut hic dies tibi candidus illuxerit.
VOLFGANGVS. Idem faciat ut talis sit tibi.
VILHELMVS. Felici omine hic dies te afficiat.
VOLFGANGVS. Te pariter.
VILHELMVS. Fortunatus praesens sit tibi dies.
VOLFGANGVS. Sit tibi non infortunatus.

---

23 istud] illud A | 33 Sit tibi] Sit et tibi A

2. SAYING GOOD MORNING

Vilhelmus and Volfgangus

VILHELMUS. Bonum mane.
VOLFGANGUS. Semper sane.
VILHELMUS. I wouldn't reply like that.
VOLFGANGUS. Why not?
VILHELMUS. Because it's barbarous and the educated disapprove of it.
VOLFGANGUS. And yet I've heard a lot of priests say that. But you tell me if you know something more elegant.
VILHELMUS. And I could say it to you, too.
VOLFGANGUS. And then afterwards I'll give the reply to your greeting.
VILHELMUS. Good day.
VOLFGANGUS. Good day to you.
VILHELMUS. I wish you a prosperous day today.
VOLFGANGUS. And I wish you the same.
VILHELMUS. May this day begin well for you.
VOLFGANGUS. And for you.
VILHELMUS. I wish you a fortunate day.
VOLFGANGUS. I wish you the same in return.
VILHELMUS. May this day be prosperous for you.
VOLFGANGUS. And for you.
VILHELMUS. I wish that today everything may turn out well for you.
VOLFGANGUS. And may the same happen to you.
VILHELMUS. I wish that no ill may befall you today.
VOLFGANGUS. And I wish you the very same.
VILHELMUS. I wish you an auspicious day.
VOLFGANGUS. And in return I wish you the same.
VILHELMUS. May God grant that this day which dawns on you is a prosperous one.
VOLFGANGUS. And may he grant that it is the same for you.
VILHELMUS. May this day affect you favourably.
VOLFGANGUS. And you too.
VILHELMUS. May this day be a lucky one for you.
VOLFGANGUS. And may it not be an unlucky one for you.

3. DE SALVTATIONE POMERIDIANA

Petrus et Cornelius

PETRVS. Salue.
CORNELIVS. Salue et tu.
PETRVS. Sis saluus.
CORNELIVS. Saluus sis tu quoque.
PETRVS. Sis salutatus.
CORNELIVS. Tu pariter.
PETRVS. Salutem tibi precor.
CORNELIVS. Eandem et tibi opto.
PETRVS. Salute te impertior.
CORNELIVS. Ego quoque te.
PETRVS. Salus sit tibi.
CORNELIVS. Et tibi non desit.
PETRVS. Salutem □pt out habeas.
CORNELIVS. Eam precor habeas et tu.
PETRVS. Adsit tibi salus.
CORNELIVS. Et tibi absit minime.
PETRVS. Iubeo te saluere.
CORNELIVS. Te quoque ego.
PETRVS. Iubeo ut saluus sis.
CORNELIVS. Talem iubeo et ego te esse.
PETRVS. Iubeo te saluti frui.
CORNELIVS. Et ea te potiri opto.
PETRVS. Salutifera sit tibi fortuna.
CORNELIVS. Et talis tibi adsit.
PETRVS. Saluam et incolumem uitam habeas.
CORNELIVS. Talem habeas et tu.
PETRVS. Salute te afficio.
CORNELIVS. Ego uicissim et te.
PETRVS. Adeo te salute.
CORNELIVS. Id facio et ego.
PETRVS. Salute te adorior.
CORNELIVS. Non aliter [A3v] et ego te.
PETRVS. Saluum te esse toto cupio animo.
CORNELIVS. Et ego infelicem te non esse desidero.
PETRVS. Felicitatis particeps sis anhelo.
CORNELIVS. Totus et tu sis felix.

3. THE AFTERNOON GREETING

Petrus and Cornelius

PETRUS. Hallo.
CORNELIUS. Hallo to you.
PETRUS. Good day.
CORNELIUS. Good day to you.
PETRUS. I greet you.
CORNELIUS. And I greet you.
PETRUS. I give you my greetings.
CORNELIUS. I do the same to you.
PETRUS. I offer you my greetings.
CORNELIUS. And I offer you mine.
PETRUS. Well-being to you!
CORNELIUS. And may you not lack it.
PETRUS. I wish that you may enjoy well-being.
CORNELIUS. And I pray that you may, too.
PETRUS. May well-being be yours.
CORNELIUS. And may you not lack it.
PETRUS. I wish you well.
CORNELIUS. And I wish the same to you.
PETRUS. I desire your well-being.
CORNELIUS. And I desire yours.
PETRUS. I wish you may enjoy well-being.
CORNELIUS. And I wish you do too.
PETRUS. May fortune be propitious for you.
CORNELIUS. And for you too.
PETRUS. I wish you a safe, secure life.
CORNELIUS. May you have the same.
PETRUS. I give you my best wishes.
CORNELIUS. I give them back to you.
PETRUS. Greetings I offer to you.
CORNELIUS. And I to you.
PETRUS. I wish you well.
CORNELIUS. And I do not wish you otherwise.
PETRUS. I wish with all my heart that you are well.
CORNELIUS. And I wish that you are not unhappy.
PETRUS. I wish you may enjoy happiness.
CORNELIUS. May you be entirely happy.

PETRVS. Secunda tibi sint omnia.
CORNELIVS. Tibi etiam secunde adueniant singula et ex sententia.

11 impertior] impartior A

4. DE SALVTATIONE VESPERTINA

Iohannes et Gisbertus

IOHANNES. Bonus uesper.
GISBERTVS. Et tibi.
IOHANNES. Bonum serum.
GISBERTVS. Sic ego non loquerer.
IOHANNES. Quare?
GISBERTVS. Quia serum significat tarde et non tempus uespertinum.
IOHANNES. Tamen Capnion in comoedia prima dicit, 'Vxor, bonum serum'.
GISBERTVS. Id ioco dicitur, et qui loquitur est homo uillanus imperitus.
IOHANNES. Estne dicendum 'Bonum uesper'?
GISBERTVS. Non, sed 'bonus'.
IOHANNES. Tamen sic olim loquebantur, et adhuc quidam senes.
GISBERTVS. Quid tum, nunc non licet apud doctos.
IOHANNES. Precor tibi felix tempus uespertinum.
GISBERTVS. Idem et tibi opto.
IOHANNES. Felicem noctem tibi opto.
GISBERTVS. Talem et tibi precor.
IOHANNES. Auspicata sit tibi nox.
GISBERTVS. Non alia sit et tibi.
IOHANNES. Faustam habeas noctem.
GISBERTVS. Tu quoque.
IOHANNES. Fortunatum tibi sit tempus nocturnum.
GISBERTVS. Et tibi non infortunatum.
IOHANNES. Candidam tibi opto noctem.
GISBERTVS. Et ego non sinistram tibi precor.
IOHANNES. Prospera sit tibi nox imminens.
GISBERTVS. Tibi etiam non infelix.

PETRUS. May everything be favourable for you.
CORNELIUS. And may everything happen for you favourably and as you would wish.

4. THE EVENING GREETING

Iohannes and Gisbertus

IOHANNES. Good evening
GISBERTUS. Good evening to you.
IOHANNES. Bonum serum.
GISBERTUS. I wouldn't talk like that.
IOHANNES. Why not?
GISBERTUS. Because 'serum' means 'late', not 'evening time'.
IOHANNES. And yet in his first comedy Reuchlin says, 'Wife, bonum serum'.
GISBERTUS. That's said as a joke, and the man who says it is an ignorant peasant.
IOHANNES. Should you say 'Bonum uesper'?
GISBERTUS. No, 'Bon*us* uesper'.
IOHANNES. And yet people talked like that in former times, and some old men still do.
GISBERTUS. So what? The learned don't allow it now.
IOHANNES. I wish you a fortunate evening-time.
GISBERTUS. And I wish you the same.
IOHANNES. I wish you a fortunate night.
GISBERTUS. And I wish you the same.
IOHANNES. May the night be auspicious for you.
GISBERTUS. And may it be the same for you.
IOHANNES. May you have a fortunate night.
GISBERTUS. And you too.
IOHANNES. May the night-time be attended by good fortune for you.
GISBERTUS. And may it not be attended by bad fortune for you.
IOHANNES. I wish you a prosperous night.
GISBERTUS. And may yours not be unfavourable.
IOHANNES. May the approaching night be propitious for you.
GISBERTUS. And may it not be unpropitious for you.

IOHANNES. Vespertinum tibi commodet tempus.
GISBERTVS. Et tibi non incommodet.

33 commodet] commodat A

5. DE VERBIS DVM CVBITVM ITVR

Valterus et Adrianus

VALTERVS. Quota est hora?
ADRIANVS. Octaua.
VALTERVS. Quotam horam sonuit?
ADRIANVS. Octauam.
VALTERVS. Quota est audita hora?
ADRIANVS. Octaua, et nona im- [A4r] minet.
VALTERVS. Id non credo.
ADRIANVS. Verum est per Herculem.
VALTERVS. Tunc eundi cubitum tempus est.
ADRIANVS. Ego nondum dormiturio.
VALTERVS. Me autem somnus oppido urget.
ADRIANVS. Ipse adhuc horam aut alteram uigilarem.
VALTERVS. Vigila tu quoad placuerit, ego cubitum ibo.
ADRIANVS. Abi tu Endymion.
VALTERVS. Ita me appellas, sed id nominis rectius tibi conuenit.
ADRIANVS. Res ipsa nunc loquitur, quis maior sit Endymion et Epimenides.
VALTERVS. Tu alias semper prius me te cubitum confers.
ADRIANVS. Istud posthac non fiet.
VALTERVS. O insigne mendacium.
ADRIANVS. Voco te in pignus quodcunque.
VALTERVS. Nihil habeo quod tecum deponam.
ADRIANVS. Nunc si unquam prior te lectum petiero, solidum pendam.
VALTERVS. Qualem solidum? An talem, qualem praeceptor noster praebet ferula?
ADRIANVS. Non, sed pecuniae solidum.

IOHANNES. May the evening-time be favourable for you.
GISBERTUS. May it not be unfavourable for you.

5. CONVERSATON WHEN GOING TO BED

Valterus and Adrianus

VALTERUS. What time is it?
ADRIANUS. Eight.
VALTERUS. What hour has the clock struck?
ADRIANUS. Eight.
VALTERUS. What time have we heard striking?
ADRIANUS. Eight, and nine's approaching.
VALTERUS. I don't believe it.
ADRIANUS. It's true, I swear.
VALTERUS. Then it's time to go to bed.
ADRIANUS. I'm not sleepy yet.
VALTERUS. But sleep's weighing really heavily on me.
ADRIANUS. I'm going to stay up another hour or two.
VALTERUS. Stay up as long as you like, I'm going to bed.
ADRIANUS. Off you go, sleepy-head.
VALTERUS. You call me that, but the name suits you better.
ADRIANUS. The facts speak for themselves as to who's the greater sleepy-head and lazy-bones.
VALTERUS. Previously you've always gone off to bed before me.
ADRIANUS. That won't happen in future.
VALTERUS. What a blatant lie!
ADRIANUS. I'll bet you something.
VALTERUS. I've got nothing that I could pledge you.
ADRIANUS. If I ever go to bed before you again, I'll pay a Schilling.
VALTERUS. What kind of Schilling? Do you mean the kind our schoolmaster gives us with his stick?
ADRIANUS. No, a Schilling coin.

VALTERVS. Age, placet, memor ero.
ADRIANVS. Istud facias.

6. DE CVBITV RESVRGENDO

Volfgangus et Georgius

VOLFGANGVS. Heus tu, expergiscere
GEORGIVS. Hui, sine ut dormiam.
VOLFGANGVS. Non sinam te dormire longius.
GEORGIVS. Quare?
VOLFGANGVS. Quia surgendi tempus est.
GEORGIVS. Nondum tamen diluxit.
VOLFGANGVS. Lux non est amplius expectanda.
GEORGIVS. Tamen ante dies octo hora sexta in luce sonuit.
VOLFGANGVS. Credo, sed interim dies diminutus est.
GEORGIVS. Quomodo tam cito?
VOLFGANGVS. Nunc pauca loquere et surge.
GEORGIVS. Surge tu prior.
VOLFGANGVS. Faciam, sed postea te non expectabo.
GEORGIVS. Fac ut lubet, et mihi ad scholam nota est uia.
VOLFGANGVS. Verum ego lucer- [A4v] nam mecum feram, tum tibi in tenebris est eundum.
GEORGIVS. Id parum refert, Lyncei mihi sunt oculi.
VOLFGANGVS. Nunc surge ut una eamus.
GEORGIVS. Ah, si liceret mihi adhuc momentum stertere!
VOLFGANGVS. Tandem tamen oporteret te calidum deserere nidum.
GEORGIVS. Post semihorulam ac lubens surgerem.
VOLFGANGVS. Surge nunc et uesperi eo citius lectum repetas.
GEORGIVS. Aestimas id consultum probe?
VOLFGANGVS. Ita mea fert opinio.
GEORGIVS. Parebo tibi ac surgam.

VALTERUS. Right, I agree. I'll remember that.
ADRIANUS. Make sure you do.

6. GETTING OUT OF BED

Volfgangus and Georgius

VOLFGANGUS. Hey you, get up!
GEORGIUS. Ow! Let me sleep.
VOLFGANGUS. I'll not let you sleep any longer.
GEORGIUS. Why not?
VOLFGANGUS. Because it's time to get up.
GEORGIUS. But it's not light yet.
VOLFGANGUS. We won't have to wait much longer for the light.
GEORGIUS. Yet a week ago it was light when six o'clock rang.
VOLFGANGUS. I believe you, but the days have got shorter since then.
GEORGIUS. How has that happened so quickly?
VOLFGANGUS. Now spare the talk and get up.
GEORGIUS. You get up first.
VOLFGANGUS. I will, but I won't wait for you afterwards.
GEORGIUS. Do what you like, I know the way to school too.
VOLFGANGUS. Well, I'm going to take my lantern with me, then you'll have to walk in the dark.
GEORGIUS. That doesn't matter, I've got eyes as sharp as Lynceus.
VOLFGANGUS. Just get up and we'll go together.
GEORGIUS. Oh, If I could just go on dozing for a while!
VOLFGANGUS. But you'll eventually have to get out of your warm nest.
GEORGIUS. Half an hour and I'll gladly get up.
VOLFGANGUS. Get up now and you can go to bed that much sooner in the evening.
GEORGIUS. Do you think that's a good idea?
VOLFGANGUS. That's my opinion.
GEORGIUS. Then I'll do what you say and get up.

7. DE IENTACVLO SVMENDO

Hermannus et Laurentius

HERMANNVS. Quid sibi uult celer tuus gressus?
LAVRENTIVS. Quid loqueris?
HERMANNVS. Quaero quo tendas tam cito gradu.
LAVRENTIVS. Domum uersus.
HERMANNVS. Quid istuc est, quod te properare cogit?
LAVRENTIVS. Ientaculum nunc ibi sumitur, quod negligam si non mox affuero.
HERMANNVS. Non expectant te serui ientando?
LAVRENTIVS. Expectant quidem, sed patina exinanita.
HERMANNVS. Non tum coquinae ministra aliud tibi parat ientaculum?
LAVRENTIVS. Minime, sed citius fustem mihi offert tam sero uenienti.
HERMANNVS. Cogeris tunc esurire ad prandium usque?
LAVRENTIVS. Non prorsus.
HERMANNVS. Quid tum ientaris?
LAVRENTIVS. Panem, cui pro obsonio addo caseum.
HERMANNVS. Non iuuat te id ientaculi?
LAVRENTIVS. Non quantum panis iurulentus.
HERMANNVS. O tu delicate et miseriae expers!
LAVRENTIVS. Nescis fruendum esse fortuna dum praesto est.
HERMANNVS. Belle scio, sed delicata iuuentus omni aetati nocet.
LAVRENTIVS. Iuuentus mea etiam non adeo laute alitur.
HERMANNVS. Nunc sat est uerborum, tu abi, ne te morer.
LAVRENTIVS. Abeo, tu uale.
HERMANNVS. Sis mei memor dum ex uoto tibi succedit.
LAVRENTIVS. Non intermittam.

14 sero] sero A C; serus B

7. EATING BREAKFAST

Hermannus and Laurentius

HERMANNUS. What's the reason you're walking so quickly?
LAURENTIUS. What are you saying?
HERMANNUS. I'm asking where you're going at such a pace.
LAURENTIUS. Home.
HERMANNUS. What is it that's forcing you to hurry?
LAURENTIUS. They're eating breakfast there now, and I'll miss it if I don't arrive soon.
HERMANNUS. Don't the servants wait for you to come to breakfast?
LAURENTIUS. They wait all right, but the plate will be emptied.
HERMANNUS. Won't the cook make you another breakfast?
LAURENTIUS. No, she'd be quicker to give me a thump if I arrived so late.
HERMANNUS. So does that mean that you're forced to go without food till lunchtime?
LAURENTIUS. No, not at all.
HERMANNUS. So what do you have for breakfast, then?
LAURENTIUS. Bread, with cheese as an accompaniment.
HERMANNUS. Don't you like that for breakfast?
LAURENTIUS. Not as much as soup.
HERMANNUS. You pernickety lad! You've never known affliction.
LAURENTIUS. You don't know that fortune should be enjoyed when it's at hand.
HERMANNUS. I do indeed, but 'a pampered youth is harmful to every age.'
LAURENTIUS. My youth isn't being fed all that luxuriously.
HERMANNUS. Enough talk now, off you go, so as I don't hold you up.
LAURENTIUS. I'm off. Goodbye.
HERMANNUS. Remember me when things turn out as you wish.
LAURENTIUS. I won't fail.

8. DE PRANDIO

Theodericus et Baptista [A5r]

THEODERICVS. Quid ita maesto es uultu?
BAPTISTA. Miraris hoc?
THEODERICVS. Quidni mirarer? Laborasne morbo?
BAPTISTA. Ita, morbo stomachi, quia fortiter esurio.
THEODERICVS. Nondum es ientatus?
BAPTISTA. Essem ientatus, cum sit ieiunium?
THEODERICVS. Seruasne tu ieiunium?
BAPTISTA. Non obseruarem? Magis certe quam lubeat.
THEODERICVS. Sis bono animo, mox aderit prandii hora.
BAPTISTA. O utinam adesset, quam ego uellem!
THEODERICVS. Expecta, iam audies horam undecimam.
BAPTISTA. Si illam audirem, hunc roderem panem.
THEODERICVS. Prandebisne ad nudum panem?
BAPTISTA. Non, sed ipsum ederem quoad melius consequerer.
THEODERICVS. Quid obsonii domi uestrae paratum est in prandium?
BAPTISTA. Aestimo holus, oua et halec unum aut alterum.
THEODERICVS. Exsaturas te etiam isto cibo?
BAPTISTA. Vtique, holere uoragines uentris impleo.
THEODERICVS. Quot oua peredis?
BAPTISTA. Nunquam plura nisi duo.
THEODERICVS. Addis ouis etiam halec unum?
BAPTISTA. Addo, et quidem integrum si tostum est.
THEODERICVS. Quid te delectat halec erutum salsugine?
BAPTISTA. Ab isto nauseo.
THEODERICVS. Qui tum iuuat te halec elixum?
BAPTISTA. Vtcunque, praefero tamen tostum.

9. DE VICTV POMERIDIANO

Ludouicus et Iohannes

LVDOVICVS. Cur ita alte suspiria ducis?
IOHANNES. Pudet me dicere causam.
LVDOVICVS. Credo quod domum cogitas.

8. LUNCH

Theodericus and Baptista

THEODERICUS. Why such a sad face?
BAPTISTA. Are you surprised at that?
THEODERICUS. Of course I am. Is an illness troubling you?
BAPTISTA. Yes, an illness of the stomach – I'm really starving.
THEODERICUS. Haven't you had breakfast yet?
BAPTISTA. Is it likely that I would have, seeing it's a fast day?
THEODERICUS. Do you keep fasts?
BAPTISTA. I do indeed, more than I'd like.
THEODERICUS. Cheer up, it'll soon be time for lunch.
BAPTISTA. Oh, I really wish it was!
THEODERICUS. Wait, you'll hear eleven o'clock strike soon.
BAPTISTA. If it did, I'd eat this piece of bread.
THEODERICUS. Will you only have bread for lunch?
BAPTISTA. No, but I'd eat that until I got something better.
THEODERICUS. What food will have been cooked for lunch at your house?
BAPTISTA. I'd guess cabbage, eggs and a herring or two.
THEODERICUS. Do you fill yourself up with that food?
BAPTISTA. Yes, I do. I fill the hollows in my stomach with cabbage.
THEODERICUS. How many eggs do you eat?
BAPTISTA. Never more than two.
THEODERICUS. Do you have a herring with the eggs?
BAPTISTA. Yes, a whole one, even, if it's grilled.
THEODERICUS. How do you like pickled herring?
BAPTISTA. I really hate it.
THEODERICUS. And how do you like boiled herring?
BAPTISTA. Very much, but I prefer it grilled.

9. THE AFTERNOON MEAL

Ludovicus and Iohannes

LUDOVICUS. Why are you sighing so deeply?
IOHANNES. I'm ashamed to tell you the reason.
LUDOVICUS. I believe you're thinking of home.

IOHANNES. Paene rem acu tetigisti.
LVDOVICVS. Vrgerisne siti?
IOHANNES. Ita, sed et fame.
LVDOVICVS. Nondum forte prandisti?
IOHANNES. Prandi utique, sed modice.
LVDOVICVS. Fuit uobis prandium adeo exiguum?
IOHANNES. Fuit, quia fo- [A5v] ris prandebant parentes.
LVDOVICVS. Non sat habuistis panis et casei?
IOHANNES. Habuimus quidem, sed isto non capior cibo.
LVDOVICVS. Sumes iam domi cibum merendinarium?
IOHANNES. Sumam, Deo fauente.
LVDOVICVS. Erit lautior quam meridiei fuit obsonium?
IOHANNES. Ita spero, si mater domi fuerit.
LVDOVICVS. Quid ipsius tu eges praesentia?
IOHANNES. E promptuario cibi aliquid carnis mihi largietur.
LVDOVICVS. Vt audio, caro domi uestrae occluditur.
IOHANNES. Occluditur, sed non prandii uel cenae tempore dum parentes adsunt.
LVDOVICVS. Sed dum absunt, forte occlusa seruatur.
IOHANNES. Nonnunquam.
LVDOVICVS. O miseram uestram familiam, cui carnes denegantur interdum.
IOHANNES. Non est misera, sat habet alimenti.
LVDOVICVS. Sed ad merendam et ientaculum nihil habet carnis.
IOHANNES. Istud facile est toleratu, nescis tenuem tunc temporis oportere esse cibum, alias in cena uel prandio nihil haberemus esuriei, neque ad edendum essemus alacres.

10. DE CENA

Petrus et Valterus

PETRVS. Salue, ut tecum agitur?
VALTERVS. Et tu salue. Agitur mecum prospere, gratia superis.
PETRVS. Id lubens audio.
VALTERVS. Gratiam habeas.

IOHANNES. You've nearly hit the nail on the head.
LUDOVICUS. Is it thirst that's troubling you?
IOHANNES. Yes, and hunger too.
LUDOVICUS. Might it be that you haven't had your lunch yet?
IOHANNES. I have, but I didn't eat much.
LUDOVICUS. Was your lunch so meagre?
IOHANNES. Yes, because my parents were having lunch somewhere else.
LUDOVICUS. Didn't you have enough bread and cheese?
IOHANNES. We did, but I'm not fond of that kind of food.
LUDOVICUS. Will you have your afternoon meal at home now?
IOHANNES. I will, if God pleases.
LUDOVICUS. Will it be more generous than your lunch was?
IOHANNES. I hope so, if my mother is at home.
LUDOVICUS. Why do you need her to be there?
IOHANNES. She'll let me have some meat from the larder.
LUDOVICUS. From what I hear the meat's locked away at your house.
IOHANNES. It is, but not at lunch or dinner-time when my parents are there.
LUDOVICUS. But when they aren't there, is it kept locked?
IOHANNES. Sometimes.
LUDOVICUS. What an unfortunate family – you're sometimes denied meat.
IOHANNES. We're not unfortunate, we have enough to eat.
LUDOVICUS. But you don't have any meat for your afternoon meal or your breakfast.
IOHANNES. That's easy to put up with. Don't you know that at that time food should be light, otherwise we wouldn't be hungry at lunch or dinner, or be keen to eat.

10. DINNER

Petrus and Valterus

PETRUS. Hallo, how are you doing?
VALTERUS. Hallo. I'm very well, thank God.
PETRUS. I'm glad to hear it.
VALTERUS. Thank you.

PETRVS. Vbi toto latuisti die?
VALTERVS. Nusquam nisi in ludo litterario.
PETRVS. Esset mihi quod tibi loquerer, si uacaret.
VALTERVS. Certe modo uacat minime.
PETRVS. Qui sic?
VALTERVS. Nox imminet, domum mihi eundum est illico.
PETRVS. Domi quid ages?
VALTERVS. Cenabo cum parentibus.
PETRVS. Non licet tibi pauxillulum morari?
VALTERVS. Non, si saltem plagas uitare uolo.
PETRVS. Fortassis tuum est mensam sternere.
VALTERVS. Est, simul et ad cyathos stare.
PETRVS. Non facit famu- [A6r] la ista munera?
VALTERVS. Non, sed in popina agenda exequitur.
PETRVS. Cenant parentes tui semper domi?
VALTERVS. Ita, uerum prandent quandoque foris.
PETRVS. Nunquam uocantur et interdum alio ad cenam?
VALTERVS. Persaepe, sed uenire renuunt.
PETRVS. Quamobrem recusant?
VALTERVS. Timent noctu plateas emetiri.
PETRVS. Vane timent.
VALTERVS. Nequaquam, nescis noctem nihil boni, sed saepe pugnos afferre.

---

20 popina] culina A | 26–29 emetiri … pugnos afferre.] emetiri. A

11. DE POSTCENIO

Cornelius et Adrianus

CORNELIVS. O utinam nox praesto esset.
ADRIANVS. Cur id uelles?
CORNELIVS. Quia delicati aliquid edulii edam.
ADRIANVS. Vbi, domi uestrae?
CORNELIVS. Non, sed alibi.
ADRIANVS. Vbinam, dic amabo, mi Corneli?
CORNELIVS. Dicam, sed tibi nil conferet.
ADRIANVS. Quid tum, gestio tamen audire.

PETRUS. Where have you been hiding all day?
VALTERUS. Just in school.
PETRUS. There's something I'd like to talk to you about, if you had the time.
VALTERUS. I really haven't.
PETRUS. Why not?
VALTERUS. It'll soon be night, I have to go home then.
PETRUS. What will you do at home?
VALTERUS. Have dinner with my parents.
PETRUS. Can't you stay for a really short time?
VALTERUS. Not if I want to avoid a beating.
PETRUS. Perhaps it's your duty to lay the table?
VALTERUS. Yes, and serve the drinks as well.
PETRUS. Doesn't your maid do those jobs?
VALTERUS. No, she takes care of what has to be done in the kitchen.
PETRUS. Do your parents always have dinner at home?
VALTERUS. Yes, though they do sometimes have lunch at other people's houses.
PETRUS. Aren't they ever invited to dinner somewhere else?
VALTERUS. Very often, but they refuse the invitation.
PETRUS. Why do they refuse?
VALTERUS. They're afraid to walk the streets at night.
PETRUS. They're wrong to be afraid of that.
VALTERUS. No they aren't. You don't know that night brings nothing good, but it often brings fights.

11. A RERE-SUPPER

Cornelius and Adrianus

CORNELIUS. I wish night would come.
ADRIANUS. Why do you wish that?
CORNELIUS. Because I'm going to have something really nice to eat.
ADRIANUS. Where? At your house?
CORNELIUS. No, elsewhere.
ADRIANUS. Where, Cornelius? Tell me, do.
CORNELIUS. I'll tell you, but it won't do you any good.
ADRIANUS. So what? I'm aching to hear nevertheless.

CORNELIVS. Arrige igitur aures.
ADRIANVS. Faciam sedulo.
CORNELIVS. Parentes mei sunt uocati ad dubiam cenam, quam postcenium appellitant.
ADRIANVS. Quid ibi tu frugis speras?
CORNELIVS. Permultum sane.
ADRIANVS. De isto me certiorem reddas.
CORNELIVS. Lucernam feram istuc, ut domum uersus reducam parentes.
ADRIANVS. Tum ibi forte ante limen tibi opperiendum erit?
CORNELIVS. Non, sed intromittor, quia aedium custodem nosco.
ADRIANVS. Intromissus quo concedis?
CORNELIVS. Mensam accedo cui parentes accumbunt, ibi bolum opiparum consequor.
ADRIANVS. E parentum manu?
CORNELIVS. Ita, et quidem largiter saccarum mellitissimumque potum.
ADRIANVS. O si tum tibi adessem. Sed oro et mihi saccari buccellam serua.
CORNELIVS. Polliceor tibi, si ipse non totum absumpsero.
ADRIANVS. Fac te amicum experiar.

12. DE POTV POSTREMO A CENA

Quirinus et Nicolaus [A6v]

QVIRINVS. Vt sic sedes nutanti capite?
NICOLAVS. Dormiturio.
QVIRINVS. Certe non dormituris, sed iam dormis.
NICOLAVS. Fortassis.
QVIRINVS. Quin surge et cubitum perge.
NICOLAVS. Congredere mihi.
QVIRINVS. Cur me comitem petis, timesne lemures?
NICOLAVS. Non, sed quia lectus friget.
QVIRINVS. Ventris anhelitu ipsum tepefac.
NICOLAVS. Nequeo, quia rapas cenatus non sum.

CORNELIUS. Listen carefully, then.
ADRIANUS. I will, very attentively.
CORNELIUS. My parents have been invited to a lavish evening meal called a 'rere-supper'.
ADRIANUS. What food are you hoping for there?
CORNELIUS. A lot, I'll tell you.
ADRIANUS. Tell me more about that.
CORNELIUS. I'll carry the lantern there, so that I can lead my parents back home.
ADRIANUS. Then I suppose you'll have to wait outside the door?
CORNELIUS. No, I'm allowed in, because I know the doorkeeper.
ADRIANUS. Where will you go when you've been let in?
CORNELIUS. To the table where my parents are sitting, and there I'll get myself something tasty to eat.
ADRIANUS. From your parents' hands?
CORNELIUS. Yes, and then sweetmeats and a drink of sweet wine.
ADRIANUS. Oh, I wish I was with you then! But keep a sweetmeat for me too, please.
CORNELIUS. I promise you – if I don't finish it all off myself.
ADRIANUS. Let me see that you're a friend.

12. AN AFTER-DINNER DRINK

Quirinus and Nicolaus

QUIRINUS. Why are you sitting nodding your head like that?
NICOLAUS. I'm falling asleep.
QUIRINUS. No, you're not falling asleep, you're asleep already.
NICOLAUS. Maybe.
QUIRINUS. Why not get up and go to bed?
NICOLAUS. Come with me.
QUIRINUS. Why do you need someone with you? Are you frightened of ghosts?
NICOLAUS. No, the bed's cold.
QUIRINUS. Warm it up with a fart.
NICOLAUS. I can't, I didn't eat turnips for dinner.

QVIRINVS. I prae, postquam denuo bibero sequar.
NICOLAVS. Mihi quoque palatum adhuc aret.
QVIRINVS. Mane, eo eductum haustum postremum a cena.
NICOLAVS. Manebo, sed uelox redi.
QVIRINVS. Promamne plusculum tui gratia?
NICOLAVS. Sic facito.
QVIRINVS. En, hic affero.
NICOLAVS. Gratum mihi est.
QVIRINVS. Sed praebibere est meum.
NICOLAVS. Non displicet mihi.
QVIRINVS. Medium tibi propino.
NICOLAVS. Prosit, sed non exhaurias totum.
QVIRINVS. Ne dubita, sat tibi reliquum sinam.
NICOLAVS. Nunc bibe actutum.
QVIRINVS. Vides plus tibi relictum quam a me potatum.
NICOLAVS. Video, rursus tecum partiar.
QVIRINVS. Non admodum moror. Si lubet, exicca.
NICOLAVS. Nimium est quam quod ebibere possem.

---

15 postremum a cena.] postremum. A

13. DE INVITATIONE AD IENTACVLVM

Crato et Michael

CRATO. O te miserum hominem.
MICHAEL. Quid me miserum uocas?
CRATO. Quia domus tua hinc longe distat, non potes ientari.
MICHAEL. Assuetus sum ad prandium usque famem suspendere.
CRATO. Id certe meo non arrideret stomacho.
MICHAEL. Tu bene in ipso nido ederes.
CRATO. Si esuris, ueni mecum ientatum. [A7r]
MICHAEL. Istud tibi cordi non est.
CRATO. Serio loquor, comitare me.
MICHAEL. Sed quid mater tua dicet?
CRATO. Ipsa aberit ab aedibus.
MICHAEL. Nunc lubet mihi congredi.

QUIRINUS. Go on ahead. I'll follow you after I've had another drink.
NICOLAUS. My throat's really dry, too.
QUIRINUS. Stay there, I'll go and pour an after-dinner drink.
NICOLAUS. I will, but come back quickly.
QUIRINUS. Will I fetch a little extra for you?
NICOLAUS. Do.
QUIRINUS. Here, I've got it.
NICOLAUS. I'm much obliged.
QUIRINUS. But I get to drink first.
NICOLAUS. I don't object.
QUIRINUS. I'll drink the half of it to your health.
NICOLAUS. Cheers! But don't drink the lot.
QUIRINUS. Don't worry, I'll leave enough for you.
NICOLAUS. Now drink it right away.
QUIRINUS. You can see that there's more left for you than there is drunk by me.
NICOLAUS. I see. I'll share it with you again.
QUIRINUS. I don't particularly care for it. Finish it off if you like.
NICOLAUS. It's more than I could drink.

13. AN INVITATION TO BREAKFAST

Crato and Michael

CRATO. O you poor man.
MICHAEL. Why are you calling me poor?
CRATO. Because your house is a long way from here, so you won't be able to have breakfast.
MICHAEL. I'm used to staving off my hunger till lunch.
CRATO. That certainly wouldn't suit my stomach.
MICHAEL. You would even eat in bed.
CRATO. If you're hungry, come and have breakfast with me.
MICHAEL. You don't really mean that.
CRATO. I'm serious, come with me.
MICHAEL. But what will your mother say?
CRATO. She'll be out of the house.
MICHAEL. Then I'm happy to go with you.

CRATO. Sed id tibi praedico, praeter panem iurulentum habebimus nihil edulii.
MICHAEL. Credo, quia fortassis caro nondum erit percocta.
CRATO. Recte coniicis.
MICHAEL. Instruit famula tam sera focum?
CRATO. Ita, quia non nisi undecima hora accumbimus mensae.
MICHAEL. Cur tam seri?
CRATO. Quia non citius pater a negotiis executis domum redit.
MICHAEL. Non prandetis nisi ipse praesto fuerit?
CRATO. Essemus adeo inciuiles, quod ipsum non opperiremur?
MICHAEL. Istud non suspicabar.
CRATO. Nunc ingrediemur, ne coquinae ministra ientaculo nos maneat.
MICHAEL. I prae, sequar.

---

20 sera] sera A; serus B; sero C | 22 seri] seri A; serus B; sero C

14. INVITANDI ALIVM AD PRANDIVM

Petrus et Georgius

PETRVS. Tempore pomeridiano gymnasio nostro non interero.
GEORGIVS. Quid te remorabitur?
PETRVS. Vocandi mihi erunt conuiuae in crastinum prandium.
GEORGIVS. Qui fit quod conuiuas inuitatis?
PETRVS. Bouem mactauimus, ad intestina hospites tractabimus.
GEORGIVS. Etiam et me?
PETRVS. Si non est tibi lautior mensa, uenias.
GEORGIVS. Vmbra sum, nolo.
PETRVS. Emaneres ideo?
GEORGIVS. Ita, nam umbris non est parata sedes.
PETRVS. Ignoras conuiuam subitum et improuisum nonnunquam uocato esse acceptiorem?
GEORGIVS. Apud paucos certe.
PETRVS. Parentes mei omnes ex aequo tractant et excipiunt conuiuas.

CRATO. But I warn you, we'll have nothing to eat except soup.
MICHAEL. I believe you, because the meat probably won't be cooked yet.
CRATO. You guess rightly.
MICHAEL. Does your maid put the fire on as late as that?
CRATO. Yes, because we only sit down to lunch at eleven o'clock.
MICHAEL. Why so late?
CRATO. Because my father doesn't come home any earlier from seeing to his business.
MICHAEL. Won't you have lunch till he's there?
CRATO. Would we be so ill-mannered as not to wait for him?
MICHAEL. I didn't imagine you would be.
CRATO. Let's go now, so that the cook doesn't have to wait for us to arrive to breakfast.
MICHAEL. On you go, I'll follow.

14. INVITING SOMEONE TO LUNCH

Petrus and Georgius

PETRUS. I won't be at our school in the afternoon.
GEORGIUS. What will keep you away?
PETRUS. I'll have to invite guests to lunch tomorrow.
GEORGIUS. How do you come to be inviting guests?
PETRUS. We've slaughtered a cow, and we'll treat the guests to the offal.
GEORGIUS. And me too?
PETRUS. If you haven't got a better meal to go to, come.
GEORGIUS. I don't want to, I'd be a hanger-on.
PETRUS. Would you stay away on that account?
GEORGIUS. Yes, because there's no place set for uninvited guests.
PETRUS. Don't you know that an unexpected guest is sometimes more welcome than one who's been invited?
GEORGIUS. But only for a few people.
PETRUS. My parents treat and welcome all their guests equally.

GEORGIVS. Nosti tu parentum cogitatus?
PETRVS. Ego [A7v] opera eorum et mentis perpendo recessus.
GEORGIVS. Saepe aliud foris et aliud corde habent homines.
PETRVS. Talia de meis desine parentibus suspicari.
GEORGIVS. Esto, faciam.
PETRVS. Actutum cras decima postquam sonuerit uenias.
GEORGIVS. In tempore adero.
PETRVS. Domi nostrae nil plus dicas quam parentes saluta.
GEORGIVS. Essem adeo inciuilis?
PETRVS. Te a me inuitatum loquitor.
GEORGIVS. Faciam, tum audacior ero, ingrediendo domum et ad mensam edendo et bibendo.

23–27 follows A; B and C read: PETRVS. Actutum cras decima postquam sonuerit uenias. GEORGIVS. Domi nostrae nil plus dicas quam parentes saluta. GEORGIVS. Essem adeo inciuilis? PETRVS. Te a me inuitatum loquitor. | 28–29 audacior ero … et bibendo.] audacior ero. A

15. VOCANDI ALIVM AD CIBVM POMERIDIANVM

Antonius et Albertus

ANTONIVS. Quid in sinu geris adeo turgidum?
ALBERTVS. Cibum merendinarium.
ANTONIVS. Certe prouidus es, quod esuriem futuram praemeditaris.
ALBERTVS. Non et tu quippiam alimenti tecum tulisti?
ANTONIVS. Mehercule, ne bolum quidem.
ALBERTVS. Forte memoriae tuae non obrepsit.
ANTONIVS. Non soleo a prandio cibum ferre mecum in ludum litterarium.
ALBERTVS. Si esuris, tecum hunc panem partiar.
ANTONIVS. Vix tibi soli sufficit.
ALBERTVS. Aestimas me uulturem esse?
ANTONIVS. Non, sed ipse ieiunus istum panem uno deuorarem rictu.
ALBERTVS. En accipe dimidiatum ipsum.
ANTONIVS. Hui, tantum non expeto.
ALBERTVS. Casei quantum lubet ede.

GEORGIUS. Do you know your parents' thoughts?
PETRUS. I can weigh up their deeds and the secret recesses of their minds.
GEORGIUS. People often behave one way outwardly and feel differently inside.
PETRUS. Stop thinking that of my parents.
GEORGIUS. Right, I will.
PETRUS. Come tomorrow, straight after ten o'clock has rung.
GEORGIUS. I'll be on time.
PETRUS. At our house, don't say anything more than a greeting to my parents.
GEORGIUS. Would I be so ill-mannered?
PETRUS. Say that you've been invited by me.
GEORGIUS. I will, then I'll be bolder and I'll go into the house and eat and drink at the table.

15. INVITING SOMEONE TO THE AFTERNOON MEAL

Antonius and Albertus

ANTONIUS. What's that lump you've got in your pocket?
ALBERTUS. My afternoon snack.
ANTONIUS. You really are provident, you've thought about being hungry later.
ALBERTUS. Haven't you brought some food with you, too?
ANTONIUS. Not a bite, damn it!
ALBERTUS. Did it slip your mind, perhaps?
ANTONIUS. I don't usually take food to school with me after lunch.
ALBERTUS. If you're hungry, I'll share this piece of bread with you.
ANTONIUS. It'll hardly be enough for you alone.
ALBERTUS. Do you think that I'm a vulture?
ANTONIUS. No, but if I hadn't eaten I'd gulp that piece of bread down in a single mouthful.
ALBERTUS. Here, take half of it.
ANTONIUS. Oh, I'm not after as much as that.
ALBERTUS. Eat as much cheese as you like.

ANTONIVS. Comede et tu.
ALBERTVS. Non admodum esurio.
ANTONIVS. Tamen edendo sis mihi comes.
ALBERTVS. Faciam, ne cibus tibi uenenatus uideatur.
ANTONIVS. Istud non soleo uereri.
ALBERTVS. Vt tuum delectat palatum caseus iste?
ANTONIVS. Optime, nam pinguedine affatim est conditus.
ALBERTVS. Paritne tibi sitim?
ANTONIVS. Paululum exiccat mihi palatum.
ALBERTVS. Ex hac lignea lagena tibi propino.
ANTONIVS. Sit felix tibi bibenti.
ALBERTVS. Cereuisia est nostra domestica.
ANTONIVS. Eam malo quam quae uulgo uenit. [A8r]

16. VOCANDI ALIVM AD CENAM

Iohannes filius ciuis, Henricus alio oriundus

IOHANNES. Condixistine alicui hodie cenam?
HENRICVS. Nemini.
IOHANNES. Neque aliquis tibi obtulit?
HENRICVS. Nemo, hercle nemo.
IOHANNES. Cenabis tum domi tuae?
HENRICVS. Domi meae non cenabo, sed ieiunabo.
IOHANNES. Qui fit hoc?
HENRICVS. Quia nihil mihi est quod edam.
IOHANNES. Parentes mei rogant ut nobiscum cenam sumas.
HENRICVS. Vellem te uera loqui.
IOHANNES. Fidem mihi habeas.
HENRICVS. Esto, do fidem.
IOHANNES. Eas igitur celerrime.
HENRICVS. Vt praecesseris, ita et sequar.
IOHANNES. Veni ocius, mensa est instructa obsoniis.
HENRICVS. Venio ac uelox.
IOHANNES. Rogo ad mensam ne quid mali de me loquaris parentibus.

ANTONIUS. You eat too.
ALBERTUS. I'm not all that hungry.
ANTONIUS. But keep me company while I eat.
ALBERTUS. I will, so as you don't think the food's poisoned.
ANTONIUS. I'm not usually afraid of that.
ALBERTUS. How does this cheese please your palate?
ANTONIUS. Very well, it's been made with plenty of fat.
ALBERTUS. Does it make you thirsty?
ANTONIUS. It makes my mouth a bit dry.
ALBERTUS. I drink to you from this wooden flagon.
ANTONIUS. Your good health.
ALBERTUS. It's the beer we brew at home.
ANTONIUS. I prefer that to the beer you buy.

16. INVITING SOMEONE TO DINNER

Iohannes, the son of a citizen, and Henricus, who comes from elsewhere

IOHANNES. Have you promised to have dinner with anyone today?
HENRICUS. No, no one.
IOHANNES. And has no one invited you?
HENRICUS. No one, no one at all.
IOHANNES. So will you eat dinner at your house?
HENRICUS. I won't eat at my house, I'll starve.
IOHANNES. How come?
HENRICUS. Because I haven't got anything to eat.
IOHANNES. My parents have asked you to have dinner with us.
HENRICUS. I wish you were telling the truth.
IOHANNES. Believe me.
HENRICUS. Right, I believe you.
IOHANNES. So go there quickly.
HENRICUS. You go ahead, and I'll follow.
IOHANNES. Come quicker, the table's been laid with food.
HENRICUS. I'm coming, and quickly.
IOHANNES. At table, please don't say anything bad about me to my parents.

HENRICVS. Securus esto, delator non sum.
IOHANNES. Si quaerent parentes an in litteris progrediar, quid dices?
HENRICVS. Asseram te omnibus aliis in litteris feruentiorem.
IOHANNES. Si secus dixeris, postremum me amicum habuisti.
HENRICVS. Ad mensam soleo non garrire sed stomachum curare.
IOHANNES. Fac edas fortiter, ne uereare ob parentum praesentiam.
HENRICVS. In mensa frontem perfrico.
IOHANNES. Sat uini tibi in calicem largiar, tu uide ut ebibas.
HENRICVS. Vinum non moror si cereuisia in promptu est.
IOHANNES. Nescis 'Vinum modice sumptum acuere ingenium'?
HENRICVS. Ingenium meum plus enecat uini potus quam excitat.
IOHANNES. Bibendo forte modum excedis? Sed ingredere, ne cenando moremur parentes.
HENRICVS. Praecede, ut dignum est.

---

32 cereuisia] ceruisia A | 33 acuere] acuit A

17. DE MODO STVDENDI

Thylmannus et Martinus [A8v]

TILMANNVS. Vbi lates, quod nusquam proripis?
MARTINVS. Semper domi ad libros.
TILMANNVS. Assides continue libris?
MARTINVS. Assideo utique.
TILMANNVS. Vide ne quid immodico te affligas studio.
MARTINVS. Id minime timeo.
TILMANNVS. Multi qui in studio modum excedunt tandem desipiunt.
MARTINVS. Id praecauebo, ne quid desipiam.
TILMANNVS. Vigilandum est tibi prouide.

HENRICUS. Don't worry, I'm not a tell-tale.
IOHANNES. If my parents ask whether I'm getting on well at school, what will you say?
HENRICUS. I'll assure them that you're keener at your lessons than everyone else.
IOHANNES. If you say anything different, that's the last of me as your friend.
HENRICUS. I'm not in the habit of gossiping at table; I look after my stomach.
IOHANNES. Do eat up, don't worry about my parents being there.
HENRICUS. When I'm at table I'm not shy.
IOHANNES. I'll pour plenty of wine into your cup; make sure you drink it all.
HENRICUS. I don't care for wine if there's beer to be had.
IOHANNES. Don't you know that wine in moderation sharpens the wits?
HENRICUS. Drinking wine dulls my wits, it doesn't stimulate them.
IOHANNES. Maybe you drink to excess. But go in, so that we don't keep my parents from their dinner.
HENRICUS. You go first, that's right and proper.

17. THE WAY TO STUDY

Tilmannus and Martinus

TILMANNUS. Where are you hiding, that you never come out?
MARTINUS. I'm always at home over my books.
TILMANNUS. Do you work at your books all the time?
MARTINUS. I certainly do.
TILMANNUS. Make sure that you don't damage yourself by studying too much.
MARTINUS. I'm really not afraid of that.
TILMANNUS. A lot of people who've studied too much have ended up by losing their minds.
MARTINUS. I'll take care not to go out of my mind.
TILMANNUS. You must watch out carefully.

MARTINVS. Non tantum me macero litteris.
TILMANNVS. Amentia illa etiam quandoque oritur ex tenui uictu.
MARTINVS. Non est mihi uictus parcus.
TILMANNVS. Assiduitatem tuam in litteris laudo.
MARTINVS. Nunc naso me suspendis.
TILMANNVS. Moriar si non ex animo loquor.
MARTINVS. Concedo.
TILMANNVS. Is optimus in studio est modus, ut quis laboret quo indies alios assequatur scientia.
MARTINVS. Id ego conor sedulo.
TILMANNVS. Pudendum est, dum scientia ab alio uincimur.
MARTINVS. Nusquam pol est maior habendus pudor.
TILMANNVS. Multos tamen nihil pudet esse indoctos.
MARTINVS. Horum est salus desperanda.
TILMANNVS. Sed quis tibi studendi est modus?
MARTINVS. Indies aliquid addisco.
TILMANNVS. Id si per annum feceris, non parum coaceruabis scientiae.
MARTINVS. Istud exitus ostendet anni.
TILMANNVS. Vide ne ante anni egressum tepescas.
MARTINVS. Istud dii auertant, quod deferueam discendo.
TILMANNVS. Accidit plerumque initio calescentibus, ut indies frigidius laborent.

18. DE EPISTOLA CONFICIENDA

Leo et Nicolaus

LEO. Vt sic sedes labia mordens?
NICOLAVS. Epistolam uulgarem uerto Latine.
LEO. Opusne est tibi conatu tanto in [B1r] epistola conficienda?
NICOLAVS. Est, et quidem perdifficili.

MARTINUS. I don't exhaust myself over my books all that much.

TILMANNUS. That kind of madness also comes from eating too little.

MARTINUS. I don't spare on food.

TILMANNUS. I praise your diligence at your studies!

MARTINUS. Now you're making fun of me.

TILMANNUS. I'll die if I'm not sincere.

MARTINUS. I accept that.

TILMANNUS. The best way in study is to work so as to outdo the others every day.

MARTINUS. I try hard to do that.

TILMANNUS. It's shameful to be outdone in knowledge by someone else.

MARTINUS. Indeed, there's nothing that should make you feel more ashamed.

TILMANNUS. And yet there are a lot of people who aren't at all ashamed to be unlearned.

MARTINUS. You have to despair of their well-being.

TILMANNUS. But what's your way of studying?

MARTINUS. I learn something new every day.

TILMANNUS. If you did that for a whole year, you'd build up a lot of knowledge.

MARTINUS. The end of the year will show that.

TILMANNUS. Make sure you don't cool down before the year ends.

MARTINUS. May the Gods prevent me from losing my enthusiasm for learning.

TILMANNUS. It happens a lot that people who start by being really keen work less and less enthusiastically as the days go by.

18. WRITING A LETTER

Leo and Nicolaus

LEO. Why are you sitting biting your lip like that?

NICOLAUS. I'm translating a German letter into Latin.

LEO. Do you need to put so much effort into writing a letter?

NICOLAUS. Yes, I do, and really hard effort, too.

LEO. Ego dicto citius epistolam in Latinum commuto.

NICOLAVS. Credo, sed admodum impolite.

LEO. Non curo an polita uel inepta sit.

NICOLAVS. Cur id paruipendis?

LEO. Quia praeceptor adhibet limam.

NICOLAVS. Tamen puderet me alios audire tam inelegantem meam epistolam.

LEO. In isto perfricui frontem.

NICOLAVS. Hui, quid loqueris? non pudet te inscitiae?

LEO. Non pudet me istius quod etiam doctis usu uenit.

NICOLAVS. Quid istud est?

LEO. Quod eorum emendantur scripta.

NICOLAVS. Vtcunque sit, dedecus est lapsum esse.

LEO. Cudis tu epistolam ubique politam?

NICOLAVS. Id certe si non facio, laboro tamen pro uiribus.

LEO. Est id satis, pro uiribus laborasse dum nihil exit egregii?

NICOLAVS. Ita, quia in magnis (ut aiunt) uoluisse sat est.

LEO. Posthac in epistola diligentior etiam ero.

NICOLAVS. Id faxit Deus.

LEO. Si lubet, certemus, quis in epistola scribenda excellat uel facundior sit.

NICOLAVS. Assumo prouinciam.

LEO. Ego glaciem secabo.

NICOLAVS. Quid hoc prouerbii est?

LEO. Adagium est, significans primus rem aliquam experiri.

NICOLAVS. Et ego te sequar, litterisque meis tibi obstrepam.

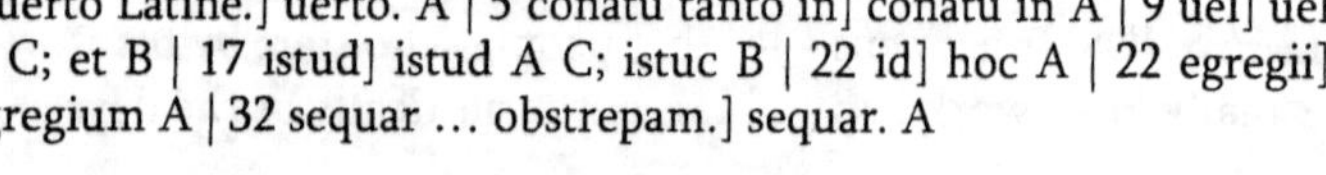

4 uerto Latine.] uerto. A | 5 conatu tanto in] conatu in A | 9 uel] uel A C; et B | 17 istud] istud A C; istuc B | 22 id] hoc A | 22 egregii] egregium A | 32 sequar … obstrepam.] sequar. A

LEO. I can put a letter into Latin faster than you could blink.

NICOLAUS. I'm sure you can – but it would be a pretty inelegant one.

LEO. I don't care whether it's elegant or slovenly.

NICOLAUS. Why don't you care about that?

LEO. Because the teacher will put the finishing touches to it.

NICOLAUS. But I'd be ashamed for others to hear a letter of mine that was as inelegant as that.

LEO. I don't give a hoot about that.

NICOLAUS. What are you saying? You're not ashamed of being ignorant?

LEO. I'm not ashamed of something that happens even to learned people.

NICOLAUS. What's that?

LEO. Their writings being corrected.

NICOLAUS. However that may be, it's shameful to have made an error.

LEO. Can you compose a letter that's elegant in all respects?

NICOLAUS. Well certainly if I don't succeed, at least I do the best I can.

LEO. Is it enough to do your best if nothing excellent comes of it?

NICOLAUS. Yes, because as the saying goes, 'in great things trying is enough'.

LEO. In future I'll try harder at writing letters too.

NICOLAUS. May God grant that.

LEO. If you like we can have a contest to see who's better or eloquent at writing letters.

NICOLAUS. I'll take that on.

LEO. I'll break the ice.

NICOLAUS. What sort of a phrase is that?

LEO. It's a saying, it means to be the first to try something.

NICOLAUS. And I'll follow you, and I'll outdo you in learning.

19. DE REPETENDA LECTIONE

Gosuinus et Matthaeus

GOSVINVS. Quid a cena tibi domi est negotii?

MATTHAEVS. Appetis id scire?

GOSVINVS. Appeto oppido, ideo sciscitor.

MATTHAEVS. Arrige aures, non te celabo.

GOSVINVS. Arrigo sedulo, effare.

MATTHAEVS. Cibo recondito expatior, uel colloquor parentibus pauculis.

GOSVINVS. Quid istis colloqueris? [B1v]

MATTHAEVS. Varia sunt uerba, et praecipue si quae iocunda per diem didici.

GOSVINVS. Vt audio, tu parentes doces uesperi quod ipse per diem didicisti.

MATTHAEVS. Non doceo eos, sed dicto aliquot lepido eos delector.

GOSVINVS. Transigis totam uesperam istis colloquiis?

MATTHAEVS. Non, sed semi fortassis horam.

GOSVINVS. Quid operis deinde tibi sumis?

MATTHAEVS. Per diem in ludo litterario audita rumino.

GOSVINVS. Quo id facis modo, cum solus sis?

MATTHAEVS. Perlego subinde, ubi ignoro sciscitor altero mane a peritiore.

GOSVINVS. Vellesne repetendo te Theseum habere?

MATTHAEVS. Mallem, si consequi possem.

GOSVINVS. Quid si me comitem susciperes?

MATTHAEVS. Arrideret mihi.

GOSVINVS. Si hospitio parentes tui me uellent immunem habere?

MATTHAEVS. Nihil lubentius facerent, mei gratia.

GOSVINVS. O quam feruide lectiones repetere uelimus.

MATTHAEVS. Certe manibus et pedibus discere uelimus.

GOSVINVS. Certaremus ante cubitum, quis eo die didicisset uberius.

19. REPEATING A LESSON

Gosuinus and Matthaeus

GOSUINUS. What do you do at your house after dinner?
MATTHAEUS. Do you want to know that?
GOSUINUS. I really do, that's why I'm asking.
MATTHAEUS. Listen carefully, then, I'll not hide it from you.
GOSUINUS. I'm listening really hard, tell me.
MATTHAEUS. When the food has been put away I converse with my parents about a few things.
GOSUINUS. What do you talk to them about?
MATTHAEUS. About lots of different things, and especially if I've learnt any pleasant things during the day.
GOSUINUS. You're saying that in the evening you teach your parents what you've learnt during the day.
MATTHAEUS. I don't teach them, I entertain them with some amusing quotation.
GOSUINUS. Do you spend the whole evening talking like that?
MATTHAEUS. No, maybe half an hour.
GOSUINUS. What work do you do then?
MATTHAEUS. I think over the things I've heard at school during the day.
GOSUINUS. How do you do that, seeing that you're alone?
MATTHAEUS. I read the lesson through repeatedly, and if there's anything I don't know I ask someone who knows more the next morning.
GOSUINUS. Would you like to have someone to do your revising with you?
MATTHAEUS. I'd prefer that, if I could find someone.
GOSUINUS. Supposing you took me on as a companion?
MATTHAEUS. I'd really like that.
GOSUINUS. Might your parents be prepared to give me free accommodation?
MATTHAEUS. They'd be delighted to do that for my sake.
GOSUINUS. Oh, how keenly we'll repeat our lessons!
MATTHAEUS. Indeed, we'll learn with all our might.
GOSUINUS. We'll have a contest before going to bed, to see who's learnt the most that day.

MATTHAEVS. Hic ego semper tibi cederem.

GOSVINVS. Quisque laborare deberet ut uinceret.

MATTHAEVS. Vtique, nam uinci turpissimum est, in litteris praecipue.

---

22 Perlego subinde, ubi] Perlego, subinde ubi A | 23 peritiore] peritiori A; peritiore B C | 31 feruide] feruide A C; feruidae B | 31 repetere uelimus] repeteremus A | 35–38 cederem … praecipue.] cederem. A

20. DE CORYCAEI METV AVSCVLTANTIS EOS QVI NON ROMANO VTVNTVR SERMONE

Erasmus et Vdalricus

ERASMVS. Hem, qui sic loqueris?

VDALRICVS. Vt loquor?

ERASMVS. Estne sic sermo habendus?

VDALRICVS. Cur non, ita mater me instituit.

ERASMVS. Nostine nobis indicta esse uerba quae a matre didicimus?

VDALRICVS. Quibus tum utemur?

ERASMVS. Latinis uel Romanis.

VDALRICVS. Quis id sanciuit?

ERASMVS. Praeceptor constituit Corycaeos in eos qui non Latine sonant. [B2r]

VDALRICVS. Quid facient illi, qui Latini sunt expertes?

ERASMVS. Hi aut silebunt, aut ut possunt Latina proferent.

VDALRICVS. Sed quid iuuat male Latine fari?

ERASMVS. Qui loquendo delirat ab eruditiore debet instrui.

VDALRICVS. Id aequum est.

ERASMVS. Timeo mihi male a clanculario illo Corycaeo.

VDALRICVS. Ego autem manum non uertero.

ERASMVS. Ipse oppido timeo, quia ferulae podicem subdere oportet.

VDALRICVS. Cutis mea ad ferulam occalluit.

ERASMVS. Aliud certe diceres si ad ferulam tibi res rediret.

VDALRICVS. Quid tum, quando corrigor dentes comprimo, quod ictus non sentio.

MATTHAEUS. I would always lose to you in that.
GOSUINUS. Everyone ought to work so as to win.
MATTHAEUS. Indeed, because it's shameful to be beaten, especially in learning.

20. THE FEAR OF THE 'CORYCEAN' WHO LISTENS FOR THOSE WHO DON'T SPEAK LATIN

Erasmus and Udalricus

ERASMUS. What? Why are you speaking like that?
UDALRICUS. Like what?
ERASMUS. Is that the language to use?
UDALRICUS. Why not? It's what my mother taught me.
ERASMUS. Do you know that we're not allowed to use the words we learnt from our mothers?
UDALRICUS. What words will we use, then?
ERASMUS. Latin ones, Roman ones.
UDALRICUS. Who made that rule?
ERASMUS. The teacher has appointed 'Coryceans' to spy on the pupils who don't speak Latin.
UDALRICUS. What'll the boys who don't know Latin do?
ERASMUS. They'll either say nothing, or speak what Latin they can.
UDALRICUS. But what use is there in speaking Latin badly?
ERASMUS. Someone who goes wrong when they're speaking should be taught by someone who knows more.
UDALRICUS. That's fair.
ERASMUS. I'm concerned for myself on account of the secret Corycean.
UDALRICUS. But I don't care.
ERASMUS. I'm really scared, because I'm bound to get the cane on the backside.
UDALRICUS. My skin has grown insensitive to the cane.
ERASMUS. It would be a different story if it came to a caning for you.
UDALRICUS. So what? When I get punished I clench my teeth, so as not to feel the blows.

ERASMVS. Ego conabor ut caligae meae ligulis sint constrictae diploidi.
VDALRICVS. Non solet praeceptor ligulas cultro soluere?
ERASMVS. Nondum uisum est mihi.
VDALRICVS. Sed mihi saepiuscule contigit.
ERASMVS. Fortassis iste praeceptor tuus fuit plagosus.
VDALRICVS. Immo saeuior Orbilio.

1, etc. Corycaei] coricei A; Coricei B C | 1 auscultantis eos] auscultantis eos A C; auscultantis in eos B | 21 uertero] uerterem A

21. DE SOMNO PLVS AEQVO EXTENSO

Vinandus et Sebastianus

VINANDVS. Hui, nos miseros, quid faciemus nunc?
SEBASTIANVS. Quid sic eiulas?
VINANDVS. Quidni eiularem? Surgendi hora praeteriit.
SEBASTIANVS. Quam horam putas?
VINANDVS. Sextam, qua schola inuisenda est.
SEBASTIANVS. Sis bono animo, ea nondum sonuit.
VINANDVS. Sonuit certe diu.
SEBASTIANVS. Id mihi non persuadebis.
VINANDVS. Si scholam accesserimus, tum ferulam nanciscemur.
SEBASTIANVS. Semel nobis indulgebit praeceptor.
VINANDVS. Indulsit mihi heri, dicens se ultra non condonaturum.
SEBASTIANVS. Nondum mihi condonauit plagam, ideo iam liber ero.
VINANDVS. Pete igitur tu scholam.
SEBASTIANVS. Non es congressurus?
VINANDVS. Non, sed tu [B2v] emanendi mihi copiam flagita.
SEBASTIANVS. Quid causae asseram?
VINANDVS. Dic me matri negotium facessere.
SEBASTIANVS. Timeo ne postea mater ambos apud praeceptorem mendacii accuset.
VINANDVS. Id ne metuas, in me sumam si quid irata fuerit.
SEBASTIANVS. Bene, tu lues, ego minime.

ERASMUS. I'll try to make sure my breeches are tied to my doublet with laces.
UDALRICUS. Doesn't the teacher usually cut the laces with a knife?
ERASMUS. I've never seen that.
UDALRICUS. But it's happened to me a good many times.
ERASMUS. It sounds as though that teacher of yours was fond of beating.
UDALRICUS. He certainly was, harsher than Orbilius.

21. SLEEPING LONGER THAN YOU SHOULD

Vinandus and Sebastianus

VINANDUS. Oh, no, poor us, what'll we do now?
SEBASTIANUS. Why are you wailing like that?
VINANDUS. Why shouldn't I wail? It's past the time for getting up.
SEBASTIANUS. What time do you think it is?
VINANDUS. Six, the time we have to go to school.
SEBASTIANUS. Don't worry, six hasn't rung yet.
VINANDUS. Oh yes it has, a while ago.
SEBASTIANUS. You'll not get me to believe that.
VINANDUS. If we go to school, we'll get the cane.
SEBASTIANUS. The teacher will let us off once.
VINANDUS. He let me off yesterday, and said that he wouldn't let me off again.
SEBASTIANUS. He's never let me off a beating, so I'll be safe.
VINANDUS. You go to school, then.
SEBASTIANUS. Aren't you going?
VINANDUS. No, you ask for permission to take the day off for me.
SEBASTIANUS. What reason will I give?
VINANDUS. Say that I have to do a job for Mum.
SEBASTIANUS. I'm afraid that afterwards Mum will tell the teacher we've both been lying.
VINANDUS. Don't worry about that, I'll take the blame if she's at all angry.
SEBASTIANUS. Right, you take the punishment, not me.

VINANDVS. Periculum faciam.
SEBASTIANVS. Iacias aleam, mea nihil refert.
VINANDVS. Tu abi, nam appetit septima hora.
SEBASTIANVS. Abeo, tu in medium dormias diem.
VINANDVS. Non hercle, pauxillulum adhuc quiescam, mox inde erumpam.
SEBASTIANVS. Ego hinc discedo, tu pigritiam edormias, sed uide ne cum periculo.
VINANDVS. Ferulae ictum non timeo, uulnera non infligit.

---

11 accesserimus, tum ferulam] accesserimus modo, ferulam A | 17 liber ero.] liber. A | 28 iacias] iaceas A B C; 33–35 discedo … non infligit.] discedo. A

22. DE MORBO SOCORDIAE QVEM SCHOLASTICIS ASCRIBVNT

Valterus et Petrus

VALTERVS. Salue tu Epimenides, cur tam diu gymnasio non interfuisti?
PETRVS. Morbus obstitit.
VALTERVS. Morbus? Cuius farinae fuit?
PETRVS. Dolor nempe capitis et uentris.
VALTERVS. Coniicio facile quid aegritudinis fuerit.
PETRVS. Qui hoc agnoscis, anne ex facie mea?
VALTERVS. Non, quia medicam artem non calleo.
PETRVS. Vnde alias percipis?
VALTERVS. Diuino.
PETRVS. Potes diuinare? Amabo dic quam putas fuisse mihi infirmitatem.
VALTERVS. Eam quam ascribunt scholasticis, scilicet desidiam.
PETRVS. Minime, toto caelo aberras.
VALTERVS. Ne infitias iueris, per Herculem is fuit morbus.
PETRVS. Peream si ille fuerit.
VALTERVS. Esto, sed isto morbo plerumque succumbunt scholastici, dum a ludo absunt.
PETRVS. Assentio, sed istius cohortis ego non sum.
VALTERVS. Ah, quasi te intus et in cute non noscerem.

VINANDUS. I'll run the risk.
SEBASTIANUS. Have a go, it doesn't affect me.
VINANDUS. Off you go, seven o'clock's approaching.
SEBASTIANUS. I'm off. You sleep till the middle of the day.
VINANDUS. No, indeed, I'll only rest a bit longer, then I'll get up soon.
SEBASTIANUS. I'm leaving. You sleep off your laziness, but make sure there's no danger to you.
VINANDUS. I'm not afraid of a blow from the cane; it doesn't cause wounds.

22. THE DISEASE OF IDLENESS FROM WHICH SCHOOLBOYS ARE SAID TO SUFFER

Valterus and Petrus

VALTERUS. Hallo, you lazy-bones. Why haven't you been at school for so long?
PETRUS. A disease prevented me.
VALTERUS. A disease? What kind was it?
PETRUS. A pain in the head and the stomach.
VALTERUS. I can easily guess what illness it was.
PETRUS. How do you know that – from my face?
VALTERUS. No, I'm not skilled in medicine.
PETRUS. What else do you see it from?
VALTERUS. I divine it.
PETRUS. You can divine things? Tell me, please, what you think my illness was.
VALTERUS. The disease they say schoolboys suffer from – idleness.
PETRUS. No, you're completely wrong.
VALTERUS. Don't deny it. That was the disease, I'll swear.
PETRUS. I'll die if it was.
VALTERUS. All right, but schoolboys usually give in to that disease when they're off school.
PETRUS. I agree, but I'm not one of that type.
VALTERUS. Oh, as though I didn't know you inside out!

PETRVS. Si talem me aestimas, nondum a uertice ad pedes me noui- [B3r] sti.

VALTERVS. Dum me hic occupat morbus, dico matri me ex intestinorum dolore laborare.

PETRVS. Adhibet tum fidem tuis dictis?

VALTERVS. Illico, et me in mollem collocat lectum, ouorumque sorbitiuncula lauta me reficiens.

PETRVS. Si talem haberem matrem saepe me aegrum simularem, ut sorbitiuncula potirer et lautis bolis.

VALTERVS. Ego nonnunquam totus sanus assero me infirmum, dum opipari aliquid meum palatum suspirat.

PETRVS. Mater mea citius fustem quam talia mihi praeberet.

VINANDVS. Per Pollucem miror cur scholastici plus aliis socordiae sint obnoxii.

PETRVS. In promptu causa est: quia a labore feriantur, eumque fugiunt et execrantur omnes.

---

13 Diuino] Diuinor A | 14 diuinare] diuinari A; 29 Illico, et me in] Illico, et me in A; Illico et in B C; | 32 sorbitiuncula] sorbiuncula A; sorbiciuncula B C | 32 potirer et lautis bolis.] potirer. A | 38–39 feriantur … omnes.] feriantur. A |

23. DE METV FERVLAE

Cornelius et Christianus

CORNELIVS. Quo tu abis?

CHRISTIANVS. Gymnasium litterarium uersus.

CORNELIVS. Istuc tibi non congrediar.

CHRISTIANVS. Quid te remoratur uel detinet?

CORNELIVS. Quia (ut nosti) lectionibus diu non interfui.

CHRISTIANVS. Emaneres ideo?

CORNELIVS. Ita, quia male mihi metuo a ferula.

CHRISTIANVS. Non est tibi quid commenti quo te excuses?

CORNELIVS. Veri nihil habeo, quod afferam.

CHRISTIANVS. Vera ubi desunt, falsis utere, quo plagas effugias.

CORNELIVS. Rogabo fortassis matrem ut praeceptorem mihi reconciliet.

CHRISTIANVS. Id age et illico redeas.

PETRUS. If you think I'm like that, you don't know me from top to bottom yet.

VALTERUS. When I'm suffering from that disease, I tell my mother I've got a pain in the guts.

PETRUS. And does she believe what you say?

VALTERUS. Right away, and she puts me into a soft bed, and feeds me with a delicious custard.

PETRUS. If I had a mother like that, I'd pretend to be ill a lot, so as to get custard and nice things to eat.

VALTERUS. Sometimes I say I'm sick even when I'm completely well, when my mouth's longing for something luxurious.

PETRUS. My mother would be quicker to let me have the stick than things like that.

VALTERUS. I really wonder why schoolboys are more prone to idleness than others.

PETRUS. The reason's obvious: they all stay away from work, avoid it and detest it.

23. FEAR OF THE CANE

Cornelius and Christianus

CORNELIUS. Where are you off to?

CHRISTIANUS. To school.

CORNELIUS. I won't go with you.

CHRISTIANUS. What's keeping you?

CORNELIUS. As you know, I've not been to lessons for a long time.

CHRISTIANUS. And you'd stay off on that account?

CORNELIUS. Yes, because I'm afraid of getting the cane.

CHRISTIANUS. Haven't you got any story you could use as an excuse?

CORNELIUS. There's nothing true I could relate.

CHRISTIANUS. When there's nothing true, make use of something false to escape a beating.

CORNELIUS. Perhaps I'll ask my mother to make it up between me and the teacher.

CHRISTIANUS. Do that and then come back.

CORNELIVS. Vereor tamen matrem petere, quia latet eam illa mea a schola absentia.

CHRISTIANVS. Fugit id matrem tuam? Ubi locorum tum egisti?

CORNELIVS. Cum nonnullis commilitonibus aues captatum.

CHRISTIANVS. Proh, quid audio? Es tu auium captator?

CORNELIVS. Non sum, sed captionis spectator.

CHRISTIANVS. [B3v] Iuxta carpendus ut captatores.

CORNELIVS. Nunc quid faciam consulis, quo ferulam euadam?

CHRISTIANVS. Certe consilio uaco.

CORNELIVS. Scio quid faciam.

CHRISTIANVS. Quid? Fac audiam.

CORNELIVS. Praeceptoris ferulam subibo, ne parentum fustes recipiam.

CHRISTIANVS. Id si feceris, prudenter ages.

CORNELIVS. Praestat molles ferulae plagas sustinere quam fustium graues morsus.

CHRISTIANVS. Istud te sapere arguit, et pituitae (ut uulgo fertur) non esse obnoxium.

CORNELIVS. Corneae fibrae homo esset, qui non acrem ferulam quam uirides fustes ferre mallet, si quid commeruisset.

---

20 aues captatum] fui captatum aues A

24. DE EXCVSATIONE ABSENTIAE A LVDO LITTERARIO

Laurentius et Crato

LAVRENTIVS. Qui fiat nescio: hodie totus a schola abhorreo.

CRATO. Ego quoque.

LAVRENTIVS. O si liceret iam a libris et lectione nos feriari.

CRATO. Id perquam uellem.

LAVRENTIVS. Periculum faciemus apud praeceptorem de impetranda uacatione.

CRATO. Aegre impetrabitur otiandi facultas, nam multi fuerunt dies celebres.

CORNELIUS. But I'm afraid to ask my mother, because she doesn't know about me being absent from school.

CHRISTIANUS. It's been kept from your mother? Whereabouts have you been?

CORNELIUS. I've been catching birds with a few classmates.

CHRISTIANUS. My God, what are you saying? Are you a bird-snarer?

CORNELIUS. No, I look on when they're being caught.

CHRISTIANUS. You're just as much to be criticized as the one who do the snaring.

CORNELIUS. Now advise me what I ought to do to escape the cane.

CHRISTIANUS. I really haven't any advice to offer.

CORNELIUS. I know what I'll do.

CHRISTIANUS. What? Let me hear.

CORNELIUS. I'll endure the teacher's cane, so as not to get the stick from my parents.

CHRISTIANUS. If you do that, you'll be acting wisely.

CORNELIUS. It's better to put up with the mild blows the cane gives than the heavy wounds that sticks inflict.

CHRISTIANUS. That shows that you've got good sense, and that you don't easily catch a cold, as the German saying goes.

CORNELIUS. It would be an insensitive person who wouldn't prefer to suffer a stinging cane than a stout stick if they were guilty of some offence.

24. EXCUSING AN ABSENCE FROM SCHOOL

Laurentius and Crato

LAURENTIUS. I don't know why, but today I have absolutely no taste for school.

CRATO. Me neither.

LAURENTIUS. It would be good if we could be allowed a holiday from books and lessons now.

CRATO. I'd like that a lot.

LAURENTIUS. We'll take the risk of asking for a day off from the teacher.

CRATO. He's hardly likely to grant us permission to stay off, because there have been a lot of holidays.

LAVRENTIVS. Dicemus posthac nos fore feruentiores in litterario labore.

CRATO. Istud uerbum apud eum nihil habebit loci.

LAVRENTIVS. Vnde hoc nosti?

CRATO. Quia illo uerbo saepe usi sumus, neque unquam facto aequauimus.

LAVRENTIVS. Pollicemur nunc, cum periculo cutis.

CRATO. Arridet mihi, si aliis.

LAVRENTIVS. Sed si ludendi copiam nobis non concedet praeceptor, ipse mihi ferias faciam.

CRATO. Vide, si feceris, ne male cadat.

LAVRENTIVS. Quomodo male caderet?

CRATO. Quia cras ferulam senties.

LAVRENTIVS. Ibi consilii sum plenus.

CRATO. Fac et nos participes si quid boni consilii nosti.

LAVRENTIVS. [B4r] Praeceptorem adeo uel ipse uel per nuntium et domi me detineri dico negotio aliquo.

CRATO. Faciemus et id nos quoque tunc, tum una expatiabimur.

LAVRENTIVS. Sanciemus inter nos foedus, ut in scholis unus alterius asserat uerbum.

CRATO. Placet, sed poena dicatur in eum qui tesseram fregerit.

LAVRENTIVS. Poena sit quod e nostro eliminetur consortio.

CRATO. Ratum sit et sancitum quod loqueris.

---

6 liceret iam a] liceret a A; 29 tunc] nunc A

25. QVARE SCHOLA DICATVR LVDVS

Eberhardus et Theodericus

EBERHARDVS. Quorundam uerbis aliquando percepi scholam dici ludum, audistine et tu?

THEODERICVS. Audiui saepiuscule.

EBERHARDVS. Quid tum censes? Aestimas uerum esse?

THEODERICVS. Neutiquam certe.

EBERHARDVS. Neque ego, cum in ea non ludatur, sed percutiatur.

LAURENTIUS. We'll say that afterwards we'll be more eager about our school work.
CRATO. That promise won't carry any weight with him.
LAURENTIUS. How do you know?
CRATO. Because we've often made that promise, but we've never matched it with actions.
LAURENTIUS. We're promising it now, pledging our hides.
CRATO. I like the idea, if others do.
LAURENTIUS. If the teacher doesn't give us leave to play, I'll take a holiday myself.
CRATO. Make sure that it doesn't turn out badly if you do.
LAURENTIUS. How might it turn out badly?
CRATO. Because tomorrow you'll feel the cane.
LAURENTIUS. I've got lots of ideas about that.
CRATO. Let us in on it, too, if you know any good plans.
LAURENTIUS. I'll go to the teacher, either myself or through a messenger, and I'll tell him that I'm kept at home by some job or other.
CRATO. We'll do that too, then we'll all go out together.
LAURENTIUS. We'll agree a pact between us, that in school one will back up what the other says.
CRATO. A good idea, but let's decide on a punishment for anyone who breaks the pact.
LAURENTIUS. The punishment should be that he's thrown out of our group.
CRATO. Let what you say be formally agreed.

25. WHY 'LUDUS', THE LATIN FOR 'SCHOOL', MEANS A 'GAME'

Eberhardus and Theodericus

EBERHARDUS. I've sometimes heard people say that school is called 'ludus', a game. Have you heard that too?
THEODERICUS. I've heard it a lot.
EBERHARDUS. So what do you reckon? Do you think it's true?
THEODERICUS. Not at all!
EBERHARDUS. Neither do I, because it's not playing that goes on there, it's beating.

THEODERICVS. Tuae accedo sententiae.

EBERHARDVS. Fortassis praeceptori est ludus, qui ad nutum nos miseros ferit?

THEODERICVS. Istud ludere Eumenides ferant.

EBERHARDVS. Hercule scholam potius pistrinum quam ludum dicerem.

THEODERICVS. Verius istud nominis ipsi conueniret Gymnasio.

EBERHARDVS. Sed age dic causam, cur credis scholam dictam esse ludum.

THEODERICVS. Eloquar, quantum ab aliis didici.

EBERHARDVS. Ero auditor sedulus.

THEODERICVS. Vt lusor suo Theseo saepe facetias praebet, ita et praeceptor animo amico tanquam ludendo docebit discipulos.

EBERHARDVS. Hoc certe perpauci scholae praefecti faciunt.

THEODERICVS. Nosco cute expertus.

EBERHARDVS. O quam lubens scholas inuiserem, si blandiens esset praeceptor.

THEODERICVS. [B4v] Oportet blandiri diligenti, non desidi et Endymioni ut tibi.

EBERHARDVS. Miror an plus prodesset discipulis benignitas uel seueritas praeceptoris.

THEODERICVS. Istud non miror uel haereo, nescis libentius nos sequi blandientem quam minantem?

EBERHARDVS. Habuistine unquam ludimagistrum, qui ludentis speciem instruendo exhibuit?

THEODERICVS. Habui, et quidem primo studii mei tempore.

EBERHARDVS. Studebas sub istius ferula apprime diligenter?

THEODERICVS. Conatum quem potui discendo adhibui ut solent elementares pueri, si laudati fuerint et non ad acres tractati uirgas.

EBERHARDVS. Mirum est, si studio incaluisti, licentia tamen et blanditiis solemus fieri deteriores, ut Terentius inquit.

THEODERICVS. Nihil sceleris nobis permisit praeceptor, sed in discendo nostros conatus laude extulit.

---

6 aestimas] aestimas ne A | 14 Hercule] Ego hercule A

THEODERICUS. I agree with what you say.
EBERHARDUS. Maybe it's a game for the teacher, because he can hit us poor boys whenever he likes?
THEODERICUS. To Hell with that kind of game!
EBERHARDUS. God, I'd call school a jail rather than a game.
THEODERICUS. That name would fit school better.
EBERHARDUS. But tell me the reason why you think school has been called a game.
THEODERICUS. I'll tell you as much as I've learnt from others.
EBERHARDUS. I'll listen very carefully.
THEODERICUS. Just as a joker will be playful with his companion, so the teacher will teach his pupils with a friendly attitude, as though he was playing.
EBERHARDUS. Very few schoolmasters indeed do that.
THEODERICUS. I know, only too well.
EBERHARDUS. How willing I'd be to go to school if the teacher was encouraging!
THEODERICUS. It's someone hard-working you need to be encouraging to, not to a lazy dreamer like you.
EBERHARDUS. I wonder whether it helps the pupils more if the teacher is kind or harsh.
THEODERICUS. I don't wonder or doubt. Don't you know that we're more willing to follow someone encouraging than someone threatening?
EBERHARDUS. Have you ever had a teacher who gave the appearance of playing when he was teaching?
THEODERICUS. Yes, I have, at the beginning of my schooldays.
EBERHARDUS. Did you learn especially keenly under him?
THEODERICUS. I made as much effort as I could, as small boys do if they're praised and not punished harshly.
EBERHARDUS. It's a wonder you grew so keen about studying, for we usually get worse when restrictions are removed and when we're flattered, as Terence says.
THEODERICUS. Our teacher didn't allow us to do anything bad; he praised our efforts at learning highly.

26. DE DIE QVA OTIATVR A LECTIONE

Iohannes et Vdalricus

IOHANNES. O simus hilares, sodales charissimi.

VDALRICVS. Vt sic gestis?

IOHANNES. Non gestirem hodie, cum a prandio sit nobis otiandum a lectionibus?

VDALRICVS. Illud et ipsi scimus.

IOHANNES. Hunc diem feliciorem omnibus aliis iudico.

VDALRICVS. Et nos non parum delectat.

IOHANNES. Belle post meridiem sol lucebit.

VDALRICVS. Ita aurora praedixit.

IOHANNES. Prandii igitur peracta fabula, si omnibus est cordi, una rusticabimur.

VDALRICVS. Cui id displiceret?

IOHANNES. Vel si nobis uisum fuerit, in pomerio ludemus.

VDALRICVS. Parum intererit quo nos recreemus loco, saltem in schola non desideamus.

IOHANNES. At adhuc incerti sumus, an a lectione uacabimus.

VDALRICVS. Isto nihil est certius.

IOHANNES. Si facultas diuagandi nobis dabitur, quid agemus scio.

VDALRICVS. Exprime.

IOHANNES. [B5r] Arcum in rus mecum feram, in columbas tela emissurus.

VDALRICVS. Si uelint sagittam tuam morari.

IOHANNES. Nonnunquam uolando ipsas enecaui.

VDALRICVS. Hoc continget perquam raro.

IOHANNES. Quicquid auium consecutus fuero, commune erit.

VDALRICVS. Age, tum conuiuabimur.

IOHANNES. Vbi? An in Platea Ouium, ubi solemus potitare a ludo?

VDALRICVS. Ibidem torrebimus aues a te enectas.

IOHANNES. Sed a symbolo per aues ego immunis ero.

VDALRICVS. Quicquid biberimus nos pendemus, tu non teruncium dabis.

26. A DAY OFF LESSONS

Iohannes and Udalricus

IOHANNES. O, my dear friends, let's be happy!

UDALRICUS. Why are you so elated?

IOHANNES. Why wouldn't I be elated today, when we're off school after lunch?

UDALRICUS. We know that too.

IOHANNES. I would say this day is happier than all the rest.

UDALRICUS. We're pretty pleased about it, too.

IOHANNES. After noon the sun is going to be shining nicely.

UDALRICUS. That's what the dawn predicted.

IOHANNES. So after we've got through lunch, if it pleases us all, we'll go off to the countryside together.

UDALRICUS. Who wouldn't want to?

IOHANNES. Or if we like the idea, we'll play in the fields outside town.

UDALRICUS. It doesn't matter much where we enjoy ourselves, at least we aren't sitting in school.

IOHANNES. But we're still not sure if we're off school.

UDALRICUS. There's nothing surer.

IOHANNES. If we're given permission to wander about, I know what we'll do.

UDALRICUS. Tell me.

IOHANNES. I'll take my bow with me to the country, and shoot at pigeons.

UDALRICUS. If they're prepared to wait for your arrow.

IOHANNES. I've sometimes killed them on the wing.

UDALRICUS. That'll hardly ever happen.

IOHANNES. We'll share however many birds I bag.

UDALRICUS. Right, then we'll have a party

IOHANNES. Where? In the Schaafenstraße, where we usually drink after school?

UDALRICUS. We'll roast the birds you've shot there.

IOHANNES. But because of the birds I won't have to pay a contribution.

UDALRICUS. We'll pay for whatever we drink, you won't have to pay a penny.

IOHANNES. Sin nihil praedae et spolii sagittae a me emissae attulerint, de impendio conpotatiunculae quid fiet?

VDALRICVS. Compotatiuncula nulla inter nos agetur.

IOHANNES. Dedeceret a deambulando siccis palatis nos digredi.

VDALRICVS. Id laudabilius, quam quod madentes potu, nutanti gressu domum parentum repeteremus.

16–17 intererit ... desideamus.] intererit. A | 27 continget] continget A B; contingit C

27. DE AESTATE

Hermannus et Gisbertus

HERMANNVS. Placetne tibi mihi congredi rusticatum?

GISBERTVS. Rusticari nondum cupio.

HERMANNVS. Ego autem anhelo maxime, quia aestatis amoenitas aduenit.

GISBERTVS. Est tibi aestas? Mihi hibernaculum adhuc immoratur.

HERMANNVS. Hui, non pudet te hibernaculo nunc insidere temporis?

GISBERTVS. Minime, cum acre sit frigus.

HERMANNVS. Rus hinc abeo, uisum quomodo campi floreant.

GISBERTVS. Abi, me comitem non habebis.

HERMANNVS. Aliquo tamen dierum, quo tibi integrum erit, rus una inuisemus.

GISBERTVS. Si uacauerit, non rennuam.

HERMANNVS. Eundum mihi est in campum, latum frondes redolentes.

GISBERTVS. Tales uix ortas reperies.

HERMANNVS. Inueniam [B5^{v}] complures, nam diu floruerunt.

GISBERTVS. Deferesne eas deinde uenum, clamando per plateas, 'Hic frondes redolentes'?

HERMANNVS. Aestimas talia me agere?

GISBERTVS. Quo alias feres ipsas?

HERMANNVS. Domum uersus, ut ibi nobis redoleant.

GISBERTVS. Hoc negotii quis tibi dedit?

IOHANNES. But if the arrows I shoot don't hit any prey, what will happen about the cost of the drinking-party?

UDALRICUS. Then we won't hold any drinking-party.

IOHANNES. It would be a disgrace for us to come back from a walk with dry throats.

UDALRICUS. It would be less of a disgrace than tottering back to our parents' houses drunk.

27. SUMMER

Hermannus and Gisbertus

HERMANNUS. Would you like to come with me on a trip to the country?

GISBERTUS. I don't want to visit the country yet.

HERMANNUS. But I'm really eager, because the delights of summer are coming.

GISBERTUS. Is it summer for you? I'm still staying in the living-room.

HERMANNUS. Gosh, aren't you ashamed to be in the living-room in this season?

GISBERTUS. Not at all, the cold is harsh.

HERMANNUS. I'm off to the country, to see how the fields are blooming.

GISBERTUS. Off you go. I won't be going with you.

HERMANNUS. But at some other time, when it's convenient for you, we'll visit the country together.

GISBERTUS. If I'm free I won't refuse.

HERMANNUS. I've got to go to the country to bring back sweet-smelling boughs.

GISBERTUS. You'll find they've hardly sprouted yet.

HERMANNUS. I'll find plenty, for they've been in blossom for a good while.

GISBERTUS. And then will you offer them for sale, crying 'buy my fragrant boughs' in the streets?

HERMANNUS. Do you reckon I do things like that?

GISBERTUS. Where else will you take them?

HERMANNUS. To our house, so that they'll make a pleasant smell there.

GISBERTUS. Who gave you that job?

HERMANNVS. Mater.
GISBERTVS. Tum uade ocius exequere.
HERMANNVS. Satis temporis ad uesperam restat.
GISBERTVS. Audin tu, hac aestate quid ages, dum nimius fuerit aestus?
HERMANNVS. Domi me in umbra continebo.
GISBERTVS. Inamoenum est domi latitare aëre calido et blandienti.
HERMANNVS. Non infitias eo.
GISBERTVS. Cur tum sub tecto domi tempus teris?
HERMANNVS. Oportet per parentes.
GISBERTVS. Plus aequo curiosi et molesti sunt parentes, qui te eo tempore domi coercent, ut nusquam proripias.
HERMANNVS. Mei commodi sunt solliciti.
GISBERTVS. Istud domi desidere, quid conferre tibi potest?
HERMANNVS. Non parum prodest.
GISBERTVS. Explica.
HERMANNVS. Domi cochleae agendo uitam calceos non detero, neque a sole exuror, ut fuscus fiam.
GISBERTVS. Per Herculem istud multum commodat.

45–46 ut fuscus fiam … commodat.] ut fuscus fiam. A.

28. DE AVTVMNO

Iaspar et Iacobus

IASPAR. Adest rursus tempus istud pestiferum et hiemem reducens.
IACOBVS. Quod tempus putas?
IASPAR. Autumnale, cuius hodie primus est dies, festum Sancti Bartholomaei.
IACOBVS. Vocas tu istud tempus pestiferum?
IASPAR. Voco, quia nunquam magis quam hoc tempore morbo succumbumt homines.
IACOBVS. Si uerum fateri uis, nullo non tempore totius anni laboratur doloribus corporis.
IASPAR. Praecipue tamen autumni diebus.

HERMANNUS. My mother.
GISBERTUS. Then go and do it quickly.
HERMANNUS. There's enough time before evening.
GISBERTUS. Tell me, what will you do this summer when the heat gets too much?
HERMANNUS. I'll stay at home in the shade.
GISBERTUS. It's not pleasant to stay shut up at home when the air is warm and gentle.
HERMANNUS. I don't deny that.
GISBERTUS. So why do you waste your time inside your house?
HERMANNUS. My parents make me.
GISBERTUS. Your parents are overly fussy and tiresome if they shut you up in the house at that time, so that you never come out.
HERMANNUS. They're concerned for my welfare.
GISBERTUS. What good can staying at home like that do you?
HERMANNUS. Quite a lot.
GISBERTUS. Explain.
HERMANNUS. By living like a snail at home I don't wear out my shoes, and I don't get burnt by the sun and go swarthy.
GISBERTUS. By heavens, that is a great help.

28. AUTUMN

Iaspar and Iacobus

IASPAR. That pestilential season is here again, the one that brings back the winter.
IACOBUS. What season do you mean?
IASPAR. The autumn. Today's the first day, the feast of St Bartholomew.
IACOBUS. Do you call that season pestilential?
IASPAR. I do, because people never fall ill so much as in this season.
IACOBUS. If you want to speak the truth, there's no time in the whole year when people aren't troubled by pains in their bodies.
IASPAR. Especially in the autumn days, though.

IACOBVS. Nescio, laus superis, ego nunquam infirmitatem sensi [B6r] in autumno.
IASPAR. Praeter istud incommodum, et frugem tamen aliquam secum affert.
IACOBVS. In quo est frugifer?
IASPAR. Quia uinum profert.
IACOBVS. In hoc certe laudem meretur.
IASPAR. Alia quoque commoda habet.
IACOBVS. Quaenam? Dic.
IASPAR. Abigit pulices suo frigore, qui nos nocte in aestate uerminarunt.
IACOBVS. Certe non omnibus illos depellit.
IASPAR. Qui sentiunt pulices in autumno?
IACOBVS. Vetulae mulieres semper sub uestibus quaeritant eos.
IASPAR. Apud illas perpetuum habent hospitium.
IACOBVS. Adde et pediculi.
IASPAR. Autumnus etiam nucum adducit messem.
IACOBVS. Istas non admodum moror.
IASPAR. Narra quid causae siet.
IACOBVS. Quia adimunt uocis sinceritatem.
IASPAR. Eam restituit aqua pura et calida.
IACOBVS. Sed a cibo abhorreo qui me aquam potare cogit.
IASPAR. Supra communem hominum sortem sapis.
IACOBVS. Nunc me naso suspendis.
IASPAR. Non, quia homines saepe aliqua edunt, etiam unde perniciem sunt accepturi; istud tu fugiturum te dicis.

---

35 a cibo abhorreo] cibum abhorreo A

29. DE HIEME

Vilhelmus et Georgius

VILHELMVS. Ah ah, quantum frigeo!
GEORGIVS. Friges nunc temporis?
VILHELMVS. Nonne et tu frigore premeris?
GEORGIVS. Non, sed totus caleo.
VILHELMVS. Praestantius me uestitus es.

IACOBUS. I don't know. Thanks be to God, I've never felt ill in autumn.
IASPAR. Apart from that disadvantage, the autumn does bring some bounty.
IACOBUS. In what way it is bountiful?
IASPAR. Because it produces wine.
IACOBUS. It definitely deserves praise for that.
IASPAR. It has other advantages too.
IACOBUS. What are they? Tell me.
IASPAR. Its cold drives away the fleas that have infested us at night during the summer.
IACOBUS. It definitely doesn't get rid of them all.
IASPAR. What people feel fleas in the autumn?
IACOBUS. Old women are always looking for them under their clothes.
IASPAR. They have a permanent lodging with them.
IACOBUS. And lice too.
IASPAR. Autumn brings the nut harvest as well.
IACOBUS. I'm not especially fond of them.
IASPAR. Tell me the reason.
IACOBUS. Because they take away the clarity of the voice.
IASPAR. Pure, hot water restores it.
IACOBUS. But I loathe food that forces me to drink water.
IASPAR. You're wise beyond the common human lot.
IACOBUS. Now you're pulling my leg.
IASPAR. No, because people often eat particular things, even when they're going to be injured by them. You say you're going to avoid that.

29. WINTER

Vilhelmus and Georgius

VILHELMUS. Oh, oh, I'm so cold!
GEORGIUS. Are you cold now?
VILHELMUS. Isn't the cold affecting you, too?
GEORGIUS. No, I'm really warm.
VILHELMUS. You're better dressed than I am.

GEORGIVS. Id sane parum est, sed crepidae me calere faciunt.

VILHELMVS. Facile frigus pellit, cui crepidae sunt et chirothecae subductae pellibus.

GEORGIVS. Oportet et corpus multis operiri indumentis.

VILHELMVS. Quid faciam, nescio, male ad hiemem instructus sum.

GEORGIVS. Qui hoc fit?

VILHELMVS. Indumenti mihi nihil est quam conspicis.

GEORGIVS. [B6v] Vere, non bene tibi cum hieme conueniet.

VILHELMVS. Si in patria agerem in caelo essem.

GEORGIVS. Quare?

VILHELMVS. Dum ibidem essem, hiemem non sensi.

GEORGIVS. Non tum scholam inuisisti?

VILHELMVS. Aestate quidem, sed hieme post fornacem latui.

GEORGIVS. Quid egisti, torrebasne poma in fornace?

VILHELMVS. Vtique, et pira quandoque.

GEORGIVS. Mirum quod parentes tibi indulserunt.

VILHELMVS. Lubentissime, sed istam non habebo hic lautitiam.

GEORGIVS. Vereor quod non.

VILHELMVS. Ah, quantum mihi ferendum erit uice delitiarum, quas in patria habui.

GEORGIVS. Tibi ipsi es uates.

VILHELMVS. Dabit Deus his quoque finem.

GEORGIVS. Sed serius fortassis quam uelles.

VILHELMVS. Et haec olim (ut inquit poeta) meminisse iuuabit.

GEORGIVS. Mehercule dulcius nihil est quam actorum recordari laborum quos superauimus.

VILHELMVS. Multos tamen quandoque uidi (ut secundo Aeneidos de Aenea scribit Vergilius) qui lacrimando habitam miseriam recensuerunt.

GEORGIVS. Stulti homines, qui uictam calamitatem lacrimis prosequuntur.

GEORGIUS. That's not much, but my shoes keep me warm.
VILHELMUS. You'll easily ward off the cold if you've got shoes and gloves lined with fur.
GEORGIUS. And your body has to be covered with lots of clothes.
VILHELMUS. I don't know what I'll do. I'm badly prepared for winter.
GEORGIUS. Why is that?
VILHELMUS. I have no clothes, apart from what you can see.
GEORGIUS. Indeed, you're not going to be well suited to the winter.
VILHELMUS. If I was in my own country, I'd be in clover.
GEORGIUS. Why?
VILHELMUS. When I was there I didn't feel the winter.
GEORGIUS. Didn't you go to school then?
VILHELMUS. I did in summer, but in winter I sat by the stove.
GEORGIUS. What did you do? Roast apples in the stove?
VILHELMUS. Oh, yes, and sometimes pears.
GEORGIUS. Your parents indulged you amazingly.
VILHELMUS. They did it gladly, but here I won't enjoy that luxury.
GEORGIUS. I'm afraid not.
VILHELMUS. Oh, I'm going to have to put up with so much instead of the pleasures I had at home!
GEORGIUS. You're your own prophet.
VILHELMUS. God will put an end to that, as well.
GEORGIUS. But maybe later than you'd like.
VILHELMUS. 'Some day we'll take pleasure in remembering even this,' as the poet says.
GEORGIUS. I swear there's nothing more agreeable than remembering the past hardships we've overcome.
VILHELMUS. And yet I've sometimes seen a lot of people in tears as they reviewed the sorrows they'd known, as Vergil writes of Aeneas in the second book of the *Aeneid*.
GEORGIUS. Foolish people, to go on crying over a misfortune they've overcome.

30. DE VERE

Gerhardus et Bruno

GERHARDVS. Vnde tanta fluuiorum copia?
BRVNO. Nix altis in montibus liquitur.
GERHARDVS. Fortassis.
BRVNO. Sic est.
GERHARDVS. Tempus expetit, quia uer adest.
BRVNO. Non adesset uer, cum simus in Martio mense?
GERHARDVS. Nunc agricolae redeunt ad agros colendos.
BRVNO. Labor etiam rursus incumbit equis.
GERHARDVS. Satis per hiemem quieuerunt.
BRVNO. Inertiam ipsis aratrum expellet.
GERHARDVS. Fuistine hisce diebus in pomeriis?
BRVNO. Istic nihil est quod agam.
GERHARDVS. [B7r] An fortassis uiolas quaesisses.
BRVNO. Non sum uiolarum, sed librorum amator.
GERHARDVS. Putabam uiolas a rusticis egestas.
BRVNO. Hae tuo naso et ori conueniunt.
GERHARDVS. Bona uerba quaeso.
BRVNO. Vt loqueris, ita et responsum accipis.
GERHARDVS. Fateor, meo ipsius gladio cado.
BRVNO. Incidisti in foueam quam fecisti.
GERHARDVS. Post aliquot dies redolebunt pomeria uiolis.
BRVNO. Post multos, non paucos certe.
GERHARDVS. Indies iam e terra erumpunt.
BRVNO. Vidistin aliquas?
GERHARDVS. Vidi compluscculas.
BRVNO. Ego hoc uere nullam.
GERHARDVS. Si quas reperero, ad te feram.
BRVNO. Id facito, si te non grauabit.
GERHARDVS. Non me grauat obsequium amico exhibendum.

30. SPRING

Gerhardus and Bruno

GERHARDUS. Why are the rivers so high?
BRUNO. The snow's melting in the high mountains.
GERHARDUS. Maybe.
BRUNO. It's true.
GERHARDUS. It fits the season, because spring's arrived.
BRUNO. You'd expect spring to have arrived; we're in March.
GERHARDUS. Now the farmers are going back to working the fields.
BRUNO. And the horses are forced to work again.
GERHARDUS. They've rested enough over the winter.
BRUNO. The plough will drive the laziness out of them.
GERHARDUS. Have you been in the fields in the last few days?
BRUNO. I have no business there.
GERHARDUS. You might have been looking for violets.
BRUNO. I'm a lover of books, not of violets.
GERHARDUS. I thought that peasants shit violets.
BRUNO. It's your humour that's shitty.
GERHARDUS. Don't talk like that!
BRUNO. You get a reply that fits the way you speak.
GERHARDUS. I agree. I fall by my own sword.
BRUNO. You've fallen into the pit you dug yourself.
GERHARDUS. In a few days the fields will be blooming with violets.
BRUNO. In a good many days, not a few.
GERHARDUS. They're already coming up from the ground as the days go by.
BRUNO. Have you seen any?
GERHARDUS. I've seen quite a few.
BRUNO. I haven't seen any this spring.
GERHARDUS. If I find any I'll bring them to you.
BRUNO. Do, if it's not an inconvenience to you.
GERHARDUS. It's not an inconvenience to render a service to a friend.

BRVNO. Facile amicos tibi parabis (teste comico) si obsequiis conferendis aliis delectaris.

GERHARDVS. Inseruire amicis mihi delicium est.

BRVNO. Id hominem decet (ut alius inquit comicus) ut homini alteri deus sit, id est, praestet auxilium et commodum.

31. DE FESTO SANCTI GALLI

Nicolaus et Vinandus

NICOLAVS. Appetit nunc dies Sancti Galli, quo scholastici delectari solent.

VINANDVS. Ego certe ipsius aduentu nunc doleo.

NICOLAVS. Solebas tamen plus aliis gaudere ob diem istum.

VINANDVS. Fateor, sed nunc secus mecum agitur.

NICOLAVS. Amabo dic, quis tibi est scrupulus?

VINANDVS. Facilis est, et tamen plurimum me male habet.

NICOLAVS. Fortassis causam probe augurarer.

VINANDVS. Si coniectura consequi potes, dicam.

NICOLAVS. Periculum coniiciendi faciam.

VINANDVS. Age, audiam.

NICOLAVS. Non licebit tibi prosternationi galli adesse.

VINANDVS. Hercule rem acu tetigisti.

NICOLAVS. Sed cedo, quid impedimenti erit? [B7^{v}]

VINANDVS. Mater aes mihi largiri recusat.

NICOLAVS. Sis animi praesentis, isti rei facile medebor.

VINANDVS. Qui mihi succurres?

NICOLAVS. Mutuum tibi solidum aeris dabo.

VINANDVS. Si feceris, non diu carebis ipso.

NICOLAVS. Estne tibi animus laborare, ut tu gallum eneces, et (ut aiunt) rex efficiaris?

VINANDVS. Istud honoris non cupio, ubi nihil est lucri.

NICOLAVS. Vellem me posse ipsius caedem peragere.

VINANDVS. Vino te donabo, si ipsi mortem intuleris.

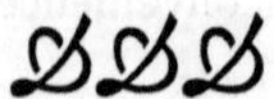

BRUNO. You'll easily make friends, as Terence says, if you please others by rendering services to them.
GERHARDUS. Serving the interests of friends is a pleasure to me.
BRUNO. As another playwright says, it's right for humans for one to be a god to another, that is to offer help and benefits.

31. ST GALL'S DAY

Nicolaus and Vinandus

NICOLAUS. St Gall's day is coming now, the day when schoolboys enjoy themselves.
VINANDUS. But I'm really sad that it's coming.
NICOLAUS. And yet you used to take more pleasure in that day than others did.
VINANDUS. True, but things are different for me now.
NICOLAUS. Do tell me what's worrying you.
VINANDUS. It's simple, yet it causes me a lot of grief.
NICOLAUS. I might be able to guess the reason correctly.
VINANDUS. If you can reach it by guesswork, I'll tell you.
NICOLAUS. I'll have a stab at guessing.
VINANDUS. Go on, I'll listen.
NICOLAUS. You won't be allowed to be at the killing of the cock.
VINANDUS. God, you've hit the nail on the head.
NICOLAUS. But tell me, what will hold you back?
VINANDUS. My mother refuses to let me have the money.
NICOLAUS. Stand firm, I'll sort that situation out easily.
VINANDUS. How will you help me?
NICOLAUS. I'll lend you a Schilling.
VINANDUS. If you do, you won't be without it for long.
NICOLAUS. Do you intend to make the effort to kill the cock, and be made the king, as they say?
VINANDUS. I've no desire for that honour, since no money goes with it.
NICOLAUS. I wish I could succeed in slaughtering the cock.
VINANDUS. I'll present you with some wine if you bring about its death.

NICOLAVS. Omne mouebo saxum, quo ipsum acerbius aliis tangam.
VINANDVS. Spectator ero.
NICOLAVS. Sed interim non obliuiscaris uini mihi modo promissi.
VINANDVS. Do fidem me praestiturum promissa.
NICOLAVS. Ego si gallum interfecero, lautum exhibebo nobis conuiuium.
VINANDVS. Quid a te immune accipiemus?
NICOLAVS. Duos gallos gallinaceos ad ueru coctos, et uini mensuras quattuor.
VINANDVS. Sat erit.
NICOLAVS. Spero quod aliquid uini mihi donabitur, tum minus impendii faciam.

---

18 medebor] medebor A C; meditebor B | 39–40 donabitur … faciam.] donabitur. A

32. DE FESTO SANCTI LAMBERTI

Paulus et Thomas

PAVLVS. Rursus matrem iratam reddam.
THOMAS. Quo ipsam offendes?
PAVLVS. Rogitando pecuniam.
THOMAS. Pecunia quid ages, cum uictum habeas?
PAVLVS. Aliis egeo quam uictu.
THOMAS. An non quibus indiges praebent tibi parentes?
PAVLVS. Quidni?
THOMAS. Cur tum aes expetis?
PAVLVS. Ludimagistro ut manus farciam.
THOMAS. Cuius rei gratia?
PAVLVS. Lamberti feriae expostulant.
THOMAS. Ecce, nisi dixisses oblitus fuissem.
PAVLVS. Nunquid et tu modico aere ipsum donabis?
THOMAS. Quod moris est, ipse non intermittam.
PAVLVS. So- [B8r] let fieri, sed ignoro an merito.
THOMAS. Forte praemii loco est?
PAVLVS. Pretium seorsum exoluitur.

NICOLAUS. I'll do everything I can to hit it harder than the others.
VINANDUS. I'll watch.
NICOLAUS. But in the meantime, don't forget the wine you've just promised me.
VINANDUS. I assure you I'll fulfil my promises.
NICOLAUS. If it's me who kills the cock, I'll provide us with a generous feast.
VINANDUS. What will you treat us to?
NICOLAUS. Two spit-roasted cocks and four measures of wine.
VINANDUS. That'll be enough.
NICOLAUS. I hope I'll be given some wine, then it'll mean less expense for me.

32. ST LAMBERT'S DAY

Paulus and Thomas

PAULUS. I'm going to make my mother angry again.
THOMAS. How are you going to annoy her?
PAULUS. By asking for money.
THOMAS. What do you need money for? You get given your food.
PAULUS. I need things apart from my food.
THOMAS. Don't your parents provide you with the things you need?
PAULUS. Of course.
THOMAS. So why are you trying to get hold of money?
PAULUS. So that I can tip the schoolmaster.
THOMAS. What's the reason?
PAULUS. You have to do it on St Lambert's day.
THOMAS. There, if you hadn't said that, I'd have forgotten.
PAULUS. Won't you be giving him a little money, too?
THOMAS. If it's the custom, I'm not going to break it.
PAULUS. It's the custom, but I'm not sure how proper it is.
THOMAS. Maybe it's in lieu of pay?
PAULUS. The school fees are paid separately.

THOMAS. Quod nunc dandum est, forte munus aestimat praeceptor.
PAVLVS. Id muneris crebrius pendimus.
THOMAS. Nostine? Saepe dandum amicis, ne intereat gratia.
PAVLVS. Praeceptor munere isto non amicus, sed inimicus redditur.
THOMAS. Exploratum unde habes?
PAVLVS. Scio aliquos qui plus ceteris ipsi conferunt munuscula, et illos acerbius aliis corrigit, et in eos animaduertit.
THOMAS. Quos saeuius tractat, illos prae aliis diligit.
PAVLVS. Istud diligere Eumenides ferant.
THOMAS. Cessa imprecari praeceptori.
PAVLVS. Quid tu ipsi dabis? Ego solido eum exhilarabo.
THOMAS. Nummum praestares quem indocti album uocant, tu opulentus es; ego obolum unum aut alterum dabo.

29 saeuius] seuius B C; seuerius A | 33–34 tu opulentus es … dabo.] tu opulentus es. A

33. DE ELIGENDO EPISCOPO

Iaspar et Melchior

IASPAR. Intererisne die Lunae gymnasio litterario?
MELCHIOR. Sic credo.
IASPAR. Cui tuam dabis uocem?
MELCHIOR. Quid hoc est, uocem dare?
IASPAR. Id est, quem eliges in episcopum?
MELCHIOR. Inconcinna est locutio.
IASPAR. Dic tu uenustiorem.
MELCHIOR. 'Cui tuum dabis suffragium?'
IASPAR. Poterisne et alio pacto eloqui?
MELCHIOR. Possum. 'In cuius personam eligendam tu consenties?'
IASPAR. Memoriae istas recondam orationes. Ego suffragabor tibi.
MELCHIOR. Ne facito.
IASPAR. Cur, istum non desideras magistratum?
MELCHIOR. Non, quia frugis nihil affert.

THOMAS. Perhaps the teacher sees the money we're going to give him now as a gift.
PAULUS. We often give him that kind of gift.
THOMAS. Don't you realise that you have to give your friends frequent presents, so that their friendship doesn't fade?
PAULUS. That gift doesn't make the teacher friendly, it makes him hostile.
THOMAS. How can you be sure of that?
PAULUS. I know a few boys who give him more presents than the others, and he punishes them more harshly than the others, and criticizes them.
THOMAS. The ones he treats more harshly are the ones he likes more than the others.
PAULUS. To Hell with that kind of liking!
THOMAS. Stop cursing the teacher.
PAULUS. What are you going to give him? I'll give him a Schilling, that'll please him.
THOMAS. You could give him an Albus, as the unlearned call it, you're well off. I'll give him a Heller or two.

33. ELECTING A 'BISHOP'

Iaspar and Melchior

IASPAR. Will you be at school on Monday?
MELCHIOR. I think so.
IASPAR. Who are you going to plump for?
MELCHIOR. What does 'plump for' mean?
IASPAR. Who will you elect as bishop?
MELCHIOR. That's an awkward expression.
IASPAR. Tell me a more graceful one.
MELCHIOR. 'Who will you vote for?'
IASPAR. Could you put it another way?
MELCHIOR. Yes. 'Which candidate will you elect?'
IASPAR. I'll commit those expressions to memory. I'm going to vote for you.
MELCHIOR. Don't.
IASPAR. Why don't you want that office?
MELCHIOR. Because it doesn't do me any good.

IASPAR. Satis praemii mihi esset honor iste.

MELCHIOR. Ipse honoris istius auidus non sum.

IASPAR. [B8v] At pulchrum est dici episcopus.

MELCHIOR. Verum, sed miserum est censum non expectare.

IASPAR. Si episcopus fierem, sperarem adhuc me in magnum euasurum uirum.

MELCHIOR. Vnde istud sperares?

IASPAR. Ex moribus gentilium.

MELCHIOR. Quos isti habuerunt mores?

IASPAR. Ab his quae in iuuentute alicui acciderunt, sumpserunt futurae fortunae condicionem.

MELCHIOR. Fiebant etiam quandoque uoti compotes, uel semper frustrabantur spe?

IASPAR. Quidni? Saepissime.

MELCHIOR. Exemplum unum eloquere.

IASPAR. Platoni in cunis dormienti apes in os mel ingesserunt, ex quo aruspices eum fore uirum facundum dixerunt, quod sic factum est.

MELCHIOR. Mirum quod audio, sed haud et aegre credibile est.

12–15: A reads: MEL. Possum. IASPAR. In cuius personam eligendam tu consenties? MEL. Memoriae istas recondam orationes. IAS. Ego sufragabor tibi. | 30–31 uoti compotes … spe?] uoti compotes? A | 37 audio … est.] audio. A

34. DE ELIGENDO REGE

Henricus et Iacobus

HENRICVS. Hodierno uesperi ubi tui cenabunt parentes?

IACOBVS. Vbi alias nisi domi nostrae?

HENRICVS. Non aliquo sunt uocati conuiuae?

IACOBVS. Quo hodie inuitati essent?

HENRICVS. Ad amicorum lances.

IACOBVS. Foris cenare eos puderet, hoc die.

HENRICVS. Apud honestos conuiuam agere non est pudendum.

IACOBVS. Fateor.

HENRICVS. Cur tum dicis quod eos puderet?

IASPAR. The honour would be enough reward for me.
MELCHIOR. I'm not eager for that honour.
IASPAR. But it's an honour to be called a bishop.
MELCHIOR. True, but it's miserable not to look forward to being wealthy.
IASPAR. If I was made bishop, I'd hope that I'd go on to become a great man.
MELCHIOR. What would make you hope that?
IASPAR. The practice of the pagans.
MELCHIOR. What was their practice?
IASPAR. From what happened to somebody in his youth they derived how his future position would turn out.
MELCHIOR. And did things sometimes turn out as they wished, or were their hopes always frustrated?
IASPAR. Often, of course.
MELCHIOR. Tell me one example.
IASPAR. When Plato was sleeping in his cradle, some bees put honey into his mouth. From that the diviners said that he would become an eloquent man, and so it turned out.
MELCHIOR. What you say's amazing, but it really is hard to believe.

34. ELECTING A 'KING'

Henricus and Iacobus

HENRICUS. Where will your parents have dinner this evening?
IACOBUS. At home, where else?
HENRICUS. Haven't they been invited somewhere as guests?
IACOBUS. Where would they have been invited today?
HENRICUS. To eat with friends.
IACOBUS. They would be ashamed to eat elsewhere today.
HENRICUS. There's no shame in being the guest of respectable people.
IACOBUS. True.
HENRICUS. So why do you say that they'd be ashamed?

IACOBVS. Quia non solent hanc uesperam sollemnem foris peragere.
HENRICVS. Qui fiat cedo?
IACOBVS. Nobiscum frontem domi exporrigunt.
HENRICVS. Ecquid uoluptatis domi habetis?
IACOBVS. Multum certe.
HENRICVS. Fortassis regem inter uos decernitis?
IACOBVS. Idipsum facimus scilicet.
HENRICVS. Delectune an sorte?
IACOBVS. Chartulis pilleo impositis.
HENRICVS. Suntne omnes inscriptae litteris?
IACOBVS. Sunt, et [C1r] quidem nominibus magistratuum.
HENRICVS. Adest etiam reginae scriptus titulus?
IACOBVS. Est, sed uel matri uel ancillis uenditatur.
HENRICVS. Fortuna quem regem fecerit quid pendet?
IACOBVS. Hodierno uesperi a sumptu est immunis.
HENRICVS. Immunis? Quis tum uini exsoluit cyathos?
IACOBVS. Potu omni nos alii regem donamus, sed ipse alio tempore suo aere geniale parat nobis conuiuium et regium.

---

25 uenditatur] uendicatur A B C | 29–30 donamus … regium.] donamus. A

35. DE FESTO NATALI CHRISTI

Georgius et Gisbertus

GEORGIVS. Ego nunquam toto anno plus gaudeo quam nunc temporis.
GISBERTVS. Ego uero nunquam magis doleo.
GEORGIVS. Doles tu, tempore adeo laeto?
GISBERTVS. Non dolerem, in tanto frigore?
GEORGIVS. Ipse totus laetor ob festorum dierum aduentum et copiam.
GISBERTVS. Quid feriae tibi commodant?
GEORGIVS. Otiabimur a lectionibus abunde.
GISBERTVS. Quot dies?

IACOBUS. Because it's not their custom to spend this holy evening away from home.
HENRICUS. Why is that, may I ask?
IACOBUS. They enjoy themselves with us at home.
HENRICUS. What amusement do you have at home?
IACOBUS. A whole lot.
HENRICUS. Do you appoint a king from amongst your number, maybe?
IACOBUS. Indeed we do.
HENRICUS. Do you choose him or is it done by lot?
IACOBUS. With slips of paper put into a hat.
HENRICUS. Have they all got things written on them?
IACOBUS. Yes, the names of the court offices.
HENRICUS. Is the title of queen written out too?
IACOBUS. Yes, but it's sold to my mother or one of the maids.
HENRICUS. What will the person who's made king by chance pay?
IACOBUS. He's let off paying tonight.
HENRICUS. Let off? So who'll pay for the wine?
IACOBUS. The rest of us give the king all he drinks, but later he gives us a festive, royal banquet with his own money.

35. THE FEAST OF CHRISTMAS

Georgius and Gisbertus

GEORGIUS. Out of the whole year, I'm never gladder than at this time.
GISBERTUS. And I'm never more miserable.
GEORGIUS. Are you miserable, at such a happy time?
GISBERTUS. Why wouldn't I be, in this cold?
GEORGIUS. I'm really happy that the festive days are coming, and that there are so many of them.
GISBERTUS. What advantage are the holidays to you?
GEORGIUS. We'll have a great deal of time off lessons.
GISBERTUS. How many days?

GEORGIVS. Ferme quattuordecim.
GISBERTVS. Quando incipientur istae uacationes nostrae?
GEORGIVS. A pridiano Thomae, et ad alterum Circumcisionis diem durant.
GISBERTVS. Et interim non uisimus scholam?
GEORGIVS. Accedimus quandoque, sed solum cantatum.
GISBERTVS. Quae cantabimus?
GEORGIVS. Reddenda istis sacris diebus in templo.
GISBERTVS. Istos cantus noui abhinc biennio.
GEORGIVS. Anni curriculo mihi exciderunt memoria.
GISBERTVS. Oportet ut sterilissima sit tibi memoria.
GEORGIVS. Talia mihi curae non sunt, diligentius lusus quam ista cogito.
GISBERTVS. Scholasticum id dedecet.
GEORGIVS. Canenda his diebus habesne scripta?
GISBERTVS. Habeo, et cum musicis concentibus.
GEORGIVS. Exscribenda mihi ipsa accommodes.
GISBERTVS. Libentissime.
GEORGIVS. [C1v] Plurimum laetor quod nunc temporis adeo mitis est aër, et non acerbum frigus.
GISBERTVS. Et ego gaudeo, alias in matutinis precibus frigore perirem.
GEORGIVS. In lecto me continerem si frigus saeuiret.
GISBERTVS. Ah, propter nouum regem natum nihil uelis pati?
GEORGIVS. Durum est a tepido nido discedere.

---

15 A pridiano Thomae, et ad] A uigilia Thomae ad A | 17 uisimus] uisemus A | 18 Accedimus] Accedemus A | 22 memoria] memoriae A | 36–37 pati? … discedere.] pati? A

36. DE TEMPORE BACCHANALI

Michael et Vilhelmus

MICHAEL. Quot hebdomadae nunc intersunt inter ferias natales Christianas et Quadragesimam?
VILHELMVS. Opinor nouem.
MICHAEL. Hui, tot?

GEORGIUS. Almost fourteen.
GISBERTUS. When do these holidays of ours start?
GEORGIUS. On the eve of St Thomas's Day, and they last till the day after the Circumcision.
GISBERTUS. And won't we have been in school in that space of time?
GEORGIUS. We go sometimes, but only to sing.
GISBERTUS. What will we sing?
GEORGIUS. The chants to be performed in church on these holy days.
GISBERTUS. I've known those chants for two years.
GEORGIUS. They've dropped out of my memory with the passing of the year.
GISBERTUS. Your memory must be really useless.
GEORGIUS. I'm not bothered about things like that. I put more effort into thinking about games than about them.
GISBERTUS. That's disgraceful for a schoolboy.
GEORGIUS. Have you got the chants to be sung on the coming feasts written down?
GISBERTUS. I have, with the music too.
GEORGIUS. Would you lend them to me so as I can write them out?
GISBERTUS. I'd be glad to.
GEORGIUS. What makes me happiest is that the air is mild at the moment, and the cold isn't intense.
GISBERTUS. I'm happy too, otherwise I'd die of cold at morning prayers.
GEORGIUS. I'd stay in bed if the cold was really fierce.
GISBERTUS. Oh, aren't you willing to suffer anything for the sake of the new-born King?
GEORGIUS. It's hard to get out of a warm bed.

36. SHROVETIDE

Michael and Vilhelmus

MICHAEL. How many weeks are there now between the Christmas holidays and Lent?
VILHELMUS. Nine, I believe.
MICHAEL. Gosh, as many as that?

VILHELMVS. Ita relatu aliorum accepi.
MICHAEL. Cuius uerbis habes?
VILHELMVS. Viri cuiusdam apprime docti.
MICHAEL. Tum longum erit Carnispriuium.
VILHELMVS. Tace, obsecro, uerbum istud barbarum.
MICHAEL. 'Carnispriuium', non est uerbum uenustum et Latinum?
VILHELMVS. Minime, sed maxime impolitum.
MICHAEL. Dic politiorem dictionem aliquam.
VILHELMVS. Tempus Bacchanale.
MICHAEL. Cur ita appellas tempus hoc?
VILHELMVS. Quia olim in sacrificiis Bacchi insaniebant ita, ut hoc tempore furunt.
MICHAEL. Insaniebant sacrificando Baccho deo gentiles?
VILHELMVS. Viuebant in omni luxu et dementia.
MICHAEL. Estne tibi aliud uerbum quo hoc tempus appelles?
VILHELMVS. Festum uel tempus Lupercale etiam potest dici.
MICHAEL. Quid noui uerbi affers?
VILHELMVS. Nouum non est, sed a ueteribus historicis proditum.
MICHAEL. A quibus?
VILHELMVS. A Valerio Maximo.
MICHAEL. Cur istud nomen huic tribuis tempori?
VILHELMVS. Ob morem gentilium.
MICHAEL. Quis is erat mos?
VILHELMVS. Pastores pecorum currebant hoc tempore nudi, habentes pelles in manibus, in honorem Panos dei pastorum.
MICHAEL. In [C2r] quod commodum isti sacrificabant?
VILHELMVS. Credebant quod ab ouibus pelleret lupos, hinc uocatum est tempus Lupercale.
MICHAEL. Fiebant etiam uoti compotes?
VILHELMVS. Ignoro, nam tum temporis uitam non egi.

10, 12 Carnispriuium] Carnisbriuium A | 19 furunt] furiunt A C

VILHELMUS. That's what I've been told by others.
MICHAEL. Whose word do you have?
VILHELMUS. Someone extremely learned.
MICHAEL. Then Shrovetide, 'Carnispriuium', will be long.
VILHELMUS. Please, please, don't say that barbarous word.
MICHAEL. Isn't 'Carnispriuium' an elegant Latin word?
VILHELMUS. No, it's a really inelegant one.
MICHAEL. Tell me some more elegant way of saying it.
VILHELMUS. The Bacchanalia.
MICHAEL. Why do you call this time by that name?
VILHELMUS. Because in the past people went mad during the holidays of Bacchus, just as they go crazy at this time.
MICHAEL. Did the pagans go mad making sacrifices to Bacchus?
VILHELMUS. They lived in utter extravagance and madness.
MICHAEL. Do you know another word that you can use for this time?
VILHELMUS. It can be called the holiday or time of Lupercal.
MICHAEL. What kind of new word are you introducing?
VILHELMUS. It's not new, it's handed down by the old historians.
MICHAEL. Who by?
VILHELMUS. Valerius Maximus.
MICHAEL. Why do you apply that name to this time?
VILHELMUS. On account of the pagans' custom.
MICHAEL. What custom was that?
VILHELMUS. At that time the shepherds ran about naked, with sheepskins in their hands, in honour of Pan, the god of shepherds.
MICHAEL. What benefit were they trying to achieve with their sacrifices?
VILHELMUS. They thought it would drive the wolves away from the sheep, and so the time was called Lupercal, from 'lupus', 'wolf'.
MICHAEL. And did things turn out as they wished?
VILHELMUS. I don't know, I wasn't alive at that time.

37. DE QVADRAGESIMA

Seuerinus et Philippus

SEVERINVS. Poetarum non semper uanae sunt fabulae.
PHILIPPVS. Certe me iudice parum habent ueri.
SEVERINVS. Habent mea sententia saepe nihil praeter ueritatem.
PHILIPPVS. Probes id, alioqui fidem tibi non habeo.
SEVERINVS. De Fortuna fabulantur quod rotae insistat.
PHILIPPVS. Notum habui diu.
SEVERINVS. Istud ueracissime dicunt.
PHILIPPVS. Fac mihi persuadeas.
SEVERINVS. Hactenus per aliquot dies curauimus cutem delicatissime.
PHILIPPVS. Praeterea quid?
SEVERINVS. Et nunc instat tempus quo corpus rursus macerabimus.
PHILIPPVS. Aestimas forte ieiunii tormentum.
SEVERINVS. Puto istud, nam carnes prohibentur, quae solae pascunt corpus.
PHILIPPVS. Etiam pisces multos saginant.
SEVERINVS. Neruos adeo non roborant, ut caro.
PHILIPPVS. Immo uideas nonnullos pinguiores ex piscibus quam alios e carnibus.
SEVERINVS. Qui isti sunt?
PHILIPPVS. Monachi in coenobiis, ubi Pythagorice mensa instruitur.
SEVERINVS. Crassa illorum capita et uentres obesi certe e piscibus non fiunt uel exurgunt.
PHILIPPVS. Forte extra limen monasteriorum uescuntur, credis, carnibus?
SEVERINVS. Scio et uidi, non solum credo.
PHILIPPVS. Et mihi uisum est creberrime.
SEVERINVS. In hisce semiseptem hebdomadibus esurialibus quo uesceris cibo?
PHILIPPVS. Pisis et piris in fornace tostis.

37. LENT

Severinus and Philippus

SEVERINUS. The stories poets tell aren't always false.

PHILIPPUS. As far as I can judge, there's very little true in them.

SEVERINUS. In my opinion they often tell nothing but the truth.

PHILIPPUS. Prove that, or else I'll not believe you.

SEVERINUS. They tell about Fortune, that she sits on a wheel.

PHILIPPUS. I've known that for a long time.

SEVERINUS. They're absolutely truthful in saying that.

PHILIPPUS. Convince me.

SEVERINUS. Up till now we've been doing ourselves extremely well for a number of days.

PHILIPPUS. Yes, and?

SEVERINUS. And now the time when we'll torment our bodies again is upon us.

PHILIPPUS. I suppose you mean the agony of fasting.

SEVERINUS. That's what I'm thinking of, because meats are forbidden, and they're the only foods that satisfy the body.

PHILIPPUS. Fish fatten a lot of people, too.

SEVERINUS. But they don't give the body strength the way meat does.

PHILIPPUS. And yet you could see some people fatter from eating fish than others are from eating meat.

SEVERINUS. Who are they?

PHILIPPUS. Monks in monasteries, where the table is set frugally.

SEVERINUS. Their fat faces and plump bellies definitely don't come from eating fish.

PHILIPPUS. Do you think, perhaps, that they eat meat outside the monastery?

SEVERINUS. I don't just think it – I know it and I've seen it.

PHILIPPUS. And I've seen it too, a lot.

SEVERINUS. In these six and a half weeks of fasting, what food will we eat?

PHILIPPUS. Peas and pears baked in the oven.

SEVERINVS. Ficubus istis, qui rusticis mel sapiunt?
PHILIPPVS. Ita, illos ad panem edo cum nucibus. [C2v]

---

3 Poetarum non semper] Poëtarum semper A

38. DE FESTO PASCHATIS

Petrus et Matthaeus

PETRVS. Appetit nunc tempus quo nullum toto anno est crudelius.
MATTHAEVS. Quod illud est adeo impium?
PETRVS. Paschatis puto dies.
MATTHAEVS. Sunt isti tibi immanes et impii?
PETRVS. Vtique, nam magna solet fieri caedes.
MATTHAEVS. Habetur tum semper bellum hoc tempore?
PETRVS. Nescis istud?
MATTHAEVS. Ignoro.
PETRVS. Nosti Thuringiam, regionem Germaniae orientalis?
MATTHAEVS. Nosco, ubi urbs Erphurdia est excellentior.
PETRVS. Ibidem duo sunt loci, unus ab halece, alter a uitulo nomen sortitus.
MATTHAEVS. Et quid postea?
PETRVS. Inter hos circa Pascha ingens bellum oritur.
MATTHAEVS. Etiam annuo?
PETRVS. Immo, quotennis duabus uicibus.
MATTHAEVS. Tempore dic quo?
PETRVS. Circa quadragesimae auspicium et ferias Paschales.
MATTHAEVS. Cuius loci incolae euadunt uictores?
PETRVS. Dum exorditur esuriale tempus, illi de halece agnominati.
MATTHAEVS. Quare illi?
PETRVS. Quia diebus ieiunii piscis iste in coquinis et patinis dominatur.
MATTHAEVS. Quando illi triumphant de praelio, quibus uitulus agnomen praebuit?
PETRVS. Paschatis tempore.
MATTHAEVS. Qui hoc?

SEVERINUS. Those 'figs', that peasants think taste like honey?
PHILIPPUS. Yes. I eat them on bread with nuts.

38. THE FEAST OF EASTER

Petrus and Matthaeus

PETRUS. And now the time's approaching that's crueller than any other time of the year.
MATTHAEUS. What really wicked time is that?
PETRUS. I'm thinking of the days of Easter.
MATTHAEUS. Do you find those days brutal and wicked?
PETRUS. Yes indeed, because there's always a huge slaughter then.
MATTHAEUS. Is there always a war at that time?
PETRUS. Don't you know that?
MATTHAEUS. No, I don't.
PETRUS. Do you know Thüringen, a region in the east of Germany?
MATTHAEUS. Yes, where the fine city of Erfurt is.
PETRUS. There are two places there; one has taken its name from the herring, the other from the calf.
MATTHAEUS. And so?
PETRUS. Around Easter, a huge war breaks out between them.
MATTHAEUS. Every year?
PETRUS. Twice every year, actually.
MATTHAEUS. Tell me at what time.
PETRUS. Around the start of Lent and at Easter time.
MATTHAEUS. The people of which town turn out the winners?
PETRUS. At the start of Lent it's the people named after the herring.
MATTHAEUS. Why them?
PETRUS. Because during the fast days that fish rules in the markets and on people's plates.
MATTHAEUS. And when do the people who take their name from the calf win the battle?
PETRUS. At Easter time.
MATTHAEUS. How?

PETRVS. Nam sequentibus diebus uictitatur carnibus.
MATTHAEVS. Lepidum audio iocum.
PETRVS. Hoc quondam Erphurdiae agens, nugari audiui.
MATTHAEVS. Satis festiuum dicterium.

2 Matthaeus] Matthias A | 16 Et quid] Ecquid A | 23 illi de halece] illi halece A

39. DE FESTO PENTECOSTES

Vinandus et Baptista

VINANDVS. Sabbato proximo pridianus erit dies festi Pentecostes.
BAPTISTA. Compertum id habeo.
VINANDVS. Ventri nostro rursus bellum afferet.
BAPTISTA. Quale bellum [C3r] narras?
VINANDVS. Corporis bellum, ieiunium scilicet.
BAPTISTA. Pulchre ieiunium uocas bellum, quia uentri odiosum est.
VINANDVS. Hactenus tranquilla fuit caro nostra.
BAPTISTA. Vnde ista sibi tranquillitas quam aestimas?
VINANDVS. Quia a Paschatis die non sensit ieiunii molestiam.
BAPTISTA. Corpus meum tum ouis, tum aliis affatim est pastum delicatis bolis.
VINANDVS. Sabbato denuo in pistrinum ibimus.
BAPTISTA. Facile est unum diem abstinentia peragere.
VINANDVS. Ipso die Pentecostes accedes sacram Synaxin?
BAPTISTA. Incertus sum.
VINANDVS. Quid sic? Ego me accingam quo gratiam Spiritus Sancti acquiram.
BAPTISTA. Facerem et id ipse quoque, sed unicum me moratur.
VINANDVS. Istud quidnam est?
BAPTISTA. Inuitus confiteor.
VINANDVS. Ego alicui ignoto mea delicta recenseo, tum plus audeo.
BAPTISTA. Parabo et me, ut tecum peccata in sacrificuli aurem murmerem.

PETRUS. Because in the days that follow people live on meat.
MATTHAEUS. That's a good joke.
PETRUS. I heard it told when I was living at Erfurt a while ago.
MATTHAEUS. It's a really amusing joke.

39. THE FEAST OF PENTECOST

Vinandus and Baptista

VINANDUS. Next Saturday it'll be the eve of the feast of Pentecost.
BAPTISTA. I know.
VINANDUS. It'll make war on our stomachs again.
BAPTISTA. What kind of war do you mean?
VINANDUS. The war of the body – fasting.
BAPTISTA. It's very apt to call fasting a war, because it's offensive to the stomach.
VINANDUS. Up till now our bodies have been at peace.
BAPTISTA. Where did the peace, as you see it, come from?
VINANDUS. Because they haven't felt the discomfort of fasting since Easter Day.
BAPTISTA. My body has been amply fed with eggs and other delicious things.
VINANDUS. On Saturday we'll be back to the grind again.
BAPTISTA. It's easy to get through one day of abstinence.
VINANDUS. Will you go to Communion on the day of Pentecost?
BAPTISTA. I'm not sure.
VINANDUS. Why not? I'm going to make an effort so as to obtain the grace of the Holy Spirit.
BAPTISTA. I'd do the same myself, but there's one thing holding me back.
VINANDUS. Tell me, what's that?
BAPTISTA. I'm not keen on going to Confession.
VINANDUS. I tell my sins to someone I don't know, then I have more courage.
BAPTISTA. I'll prepare myself too, and join you in muttering my sins into some priest's ear.

VINANDVS. His Spiritus Sancti feriis nobis scholasticis imprimis est scelerum faex eiicienda.
BAPTISTA. Vere dicis, ut Spiritus Sanctus nos inuisat.
VINANDVS. Si is nobis praesto fuerit sine sudore discemus.
BAPTISTA. O utinam tum mihi adesset.
VINANDVS. Peccata exue, poenitentiam age, certe te suo donabit munere.
BAPTISTA. Enitar pro uiribus.
VINANDVS. Sic facias, et litteris fias aptior alumnus.

---

13 Quia a Paschatis] Quia Paschatis A | 31 inuisat] inuisat C; inuiset A B | 36–37 Enitar pro uiribus … fias aptior alumnus.] Enitar pro uiribus. A

40. DE FESTO SANCTI MARTINI

Hieronymus et Hermannus

HIERONYMVS. Quot nam dies ab hinc absunt feriae sancti Martini?
HERMANNVS. Opinor octo.
HIERONYMVS. Quo die peragentur?
HERMANNVS. In macra die, scilicet Veneris.
HIERONYMVS. Vespera tamen erit ipso die Iouis.
HERMANNVS. Erit, ni fallor.
HIERONYMVS. O tum adhuc bene nobiscum agetur.
HERMANNVS. Vnde illud coniicis?
HIERONYMVS. Nam tunc carni- [C3v] bus uescentur homines.
HERMANNVS. Illud nostro stomacho nihil commodabit.
HIERONYMVS. Immo plurimum proderit.
HERMANNVS. Effare quomodo.
HIERONYMVS. Quicquid iusculi uel carnis a mensis leuarint nobis ad fores cantantibus impartient.
HERMANNVS. Ad istud certe ollam mihi parabo.
HIERONYMVS. Si tibi placuerit, inuicem tunc temporis ostiatim canemus?
HERMANNVS. Oppido mihi arridet.

VINANDUS. During these days sacred to the Holy Spirit, the most important thing for us schoolboys to do is to get rid of the dregs of sin.
BAPTISTA. You're right, if the Holy Spirit will watch over us.
VINANDUS. If he's with us, we'll learn effortlessly.
BAPTISTA. Then I wish he would be with me!
VINANDUS. Throw off your sins and do penance, he'll certainly give you his gift.
BAPTISTA. I'll make the very best effort I can.
VINANDUS. Do that, and become better at your studies.

40. ST MARTIN'S DAY

Hieronymus and Hermannus

HIERONYMUS. How many days from now is St Martin's Day?
HERMANNUS. Eight, I think.
HIERONYMUS. What day does it fall on?
HERMANNUS. On a day of abstinence, Friday.
HIERONYMUS. But the eve will be on Thursday.
HERMANNUS. It will, if I'm not mistaken.
HIERONYMUS. Oh, then it'll be good for us.
HERMANNUS. What makes you say that?
HIERONYMUS. Because then people eat meat.
HERMANNUS. That won't do our stomachs any good.
HIERONYMUS. Oh yes it will – a lot.
HERMANNUS. How, tell me?
HIERONYMUS. They'll make us a present of whatever sauce or meat they've taken from their tables when we sing at their doors.
HERMANNUS. I'll certainly get my bowl ready for that.
HIERONYMUS. If you like, we'll take turns at singing at people's doors then.
HERMANNUS. I'd really like that.

HIERONYMVS. Sed quidquid obsonii, uel aeris, nobis datum fuerit, commune erit.

HERMANNVS. Conferetur in illius uesperae nostrum conuiuium.

HIERONYMVS. Sed qua hora egrediemur precatum stipem?

HERMANNVS. Postquam octaua sonuerit.

HIERONYMVS. Illud temporis plane integrum erit nostrae precationi.

HERMANNVS. Conueniet maxime, nam eo tempore de mensa tolluntur patinae.

HIERONYMVS. Anno ab hinc proximo tantum accepi alimenti quo octo uictitabam dies.

HERMANNVS. O si ea nunc rediret fortuna.

HIERONYMVS. Sperandum est, et Deo confidendum.

HERMANNVS. Quis illius non anhelaret adminiculum?

HIERONYMVS. Multi suum exoptant praesidium, uerum inseruiunt ipsi inique.

HERMANNVS. Hi consequentur gratiam eius ad Graecorum Kalendas.

---

24 Conferetur] Conferetur C; Conferretur A B

41. DE XENIIS MITTENDIS

Kilianus et Theodericus

KILIANVS. Precor tibi diem candidum.

THEODERICVS. Talem et tibi opto.

KILIANVS. Xenium fac mihi praebeas.

THEODERICVS. Hui, tam cito? Vix noui anni dies illuxit.

KILIANVS. Hodie uerum est tempus dandi xeniola.

THEODERICVS. Hodie incipit, sed diu durat.

KILIANVS. Fateor, sed tantum qui alteri dare uolunt non diuturnam moram agunt.

THEODERICVS. Expecta quoad ipsum struxero.

KILIANVS. Non opto strenam farinaceam.

THEODERICVS. Lautior mihi non est alia.

HIERONYMUS. But whatever food or money we're given, we'll share.
HERMANNUS. It'll be taken to the banquet we'll have that evening
HIERONYMUS. But what time will we go out and beg for our alms?
HERMANNUS. After eight.
HIERONYMUS. That time will be just right for our begging.
HERMANNUS. It'll be really suitable, because that's the time the plates are cleared from the table.
HIERONYMUS. Last year I got enough food to live on for a week.
HERMANNUS. If we had the same good fortune again this time!
HIERONYMUS. We must hope, and trust in God.
HERMANNUS. Who wouldn't long for support from him?
HIERONYMUS. There are lots of people who long for his assistance, but whose devotion to him is very grudging.
HERMANNUS. They'll never ever obtain his grace.

41. SENDING NEW YEAR'S GIFTS

Kilianus and Theodoricus

KILIANUS. I wish you a prosperous day.
THEODORICUS. And I wish you the same.
KILIANUS. Give me a present.
THEODORICUS. What, as quickly as that? New Year's Day has hardly dawned.
KILIANUS. This is the right time for giving presents.
THEODORICUS. It begins today, but it lasts for a long while.
KILIANUS. True, but people who want to give something to someone else don't delay it for a long time.
THEODORICUS. Wait till I've made it.
KILIANUS. I don't want a pastry as a present.
THEODORICUS. I haven't got anything finer.

KILIANVS. [C4r] Sed puderet me amicum mellito munusculo salutare.

THEODERICVS. Qui id fit?

KILIANVS. Quia timerem ne ab ipso nausearet.

THEODERICVS. Vanum metuis, si bonus esset, boni consuleret.

KILIANVS. Verbis fortassis, at corde sperneret.

THEODERICVS. Is personatus amicus esset.

KILIANVS. Honestius est panniculum emunctiorum largiri uice xenii.

THEODERICVS. Est quidem, sed tale munus non omnibus in promptu est.

KILIANVS. De interula aut panni ulna plura conficiuntur.

THEODERICVS. Sed saepe pluris constat conficiendi sumptus quam pannus.

KILIANVS. Cultros uidi quandoque inter amicos missitari.

THEODERICVS. Illos ego non mitterem.

KILIANVS. Cur?

THEODERICVS. Quia uulgo dicitur, cultros amicitiam rumpere.

KILIANVS. Stolide, isti tu accedis dicto?

THEODERICVS. Non totus consentio.

KILIANVS. Attamen nonnihil ipsi fidem praebes.

THEODERICVS. Facio ut solent hi qui quicquid audiunt, ex oraculo prolatum putant.

KILIANVS. Es tu illius farinae homo?

THEODERICVS. Nescio, me ipsum non nosco.

KILIANVS. Sed strenulam mihi fac mittas.

THEODERICVS. Cras ultro tibi conferam, interim spe uiuas.

2, etc. Theodericus] Theodolus A | 37 Facio] Facio A C; Facito B

KILIANUS. But I'd be ashamed to present a friend with a honey-cake as a gift.
THEODORICUS. Why?
KILIANUS. Because I'd be afraid he might hate it.
THEODORICUS. You're wrong to worry. If he was good, he'd take it in good part.
KILIANUS. He might say he did, but in his heart he'd disdain it.
THEODORICUS. He would only be pretending to be a friend.
KILIANUS. It's more becoming to give a handkerchief as a present.
THEODORICUS. It is, but not everyone has that sort of gift to hand.
KILIANUS. You can make several out of a shirt or an ell of cloth.
THEODORICUS. But making them often costs more than the cloth.
KILIANUS. I've sometimes seen knives being sent as presents between friends.
THEODORICUS. I wouldn't give them.
KILIANUS. Why not?
THEODORICUS. Because there's a popular saying that knives break friendships.
KILIANUS. You stupid boy, do you go along with that saying?
THEODORICUS. I don't entirely agree.
KILIANUS. And yet you believe it to a certain extent.
THEODORICUS. I do what people do who think that anything they hear has been spoken by an oracle.
KILIANUS. Are you that sort of person?
THEODORICUS. I don't know; I don't know myself.
KILIANUS. But do send me a present.
THEODORICUS. I'll willingly send you one tomorrow. In the meantime, live in hope.

42. DE PECVNIA DANDA IN NOVAE SCHOLAE INGRESSV

Martinus et Nicolaus

MARTINVS. Feriabimurne post meridiem a lectionibus?
NICOLAVS. Non compertum habeo.
MARTINVS. Ego ea spe ducor.
NICOLAVS. Vide ne uanam spem foueas.
MARTINVS. Certus sum, spe non frustrabor.
NICOLAVS. Praestaret fideiussorem habere.
MARTINVS. Tam scio quam nomen meum.
NICOLAVS. Eloquere, qui scias.
MARTINVS. Est mihi adolescens domi, qui primus iam scholam inuiset.
NICOLAVS. Hoc quid afferet nobis?
MARTINVS. Ipse a praeceptore copiam otiandi nobis impetrabit.
NICOLAVS. Qua arte?
MARTINVS. Largiendo ipsi pauxillulum nummorum.
NICOLAVS. Putas illud quod introitum [C4v] uulgo appellitant?
MARTINVS. Istud ipsum uolo.
NICOLAVS. Sat habeo.
MARTINVS. Verum, nostin unde mos ille prouenerit?
NICOLAVS. Audiui nunquam originem.
MARTINVS. Dicam huius consuetudinis fontem, si te audire non taeduerit.
NICOLAVS. Audire gestio.
MARTINVS. Qui apud artifices mechanicos tirones sunt, istius artificii classi aliquid pendere coguntur.
NICOLAVS. Vidi quandoque in ipsorum artificum conciliabulo.
MARTINVS. Isto munusculo fauorem sibi uindicant aliorum.
NICOLAVS. Etiam in ipsorum album referuntur.
MARTINVS. Non secus et nouus litterarum tiro et praeceptorem et nos demeretur.

42. PAYING MONEY ON STARTING AT A NEW SCHOOL

Martinus and Nicolaus

MARTINUS. Will we get off lessons in the afternoon?
NICOLAUS. I'm not certain.
MARTINUS. That's what I'm hoping for.
NICOLAUS. Be careful that you're not nursing a vain hope.
MARTINUS. I'm sure. My hopes won't be disappointed.
NICOLAUS. It would be better to have someone who would guarantee it.
MARTINUS. I know it as well as I know my own name.
NICOLAUS. Tell me how you know.
MARTINUS. There's a young lad at home who's coming to school for the first time today.
NICOLAUS. What good will that do us?
MARTINUS. He'll get the teacher to allow us off school.
NICOLAUS. How will he manage that?
MARTINUS. By presenting him with a small amount of money.
NICOLAUS. Do you mean what's commonly called an entrance fee?
MARTINUS. That's exactly what I mean.
NICOLAUS. I'm content with that.
MARTINUS. But do you know where that practice came from?
NICOLAUS. I've never heard how it began.
MARTINUS. I'll tell you the origin of the custom, if it won't bore you to listen.
NICOLAUS. I'm eager to hear.
MARTINUS. Craft apprentices are required to pay something to the relevant craft guild.
NICOLAUS. I've seen that sometimes, in the craftsmen's meetings.
MARTINUS. They secure the others' goodwill with that gift.
NICOLAUS. And they're included amongst their members.
MARTINUS. In just the same way, the new boy at school will win the teacher's goodwill as well as ours.

NICOLAVS. Quo?
MARTINVS. Praeceptorem pauxillulo aeris, nos uero otio medii diei.

---

27 tirones] Tirones B; Tyrones A; tyrones C | 30 uindicant] uendicant A B C | 32 tiro] Tyro A B; tyro C

43. NON SEMPER ESSE STVDENDVM

Vincentius et Vilhelmus

VINCENTIVS. Heus tu, paucis te uolo.
VILHELMVS. Quis me uocat?
VINCENTIVS. En, ego te uoco.
VILHELMVS. Quid est, quod me uis?
VINCENTIVS. Facilis res est.
VILHELMVS. Exprime ocius.
VINCENTIVS. Qui fit quod ita palles?
VILHELMVS. Palleo? Id ipse ignoro.
VINCENTIVS. Palles non secus ac aegrotares.
VILHELMVS. Sane nihil sentio doloris, gratia Deo.
VINCENTIVS. Vnde tum pallor ille oritur?
VILHELMVS. Color hic mihi est natiuus.
VINCENTIVS. Non adeo pallescunt homines a natura.
VILHELMVS. Qui nosti? Esne medicus?
VINCENTIVS. Non, sed coniectura consequor, te chartis nimium addictum.
VILHELMVS. Litteris totum transigo otium quod habeo.
VINCENTIVS. Si id agis, tibi ipsi obes.
VILHELMVS. Hoc non spero, quod mihi desim studendo.
VINCENTIVS. Prodes forte animae, sed corpori noces.
VILHELMVS. Malo animae quam corporis profectum.
VINCENTIVS. Belle dicis, sed corpore debili et animae tandem uis perimitur.
VILHELMVS. Periti istud non asserunt.
VINCENTIVS. Quid tum dicunt?
VILHELMVS. Ad tenuem lancem [C5r] litteras melius imbibi.
VINCENTIVS. Concedo, sed tamen oportet corporis curam non totam omittere.

NICOLAUS. How?
MARTINUS. The teacher's with a little money, and ours with a half-holiday.

43. YOU SHOULDN'T STUDY ALL THE TIME

Vincentius and Vilhelmus

VINCENTIUS. Hey you, I want you for a moment.
VILHELMUS. Who's calling me?
VINCENTIUS. I am.
VILHELMUS. What is it you want with me?
VINCENTIUS. It's something simple.
VILHELMUS. Tell me quickly.
VINCENTIUS. What's the reason you're so pale?
VILHELMUS. I'm pale? I don't know myself.
VINCENTIUS. You're as pale as if you were ill.
VILHELMUS. At any rate I don't feel any pain, thank God.
VINCENTIUS. So where does your pallor come from?
VILHELMUS. It's my natural colour.
VINCENTIUS. People aren't as pale as that naturally.
VILHELMUS. How do you know? Are you a doctor?
VINCENTIUS. No, but my guess is that you're too devoted to your books.
VILHELMUS. I spend all the free time I have studying.
VINCENTIUS. If you do that, you're damaging yourself.
VILHELMUS. I hope I'm not neglecting myself by studying.
VINCENTIUS. You may do your mind good, but you're harming your body.
VILHELMUS. I'd rather the mind advanced than the body.
VINCENTIUS. Well said; but if the body's weak, the power of the mind is eventually destroyed too.
VILHELMUS. The experts don't say that.
VINCENTIUS. What do they say, then?
VILHELMUS. That learning is best taken in on a meagre diet.
VINCENTIUS. That's true, and yet you mustn't completely neglect caring for the body.

VILHELMVS. Neque hoc facio.
VINCENTIVS. Extremum dementiae esset abstinentia immodica suum fraudare genium.
VILHELMVS. Praestat tamen alimonia animae quam corporis.
VINCENTIVS. Eneruatis autem corporis uiribus, fulcimentum animae et uirtutibus tollitur.
VILHELMVS. Infitias non eo, quum corpus sit animae promptuarium.

---

36 animae et uirtutibus] animae uirtutibus A

44. QVEM LVDVM DEBEANT IVVENES EXERCERE

Antonius et Laurentius

ANTONIVS. Hui, ludis tu tesseris?
LAVRENTIVS. Hoc tua quid refert?
ANTONIVS. Ludus iste non scholasticorum est.
LAVRENTIVS. Quorum tum est?
ANTONIVS. Nebulonum, helluonum et histrionum.
LAVRENTIVS. Vidi ego complures litterarum tirones hoc uti ludo.
ANTONIVS. Nihilo fuere meliores.
LAVRENTIVS. Anne peiores eos fuisse censes?
ANTONIVS. Hercule, non solum peiores, sed et pessimi.
LAVRENTIVS. Tu nosti, quia tertius Cato es.
ANTONIVS. Ride ut lubet, uera loquor.
LAVRENTIVS. Nihil ludendum scholasticis arbitraris?
ANTONIVS. Ludendum et ipsis quandoque, sed aliud lusus genus.
LAVRENTIVS. Age, qui ludus?
ANTONIVS. Ludi nempe honesti et uerecundi.
LAVRENTIVS. Qui illi sunt?
ANTONIVS. Quos olim Romani suos docuerunt liberos.
LAVRENTIVS. Quales isti tradiderunt pueris?
ANTONIVS. Natare, dimicare et certare luctando.

VILHELMUS. And I don't.
VINCENTIUS. It would be the height of madness to weaken yourself by being overly abstemious.
VILHELMUS. And yet feeding the mind is preferable to feeding the body.
VINCENTIUS. But if the body's strength is weakened, the support is removed from the mind and the virtues.
VILHELMUS. You're right, because the body is the chamber of the soul.

44. WHAT GAME BOYS OUGHT TO PLAY

Antonius and Laurentius

ANTONIUS. What, are you playing dice?
LAURENTIUS. What difference does it make to you?
ANTONIUS. That's not a game for schoolboys.
LAURENTIUS. Who's it for, then?
ANTONIUS. Scoundrels, spendthrifts and buffoons.
LAURENTIUS. I've seen a lot of young schoolboys playing this game.
ANTONIUS. They were none the better for it.
LAURENTIUS. Do you think they were any the worse?
ANTONIUS. Good Lord, not just the worse – the very worst.
LAURENTIUS. You know, because you're a third Cato.
ANTONIUS. Laugh if you like, what I say is true.
LAURENTIUS. Don't you think schoolboys should play anything?
ANTONIUS. They should play sometimes, too, but a different kind of game.
LAURENTIUS. What game, tell me?
ANTONIUS. Respectable, seemly games, of course.
LAURENTIUS. What ones are they?
ANTONIUS. The ones the Romans taught their children in the past.
LAURENTIUS. What sort of games did they pass on to their children?
ANTONIUS. Swimming, fencing and wrestling.

LAVRENTIVS. Nullos alios?

ANTONIVS. Nullos, quod audiero.

LAVRENTIVS. Nunquam charta lusoria, uel talis?

ANTONIVS. Minime gentium.

LAVRENTIVS. Etiamne inter conuiuia cum amiculo?

ANTONIVS. Nusquam locorum.

LAVRENTIVS. Nimium sapuerint.

ANTONIVS. Si semel et iterum concessissent, male cecidisset.

LAVRENTIVS. Nonnunquam [C5v] ludere, ferendum esset.

ANTONIVS. Audistin Platonem dicentem, non paruum incommodum esse consuetudinem iniquam?

LAVRENTIVS. Consuetudo diutino et frequenti conatu fit, non raro tentando.

---

8 tirones] Tyrones A; tyrones B C | 15 Ludendum scholasticis] ludendum scholasticis A; ludendum et scholasticis B

45. DE ELEEMOSYNIS COLLIGENDIS

Ludouicus et Pantaleon

LVDOVICVS. Placetne tibi mihi congredi?

PANTALEON. Quo?

LVDOVICVS. Ignoras? Ostiatim, petitum decimas nostras.

PANTALEON. Decimas quid uocas?

LVDOVICVS. Stipem, quae nobis pauperibus a diuitibus erogatur.

PANTALEON. Est illa nobis uice decimarum?

LVDOVICVS. Vtique est.

PANTALEON. Mihi non fit uerisimile.

LVDOVICVS. Pinguis Mineruae homo es, quod ista non capis.

PANTALEON. Haud capio, rogo apertius mihi dicas.

LVDOVICVS. Obsecundabor, tu ausculta.

PANTALEON. Aduertam diligenter.

LVDOVICVS. Nosti agrorum dominos oportere suis aut paroecianis aut principibus pendere decimas?

PANTALEON. Nosco per parentes meos.

LAURENTIUS. No others?
ANTONIUS. None that I heard of.
LAURENTIUS. Never cards or dice?
ANTONIUS. Absolutely never.
LAURENTIUS. Not even at a meal with a friend?
ANTONIUS. Never at all.
LAURENTIUS. They were *too* sensible.
ANTONIUS. If they'd allowed those games once or twice, the consequences would have been bad.
LAURENTIUS. It would be acceptable to gamble sometimes.
ANTONIUS. Have you heard Plato's saying that an excessive habit does considerable harm?
LAURENTIUS. A habit comes from practising things often over a long period, not from trying them rarely.

45. COLLECTING ALMS

Ludovicus and Pantaleon

LUDOVICUS. Would you like to come with me?
PANTALEON. Where to?
LUDOVICUS. Don't you know? Round the houses, to ask for our tithes.
PANTALEON. What do you call 'tithes'?
LUDOVICUS. The alms paid by the rich to us poor boys.
PANTALEON. Is that what we get instead of tithes?
LUDOVICUS. It certainly is.
PANTALEON. It doesn't sound probable to me.
LUDOVICUS. You must be dim not to understand that.
PANTALEON. I don't understand it. Tell me more clearly, please.
LUDOVICUS. I'll do as you ask, you listen.
PANTALEON. I'll pay careful attention.
LUDOVICUS. You know that landowners have to pay tithes either to their parish priests or to their lords?
PANTALEON. My parents have told me.

LVDOVICVS. Non secus oportet et diuites illos, de suis bonis pendere nobis stipem.

PANTALEON. Certe si oporteret eos, tum nunquam recusarent.

LVDOVICVS. Dum renuunt, ipsis luditur.

PANTALEON. Immo plus luditur nobis quam ipsis.

LVDOVICVS. Longe aberras.

PANTALEON. Deliro, dicis? Venter mihi fame perit.

LVDOVICVS. Diuitum incommodum longe est grauius.

PANTALEON. Dic quod illud est.

LVDOVICVS. Dei incidunt iram, quod pietatis non sunt cultores.

PANTALEON. Istud non aestimant.

LVDOVICVS. Sed olim ante iudicem Deum acerbe sentient.

PANTALEON. Interim induciis fruuntur.

LVDOVICVS. Miserae induciae sunt, quas certum sequitur tormentum.

PANTALEON. Solacium tamen est, dilatione frui, etiam momentanea. [C6^{r}]

---

1 Eleemosynis] Eleemosinis A C | 2, etc. Pantaleon] Pantaleon C; Panthaleon A B | 17 paroecianis] parrecianis B C; parretianis A

46. DE LVDO PILAE

Gisbertus et Petrus

GISBERTVS. Vt sic desidetis? Surgite, pigerrimi.

PETRVS. Quid conabimur?

GISBERTVS. Colludemus nonnihil?

PETRVS. Malumus hic in gramine uiridi quiescere.

GISBERTVS. Endymionum est, non adolescentum, ita gramini incumbere.

PETRVS. Attamen dulce est.

GISBERTVS. Iucundius mihi est ludere quam torpere.

PETRVS. Age, ludendo concertemus.

GISBERTVS. Pilamne iaciendo inuicem?

LUDOVICUS. In just the same way those rich people have to pay us our alms out of their possessions.
PANTALEON. If they really had to, they'd never refuse.
LUDOVICUS. If they refuse, the joke's on them.
PANTALEON. No, the joke's more on us than on them.
LUDOVICUS. You're completely mistaken.
PANTALEON. You're saying I'm crazy? My stomach's aching with hunger.
LUDOVICUS. The disadvantage to the rich is far greater.
PANTALEON. Tell me what it is.
LUDOVICUS. They incur the wrath of God, because they don't observe their religious duty.
PANTALEON. They don't care about that.
LUDOVICUS. But one day they'll feel it bitterly before God as their judge.
PANTALEON. In the meantime, they're enjoying a period of grace.
LUDOVICUS. It's a pitiable period of grace that's followed by certain torment.
PANTALEON. Yet it's a comfort to enjoy a postponement, even a short-lived one.

46. PLAYING BALL

Gisbertus and Petrus

GISBERTUS. What are you lying around like that for? Get up, you lazy lot.
PETRUS. What'll we do?
GISBERTUS. Shall we play together a bit?
PETRUS. We prefer to rest here on this green grass.
GISBERTUS. Lying on the grass like that's for layabouts, not boys.
PETRUS. But it's pleasant.
GISBERTUS. I find it's more enjoyable to play than to laze about.
PETRUS. All right, let's play against one another.
GISBERTUS. Throwing the ball to one another?

PETRVS. Cui est pila? Nobis deest.
GISBERTVS. En, hic duas habeo.
PETRVS. Molliorem et leuiorem accipiemus.
GISBERTVS. Belle dicis, nam ista minus afferet doloris.
PETRVS. Sed sortiemur periculi et ludi comites.
GISBERTVS. Ludemus, ut pila scrobibus impellatur.
PETRVS. Tum sors mittatur, quis incipiat.
GISBERTVS. Scrobs prius ascribatur cuilibet.
PETRVS. Quisque accipiat quam uelit, suprema erit mea.
GISBERTVS. Aduolue pilam, in cuius scrobem ceciderit, eam in alios proiiciet.
PETRVS. Papae, meam incidit, fugite hinc.
GISBERTVS. Ho, ho, neminem tetigisti, notula tibi appingatur creta
PETRVS. In calceum fige mihi cretae lineam.
GISBERTVS. Demum adiice foueis pilam.
PETRVS. Nunc tuae intrudam foueae.
GISBERTVS. Si feceris, te primum proiiciam.
PETRVS. Viden? Age quae lubet.
GISBERTVS. Fuge, aut te iactu petam.
PETRVS. Si audes, iacias.
GISBERTVS. Audeo maiora, en tactus es.
PETRVS. Et te rursus ad suras laesi.
GISBERTVS. Vix credo, nam sensi penitus nihil.

---

24 Papae] Papae A; Pape B C | 32 iactu] iactu A C; tactu B

47. DE LVDO GLOBORVM MISSILIVM, QUOS 'OMNIA' VOCANT COLONIENSES TIRVNCVLI LITTERARII

Cornelius et Iacobus [C6v]

CORNELIVS. Non decet aliis ludentibus nos ita desidere.
IACOBVS. Praestat spectatorem esse quam ignauum collusorem.
CORNELIVS. Auspicemur et nos duo ludum cognitum.
IACOBVS. Quem agemus consulis ludum?
CORNELIVS. Globularem.

PETRUS. Who's got a ball? We haven't got one.
GISBERTUS. Look, I've got two here.
PETRUS. We'll take the one that's softer and lighter.
GISBERTUS. You're right there, because that one will hurt less.
PETRUS. But we'll draw lots to see who's going to be whose partner.
GISBERTUS. We'll play at throwing the ball into holes.
PETRUS. Then let's cast lots for who begins.
GISBERTUS. First, allot a hole to each player.
PETRUS. Everyone can take the one he wants. The last one will be mine.
GISBERTUS. Roll the ball. The player whose hole it falls into will throw it at others.
PETRUS. Wow, it's fallen into mine. Run!
GISBERTUS. Ha ha, you haven't got anyone. You've got to have a chalk mark drawn on you.
PETRUS. Draw a chalk line on my shoe.
GISBERTUS. And now throw the ball at the holes.
PETRUS. Now I'll get it into your hole.
GISBERTUS. If you do, I'll throw it at you first.
PETRUS. See? Do what you like.
GISBERTUS. Run, or I'll get you with my throw.
PETRUS. Throw if you dare.
GISBERTUS. I dare plenty; look, you're hit.
PETRUS. And I've hit you back, on the calves.
GISBERTUS. I don't really believe you, because I felt absolutely nothing.

47. THE GAME OF MARBLES, WHICH COLOGNE SCHOOLBOYS CALL 'OMNIA'

Cornelius and Iacobus

CORNELIUS. When others are playing, it's not right for us to sit around like this.
IACOBUS. It's better to be a spectator than a lazy player.
CORNELIUS. The two of us should start a game we know, too.
IACOBUS. Tell me what game we'll play.
CORNELIUS. Marbles.

IACOBVS. Cum globulis, quos 'omnia' uocant?
CORNELIVS. Impolitum istud est uerbum.
IACOBVS. Nosti tu aliud uenustius?
CORNELIVS. Ipse dicerem globulos missiles per pollices.
IACOBVS. Et istam memoriae recondam orationem.
CORNELIVS. Fiat fossiculus, in quem globuli mittantur.
IACOBVS. Tibi culter est, effode terram.
CORNELIVS. Praescribe tu ludi carceres.
IACOBVS. Hic signo ligneolo.
CORNELIVS. Praemitte tu globulum, ego deinde.
IACOBVS. En, istic me ferias.
CORNELIVS. Si possum, non sinam te ibidem durare.
IACOBVS. Te expectabit globulus.
CORNELIVS. Vides? Vbi nunc sistis?
IACOBVS. Semel sum a te propulsus, id nihilo aestimo.
CORNELIVS. Denique tria uici, tu nondum lucratus es.
IACOBVS. Istis tribus nihil addes lucri.
CORNELIVS. Res ipsa loquetur.
IACOBVS. Quibus fortuna prius aspirat, tandem aduersatur.
CORNELIVS. Mox sex numerabo.
IACOBVS. Ipse praeueniam te.
CORNELIVS. Ah, nunc mihi timeo.
IACOBVS. Ecce et mihi tria sunt.
CORNELIVS. Ego rursus tribus te excello.
IACOBVS. Non diu numero superior manebis.
CORNELIVS. Istud experiar.
IACOBVS. Tuis conatibus ipse obsistam.
CORNELIVS. Enitere quantum potes.

35–37 experiar … potes.] experiar. A

48. DE LVDO GLOBORVM QVI TORQVENTVR PER ANNVLVM

Vdalricus et Vinandus

VDALRICVS. Eamus deambulatum rus uersus.
VINANDVS. Ruri quid tractabimus?

IACOBUS. With the marbles they call 'omnia'?
CORNELIUS. That's an inelegant word.
IACOBUS. Do you know another more elegant one?
CORNELIUS. I would say 'little balls flicked with the thumb'.
IACOBUS. I'll commit that expression to memory too.
CORNELIUS. We need to make a hole for the marbles to be flicked into.
IACOBUS. You've got a knife, dig up the ground.
CORNELIUS. You mark the limit of the playing area.
IACOBUS. I'm marking it here with this little piece of wood.
CORNELIUS. You flick your marble first, then I will.
IACOBUS. Now, try to hit me over there!
CORNELIUS. If I can, I won't let you stay there long.
IACOBUS. My marble will wait for you.
CORNELIUS. Look! Where are you stuck now?
IACOBUS. I've been knocked away by you once, that doesn't bother me.
CORNELIUS. The point is that I've won three times, you haven't won yet.
IACOBUS. You won't add any more winnings to those three.
CORNELIUS. The facts will speak for themselves.
IACOBUS. The people fortune favours at first, she eventually opposes.
CORNELIUS. I'll soon have six.
IACOBUS. I'll get ahead of you.
CORNELIUS. Oh, now I'm afraid for myself.
IACOBUS. Now I've got three too.
CORNELIUS. And now I've got three more than you again.
IACOBUS. You won't have more for long.
CORNELIUS. We'll see about that.
IACOBUS. I'll resist your efforts.
CORNELIUS. Try as hard as you can.

48. THE GAME OF KNOCKING BALLS THROUGH A RING

Udalricus and Vinandus

UDALRICUS. Let's go for a walk into the country.
VINANDUS. What will we do in the country?

VDALRICVS. Ibi et ambulando et colludendo nos oblectabimus.
VINANDVS. Quod ludi genus exercebimus?
VDALRICVS. Torquebimus globum per annulum ferreum.
VINANDVS. Si tibi lubet, ipse recusabo nihil.
VDALRICVS. In me nihil erit morae. [C7r]
VINANDVS. Age, propere eamus.
VDALRICVS. Sed audi, in ludo globi annularis peritior me es.
VINANDVS. Rarus certe ipsum exerceo.
VDALRICVS. Attamen videbo quid et ego possim.
VINANDVS. Globum prome.
VDALRICVS. En tibi ferreum annulum, terrae infige.
VINANDVS. Flagellum et mihi praebe.
VDALRICVS. Sortiemur quis prius ludet.
VINANDVS. Ego cultrum sursum iaciam, tu elige.
VDALRICVS. Seligam alterum culelli latus, signum ubi impressum est.
VINANDVS. Latus planum sursum uergit, exordiri est meum.
VDALRICVS. Age, placet, incipe.
VINANDVS. Ictu primo globum per annulum pellam.
VDALRICVS. Si feceris, eris mihi magnus Apollo.
VINANDVS. Ridere sine, videbis me uirum.
VDALRICVS. Ah, ah, nondum te expertum aspicio.
VINANDVS. Nescis uerbum Vergilii, neminem ubique felici ludere dextra?
VDALRICVS. Vt ego, ita per annulum agitares globum.
VINANDVS. Robur tibi est maius quam mihi.
VDALRICVS. Hic non robur, sed et promptitudo ualet.
VINANDVS. Nunc belle annulum penetrabit.
VDALRICVS. Vel a latere praeteribit.
VINANDVS. Istud ipsi prohibebo.
VDALRICVS. Clausis oculis aptius te luderem.
VINANDVS. Verbis tu magnus es, sed factis nullus.

9–10 in A only | 36–37 luderem … nullus.] luderem. A

UDALRICUS. We'll amuse ourselves walking and playing together.
VINANDUS. What kind of game will we play?
UDALRICUS. We'll hit the ball through the iron ring.
VINANDUS. Right, let's go quickly.
UDALRICUS. But listen, you're more experienced at the game of the ball and the ring than I am.
VINANDUS. I really don't play it often.
UDALRICUS. Nonetheless, I'll see what I can do too.
VINANDUS. Take out the ball.
UDALRICUS. You take the iron ring and stick it into the ground.
VINANDUS. Give me a stick, too.
UDALRICUS. We'll toss for who plays first.
VINANDUS. I'll throw the knife up, you choose.
UDALRICUS. I'll choose the other side of the knife, where the sign is stamped.
VINANDUS. It's fallen plain side up, I get to start.
UDALRICUS. All right, begin.
VINANDUS. I'll hit the ball through the ring with my first stroke.
UDALRICUS. If you do, you'll be my great Apollo.
VINANDUS. Stop laughing, you'll see I'm a true man.
UDALRICUS. Ah, ah, I see you're not an expert yet.
VINANDUS. Don't you know what Vergil says, that 'no one can make a good shot in all circumstances'?
UDALRICUS. You should hit the ball through the ring like I do.
VINANDUS. You've got more strength than I have.
UDALRICUS. It's not just strength that counts here, it's facility too.
VINANDUS. It'll go through the ring nicely now.
UDALRICUS. Or pass to one side.
VINANDUS. I'll make sure it doesn't do that.
UDALRICUS. I could play better than you with my eyes closed.
VINANDUS. You're all words and no deeds.

49. DE LVDO SALTVS

Georgius et Volfgangus

GEORGIVS. O uos ciconiarum proles.

VOLFGANGVS. Sumus proles ciconiarum?

GEORGIVS. Estis, quia longissima habetis crura.

VOLFGANGVS. Hoc tua nihil refert.

GEORGIVS. Si audetis, ego pumilio unumquemuis uestrum ad saltandum lacesso et prouoco.

VOLFGANGVS. Et ipse in harenam tecum descendam.

GEORGIVS. Hoc saltandi more me imitare.

VOLFGANGVS. Praesilias, faciam periculum.

GEORGIVS. Ter solum salias post cursum factum. [C7v]

VOLFGANGVS. Metam signa lapide aut ligno.

GEORGIVS. En, hic constiti.

VOLFGANGVS. Eam facile assequar metam.

GEORGIVS. Id post cursum iactita.

VOLFGANGVS. Nunc uiri aspice saltum.

GEORGIVS. Ah, saltum indignum iuuene tali.

VOLFGANGVS. Pro uiribus conatus sum.

GEORGIVS. Vires tibi (ut uideo) sunt imbecilles.

VOLFGANGVS. Rursus experiar quid possim.

GEORGIVS. Semel uici, non alterum tibi concedam saltum.

VOLFGANGVS. Si nunc non assequar metam, palmam dabo.

GEORGIVS. Lubens permitto, tandem tenta.

VOLFGANGVS. Vides me paene assecutum metam tuam?

GEORGIVS. Assecutus es, sed non longius transponis.

VOLFGANGVS. Sat est quod attigi.

GEORGIVS. Denuo tibi consequendam ponam metam aliam.

VOLFGANGVS. Vix remotius collocabis.

GEORGIVS. Puderet me si non qualibet uice distantius saltarem.

VOLFGANGVS. Te uirum dicam, si ostenderis.

GEORGIVS. Vides? Paene prolongassem.

VOLFGANGVS. Quod paene fit (ut uulgo dicitur), id tamen non consequitur uotum.

---

7 pumilio] Pomilio A; pomilio B C | 21 possim] possim A C; possem B

49. JUMPING

Georgius and Volfgangus

GEORGIUS. You stork's brood!
VOLFGANGUS. Us – stork's brood?
GEORGIUS. Yes, because you've got long legs.
VOLFGANGUS. That's no business of yours.
GEORGIUS. If you dare, I challenge any one of you to a jumping contest, though I'm so small.
VOLFGANGUS. And I'll take up your challenge.
GEORGIUS. Imitate the way I'm jumping.
VOLFGANGUS. Jump first, I'll try.
GEORGIUS. You jump just three times after a run-up.
VOLFGANGUS. Draw a goal with a stone or a stick.
GEORGIUS. Right, I've put it here.
VOLFGANGUS. I'll easily reach that mark.
GEORGIUS. Boast after you've run.
VOLFGANGUS. Now look at how a real man jumps.
GEORGIUS. Oh, it's a jump unworthy of a boy like you.
VOLFGANGUS. I tried with all my strength.
GEORGIUS. Your strength is lacking, I can see.
VOLFGANGUS. I'll try what I can do again.
GEORGIUS. I've won once, I'm not going to allow you another jump.
VOLFGANGUS. If I don't reach the mark now, I'll admit defeat.
GEORGIUS. I'm happy to allow that, just get on and try.
VOLFGANGUS. Do you see I almost reached your mark?
GEORGIUS. You reached it, but you haven't shifted the mark further on.
VOLFGANGUS. It's enough that I reached it.
GEORGIUS. I'll make another mark for you to reach a second time.
VOLFGANGUS. You could hardly move it any farther away!
GEORGIUS. I'd be ashamed if I didn't jump farther than that some time.
VOLFGANGUS. I'll call you a real man if you show me.
GEORGIUS. You see? I nearly jumped farther.
VOLFGANGUS. As the saying goes, nearly doesn't do the job.

50. DE CERTAMINE CVRSVS

Gerhardus et Crato

GERHARDVS. Cessemus, oro, de hoc ludo torquendi globum per annulum.
CRATO. Repetemus tum aedes nostras?
GERHARDVS. Vt uisum fuerit uobis.
CRATO. Esset nimis tempestiuum.
GERHARDVS. Ludi aliud genus incipiamus.
CRATO. Quale aestimas auspicandum?
GERHARDVS. Mihi ex diutino inflexu genua dolent.
CRATO. Eo praestaret in gramine decumbere.
GERHARDVS. Id me puderet, sed currendo ipsa reficiam.
CRATO. Hoc fatigat, non recreat.
GERHARDVS. Currere uires excitat, quas eneruauit torpor.
CRATO. Multi currendo crura infregerunt, qui torpendo tuti fuissent.
GERHARDVS. Equi in stabulis diutius sistendo crurum uires amittunt. [C8r]
CRATO. Aliud equis, et homini competit.
GERHARDVS. Quemlibet uestrum ad parem cursum irrito.
CRATO. Et ego currendo tecum palaestram ineo.
GERHARDVS. At aliquo pretiolo curremus.
CRATO. Quid deponemus?
GERHARDVS. Victus pendet binas uini mensuras.
CRATO. Mensuras cereuisiae, non uini exsoluet.
GERHARDVS. Vt lubet, qui primus portae adfuerit, uicit.
CRATO. Sed una cursum inchoemus.
GERHARDVS. Adsis, meo adsta lateri, dum clamauero, curremus alacriter.
CRATO. Adsto, curre, non retine me ueste.
GERHARDVS. Ho, ho, uici, uici.
CRATO. Nisi cecidissem, non me praecurrisses
GERHARDVS. Gaudeo me euicisse te, utcunque primus attigi metam, id refert nihil.

50. A RUNNING RACE

Gerhardus and Crato

GERHARDUS. Please let's stop playing knocking the ball through the ring.

CRATO. Will we go back home, then?

GERHARDUS. As the rest of you like.

CRATO. It would be too early.

GERHARDUS. Let's start another kind of game.

CRATO. What do you think we should start?

GERHARDUS. My knees are hurting from bending them so long.

CRATO. Then it would be better to lie on the grass.

GERHARDUS. I'd be ashamed to do that. I'll cure them by running.

CRATO. That's tiring, not reviving.

GERHARDUS. Running revives the forces that have been weakened by inactivity.

CRATO. Lots of people have broken their legs running, when they'd have been safe hitting the ball.

GERHARDUS. Horses that stand in the stables too long lose the strength of their legs.

CRATO. It's one thing for horses and another for humans.

GERHARDUS. I challenge any of you to a race against me.

CRATO. I'll take you on at running.

GERHARDUS. But we'll run for a small prize of some kind.

CRATO. What'll we wager?

GERHARDUS. The loser pays for two measures of wine.

CRATO. Two measures of beer, not wine.

GERHARDUS. Whatever you like. The first to reach the gate wins.

CRATO. But let's start the race together.

GERHARDUS. Come here, stand beside me. When I shout, we'll run quickly.

CRATO. I'm ready. Run, don't hold me back by my clothes.

GERHARDUS. Ho, ho, I've won, I've won!

CRATO. If I hadn't fallen you wouldn't have beaten me.

GERHARDUS. I'm glad I beat you. The way I reached the finish first doesn't matter.

CRATO. Facile est uincere solus currentem.
GERHARDVS. Fortuna uictoriam largiri solet.

---

3 de] te A | 15 infregerunt, qui torpendo] infregerunt, torpendo A

51. AN ILLE SIT DOCTUS SEMPER (VT PVTANT RVSTICI) QVI MAGNOS POTEST LEGERE LIBROS

Philippus et Hieronymus

PHILIPPVS. In doctissimi hominis aedibus nunc fui.
HIERONYMVS. Doctissimi? Age, quis iste est?
PHILIPPVS. Ecclesiae nostrae rector, quem uulgus pastorem appellitat.
HIERONYMVS. Proh, istum doctissimum aestimas?
PHILIPPVS. Non magnae esset eruditionis, cum grandes legat et habeat libros?
HIERONYMVS. Librorum aceruus et pretiositas doctum non arguit uirum.
PHILIPPVS. Vulgus tamen persuasum habet, grandium librorum lectorem peritum admodum esse.
HIERONYMVS. Toto errat caelo id credendo.
PHILIPPVS. Errorem illum mihi ostende.
HIERONYMVS. Multi libros habent, quos neque legunt, neque lectos intelligunt.
PHILIPPVS. Quare tum eos mercati sunt?
HIERONYMVS. Vt se exornent, tamquam oppido gnaros.
PHILIPPVS. Stulti, qui pecuniam non retinent.
HIERONYMVS. [C8v] Emendo librorum suppellectilem docti sibi nomen conciliant.
PHILIPPVS. Si hoc scirem, doctum me uocatum iri, tota re paterna libros emerem.
HIERONYMVS. Apud populum philosophus dicereris.
PHILIPPVS. Vtrum praestare credis complures habere libros et indoctum esse, uel peritum et pauculos libros?
HIERONYMVS. Peritum esse praeualet et modicos possidere codices.
PHILIPPVS. Peritia e memoria cito elabitur, in libris autem diutius durat.

CRATO. It's easy to beat someone at running on your own.
GERHARDUS. It's usually Fortune who bestows victory.

51. IS THE PERSON WHO CAN READ LONG BOOKS ALWAYS LEARNED, AS PEASANTS THINK?

Philippus and Hieronymus

PHILIPPUS. I've just been in the house of a really learned man.
HIERONYMUS. A really learned one? Who's that, then?
PHILIPPUS. The parish priest of our church; the common people call him the pastor.
HIERONYMUS. Good God do you think he's really learned?
PHILIPPUS. Don't you think he's a man of great learning, seeing that he's got big books and reads them?
HIERONYMUS. A large number of books, and the fact that they cost a lot of money, doesn't prove a man is learned.
PHILIPPUS. And yet the common people are convinced that someone who reads big books is really knowledgeable.
HIERONYMUS. They're absolutely wrong to think that.
PHILIPPUS. Show me how they're wrong.
HIERONYMUS. There are lots of people who have books that they don't read, or understand them if they do.
PHILIPPUS. So why did they buy them?
HIERONYMUS. To distinguish themselves, as if they were extremely knowledgeable.
PHILIPPUS. They're stupid not to keep their money.
HIERONYMUS. By buying books as furniture they acquire the reputation of being learned.
PHILIPPUS. If I knew that I would be called learned, I'd buy books with all my father's money.
HIERONYMUS. Amongst the common people you'd be called a philosopher.
PHILIPPUS. Do you think it's better to have a lot of books and not be learned, or to be knowledgeable and have a few books?
HIERONYMUS. It's better to be knowledgeable and have a moderate number of books.
PHILIPPUS. Knowledge slips out of the memory quickly, but it lasts longer in books.

HIERONYMVS. Praestantius tamen est (ut inquit Erasmus) ingenium habere doctum, quam libros eruditos.

PHILIPPVS. Sed e memoria elapsa scientia, ubi rursus acquiretur, si copia librorum deerit?

HIERONYMVS. Vbique extant bibliothecae litterariae.

---

2 magnos potest] potest magnos A | 33 inquit Erasmus] Erasmus inquit A | 37 litterariae] literariae C; literatae A B

52. DE PRAECEPTORE ELIGENDO

Antonius et Iohannes

ANTONIVS. Es tu in hoc ludo litterario duraturus longius?

IOHANNES. Minime, sed alio me conferam.

ANTONIVS. Quo locorum?

IOHANNES. Vbi melius erit consultum meo profectui in litteris.

ANTONIVS. Vide ne praestantiora quaerens uiliora incidas.

IOHANNES. Prouidebo strenue.

ANTONIVS. Sed nosti quis sit praeceptor eligendus?

IOHANNES. Instar caeci, qui mihi arridet, illi me subdo.

ANTONIVS. Ementium haberes morem. qui nihil emunt, nisi diu ante perspectum habeant.

IOHANNES. Praeceptorem ut rem uenum expositam licetne perspicere?

ANTONIVS. Duo sunt per quae praeceptor utrisque (ut aiunt) brachiis amplexandus cognoscitur.

IOHANNES. Quae illa sunt edissere precor.

ANTONIVS. Si erudite docet, et discipulos litteratos reddit.

IOHANNES. Eruditionem praeceptoris ignoti, quomodo percipiam?

ANTONIVS. Audiendo eum docentem, uel alios de ipso con- [D1r] sulendo.

IOHANNES. Ego indoctus iudicii sum expers.

ANTONIVS. Peritiores qui uir sit, facile tibi ostendent.

IOHANNES. Iudicantne etiam discipuli de praeceptoris industria?

HIERONYMUS. And yet, as Erasmus says, it's better to have a learned mind than learned books.

PHILIPPUS. But where do you get hold of knowledge that's slipped out of your memory if you haven't got enough books?

HIERONYMUS. There are scholarly libraries everywhere.

52. CHOOSING A TEACHER

Antonius and Iohannes

ANTONIUS. Are you going to stay at this school for some time?

IOHANNES. No, I'm going to go somewhere else.

ANTONIUS. Whereabouts?

IOHANNES. Where it'll be better-advised for my academic progress.

ANTONIUS. Be careful that when you look for something more excellent you don't come upon something inferior.

IOHANNES. I'll take extremely good care.

ANTONIUS. But do you know who you should choose as your teacher?

IOHANNES. Like a blind man, if someone pleases me, I become their pupil.

ANTONIUS. You should be like buyers who won't buy anything unless they've had a long look at it beforehand.

IOHANNES. Can you examine a teacher like something set out for sale?

ANTONIUS. There are two ways you can tell a teacher who ought to be 'embraced with open arms', as the saying goes.

IOHANNES. What are they? Please tell me.

ANTONIUS. If his teaching is learned, and if he turns his pupils into cultured people.

IOHANNES. How can I tell how learned a teacher is if I don't know him?

ANTONIUS. By listening to him teaching, or inquiring about him from others.

IOHANNES. I'm unlearned, I've got no ability to judge.

ANTONIUS. More experienced people will easily be able to tell you what kind of man he is.

IOHANNES. Can pupils judge how diligent their teacher is?

ANTONIVS. Haeres in illo? Nescis prouerbium uulgo usurpatum, discipuli doctrinam ex praeceptoris pendere peritia?
IOHANNES. Audiui interdum, qualis praeceptor, tales et fieri discipulos.
ANTONIVS. Quid tum adhuc suspenso es animo?

---

18 Quae illa sunt edissere precor] Quae illa sunt, edissere, praecor? A; Quae illa sunt? edissere, precor? B C | 32–33 discipulos … animo?] discipulos. A

53. AN PRAECEPTOR LITTERARIVS SIT COLENDVS TAMQUAM PARENTES

Iacobus et Laurentius

IACOBVS. Vt ita erga praeceptorem te habes?
LAVRENTIVS. Tua quid refert?
IACOBVS. Nihil.
LAVRENTIVS. Quidni tum siles?
IACOBVS. Iniquum uidens, tacere nequeo.
LAVRENTIVS. Est istud iniquum obloqui praeceptori?
IACOBVS. Certe parum decet.
LAVRENTIVS. Par pari referre licet.
IACOBVS. Praeceptori non reluctandum, sed tacendum est.
LAVRENTIVS. Dico ut tu, iniquo obticere nequeo.
IACOBVS. Taciturnitas decorat iuuenem, praecipue ad praeceptoris uerba.
LAVRENTIVS. Vecors esset, qui ad plagas obmutesceret.
IACOBVS. Qui obmurmurat plus ictuum recipit.
LAVRENTIVS. Iuuat me tamen uerbis ulcisci, si factis non conceditur.
IACOBVS. At miserum est uerbis emere uerbera.
LAVRENTIVS. Istas paruipendo plagas.
IACOBVS. Illi infeliciter succedit, qui praeceptorem non ueneratur.
LAVRENTIVS. Talem hominem quis ueneraretur?
IACOBVS. Sit fortunae cuiuscunque, denique praeceptor noster est.

ANTONIUS. Do you doubt it? Don't you know the proverb taken from the vernacular, that 'pupils' learning depends on their teacher's knowledge'?

IOHANNES. I've occasionally heard, 'like teacher, like pupils'.

ANTONIUS. So why are you still uncertain?

53. SHOULD A SCHOOLMASTER BE RESPECTED LIKE ONE'S PARENTS?

Iacobus and Laurentius

IACOBUS. Why do you behave towards your teacher like that?

LAURENTIUS. What's it got to do with you?

IACOBUS. Nothing.

LAURENTIUS. So why not shut up, then?

IACOBUS. If I see something wrong, I can't keep quiet about it.

LAURENTIUS. Is it wrong to interrupt your teacher?

IACOBUS. It's not proper at all.

LAURENTIUS. It's all right to give as good as you get.

IACOBUS. You shouldn't show resistance to your teacher, you should say nothing.

LAURENTIUS. I say the same as you: I can't keep quiet about something wrong.

IACOBUS. Silence becomes a boy, especially when the teacher speaks.

LAURENTIUS. Someone who said nothing when he was beaten would be crazy.

IACOBUS. If you protest you get more strokes.

LAURENTIUS. But I enjoy getting my own back in words, if it can't be done in actions.

IACOBUS. But it's miserable for your words to earn you a beating.

LAURENTIUS. I don't care about being beaten.

IACOBUS. Things go badly for the boy who doesn't admire his teacher.

LAURENTIUS. Who would admire a man like that?

IACOBUS. No matter what kind of man he is, he's still our teacher.

LAVRENTIVS. Non diu sibi discipulus ero.

IACOBVS. De tuo non plorabit discessu.

LAVRENTIVS. Et ego gaudebo me ab eo liberari.

IACOBVS. Praeceptores non secus ac parentes sunt colendi.

LAVRENTIVS. Sane per Herculem, id [D1v] ego feci nunquam.

IACOBVS. Ego autem maiori amore praeceptorem quam parentes sum prosecutus.

LAVRENTIVS. O ingrate parentibus.

IACOBVS. Praeceptor scientiam mihi praebet, quod nequeunt parentes.

LAVRENTIVS. Ab ipsis autem uitam habes, et quod homo es.

IACOBVS. Id parum est, quid enim uita est sine litterarum peritia?

LAVRENTIVS. Nescis, uita nihil est nobilius.

IACOBVS. Sed uita nostra imperiti si fuerimus, non uita sed mors est uerius, si quid Aristoteli fidei datur.

54. DE NVNDINIS ET MVNERVM NVNDINARIORVM EMPTIONE

Seuerinus et Balthasar

SEVERINVS. Vidisti quam feruide tentoria erigunt mercatores?

BALTHASAR. Vidi, quid deinde?

SEVERINVS. Nundinarum appetunt feriae.

BALTHASAR. In illo mihi nihil metitur.

SEVERINVS. Sed ipse nonnihil commode spero.

BALTHASAR. Quo nomine?

SEVERINVS. Ab amicis munera nundinaria expecto.

BALTHASAR. Ah, expectare miserum est.

SEVERINVS. Satius tamen est expectare quam nihil habere spei.

BALTHASAR. Qui spe uiuit, miseram agit uitam.

SEVERINVS. Non omnes spe frustrantur.

BALTHASAR. Plures certe quam uoti compotes fiunt.

SEVERINVS. Nundinaria munera quotannis his nundinis mihi largiuntur affatim.

BALTHASAR. Fortunatior me es, cui non teruncius datur.

LAURENTIUS. I won't be his pupil much longer.
IACOBUS. He won't cry when you leave.
LAURENTIUS. And I'll be glad to be free of him.
IACOBUS. Teachers should be respected exactly like parents.
LAURENTIUS. Good God, I've never done that.
IACOBUS. But *I've* shown greater love to my teacher than to my parents.
LAURENTIUS. You're ungrateful to your parents!
IACOBUS. The teacher provides me with knowledge, something my parents can't do.
LAURENTIUS. But you've got life from them, and the fact that you're a human being.
IACOBUS. That's not much – what's life without learning?
LAURENTIUS. Don't you know that nothing is more important than life?
IACOBUS. But if you believe Aristotle, if we're ignorant, our life isn't life but rather death.

54. FAIRS, AND BUYING FAIR PRESENTS

Severinus and Balthasar

SEVERINUS. Have you seen how busily the merchants are putting up their stalls?
BALTHASAR. Yes, so what?
SEVERINUS. The fair time is coming.
BALTHASAR. There's nothing in it for me.
SEVERINUS. But I'm hoping for something to my advantage.
BALTHASAR. What's the reason?
SEVERINUS. I'm hoping for fair presents from my friends.
BALTHASAR. Oh, hoping's a miserable business.
SEVERINUS. But it's better to have some hope than none at all.
BALTHASAR. To live in hope is to lead a miserable life.
SEVERINUS. Not everyone has their hopes disappointed.
BALTHASAR. There are more people who are disappointed than there are who get what they wish.
SEVERINUS. At this fair every year I get given lots of fair presents.
BALTHASAR. You're luckier than I am, I don't get a penny.

SEVERINVS. Tu alienus es, ego incola et ciuis sum.

BALTHASAR. Si in patria agerem etiam de nundinis gauderem.

SEVERINVS. Expecto nunc et calceos et tiaram me accepturum.

BALTHASAR. Quis ista tibi mercabitur?

SEVERINVS. Cognati et agnati mei, qui ex alienis adsunt oppidis.

BALTHASAR. Vide ne mercimoniis impediti tui obliuiscentur.

SEVERINVS. Ego ipsos saepe admoneo et interpello.

BALTHASAR. Rogare mendicorum est.

SEVERINVS. Non stipem rogo, sed munus nundi- [D2r] narium.

BALTHASAR. Parum interest.

SEVERINVS. Sit utcunque, ego lubens accipio ea munuscula.

BALTHASAR. Certe desiperes, si data recusares.

55. DE NVNDINIS FRANCFORDIENSIBVS

Gisbertus et Andreas

GISBERTVS. Nautae nunc suas instruunt naves passim.

ANDREAS. Quo concessuri sunt?

GISBERTVS. Francfordiam uersus.

ANDREAS. Appropinquatne tempus nundinarum?

GISBERTVS. Mox in foribus erit, antea quam istuc uenient.

ANDREAS. Non putassem adhuc eas pulsare fores.

GISBERTVS. O quam uellem et me istuc posse concedere.

ANDREAS. Ibidem tibi quid exequendum esset?

GISBERTVS. Praeter quam ignota perlustrarem loca, prorsus nihil.

ANDREAS. Pigrior ego essem, quam quod eo tenderem, ubi nihil esset quod agerem.

GISBERTVS. Dulce est peragrasse uarias urbes.

ANDREAS. Praestat tamen quandoque in patria manisse.

GISBERTVS. Francfordiam me hercule accederem, nisi aliqua me morarentur.

ANDREAS. Quae te detinent?

SEVERINUS. You're not from this city. I'm a native of here and a citizen.

BALTHASAR. If I was in my own region I'd be pleased about the fair too.

SEVERINUS. Now I'm expecting that I'll get shoes and a hat.

BALTHASAR. Who's going to buy you those?

SEVERINUS. Relatives of mine who've come from other towns.

BALTHASAR. Make sure that they don't forget you because they're hindered by their business.

SEVERINUS. I often remind them and ask them.

BALTHASAR. Asking is for beggars.

SEVERINUS. I'm not asking for alms, I'm asking for a fair present.

BALTHASAR. There's not a lot of difference.

SEVERINUS. No matter, I love getting those presents.

BALTHASAR. You'd certainly be mad to refuse what you were given.

55. THE FRANKFURT FAIR

Gisbertus and Andreas

GISBERTUS. The sailors are getting their ships ready all over the place now.

ANDREAS. Where are they off to?

GISBERTUS. Towards Frankfurt.

ANDREAS. Is the fair time approaching?

GISBERTUS. It'll arrive soon, before they get there.

ANDREAS. I wouldn't have thought it was as close as that.

GISBERTUS. I wish I could go there too.

ANDREAS. What would you have to do there?

GISBERTUS. Nothing at all, other than going round places I haven't seen.

ANDREAS. I'd be too lazy to go somewhere where there was nothing for me to do.

GISBERTUS. It's enjoyable to travel round different cities.

ANDREAS. But sometimes it's better to stay at home.

GISBERTUS. I tell you, I'd go to Frankfurt if there weren't a few things holding me back.

ANDREAS. What's keeping you?

GISBERTVS. Sane multa, praecipue tamen duo.
ANDREAS. Quae illa sunt?
GISBERTVS. Primum uiatici carentia.
ANDREAS. Num id pater tibi suppeditaret?
GISBERTVS. Nimio constat, ego iuuenis quantum ipse sumptus in diuersoriis facerem.
ANDREAS. Fidem do, sed quod est alterum impedimentum?
GISBERTVS. Dicunt in itinere eum cui nunquam uisa est Francfordia, tractare ut asinum inter simias.
ANDREAS. Et istud nonnunquam uidi quomodo aquae immergebantur.
GISBERTVS. Post illud et mulctantur credo pecunia.
ANDREAS. Forte aureum insumunt conuiuio, id parum est.
GISBERTVS. Certe non parum est, quia difficilis acquisitu est pecunia.
ANDREAS. Tibi et tui similibus nihil obest. [D2v]

---

7 antequam] antea quam A C | 8 missing in C; thereafter speakers are reversed for the rest of the colloquy. | 17–18 me morarentur] me non morarentur A | 23 tibi suppeditaret] tibi non suppeditaret A | 25 diuersoriis] diuerticulo A | 28 tractare] tractare A; tractari B C

56. DE VITANDO MENDACIO

Euergislus et Hermannus

EVERGISLVS. Nostra non diu amicitia constabit.
HERMANNVS. Mali quid ipsam infringeret?
EVERGISLVS. Mentiri assuescis.
HERMANNVS. Mentiri ioco ferendum est.
EVERGISLVS. Anguem minus odi quam mendacium.
HERMANNVS. Loqueris tu semper certa?
EVERGISLVS. Aut sileo, aut quae mihi constant loquor.
HERMANNVS. Iocarisne interdum?
EVERGISLVS. Etiam saepissime.
HERMANNVS. Qui iocari potes, si uero inniteris?
EVERGISLVS. Nequit iocus per uerum credis fieri?

GISBERTUS. Lots of things, but two in particular.
ANDREAS. What are they?
GISBERTUS. First the lack of money for the journey.
ANDREAS. But surely your father would provide you with that?
GISBERTUS. I'm a boy; it's very clear how much I'd spend in the inns.
ANDREAS. I believe you, but what's the other hindrance?
GISBERTUS. They say that on the journey, they treat anyone who's never seen Frankfurt 'like an ass amongst monkeys'.
ANDREAS. And I've sometimes seen them being ducked in the water.
GISBERTUS. And after that, I think they're made to forfeit money.
ANDREAS. They maybe spend a Gulden on a party, that's not a lot.
GISBERTUS. It most certainly is, money's hard to come by.
ANDREAS. Nothing would hurt you and people like you.

56. LYING SHOULD BE AVOIDED

Evergislus and Hermannus

EVERGISLUS. Our friendship won't last long.
HERMANNUS. What evil might break it?
EVERGISLUS. You're getting used to lying.
HERMANNUS. I lie for a joke, that's allowable.
EVERGISLUS. I hate snakes less than lies.
HERMANNUS. Do you always speak the truth?
EVERGISLUS. Either I say nothing, or I say what I know is true.
HERMANNUS. Do you sometimes joke?
EVERGISLUS. I do, very often.
HERMANNUS. How can you joke, if you rely on the truth?
EVERGISLUS. Can't you make a joke using the truth?

HERMANNVS. Verum mordere solet et odium parere.
EVERGISLVS. Delectatne tum sermo falsus?
HERMANNVS. Nugae quanto maiores, tanto exhilarant uberius.
EVERGISLVS. Frugi homines falsitate et mendacio non capiuntur.
HERMANNVS. Non omnes sunt Solones, ut tu.
EVERGISLVS. Probi ueritate sola tenentur.
HERMANNVS. Attamen quandoque dum carpuntur inuiti eam recipiunt.
EVERGISLVS. Mendacio detestabilius in homine nihil esse potest.
HERMANNVS. Lusorem, uel furem, uel latronem esse adhuc grauius est.
EVERGISLVS. Ah minime, longe ista excedit mentiri ipsum.
HERMANNVS. Credat hoc Iudaeus Apella.
EVERGISLVS. Qui mentiri audet, nihil sceleris intentatum relinquit.
HERMANNVS. O tu mendacii contemptor.
EVERGISLVS. Vulgo fertur, 'Furari mendacium comitatur'.
HERMANNVS. Vulgi non est innitendum sententiae.

2, etc. Euergislus] Euergisilus A; Euergissus C | 21 inuiti] inuitus A C | 28 Apella] appella A | 32 mendacium comitatur] comitatur mendacium A

57. DE CONFESSIONE

Thomas et Iodocus

THOMAS. Recensuistine sacerdoti peccata tua?
IODOCVS. Nondum.
THOMAS. Quando exequeris istud muneris?
IODOCVS. Adhuc sat restat temporis.
THOMAS. Peracto autem [D3r] opere dulce est quiescere.
IODOCVS. Etiam ante laborem quies est iucunda.
THOMAS. Sed non adeo delectat ut negotio executo.
IODOCVS. Assentio.
THOMAS. Ego nunc confessum eo.

HERMANNUS. The truth generally hurts and makes you unpopular.
EVERGISLUS. Are lies pleasing, then?
HERMANNUS. The more frivolous the talk, the greater the amusement.
EVERGISLUS. Honest people aren't fond of lies and falsehood.
HERMANNUS. Not everyone's a Solon like you.
EVERGISLUS. Decent people are only influenced by truth.
HERMANNUS. And yet sometimes, when they're criticized, they're reluctant to accept it.
EVERGISLUS. Nothing can be more abominable in a man than lying.
HERMANNUS. It's worse to be a gambler or a thief or a brigand.
EVERGISLUS. Oh, not at all, lying is far worse than that.
HERMANNUS. That I just can't believe.
EVERGISLUS. Someone who dares to lie won't leave any kind of wickedness untried.
HERMANNUS. O you despiser of lies!
EVERGISLUS. People say, 'Stealing goes hand in hand with lying'.
HERMANNUS. You shouldn't rely on what people say.

57. CONFESSION

Thomas and Iodocus

THOMAS. Have you told your sins to a priest?
IODOCUS. Not yet.
THOMAS. When will you perform that duty?
IODOCUS. There's still plenty of time.
THOMAS. But it's pleasant to rest after a task completed.
IODOCUS. Rest is agreeable even before work.
THOMAS. But it isn't as delightful as after finishing your business.
IODOCUS. That's true.
THOMAS. I'm going to confession now.

IODOCVS. Comitabor te.
THOMAS. Cui soles delicta enarrare, an plebeiario nostro?
IODOCVS. Feci nunquam, sed semper cuipiam monachorum.
THOMAS. Istud et mihi est moris.
IODOCVS. Apud illos plus mihi est deuotionis.
THOMAS. Et illi ipsi pecuniae nihil expetunt.
IODOCVS. Aliqui eorum tamen acciperent, si daretur.
THOMAS. Timesne etiam sacerdoti peccata denudare?
IODOCVS. Metuebam olim puer, nunc non.
THOMAS. Metum quid tibi incutiebat?
IODOCVS. Dicebatur passim, quod uni a confessore fronti clauus infigeretur.
THOMAS. Istud et ipse audiui, sed credebam nunquam.
IODOCVS. Confiteris tu ex chartula?
THOMAS. Confiteor, alias timor omnium mihi induceret peccatorum obliuionem.
IODOCVS. Prohibent tamen istud nonnulli confessionem audientes.
THOMAS. Timent ne perdatur schedula, uerum eam deinde illico comburo.
IODOCVS. Latinene reddis confessionem?
THOMAS. Non, sed Germanice loquor.
IODOCVS. Confessor quadam uice nolebat a me Romanum audire sermonem.
THOMAS. Fortassis pessime intellexit.
IODOCVS. Certe parum doctus fuit.

---

13 plebeiario] plebiario A B C | 14 cuipiam] cuiquam A

58. DE CENA SVPREMA CHRISTI CVM DISCIPVLIS ET DIE PARASCEVES

Vincentius et Matthias

VINCENTIVS. Nunc post triduum Pascha praesto erit.
MATTHIAS. Verum, sed illud triduum nondum lapsum est.
VINCENTIVS. Elabetur denique citius, quam dies esuriales hactenus acti.
MATTHIAS. Magis autem et acerbius nunc esuriendum est.

IODOCUS. I'll come with you.
THOMAS. Who do you usually confess your sins to – our parish priest?
IODOCUS. I've never done that. It's always been one of the monks.
THOMAS. That's what I do, too.
IODOCUS. With them I feel more devotion.
THOMAS. And they don't demand any money.
IODOCUS. Some of them would accept it, though, if they were given it.
THOMAS. Are you afraid to reveal your sins to a priest?
IODOCUS. I was previously, when I was a boy, not now.
THOMAS. What struck that fear into you?
IODOCUS. Everyone was saying that someone had had a nail driven into their forehead by a confessor.
THOMAS. I heard that one too, but I never believed it.
IODOCUS. Do you confess from a list?
THOMAS. Yes, otherwise fear would make me forget all my sins.
IODOCUS. But some confessors don't allow that.
THOMAS. They're afraid that you'll lose the list. But I burn it straight afterwards.
IODOCUS. Do you make your confession in Latin?
THOMAS. No, I speak German.
IODOCUS. A confessor once refused to listen to me in Latin.
THOMAS. He probably could hardly understood it.
IODOCUS. He definitely wasn't very learned.

58. THE LAST SUPPER OF CHRIST WITH HIS DISCIPLES AND GOOD FRIDAY

Vincentius and Matthias

VINCENTIUS. In three days' time now it'll be Easter.
MATTHIAS. True, but those three days haven't passed yet.
VINCENTIUS. In the end they'll go more quickly than the fast days we've lived through so far.
MATTHIAS. Yet now we have to fast more, and more harshly.

VINCENTIVS. Id refert nihil, carceri incluso egendum [D3v] esset cibo.
MATTHIAS. Ibi necessitas eum urgeret.
VINCENTIVS. Hi dies tres mihi abibunt pernicissime.
MATTHIAS. Quo delicio eos transiges?
VINCENTIVS. Spe uescendi ouis Paschalibus (ut uulgo fertur) post ipsos.
MATTHIAS. Pulchre dicis, nam spes quandoque leuat aduersa.
VINCENTIVS. Vbi hodie intereris pedum lotioni?
MATTHIAS. Coenobium aliquod religiosorum accedam.
VINCENTIVS. Quorum?
MATTHIAS. Incertus sum, quocunque uenero.
VINCENTIVS. Expectas aliquem bolum opiparum?
MATTHIAS. Vtique, in quibusdam coenobiis mensae accumbitur.
VINCENTIVS. Cui monasterio soles interesse hoc die?
MATTHIAS. Antonio diuo dicatis aedibus.
VINCENTIVS. Ibidem quid consequeris lucri?
MATTHIAS. Placentas duas triticeas.
VINCENTIVS. Accumbit quilibet istuc ueniens mensae?
MATTHIAS. Assidet, et ante ipsum calix uini ponitur.
VINCENTIVS. Et quot placentae?
MATTHIAS. Cuilibet duae, et deinde una inter duos, de qua rodunt ut sitim excitent.
VINCENTIVS. Defert quisque duas secum domi?
MATTHIAS. Quidni?
VINCENTIVS. Quoties calices uino replentur?
MATTHIAS. Tribus (ni fallor) uicibus.
VINCENTIVS. Lauanturne ibi pedes?
MATTHIAS. Religiosis, sed aduenis dextera manus.
VINCENTIVS. Quis Christi munus exequitur?
MATTHIAS. Coenobii antistes, uulgus Praeceptorem appellat, uir nostra aetate uere litteratorum Maecenas.

---

38 Religiosis, sed] Religiosis solis, sed A | 41 Maecenas] mecoenas A; mecaenas B C

VINCENTIUS. That doesn't matter. Someone in jail would have to do without food.

MATTHIAS. There he'd be forced by necessity.

VINCENTIUS. For me these three days will go by really quickly.

MATTHIAS. In what pleasures will you spend them?

VINCENTIUS. The hope of eating Easter eggs, as they're popularly called, when they're past.

MATTHIAS. Well said, because hope always relieves adversity.

VINCENTIUS. Where will you attend the foot-washing today?

MATTHIAS. I'll go to some monastery or other.

VINCENTIUS. Which one?

MATTHIAS. I'm not sure; wherever I end up.

VINCENTIUS. Are you hoping for some tasty bite?

MATTHIAS. Indeed I am. In some monasteries they serve food.

VINCENTIUS. Which monastery do you usually go to today?

MATTHIAS. St Anthony's.

VINCENTIUS. And what will you get given there?

MATTHIAS. Two wheaten cakes.

VINCENTIUS. Can anyone who arrives there sit down at the table?

MATTHIAS. Yes, and they put a cup of wine in front of him.

VINCENTIUS. And how many cakes?

MATTHIAS. Everyone gets two, and then one between two, which they nibble to work up a thirst.

VINCENTIUS. Can anyone take the two home with him?

MATTHIAS. Of course he can.

VINCENTIUS. How many times are the cups refilled with wine?

MATTHIAS. Three times, if I'm not mistaken.

VINCENTIUS. Are feet washed there?

MATTHIAS. The monks' feet are, but in the case of visitors it's their right hand.

VINCENTIUS. Who performs the office of Christ?

MATTHIAS. The superior of the monastery; he's commonly called the Preceptor. The man's a true patron of scholars in our time.

59. DE SVMPTIONIS EVCHARISTIAE PRAEPARATIONE

Antonius et Michael

ANTONIVS. Hoc uesperi, si lubet tibi, una modice bolum unum aut alterum edemus?

MICHAEL. Edere mihi non licet.

ANTONIVS. Es forte cras sacrum Christi corpus manducaturus?

MICHAEL. Ita stat sententia, si digne possem.

ANTONIVS. Bolus ac haustus unus uini te nihil impediet.

MICHAEL. Nonnihil edam ne deficiam corpore.

ANTONIVS. Quomodo te [D4r] parare soles ad Synaxim sumendam?

MICHAEL. Vesperi os colluo aqua et eximo si quid cibi inhaeret dentibus.

ANTONIVS. Praestaret cor a peccandi uoluntate purgare.

MICHAEL. Quantum possum, neque id negligo.

ANTONIVS. Ad digne manducandum id confert oppido.

MICHAEL. Compertum habeo.

ANTONIVS. Difficillimum est uoluntatem peccandi radicitus excutere.

MICHAEL. Fit facile si Dei precati fuerimus opitulamen.

ANTONIVS. Istud sedulo inuoco.

MICHAEL. Tum confide sacramenti sumptionem tibi saluti futuram.

ANTONIVS. Nosti quid facies, si hostia summo adhaeserit palato?

MICHAEL. Scio, potu depono, non digito detraho.

ANTONIVS. At quam diu corpus Christi in nostro manet uentre?

MICHAEL. Quousque hostiae materia fuerit decocta.

ANTONIVS. Estne expuendum illo die in terram?

MICHAEL. Ante cibum sumptum uitandum est.

ANTONIVS. Licebit tum prandio peracto?

59. PREPARING TO RECEIVE THE EUCHARIST

Antonius and Michael

ANTONIUS. This evening, if you like, shall we eat a little bite or two together?

MICHAEL. I can't eat.

ANTONIUS. Are you by any chance going to eat the sacred body of Christ tomorrow?

MICHAEL. That's what I intend to do, if I can do it worthily.

ANTONIUS. A mouthful of food and a drink of wine won't prevent you at all.

MICHAEL. I'll eat something so as not to feel physically weak.

ANTONIUS. How do you usually prepare yourself to receive the Eucharist?

MICHAEL. In the evening I wash my mouth out with water and if there's any food stuck between my teeth I remove it.

ANTONIUS. It would be better to purify your heart from the will to sin.

MICHAEL. I don't neglect that either, as best I can.

ANTONIUS. That makes a great contribution towards receiving the sacrament worthily.

MICHAEL. I realize that.

ANTONIUS. It's extremely hard to drive out the will to sin completely.

MICHAEL. It's easily done if we pray for God's assistance.

ANTONIUS. I beg for that earnestly.

MICHAEL. Then trust that receiving the sacrament will bring you salvation.

ANTONIUS. Do you know what to do if the host sticks to the roof of your mouth?

MICHAEL. Yes. I wash it off with a drink, I don't pick it off with my finger.

ANTONIUS. But how long does the body of Christ remain in our stomach?

MICHAEL. Until the matter of the host has been digested.

ANTONIUS. Should you spit on the ground that day?

MICHAEL. You should avoid it until you've had some food.

ANTONIUS. So is it all right after lunch?

MICHAEL. Concedetur, satius tamen esset (uulgi sententia) in parietem sputum emittere.

---

16 neque] neque A; ne B C

60. DE MORE POST GYMNASIA TRIVIALIA ACCEDENDI SCHOLAS PRAECELSAS, QVAS BVRSAS APPELLANT

Vinandus et Crato

VINANDVS. Praeceptor erit nobis in prandio conuiua.

CRATO. Vocarunt eum parentes tui?

VINANDVS. Ego ipsum heri nomine parentum inuitaui.

CRATO. Cuius rei gratia?

VINANDVS. Id homo linguax mox dixisset.

CRATO. Tu loquace non es praestantior.

VINANDVS. Expetis scire causam?

CRATO. Vtique cupio.

VINANDVS. Mea fit causa.

CRATO. Facile persuadebis mihi.

VINANDVS. Mercedem meae instructionis ei pendet pater.

CRATO. Hoc ipsum oblectabit.

VINANDVS. Sed aliud audiet unde dolebit.

CRATO. Loquenturne ei parentes tui lapides?

VINANDVS. Dicent me ferulae alterius subdi- [D4v] turum manus.

CRATO. In quonam gymnasio militabis?

VINANDVS. Non in triuiali, sed ubi studentes agunt nudis capitibus.

CRATO. In bursane?

VINANDVS. Ibidem scilicet.

CRATO. Cur nostram deseris palaestram litterariam?

VINANDVS. Pudet me grandaeuum assidere tirunculis litterariis.

CRATO. Non puduit tamen Iudaeos adsidere puero Iesu.

VINANDVS. Etiam aetas mea exigit, ut grauiora petam studia.

CRATO. Vide ut primam et rudem prius calleas eruditionem.

MICHAEL. It's permitted, but people generally say that it's better to spit on a wall.

60. THE PRACTICE OF GOING ON, AFTER THE GRAMMAR SCHOOL, TO ADVANCED SCHOOLS CALLED *BURSAE*

Vinandus and Crato

VINANDUS. Our teacher's going to come to lunch with us.
CRATO. Have your parents invited him?
VINANDUS. I invited him yesterday on my parents' behalf.
CRATO. What's the reason?
VINANDUS. A talkative person would soon have told you.
CRATO. You're a gossip, you're no better.
VINANDUS. Do you want to know the reason?
CRATO. I certainly do.
VINANDUS. It's on account of me.
CRATO. You'll easily convince me of that.
VINANDUS. My father's going to pay him my tuition fees.
CRATO. He'll be delighted by that.
VINANDUS. But he's going to be told something else that'll make him sad.
CRATO. Are your parents going to say things that will wound him?
VINANDUS. They're going to tell him that I'm going to be the pupil of another teacher.
CRATO. Which school will you go to?
VINANDUS. Not to a grammar school, I'll be where the students work bare-headed.
CRATO. In a *bursa*?
VINANDUS. That's the very place.
CRATO. Why are you abandoning our school?
VINANDUS. I'm a big boy, and I'm ashamed to sit alongside beginners.
CRATO. And yet the Jews weren't ashamed to sit alongside the boy Jesus.
VINANDUS. And then my age demands that I should pursue more serious studies.
CRATO. Make sure you understand the basics of learning first.

VINANDVS. Si quid meis defuerit rudimentis, tempus addet.
CRATO. Sed forsan non omnis schola.
VINANDVS. Noli mihi tutor esse.
CRATO. Nostine, cur gymnasia ista philosophica bursae uocentur?
VINANDVS. Doceas me, auscultabo.
CRATO. A bursa (quod nonnullis crumena est) quia crumenam exigunt.
VINANDVS. Qui hoc?
CRATO. Quia gradus inanium nominum magno in ipsis ueneunt.

---

27 tirunculis] tyrunculis A C | 42 ueneunt] ueneunt C; ueniunt A B

61. DE DEPONENDIS (VT AIVNT) CORNIBVS BEANITATIS

Petrus et Vrbanus

PETRVS. Heus tu, audistine unquam prouerbium, 'Odit figulus figulum'?
VRBANVS. Hisce hausi auribus saepiuscule.
PETRVS. Nosti quid uelit?
VRBANVS. Noui diutissime.
PETRVS. Explica ut audiam.
VRBANVS. Id est, quisque artis suae odit riualem.
PETRVS. Haec inter deditos litteris etiam est simultas?
VRBANVS. Est inter studentes et nos, quos beanos uocant.
PETRVS. Credisne tu cornua nos gerere, ut ipsi garriunt?
VRBANVS. Ignoro, nam me ipsum non nosco.
PETRVS. Nemo persuadebit mihi.
VRBANVS. Ipsi tamen dicunt et se olim ea habuisse.
PETRVS. Nugantur et nos hircum olere.
VRBANVS. Istud est facilius creditu.
PETRVS. Ais et tu? Vnde coniicis?
VRBANVS. Sordemus a frustis panis delinitis, quae saepe [D5r] ad diem in sinu gessimus.
PETRVS. An nos liberent de his duobus uitiis, dum cornua nobis tollunt?
VRBANVS. Sic habet fides ipsorum.

VINANDUS. If I'm lacking in any of the rudiments, time will add them.
CRATO. But maybe not any school will.
VINANDUS. Don't try to be my guardian.
CRATO. Do you know why those philosophical schools are called *bursae*?
VINANDUS. Tell me, I'll listen.
CRATO. From the word 'bursa', a moneybag – because they charge bags of money.
VINANDUS. Why's that?
CRATO. Because they charge a lot for degrees with meaningless names.

61. 'REMOVING THE FRESHMAN'S HORNS'

Petrus and Urbanus

PETRUS. Hey, you! Have you ever heard the proverb 'One potter hates another'?
URBANUS. I've heard it myself quite often.
PETRUS. Do you know what it means?
URBANUS. I've known for a long time.
PETRUS. Explain it, so as I can hear.
URBANUS. It means that everyone hates a rival in his own profession.
PETRUS. Does that animosity exist between scholars?
URBANUS. It does between the students and us, the people they call freshman.
PETRUS. Do you think we have horns, as their jabbering has it?
URBANUS. I don't know, because I don't know myself.
PETRUS. No one will convince me.
URBANUS. And yet they say that they used to have them too.
PETRUS. They also joke that we smell like goats.
URBANUS. That's easier to believe.
PETRUS. Do you say so too? Why do you say that?
URBANUS. We're dirty because of the crusts of bread and butter we often carry around for the day in our pockets.
PETRUS. Do they free us from both of those defects when they remove our horns?
URBANUS. That's what they believe.

PETRVS. Fides ista uanior est mulierum credulitate.
VRBANVS. Ipse fortassis breui experiar.
PETRVS. Tollentur tibi cornua?
VRBANVS. Auferentur, simul et sordities.
PETRVS. O, si liceret me esse spectatorem.
VRBANVS. Ego quoque spectare mallem quam ferre.
PETRVS. Vidistin quandoque spectaculum istud?
VRBANVS. Nusquam integre.
PETRVS. Tractabunt te ut asinum inter simias.
VRBANVS. Iaciam aleam, non tamen de capite agitur.

34 iaciam] iaceam A B C

62. QVOD DIFFICILE ET AMARVM SIT A TEPEFACTO SVRGERE LECTO

Cornelius et Petrus

CORNELIVS. Ah, si liceret nobis diutius stertere!
PETRVS. Hoc et ego optarem.
CORNELIVS. Me sopor oppido adhuc grauat.
PETRVS. Et mihi oculi sunt constricti.
CORNELIVS. Sputo ipsas linias et aperientur.
PETRVS. Proderitne?
CORNELIVS. Fac periculum et percipies.
PETRVS. Incipio uti uisu.
CORNELIVS. Sed surgemusne?
PETRVS. Tuae me subscribam sententiae.
CORNELIVS. Frigus est acre.
PETRVS. Sensi dum e lodice extendi manum.
CORNELIVS. Praestaret nido tepido immorari, quam a cubitu resurgere.
PETRVS. Probe mones.
CORNELIVS. Frigus non minus ac culter laedit.
PETRVS. Istud nasus meus et manus loquuntur.
CORNELIVS. Pauxillulum temporis adhuc sub centone agemus.
PETRVS. Hoc si tacuisses, protulissem.
CORNELIVS. Interulam et caligas sub lodicem pone quo incalescant.
PETRVS. Hac nocte indusio indormiui.

PETRUS. That belief is emptier than an old wives' tale.
URBANUS. Perhaps I'll find out shortly.
PETRUS. Are your horns going to be removed?
URBANUS. Yes, and my dirt too.
PETRUS. Oh, I wish I could watch.
URBANUS. I'd prefer to be the spectator rather than the victim, too.
PETRUS. Have you seen the sight sometimes?
URBANUS. I've never seen it all.
PETRUS. They'll treat you 'like an ass amongst monkeys'.
URBANUS. I'll take the chance; after all, my head's not at stake.

62. HOW HARD AND UNPLEASANT IT IS TO GET OUT OF A WARM BED

Cornelius and Petrus

CORNELIUS. If only we could doze for longer!
PETRUS. I'd like that too.
CORNELIUS. Sleep is still weighing heavily on me.
PETRUS. And my eyes are stuck closed.
CORNELIUS. Rub spittle on them and they'll open.
PETRUS. Will it help?
CORNELIUS. Try it and you'll see.
PETRUS. I'm starting to be able to see.
CORNELIUS. But shall we get up?
PETRUS. I'll go along with your opinion.
CORNELIUS. The cold is fierce.
PETRUS. I felt it when I stuck my hand out from under the blanket.
CORNELIUS. It would be better to stay in the warm bed than to get out of it.
PETRUS. You're quite right.
CORNELIUS. The cold cuts like a knife.
PETRUS. My nose and my hands can testify to that.
CORNELIUS. Let's spend a little more time under the quilt.
PETRUS. If you hadn't said that, I would have.
CORNELIUS. Put your shirt and your breeches under the blanket to warm up.
PETRUS. I slept in my vest last night.

CORNELIVS. Nequeo somnium capere, nisi totus me exuero.
PETRVS. O delicias hominis!
CORNELIVS. Aiunt inde uermes gigni si diu noctuque ue- [D5v] stes corpori adhaeserint.
PETRVS. Expers metus illius sum, quia saepe muto lineum indumentum.
CORNELIVS. Sat nugatum est, surgendum est tandem.
PETRVS. Hui, uellem me indutum esse.
CORNELIVS. Festinemus nos cingendo uestibus.
PETRVS. Age uter citius erit instructus.
CORNELIVS. Caligae me morantur.
PETRVS. Et ego calceos non reperio.

---

4 liceret] liceret A C; licet B | 32 nugatum] nugarum A | 36 me morantur] memorantur A

63. DE PROFECTIONE IN PEREGRINAE VRBIS GYMNASIVM LITTERARIVM

Erasmus et Adolphus

ERASMVS. Salue sodalium iucundissime.
ADOLPHVS. Salue et tu quoque.
ERASMVS. Quomodo tibi conuenit cum parentibus tuis?
ADOLPHVS. Qui istud quaeritas?
ERASMVS. Eo quia ipse apud meos longius durare nequeo.
ADOLPHVS. Nolunt te alere?
ERASMVS. Alerent me bene, sed nunquam tranquille.
ADOLPHVS. Forte plagis te saepe domant.
ERASMVS. Non, sed me semper inscitiae arguunt.
ADOLPHVS. Vnde ipsi tuae peritiae periculum habent?
ERASMVS. Mater aestimat me iuxta inscium manere.
ADOLPHVS. More andabatarum id fortassis coniicit.
ERASMVS. Ideo alio me conferam e patria.
ADOLPHVS. Exulabisne?
ERASMVS. Inuisam quid aliis in urbibus rerum geratur.
ADOLPHVS. Sed fac ut eruditior redeas.
ERASMVS. Omne mouebo saxum.
ADOLPHVS. Id decet, nam patriam regredi imperitum extremum est uitiorum.

CORNELIUS. I can't get to sleep unless I take all my clothes off.
PETRUS. O you sensitive soul!
CORNELIUS. They say that worms are caused by your clothes sticking to your body day and night.
PETRUS. I needn't be afraid of that, because I often change my linen.
CORNELIUS. Enough idle chat, we must get up at last.
PETRUS. Oh, I wish I was dressed.
CORNELIUS. Let's put our clothes on really fast.
PETRUS. See who's ready quickest.
CORNELIUS. My breeches are holding me up.
PETRUS. And I can't find my shoes.

63. GOING OFF TO SCHOOL IN ANOTHER CITY

Erasmus and Adolphus

ERASMUS. Greetings, most congenial of my companions!
ADOLPHUS. And the same to you.
ERASMUS. How well do you get on with your parents?
ADOLPHUS. Why do you ask?
ERASMUS. Because I can't stay with mine any longer.
ADOLPHUS. Do they refuse to maintain you?
ERASMUS. They're prepared to maintain me, but they never leave me in peace.
ADOLPHUS. Do they often control you by beating you?
ERASMUS. No, but they're always saying that I know nothing.
ADOLPHUS. How do they have any proof of your knowledge?
ERASMUS. My mother reckons that I'm staying ignorant.
ADOLPHUS. Perhaps she's made a blind guess at that.
ERASMUS. So I'm leaving home and going somewhere else.
ADOLPHUS. Will you stay away from home?
ERASMUS. I'll go and see what's going on in other cities.
ADOLPHUS. But make sure you come back more learned.
ERASMUS. I'll make every effort.
ADOLPHUS. That's right and proper, because coming back home ignorant is the most serious of faults.

ERASMVS. Accinge te, et mecum proficiscere.
ADOLPHVS. Placaret mihi, si parentibus uisum esset.
ERASMVS. Non posses, scio, a matre abesse.
ADOLPHVS. Qui hoc nosti?
ERASMVS. Nonnunquam mammillas te sugere oportet.
ADOLPHVS. Assem sumerem et matris deuouerem conspectum.
ERASMVS. Si tibi liberum fuerit, hoc [D6r] uesperi mihi adsis.
ADOLPHVS. Dabis nobis monumentum discessus?
ERASMVS. Largiar, et cras prima luce hinc anchoram soluam.
ADOLPHVS. Precabor parentes meos, quo conuenire liceat.
ERASMVS. Istud facito et uenias, bellos homunculos agemus.
ADOLPHVS. Si per parentes potuero, non emanebo.

64. QVANDO QVIS SATIS SCIENTIAE HABEAT, VEL SCIAT

Iohannes et Iacobus

IOHANNES. Tu ueterane miles assides adhuc libris?
IACOBVS. Aliud nihil agere possum commodius.
IOHANNES. Tranquillam nunc sumeres uitam otiando et potando.
IACOBVS. Nulla mihi tranquillior est uita quam litteraria.
IOHANNES. Satis nunc scientiae habes.
IACOBVS. Scientias uix prioribus labiis attigi.
IOHANNES. Nunc tuum ipsius encomium taces.
IACOBVS. Loquor quod res est.
IOHANNES. Tamen omnes tuos commilitones peritia excellis.
IACOBVS. Facile est amusos praecellere.
IOHANNES. Si tua mihi esset eruditio, libros raro salutarem.
IACOBVS. Tum certe tibi ipsi imponeres.
IOHANNES. Non moror philosophiae fastigium.
IACOBVS. Et ego nollem aliis esse imperitior.
IOHANNES. Precor edissere quando quis satis scientiae habeat.

ERASMUS. Get yourself ready and come with me.
ADOLPHUS. I'd like to, if my parents agreed.
ERASMUS. I know you couldn't leave your mother.
ADOLPHUS. How do you know that?
ERASMUS. You sometimes have to suck her breasts.
ADOLPHUS. I'd happily take my money and renounce the sight of my mother.
ERASMUS. If you're given permission, join me this evening.
ADOLPHUS. Will you give us a party to mark your departure?
ERASMUS. Yes, and at first light tomorrow I'll be off.
ADOLPHUS. I'll beg my parents to be allowed to come too.
ERASMUS. Do that and come, we'll be the fine fellows.
ADOLPHUS. If my parents allow me, I'll be there.

64. WHEN DOES SOMEONE POSSESS ENOUGH KNOWLEDGE?

Iohannes and Iacobus

IOHANNES. You hardened soldier, still at your books?
IACOBUS. There's nothing more pleasant I can do.
IOHANNES. You could take up a tranquil life, idling and drinking.
IACOBUS. I don't find any life more tranquil than a life of scholarship.
IOHANNES. You've got enough knowledge now.
IACOBUS. I've hardly scratched the surface of learning.
IOHANNES. Now you're just being modest.
IACOBUS. I'm saying what's true.
IOHANNES. And yet you excel all your classmates in knowledge.
IACOBUS. It's easy to be better than ignoramuses.
IOHANNES. If I had your learning, I'd hardly ever open a book.
IACOBUS. Then you'd definitely be deceiving yourself.
IOHANNES. I've no taste for the dizzy heights of philosophy.
IACOBUS. And I wouldn't want to be more ignorant than other people.
IOHANNES. Tell me, please, when someone has enough knowledge.

IACOBVS. Quod quaeris mei ingenii uires excedit.

IOHANNES. Respondeas saltem, quantum per Mineruam potueris.

IACOBVS. Respondeo, quando nihil ignorat.

IOHANNES. Tuo iudicio (ut audio) nullus fieret doctus.

IACOBVS. Non capio quid uelis.

IOHANNES. Quia illi qui habentur passim eruditi adhuc multa ignorant, ut artes ipsas manuarias.

IACOBVS. Nescire illas litteris deditum refert nihil.

IOHANNES. Speras etiam te olim consecuturum scientiae metam?

IACOBVS. Si Nestoris audio sententiam, tunc nunquam.

IOHANNES. [D6v] Quid Nestor dixit de scientiarum meta?

IACOBVS. Retulit se et senem fieri et indies prius ignota discere.

IOHANNES. Quem Plato litteratum censuit?

IACOBVS. Eum qui omnium scientiarum esset utcunque gnarus.

65. DE MORE STANDI AD CYATHOS

Adrianus et Christophorus

ADRIANVS. O quam occupatissimi omnes cras erimus domi nostrae!

CHRISTOPHORVS. Vnde istae occupationes?

ADRIANVS. Permulti apud nos prandebunt.

CHRISTOPHORVS. Facient tui parentes soli sumptum?

ADRIANVS. Vtique, solemus hoc die annuo uicinos excipere conuiuio.

CHRISTOPHORVS. Gentiles Romanos imitamini.

ADRIANVS. Solebantne et illi inter se sollemne agitare conuiuium?

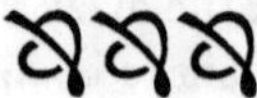

IACOBUS. What you're asking is more that my intellect can cope with.
IOHANNES. Just answer as best as your intellect allows.
IACOBUS. My answer is – when there's nothing he doesn't know.
IOHANNES. I see that in your opinion no one would become learned.
IACOBUS. I don't understand what you mean.
IOHANNES. Because people generally regarded as learned still don't know a lot of things, like the manual trades.
IACOBUS. It doesn't matter if scholars don't know *them*.
IOHANNES. Do you hope that one day you'll master the whole of knowledge yourself?
IACOBUS. Never, if I accept Nestor's opinion.
IOHANNES. What did Nestor say about the whole of knowledge?
IACOBUS. He reported that he was becoming an old man, and that every day he was still learning things he hadn't known before.
IOHANNES. Who did Plato consider was learned?
IACOBUS. The person as familiar as possible with every branch of learning.

65. HOW TO SERVE DRINKS AT TABLE

Adrianus and Christophorus

ADRIANUS. We're all going to be really busy at our house tomorrow!
CHRISTOPHORUS. What will make you so busy?
ADRIANUS. There are going to be lots of people having lunch with us.
CHRISTOPHORUS. Will your parents pay for it all by themselves?
ADRIANUS. They will indeed. On this day every year we treat our neighbours to a meal.
CHRISTOPHORUS. You're imitating the pagan Romans.
ADRIANUS. Did they hold formal banquets amongst themselves, too?

CHRISTOPHORVS. Solebant, si Valerio Maximo creditur.

ADRIANVS. Et quos inuitabant?

CHRISTOPHORVS. Solos amicos.

ADRIANVS. Apud pocula quid tractabant?

CHRISTOPHORVS. Anni spatio inter se ortam inuidiam leniebant.

ADRIANVS. Ni fallor et ea gratia nobis mos ille est.

CHRISTOPHORVS. Facile credidero.

ADRIANVS. Mihi autem cras plus aliis sudandum erit.

CHRISTOPHORVS. Quod tibi committetur munus?

ADRIANVS. Aliis accumbentibus standum mihi erit ad cyathos.

CHRISTOPHORVS. Est illud tibi molestum?

ADRIANVS. Non molestum admodum, sed laboriosum.

CHRISTOPHORVS. Conuiuae tibi interdum calices exsorbendos dabunt.

ADRIANVS. Certe istas delicias non efflagito.

CHRISTOPHORVS. Tamen aliquorum palata iuuant.

ADRIANVS. Cantharus quo pocula implebo et patinarum tollere me onerabunt.

CHRISTOPHORVS. Non licebit tibi fesso alteri tradere in decursu lampadem?

ADRIANVS. Tum omnes me incusarent desidiae.

CHRISTOPHORVS. Simulares te aegrotare.

ADRIANVS. Absit istud, quia tunc lautis priuarer bolis. [D7r]

CHRISTOPHORVS. Minime, nescis delicatiora porrigi aegris?

66. QVIBVS VTENDVM VERBIS, DVM VINVM FORIS EMPTVM MENSAE AFFERTVR

Emmericus et Chrysantus

EMMERICVS. Quippiam te rogarem, si scirem non recusaturum.

CHRYSANTVS. Si potuero, haud difficilis ero.

CHRISTOPHORUS. They did, if you believe Valerius Maximus.
ADRIANUS. And who did they invite?
CHRISTOPHORUS. Just their friends.
ADRIANUS. What did they talk about at table?
CHRISTOPHORUS. They softened the ill-feeling that had grown up amongst them over the year.
ADRIANUS. If I'm not mistaken, that's our reason for the custom, too.
CHRISTOPHORUS. I can well believe it.
ADRIANUS. But tomorrow I'll have to slog harder than the others.
CHRISTOPHORUS. What duty will you be given?
ADRIANUS. While the others sit down to eat, I'll have to serve the drinks.
CHRISTOPHORUS. Do you find that tiresome?
ADRIANUS. Not particularly tiresome, but it is hard work.
CHRISTOPHORUS. Now and again the guests will give you their cups to drink off.
ADRIANUS. I don't ask for those pleasures, I assure you.
CHRISTOPHORUS. But they delight some people's palates.
ADRIANUS. The jug I fill the cups from, and removing the plates, will be very heavy for me.
CHRISTOPHORUS. Won't you be allowed to hand over to someone else when you're tired?
ADRIANUS. Then everyone would accuse me of being lazy.
CHRISTOPHORUS. You could pretend you're ill.
ADRIANUS. Certainly not – I wouldn't get any tasty treats then.
CHRISTOPHORUS. That's not true. Don't you know that sick people get given dainty things?

66. WHAT TO SAY WHEN WINE BOUGHT OUTSIDE THE HOUSE IS BROUGHT TO THE TABLE

Emmericus and Chrysantus

EMMERICUS. I'd like to ask you something, if I knew you wouldn't refuse.
CHRYSANTUS. If I can, I won't be reluctant.

EMMERICVS. Poteris facile, si te non grauauerit.
CHRYSANTVS. Grauabit me nequaquam, si praestare possum.
EMMERICVS. Doceas me oro quibus uerbis uinum afferam mensae mercatum uel latum foris.
CHRYSANTVS. Nihil ac lubens fecero.
EMMERICVS. Loquere tu ut uinum afferens, ego ac mensae accumbens respondebo.
CHRYSANTVS. Faciam, tu uide commode respondeas.
EMMERICVS. Auspicare.
CHRYSANTVS. Hoc uini prosit bibentibus.
EMMERICVS. Et tibi afferenti.
CHRYSANTVS. Istud uini bibentibus non obsit.
EMMERICVS. Neque tibi adducenti.
CHRYSANTVS. Vinum quod apporto sit uobis omnibus salutiferum.
EMMERICVS. Et tibi apportanti salutem praebeat.
CHRYSANTVS. Merum hoc quod foris tuli, felix sit uobis potus.
EMMERICVS. Neque infelix sit tibi nuntio.
CHRYSANTVS. Hic Bacchicus potus uobis omnibus fortunatus sit.
EMMERICVS. Talis sit et tibi id nobis precanti.
CHRYSANTVS. Hoc uini Deus salubre faciat.
EMMERICVS. Idem et tibi reddat.
CHRYSANTVS. Felicissimo omine haec Bacchica bibite munera.
EMMERICVS. Et tu quoque felici auspicio de ipsis sumito.
CHRYSANTVS. Has uineae dotes opto uobis omnibus secundas.
EMMERICVS. Gratiam habe, neque tibi sint minus salutiferae.

---

26 sit] sit A C; fit B

67. DE MODO STERNENDI MENSAM

Crato et Valterus

CRATO. Audin tu horologium?
VALTERVS. Audio, quid inde?
CRATO. Scis quota sonat hora?

EMMERICUS. You'll easily be able to, if you don't find it a nuisance.

CHRYSANTUS. It won't be a nuisance at all, if I can do it.

EMMERICUS. Teach me, please, the words to use when I bring wine that's been bought or fetched outside the house to the table.

CHRYSANTUS. There's nothing I'd rather do.

EMMERICUS. You speak like the person bringing the wine, and I'll reply like the person sitting at table.

CHRYSANTUS. All right, and you make sure that you give a suitable reply.

EMMERICUS. Begin.

CHRYSANTUS. May this wine do good to you who drink it.

EMMERICUS. And to you who bring it.

CHRYSANTUS. May this wine not harm you who drink it.

EMMERICUS. Nor you who bring it.

CHRYSANTUS. May the wine I bring give health to you all.

EMMERICUS. And may it do the same to you who bring it.

CHRYSANTUS. May this wine I've fetched from outside the house be a fortunate drink for you.

EMMERICUS. And may it be fortunate to you the bearer.

CHRYSANTUS. May this drink of Bacchus be auspicious to you all.

EMMERICUS. And may it be the same for you for wishing us that.

CHRYSANTUS. May God make this wine health-giving.

EMMERICUS. And may he do the same for you.

CHRYSANTUS. Drink these gifts of Bacchus to your good fortune.

EMMERICUS. And you too, drink them to yours.

CHRYSANTUS. I wish that these fruits of the vine may be favourable to you all.

EMMERICUS. Thank you, and may they be no less health-giving to you.

67. HOW TO SET THE TABLE

Crato and Valterus

CRATO. Do you hear the clock?

VALTERUS. Yes, so what?

CRATO. Do you know what time it's striking?

VALTERVS. Aestimo nona.
CRATO. Si addideris unum, ue- [D7v] rum loqueris.
VALTERVS. Sonat decimam?
CRATO. Accelera tu domum uersus.
VALTERVS. Tardus non ibo.
CRATO. Appara mensam ante patris aduentum.
VALTERVS. Timeo ne tam cito possim.
CRATO. Veni, iuuabo te.
VALTERVS. Ah, leua mihi laborem.
CRATO. Faciam, sed alia uice et me auxilio afficies.
VALTERVS. Experieris me diligentiorem quam putas.
CRATO. Linteum quo mensa sternitur feras, ego panem quaeram.
VALTERVS. Linteum nondum ab hesterna cena euacuatum est.
CRATO. Illico effunde, si quid intus est quisquiliarum.
VALTERVS. En feci, mensam sterno.
CRATO. Panis nondum est decorticatus.
VALTERVS. Ego celerrime ipsum perpoliam.
CRATO. Confero me eductum cereuisiam.
VALTERVS. Vade uorans uiam.
CRATO. Rursum praesto sum.
VALTERVS. Quadras porrige.
CRATO. Aereas uel ligneas?
VALTERVS. Ligneas primum.
CRATO. Circinum in medium mensae ponas.
VALTERVS. Tu salis sis memor.
CRATO. Cuilibet quadrae frustum panis appone.
VALTERVS. Et tu singulis poculum adde cereuisiae.
CRATO. Quid nunc restat?
VALTERVS. Calices uini elue.
CRATO. Satis mature istud fiet uino allato.
VALTERVS. Mox aderit qui uinum afferet.

---

15 auxilio afficies] auxilio tuo afficies A | 32 frustum] frusta A

VALTERUS. Nine, I reckon.
CRATO. If you add one you'll be right.
VALTERUS. It's striking ten?
CRATO. Hurry off home!
VALTERUS. I won't be slow.
CRATO. Set the table before Dad arrives.
VALTERUS. I don't think I'll be able to do it as quickly as that.
CRATO. Come on, I'll help you.
VALTERUS. Oh, do give me a hand!
CRATO. I will, but another time you can give me the benefit of your help.
VALTERUS. You'll find me more attentive than you think.
CRATO. You bring the cloth the table's spread with, I'll get the bread.
VALTERUS. The cloth hasn't been emptied out after dinner yesterday.
CRATO. Shake it out, in that case, if there are any crumbs in it.
VALTERUS. Right, I've done that, I'm spreading it on the table.
CRATO. The crust hasn't been cut off the bread yet.
VALTERUS. I'll take it off really quickly.
CRATO. I'm off to draw some beer.
VALTERUS. Run like the wind!
CRATO. I'm back again.
VALTERUS. Put out the plates.
CRATO. The bronze ones or the wooden ones?
VALTERUS. The wooden ones first.
CRATO. Put a dish-ring in the centre of the table.
VALTERUS. And you remember the salt.
CRATO. Put a piece of bread on every plate.
VALTERUS. And you set a cup of beer beside each one.
CRATO. What's left now?
VALTERUS. Wash out the wine-goblets.
CRATO. It'll be time enough to do that when the wine has been brought.
VALTERUS. The person who'll bring the wine will soon be here.

68. MISERVM ESSE IN PRANDIO VENIRE PERACTA FABVLA

Balthasar et Liborius

BALTHASAR. Tu saltas nunc, ego potius flerem.
LIBORIVS. Fleres forte siccis oculis.
BALTHASAR. Certe oculis madentibus.
LIBORIVS. Non tamen uapulas.
BALTHASAR. Aliud est quod mihi lacrimas excuteret.
LIBORIVS. Dum nihil est secreti, effare.
BALTHASAR. Esurie mihi crepitat uenter.
LIBORIVS. Esuris tu a prandio?
BALTHASAR. Ieiuni est esurire. [D8r]
LIBORIVS. Forte nondum es pransus?
BALTHASAR. Non tantillum.
LIBORIVS. Denegabant tibi parentes uictum?
BALTHASAR. Et a cibo et potu me arcebant.
LIBORIVS. Grauiterne eos offendisti?
BALTHASAR. Nihil commerui, nisi quod mensa sublata domum ueni.
LIBORIVS. Vbi tam serus fuisti moratus?
BALTHASAR. Templa diuersa obambulaui orandi gratia.
LIBORIVS. Vix tantum religionis tibi esse credo.
BALTHASAR. Deuotionis nihil mihi uindico.
LIBORIVS. Sed age, cogitur ille esurire qui post sumptum prandium uenerit?
BALTHASAR. Aedes nostrae peracta prandii fabula nulli uictum praebent.
LIBORIVS. Certe tum post 'plaudite' apud uos uenire miserum est.
BALTHASAR. Me hodie ueniente domum de prandio conclamatum fuit.
LIBORIVS. Non rursus tibi sternebatur mensa?
BALTHASAR. Nequaquam, sed fuste ego sternebar terram uersus.

68. IT'S DREADFUL TO ARRIVE AT LUNCH WHEN IT'S OVER

Balthasar and Liborius

BALTHASAR. You're dancing for joy now, but as for me, I could cry.
LIBORIUS. I think you might cry with dry eyes.
BALTHASAR. No, my eyes would be wet.
LIBORIUS. But you're not being beaten.
BALTHASAR. It's something else that might force the tears out of me.
LIBORIUS. Nothing's secret, so tell me.
BALTHASAR. My stomach's rumbling with hunger.
LIBORIUS. Are you hungry after lunch?
BALTHASAR. If you haven't eaten, you feel hungry.
LIBORIUS. Haven't you had lunch yet?
BALTHASAR. Not a bite.
LIBORIUS. Did your parents deny you food?
BALTHASAR. They deprived me of food and drink.
LIBORIUS. Did you offend them seriously?
BALTHASAR. I didn't do anything wrong, other than come home when the table had been cleared after lunch.
LIBORIUS. Where had you been dallying so late?
BALTHASAR. I went round a number of churches to pray.
LIBORIUS. I can hardly believe you're so devout.
BALTHASAR. I don't claim to be devout.
LIBORIUS. But tell me, is someone forced to go hungry if they arrive home after lunch has been eaten?
BALTHASAR. At our house they don't let anyone have food after lunch is over and done with.
LIBORIUS. It's obviously dreadful to arrive at your house after it's over.
BALTHASAR. When I got home today it was all over as far as lunch was concerned.
LIBORIUS. Didn't they lay the table for you again?
BALTHASAR. Not at all – they laid me out on the ground with a stick.

LIBORIVS. Saturabaris etiam inde?
BALTHASAR. Non in stomacho, sed in corpore plagis.
LIBORIVS. Ita nollem saturari.
BALTHASAR. Et ego esurire malo quam saepe illo pasci cibo.

---

23 uindico] uendico A B C | 37–38 saturari … cibo.] saturari. A

69. DE VVIS CARPENDIS

Petrus et Cornelius

PETRVS. Nosti quid sequenti hebdomada nobis incumbit laboris?
CORNELIVS. Carpemus uuas, ut opinor.
PETRVS. Lubens faciam.
CORNELIVS. O quantum uuarum ego deuorabo.
PETRVS. Et ipse illis non abstinebo.
CORNELIVS. Videndum tamen est ne earum esus nobis male cadat.
PETRVS. Qui male caderet?
CORNELIVS. Multi nocte lectum concacant.
PETRVS. Noui aliquos qui caligas impleuerunt uentris oleto.
CORNELIVS. Ego in die saepe exonerabo aluum.
PETRVS. [D8v] Eris tum nocte liber, credis?
CORNELIVS. Spero.
PETRVS. At in nocte primum fit digestio.
CORNELIVS. Ego postquam cunas deserui, nunquam lectum oleto foedaui.
PETRVS. Neque ipse, ut mater testis est.
CORNELIVS. Acuisti cultrum tuum?
PETRVS. Heri subegi in coticula.
CORNELIVS. Per quot dies carpemus uuas?
PETRVS. Nescio, istud copia uel turba decerpentium admonebit.
CORNELIVS. Si mensis spatio duraret, non me grauaret.
PETRVS. Quid ais? Omnium rerum est satietas.
CORNELIVS. Aliquot uuas celabo sub uestem et domi deponam.
PETRVS. Quo? Ad arculam tuam?

LIBORIUS. And then did you have your fill?
BALTHASAR. My stomach didn't, but my body had its fill of blows.
LIBORIUS. I wouldn't like to have my fill of those.
BALTHASAR. And I prefer to go hungry than to swallow that sort of food too often.

69. GRAPE-PICKING

Petrus and Cornelius

PETRUS. Do you know what work we have to do next week?
CORNELIUS. We're picking grapes, I believe.
PETRUS. I'll enjoy doing that.
CORNELIUS. I'm going to eat *so* many grapes!
PETRUS. And I won't abstain from them either.
CORNELIUS. But we must take care that eating them doesn't do us any harm.
PETRUS. How might it harm us?
CORNELIUS. Lots of people shit the bed at night.
PETRUS. I know some who've filled their breeches with shit.
CORNELIUS. I'll empty my bowels often during the day.
PETRUS. Do you think you'll you be safe at night, then?
CORNELIUS. I hope so.
PETRUS. But it's at night that digestion begins.
CORNELIUS. Since I've been out of nappies, I've never fouled the bed.
PETRUS. Nor me, as my mother can tell you.
CORNELIUS. Have you sharpened your knife?
PETRUS. I sharpened it on a stone yesterday.
CORNELIUS. How many days will we pick grapes for?
PETRUS. I don't know. The number of pickers will decide that.
CORNELIUS. If it went on for a month it wouldn't bother me.
PETRUS. What are you saying? You can get enough of anything.
CORNELIUS. I'm going to hide some grapes under my clothes and put them them aside at home.
PETRUS. Where? In your chest?

CORNELIVS. Sic, et dum cubitum ibo semper unam aut alteram edam.
PETRVS. O tu delicati palati homo.
CORNELIVS. Partiar tecum, si apud matrem me non prodes.
PETRVS. Harpocratem agam bellissime.
CORNELIVS. Quam diu forte solus fueris.
PETRVS. Silebo bellissime.

18–19 lectum oleto foedaui] lectum concacaui A | 27 ais] agis A | 35–37 agam bellissime … Silebo bellissime.] agam bellissime. A

70. DE CERASIS

Bartholomaeus et Aegidius

BARTHOLOMAEVS. Ho, ho, quid ego noui uidi.
AEGIDIVS. Quid, quid? Exprime.
BARTHOLOMAEVS. In foro quippiam uidi, quo gaudebam.
AEGIDIVS. Audiam quid.
BARTHOLOMAEVS. Matura cerasa.
AEGIDIVS. Vix credo.
BARTHOLOMAEVS. Sane, erant ligneolo circumligata.
AEGIDIVS. Quanti ueniebant?
BARTHOLOMAEVS. Ligneolum forte uiginti continens cerasa teruncio uendebatur.
AEGIDIVS. Tanti ego non edam cerasa.
BARTHOLOMAEVS. Si mihi nummulus esset, mercarer illico.
AEGIDIVS. Expecta, mox uilius uenient.
BARTHOLOMAEVS. Expectare uix queo, ita gula mihi prurit.
AEGIDIVS. Eme ipsa, si aes in numerato habes.
BARTHOLOMAEVS. Coemamus, rogo, solido.
AEGIDIVS. Fiet, posthac, dum minoris uendentur.
BARTHOLOMAEVS. Timeo desinat cerasorum messis antequam me ipsis exsaturauero. [E1r]
AEGIDIVS. Metuis ne caelum ruat.
BARTHOLOMAEVS. Quam diu credis adhuc erit ipsorum mercatus?
AEGIDIVS. Ad sesquimensem.
BARTHOLOMAEVS. Nunc in caelo sum, interim nummatus euadam.

CORNELIUS. Yes, and every time I go to bed I'll eat one or two.
PETRUS. You self-indulgent man!
CORNELIUS. I'll share them with you, if you don't tell my mother on me.
PETRUS. I'll be as silent as the grave.
CORNELIUS. Maybe – as long as you're on your own.
PETRUS. I'll keep really quiet.

70. DE CERASIS

Bartholomaeus and Aegidius

BARTHOLOMAEUS. I say, I've seen something new!
AEGIDIUS. What? What? Tell me.
BARTHOLOMAEUS. I saw something in the market that really delighted me.
AEGIDIUS. Tell me what.
BARTHOLOMAEUS. Ripe cherries.
AEGIDIUS. I can hardly believe you.
BARTHOLOMAEUS. Yes, they were tied up with a sliver of wood.
AEGIDIUS. What price were they?
BARTHOLOMAEUS. A bundle holding about twenty cherries was going for a Pfennig.
AEGIDIUS. I wouldn't eat as many cherries as that.
BARTHOLOMAEUS. If I had money, I'd buy them straight away.
AEGIDIUS. Wait, they'll soon get cheaper.
BARTHOLOMAEUS. I can hardly wait, my mouth's watering so much.
AEGIDIUS. Buy them, if you have the ready cash.
BARTHOLOMAEUS. Let's buy a Schilling's worth together.
AEGIDIUS. All right, afterwards, when they're cheaper.
BARTHOLOMAEUS. I'm afraid the cherry season will be over before I've eaten my fill of them.
AEGIDIUS. That's a needless fear.
BARTHOLOMAEUS. How long do you think they'll go on selling them?
AEGIDIUS. For six weeks.
BARTHOLOMAEUS. Now I'm in clover: before then I'm going to have money.

AEGIDIVS. Istud mihi non est sperandum.
BARTHOLOMAEVS. Colligis tu e cerasis nucleos?
AEGIDIVS. Conseruo utique.
BARTHOLOMAEVS. At in quem usum? An ut par uel impar ludas?
AEGIDIVS. Non, sed ut ipsos dem praeceptori.
BARTHOLOMAEVS. Locum tibi dicam ubi permultos reperies nucleos ceraseos.
AEGIDIVS. Vbinam?
BARTHOLOMAEVS. In oleti reconditorio.
AEGIDIVS. Istic tu eos lege.
BARTHOLOMAEVS. Ego ipsis non egeo.
AEGIDIVS. Et mihi satis magna illorum est copia.

2, etc. Aegidius] Egydius A B C

71. DE FABIS, ET CVR SIT PROVERBIVM 'FABIS VIRENTIBVS FVRVNT MORI'

Franciscus et Augustinus

FRANCISCVS. Nunc uirent campi, nunc formosissimus annus.
AVGVSTINVS. Haud falsa narras.
FRANCISCVS. Segetes nunc adolescunt.
AVGVSTINVS. Mox adoleuerunt.
FRANCISCVS. Vidisti etiam et fabas uirere?
AVGVSTINVS. Vtique, ante dies complusculos.
FRANCISCVS. Sensisti etiam ipsarum florere in capite tuo?
AVGVSTINVS. Quomodo fabarum germen caput meum perciperet?
FRANCISCVS. Miraris hoc?
AVGVSTINVS. Admiror maxime, cum in agris, non meo crescant capite.
FRANCISCVS. Ah, certe uis fabarum nunquam magis quam in tuo cerebro oritur.
AVGVSTINVS. Cerebrum meum tamen non est satum fabis.
FRANCISCVS. Aeque uis ipsarum ibidem residet.
AVGVSTINVS. Quid uocas uim fabarum?
FRANCISCVS. Vis earum est obtusum reddere quod tangunt.

AEGIDIUS. I've no hope of that.
BARTHOLOMAEUS. Do you collect the cherry-stones?
AEGIDIUS. Yes, indeed I keep them.
BARTHOLOMAEUS. But what for? To play 'odd or even'?
AEGIDIUS. No, to give them to the teacher.
BARTHOLOMAEUS. I'll tell you a spot where you'll find lots of cherry-stones.
AEGIDIUS. Where's that?
BARTHOLOMAEUS. In the cess-pit.
AEGIDIUS. *You* can pick them out of there!
BARTHOLOMAEUS. I have no need of them.
AEGIDIUS. And I've got a big enough supply of them.

71. BEANS, AND WHY WE HAVE THE PROVERB 'WHEN THE BEANS SPROUT, FOOLS GO CRAZY'

Franciscus and Augustinus

FRANCISCUS. Now the fields are green, and the year's at its most beautiful.
AUGUSTINUS. You're quite right.
FRANCISCUS. The crops are ripening.
AUGUSTINUS. Soon they'll be ripe.
FRANCISCUS. Have you seen the beans sprout too?
AUGUSTINUS. Oh, yes, several days ago.
FRANCISCUS. Have you felt them blossoming in your head as well?
AUGUSTINUS. How could a bean-seed take root in my head?
FRANCISCUS. Do you wonder at that?
AUGUSTINUS. A lot, because they grow in the fields, not in my head.
FRANCISCUS. Oh, the power of beans sprouts nowhere more than in your brain.
AUGUSTINUS. Yet my brain isn't sown with beans.
FRANCISCUS Their power resides there just as much as if it were.
AUGUSTINUS. What do you mean by the power of beans?
FRANCISCUS They have the power of dulling whatever they touch.

AVGVSTINVS. Forte ingenia eorum qui ipsis uescuntur?
FRANCISCVS. Sic, ideo Pythagoras iussit abstinere ab illis.
AVGVSTINVS. Vero non dissonat.
FRANCISCVS. Habes compertum cur dicatur fabis uirentibus furere moros?
AVGVSTINVS. [E1v] Prouerbium scio, sed non causam.
FRANCISCVS. Haec est causa, quia per ipsa infatuata cerebra homines faciunt furere.
AVGVSTINVS. Tunc eas nunquam degustabo.
FRANCISCVS. Etiam odore perceptae gestire faciunt moros.
AVGVSTINVS. Nunc tutus esse nequeo.
FRANCISCVS. Olfactum occlude alterius rei odore.
AVGVSTINVS. Cuius rei suades?
FRANCISCVS. Oleti uetulae aniculae.
AVGVSTINVS. Id facito uice mea.
FRANCISCVS. Ipse a moris sum liber.
AVGVSTINVS. Qui hoc?
FRANCISCVS. Saepe nauigo Anticyras, et edo nasturtium.

36–39 mea … nasturtium.] mea. A | 39 Anticyras] Antyciras B C

72. DE MISSA INDIES AVDIENDA

Bernardus et Conradus

BERNARDVS. Quando e lecto tuo tu te mane corripis?
CONRADVS. Statutum mihi tempus non habeo.
BERNARDVS. Licet dum tibi ad tuum dormire nutum?
CONRADVS. Hisce diebus quos sacros habemus.
BERNARDVS. Transigis tunc cubando longius tempus quam alio die?
CONRADVS. Etiam, quia plus per scholam uacat.
BERNARDVS. Matutinis sacrificiis non soles interesse?
CONRADVS. Soleo, sed non nisi in praecipuis sanctorum festis et summis.
BERNARDVS. Diebus autem operosis quando a cubitu surgis?
CONRADVS. Ad horam quintam.

AUGUSTINUS. Does that include the intellects of the people who eat them?
FRANCISCUS Yes, that's why Pythagoras ordered people to avoid them.
AUGUSTINUS. That sounds plausible.
FRANCISCUS Do you know why people say that 'when the beans sprout fools go crazy'?
AUGUSTINUS. I know the proverb, but not the reason.
FRANCISCUS The reason is that brains softened by beans make people go mad.
AUGUSTINUS. Then I'll never eat them.
FRANCISCUS Even just smelling them makes fools lose control.
AUGUSTINUS. Now I can't be safe.
FRANCISCUS Block out the smell with the scent of something else.
AUGUSTINUS. What would you suggest?
FRANCISCUS An old woman's crap.
AUGUSTINUS. You do that for me.
FRANCISCUS I'm not bothered by fools.
AUGUSTINUS. How?
FRANCISCUS I often sail to Anticyra, and I eat watercress.

72. GOING TO MASS EVERY DAY

Bernardus and Conradus

BERNARDUS. When do you get out of your bed in the morning?
CONRADUS. I haven't got a fixed time.
BERNARDUS. So are you allowed to sleep as long as you like?
CONRADUS. During these religious holidays.
BERNARDUS. So do you spend a longer time in bed now than on other days?
CONRADUS. Yes, because I have more time to, thanks to school being out.
BERNARDUS. Don't you go to morning Mass?
CONRADUS. I do, but only on the most important saints' days.
BERNARDUS. But when do you get out of bed on workdays?
CONRADUS. At five.

BERNARDVS. Inuisis ea hora scholam?
CONRADVS. Non, sed templum accedo.
BERNARDVS. In templo quid exequeris?
CONRADVS. Sacrificio missae intersum.
BERNARDVS. Quotidiene audis missam?
CONRADVS. Indies certe, si licet per negotia.
BERNARDVS. Ego nunquam, nisi die festo uel Dominico.
CONRADVS. Ideo etiam in litteris nequis progredi.
BERNARDVS. Aestimas id esse causae?
CONRADVS. Scio ueracissime.
BERNARDVS. Vnde nosti?
CONRADVS. Euangelium dicit, si primum quaesierimus regnum Dei, omnia nobis dabuntur.
BERNARDVS. Nonnullos tamen uidi peritissimos euadere, et rarissime aedem sacram inuiserunt. [E2v]
CONRADVS. Fortuna illorum diu non durabit.
BERNARDVS. Quantumuis autem sciuerunt, inopes tamen usque mansere.
CONRADVS. Sint tibi exemplo, et tu frequentius ora.
BERNARDVS. Faciam, tu tuae admonitionis gratiam habeas.
CONRADVS. Videbis pauxillulo temporis progressum ubique feliciorem te habiturum.
BERNARDVS. Parebo tuis iussis.

---

34 tu tuae admonitionis] tu admonitionis A | 34–37 habeas … iussis.] habeas. A

73. QVOMODO IVVENIS IN LITTERIS PROFECTVRVS SE GERERE DEBEAT

Albanus et Lycurgus

ALBANVS. Salue.
LYCVRGVS. Et tu quoque.
ALBANVS. Negotii quid geris?
LYCVRGVS. Equidem otium, non negotium ago.
ALBANVS. Tu rarus libros tractas.
LYCVRGVS. Non semper eadem sunt agenda.
ALBANVS. Credebam te nihil quam chartas reuoluere.
LYCVRGVS. Cur id persuasum habuisti?

BERNARDUS. Do you go to school then?
CONRADUS. No, I go to church.
BERNARDUS. What do you do in church?
CONRADUS. I go to Mass.
BERNARDUS. You hear Mass every day?
CONRADUS. Every day, indeed, if my business allows me.
BERNARDUS. I never do, apart from holidays and Sundays.
CONRADUS. And so you're not able to make any progress in your studies.
BERNARDUS. Do you reckon that's the reason?
CONRADUS. I know it, very truthfully.
BERNARDUS. How do you know?
CONRADUS. The Gospel says that if we seek first the Kingdom of God, all things will be given to us.
BERNARDUS. Yet I've seen some people become very learned, and they hardly ever went to church.
CONRADUS. Their good fortune won't last.
BERNARDUS. However much they knew, they've still stayed poor up to now.
CONRADUS. Let them be an example to you, and pray more often.
BERNARDUS. I will, and thanks for your advice.
CONRADUS. You'll see that in a short time you'll make good all-round progress.
BERNARDUS. I'll do what you say.

73. HOW A BOY AIMING TO MAKE PROGRESS IN HIS STUDIES SHOULD BEHAVE

Albanus and Lycurgus

ALBANUS. Hallo.
LYCURGUS. Hallo to you.
ALBANUS. What work are you engaged in?
LYCURGUS. I'm engaged in leisure, not work.
ALBANUS. You rarely work at your books.
LYCURGUS. You shouldn't do the same thing all the time.
ALBANUS. I thought you did nothing but read books.
LYCURGUS. Why did you think that?

ALBANVS. Quia longe praecellis alios peritia.
LYCVRGVS. Scientia non solum legendo acquiritur.
ALBANVS. Quo tum alio modo?
LYCVRGVS. Etiam precando et gratiam diuinam implorando.
ALBANVS. Tamen raro templis intersunt feruentes studio.
LYCVRGVS. Mane, dum tu stertis in nido calido, ipsi Deo seruiunt.
ALBANVS. Ego etiam singulis diebus oro, et perlego folia multa.
LYCVRGVS. Labiis forte murmuras, sed cor aliud uoluit.
ALBANVS. Et corde oro quantum conceditur.
LYCVRGVS. Et orare et studere simul oportet.
ALBANVS. Putabam habita gratia diuina labore opus non esse.
LYCVRGVS. Minime, prouerbium est: ‘Cum diis manum admoue’.
ALBANVS. Quid illud sibi uult adagium?
LYCVRGVS. Id est, cum gratia diuina etiam laborandum esse.
ALBANVS. Posthac igitur feruentius et orabo, et chartis impallescam.
LYCVRGVS. Scientia datur a praeceptoribus, a libris et gratia diuina. [E2v]

29–31 impallescam … diuina.] impallescam. A

74. CVR SCHOLASTICI TAM DESIDES SINT AD LABOREM

Theophilus et Parmeno

THEOPHILVS. Cur tu ita desides manibus insinuatis?
PARMENO. Quid agerem?
THEOPHILVS. Admoue manum nostro operi.
PARMENO. Labore non capior.
THEOPHILVS. Quo tum? Delectarisne otio?
PARMENO. Sic, potius quam opere.
THEOPHILVS. Facile mihi persuaseris.

ALBANUS. Because you're far ahead of the others in knowledge.

LYCURGUS. Knowledge isn't only acquired by reading.

ALBANUS. What other way is it acquired, then?

LYCURGUS. By praying, too, and by imploring divine grace.

ALBANUS. Yet people who are enthusiastic about study aren't at church very often.

LYCURGUS. In the morning, whilst you're snoring in a warm bed, they're serving God.

ALBANUS. I pray every day too, and I read lots of books.

LYCURGUS. You probably murmur with your lips, but your heart has been somewhere else.

ALBANUS. I pray with my heart as well, as much as I can manage.

LYCURGUS. You have to pray and study at the same time.

ALBANUS. I thought that when you had divine grace there was no need for effort.

LYCURGUS. No, the proverb goes, 'Move your hand along with the gods.'

ALBANUS. What does that proverb mean?

LYCURGUS. It means that even if you have divine grace you still have to work.

ALBANUS. So in future I'll both pray more fervently, and work hard at my books.

LYCURGUS. Knowledge is imparted by teachers, books and the grace of God.

74. WHY SCHOOLBOYS ARE SO LAZY ABOUT THEIR WORK

Theophilus and Parmeno

THEOPHILUS. Why are you lounging about like that?

PARMENO. What should I do?

THEOPHILUS. Apply yourself to our work.

PARMENO. I'm not fond of work.

THEOPHILUS. Well then, does leisure please you?

PARMENO. Yes, more than work.

THEOPHILUS. You'll easily convince me of that.

PARMENO. Credis ita celerrime?
THEOPHILVS. Vbi uera audio, non dubito.
PARMENO. Et falsis ego quandoque fidem praebeo.
THEOPHILVS. Compertumne habes cur scholastici plus aliis torpeant?
PARMENO. Causam ignoro.
THEOPHILVS. Otiando torpor adipiscitur.
PARMENO. Torpent interdum et laborantes.
THEOPHILVS. Citius tamen otiosi, quia non sunt assueti labore.
PARMENO. Etiam et laboriosi eneruati nonnunquam sudando.
THEOPHILVS. Torpor praecipue tamen scholasticis ascribitur.
PARMENO. Miror cur fiat.
THEOPHILVS. Hanc uulgus adhibet causam, quia in die diui Gregorii omnibus priuantur uiribus.
PARMENO. Dum primum in scholam feruntur? At quis ipsis uires adimeret?
THEOPHILVS. Aiunt quod beatus Gregorius.
PARMENO. Vanum est, iste scientiae est praeses, non uirium spoliator.
THEOPHILVS. Per Pollucem, me censore socordiae scholasticae longe alia est causa.
PARMENO. Amabo, dic quae.
THEOPHILVS. Assuescunt mollem ducere pennam, et onera grauiora fugiunt.
PARMENO. Assuefactio efficacissima est, et altera ferme natura.

---

28 uirium] uirum A; 33 onera] onera C; onere A B | 35–36 est … natura.] est. A

75. QVOD PROMISSA STVLTOS EXHILARANT

Dauus et Pamphilus

DAVVS. Ipse nunc in portu nauigabo, scisne?
PAMPHILVS. Mutabitur tecum fortuna?
DAVVS. Ita sperare iussus sum.
PAMPHILVS. Caue uel uide ne lupus hians deludaris.

PARMENO. Do you believe me as readily as that?
THEOPHILUS. When I hear the truth I'm in no doubt.
PARMENO. I sometimes believe lies, too.
THEOPHILUS. Do you know why schoolboys are more lethargic than other people?
PARMENO. I don't know the reason.
THEOPHILUS. By being idle, they acquire sloth.
PARMENO. But they sometimes slack even when they're working.
THEOPHILUS. But they do so more quickly when they're idle, because they're not used to work.
PARMENO. But even hard-working people are sometimes exhausted by their exertions.
THEOPHILUS. Yet lethargy's ascribed particularly to schoolboys.
PARMENO. I wonder why that's so.
THEOPHILUS. People say the reason is that on St Gregory's day they're deprived of all their strength.
PARMENO. When they're first taken to school? But who would take away their strength?
THEOPHILUS. People say it's St Gregory.
PARMENO. That's wrong. He's the patron of knowledge, not someone who robs you of your strength.
THEOPHILUS. Heavens, in my view the reason for schoolboys' slackness is completely different.
PARMENO. Tell me what it is, please.
THEOPHILUS. They're used to wielding a supple pen, and they avoid heavier tasks.
PARMENO. Being used to something is very effective, it's almost a second nature.

75. FOOLS ARE DELIGHTED BY PROMISES

Davus and Pamphilus

DAVUS. I'm all right now, let me tell you.
PAMPHILUS. Is your luck going to change?
DAVUS. That's what I've been told to hope.
PAMPHILUS. Take care, make sure you're not duped like a wolf with gaping jaws.

DAVVS. Ab isto non timeo, nam aurei montes mihi sunt [E3r] promissi.

PAMPHILVS. Polliciti forte, sed nondum praestiti.

DAVVS. Certus sum ac si accepissem.

PAMPHILVS. Fatue, quid loqueris?

DAVVS. Qui mihi promisit homo fallere non solet.

PAMPHILVS. Est ipse tibi intus et in cute notus?

DAVVS. A pedibus usque ad uerticem mihi cognitus est.

PAMPHILVS. Spem igitur foueas.

DAVVS. Pollicitus est mihi ultro.

PAMPHILVS. Promissa ultronea saepe non dantur.

DAVVS. Cur minus dantur quam precata?

PAMPHILVS. Quia uulgo dicitur, 'Promisisse sat est, praestare opus non est.'

DAVVS. Spe uiuam, hominem ipsum exploraturus.

PAMPHILVS. Ita facito, sed interim eum saepe moneto.

DAVVS. Crebrius monere molestum reddit cui supplicatur.

PAMPHILVS. At ueteri prouerbio, 'Bona nomina nonnunquam fiunt mala, si nunquam interpellas.'

DAVVS. Dicterio isto quid significatur?

PAMPHILVS. Obliuisci nostri si nunquam interloquimur amicum.

DAVVS. Indies conspectui istius obuersor.

PAMPHILVS. Fias uoti compos, precor.

DAVVS. Si promissa factis mihi aequantur, efficiar egregius.

PAMPHILVS. Tum me non agnosces.

76. DE OMASIS VICINIS DEPORTANDIS POST BOVEM MACTATVM

Eusebius et Thylmannus

EVSEBIVS. Quo uadis?

TILMANNVS. Hanc patinam latum amicis.

EVSEBIVS. Quid in ipsa geris tecti?

DAVUS. I've no fear of that, for I've been promised mountains of gold.
PAMPHILUS. Promised, maybe, but you haven't been given them yet.
DAVUS. I'm as sure as if I had received them.
PAMPHILUS. You fool, what are you saying?
DAVUS. The person who promised me isn't in the habit of deceiving.
PAMPHILUS. Do you know him inside and out?
DAVUS. I know him from top to toe.
PAMPHILUS. So you can live in hope.
DAVUS. He promised me spontaneously.
PAMPHILUS. Spontaneous promises often aren't kept.
DAVUS. Why are they kept any less than promises obtained by entreaties?
PAMPHILUS. Because the saying goes that it's enough to promise, you don't have to deliver.
DAVUS. I'll live in hope, I'll be putting that man to the test.
PAMPHILUS. Do, but in the meantime, remind him often.
DAVUS. Frequent reminders make you a nuisance to the person you're petitioning.
PAMPHILUS. But as the old proverb has it, 'Good debts often turn bad, if you never call them in.'
DAVUS. What's the meaning of that saying?
PAMPHILUS. That a friend will forget us if we never talk to him.
DAVUS. I cross his path every day.
PAMPHILUS. I hope your wish comes true.
DAVUS. If what's promised is delivered, I'll be made into a splendid person.
PAMPHILUS. Then you won't acknowledge me.

76. TAKING THE TRIPE TO NEIGHBOURS AFTER SLAUGHTERING AN OX

Eusebius and Tilmannus

EUSEBIUS. Where are you going?
TILMANNUS. I'm taking this dish to our friends.
EUSEBIUS. What have you got covered up in it?

TILMANNVS. Quippiam opipari.

EVSEBIVS. Sine aspiciam quid sit.

TILMANNVS. Quid uidere tibi proderit?

EVSEBIVS. Forte omasa sunt et farcimina.

TILMANNVS. Ea ipsa sunt, aspice.

EVSEBIVS. Feres ipsa uni domui?

TILMANNVS. Diuiderem, quum modica sunt?

EVSEBIVS. Tantum carnis et ego boni consulerem.

TILMANNVS. Tibi iniurato do fidem.

EVSEBIVS. Num et me intestinorum portiuncula donabis?

TILMANNVS. Si pusillum tibi gratum esset, a parentibus buccellam unam uel alteram intestinorum bouillorum impetrarem tuae gulae. [E3v]

EVSEBIVS. Farcimine etiam admodum exiguo me delectare poteris.

TILMANNVS. Non tantum farcimine te donabo, sed et omasorum duobus uerubus.

EVSEBIVS. Belle promittis, si praestares facto.

TILMANNVS. Vt primum domum rediero, matrem rogabo tuo nomine.

EVSEBIVS. Mei gratia nemini sis molestus.

TILMANNVS. Hoc non metuas, adamat omnes qui mihi sunt socii.

EVSEBIVS. Si potes, egestati meae subuenias.

TILMANNVS. Faciam, uide ut domi sis.

EVSEBIVS. Digitulo appulses ianuam, ubi ueneris.

TILMANNVS. Tum et actutum aperi.

EVSEBIVS. Confestim aperire soleo afferenti.

TILMANNVS. Occludesne ostium petenti?

EVSEBIVS. Istius pulsare non audio.

TILMANNVS. Vnde percipis pulsantem uel afferre uel exigere?

EVSEBIVS. Per rimulam ianuae uideo quis homo sit.

---

13 sunt] sint A | 19 E3] D3 B | 28 mihi] mei A |

TILMANNUS. Something tasty.
EUSEBIUS. Let me look at what it is.
TILMANNUS. What good will seeing it do you?
EUSEBIUS. It might be tripe and sausages.
TILMANNUS. That's what it is, look.
EUSEBIUS. Will you take those all to a single household?
TILMANNUS. Would you expect me to divide them, seeing that there's not much of them?
EUSEBIUS. I'd be satisfied with as much meat as that.
TILMANNUS. I believe you, you don't have to swear it.
EUSEBIUS. Won't you give me a little portion of the offal, too?
TILMANNUS. If you'd welcome a little bit, I'd ask my parents for a mouthful or two of beef offal for you to eat.
EUSEBIUS. You could please me with a tiny little sausage, too.
TILMANNUS. I won't only give you a sausage, I'll give you two skewers of tripe, too.
EUSEBIUS. A fine promise, if you keep it.
TILMANNUS. As soon as I get home I'll ask my mother on your behalf.
EUSEBIUS. Don't bother anyone for my sake.
TILMANNUS. Don't worry about that, she loves everyone who's a friend of mine.
EUSEBIUS. Relieve my poverty if you can.
TILMANNUS. I will, make sure you're at home.
EUSEBIUS. Knock on the door with your finger when you come.
TILMANNUS. Then open up immediately.
EUSEBIUS. I always open up right away to someone who's bringing me something.
TILMANNUS. Do you close the door to people asking for something?
EUSEBIUS. I don't hear their knocking.
TILMANNUS. How can you tell if the person who's knocking is bringing you something, or asking for something?
EUSEBIUS. I see what sort of person it is through a crack in the door.

77. DE CONVIVIO OPIPARO ET LAVTO

Hospes et Conuiuae et Puer

HOSPES. Acceptus est mihi uester aduentus.
CONVIVAE. Gratia tibi sit, o hospes.
HOSPES. Perplacet quod in tempore adestis.
CONVIVAE. Gaudemus.
HOSPES. Hibernaculum ingrediemini.
CONVIVAE. Non admodum frigemus.
HOSPES. Aeque intus ac hic in frigido eritis.
CONVIVAE. Obsequemur tuis iussis.
HOSPES. Si cupitis, feruidius instruetur fornax.
CONVIVAE. Non, nam calet temperate.
HOSPES. Ipse nequeo ferre dum nimio calore aestuat.
CONVIVAE. Insalubre etiam est.
HOSPES. Mox erit coquinae ministra parata, tum eduliis onerabimus mensam.
CONVIVAE. Nil properes nostra causa, non uehementi premimur fame.
HOSPES. Feram bolum aliquem unde procenium facietis.
CONVIVAE. Ah, noli, tum prandere cupide nobis non libebit.
HOSPES. Parebo. Lauetis manus et accumbite mensae.
CONVIVAE. Discumbe tu prior, ut decet.
HOSPES. [E4r] Domi meae sum, stabo uel assidebo mensae.
CONVIVAE. Aduenias tamen nobis.
HOSPES. Consecra cenam puer.
PVER. Benedicite.
CONVIVAE. Dominus.
PVER. Quicquid appositum est et apponetur, per uerbum Dei sanctificetur, in nomine Patris, et Filii, et Spiritus Sancti.
CONVIVAE. Amen.
HOSPES. Nunc uos amici haec attingite obsonia, et eorum uilitatem boni consulite.
CONVIVAE. Sunt haec uilia? Principis decerent patinas et conspectum.

77. A SPLENDID, LUXURIOUS DINNER-PARTY

Host, Guests and Boy

HOST. I'm glad that you've arrived.
GUESTS. Thank you, our host.
HOST. It's very pleasing that you're here on time.
GUESTS. We're delighted.
HOST. Go into the sitting-room.
GUESTS. We're not particularly cold.
HOST. You'll be equally cool inside and here.
GUESTS. We'll do as you say.
HOST. If you like, the stove can be stoked up higher.
GUESTS. No, it's pleasantly warm.
HOST. I can't stand it when it's burning too high.
GUESTS. It's unhealthy, too.
HOST. The cook will be ready soon, then we'll put the food out on the table.
GUESTS. Don't hurry on our account, we're not excessively hungry.
HOST. I'll bring a bite of something that you can have as an hors d'œuvre.
GUESTS. Oh, no, then we won't be eager to eat the meal.
HOST. Very well. Wash your hands and sit down.
GUESTS. You sit down first, as is proper.
HOST. I'm in my own house, I'll stand or sit at the table.
GUESTS. Join us, all the same.
HOST. Boy, say a blessing.
BOY. Benedicite.
GUESTS. Dominus.
HOST. May what is served, and what is yet to be served, be sanctified by the word of God. In the name of the Father, and of the Son, and of the Holy Spirit.
GUESTS. Amen.
HOST. Now, friends, help yourselves to these dishes, and excuse their ordinariness.
GUESTS. Are these ordinary? They'd be fit for a prince to eat, and to look at.

HOSPES. Sunt talia, quae plebeiorum focus fert, et infimae fortunae homines edunt.

---

17 causa] gratia A | 20 cupide] inde A | 22 prior, ut decet.] prior. A | 23 stabo uel assidebo] uel assidebo uel astabo A | 29 Filii, et Spiritus Sancti] filii, et spiritussancti A C; filii spiritus sancti B

78. DE CONVIVIO TENVI ET FRVGALI

Hospes, Puer et Conuiuae

HOSPES. Serue, curre adductum conuiuas.
PVER. Facesso iussum.
HOSPES. Dic instructa omnia.
PVER. Exequar.
HOSPES. Et ut maturent gressus.
PVER. Iubebo.
HOSPES. Me eos expectare nuncia.
PVER. Faciam.
HOSPES. En mei conuiuae, gratulor uestro aduentui.
CONVIVAE. Habemus tibi gratiam.
HOSPES. Cur tam seri adestis? Quid uos detinuit?
CONVIVAE. Timuimus nondum hic instructum esse prandium.
HOSPES. Omnia diu instructa fuere.
CONVIVAE. Tam seri quod adsumus tibi non tamen displiceat precamur
HOSPES. Non, sed stomacho meo amarum fuit.
CONVIVAE. Cur non ientabaris?
HOSPES. Credebam uos semper propediem affuturos.
CONVIVAE. En, iam adsumus ipsi.
HOSPES. Gaudeo, si diutius emansissetis, edissem.
CONVIVAE. Nunc alacrius prandebis nobiscum.
HOSPES. Praedico uobis, mei conuiuae, tenuis hic erit ciborum apparatus.
CONVIVAE. Facile contenti erimus obsoniis, non uulturis aut lupi stomachum habemus.
HOSPES. Patina holusculi et porcina carne uos tractabo.
CONVIVAE. [E4v] Nihil super istud expeteremus.
HOSPES. Aqua igitur manus abluite, et quisque mensae assideat.
CONVIVAE. Faciemus ut iubes.

HOST. They're the sort prepared by common people, and eaten by the humblest sort.

78. A MODEST, FRUGAL DINNER-PARTY

Host, Boy and Guests

HOST. Boy, run and fetch the guests.
BOY. I'll do as you say.
HOST. Tell them that everything is ready.
BOY. I will.
HOST. And that they should hurry.
BOY. I'll tell them.
HOST. Tell them I'm waiting for them.
BOY. I will.
HOST. Ah, my guests, I'm glad you've arrived.
GUESTS. Thank you.
HOST. Why have you come so late? What held you up?
GUESTS. We were afraid the meal wouldn't be ready here yet.
HOST. Everything has been ready for a long time.
GUESTS. We beg you not to be displeased that we've joined you so late.
HOST. I'm not, but it's been hard on my stomach.
GUESTS. Why didn't you eat something?
HOST. I thought you were going to arrive before long.
GUESTS. Well, here we are now.
HOST. I'm pleased. If you'd stayed away any longer I'd have eaten.
GUESTS. Now you'll eat with us all the more eagerly.
HOST. My guests, I must warn you that this will be a modest spread.
GUESTS. We'll be readily contented with the food, we haven't got the stomachs of vultures or wolves.
HOST. I'm going to serve you a dish of cabbage and pork.
GUESTS. We wouldn't ask for anything more than that.
HOST. Wash your hands with water, then, and sit down at table, each of you.
GUESTS. We'll do as you say.

HOSPES. Praelegamus nunc hymnum.
CONVIVAE. Ipsum enarra hospes, nos respondebimus.

11, 24 mei] mi A B C | 13, 16 seri] seri A; serus B; sero C | 24 Praedico uobis, mei] Praedico uobis mi A C; Praedico mi B | 32 Praelegamus] Prelegemus A

79. DE AVIBVS, COLVMBIS ET PISCIBVS CAPIENDIS

Georgius et Valterus

GEORGIVS. Quid negotii tibi sumis a labore litterario?
VALTERVS. Aues, columbas et pisces insequor.
GEORGIVS. Insequeris tu ista? Non usque libris insudas?
VALTERVS. Nequeo semper incumbere chartis.
GEORGIVS. Proficies in litteris, timeo, nunquam.
VALTERVS. Auguraberis, spero, falso.
GEORGIVS. Memoriae teneas quod tibi uaticinor.
VALTERVS. Elaborabo ne uerax sies.
GEORGIVS. Vulgatum audistine prouerbium?
VALTERVS. Quod?
GEORGIVS. Per auium, piscium et columbarum studia multa interiisse ingenia.
VALTERVS. Saepissime audiui, non tamen assensi.
GEORGIVS. Non conuenit simul insequi aues et pisces, ac litteras amplecti.
VALTERVS. Dum otiamur a lectionibus licebit talia quandoque agere.
GEORGIVS. At tu nimis saepe aues et columbas, raro libros tractas.
VALTERVS. Hoc me plus delectat.
GEORGIVS. Verum minus proderit: nauseas, timeo, a labore litterario.
VALTERVS. Praefero aucupium et piscationem.
GEORGIVS. Serus uide ne sapias.
VALTERVS. Satis sapio mihi, non opto Catonis prudentiam.
GEORGIVS. Viue tuo more, nolo tibi esse tutor.

HOST. Now let's say grace.
GUESTS. You begin it, and we'll say the response.

79. CATCHING BIRDS, PIGEONS AND FISH

Georgius and Valterus

GEORGIUS. How do you occupy yourself after school?
VALTERUS. I catch birds, pigeons and fish.
GEORGIUS. You go after those creatures? You don't go on slogging at your books?
VALTERUS. I can't always be at my books.
GEORGIUS. I'm afraid you'll never make any progress in your studies.
VALTERUS. Your prophecy will be wrong, I hope.
GEORGIUS. Keep in mind what I predict for you.
VALTERUS. I'll strive to prove you wrong.
GEORGIUS. Have you heard the well-known proverb?
VALTERUS. Which one?
GEORGIUS. That many a mind has been ruined by the pursuit of birds, fish and pigeons.
VALTERUS. I've heard it very often, but I haven't agreed with it.
GEORGIUS. It's not possible to pursue birds and fish, as well as learning.
VALTERUS. When we haven't got lessons it's all right to do things like that sometimes.
GEORGIUS. But you concern yourself with birds and pigeons too often, and seldom with your books.
VALTERUS. I like doing that better.
GEORGIUS. But it's less good for you. I'm afraid you loathe your studies.
VALTERUS. I prefer bird-catching and fishing.
GEORGIUS. Take care that you don't leave it too late to develop sense.
VALTERUS. I have sense enough for me, I don't want to be as wise as Cato.
GEORGIUS. Live your own way, I don't want to be your guardian.

VALTERVS. Non intermitto penitus studium litterarum, ut tu aestimas.
GEORGIVS. Animum oportet habeas liberum, non talia cogitantem, si profectum eruditionis desideras.
VALTERVS. Sentio quod quicquid ago, cogito de piscibus.
GEORGIVS. litteris solum te dedas, et istas desere nugas.
VALTERVS. Aegre possum, attamen conabor. [E5r]

33–35 piscibus … conabor.] piscibus. A

80. DE BALNEIS INGREDIENDIS

Petrus et Hermannus

PETRVS. Vt ita oles hircum!
HERMANNVS. Arguis me foetoris beanorum?
PETRVS. Non beanum te uoco, sed grauiter oles.
HERMANNVS. Forte pituita laboras.
PETRVS. Sordes tamquam diu balneis non interfuisses.
HERMANNVS. Balnea ut Sirenes fugio.
PETRVS. Malene tibi cum balneis conuenit?
HERMANNVS. Scabie infectus sum, ideo uereor conspici nudus.
PETRVS. Tanto crebrius te ablueres, quo purgareris.
HERMANNVS. In balneis non omnes purgantur.
PETRVS. Qui non?
HERMANNVS. Multi ingressi mundi exeunt ulcerosi.
PETRVS. Scabiem talem plerunque istic tollunt homines.
HERMANNVS. Credo, sed et deridetur et uitatur ab omnibus scabie confectus.
PETRVS. Mallem istud deridere ferre quam semper scabie affligi.
HERMANNVS. Facile consilium praebes (sententia Terentii) quia tu cute purus es.
PETRVS. Consulo tibi quod et ego agerem.
HERMANNVS. Vereor apprime conspici scabiosus.

VALTERUS. I'm not dropping my studies completely, as you think.
GEORGIUS. Your mind needs to be unencumbered, not occupied with things like that, if you want to make progress in learning.
VALTERUS. I agree that whatever I'm doing I'm thinking about fish.
GEORGIUS. Devote yourself to study, and give up those useless pursuits.
VALTERUS. I can scarcely manage it, but I'll try.

80. GOING TO THE BATHS

Petrus and Hermannus

PETRUS. You smell revolting!
HERMANNUS. Are you saying I smell like a freshman?
PETRUS. I'm not calling you a freshman, but you do smell foul.
HERMANNUS. Maybe you've got catarrh.
PETRUS. You're as dirty as if you hadn't been to the baths for a long time.
HERMANNUS. I avoid the baths like the Sirens.
PETRUS. Don't baths agree with you?
HERMANNUS. I've got eczema, so I'm afraid to be seen naked.
PETRUS. You should wash yourself more often, so as to get rid of it.
HERMANNUS. Not everyone is cleansed in the baths.
PETRUS. How come?
HERMANNUS. Lots of people go in clean and come out covered with sores.
PETRUS. People generally get rid of that kind of skin disease there.
HERMANNUS. I believe you, but someone with eczema is laughed at and avoided by everyone.
PETRUS. I'd rather put up with being laughed at than always suffer from eczema.
HERMANNUS. It's easy for you to offer advice, as Terence says, because your skin's clear.
PETRUS. I'm advising you to do what I'd do myself.
HERMANNUS. I'm really afraid to be seen with eczema.

PETRVS. Frontem perfrica, ac mihi in balneum congredere, mea crumena.
HERMANNVS. Exolues tu lotionis meae symbolum?
PETRVS. Promitto, immunis meo balneabis aere.
HERMANNVS. Congrediar, posthac et te ab impendio balnei habebo liberum.
PETRVS. Id non expeto, accinge ut coeamus.
HERMANNVS. Ibo prius domum, indutum interulam mundam uel lotam.
PETRVS. I propere, hic in aedibus te manebo.
HERMANNVS. Mox rursus adero.
PETRVS. I Pegaseo gradu et uorans uiam.

35–36 adero … uiam.] adero. A

81. DE PESTIS SAEVITIA

Arnoldus et Theodolus

ARNOLDVS. Cur iam a patria exulas?
THEODOLVS. Patriam iam fugio ut aues Auernum.
ARNOLDVS. Quomodo istae Auernum fugiunt?
THEODOLVS. Auernus locus est, [E5v] quem propter foetorem nequeunt aues incolere.
ARNOLDVS. Fugis tu etiam ita nunc solum tuum natale?
THEODOLVS. Vtique.
ARNOLDVS. Qui fit istud?
THEODOLVS. Quia ibi nunc foetor pestifer imperat.
ARNOLDVS. Ah, tu perfide.
THEODOLVS. Perfidiae quid me insimulas?
ARNOLDVS. Tu peruerse Menalca, qui deseris in miseria patriam.
THEODOLVS. Traherem ibi moram, ubi de meo capite ageretur?
ARNOLDVS. Amicus in neutra est deserendus fortuna.
THEODOLVS. Infitias non eo, tamen sibi ipsi est cauendum.
ARNOLDVS. In amicitia uera, cura propria non est amico praeferenda.

PETRUS. Stop worrying about it and come to the baths with me, I'll pay.
HERMANNUS. You'll pay the cost of my bath?
PETRUS. You'll have a free bath on me, I promise.
HERMANNUS. I'll go with you, and later I'll treat you to a free bath.
PETRUS. I'm not looking for that. Get ready so as we can go.
HERMANNUS. I'll go home first, and put on a clean shirt.
PETRUS. Go quickly, I'll wait for you here in the house.
HERMANNUS. I'll be back soon.
PETRUS. Go like Pegasus; run like the wind!

81. THE SEVERITY OF THE PLAGUE

Arnoldus and Theodolus

ARNOLDUS. Why are you leaving the country now?
THEODOLUS. I'm fleeing the country as the birds avoid Avernus.
ARNOLDUS. How do you mean, they avoid Avernus?
THEODOLUS. Avernus is a place where birds can't stay because of its foul smell.
ARNOLDUS. Is that the way that you're leaving your native land now?
THEODOLUS. It is indeed.
ARNOLDUS. What's the reason for that?
THEODOLUS. The noxious stench there now forces me to.
ARNOLDUS. Oh, you treacherous person!
THEODOLUS. Why are you accusing me of treachery?
ARNOLDUS. You faithless shepherd, deserting your country in its distress.
THEODOLUS. Why should I stay there, where my life's at stake?
ARNOLDUS. You shouldn't desert a friend in good or bad fortune.
THEODOLUS. I don't deny that – but you have to look out for yourself.
ARNOLDUS. In true friendship, you shouldn't put looking after yourself before your friend.

THEODOLVS. Credo, sed tamen genu cruri propius est.

ARNOLDVS. Iuuares consolando amicos peste infectos.

THEODOLVS. Sat istic habent consolatorum ex cucullatis monachis.

ARNOLDVS. Adsunt ibidem aegrotis monachi?

THEODOLVS. Ita, ordinis Sancti Alexii, non autem sacerdotes sunt.

ARNOLDVS. Sunt etiam illi infirmis mulieribus praesto?

THEODOLVS. Mulieribus adsunt moniales, siue uirgines uestales.

ARNOLDVS. Saeuit apud uestrates adeo atrociter pestis?

THEODOLVS. Homines indies agminatim moriuntur.

ARNOLDVS. Quanta funerum indies est turba?

THEODOLVS. Nonnunquam una die uiginti condiebantur humo me praesente.

ARNOLDVS. Miserum et lamentabile est spectaculum, tot sepelire eodem tempore.

THEODOLVS. Extremum tristitiae est illis quorum amici animam agunt.

ARNOLDVS. Istud expertus sum, dum mei parentes uita defungebantur.

THEODOLVS. In paterno meo solo homines penitus erant consternati animis.

ARNOLDVS. Quis animo non esset perturbato, dum periculo capitis adest?

THEODOLVS. Satius tamen est in culcitra, quam alio mortis genere occumbere.

ARNOLDVS. Vergilius eos uocat terque quaterque beatos, quibus contingit Troiae ante ora pa- [E6r] trum mori.

THEODOLVS. Istud ex oraculo Apollinis protulit dictum, nam mortem leuat patria et amicorum praesentia.

51–52 dictum … praesentia.] dictum. A

82. DE BELLORVM INCOMMODO

Martinus et Valerius

MARTINVS. O quam misere ista natio est deuastata.

THEODOLUS. I believe you, but 'the knee is closer than the calf.'

ARNOLDUS. You could be of use to your friends who have the plague by consoling them.

THEODOLUS. They have enough comforters there in the monks.

ARNOLDUS. Are there monks attending the sick there?

THEODOLUS. Yes, monks of the Alexian order; but they're not priests.

ARNOLDUS. Do they attend sick women too?

THEODOLUS. Women are attended by nuns.

ARNOLDUS. Is the plague raging really fiercely in your part of the world?

THEODOLUS. People are dying every day in droves.

ARNOLDUS. How many funerals are there each day?

THEODOLUS. Sometimes I've been there when twenty people have been buried in a single day.

ARNOLDUS. It's a doleful, distressing sight to see so many people buried at the same time.

THEODOLUS. It's the height of sadness to those whose friends are breathing their last.

ARNOLDUS. I experienced that when my parents passed on.

THEODOLUS. Where I come from people were utterly frantic.

ARNOLDUS. Who could fail to be unsettled when he's exposed to the danger of death?

THEODOLUS. Yet it's better to die in your bed than to suffer another kind of death.

ARNOLDUS. Vergil calls the people whose fate it was to die at Troy in the sight of their fathers 'thrice and four times happy'.

THEODOLUS. That was divinely inspired, for your own country, and the presence of your friends, makes death easier to bear.

82. THE HARM DONE BY WAR

Martinus and Valerius

MARTINUS. Oh, how pitifully that country has been laid waste!

VALERIVS. Vnde ista miseria?
MARTINVS. E bellorum tyrannide.
VALERIVS. Solet bellum tantum afferre ruinae?
MARTINVS. Reparat nihil, sed omnia solo aequat.
VALERIVS. O rem execrabilem.
MARTINVS. Pacis est quaeque salua reddere, ita belli omnia dissipare.
VALERIVS. Longe (ut uideo) praestabit pace frui.
MARTINVS. Experientia istud persuadet.
VALERIVS. Felices terque quaterque qui armis nunquam obruuntur.
MARTINVS. Bellum agendi quis tamen auctor extitit?
VALERIVS. Nullus, nisi Eumenides et Furiae.
MARTINVS. Ego aestimo eos esse auctores, qui primi belli inuenerunt tormenta.
VALERIVS. Haud male iudicas.
MARTINVS. Sed apud quam nationem illa sunt exorta?
VALERIVS. Aiunt in Germania.
MARTINVS. A nostris Germanis multa mira sunt reperta.
VALERIVS. Tamen illa tormenta praestaret nunquam excogitata.
MARTINVS. Res bellica etiam crebro armis et satellitibus, non istis geritur ferocibus instrumentis.
VALERIVS. Arma et satellites urbem soli non expugnarent.
MARTINVS. Obsiderent tamen, et tandem esurie uincerent eam.
VALERIVS. Forte et ipsi fame compulsi demum abirent ante uictoriam.

---

1 incommodo] incommodis A

83. DE ANNONAE CARITATE

Dauid et Lucas [E6v]

DAVID. Quid sibi uult macies ista tua?
LVCAS. Quod macer appareo mirum non est.
DAVID. Forte pasceris aride et tenuiter.
LVCAS. Tenacissime alunt me parentes.
DAVID. In rem tuam forte faciunt.

VALERIUS. What has caused its plight?
MARTINUS. The tyranny of war.
VALERIUS. Does war usually bring such destruction?
MARTINUS. It restores nothing; it razes everything to the ground.
VALERIUS. What a detestable business!
MARTINUS. Just as peace makes all well, war destroys everything.
VALERIUS. As I see, it's far better to enjoy peace.
MARTINUS. Experience convinces us of that.
VALERIUS. How very fortunate are those who've never been overwhelmed by an army.
MARTINUS. Who's recorded as the inventor of war?
VALERIUS. No one, other than the Furies.
MARTINUS. I think the inventors were the people who first invented engines of war.
VALERIUS. You're right to think that.
MARTINUS. But what country did they originate in?
VALERIUS. In Germany, they say.
MARTINUS. A lot of wonderful things have been invented by us Germans.
VALERIUS. Yet it would be better if those engines had never been thought up.
MARTINUS. Yet war's often fought by armed soldiers, not with those violent machines.
VALERIUS. Armed soldiers wouldn't take a city on their own.
MARTINUS. But they'd lay siege to it, and eventually they'd conquer it by starving it.
VALERIUS. Maybe hunger would force them to go away before the victory.

83. FOOD IS DEAR

David and Lucas

DAVID. What's the reason you're so thin?
LUCAS. It's no wonder that I look thin.
DAVID. Are you eating sparely and meagrely?
LUCAS. My parents are feeding me very meanly.
DAVID. Maybe they're doing it for your good.

LVCAS. Est illud commodum, parce ali?
DAVID. Libris incumbenti non conuenit saturitas.
LVCAS. Certe et uenter ieiunus chartis non gaudet.
DAVID. Cibus mediocris commodat litteris dedito.
LVCAS. Eo contentus essem, si daretur.
DAVID. Cur tam modicum tibi praebent cibi?
LVCAS. Ob annonae caritatem.
DAVID. Est ideo ieiunandum, quia omnia ueneunt care?
LVCAS. Est egenti pecunia.
DAVID. Nobis adhuc in annum de frugibus prospectum est.
LVCAS. Feliciores nobis estis.
DAVID. Quanti nunc uenit siligo?
LVCAS. Aureo nummo credo.
DAVID. Tolerandus adhuc est iste mercatus.
LVCAS. Certe non inopibus, sed opulentis.
DAVID. Audiui in Gallia in quadam urbe uendi quinque coronis (ut uocant) aureis.
LVCAS. Hui, mentiris nimium.
DAVID. Inde huc scriptum est.
LVCAS. Per quem?
DAVID. Per filium cuiusdam senatoris huius urbis.
LVCAS. Nollem me istuc nunc temporis agere.
DAVID. Et ego laetor me istic praesto non esse.
LVCAS. Gratia Deo, quod hic adhuc asse tolerando uenditur.

---

15 ueneunt] ueniunt A | 30–31 esse … uenditur.] esse. A

84. QVAM DELICATE IN OPPIDIS, ET QVAM MISERE AC TENVITER VICTITENT IN AGRIS

Eobanus et Adelarius

EOBANVS. O magne Apollo, quam inique inter homines uiuitur!
ADELARIVS. Vt istud coniicis?
EOBANVS. Nam multi delicate, aliqui tenuiuscule uictitant.
ADELARIVS. Es tu expertus fortunam uitae aliorum?
EOBANVS. Res ipsa lo- [E7r] quitur passim.

LUCAS. Is it good to be given very little to eat?
DAVID. Being full isn't good for someone working at books.
LUCAS. An empty stomach takes no pleasure in books, either.
DAVID. A medium amount of food is right for someone engaged in learning.
LUCAS. I'd be happy with that, if I was given it.
DAVID. Why are they giving you so little food?
LUCAS. Because food is dear.
DAVID. Do you have to do without food because everything is expensive?
LUCAS. You do if you don't have any money.
DAVID. We have enough grain provisions for a year yet.
LUCAS. You're better off than we are.
DAVID. How much is wheat now?
LUCAS. A Gulden, I believe.
DAVID. That's still an affordable price.
LUCAS. To the rich it is, but not to the poor.
DAVID. I heard that in some town in France it costs five golden crowns, as they call them.
LUCAS. Oh, you're really lying!
DAVID. It was in a letter sent here from there.
LUCAS. Who by?
DAVID. The son of a councillor of this city.
LUCAS. I wouldn't like to be living there now.
DAVID. I'm glad I'm not there either.
LUCAS. Thanks be to God that prices here are still tolerable.

84. HOW LUXURIOUSLY PEOPLE LIVE IN CITIES, AND HOW WRETCHEDLY AND MEAGRELY THEY LIVE IN THE COUNTRY

Eobanus and Adelarius

EOBANUS. Oh, good Lord, what unequal lives humans lead!
ADELARIUS. How do you reach that conclusion?
EOBANUS. Because many live luxuriously, and others live very meagrely.
ADELARIUS. Do you have experience of other people's living conditions?
EOBANUS. It's obvious everywhere.

ADELARIVS. Apertius istud loquere.
EOBANVS. Rustici ut edant uidistin?
ADELARIVS. Vidi, pulmentis hordeaceis pascuntur.
EOBANVS. Vrbani autem omni utuntur ciborum lautitia.
ADELARIVS. Aliqui eorum etiam nudum rodunt panem.
EOBANVS. Quandoque tamen curant cuticulam et uiuunt genialiter.
ADELARIVS. Vt possunt illud, cum aes ipsis desit?
EOBANVS. Vestes uel alia oppignorant.
ADELARIVS. Tum oporteret eos nudos incedere.
EOBANVS. Domi se continent quousque redemerint.
ADELARIVS. Fortassis accommodatis indumentis utuntur?
EOBANVS. Nonnunquam certe, uel aes credito accipiunt, unde redimant uestes.
ADELARIVS. Tum uorsuram soluunt.
EOBANVS. Quid est uorsuram soluere?
ADELARIVS. Est creditorem soluere pecunia credito accepta ab alio.
EOBANVS. Viuitur adeo opipare et magno in urbibus?
ADELARIVS. Vtique, quicquid labore acquiritur, festo die prodigitur.
EOBANVS. Quo uictitant deinde diebus operosis?
ADELARIVS. Pane et raparum quisquiliis.
EOBANVS. Stulti homines, qui crapula famem emunt.
ADELARIVS. Ipsi super choenice non sedent.

---

18 oppignorant] oppignorant A C; oppignerunt B | 34 choenice] Chenice A C; Chenicae B

85. FACILE EMERGI EOS QVI OPVLENTI SVNT

Matthias et Virgilius

MATTHIAS. Subito iste in uirum euasit.
VIRGILIVS. Dignum non est admiratione.
MATTHIAS. Ego uehementer miror.
VIRGILIVS. Ego nihil, quia facile potuit.
MATTHIAS. Qui facile potuit?
VIRGILIVS. Quia opulentus fuit.

ADELARIUS. Say that more clearly.
EOBANUS. Have you seen how peasants eat?
ADELARIUS. Yes, they live on barley pottage.
EOBANUS. But people who live in towns enjoy the best of everything to eat.
ADELARIUS. Some of them eat dry bread, too.
EOBANUS. But sometimes they do themselves well, and live luxuriously.
ADELARIUS. How can they do that when they have no money?
EOBANUS. They pawn their clothes or other things.
ADELARIUS. Then they'd have to go around naked.
EOBANUS. They stay at home till they've redeemed them.
ADELARIUS. Do they use patched clothes?
EOBANUS. Indeed they do, sometimes, or they borrow money to redeem their clothes.
ADELARIUS. Then they're robbing Peter to pay Paul.
EOBANUS. What's that?
ADELARIUS. It means paying one creditor with money borrowed from another.
EOBANUS. Is life really rich and lavish in cities?
ADELARIUS. It is indeed. Whatever they get by working they spend on holidays.
EOBANUS. Then how do they live on workdays?
ADELARIUS. On bread and turnip-skins.
EOBANUS. They're stupid to pay for their blow-outs with hunger.
ADELARIUS. They take no care for the morrow.

85. THOSE WHO ARE WEALTHY FIND IT EASY TO DO WELL IN LIFE

Matthias and Virgilius

MATTHIAS. He's quickly turned out as a fine man.
VIRGILIUS. That's not worth being amazed at.
MATTHIAS. It amazes me a great deal.
VIRGILIUS. I don't at all, because it was easy for him.
MATTHIAS. How was it easy for him?
VIRGILIUS. Because he was wealthy.

MATTHIAS. Emergunt illi omnes qui diuites sunt?
VIRGILIVS. Dubitas? Anne indies istud uides?
MATTHIAS. Pauperibus ut succedit?
VIRGILIVS. Iacent et pessundantur ubique.
MATTHIAS. Prospice quid dicas.
VIRGILIVS. Dico Apolli- [E7v] nis oraculum.
MATTHIAS. Non raro pauper in uirum euadit egregium, diues semper humi repit.
VIRGILIVS. Raro uisum est quod dicis.
MATTHIAS. Eruditorum turbam et classem aspice, omnes ferme inopes fuere.
VIRGILIVS. Adiuti tamen aliorum opibus.
MATTHIAS. Saepe et sibi ipsis opitulantur ingeniis et scientiis.
VIRGILIVS. Per illa ipsis applauditur ab opulentis.
MATTHIAS. Phoenice rariorem reperies doctum, qui rerum est educatus copia.
VIRGILIVS. Qui illud fiat admiror.
MATTHIAS. Qui abundant aestimant se non egere doctrina.
VIRGILIVS. Tales complures audiui suas iactitantes opes.
MATTHIAS. Nonnulli etiam abundantes aere, scientia nequeunt pollere, ob ingenii ruditatem.
VIRGILIVS. Vere dicis, nam non omnia dii uni dedere: uni ingenium, alteri opes, ceteris formam corporis uenustissimam et cetera.
MATTHIAS. Tanta uarietate mortales differre uoluit uerus ipse Iupiter.

30–34 dedere … Iupiter.] dedere. A

86. DE NVPTIIS

Herebertus et Hylgerus

HEREBERTVS. Ad proximum diem festum indulgebo genio.
HYLGERVS. Vbi locorum?
HEREBERTVS. In aedibus nostris.

MATTHIAS. Does everyone who's wealthy do well in life?
VIRGILIUS. Do you doubt it? Don't you see it every day?
MATTHIAS. What happens to the poor?
VIRGILIUS. Everywhere they're forced to the bottom of the heap.
MATTHIAS. Think carefully about what you say.
VIRGILIUS. What I'm saying is the Gospel truth.
MATTHIAS. It's not rare for a poor man to become an illustrious person, and for a rich one to stay in a lowly position.
VIRGILIUS. What you say is rarely seen.
MATTHIAS. Look at the group of learned men; nearly all of them were poor.
VIRGILIUS. But they were helped by other people's money.
MATTHIAS. Often they've helped themselves with their own brains and knowledge.
VIRGILIUS. The rich applaud them for that.
MATTHIAS. You'll find that a learned man who was brought up in wealthy circumstances is rarer than the Phoenix.
VIRGILIUS. I wonder how that comes about.
MATTHIAS. People who have lots of money don't think they need learning.
VIRGILIUS. I've heard lots of people like that boasting about their wealth.
MATTHIAS. Some who have lots of money can't do well at learning, because their intellects are dull.
VIRGILIUS. You're right, for the gods haven't given everything to a single person. They've given brains to some, wealth to others, physical beauty to others, and so on.
MATTHIAS. God intended mortals to be so very different from one another.

86. A WEDDING

Herebertus and Hilgerus

HEREBERTUS. On the next holiday I'll really spoil myself.
HILGERUS. Where?
HEREBERTUS. At our house.

HYLGERVS. Habebitis aliquid apparatum lautius?
HEREBERTVS. Conuiuium habebimus geniale et lautissimum.
HYLGERVS. Tantos cur facietis sumptus?
HEREBERTVS. Nuptiae peragentur domi nostrae.
HYLGERVS. Inter quos fiet uinculum maritale?
HEREBERTVS. Inter sororem meam et filium alterius ciuis.
HYLGERVS. Sponsus estne locuples?
HEREBERTVS. Nescio, arculam suam non sum exploratus.
HYLGERVS. Quantam dotem afferet?
HEREBERTVS. Aiunt duo millia aureorum.
HYLGERVS. Ho, ho, satis abundat. [E8r]
HEREBERTVS. Contenta est soror mea dote ista.
HYLGERVS. Quantum ipsa afferet?
HEREBERTVS. Nescio, mihi non retulerunt parentes.
HYLGERVS. Duces tu sponsam?
HEREBERTVS. Ad templum ducam, sed non rursus educam.
HYLGERVS. Qui tum sunt educturi? Vel immorabitur usque ecclesiae?
HEREBERTVS. Cognati ipsius sponsi cui in templo committetur in manus.
HYLGERVS. A prandio habebitisne choreas?
HEREBERTVS. Saliemus mire ad tibiam et tympanum.
HYLGERVS. In tanta laetitia et mei recorderis.
HEREBERTVS. Venias ad nos, impartiam tibi quippiam lauti e sponsa.
HYLGERVS. E sponsa nihil cupio.
HEREBERTVS. Hem, lapsus sum lingua, e nuptiis dixissem.
HYLGERVS. Nasum tuum nosco.

22 educturi?] educturi eam? A

87. DE VINO DANDO IN ILLIVS SANCTI DIE, CVIVS NOS NOMEN GERIMVS

Nicolaus et Iohannes

NICOLAVS. Vt praesentes tibi sint nummi facito.
IOHANNES. Praesenti quid agam pecunia?

HILGERUS. Are you going to have some splendid food?
HEREBERTUS. We're going to have a really fine festive banquet.
HILGERUS. Why are you spending so much money?
HEREBERTUS. There's going to be a wedding at our house.
HILGERUS. Who are going to be joined in marriage?
HEREBERTUS. My sister and the son of another citizen.
HILGERUS. Is the groom wealthy?
HEREBERTUS. I don't know, I haven't inspected his money-box.
HILGERUS. What size of settlement will he bring?
HEREBERTUS. Two thousand Gulden, they say.
HILGERUS. Oh, he's got plenty!
HEREBERTUS. My sister's happy with that settlement.
HILGERUS. How much will she bring?
HEREBERTUS. I don't know, my parents haven't told me.
HILGERUS. Are you going to walk ahead of the bride?
HEREBERTUS. I'll lead her to church, but not back out again.
HILGERUS. So who will? Or is she just going to stay inside the church?
HEREBERTUS. Relatives of the bridegroom she'll be handed over to in church.
HILGERUS. Will you have dancing after the meal?
HEREBERTUS. We'll really leap about to the fife and drum.
HILGERUS. While you're having so much pleasure, remember me.
HEREBERTUS. Come to us, I'll let you have something really nice from the bride.
HILGERUS. I don't want anything from the bride.
HEREBERTUS. Oh, that was a slip of the tongue – from the *wedding*, I meant to say.
HILGERUS. I know your wit.

87. PAYING FOR WINE ON OUR SAINT'S DAY

Nicolaus and Iohannes

NICOLAUS. Make sure that you have money on you.
IOHANNES. What'll I do with ready cash?

NICOLAVS. Istud experieris.
IOHANNES. Quando experiar?
NICOLAVS. Die festo illius sancti, cuius nomen refers.
IOHANNES. An tum plus egebo aere quam nunc?
NICOLAVS. Sumptum oportet facias.
IOHANNES. Quas haberem expensas?
NICOLAVS. Pendes uinum ob tuum nomen, quo isti sancto es cognominis.
IOHANNES. Spem frustra fouebitis.
NICOLAVS. Recusares? Nonne et ego nomen meum uino celebraui?
IOHANNES. Potationi ego autem non adfui.
NICOLAVS. Si praesto fuisses, conbibisses, non potuimus te expectare.
IOHANNES. Iniquum esset me tingere te uino quum tuum non degustaui.
NICOLAVS. Anno abhinc proximo largius bibe, ubi redierunt feriae sancti illius, cui nomine ego consono.
IOHANNES. Incertus sum an uita superstes manebo. [E8v]
NICOLAVS. Dabis uinum necne?
IOHANNES. Experiemini, ubi dies ille aduenerit.
NICOLAVS. Memores erimus, non obliuiscemur.
IOHANNES. Praeter binas uini mensuras dabo nihil.
NICOLAVS. Sat erit, ultra non postulabimus.
IOHANNES. Vnde exortus sit mos ille miror maxime.
NICOLAVS. Ex gentilium consuetudine, qui solebant diem natalem conuiuando celebrare.
IOHANNES. Verisimile est, nam multa uestigia ethnicorum nostrae consuetudines referunt.

---

20 tingere te] te tingere A | 33–34 est … referunt] est. A

88. DE PRIMO SACERDOTIS SACRIFICIO

Bonifacius et Brictius

BONIFACIVS. Quando sacris initiaberis ordinis?
BRICTIVS. Proximo Paschate spero.
BONIFACIVS. Est tibi matura aetas?
BRICTIVS. Ago nunc annum uigesimum quartum.

NICOLAUS. You'll find out.
IOHANNES. When will I find out?
NICOLAUS. On the feast of the saint whose name you bear.
IOHANNES. Won't I have less money then than now?
NICOLAUS. You'll have to spend money.
IOHANNES. What expense am I going to have?
NICOLAUS. You'll pay for wine in your name, on the day of the saint you're named after.
IOHANNES. Your hopes are going to be in vain.
NICOLAUS. Would you refuse me? Didn't I celebrate my name-day with wine?
IOHANNES. But I wasn't at the party.
NICOLAUS. If you'd been there you'd have drunk with us; we couldn't wait for you.
IOHANNES. It wouldn't be fair to treat you to wine since I haven't drunk yours.
NICOLAUS. Drink more next year, when the feast of the saint I'm named after comes around again.
IOHANNES. I'm not sure if I'll still be alive.
NICOLAUS. Will you give us wine or won't you?
IOHANNES. You'll find out, when that day arrives.
NICOLAUS. We'll remember, we won't forget.
IOHANNES. I won't pay for any more than two measures.
NICOLAUS. That'll be enough, we won't ask for more.
IOHANNES. I really wonder where that practice had its origin.
NICOLAUS. From the customs of the pagans, who used to celebrate their birthday with a feast.
IOHANNES. That seems likely, for our customs show a lot of pagan traces.

88. A PRIEST'S FIRST MASS

Bonifacius and Brictius

BONIFACIUS. When will you take Holy Orders?
BRICTIUS. Next Easter, I hope.
BONIFACIUS. Are you old enough?
BRICTIUS. I'm in my twenty-fourth year now.

BONIFACIVS. Ordinibus suscipiendis isti conueniunt anni.

BRICTIVS. Aetas mihi tantum est, uerum minor sapientia.

BONIFACIVS. Addisce tandem spargere nuces, si hactenus puerum egisti.

BRICTIVS. Ad uires laborabo.

BONIFACIVS. Census quid habes? Cuius ope uiues in ordinibus sumptis?

BRICTIVS. Parentum uiuam praediis.

BONIFACIVS. Poteris de illorum opibus sacerdotis ducere uitam?

BRICTIVS. Confido, nam unicus sum filius.

BONIFACIVS. Ipse nollem ordinibus sacris initiari, si sacerdotii nihil mihi esset.

BRICTIVS. Eleemosynarum non sum cupidus.

BONIFACIVS. Etiam praeter sacerdotis uitam posses patrimonio uti.

BRICTIVS. Possem, at sacerdos effici ardeo.

BONIFACIVS. Nunc temporis miserrimum est sacerdotem esse.

BRICTIVS. Cur est calamitosum?

BONIFACIVS. Quia passim odio prosequuntur ab his qui Luthero accedunt.

BRICTIVS. Id si ferent aequo animo, magnam accipient mercedem.

BONIFACIVS. Exploduntur quibusdam in locis, tractanturque uti Iudaei forent.

BRICTIVS. Omnium rerum est uicissitudo, sic et illud [F1r] tandem cessabit.

BONIFACIVS. At fortassis serius quam proderit.

---

4 Paschate spero] spero paschate A | 17 unicus] solus A

89. DE EXEQVIIS DEFVNCTORVM PERAGENDIS

Bernardus et Leonardus

BERNARDVS. Hodie rursus ecclesiae nostrae plebeiarius messem suam exercebit.

LEONARDVS. Non est tamen messor uel agricola.

BERNARDVS. Plures metunt qui tamen agricolae non sunt.

BONIFACIUS. That's the right age for being ordained.
BRICTIUS. I'm old enough, but I haven't got much wisdom.
BONIFACIUS. Learn to give up childish ways, if you've been childish up to now.
BRICTIUS. I'll do my best.
BONIFACIUS. How much money have you? Whose resources will you live on when you're a priest?
BRICTIUS. I'll live on my parents' earnings.
BONIFACIUS. Will you be able to live the life of a priest on their money?
BRICTIUS. I believe so, because I'm an only child.
BONIFACIUS. I wouldn't want to be ordained if being a priest didn't bring me in any money.
BRICTIUS. I'm not greedy for offerings.
BONIFACIUS. Even without being a priest you could live on your parents' money.
BRICTIUS. I could, but I'm eager to be a priest.
BONIFACIUS. Being a priest is really wretched these days.
BRICTIUS. Whys is it miserable?
BONIFACIUS. Because everywhere they're the object of hate on the part of those who support Luther.
BRICTIUS. If they bear that patiently they'll receive a great reward.
BONIFACIUS. In some places they're ostracized, and treated as if they were Jews.
BRICTIUS. Everything changes, and in the same way that will eventually stop, too.
BONIFACIUS. But it may be later than would be good for us.

89. CELEBRATING A REQUIEM FOR THE DEAD

Bernardus and Leonardus

BERNARDUS. Our parish priest will be bringing in his harvest again today.
LEONARDUS. But he's not a reaper or a farmer.
BERNARDUS. There are lots of people who reap without being farmers.

LEONARDVS. Nunquam uidi etiam doctum hominem metere.
BERNARDVS. Aliud mihi significat metere quam tibi.
LEONARDVS. Quid per ipsum uerbum intelligis?
BERNARDVS. Metere, id est commodum et lucrum accipere.
LEONARDVS. Melius te nunc capiam loquendo.
BERNARDVS. Plebeiarius noster hodie metet in altari oblatam pecuniam.
LEONARDVS. Fiet hodie tanta immolatio nummorum?
BERNARDVS. Exequiae agentur cuidam meorum cognatorum.
LEONARDVS. Intereris etiam et tu?
BERNARDVS. Praesto ero, et cum aliis meos altari offeram nummulos.
LEONARDVS. Quot nummorum receptum est immolare?
BERNARDVS. Tres, in tribus altaribus.
LEONARDVS. Retinet pastor sibi istud soli?
BERNARDVS. Cum sacellanis (credo) partitur.
LEONARDVS. Quanti constabit candelarum emptio?
BERNARDVS. Conducimus eas, et quantum combusserimus cerae, tantum exsoluimus.
LEONARDVS. Praeter ista, quid plebeiario datis?
BERNARDVS. Incertum est mihi, sat scio pecuniae.
LEONARDVS. Ditescere eum oportet.
BERNARDVS. Nunquam aliquem sortis suae audiui, qui se non egere diceret.

90. DE SEPVLTVRA

Eberhardus et Iodocus

EBERHARDVS. Candelae per fenestras extensae quid portendunt?
IODOCVS. Cadauer hominis aedibus interesse.
EBERHARDVS. Apud nostrates istud moris non est.
IODOCVS. Nullo signo praetere- [F1v] unti ostenditur in domo defunctum iacere hominem?
EBERHARDVS. Ostium patet et in domo cum candelis ardentibus ponitur funus.
IODOCVS. Cuique nationi suus est ritus.

LEONARDUS. I've never seen a learned man reaping.
BERNARDUS. To me, 'reaping' means something different than it does to you.
LEONARDUS. What do you understand by the word?
BERNARDUS. Reaping means receiving benefits and cash.
LEONARDUS. Now I understand what you're saying better.
BERNARDUS. Today our parish priest is going to reap money offered on the altar.
LEONARDUS. Will there be a huge sacrifice of coins today?
BERNARDUS. The requiem Mass for one of my relatives is being held.
LEONARDUS. Will you be there too?
BERNARDUS. Yes, and I'll offer my coins along with the others.
LEONARDUS. How many coins is it the custom to offer?
BERNARDUS. Three, on three altars.
LEONARDUS. Does the priest keep the money for himself?
BERNARDUS. I think they're shared with the curates.
LEONARDUS. How much will it cost to buy the candles?
BERNARDUS. We hire them, and pay for the amount of wax we burn.
LEONARDUS. Apart from that, what do you give the priest?
BERNARDUS. I'm not sure. It's a lot of money, I know.
LEONARDUS. He must be rich.
BERNARDUS. I've never heard anyone of his profession who didn't say they were poor.

90. BURIAL

Eberhardus and Iodocus

EBERHARDUS. What do the candles sticking out of the windows mean?
IODOCUS. That there's a corpse in the house.
EBERHARDUS. That's not the custom where I come from.
IODOCUS. Is there no sign to tell passers-by that there's a dead body lying in the house?
EBERHARDUS. The door is open, and a bier is placed in the house with burning candles.
IODOCUS. Each country has its custom.

EBERHARDVS. Emuntne omnes istas candelas quas fenestris extendunt?

IODOCVS. Conducunt eas, non mercantur.

EBERHARDVS. Quanti?

IODOCVS. Quamlibet solido opinor.

EBERHARDVS. Praeferuntur funeri ad sepulchrum?

IODOCVS. Etiam et accenduntur.

EBERHARDVS. Sepultura quanti hic constat?

IODOCVS. Certe maximo aere.

EBERHARDVS. Dic mihi cur sepultura sit adeo pretiosa.

IODOCVS. Terra coemiterii emenda est, qua corpus conditur.

EBERHARDVS. Illa a quo uenditur?

IODOCVS. Puto a plebeiario, uel aedituo.

EBERHARDVS. Qua fronte audent terram uendere?

IODOCVS. Quidni auderent?

EBERHARDVS. Ad ipsos non pertinet, cur tum aliena uenditant?

IODOCVS. Cuius est humus, si non ipsorum est?

EBERHARDVS. In Psalmo scriptum est, 'Domini est terra et plenitudo eius.'

IODOCVS. Si est Domini, ergo et pastorum, quia Domini sunt uicarii.

EBERHARDVS. Quod Domini est, non aere, sed praecordiis deuotis impetratur.

IODOCVS. Precibus etiam plebani coemiterium uendunt, sed pecunia addita.

2, etc. Iodocus] Iodocus A; Iodouicus B C | 22 coemiterii] cimiterii A B C | 36 coemiterium] cimiterium A B C

91. DE ANNO IVBILAEO

Paschasius et Alexius

PASCHASIVS. Accingam me hac hieme profectioni longissimae.

ALEXIVS. Quo diriges gressus?

PASCHASIVS. Romam uersus.

ALEXIVS. Impetratum forte sacerdotium fertile?

PASCHASIVS. Minime, sed depositum istic peccata pergam.

EBERHARDUS. Do they buy all the candles they stick out of the windows?

IODOCUS. They hire them, they don't buy them.

EBERHARDUS. How much for?

IODOCUS. About a Schilling, I think.

EBERHARDUS. Are they carried before the bier to the grave?

IODOCUS. Yes, and they're lit, too.

EBERHARDUS. How much does burial cost here?

IODOCUS. A very great deal of money.

EBERHARDUS. Tell me why burial's so expensive.

IODOCUS. You have to buy the ground in the cemetery where the corpse is buried.

EBERHARDUS. Who's it sold by?

IODOCUS. By the parish priest, I think, or the parish clerk.

EBERHARDUS. How do they dare to sell the earth?

IODOCUS. Why wouldn't they dare to?

EBERHARDUS. It doesn't belong to them, so why do they sell what's someone else's?

IODOCUS. Whose is the earth, if it isn't theirs?

EBERHARDUS. It's written in the Psalm that 'the earth is the Lord's, and its fullness'.

IODOCUS. If it belongs to the Lord, then it belongs to the priests, because they're the Lord's representatives.

EBERHARDUS. What belongs to the Lord is gained not with money but with devout prayers.

IODOCUS. The priests do sell the cemetery for prayers – but with money added.

91. THE JUBILEE YEAR

Paschasius and Alexius

PASCHASIUS. This winter, I'm going to get ready for a long journey.

ALEXIUS. Where are you bound for?

PASCHASIUS. To Rome.

ALEXIUS. Would that be to get hold of a fat living?

PASCHASIUS. No, I'm going to leave my sins there.

ALEXIVS. Depositurus es ibi delicta?
PASCHASIVS. Confore spero.
ALEXIVS. Fidem non habeo.
PASCHASIVS. Non fit tibi uerisimile?
ALEXIVS. Dicis istud tuo ingenio, uel ab alio relatum habes?
PASCHASIVS. In litteris Pontificis Romani ita legi.
ALEXIVS. [F2r] Quid continebant?
PASCHASIVS. Cuilibet uere paenitenti et Romam hoc anno accedenti condonari scelera et poenam.
ALEXIVS. Istud et his in terris consequi potes.
PASCHASIVS. Qui hoc fieret?
ALEXIVS. Vbicunque locorum homo pro suis ingemuerit peccatis, remittuntur ipsi, ut Euangelii fides nos instruit.
PASCHASIVS. Si istud Euangelium permittit, tum hic domi me continebo et sumptibus parcam.
ALEXIVS. Verum nosti originem anni Iubilaei?
PASCHASIVS. Audiui exortum istum morem celebrandi annum Iubilaeum a ueteribus Iudaeis, apud quos quinquagesimus quisque annus sacrosanctus habebatur.

18 potes] potest A | 22 tum] dum A

92. DE TEMPORE QVO LIBRORVM LECTIONES AVSPICANTVR

Gregorius et Ambrosius

GREGORIVS. Ho, ho, sodales optimi, cor nunc est comedendum nobis.
AMBROSIVS. Delirasne?
GREGORIVS. Cur delirarem?
AMBROSIVS. Quod cor esse nobis comedendum dicis, in nobis inclusum.
GREGORIVS. Prouerbii uicem habet, significans contristari.
AMBROSIVS. Est nunc moerendi tempus?
GREGORIVS. Latet uos istud?
AMBROSIVS. Ignoramus, fac tu nos certiores.
GREGORIVS. Appetit tempus quod nos a matre rursum in exilium uocat.
AMBROSIVS. Quo?

ALEXIUS. You'll leave your offences there?
PASCHASIUS. I hope that'll be the case.
ALEXIUS. I don't believe that.
PASCHASIUS. Doesn't it seem likely to you?
ALEXIUS. Are you saying that from your own knowledge, or were you told by someone else?
PASCHASIUS. I read it in a letter of the Roman Pontiff.
ALEXIUS. What did it say?
PASCHASIUS. That anyone who is truly penitent and who goes to Rome this year will be pardoned their offences and the punishment for them.
ALEXIUS. You could achieve that in this part of the world, too.
PASCHASIUS. How could that be?
ALEXIUS. Wherever a person regrets his sins, they're forgiven him, as the Gospel faith tells us.
PASCHASIUS. If the Gospel promises that, then I'll stay at home and save the expense.
ALEXIUS. Tell me, do you know the origin of the Jubilee year?
PASCHASIUS. I've heard that that manner of celebrating the Jubilee year began with the ancient Jews, amongst whom every fiftieth year was regarded as holy.

92. THE TIME WHEN CLASSES START

Gregorius and Ambrosius

GREGORIUS. Oh, my good companions, now we can eat our hearts out!
AMBROSIUS. Are you crazy?
GREGORIUS. Why should I be crazy?
AMBROSIUS. Because you're saying that we have to eat our hearts, but they're inside us.
GREGORIUS. It functions as a proverb, meaning to be sad.
AMBROSIUS. Is this the time for sorrow?
GREGORIUS. Don't you know that?
AMBROSIUS. No, we don't. Tell us about it.
GREGORIUS. The time is coming that calls us back into exile away from our mothers.
AMBROSIUS. Where to?

GREGORIVS. Ad peregrinas urbes, nam lectiones auspicabuntur illico.
AMBROSIVS. Alio concedens ne tantillum flere soleo.
GREGORIVS. Sed ego lugeo affatim.
AMBROSIVS. An ob digressum a matre?
GREGORIVS. Non, sed ob discessum a lauta culina.
AMBROSIVS. Coquinam semper iuxta opiparam non optarem.
GREGORIVS. Alienis in terris est mihi precaria dape uiuendum.
AMBROSIVS. Id dulce est, pati in iuuentute ut in senio abundemus.
GREGORIVS. Isto pati mallem carere.
AMBROSIVS. Haec olim dulce et iucundum erit meminisse. [F2v]
GREGORIVS. Multum caseorum et carnis porcinae mecum profecturus deferam.
AMBROSIVS. At ego opimam aere crumenam malo.
GREGORIVS. Parce mihi aes praebent parentes.
AMBROSIVS. Timent ne prodigas.

---

1 librorum lectiones] lectiones librorum A

93. DE TEMPORE QVO LECTIONIBVS LIBRORVM COLOPHON IMPONITVR

Lucius et Vdalricus

LVCIVS. In articulis quid tecum computas adeo solicite?
VDALRICVS. Dies quot restant ad ferias diui Bartholomaei?
LVCIVS. Etiam si scires, conferretne tibi?
VDALRICVS. Exhilararer oppido si istae adessent feriae.
LVCIVS. Eloquere cur, ut tibi congratularer.
VDALRICVS. Ad umbilicum tum ducentur scholae lectiones.
LVCIVS. Optimum esset eas et nostro inhaerere ingenio.
VDALRICVS. Id floccipendo.
LVCIVS. Remigrabis tu patriam uersus?
VDALRICVS. Nisi aliud litteris iusserint parentes, hic non durabo.
LVCIVS. Vestieris recens?

GREGORIUS. To other towns, for school will be beginning there.
AMBROSIUS. I don't usually weep the tiniest bit when I go somewhere else.
GREGORIUS. But I grieve a lot.
AMBROSIUS. Because of parting from your mother?
GREGORIUS. No, because of saying goodbye to good cooking.
AMBROSIUS. I wouldn't always like to have rich cooking.
GREGORIUS. When I'm abroad I'm not sure where the next meal is coming from.
AMBROSIUS. It's agreeable to suffer in youth, so that we'll have plenty in our old age.
GREGORIUS. I'd prefer to do without that kind of suffering.
AMBROSIUS. One day it'll be pleasant and agreeable to remember this.
GREGORIUS. I'm going to take a lot of cheeses and pork with me when I go.
AMBROSIUS. But I prefer a purse with plenty of money in it.
GREGORIUS. My parents provide me with money sparingly.
AMBROSIUS. They're afraid you'll squander it.

93. THE TIME WHEN CLASSES ARE FINISHED OFF

Lucius and Udalricus

LUCIUS. What are you counting on your fingers to yourself so carefully?
UDALRICUS. How many days are left till St Bartholomew's day?
LUCIUS. Even if you knew, would it do you any good?
UDALRICUS. I'd be really glad if that day were here.
LUCIUS. Tell me why, so as I can congratulate you.
UDALRICUS. School lessons finish then.
LUCIUS. It would be really good if they stayed in our minds.
UDALRICUS. I don't give a hoot about that.
LUCIUS. Are you going back to your parents?
UDALRICUS. Unless my parents write to me giving me other instructions, I won't stay here.
LUCIUS. Will you be given a new suit of clothes?

VDALRICVS. Ista spe uiuo.
LVCIVS. Sed age, libri suntne paene finiti?
VDALRICVS. Non longe abest 'plaudite'.
LVCIVS. 'Plaudite' quid uocas?
VDALRICVS. Id est finis, in quo plaudimus libris.
LVCIVS. Audiuisti unquam causam, cur pulsemus libris dum sunt perlecti?
VDALRICVS. Facile liceat coniicere quae sit.
LVCIVS. Coniectura ego nequeo assequi.
VDALRICVS. Ex more lusus comoediarum credo ortum.
LVCIVS. In ludo comoediarum quid fieri solet?
VDALRICVS. In fine comploditur manibus.
LVCIVS. Vis conferre scholae lectiones ludo comoediarum?
VDALRICVS. Quidni? Lectores sunt actores, nos spectatores, libri uero comoediae.
LVCIVS. Hactenus credidi per librorum ad caput allisionem cerebro scientiam imprimi.
VDALRICVS. Ah, nimium delirasti.

5 restant … Bartholomaei?] restent … Bartholomaei. A

94. DE EBRIETATE VITANDA [F3r]

Demea et Helluo

DEMEA. Pudetne te hominem inebriari, et in bestiae degenerare mores?
HELLVO. Pudet utique, sed uitare nequeo.
DEMEA. Mirum esset si cauere non posses.
HELLVO. Per Pollucem non queo.
DEMEA. Auscultare si uelis, docerem te uitandi modum.
HELLVO. Age, parebo.
DEMEA. Fugias haustus ingentes.
HELLVO. Vix potero.
DEMEA. Nequis istud, saltem paucos bibas.
HELLVO. Pauci exsorpti calices non opprimunt, credis, hominem?
DEMEA. Haud facile, nisi immodicum contineant potus.
HELLVO. Quot cyathos mihi permittis exsiccandos?
DEMEA. Ternarium caueas transgredi.

UDALRICUS. I'm living in hope of that.
LUCIUS. But tell me, are the books nearly finished?
UDALRICUS. The 'applause' isn't far off.
LUCIUS. What do you call the 'applause'?
UDALRICUS. That's the end, when we applaud the books.
LUCIUS. Have you ever heard the reason why we thump with the books when we've read them to the end?
UDALRICUS. It's easy to guess what it is.
LUCIUS. I can't guess it.
UDALRICUS. I think it came from the custom in stage-plays.
LUCIUS. What is done in a play?
UDALRICUS. At the end people clap their hands.
LUCIUS. Do you mean to compare school lessons with plays?
UDALRICUS. Why not? The teachers are the actors, we're the audience, and the books are the plays.
LUCIUS. Up till now I thought that by banging the books against our heads knowledge was impressed on the brain.
UDALRICUS. Oh, you were really wide of the mark.

94. AVOIDING DRUNKENNESS

Demea and Helluo

DEMEA. Aren't you ashamed as a human being to get drunk and descend to the behaviour of animals?
HELLUO. I certainly am, but I can't avoid it.
DEMEA. It would be remarkable if you weren't able to avoid it.
HELLUO. I can't, I swear.
DEMEA. If you'll listen, I'll teach you the way to avoid it.
HELLUO. Right, I'll do what you say.
DEMEA. Avoid drinking huge draughts.
HELLUO. I'll hardly be able to do that.
DEMEA. If you can't do that, at least don't drink many.
HELLUO. You don't think that drinking a few glasses will overcome someone?
DEMEA. Not easily, unless they hold a vast amount of drink.
HELLUO. How many glasses will you let me drain?
DEMEA. Take care not to go beyond three.

HELLVO. Hui, nimium palatum meum fraudare conaris.

DEMEA. Audisti unquam uerbum (ni fallor) Thaletis philosophi, primam crateram | ad sitim, secundam ad hilaritatem, tertiam ad uoluptatem, quartam ad insaniam pertinere?

HELLVO. Antiqui abeant, sequemur tempora nostra.

DEMEA. Si a mea aberraueris sententia, bestiam indues.

HELLVO. Fierem ob id bestia, si potu maderem?

DEMEA. Moribus non hominem sed bestiam prae te ferres.

HELLVO. Ah, tace, probi sunt homines, qui inebriantur.

DEMEA. Habentur isti probi? Quo auctore?

HELLVO. Vulgo ipso, quod dicit scelestos non audere potu madere.

DEMEA. Ita aiunt populares, non tamen nimium et ebrios laudant.

HELLVO. Tamen ipsis delectantur, et ab eis risum captant.

---

24 aberraueris] aberrabis A | 26 ferres] ferres A; feres B C

95. DE CEREIS GERENDIS IN FESTO PVRIFICATIONIS MARIAE

Theophilus et Germanus

THEOPHILVS. Quo te confers?

GERMANVS. Forum uersus.

THEOPHILVS. Obsonatumne?

GERMANVS. Non.

THEOPHILVS. Executum aliquid negotii?

GERMANVS. Mercatum candelam [F3v] ceream.

THEOPHILVS. At in quem usum?

GERMANVS. Vt cras eam in templo feram.

THEOPHILVS. Adulterorum est candelas ferre.

GERMANVS. Alio modo autem, lapidibus additis.

THEOPHILVS. Quantum emes cereum?

GERMANVS. Vnius talenti.

THEOPHILVS. Sufficeret semilibrae.

GERMANVS. Inter alios puderet me minutiorem gerere candelam.

HELLUO. Oh, you're really trying to cheat my throat!
DEMEA. Have you ever heard the quotation from the philosopher Thales (If I'm not mistaken)? The first bowl is for thirst, the second for cheerfulness, the third for pleasure, and the fourth for madness.
HELLUO. Forget the ancients, let's be guided by our own times.
DEMEA. If you don't stick to my advice, you'll become like a beast.
HELLUO. Would being drunk make me into a beast?
DEMEA. You'd show yourself an animal, not a man, in your behaviour.
HELLUO. Oh, stop it! The people who get drunk are good.
DEMEA. Are they considered good? By what authority?
HELLUO. The people, who say that wicked men don't dare to get drunk.
DEMEA. That's what the common people say, but they don't praise drunk people all that much.
HELLUO. But they're amused by them, and they get a laugh from them.

95. CARRYING CANDLES ON THE FEAST OF THE PURIFICATION OF THE VIRGIN MARY

Theophilus and Germanus

THEOPHILUS. Where are you off to?
GERMANUS. To the market-place.
THEOPHILUS. To buy food?
GERMANUS. No.
THEOPHILUS. To do some business?
GERMANUS. To buy a wax candle.
THEOPHILUS. But what for?
GERMANUS. For me to carry in church tomorrow.
THEOPHILUS. It's adulterers who carry candles.
GERMANUS. But in a different way, with stones added.
THEOPHILUS. What size of candle will you buy?
GERMANUS. A pound one.
THEOPHILUS. A half-pound one would be enough.
GERMANUS. Amongst the other people, I'd be ashamed to carry a smaller candle.

THEOPHILVS. Vt audio, tua candela uideri cupis.
GERMANVS. Cupio, sed ad honorem Mariae Virginis, non meum.
THEOPHILVS. Plus placet Deo cor humile, quam celebris pompa.
GERMANVS. Animo pio in Deum facio quicquid agam.
THEOPHILVS. In manibus ego tenebo candelam sebaciam, non ceream.
GERMANVS. Nulla solet deferri nisi cerea, sed prouerbium est, 'Pauperes et uilia offerunt.' Verum solido mercaberis cereum lumen.
THEOPHILVS. Locupletius orabo Mariae Virgini.
GERMANVS. Attamen consuetudini non satages.
THEOPHILVS. Malo placere Deo quam hominibus.
GERMANVS. Platonis tamen uerbum est, oportere placere hominibus.
THEOPHILVS. At contra Diui Pauli uerbum est, 'Si hominibus placerem, Christi seruus non essem.'
GERMANVS. Istud intelligitur in factis malis, non bonis.

25–26 sebaciam, non ceream.] sepatiam. A | 35–36 Diui … essem] diu isti seruus non essem. A

96. DE SERTIS IN DIE CELEBRI FERENDIS

Kilianus et Marcus

KILIANVS. Ancillae uestrae quid a prandio agent?
MARCVS. Quare sciscitaris?
KILIANVS. Est cur quaeram.
MARCVS. Audiam, tum respondebo.
KILIANVS. Capitis sertum mihi concinnarent.
MARCVS. In foro uenustius emes.
KILIANVS. Mercari non soleo nugas istas.
MARCVS. Et nos rosas tibi non donabimus nihilo.
KILIANVS. Sat florum tamen uobis in horto sunt, qui pereunt.
MARCVS. Isti mihi hac aestate uix coronas praebebunt.
KILIANVS. Vna uestrarum ancillarum mihi sertum debet. [F4^{r}]
MARCVS. Debet? Dic unde.

THEOPHILUS. From what I hear, you want to make a good impression with your candle.
GERMANUS. I do, but in honour of the Virgin Mary, not of myself.
THEOPHILUS. A humble heart is more pleasing to God than the display of a religious festival.
GERMANUS. Whatever I do, I do it with a soul devoted to God.
THEOPHILUS. I'll have a tallow candle in my hands, not a wax one.
GERMANUS. Nothing but wax candles are usually carried, but as the proverb says, 'The poor make cheap offerings.' But you could buy a wax candle for a Schilling.
THEOPHILUS. I'll pray to the Virgin Mary at greater length.
GERMANUS. But you won't fulfil the custom.
THEOPHILUS. I prefer to please God than people.
GERMANUS. Yet Plato says that we should please people.
THEOPHILUS. But against that St Paul says, 'If I were pleasing to men, I would not be the servant of Christ.'
GERMANUS. That's to be understood with reference to bad deeds, not good ones.

96. WEARING WREATHS ON A HOLIDAY

Kilianus and Marcus

KILIANUS. What are your maids doing after lunch?
MARCUS. Why do you want to know?
KILIANUS. I have a reason for asking.
MARCUS. I'll listen, then I'll answer.
KILIANUS. They might make me up a wreath to wear on my head.
MARCUS. You'd buy a better-looking one in the market.
KILIANUS. I'm not in the habit of buying silly things like that.
MARCUS. And we won't give you the roses free.
KILIANUS. But you've got plenty of flowers in your garden that are dying.
MARCUS. They'll hardly provide enough wreaths for me this summer.
KILIANUS. One of your maids owes me a wreath.
MARCUS. Owes you one? Why?

KILIANVS. Ex promisso mihi facto.

MARCVS. Sufficit promisisse, reddere non oportet.

KILIANVS. Si nequeo rosaceum sertum consequi, ex frondibus unum conficiam.

MARCVS. Receptum non est tales gerere coronas.

KILIANVS. Morem ipse mihi ita faciam.

MARCVS. Noui moris auctor exsibilatur passim.

KILIANVS. Spero quod ancilla uestra me non deseret.

MARCVS. Faciam ut te donet rosis, tu deinde sertum connecte.

KILIANVS. Aut unum in foro mercabor.

MARCVS. Solido ibidem emes.

KILIANVS. Tribus nummis comparabo mihi sat pulchrum.

MARCVS. Laborabo quo te uenustius habeam.

KILIANVS. Non pudet me in talibus nugis superari.

MARCVS. Ego malo pulchrior quam deformior conspici.

---

20 faciam] facerem A | 29 conspici] contueri A

97. DE CONVIVIO INTER CEREVISIAE BARATRA CELBRANDO

Strophylus et Lyconides

STROPHYLVS. Saluus sis, sodalium meorum optime.

LYCONIDES. Quid adeo blande me appellas?

STROPHYLVS. Quia diu mihi uisus non es.

LYCONIDES. Neque tu mihi.

STROPHYLVS. Latuisti semper domi instar testudinis?

LYCONIDES. Domi raro fui, semper foris negotia parentum executus sum.

STROPHYLVS. Tanto in tempore cur me non salutasti?

LYCONIDES. Licuit mihi nunquam per occupationes.

STROPHYLVS. Resarciemusne intermissam amicitiam et sodalitatem?

LYCONIDES. Ad tuum nutum obsequar.

STROPHYLVS. Id ego ferrem consilii, ut compotaremus pauxillulum.

KILIANUS. Because she promised me.
MARCUS. Promising is enough, you don't have to deliver.
KILIANUS. If I can't get a wreath of roses, I'll make one of foliage.
MARCUS. It's not the custom to wear wreaths like that.
KILIANUS. I'll start my own custom.
MARCUS. People who start new customs are ridiculed everywhere.
KILIANUS. I hope your maid won't let me down.
MARCUS. I'll get her to give you some roses, then you can make up a wreath.
KILIANUS. Or else I'll buy one in the market.
MARCUS. You'll get one there for a Schilling.
KILIANUS. I'll buy myself quite a nice one for very little.
MARCUS. I'll do my best to have a better-looking one than yours.
KILIANUS. I'm not ashamed to be beaten in trivial things like that.
MARCUS. I prefer to be regarded as attractive than as ugly.

97. TOPERS HOLDING A PARTY

Strophylus and Lyconides

STROPHYLUS. Greetings, my favourite companion!
LYCONIDES. Why are you speaking to me in such a flattering way?
STROPHYLUS. Because I haven't seen you for a long time.
LYCONIDES. Nor I you.
STROPHYLUS. Have you been hiding at home all the time like a tortoise?
LYCONIDES. I haven't been at home much, I've been doing things for my parents outside the house.
STROPHYLUS. Why haven't you called on me all this time?
LYCONIDES. I was so busy I never could.
STROPHYLUS. Shall we renew our interrupted friendship and companionship?
LYCONIDES. I'll obey your every command.
STROPHYLUS. My advice is that we should have a little drink together.

LYCONIDES. Renitar nihil.
STROPHYLVS. Potatoriamne domum aliquam nosti?
LYCONIDES. Rarus soleo esse aliorum compotor, quod tabernas nescio.
STROPHYLVS. Mihi est compertum ubi bibuli scholastici latere solent.
LYCONIDES. Forte et frequens ipsis ades?
STROPHYLVS. [F4v] Interdum, cum per crumenam licet.
LYCONIDES. Non te immunem poculis tingunt?
STROPHYLVS. Pari asse impendium soluo.
LYCONIDES. Non donarent te pauperem symbolo?
STROPHYLVS. Vis scire ubi sit situm diuerticulum nostrum cereuisiarium?
LYCONIDES. Percupio.
STROPHYLVS. In Platea (quam uocant) Ouium.
LYCONIDES. Tranquillum et solitarium locum elegistis.
STROPHYLVS. Latebris solemus gaudere.
LYCONIDES. Id prudentiae est.
STROPHYLVS. Concedamus istuc, uisum an aliquot nostrum ibi pocula tractent.
LYCONIDES. Congredior.

---

30 cereuisiarium] cereuisiarum A

98. DE CONVIVIO VICISSITVDINARIO, QVOD SACERDOTES INTER SE AGVNT

Burchardus et Conradus

BVRCHARDVS. Domi uestrae cur adeo lautus instruitur focus?
CONRADVS. Conuiuium nobiscum agetur festiuum.
BVRCHARDVS. Qualenam erit illud?
CONRADVS. Nequeo Latine reddere.
BVRCHARDVS. Effare ut potes.
CONRADVS. Canonici inter se conuiuium agunt, quod a serto capitis uocitant.
BVRCHARDVS. Scio, conuiuium uicissitudinarium Latine dices.
CONRADVS. Quare?

LYCONIDES. I won't resist that at all.
STROPHYLUS. Do you know of any ale-house?
LYCONIDES. I don't go drinking with others much, so I don't know the pubs.
STROPHYLUS. I know exactly where the schoolboys who are fond of a drink hang out.
LYCONIDES. Does that mean you're often with them?
STROPHYLUS. Now and again, when funds permit.
LYCONIDES. Do they treat you to free drink?
STROPHYLUS. I pay my full amount.
LYCONIDES. You're poor, wouldn't they pay for your share?
STROPHYLUS. Would you like to know where our alehouse is?
LYCONIDES. Very much.
STROPHYLUS. In the Schaafenstraße.
LYCONIDES. That's a quiet, isolated spot you've chosen.
STROPHYLUS. We like to have our hideouts.
LYCONIDES. That's a sensible idea.
STROPHYLUS. Let's go there and see if any of our gang are drinking there.
LYCONIDES. I'll come with you.

98. THE ROTATING DINNER-PARTY THE PRIESTS HOLD AMONGST THEMSELVES

Burchardus and Conradus

BURCHARDUS. Why's such a splendid fire being stoked up at your house?
CONRADUS. We're having a special dinner-party.
BURCHARDUS. What kind is it going to be?
CONRADUS. I can't say it in Latin.
BURCHARDUS. Express it as best you can.
CONRADUS. The canons hold a dinner amongst themselves; they call it a 'Kränzchen'.
BURCHARDUS. I know. In Latin you'd say 'conuiuium uicissitudinarium', a 'rotating dinner-party'.
CONRADUS. Why?

BVRCHARDVS. Quia per uices nunc ab hoc, nunc ab illo sumptus ipsius fiunt.
CONRADVS. Verum est, alternatim faciunt impendia.
BVRCHARDVS. Fiet istud nunc aere tui domini?
CONRADVS. Fiet, quia ordine sequitur eum qui ultimo expensas dedit.
BVRCHARDVS. Quanti constabit, credis, prandium istud?
CONRADVS. Insumet forte decem aureos nummos.
BVRCHARDVS. Hui, tanti?
CONRADVS. Et alii suo tempore non minus in obsoniis exponunt.
BVRCHARDVS. Exporrigunt etiam frontem basilice?
CONRADVS. Omnibus numeris sese exhilarant.
BVRCHARDVS. Edunt etiam carnes ueru paratas?
CONRADVS. Carnem elixam ac assam simul, et uinum hornum et bimum.
BVRCHARDVS. Quam [F5r] crebro istud conuiuium agunt?
CONRADVS. Ni fallor, quolibet mense.
BVRCHARDVS. Quisque forte semel est conuiuator?
CONRADVS. Toties quoties numero succedit.

---

10 uocitant] uocant A | 14 illo] alio A | 28 assam simul, et] assam, simul et A | 30 Quam] Quam A C; Quantum [?] B ('Quā' followed by 2 or 3 letters struck out by hand, and now indecipherable).

99. CVR CONVIVIVM ISTVD INSTITVERVNT SACERDOTES VEL ALII

Zacharias et Ferdinandus

ZACHARIAS. Prouerbium uulgo est, 'Nihil sine causa.'
FERDINANDVS. Quid tum?
ZACHARIAS. Hoc mihi probatur maxime.
FERDINANDVS. Etiam si detestari uelles, salua fronte non posses.
ZACHARIAS. Conuiuii uicissitudinarii precor causam profer.
FERDINANDVS. Vnde radices ceperit facile est cognitu.
ZACHARIAS. Mihi est quam ignotissimum.
FERDINANDVS. In conuiuiis sarcitur amicitia, nonne?
ZACHARIAS. Hercule non dissentio.

BURCHARDUS. Because the cost is borne first by this person, then that one, in turn.
CONRADUS. That's true, they take it in turns to foot the bill.
BURCHARDUS. Is this one being paid for by your master?
CONRADUS. Yes, because he's next in line after the one who paid for it the last time.
BURCHARDUS. How much do you think the meal will cost?
CONRADUS. Probably about ten Gulden.
BURCHARDUS. Gosh, as much as that?
CONRADUS. And when it's their turn the others spend just as much on the food.
BURCHARDUS. Do they enjoy themselves in a right royal way?
CONRADUS. They amuse themselves to the full.
BURCHARDUS. Do they eat spit-roasted meat, too?
CONRADUS. Boiled and roast meat together, new wine and wine from last year.
BURCHARDUS. How often do they hold these feasts?
CONRADUS. Every month, if I'm not mistaken.
BURCHARDUS. And I presume everyone is the host once?
CONRADUS. As often as their turn comes up.

99. WHY THIS DINNER-PARTY WAS STARTED BY PRIESTS OR OTHERS

Zacharias and Ferdinandus

ZACHARIAS. There's a common proverb, 'Nothing without a cause'.
FERDINANDUS. So?
ZACHARIAS. I approve of it highly.
FERDINANDUS. Even if you wanted to condemn it, you couldn't possibly.
ZACHARIAS. Will you please inform me of the origin of the rotating dinner-party?
FERDINANDUS. It's easy to know where its roots are.
ZACHARIAS. It's completely unknown to me.
FERDINANDUS. Friendship is restored at dinner-parties, isn't it?
ZACHARIAS. By Heavens, I wouldn't disagree.

FERDINANDVS. Et sancitur solidius, saepius inuicem conuiuando.
ZACHARIAS. Esset inde uicissitudo illa conuiuii nata?
FERDINANDVS. Persuasum ita habeo.
ZACHARIAS. Vix mihi persuaseris.
FERDINANDVS. Es adeo incredulus?
ZACHARIAS. Ad istud dictum difficilis sum fide.
FERDINANDVS. Scrupulum in eo quem habeas, cedo?
ZACHARIAS. Scio, 'Vulgus amicitias utilitate probat.'
FERDINANDVS. Ita Horatius in Odis refert.
ZACHARIAS. Est Horatii uerbum, sed et uulgi probatum calculo.
FERDINANDVS. Non infitiabor istum diligi, unde commodum datur.
ZACHARIAS. Sed conuiuium illud incommodat conuiuatori, ideo non est ob amicitiam natum.
FERDINANDVS. Canonici opulenti amicitiam non commodo sed corde pensitant.
ZACHARIAS. Malunt tamen accipere quam praebere.
FERDINANDVS. Dando etiam non sunt difficiles.

100. EXEMPLO SACERDOTVM ETIAM CONVIVIORVM INEVNT CIRCVLVM Gerardus et Henricus [F5v]

GERARDVS. Seniorum uita, audiui quondam, est iuniorum instructio.
HENRICVS. Debet esse, si fuerit bona.
GERARDVS. Sin autem fuerit mala, quid tum fiet?
HENRICVS. Non erit imitanda.
GERARDVS. Vicissitudo conuiuiorum frequens sacerdotibus estne sequenda?
HENRICVS. Est, sed opulentis.
GERARDVS. Nobisne fugienda?
HENRICVS. Inopia nostra satis docet.

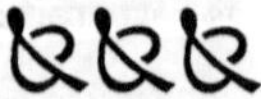

FERDINANDUS. And it's confirmed in a more lasting way by eating together often.
ZACHARIAS. Might that be what gave rise to taking it in turns to give that dinner?
FERDINANDUS. I'm convinced of it.
ZACHARIAS. You won't convince me.
FERDINANDUS. Are you that incredulous?
ZACHARIAS. I find it hard to credit what you say.
FERDINANDUS. What misgivings do you have about it, may I ask?
ZACHARIAS. I know that 'The common herd judges friendships by the advantage they bring'.
FERDINANDUS. That's what Horace writes in the *Odes*.
ZACHARIAS. It's a quotation from Horace, but it's generally approved, too.
FERDINANDUS. I won't deny that people like what is to their advantage.
ZACHARIAS. But that dinner-party is inconvenient to the host, so it hasn't arisen because of friendship.
FERDINANDUS. Rich canons don't weigh friendship by advantage, but by affection.
ZACHARIAS. But they prefer to receive than to give.
FERDINANDUS. They're not reluctant to give, either.

100. FOLLOWING THE PRIESTS' EXAMPLE, A ROUND OF DINNER-PARTIES IS STARTED by Gerardus and Henricus

GERARDUS. 'The lives of older people,' I've sometimes heard, 'are there to instruct the young.'
HENRICUS. They should be, if they're good.
GERARDUS. But if they should be bad, what happens then?
HENRICUS. They shouldn't be imitated.
GERARDUS. Should the way priests take it in turn to have frequent dinner-parties be imitated?
HENRICUS. Yes, but by rich people.
GERARDUS. Should we avoid it?
HENRICUS. Our lack of money tells us that clearly.

GERARDVS. Pulchrum tamen esset inter nos orbem agi conuiuiorum.

HENRICVS. Quam pulchrum fuerit ignoro, parum quaestuosum certe.

GERARDVS. Nescis ob sumptum pulchra non intermittenda?

HENRICVS. Fateor, pulchra et honesta.

GERARDVS. Non indecorum est inuicem potitare modice.

HENRICVS. Sed nequimus abstinere, ubi amplexi fuerimus pocula.

GERARDVS. Cessabimus una aut altera epota mensura.

HENRICVS. Tum unusquisque uix labia humectaret.

GERARDVS. Ineamus precor foedus agendi inter nos mutuas interdum compotationes.

HENRICVS. At quis sumptus feret?

GERARDVS. Vicissim omnes.

HENRICVS. Quantum impendet potationis princeps?

GERARDVS. Exiguum, nam praeter cereuisiam et bolum panis (nisi liberalior fuerit) dabit nihil.

HENRICVS. Si uinum appeteremus, unde istud compararetur?

GERARDVS. Quisque suo apponeret nomine.

HENRICVS. Nunc consentio.

101. DE MORIBVS MENSAE

Iulius et Morus

IVLIVS. 'Iuuenem nihil tam exornat quam ingenui mores,' dixit hodie praeceptor noster.

MORVS. E tripode locutus est.

IVLIVS. Hactenus credidi quod plus scientia nos decoraret.

MORVS. Toto caelo aberrasti.

IVLIVS. Pluris tamen constat scientia quam uirtus.

MORVS. Nonnunquam scientia facili- [F6r] us adipiscitur, sed sine moribus probis scientia nihil habet laudis.

IVLIVS. Nescius sum istius.

GERARDUS. But it would be splendid to have a round of dinner-parties amongst ourselves.

HENRICUS. I don't know how splendid it would be, but it certainly wouldn't be financially good for us.

GERARDUS. Don't you know that you shouldn't stop doing fine things because of the expense?

HENRICUS. I agree – fine and honourable things.

GERARDUS. It's not improper to have the odd drink together.

HENRICUS. But we can't stop once we have a glass in our hands.

GERARDUS. We'll stop once we've drunk a measure or two.

HENRICUS. Then each of us would hardly wet his lips.

GERARDUS. Please let's make an agreement to have drinking-parties amongst ourselves in turn.

HENRICUS. But who'll bear the expense?

GERARDUS. All of us in turn.

HENRICUS. How much will the person giving the party pay?

GERARDUS. A small amount, because he'll offer nothing more than beer and a mouthful of bread, unless he's more generous.

HENRICUS. If we wanted wine, what would that be bought with?

GERARDUS. Everyone would contribute his own.

HENRICUS. Now I agree.

101. TABLE MANNERS

Iulius and Morus

IULIUS. 'Nothing becomes a boy as well as good conduct,' our teacher told us today.

MORUS. That was a true word he spoke.

IULIUS. Up to now I've thought that knowledge did us more credit.

MORUS. You were completely wrong.

IULIUS. But knowledge is worth more than virtue.

MORUS. Knowledge can sometimes be easily come by, but without upright conduct knowledge isn't praiseworthy.

IULIUS. I'm not sure about that.

MORVS. Quantumuis peritus sit, si moribus uacauerit candidis, nihili homo erit.

IVLIVS. Tantine fiunt mores?

MORVS. Aestimantur magni, ubiuis locorum, maxime tamen ad mensam.

IVLIVS. Ad lances ego frontem perfrico, morum omnium ignarus.

MORVS. Non pudet te absque fronte esse hominem?

IVLIVS. Prouerbium uulgi sequor, ad mensam uerecundari decere neminem.

MORVS. Non satis intelligis dicterium illud.

IVLIVS. Quid sibi uelit tu apertius dicas.

MORVS. Neminem a cibis debere abstinere, iuxta tamen mores seruandi.

IVLIVS. Admones me hactenus ignoti.

MORVS. Nusquam magis quam ad mensam rusticitas aduertitur hominis.

IVLIVS. Estne adeo facile ad mensam delinquere?

MORVS. Facillime, si uel indecore biberis, comederis, uel cibum attigeris.

IVLIVS. Posthac me instar assidentium geram, ne quid committam indignum.

---

6 credidi quod plus] credidi plus A B C | 23 uelit tu apertius dicas.] uult, tu apertius dicas? A | 26 admones] admoneas A | 9–33 follows C. 9–10 in A and B read: MOR. Nonnunquam scientia facilius adipiscitur. IVLI. Sed sine moribus probis scientia nihil habet laudis. Then speakers are reversed for the rest of the dialogue.

102. DE FERIIS DIVI BLASII

Osualdus et Paschasius

OSVALDVS. In quem usum paras cuspidem illam?

PASCHASIVS. Quasi tu nescires.

OSVALDVS. Quid ego scirem tua negotia?

PASCHASIVS. Id quod molior commune hic locorum est.

OSVALDVS. Age et me istius certiorem redde.

PASCHASIVS. Crastino die oculis cernes.

OSVALDVS. Spectaculum forte aliquod erit?

MORUS. However learned a man may be, without upright behaviour he's worthless.
IULIUS. Is behaviour so highly regarded?
MORUS. It's held in high esteem everywhere, but especially at table.
IULIUS. When I'm eating I don't worry about manners; I know nothing about them.
MORUS. Aren't you ashamed not to have any sense of propriety?
IULIUS. I follow the common saying that no one should be shy at table.
MORUS. You don't understand the saying properly.
IULIUS. Tell me more clearly what it means.
MORUS. That no one should hold back from eating – as long as they respect the manners for serving food.
IULIUS. You're telling me about something I didn't know up till now.
MORUS. People's uncouthness is nowhere more obvious than at table.
IULIUS. Is it very easy to do something wrong at table?
MORUS. Very easy, if you eat, drink or touch food in an unseemly way.
IULIUS. From now on I'll behave in the way the others at table do, so as not to do anything unacceptable.

102. ST BLASIUS'S DAY

Osualdus and Paschasius

OSUALDUS. What are you making that pointed stick for?
PASCHASIUS. As though you didn't know!
OSUALDUS. How would I know your business?
PASCHASIUS. What I'm making is common hereabouts.
OSUALDUS. Go on, tell me about it.
PASCHASIUS. You'll see it for yourself tomorrow.
OSUALDUS. Will there be some kind of performance?

PASCHASIVS. Spectaculum erit non ludi, sed cursus.
OSVALDVS. Qui current? Et quorsum?
PASCHASIVS. Receptum est, puerulos cras ostiatim cursitare.
OSVALDVS. Quid ostiatim petent?
PASCHASIVS. Aliquid muneris in Diui Blasii nomine.
OSVALDVS. Ecquid precantibus erogatur?
PASCHASIVS. Frustum carnis suillae, uel panis triticeus unius teruncii.
OSVALDVS. Vnde natus est mos iste?
PASCHASIVS. Fugit me per Her- [F6v] culem.
OSVALDVS. Coniicio eius originem.
PASCHASIVS. Enarra unde aestimas.
OSVALDVS. In templo memini me uidisse Diui Blasii simulachrum.
PASCHASIVS. At qua effigie uel forma?
OSVALDVS. Habens caput porcinum baculo infixum.
PASCHASIVS. Ista est uero similis coniectura.
OSVALDVS. Ipse credo inde esse ortum morem quem dicis.
PASCHASIVS. Origo sit quaecunque, ego praedam me facturum spero.

---

3 illam] illum A

103. DE ELOQVENTIA ET BARBARIE

Quirinus et Romulus

QVIRINVS. Mirum est, quantum loquendo discrepant homines.
ROMVLVS. Quomodo dissonant?
QVIRINVS. Vnus culte, alius foetide Latine loquitur.
ROMVLVS. Vnde ista sermonis diuersitas?
QVIRINVS. A uario praeceptorum genere.
ROMVLVS. Non sunt praeceptores eiusdem farinae?
QVIRINVS. Ah, inter coruum et cygnum colore plus conuenit quam inter praeceptores litterarios
ROMVLVS. In quo dissimiles sunt?
QVIRINVS. In eruditione: peritus est unus, alter amusus.
ROMVLVS. Praeceptor indoctus esse nequit si instruit.

PASCHASIUS. Not a play, a run.
OSUALDUS. Who's going to run, and where to?
PASCHASIUS. There's a tradition that boys run from door to door tomorrow.
OSUALDUS. What do they ask for at the houses?
PASCHASIUS. A gift of some kind in the name of St Blasius.
OSUALDUS. And what do they get given when they beg?
PASCHASIUS. A piece of pork, or a Pfennig's worth of wheaten bread.
OSUALDUS. Where did that custom originate?
PASCHASIUS. Good Lord, that's more than I can say.
OSUALDUS. I can guess the origin.
PASCHASIUS. Tell me where you reckon it came from.
OSUALDUS. I remember seeing an image of St Blasius in church.
PASCHASIUS. What shape or likeness did he have?
OSUALDUS. He had a pig's head on a stick.
PASCHASIUS. That's a likely conclusion.
OSUALDUS. I think the custom you're talking about had its origin from there.
PASCHASIUS. Whatever the origin is, I'm hoping to make a good haul.

103. ELOQUENCE AND BARBARISM

Quirinus and Romulus

QUIRINUS. It's amazing how differently people speak.
ROMULUS. How do they differ?
QUIRINUS. One person speaks Latin stylishly, another speaks it offensively.
ROMULUS. What causes that difference in speaking?
QUIRINUS. Different kinds of schoolteacher.
ROMULUS. Aren't all teachers of the same sort?
QUIRINUS. Oh, a crow and a swan are more alike in colour than teachers are to one another.
ROMULUS. In what way do they differ?
QUIRINUS. In knowledge: one is learned, another is ignorant.
ROMULUS. A teacher can't be ignorant if he teaches.

QVIRINVS. Magistratum praeceptoris multi gerunt, sed prouinciae non satagunt.
ROMVLVS. Omnes discipulos docent.
QVIRINVS. Docere uarium est.
ROMVLVS. Quomodo est uarium?
QVIRINVS. Aliqui docent uana, inutilia et auditu iniucunda.
ROMVLVS. Quae uocas iniucunda auditu?
QVIRINVS. Latinum impolitum, forte in aliqua coquorum officina effictum.
ROMVLVS. Talem sermonem nullus docet discipulos.
QVIRINVS. Ah, nunc mihi cerebrum excutis.
ROMVLVS. Loquor ut qui ignorat.
QVIRINVS. De te uere iudicas.
ROMVLVS. Doceas tamen quid barbaries sit, et quid eloquentia.
QVIRINVS. Barbaries est sermo inculta habens uerba et impolitam compositionem.
ROMVLVS. Quid eloquentia?
QVIRINVS. Est sermo ornatum habens tum uerbis tum compositione. [F7r]

---

16 Omnes discipulos] Omnes tamen discipulos A

104. AN OMNE PERDATVR TEMPVS QVOD STVDIO NON IMPARTITVR, VT DIXIT PLINIVS

Stephanus et Theodorus

STEPHANVS. Historici admiror an semper uera afferant.
THEODORVS. Istud credendum audaci animo.
STEPHANVS. Tamen Graeci a multis mendacii arguuntur in historiis.
THEODORVS. Latinorum ego tutelam gero.
STEPHANVS. Plinii Iunioris uerbum fuit, id perire tempus quod studio uacaret litterario, credis tu illud?
THEODORVS. Non crederem? Experior indies.
STEPHANVS. Aliud agendo nonne etiam bene collocant tempus homines?

QUIRINUS. A lot of people hold the position of teacher, but they aren't up to the job.
ROMULUS. They all teach pupils.
QUIRINUS. Teaching varies.
ROMULUS. In what way?
QUIRINUS. Some people teach things that are false, useless and unpleasant to hear.
ROMULUS. What do you call unpleasant to hear?
QUIRINUS. Inelegant Latin that was probably composed in some kitchen or other.
ROMULUS. Nobody teaches language like that to his pupils.
QUIRINUS. Oh, now you're beating my brains out!
ROMULUS. I'm speaking from a position of ignorance.
QUIRINUS. You're right about that.
ROMULUS. But teach me what barbarism and eloquence are.
QUIRINUS. Barbarism is language uncouth in vocabulary and inelegant in composition.
ROMULUS. And eloquence?
QUIRINUS. Language distinguished in vocabulary and composition.

104. IS ALL TIME NOT DEVOTED TO STUDY WASTED, AS PLINY SAID?

Stephanus and Theodorus

STEPHANUS. I wonder whether historians always relate the truth.
THEODORUS. You'd be a bold person to believe that.
STEPHANUS. And yet the Greeks are accused by many of lying in their histories.
THEODORUS. I support the Latins.
STEPHANUS. Pliny the Younger said that any time not occupied by the study of literature was wasted; do you believe that?
THEODORUS. Not believe it? I experience it every day.
STEPHANUS. Don't people spend their time well doing other things too?

THEODORVS. Audiam, quid operis putes?

STEPHANVS. Potitando, edendo, et uentrem iuuando.

THEODORVS. Hoc aliud est nihil quam tempus perdere.

STEPHANVS. Tamen inde commodum sequitur corpori.

THEODORVS. Sed interim negligitur anima, quae est nobilior.

STEPHANVS. Qui manibus laborant artifices, perdunt isti etiam tempus?

THEODORVS. Id non reor.

STEPHANVS. Tamen Plinius istud uidetur uelle.

THEODORVS. Plinius de litteris deditis loquitur.

STEPHANVS. Litterarum alumni nequeunt semper incumbere chartis.

THEODORVS. Dic quando non.

STEPHANVS. Dicam. Plinius Secundus in epistolis dicit de Plinio Iuniori quod tempus balneo eximebat studio, ergo et illud perdidit.

THEODORVS. Vane loqueris; etsi libros non tractabat, tamen semper de suis meditabatur scientiis.

STEPHANVS. Forte dicere uis istud bene collocari tempus quod in libris uel colloquiis de scientia teritur.

THEODORVS. Rem ipsam tenes.

32–33 quod in libris] quod libris A | 33 colloquiis de scientia] colloquiis scientiarum A

105. CVM AETATE ESSE SAPIENDVM

Antonius et Burchardus

ANTONIVS. Non pudet te adultum ita gerere?

BVRCHARDVS. Qui ago?

ANTONIVS. Instar pueri.

BVRCHARDVS. Das id mihi uitio?

ANTONIVS. Quis uitio tibi non ascriberet?

BVRCHARDVS. Nescis, nemo ubique iuxta sapit. [F7v]

ANTONIVS. Scio dulce esse quandoque desipere in loco.

BVRCHARDVS. Cur tum me increpas?

ANTONIVS. Tu nunquam non desipis.

BVRCHARDVS. Vt sapiam me instrue.

ANTONIVS. Si audire me uelis.

THEODORUS. What kind of things are you thinking of? I'm listening.
STEPHANUS. Drinking, eating and indulging their stomachs.
THEODORUS. That's nothing but a waste of time.
STEPHANUS. And yet the body benefits as a result.
THEODORUS. But while doing that they neglect the soul, and it's superior.
STEPHANUS. Do manual workers waste their time too?
THEODORUS. I don't think so.
STEPHANUS. Yet Pliny seems to mean that.
THEODORUS. Pliny's talking of people devoted to scholarship.
STEPHANUS. Students can't always be at their books.
THEODORUS. Tell me when they can't.
STEPHANUS. Right. In his letters, Pliny the Younger says of Pliny the Elder that he took the time for his bath off from study – so he wasted that.
THEODORUS. You're wrong. He may not have been reading books, but he was still reflecting on what he knew.
STEPHANUS. What you mean, perhaps, is that time taken up by books or scholarly discussions is well spent.
THEODORUS. You're exactly right.

105. SENSE SHOULD COME WITH AGE

Antonius and Burchardus

ANTONIUS. Aren't you ashamed to behave like that as an adult?
BURCHARDUS. How am I acting?
ANTONIUS. Like a child.
BURCHARDUS. Do you see that as a fault in me?
ANTONIUS. Who wouldn't see it as one?
BURCHARDUS. Don't you know that no one can be equally sensible everywhere?
ANTONIUS. I know that 'Folly is delightful in its place'.
BURCHARDUS. So why are you reproving me?
ANTONIUS. You *never* stop behaving stupidly.
BURCHARDUS. Teach me, so that I'll gain wisdom.
ANTONIUS. If you'll listen to me.

BVRCHARDVS. Auscultabo.
ANTONIVS. Duo sunt sapientiae praecepta.
BVRCHARDVS. Quae illa sunt?
ANTONIVS. Primum est posse tacere.
BVRCHARDVS. Alterum quod est?
ANTONIVS. Discere quid sit loquendum.
BVRCHARDVS. Ista memoriae recondam.
ANTONIVS. Sed scis quando uel ubi sit tacendum?
BVRCHARDVS. Non, et id me doceas.
ANTONIVS. Tacendum est, ubi taciturnitas plus confert quam loquacitas.
BVRCHARDVS. Istud praescire quis potest?
ANTONIVS. Praemeditandum istud est, ante quam lingua moueatur.
BVRCHARDVS. Quando loquendum est?
ANTONIVS. Dum taciturnitas est obfutura.
BVRCHARDVS. Obestne aliquando silere?
ANTONIVS. Nescis Amyclas tacendo periisse?
BVRCHARDVS. A quo discam quid loquendum sit?
ANTONIVS. Sapientum aduerte uerba, et plus audias quam loquere.
BVRCHARDVS. Vix illa tenere potuero.
ANTONIVS. In mente habeas praeceptum Periandri Corinthii, quod meditatio totum continet.
BVRCHARDVS. Posthac non hiscam, nisi enixe praemeditatus quo uerba uergant.

---

3 gerere] agere A

106. DE NOVIS INDVMENTIS COLLOQVVNTVR Carolus et Daniel

CAROLVS. Hodie me noscis, cras non agnosces.
DANIEL. Mutaberis in aliud animal?
CAROLVS. Non, sed alio modo totus uariabor.
DANIEL. Forte incantamentis.
CAROLVS. Non, sed uestitu nouo.

BURCHARDUS. I'll listen.
ANTONIUS. There are two principles of wisdom.
BURCHARDUS. What are they?
ANTONIUS. The first is to be able to be silent.
BURCHARDUS. What's the second?
ANTONIUS. To learn what ought to be said.
BURCHARDUS. I'll commit them to memory.
ANTONIUS. But do you know when or where you should be silent?
BURCHARDUS. No, teach me that too.
ANTONIUS. You should be silent when silence is more beneficial than talkativeness.
BURCHARDUS. Who can know when that will be?
ANTONIUS. You should think about that before your tongue moves.
BURCHARDUS. When should you speak?
ANTONIUS. When being silent is going to be harmful.
BURCHARDUS. Is it sometimes harmful to be silent?
ANTONIUS. Don't you know that Amyclas was ruined by silence?
BURCHARDUS. Who will I learn what should be said from?
ANTONIUS. Pay attention to what wise people say, and listen more than you speak.
BURCHARDUS. I'll hardly be able to keep those rules.
ANTONIUS. Keep in mind Periander of Corinth's maxim that thinking things out is the basis of everything.
BURCHARDUS. In future I won't open my mouth unless I've assiduously thought over where my words are tending.

106. NEW CLOTHES

Carolus and Daniel

CAROLUS. Today you know me, tomorrow you won't.
DANIEL. Are you going to change into a different animal?
CAROLUS. No, I'm going to change completely in another way.
DANIEL. The effect of spells, perhaps?
CAROLUS. No, the effect of new clothes.

DANIEL. Vestieris recens?
CAROLVS. Vtique nouus a talis usque ad uerticem.
DANIEL. Tuo aere, uel parentum?
CAROLVS. Parentum, non meo sumptu.
DANIEL. Qui id es meritus?
CAROLVS. Diu est quod polliciti sunt mihi.
DANIEL. Cuius rei gratia?
CAROLVS. Si uiderint me in litteris progredi.
DANIEL. Certe tui profectus sunt auidi.
CAROLVS. [F8v] Commodum meum plus quam ego ahhelant.
DANIEL. Ista uera est parentum pietas.
CAROLVS. Laborabo omni conatu ut talis efficiar, qualem me cupiunt ipsi.
DANIEL. Nunc tempus esset ut nuces spargeres.
CAROLVS. Cum isto recenti amictu feruidior fiam litterarum alumnus.
DANIEL. Faxit id magnus Apollo.
CAROLVS. Ludibrio tu habes quae dico, sed meliora praestiturum me uidebis.
DANIEL. Vt primum uidero credam.
CAROLVS. Ignoras muneribus illectari iuuenes ad studia?
DANIEL. Horatii ista sententia est.
CAROLVS. Non secus ac ego nouis uestibus donatus discendo feruescam.
DANIEL. Ardor ille uereor peribit propediem.
CAROLVS. Id dii auertant.
DANIEL. Ero tibi augur, uestibus ueterascentibus exarescet et in te discendi cupiditas.
CAROLVS. Hoc in plerisque accidit, sed in me locum non habebit, id exitus ostendet.
DANIEL. Si perduraueris diligentia, eris mihi magnus Apollo.

---

14 Cuius rei gratia?] Cuius rei gratia? C; Cuius gratia? A B | 15 me in litteris] me literis A | 17 meum plus] meum illi plus A | 26 praestiturum] praestaturum A | 37–38 ostendet ... Apollo.] ostendet. A

DANIEL. Are you going to get a new suit of clothes?
CAROLUS. Completely new, from head to toe.
DANIEL. With your money or your parents'?
CAROLUS. At my parents' expense, not mine.
DANIEL. How did you deserve that?
CAROLUS. They've been promising them to me for a long time.
DANIEL. What for?
CAROLUS. If they saw me making progress at school.
DANIEL. They're certainly eager for you to make progress.
CAROLUS. They desire my advantage more than I do.
DANIEL. That's true parental concern.
CAROLUS. I'll work as hard as I can to turn out the way they want me to be.
DANIEL. Now it's time for you to put away childish things.
CAROLUS. As a result of the new clothes I'll become a keener scholar.
DANIEL. May great Apollo grant that.
CAROLUS. You're mocking what I say, but you'll see that I'll do better in future.
DANIEL. I'll believe that as soon as I see it.
CAROLUS. Don't you know that boys are enticed to study by presents?
DANIEL. It's an observation of Horace.
CAROLUS. And in the same way I'll become keener about learning when I'm given my new clothes.
DANIEL. I fear that enthusiasm will fade before long.
CAROLUS. Heaven forbid!
DANIEL. I predict that as your clothes get old, the will to learn will dry up in you too.
CAROLUS. That happens in most cases, but it won't apply to me, as the outcome will show.
DANIEL. If you persist in your diligence, you'll be my great Apollo.

107. TRACTARE DICVNT FABRILIA FABROS

Eberhardus et Fabricius.

EBERHARDVS. Quae conuiuii uestri fuerunt colloquia?
FABRICIVS. Talia, quales fuere hospites.
EBERHARDVS. Cuius tum farinae isti erant?
FABRICIVS. Negotiatores et mercatores ac faeneratores.
EBERHARDVS. Hi quid inuicem nugabantur?
FABRICIVS. De faenore quod exercent.
EBERHARDVS. Sperant nunc quaestum aliquem?
FABRICIVS. Spe lucri iam fouentur.
EBERHARDVS. Sed qua re lucrum facient nunc temporis?
FABRICIVS. Annonam uenundando.
EBERHARDVS. Frugum uenditio nunc tempestiua est.
FABRICIVS. Id et ipsi norunt, quia pretiose ueneunt.
EBERHARDVS. Hui, pereant cum eorum auiditate illi hominum et pauperum tortores.
FABRICIVS. Faxit Deus ut mercatus annonae uilior fiat.
EBERHARDVS. Vereor, ante proximam [F8v] messem uilius non uendetur frumentum.
FABRICIVS. Fidendum est Deo, qui omnia uertere potest.
EBERHARDVS. Ferendum adhuc esset, si non carior fieret emptio frugum.
FABRICIVS. Id dii prohibeant.
EBERHARDVS. Non alii adfuere conuiuae?
FABRICIVS. Praesto erant et sacerdotes nonnulli.
EBERHARDVS. An isti, qui mercede conducti missas celebrant, quos praesentionarios uulgus uocat?
FABRICIVS. Eiusmodi erant sacrificuli.
EBERHARDVS. Qualis ipsis fuit sermo?
FABRICIVS. Nusquam iam, uel raro, defunctis exequias fieri.
EBERHARDVS. Quid causae putabant esse?
FABRICIVS. Quod Luthero accederent homines.
EBERHARDVS. Altera et haec est ratio, quod egent plerique.
FABRICIVS. Certum est, egestate ubique laboratur.

2, etc. Fabricius] Fabricius C; Fabritius A B | 14 ueneunt] ueniunt A; uenit B C

107. 'SMITHS WORK IN METAL'

Eberhardus and Fabricius.

EBERHARDUS. What talk was there at your dinner-party?
FABRICIUS. The talk reflected the guests.
EBERHARDUS. And what kind of people were they?
FABRICIUS. Businessmen and merchants and moneylenders.
EBERHARDUS. What did they chat to one another about?
FABRICIUS. About the money they're lending.
EBERHARDUS. Are they hoping for some kind of profit now?
FABRICIUS. They're comforted by the hope of gain.
EBERHARDUS. But what do they make money from these days?
FABRICIUS. Selling grain.
EBERHARDUS. Now's the season for selling grain.
FABRICIUS. And they know that, for it's very expensive.
EBERHARDUS. Oh, curse those torturers of people and the poor, and their greed!
FABRICIUS. God grant that the price of grain gets cheaper.
EBERHARDUS. I'm afraid that wheat won't get any cheaper before the next harvest.
FABRICIUS. We must trust God, who can change the course of all affairs.
EBERHARDUS. It would be tolerable for a while yet if grain didn't get any dearer.
FABRICIUS. Heaven forbid!
EBERHARDUS. Were there no other guests present?
FABRICIUS. There were a few priests there too.
EBERHARDUS. The ones who say masses for a fee, commonly known as 'praesentionarii'?
FABRICIUS. They were priests of that kind.
EBERHARDUS. What did they talk about?
FABRICIUS. The fact that now there are never, or hardly ever, masses for the dead.
EBERHARDUS. What did they think the reason was?
FABRICIUS. The fact that people are siding with Luther.
EBERHARDUS. There's this reason too – that most people have no money.
FABRICIUS. That's true; there's poverty everywhere.

108. AD MENSAM LAETA ET NON TRISTIA DEBERE ESSE COLLOQVIA

Hero et Iulianus

HERO. Abeant uerba illa.

IVLIANVS. Quare?

HERO. Tristia sunt, quae huic loco et tempori non conueniunt.

IVLIANVS. Quae tum uerba hic apta erunt?

HERO. Dulcia et iucunda dicteria.

IVLIANVS. Quis hic est, qui aliquod scomma proferet?

HERO. Sales dicantur inter nos uicissim.

IVLIANVS. Cuius erit auspicari?

HERO. Hospitis istud est munus.

IVLIANVS. Placet, deinde et propius assidentes aliquid ioci afferent.

HERO. Vel si uisum est hospiti, sortiemur quis incipiat.

IVLIANVS. Incipere ipse essem instructus.

HERO. Lepidi igitur aliquid recense.

IVLIANVS. Sed sileant prius omnes.

HERO. Tenebimus ora intenti omnes, ut inquit Vergilius.

IVLIANVS. Prouerbium est et multorum in ore, ad mensam sedendo iuuenescere homines, idne uobis uerisimile uidetur?

HERO. Fertur, sed certum est quod false.

IVLIANVS. Cur fictum esse creditis?

HERO. Quia tempore senescimus, ubicumque locorum simus.

IVLIANVS. Diffiteri nequeo, attamen ad mensam iuuenescimus.

HERO. Consonum uero non credi- [G1r] mus esse.

IVLIANVS. Aduertite, uobis persuadebo.

HERO. Age, facias, et Phyllida solus habebis.

IVLIANVS. Sententia Horatii est, uinum hominem reddere iuuenem.

HERO. Aeque tamen senes manent ebrii.

IVLIANVS. Fiunt iuuenes animo et hilaritate.

HERO. Id uerum est, quia uinum curas abigit.

IVLIANVS. Et iuuenum est curis uacare.

HERO. Ipsi non curant quanti annona ueneat.

108. CONVERSATION AT TABLE SHOULD BE HAPPY, NOT SAD

Hero and Iulianus

HERO. Let's have no more talk like that!
IULIANUS. Why?
HERO. It's sad, and doesn't suit this time and place.
IULIANUS. So what talk would be fitting here?
HERO. Pleasant, delightful, witty remarks.
IULIANUS. Who here will tell a few jokes?
HERO. Let's take turns to tell jokes.
IULIANUS. Who'll begin?
HERO. That's the host's duty.
IULIANUS. All right, then the people sitting near me will tell some jokes.
HERO. Or, if the host likes, we'll draw lots for who begins.
IULIANUS. I'm ready to begin.
HERO. Tell us something amusing, then.
IULIANUS. But first everyone has to be quiet.
HERO. We'll 'gaze intently on you', as Vergil says.
IULIANUS. There's a saying used by many, that people grow younger sitting at table; does that seem likely to you?
HERO. That's what they say, but it's definitely untrue.
IULIANUS. Why do you think it's false?
HERO. Because we grow older with time, wherever we are.
IULIANUS. I can't deny that, and yet we do grow younger at table.
HERO. We don't think that accords with the truth.
IULIANUS. Listen, I'll convince you.
HERO. Go on, do that and you'll have Phyllis to yourself.
IULIANUS. There's a saying of Horace's that wine makes man young.
HERO. But old men stay just as old when they're drunk.
IULIANUS. They become young in mind and expression.
HERO. That's true, because wine drives cares away.
IULIANUS. And it's in the nature of boys to be without cares.
HERO. They're not concerned about the price of corn.

IVLIANVS. Ideo ad mensam sinite et nos iuuenescere largius bibendo.

---

1 laeta et non] laeta non A | 29 habebis] habeto A

109. ANTE ET POST CIBVM HYMNVM ESSE DICENDVM

Lucanus et Mauritius

LVCANVS. Homines sitis an bestiae, dubito.

MAVRITIVS. Formam nostram aspice.

LVCANVS. Species est humana, sed uita non.

MAVRITIVS. Viuimus tum bruta?

LVCANVS. Agitis mores beluinos.

MAVRITIVS. Hui, bona uerba.

LVCANVS. Porcorum est edere nullis precibus dictis.

MAVRITIVS. Oraremus usque?

LVCANVS. Decet hominem orando cibum adire et deserere.

MAVRITIVS. In aede sacra sat precum diximus.

LVCANVS. Fortassis ibidem fabulis transegistis tempus?

MAVRITIVS. Confabulari illic non solemus.

LVCANVS. Etiam non ad Deum preces funditis scio.

MAVRITIVS. Obseruasti tu in templo quid ageremus?

LVCANVS. Saepenumero.

MAVRITIVS. Tecum habita, si nos mordere intendis.

LVCANVS. Reprehendite uos et me, si quid scitis male per me gestum.

MAVRITIVS. Sapientiores sumus quam quod litem auspicaremur.

LVCANVS. Oretis, deinde cibo fruamini.

MAVRITIVS. Omittemus posthac nunquam preces ad cibum solitas.

LVCANVS. Nihil inciuilius est hominem edere sine hymno dicto, cum id Christus fecerit.

MAVRITIVS. Obliuiscimur quandoque, aliarum dum sumus solliciti rerum.

LVCANVS. Sollicitus sum nunquam adeo ut Dei obliuiscar.

MAVRITIVS. Felix, qui istam habeas gratiam.

IULIANUS. And so let yourselves grow younger at table by drinking copiously.

109. GRACE SHOULD BE SAID BEFORE AND AFTER MEALS

Lucanus and Mauritius

LUCANUS. I wonder whether you're humans or animals.
MAURITIUS. Look at our appearance.
LUCANUS. Your appearance is human, but not the way you live.
MAURITIUS. Do we live like animals?
LUCANUS. You have the manners of beasts.
MAURITIUS. Oh, watch what you're saying!
LUCANUS. It's pigs who eat without saying any prayers.
MAURITIUS. Should we pray so much?
LUCANUS. It becomes a person to start and finish a meal with a prayer.
MAURITIUS. We've said enough prayers in church.
LUCANUS. Did you perhaps spend the time there talking?
MAURITIUS. We don't talk there.
LUCANUS. I know you don't utter prayers to God there, either.
MAURITIUS. Have you watched what we were doing in church?
LUCANUS. Many's the time.
MAURITIUS. If you're out to criticize us, examine yourself.
LUCANUS. You censure me too, if you know of anything bad I've done.
MAURITIUS. We have more sense than to start a quarrel.
LUCANUS. Pray, then enjoy your food.
MAURITIUS. In future we'll never leave out the customary prayers at meals.
LUCANUS. There's nothing more ill-mannered than for a person to eat without saying grace, seeing that Christ said it.
MAURITIUS. We forget sometimes, when we're concerned about other things.
LUCANUS. I'm never so concerned that I forget God.
MAURITIUS. You're fortunate to have that grace.

LVCANVS. Precantibus ad mensam uictus suppeditatur a Deo.

MAVRITIVS. Facile credimus.

LVCANVS. Facite igitur ut [G1v] hoc praecepto mei semper sitis memores.

MAVRITIVS. Fiet, tibi gratiam habemus.

2, etc. Mauritius] Mauricius A B C | 29 Obliuiscimur] Obliuiscemur A

110. DE CAPITE APERIENDO

Nestor sapiens et Othmarus

NESTOR. Rustice, ubi egisti uitam? An inter bestias?

OTHMARVS. Mihi cum beluis non conuenit.

NESTOR. Plus cum bestiis quam hominibus tibi est similitudo.

OTHMARVS. Causam indica.

NESTOR. Apud honestos uiros sine moribus es.

OTHMARVS. Mores quos haberem?

NESTOR. Honestiori te aperiendo caput loquereris.

OTHMARVS. Caput aperire crebro molestum est.

NESTOR. Optime decet, quia datur uirtuti.

OTHMARVS. At caput nudum frigus mordet.

NESTOR. Quantumuis acre sit frigus, nequit cito laedere detectum caput.

OTHMARVS. Ipse doleo capite, dum frigus sentio.

NESTOR. Nihil plus decorat iuuenem quam dignioribus adesse non operto capite.

OTHMARVS. Admiror, nihil tamen prodest illis quibus illud fit?

NESTOR. Honor non accipientium, sed exhibentium est.

OTHMARVS. Vt audio, honor est meus, non quibus ipsum facio?

NESTOR. Sentis ueraciter.

OTHMARVS. Si praesciuissem, aperuissem caput crebrius.

NESTOR. Ingenuos indicat mores adolescentis.

LUCANUS. God supplies the food to the people praying at table.
MAURITIUS. We can well believe that.
LUCANUS. So make sure that you always remember me by keeping to this principle.
MAURITIUS. We will. Thank you.

110. DOFFING YOUR CAP

Nestor, the sensible boy, and Othmarus

NESTOR. You peasant, where have you spent your life – amongst animals?
OTHMARUS. I've nothing in common with the animals.
NESTOR. You have more of a resemblance to animals than to humans.
OTHMARUS. Tell me the reason.
NESTOR. You have no manners when you're with respectable people.
OTHMARUS. What kind of manners should I have?
NESTOR. You should bare your head when you talk to someone more honourable than you.
OTHMARUS. Taking your hat off a lot is a nuisance.
NESTOR. But it's very proper, because it's a tribute to virtue.
OTHMARUS. But the cold hurts your bare head.
NESTOR. However fierce the cold is, it can't hurt your uncovered head quickly.
OTHMARUS. *My* head hurts when I feel the cold.
NESTOR. Nothing does more credit to a boy than to have his head uncovered when he's with more honourable people.
OTHMARUS. I'm amazed, because it doesn't do any good to those you do it to.
NESTOR. The honour belongs to those who show it, not to those who receive it.
OTHMARUS. What you're saying is that the honour belongs to me, not to those I do to?
NESTOR. You think right.
OTHMARUS. If I'd known, I'd have taken off my hat more often.
NESTOR. It's a sign of good manners in a boy.

OTHMARVS. Tum facillime moratus efficiar.

NESTOR. Audisti unquam Romanorum morem de capite nudando?

OTHMARVS. Non, recense tu mihi.

NESTOR. Lex erat apud eos, quod capite plecteretur qui seniorem praeteriret coopertis capillis.

OTHMARVS. Nollem tunc temporis apud illos me uixisse.

NESTOR. Ipse si ibidem uitam egissem, nunquam operimento uerticis fuissem usus.

OTHMARVS. Istud et ego non omisissem.

---

2 Othmarus] Othmarus fatuus] A | 18–19 quibus illud fit?] quibus fit? A

111. DE FERTILI SACERDOTIO

Patris et Quirinus [G2r]

PATRIS. Ad uitam agendam sat mihi nunc est commeatus.

QVIRINVS. Gratiam Deo habeas.

PATRIS. Sed nostine unde uictitabo?

QVIRINVS. Tu me certiorem redde.

PATRIS. Optimum mihi est sacerdotium.

QVIRINVS. Tale et mihi esse uellem.

PATRIS. Piscare undique, forte reperies simile meo.

QVIRINVS. Aureo hamo careo.

PATRIS. Argenteum ut habeas hamum oportet.

QVIRINVS. Fortassis et tibi aere adeptum est sacerdotium.

PATRIS. Crede mihi, non inani ipsum sum nactus manu.

QVIRINVS. Id tibi iniurato credo.

PATRIS. Pendet mihi singulis annis centum aureos nummos.

QVIRINVS. Sufficiet et tibi et nymphae quam ales.

PATRIS. Puellam educabo nullam, sed parentibus commorabor.

QVIRINVS. Sapies in rem tuam, si feceris.

PATRIS. Graue esset, me et domum, et ancillam, et coquinam fouere.

QVIRINVS. Dicto citius multum prodigitur.

PATRIS. Parentibus uiuis impendiis largis parcam.

OTHMARUS. Then I'll become well-mannered very easily.
NESTOR. Have you ever heard about the Roman practice concerning taking off hats?
OTHMARUS. No, tell me about it.
NESTOR. They had a law that anyone who passed someone older with his head covered would be hit on the head.
OTHMARUS. I wouldn't like to have lived amongst the Romans at that time.
NESTOR. If I'd lived there I'd never have worn anything on my head.
OTHMARUS. And I would never have been without headgear.

111. A RICH BENEFICE

Patris and Quirinus

PATRIS. I'm now provided for for life.
QUIRINUS. You should be grateful to God.
PATRIS. But do you know what I'm going to live on?
QUIRINUS. Tell me.
PATRIS. I've got a fine benefice.
QUIRINUS. I wish I had one like that, too.
PATRIS. Fish everywhere, you may find one like mine.
QUIRINUS. I haven't got a golden hook.
PATRIS. A silver hook *is* what you need.
QUIRINUS. It may have been money that acquired the living in your case, too.
PATRIS. I didn't get it with empty hands, believe me.
QUIRINUS. I believe you, you don't have to swear it.
PATRIS. It's going to pay me a hundred Gulden a year.
QUIRINUS. That'll be enough for yourself and the girl you're going to support
PATRIS. I'm not going to support a girl, I'm going to stay with my parents.
QUIRINUS. If you do, you'll know what's good for you.
PATRIS. It would be too much for me to keep a house, a maid and a cook.
QUIRINUS. A lot gets spent in no time at all.
PATRIS. Whilst my parents are alive I'll save major expenses.

QVIRINVS. Viaticum ad senium tibi compara.
PATRIS. Vellem et tibi esse fecundum sacerdotium.
QVIRINVS. Ipse quoque percuperem.
PATRIS. Reperies aliquos pios, qui tui miserebuntur.
QVIRINVS. O utinam, quam gratus esse uellem.
PATRIS. Suborna amicos qui pro te diuites precentur.
QVIRINVS. Tentarem sedulo si profuturum scirem.
PATRIS. Periculum faciendum quippiam cupienti.
QVIRINVS. Verum est, audaces Fortuna iuuat. Et desidenti (ut uulgo fertur) assa non aduolat columba.

2, etc. Quirinus] Quintinus A | 7 Optimum] Opimum A | 24 fecundum] ubere A | 26 tui miserebuntur] tui se miserabuntur A | 31–32 iuuat ... columba.] iuuat. A

112. DE OFFICIO MECHANICO ADDISCENDO

Romulus et Scipio

ROMVLVS. Nunc temporis nouus mos inoleuit.
SCIPIO. Quem morem putas?
ROMVLVS. Quod a plerisque litterae deseruntur.
SCIPIO. Quid tum susceptant?
ROMVLVS. [G2v] Manibus operando uictitant.
SCIPIO. Poenitebit ipsos olim.
ROMVLVS. Illud quam multis praedixi, sed lapidi loquebar et mortuo uerba feci.
SCIPIO. Sapient nimis sero.
ROMVLVS. Laboriosos dies non diu tolerabunt.
SCIPIO. Gustata laboris amaritudine ad litteras recurrent.
ROMVLVS. Regredi ipsis non licebit ad deserta studia.
SCIPIO. Reditum quid morabitur?
ROMVLVS. Parentes, et aliorum hominum nasi suspensio.
SCIPIO. Satis amarum est ciconia affici et depingi.
ROMVLVS. Quid agent, credis, postquam eos laboris taeduerit?
SCIPIO. Crumenas amputabunt et iugulabunt homines.

QUIRINUS. Buy yourself a pension for your old age.
PATRIS. I wish you had a fat benefice too.
QUIRINUS. I really wish that myself.
PATRIS. You'll find a few good souls who'll take pity on you.
QUIRINUS. Oh, I hope so; how grateful I'd be!
PATRIS. Instruct some friends who'll make entreaties to rich people on your behalf.
QUIRINUS. I'd work hard on that if I knew it would do me any good.
PATRIS. Anyone who wants something has to try things out.
QUIRINUS. That's true; fortune favours the bold. And as the saying goes, roast pigeons don't fly into your mouth when you're sitting down.

112. LEARNING A CRAFT

Romulus and Scipio

ROMULUS. A new fashion has developed these days.
SCIPIO. What fashion are you thinking of?
ROMULUS. That lots of people are dropping out of school.
SCIPIO. What are they taking up instead?
ROMULUS. They're living by working with their hands.
SCIPIO. They'll regret it one day.
ROMULUS. I've said that to lots of people, but it was like speaking to a stone or talking to a dead man.
SCIPIO. They'll come to their senses too late.
ROMULUS. They won't put up with the days of hard work for long.
SCIPIO. When they've tasted the harshness of work they'll go back to school.
ROMULUS. They won't be allowed to go back to the studies they've given up.
SCIPIO. What'll prevent them going back?
ROMULUS. Their parents, and being made fun of by others.
SCIPIO. It's pretty distressing to be mocked behind your back.
ROMULUS. So what do you think they'll do after they've got fed up with work?
SCIPIO. They'll cut people's purses, and slit their throats.

ROMVLVS. Bellorum satellites fient etiam strenui.

SCIPIO. Fieri potest, nam et animam et uitam uenum habent.

ROMVLVS. Monachorum et quorundam diuitum admiror dementiam.

SCIPIO. Ah, admirari desine, nequeunt opiparos ferre dies.

ROMVLVS. Stolidi, qui luxuriosam uitam commutant miseria.

SCIPIO. Ignoras? 'Optat ephippia bos piger, optat arare caballus.'

ROMVLVS. Horatius isto uerbo quid dicere uolebat?

SCIPIO. Quemque suae sortis poenitere, optare alienam.

113. EOS RARO PROBOS FIERI, QVIBVS IN TENERIS PARENTES NIMIVM INDVLGENT

Telesphorus et Vdo

TELESPHORVS. O iuuenis, iuuenis, melior uirtute euades nunquam.

VDO. Nosti tu fortunas hominum?

TELESPHORVS. Tantum nosco sortem tuam, quod in melius non proficies.

VDO. Deus adhuc successum felicem mihi, spero, non denegauit.

TELESPHORVS. Tenera aetas de tota iudicat uita.

VDO. Hercule fallit saepissime.

TELESPHORVS. In teneris molliter, ut tu, educati omnium euadunt pessimi.

VDO. Tum nulli fierent principes probi, quia laute aluntur.

TELESPHORVS. Principem probum nigro cygno inuenies rariorem.

VDO. [G3r] Contine linguam, audire fastidio.

TELESPHORVS. Veterum perlustra historias, inuenies egisse tyrannos fere omnes.

ঔঔঔ

ROMULUS. They'll become violent mercenaries.
SCIPIO. They might, because their souls and their lives are for sale.
ROMULUS. I'm amazed at the madness of monks and of some rich people.
SCIPIO. Oh, don't be amazed, they can't put up with a rich life.
ROMULUS. People who exchange a life of luxury for poverty are stupid.
SCIPIO. Don't you know that 'the lazy ox would like to race, the horse would like to plough'?
ROMULUS. What did Horace mean by that statement?
SCIPIO. That everyone is dissatisfied with his own lot and wishes for someone else's.

113. THOSE WHOSE PARENTS INDULGE THEM TOO MUCH IN THEIR CHILDHOOD RARELY BECOME VIRTUOUS PEOPLE

Telesphorus and Udo

TELESPHORUS. Oh, my boy, you'll never turn out any more virtuous.
UDO. Can you tell people's fortune?
TELESPHORUS. I know enough about your fortune to say that you won't improve.
UDO. I hope that God hasn't denied me a favourable outcome yet.
TELESPHORUS. The early years decide the whole of your life.
UDO. God knows, they're very often misleading.
TELESPHORUS. Everyone who has a soft upbringing in their childhood, like you, turns out very badly.
UDO. Then no princes would become virtuous, because they're luxuriously brought up.
TELESPHORUS. You'll find a virtuous prince is rarer than a black swan.
UDO. Restrain your tongue, I don't care to hear.
TELESPHORUS. Look through the stories of the ancients, you'll find that they nearly all behaved like tyrants.

VDO. Abeant prisca tempora, aetate nostra reges et duces trutinemus.

TELESPHORVS. Hac tempestate diues probus albo coruo est rarior.

VDO. Tertius tu Cato es, omnia nosti.

TELESPHORVS. Sim qui sim, Quintiliani sequor sententiam.

VDO. Quae illa est?

TELESPHORVS. Virtute eum nunquam adolescere qui in purpura repserit.

VDO. Ita uisum est Quintiliano forte inopi.

TELESPHORVS. Censura est sua, et experientia ueracissimum esse probat.

VDO. Perpauci probi essent si uera diceres.

TELESPHORVS. Loquor de illis quorum laute alitur iuuentus.

VDO. Omnis ferme mater molliter alit filium.

TELESPHORVS. Facerent quidem istud omnes nutrices, sed multis reclamat indigentia.

VDO. Ideo Deus pauperibus, non diuitibus prolem concedit.

3, etc. Telesphorus] Thelesphorus A; Thelsephorus B C | 9 felicem mihi, spero] felicem spero A | 11 iudicat] indicat A | 23–24 coruo est rarior] coruo rarior A | 37–38 indigentia … concedit.] indigentia. A

114. QVI PARENTES SVOS DILIGANT FILIOS

Xenophon et Cyprianus

XENOPHON. Vellem tales mihi contigisse parentes.

CYPRIANVS. Quales optares?

XENOPHON. Vt ille est sortitus.

CYPRIANVS. Fatue, nescis quid desideras.

XENOPHON. Oppido bene scio.

CYPRIANVS. Si perpenderes uotum, taceres.

XENOPHON. Dies delicatos cupio.

CYPRIANVS. Tales si haberes, commodarentne tibi?

XENOPHON. Frugiferi essent, nam nulla re egerem.

CYPRIANVS. Vnde tum omnium rerum haberes copiam?

UDO. Forget the olden days, let's assess the kings and rulers of our age.

TELESPHORUS. These days a virtuous rich man is rarer than a white crow.

UDO. You're a third Cato, you know everything.

TELESPHORUS. Whoever I am, I follow Quintilian's opinion.

UDO. What is that?

TELESPHORUS. That someone who has 'crawled around in purple' as a child will never grow up virtuous.

UDO. That's probably how it seemed to Quintilian, as a poor man.

TELESPHORUS. That's his assessment, and experience proves that it's absolutely true.

UDO. Very few people would be upright if you were telling the truth.

TELESPHORUS. I'm talking about those who've had a luxurious upbringing in their youth.

UDO. Nearly every mother gives her child a soft upbringing.

TELESPHORUS. And in fact all nurses would do the same, but a lot of them are prevented by poverty.

UDO. And so God grants children to poor people, not to rich ones.

114. WHICH PARENTS LOVE THEIR CHILDREN

Xenophon and Cyprianus

XENOPHON. I wish I'd chanced to have parents like that.

CYPRIANUS. What kind would you like?

XENOPHON. Ones like fate has given him.

CYPRIANUS. You fool, you don't know what you're wishing for.

XENOPHON. I know very well.

CYPRIANUS. If you thought carefully about what you're wishing for, you wouldn't say it.

XENOPHON. I want an easy life.

CYPRIANUS. If you had one, would it be good for you?

XENOPHON. It would, because I wouldn't lack for anything.

CYPRIANUS. So where would you get such abundance from?

XENOPHON. Ab opulentis parentibus.
CYPRIANVS. Ah, ah, quid loqueris, stolide?
XENOPHON. Loquor quod res est.
CYPRIANVS. Parentes diuites plus surripiunt quam largiuntur filiis.
XENOPHON. Ipsis quid auferunt?
CYPRIANVS. Omnem laudem et commoditatem.
XENOPHON. Parentes darent filiis citius quam adimerent.
CYPRIANVS. Vt tu reris.
XENOPHON. Amabo, effare quid filiis demunt.
CYPRIANVS. Virtutem, qua nihil [G3v] est in mundo praestantius.
XENOPHON. Dicta tua non teneo.
CYPRIANVS. Vis ut tibi tanquam Dauo Terentiano apertius loquar?
XENOPHON. Volo et desidero.
CYPRIANVS. Diuites suis filiis plus aequo indulgent.
XENOPHON. Indulgentia ista quid obesse potest?
CYPRIANVS. Quintilianus inquit quod et corporis et animi neruos omnes corrumpit mollis illa educatio.
XENOPHON. Age, quomodo indulgent?
CYPRIANVS. Errantes non puniunt, neque a praeceptoribus eos corrigi uolunt.

115. QVIS NOSTER SIT AMICVS

Albertus et Bruno

ALBERTVS. Miser homo nunc est, qui rerum est expers humanarum.
BRVNO. Quis esset illarum rerum rudis?
ALBERTVS. Proh dolor, tales reperies complures.
BRVNO. Quos uocas tu humanarum rerum ignaros?
ALBERTVS. Hosce quibus facile imponitur.
BRVNO. Nonnunquam prudentissimo cuique dantur uerba.

ꙮꙮꙮ

XENOPHON. From wealthy parents.
CYPRIANUS. Oh, oh, what are you saying, you fool?
XENOPHON. I'm speaking the truth.
CYPRIANUS. Rich parents take more away from their children than they bestow on them.
XENOPHON. What do they take away from them?
CYPRIANUS. All merit and advantage.
XENOPHON. Parents would be more ready to give things to their children than to take them away.
CYPRIANUS. That's what you think.
XENOPHON. Tell me, please, what they take away from their children?
CYPRIANUS. Virtue, and there's nothing more admirable in the world.
XENOPHON. I can't understand what you say.
CYPRIANUS. Do you want me to speak more clearly to you, as though you were Terence's Davus?
XENOPHON. I do indeed.
CYPRIANUS. Rich people indulge their children more than is reasonable.
XENOPHON. How can that kind of indulgence be harmful?
CYPRIANUS. Quintilian says that that soft upbringing corrupts all the sinews of the body and the mind.
XENOPHON. Come on, how do they indulge them?
CYPRIANUS. They don't punish them when they go wrong, and they don't want them to be punished by their teachers.

115. WHO IS OUR FRIEND?

Albertus and Bruno

ALBERTUS. The person who knows nothing of human affairs now is miserable.
BRUNO. Who would be ignorant of affairs of that kind?
ALBERTUS. Goodness, you'll find lots of people like that.
BRUNO. Who do you call ignorant of human affairs?
ALBERTUS. Those who can easily be deceived.
BRUNO. Sometimes even the most careful person is tricked.

ALBERTVS. Sortem mundi qui calluerit, pulchre sibi cauebit.
BRVNO. Nostine dicterium, Homerum quandoque dormitare?
ALBERTVS. Inter homines agenti uigilandum est strenue.
BRVNO. Tenduntur tum nobis semper insidiae?
ALBERTVS. A multis nobis insidiatur, etiam quos amicissimos credimus.
BRVNO. Amici illi personati sunt.
ALBERTVS. Apparent fautores coram, sed clam mordent et pungunt instar felium.
BRVNO. Effingunt pulchre naturam felis.
ALBERTVS. Amicus est res nobilissima, sed rarissima.
BRVNO. Vnico tamen munusculo amicus adipiscitur.
ALBERTVS. Iste muneris, non nostri est amicus.
BRVNO. Verum quem aestimabimus amicum?
ALBERTVS. Neminem festinanter et temere.
BRVNO. Quando? Oro, instrue me.
ALBERTVS. Quem diutino conuictu intus et in cute nouerimus.
BRVNO. In- [G4r] tus aliquem noscere difficillimum est.
ALBERTVS. Longa consuetudo arguit qualis sit a talis ad uerticem, albus an ater.
BRVNO. Multi crocodili naturam habent, aliud uultu, aliud corde gerentes.
ALBERTVS. Verum est, immo Momus deus reprehensorius carpebat naturam quod hominem occluso pectore creauit, quod cordis alterius nos lateret cogitatus.
BRVNO. Cordium si quis explorator esse posset, facile amicum uerum agnosceret.

---

26 nouerimus] nouerimus A; uouerimus B | 31–36 gerentes … agnosceret.] gerentes. A

116. QVIS NOBIS SIT INIMICVS

Critolaus et Dauid

CRITOLAVS. O tu hominis somnium, non homo.
DAVID. Tu me hominem esse negas?
CRITOLAVS. Nego et manibus et pedibus.

ALBERTUS. Anyone who knows the ways of the world will be really on his guard.
BRUNO. Do you know the saying that Homer sometimes nods?
ALBERTUS. Someone whose business is amongst people has to watch out keenly.
BRUNO. Are traps always being set for us?
ALBERTUS. A lot of people are out to get us, even those we think are really friendly.
BRUNO. They're just pretending to be friends.
ALBERTUS. On the surface they seem like allies, but secretly they bite and scratch like cats.
BRUNO. They imitate the nature of cats very well.
ALBERTUS. A friend is a very fine thing, but a very rare one.
BRUNO. And yet a friend can be won with one little present.
ALBERTUS. That's someone who likes our gift, not us.
BRUNO. So who will we reckon as a friend?
ALBERTUS. We shoudn't count anyone rashly and in a hurry.
BRUNO. When? Teach me, please.
ALBERTUS. Someone we know inside out from being in their company for a long time.
BRUNO. To know someone inside is extremely difficult.
ALBERTUS. Long acquaintance will reveal what he's like from top to bottom, black or white.
BRUNO. A lot of people are like the crocodile: one thing on their faces and another in their hearts.
ALBERTUS. That's true. Indeed Momus the fault-finding god complained at Nature because she had made man with his breast closed, so that the thoughts of another person's heart would remain concealed from us.
BRUNO. If anyone could search out hearts, he'd easily recognize a true friend.

116. WHO IS OUR ENEMY?

Critolaus and David

CRITOLAUS. Oh you mere illusion of a man!
DAVID. Are you denying I'm a human being?
CRITOLAUS. I am, completely and utterly.

DAVID. Confirma quod dicere audes.
CRITOLAVS. Quia brutis minus sapis.
DAVID. Bruta sapiuntne?
CRITOLAVS. Prouident diligentius sibi quam tu tibi.
DAVID. Curam mei quantum possum gero.
CRITOLAVS. Factis istud uerbi non praestas.
DAVID. Vbi tum mihi incommodo?
CRITOLAVS. Quod cuilibet homini aeque credis.
DAVID. Non crederem amicis?
CRITOLAVS. Amicos quos aestimas inimici ueri sunt.
DAVID. Id dii prohibeant.
CRITOLAVS. Coram tibi blandiuntur, rodunt a tergo.
DAVID. Hoc si agnouero deseram eos.
CRITOLAVS. Percipies uereor non sine periculo.
DAVID. Argus ero, quo me non fallant.
CRITOLAVS. Actum est, diu casses eorum incidisti.
DAVID. Adhuc tamen liber sum.
CRITOLAVS. Corpore liber es, sed emolumento captus.
DAVID. Nocumenti adhuc sentio prorsus nihil.
CRITOLAVS. Percipies more Phrygum serus nimium.
DAVID. Tu si amicus es, praemoneas, quo mihi caueam commodius.
CRITOLAVS. Sed me apud eos non prodas uelim.
DAVID. Silebo ac lapis iste.
CRITOLAVS. [G4v] Foedus inierunt te deplumandi, quoad possint.
DAVID. Id ipsis prohibebitur, quia parum mihi restat quod dem.
CRITOLAVS. Id modicum si perdideris nudus esses totus, ipsos desere.
DAVID. Diutius eis non conuiuam.

---

11 Factis istud uerbi] Factis istud uerbi A; Factis istud uerbis B; Facis istud uerbis C | 18 agnouero] sciscitauero A | 31 possint] possint A; possent B C | 32 prohibebitur] prohibetur A

DAVID. Back up what you dare to say.
CRITOLAUS. Because you have less sense than the animals.
DAVID. Do animals have sense?
CRITOLAUS. They take better care of themselves than you do.
DAVID. I look after myself as best I can.
CRITOLAUS. That's what you say, but not what you do.
DAVID. So how do I disadvantage myself?
CRITOLAUS. Because you believe everyone equally.
DAVID. Shouldn't I trust my friends?
CRITOLAUS. Those you think are friends are really enemies.
DAVID. Heaven forbid!
CRITOLAUS. When they're with you they flatter you, but they slander you behind your back.
DAVID. If I find that out I'll leave them.
CRITOLAUS. I'm afraid you won't find it out without endangering yourself.
DAVID. I'll be like Argus, so that they won't deceive me.
CRITOLAUS. It's too late, you've already fallen into their trap.
DAVID. But I'm still free.
CRITOLAUS. You're physically free, but financially trapped.
DAVID. I don't feel any injury at all yet.
CRITOLAUS. You'll notice it like the Trojans, too late.
DAVID. If you're a friend, tell me how I can be on my guard more satisfactorily.
CRITOLAUS. But please don't give me away to them.
DAVID. I'll be as quiet as that stone.
CRITOLAUS. They've made a pact to fleece you as much as they can.
DAVID. They'll be prevented from doing that, because I've got very little left to give.
CRITOLAUS. If you lose that little bit you'd be completely ruined. Leave them.
DAVID. I won't associate with them any longer.

117. DE MONASTERIO ET RELIGIONIS INGRESSV

Georgius et Hermannus

GEORGIVS. Estne tibi praefixum, quo pacto senium ages?
HERMANNVS. Est praescriptum diutissime.
GEORGIVS. Ipse adhuc incertus sum, quam subeam senii conditionem.
HERMANNVS. Praescire illud deceret tanquam metam in quam curritur.
GEORGIVS. Quo studio senectutem tu transiges?
HERMANNVS. Pietatis studio et religionis.
GEORGIVS. Fouebis in senio cultum religionis?
HERMANNVS. Sic stat sententia.
GEORGIVS. Monachine assumes personam?
HERMANNVS. Cuculla me uestiam.
GEORGIVS. Habitus maxime conuenit senili corpori.
HERMANNVS. Qui id putas?
GEORGIVS. Nam senectutem frigidam calere facit.
HERMANNVS. Ob id eam non induam.
GEORGIVS. Qua spe ductus religionem ingredieris?
HERMANNVS. Ob uitae consequendum commeatum.
GEORGIVS. Pessimam habes propositi metam.
HERMANNVS. Plurimi tamen ducti ea causa mundo se abdicant.
GEORGIVS. Satius esset coenobia illos non inuisere.
HERMANNVS. Emanere eorum gulae non conferret.
GEORGIVS. Prodesset autem animae.
HERMANNVS. Corporis gerunt curam, animam Deo committunt.
GEORGIVS. Deo, non uentri ut seruiatur, monasterium est ingrediendum.
HERMANNVS. Hui, indulgendum est nonnihil et gulae.
GEORGIVS. Quae te Erinys agitat, quod nunc temporis monachatum cogitas?

117. THE MONASTERY, AND ENTERING THE RELIGIOUS LIFE

Georgius and Hermannus

GEORGIUS. Have you decided how you'll spend your old age?
HERMANNUS. It's been determined for a long time.
GEORGIUS. I'm still unsure what circumstances I'll spend my old age in.
HERMANNUS. It would be good to know that, it's the goal we're running towards.
GEORGIUS. What way will you pass your old age?
HERMANNUS. I'll devote myself to holiness and religion.
GEORGIUS. Are you going to cultivate religion in your old age?
HERMANNUS. That's what I intend.
GEORGIUS. Will you become a monk?
HERMANNUS. I'll put on the cowl.
GEORGIUS. The clothing is very well suited to the ageing body.
HERMANNUS. Why do you think that?
GEORGIUS. Because it warms up cold old age.
HERMANNUS. That's not the reason I'm going to put it on.
GEORGIUS. What hope is leading you to enter religion?
HERMANNUS. The hope of getting enough to live on.
GEORGIUS. That's the worst reason for that way of life.
HERMANNUS. And yet many people leave the world influenced by that reason.
GEORGIUS. It would be better for them not to enter monasteries.
HERMANNUS. Staying out wouldn't help their stomachs.
GEORGIUS. But it would be good for their souls.
HERMANNUS. They take care of their bodies, and commit their souls to God.
GEORGIUS. You should go into monastery to serve God, not your stomach.
HERMANNUS. Oh, your stomach has to be indulged sometimes too!
GEORGIUS. What madness has possessed you that you're thinking of the monastery now?

HERMANNVS. Ardeo illius uitae desiderio, qui fiat ignoro.

GEORGIVS. Conspicisne quomodo passim nunc monachi solitas deponunt personas?

HERMANNVS. [G5r] Audio quod undique se nudant cucullis.

GEORGIVS. Non frueris illorum insania, et detestaris monasticam uitam?

HERMANNVS. Non cito fugiendum est, quod execrantur homines nihili.

GEORGIVS. At expertis credendum, religiosam uitam commutant mundana, tanquam meliori.

HERMANNVS. Ipsi uoluptate delectantur, ideo in mundum redeunt, quo ipsa potiantur uberius.

---

1 monasterio] monasterii A C | 7 Praescire] Prescrire A | 15 Habitus] Is habitus A | 24 illos] illa A | 41–45 nihili … uberius.] nihili. A

118. NON OMNES DOCTOS ESSE, QUI CAPITE REDIMITI SUNT RUBEO TEGMINE

Iupiter et Ludolphus

IVPITER. Hodie aliquid uidi, quod portenti loco habeo.

LVDOLPHVS. Ecquid istud fuit?

IVPITER. Fortassis tibi non nouum.

LVDOLPHVS. Dicam, postquam audiero.

IVPITER. Imberbem adolescentem, magistri opertum diademate.

LVDOLPHVS. Quid tecum tacitus cogitabas?

IVPITER. Vix adultum in litteris tantum profecisse.

LVDOLPHVS. Stultus cogitatus fuit.

IVPITER. Prudenter uoluebam hoc mente, nam multos noui annis pluribus confectos, et nondum illum erant magistratum adepti.

LVDOLPHVS. Vnde sciebas istum in peritia longe progressum?

IVPITER. Capitis redimiculum id me docuit.

LVDOLPHVS. Aestimas tu ab amictu eruditum?

HERMANNUS. I have a really burning desire for that life, I don't know why.
GEORGIUS. Don't you see how monks everywhere now are giving up the state of life they've been accustomed to?
HERMANNUS. I hear they're putting off their cowls everywhere.
GEORGIUS. Won't you profit from their folly and abjure the monastic life?
HERMANNUS. You shouldn't avoid what worthless people detest.
GEORGIUS. But you have to trust those who've tried it; they're exchanging the religious life for life in the world, as being the better life.
HERMANNUS. They're attracted by pleasure, so they go back into the world so as to have it.

118. NOT EVERYONE WHO WEARS A RED CAP IS LEARNED

Jupiter and Ludolphus

JUPITER. I saw something today that I thought was quite extraordinary.
LUDOLPHUS. And what was that?
JUPITER. It may not be new to you.
LUDOLPHUS. I'll tell you after I've heard it.
JUPITER. A beardless youth, wearing a master's cap.
LUDOLPHUS. What did you think to yourself about that?
JUPITER. That somebody not grown up had made great progress in his studies.
LUDOLPHUS. That was a stupid thing to think.
JUPITER. I thought about it carefully, because I know a lot of people who are quite old and who still haven't got their MA.
LUDOLPHUS. How did you know that he had made great progress in knowledge?
JUPITER. His headgear told me.
LUDOLPHUS. Do you judge people to be learned on the basis of what they wear?

IVPITER. Quid alias loquitur illud capitis uelamen, quam hominis ingenuam doctrinam?

LVDOLPHVS. Saepe inscitiae est lenocinium, non eruditionis index.

IVPITER. O quantum hactenus spe uana me lactatum uideo.

LVDOLPHVS. Quomodo tibi impositum est?

IVPITER. Prosequutus sum honore et laude omnes capite uelatos insigniter.

LVDOLPHVS. Ah, rerum humanarum rudis es.

IVPITER. Qui ipse sciuissem eos inscios, quum tiara prodirent erudita?

LVDOLPHVS. Nostin adagium, 'Narthecophori multi, Bacchi uero pauci'?

IVPITER. Prouerbii quid istud est?

LVDOLPHVS. Multi aliud apparent quam intus sunt.

IVPITER. Vnde tu pe- [G5v] riculum sumis alterius eruditionis?

LVDOLPHVS. Si multa docet uel docte agit.

IVPITER. Etiamsi magisterii pilleolo non sit opertus?

LVDOLPHVS. Hedera uiridis uinum nihil commendat, ita neque amictus pretiosus animi nobilitatem.

---

1 rubeo tegmine.] rubeo. A | 11 profecisse] profecisse potuisse A | 13 hoc mente] hoc in mente A | 37–38 nihil commendat, ita … nobilitatem.] nihil commendat. A

119. QVIBVS SIT VTENDVM VERBIS DVM ALIQVID A PRAECEPTORE FLAGITATVR

Marcus et Nero

MARCVS. Instar folii trepido dum praeceptor mihi est conueniendus.

NERO. Cur tremis? Estne tantus tyrannis?

MARCVS. Non, sed aliud mihi tremorem incutit.

NERO. Audaculus tamen homo soles esse.

MARCVS. Apud praeceptorem mihi semper animus in pedes labitur.

NERO. Verecundari decet discipulum apud instructorem suum.

JUPITER. What does that headgear mean, if not that the person is educated?

LUDOLPHUS. It often conceals ignorance, rather than denoting learning.

JUPITER. Oh, I've really been led on by false expectations!

LUDOLPHUS. How have you been deceived?

JUPITER. I've honoured and praised everyone who wears distinguished headgear.

LUDOLPHUS. Oh, you're ignorant in the ways of the world!

JUPITER. How could I have known that they're ignorant, if they go about with an academic cap on?

LUDOLPHUS. Do you know the proverb, 'There are plenty of Bacchantes, but not many Bacchuses'?

JUPITER. What does that proverb mean?

LUDOLPHUS. That a lot of people look different from what they are inside.

JUPITER. How do you judge how learned someone is?

LUDOLPHUS. If he can teach you a lot, or behaves in a learned way.

JUPITER. Even if he doesn't wear a master's cap?

LUDOLPHUS. Green ivy doesn't mean good wine, and in the same way, distinguished clothing doesn't mean that someone is distinguished in mind.

119. WHAT WORDS TO USE WHEN ASKING THE TEACHER FOR SOMETHING

Marcus and Nero

MARCUS. I shake like a leaf whenever I have to go up to the teacher.

NERO. Why do you tremble? Is he a real tyrant?

MARCUS. No, it's something else that strikes terror into me.

NERO. Yet you're normally a courageous fellow.

MARCUS. When I'm with the teacher my heart always sinks into my boots.

NERO. It's right for a pupil to show modesty in the presence of his teacher.

MARCVS. Vereor ideo, Latine nescio ut decet loqui.
NERO. Non te labentem lingua secus docet?
MARCVS. Instruit quidem, sed semper asinum me uocat, ubi loquendo cado.
NERO. Sic incutit tibi inscitiae pudorem.
MARCVS. Verax es, nusquam nisi apud eum sermonis sollicitus sum.
NERO. Eo pacto quandoque integre Latine loqui disces, et minus errare.
MARCVS. Ea spe ducor.
NERO. Ista non frustraberis confidentia.
MARCVS. Certiorem me redde quomodo precabor ab ipso exeundi ueniam dum cacaturio?
NERO. 'Rogo ueniam exonerandi uentrem.'
MARCVS. Dum urina urgeor?
NERO. 'Precor facultatem ad euacuandam uesicam.'
MARCVS. Quando domi mihi est manendum?
NERO. 'Opto consensum emanendi e gymnasio, per occupationes adesse nequeo.'
MARCVS. Si mihi ad prandium est uocandus praeceptor?
NERO. 'Colende praeceptor, parentes mei te in prandium, uel [G6r] cenam, conuiuam petunt.'
MARCVS. Excusaturus me quod non interfui lectioni per parentum iussa?
NERO. 'Ignoscas, oro, colende praeceptor, meae absentiae, quia praesto esse non potui, per parentum negotia.'

19–20 disces … errare.] disces. A

120. DE OVIS COLLIGENDIS CIRCA PASCHATIS FERIAS

Aristophorus et Buttubatta

ARISTOPHORVS. Quid struis? Suppingis tu calceos?
BVTTVBATTA. Suppingo, ita pecuniam mihi seruo.
ARISTOPHORVS. Quam pecuniam?
BVTTVBATTA. Dandam suppactori calceario.

MARCUS. That's why I'm frightened, I can't speak Latin properly.
NERO. Doesn't he correct you when you make a mistake?
MARCUS. He does, but he always calls me an ass when I make a mistake in talking.
NERO. That way he drives the shame of being ignorant into you.
MARCUS. You're right, I'm never anxious about what to say unless I'm with him.
NERO. That way you'll learn to speak Latin faultlessly some day, and make fewer mistakes.
MARCUS. That's the hope that encourages me.
NERO. That belief won't be in vain.
MARCUS. Tell me how I ask him for permission to go out when I need a crap.
NERO. 'I beg leave to empty my bowels.'
MARCUS. And when I need to urinate?
NERO. 'I ask permission to empty my bladder.'
MARCUS. And when I have to stay at home?
NERO. 'I would like you to allow me to stay away from school; my business does not allow me to be present.'
MARCUS. If I have to invite the teacher to lunch?
NERO. 'Respected teacher, my parents ask you to be their guest at lunch, or at dinner.'
MARCUS. If I'm excusing myself for not being at my lessons because of what my parents told me to do?
NERO. 'Respected teacher, please forgive my absence, because I was unable to be present, owing to my parents' business.'

120. COLLECTING EGGS AT EASTER TIME

Aristophorus and Buttubatta

ARISTOPHORUS. What are you making? Are you repairing your shoes?
BUTTUBATTA. Yes, that way I'll save the money.
ARISTOPHORUS. What money?
BUTTUBATTA. The money to give the cobbler.

ARISTOPHORVS. Veteres quid resarcis calceos? Mercare nouos.
BVTTVBATTA. Aere laboro.
ARISTOPHORVS. Tantum bene haberes argenti.
BVTTVBATTA. Crumenam meam potius te nosco.
ARISTOPHORVS. Est tibi animus aliquo proficiscendi, quod calceos reficis?
BVTTVBATTA. Faciam iter rus uersus ad dies aliquot.
ARISTOPHORVS. Ruri quid exequeris?
BVTTVBATTA. Hoc tempore annuo rusticari soleo.
ARISTOPHORVS. Etiam emolumentum consequi?
BVTTVBATTA. Immo, integri mensis uictum.
ARISTOPHORVS. Commeatus iste quis est?
BVTTVBATTA. Ouorum magnam copiam congrego.
ARISTOPHORVS. Multitudinem ouorum, an apud saepes olentium?
BVTTVBATTA. Ista palatum meum non delectant.
ARISTOPHORVS. Colligisne oua gallinacea?
BVTTVBATTA. Coaceruo utique a rusticanis mulierculis.
ARISTOPHORVS. Cantas ante fores? Vel precaris instar mendici?
BVTTVBATTA. Cano hymnum, quem uocant 'Christe qui lux'.
ARISTOPHORVS. Iubent etiam quandoque ab ostio te abire immunem?
BVTTVBATTA. Saepe, sed blandior ipsis, quousque stipem porrigunt.
ARISTOPHORVS. Nihil praeter oua tibi praebent?
BVTTVBATTA. Nonnunquam et pingue farcimen.
ARISTOPHORVS. Solesne comitatus ire collectum oua?
BVTTVBATTA. Interdum solus, ubi Theseus mihi defuerit.
ARISTOPHORVS. Quid si me socium sumeres itineris?
BVTTVBATTA. Placebit mihi.
ARISTOPHORVS. Animo et meo arridet. [G6v]

---

7 suppactori] suppactatori A | 37 Theseus] Thaeseus A B C

ARISTOPHORUS. Why are you mending old shoes? Buy new ones.
BUTTUBATTA. I'm strapped for cash.
ARISTOPHORUS. You ought to have enough money for that.
BUTTUBATTA. I know my purse better than you do.
ARISTOPHORUS. Are you intending to go off somewhere, that you're repairing your shoes?
BUTTUBATTA. I'm making a trip to the country for a few days.
ARISTOPHORUS. What will you do in the country?
BUTTUBATTA. I go to the country at this time every year.
ARISTOPHORUS. Is that to make money?
BUTTUBATTA. Indeed – a whole month's food.
ARISTOPHORUS. What kind of provisions are they?
BUTTUBATTA. I gather a great number of eggs.
ARISTOPHORUS. A great quantity of eggs – on the dungheaps?
BUTTUBATTA. Those 'eggs' don't appeal to my taste.
ARISTOPHORUS. Do you collect hens' eggs?
BUTTUBATTA. Indeed I do; I collect them from peasant women.
ARISTOPHORUS. Do you sing at the doors, or do you beg like a beggar?
BUTTUBATTA. I sing the hymn called 'Christ, who art the light and day'.
ARISTOPHORUS. Do they sometimes tell you to go away from their doors empty-handed?
BUTTUBATTA. Often, but I flatter them until they offer me something.
ARISTOPHORUS. Don't they give you anything apart from eggs?
BUTTUBATTA. Sometimes a fat sausage as well.
ARISTOPHORUS. Do you usually go with someone else to collect your eggs?
BUTTUBATTA. I sometimes go alone, if I have no companion.
ARISTOPHORUS. What about taking me as a travelling-companion?
BUTTUBATTA. I'd like that.
ARISTOPHORUS. It attracts me, too.

121. NUSQVAM NVNC TVTAM ESSE FIDEM

Iodocus et Matthaeus

IODOCVS. Lamentarisne?

MATTHAEVS. Non lamentarer? Sanguinem paene flerem.

IODOCVS. Accidit tibi quippiam exitii?

MATTHAEVS. Ah, mali magna turba.

IODOCVS. Impartias mihi uerbis ut tibi condoleam.

MATTHAEVS. Tuum nihil mihi proderit condolere.

IODOCVS. Solacium est in miseriis amicus compatiens.

MATTHAEVS. Mallem ego iuuantem quam contristantem.

IODOCVS. Detege mihi moerorem.

MATTHAEVS. Fides pollicita mihi non seruatur.

IODOCVS. Quid promissi tibi est factum?

MATTHAEVS. Adminiculum uictus totius uitae meae.

IODOCVS. Ecastor, si factum fuisset secutum uerba, in caelo esses.

MATTHAEVS. Nunc autem et a spe et promisso decidi.

IODOCVS. Animum ne despondeas, si quid pollicitum est, forte belle seruabitur.

MATTHAEVS. Quantum intelligo, facta non sequentur uerba.

IODOCVS. Nescis diuitum animos? Volunt sibi supplicari.

MATTHAEVS. Precatus sat sum.

IODOCVS. Ores demum per amiculos, isti ocius exaudientur.

MATTHAEVS. Rete tendam per amicissimos.

IODOCVS. Eos mitte qui isti sunt intimi qui promisit.

MATTHAEVS. Cogitaram id antea diu.

IODOCVS. Verum ne differas, nam semper nocuit differre paratis, et mora sua cuilibet est nociua.

121. NO ONE EVER KEEPS PROMISES NOW

Iodocus and Matthaeus

IODOCUS. Are you wailing?
MATTHAEUS. Why shouldn't I? I could almost weep blood.
IODOCUS. Has something disastrous happened to you?
MATTHAEUS. Oh, a great deal of evil.
IODOCUS. Tell me about it so as I can sympathize with you.
MATTHAEUS. Your sympathy won't be any help to me.
IODOCUS. A sympathetic friend is a consolation in sadness.
MATTHAEUS. I'd prefer someone who would help me to someone who would sadden me.
IODOCUS. Tell me why you're sad.
MATTHAEUS. A promise that was made to me isn't being kept.
IODOCUS. What kind of promise was made to you?
MATTHAEUS. A contribution towards my living expenses for the whole of my life.
IODOCUS. Good Lord, if what was said was delivered, you'd be in clover.
MATTHAEUS. But now my hopes of the promise have been dashed.
IODOCUS. Don't be downhearted, if you've been promised something the promise may actually be kept.
MATTHAEUS. As far as I understand, the deeds are not going to match the words.
IODOCUS. Don't you know what rich people are like? They want to be entreated.
MATTHAEUS. I've begged enough.
IODOCUS. Then ask through your friends, they'll be listened to more readily.
MATTHAEUS. I'll cast a net, using people I'm very friendly with.
IODOCUS. Send those who are really close to the person who made the promise.
MATTHAEUS. I'd already thought about that.
IODOCUS. But don't put it off, for 'delay is ever fatal to those who are prepared', and 'anyone who delays harms himself'.

MATHAEVS. Quamprimum opportunum fuerit, periculum faciam.

IODOCVS. Faxit Deus ut alea tibi prospere cadat.

MATHAEVS. De isto mihi optato gratiam habe.

---

10 iuuantem] inuantem A

122. QVOD OBSEQVIVM AMICOS, VERITAS ODIVM PARIAT

Gisbertus et Cornelius

GISBERTVS. Terentii comoediae suntne unquam tibi lectae?

CORNELIVS. Saepiuscule, et adhuc indies leguntur.

GISBERTVS. Excerpis etiam elegantiora quaedam dicta? [G7r]

CORNELIVS. In hoc raptitius est mihi liber.

GISBERTVS. 'Obsequium amicos, ueritas odium parit', cuius comoediae est uerbum?

CORNELIVS. Primae, scilicet *Andriae.*

GISBERTVS. Videturne tibi esse poeticum dictum?

CORNELIVS. Nequaquam, sed Delphicum oraculum.

GISBERTVS. Paris tu semper amicos obsequendo?

CORNELIVS. Inimicos nunquam nactus sum officio.

GISBERTVS. Obsequia tamen saepe ingrata sunt.

CORNELIVS. Ingrata quae sunt, non merentur obsequia dici.

GISBERTVS. Verum pessimi sunt homines, qui obsequiis irritantur ad nocendum, ut inquit Cicero.

CORNELIVS. Istos bestias, non homines dicerem.

GISBERTVS. Ego ipsis beluam praeponerem.

CORNELIVS. Quare?

GISBERTVS. Bestiae agnoscunt pietatem exhibitam eis.

CORNELIVS. Canes praecipue grati sunt.

GISBERTVS. Miserum est sane homini obsequendo operam ludere.

CORNELIVS. Praestaret otiosum fuisse.

GISBERTVS. Sed quo modo ueritas parit odium?

CORNELIVS. Dum alteri dicitur quod ipsum aceto perfundit.

GISBERTVS. Tangitur hominibus ulcus ueritate?

MATTHAEUS. I'll make the attempt as soon as the time is right.
IODOCUS. May God grant that it works out favourably for you.
MATTHAEUS. Thanks for those good wishes.

122. THAT COMPLAISANCE MAKES FRIENDS, AND TRUTH PRODUCES HATE

Gisbertus and Cornelius

GISBERTUS. Have you ever read Terence's comedies?
CORNELIUS. I have, pretty often, and I still read them every day.
GISBERTUS. Do you write out any particularly elegant phrases?
CORNELIUS. I have a notebook for that.
GISBERTUS. Which comedy does 'Complaisance makes friends, and truth produces hate' come from?
CORNELIUS. From the first, *Andria*.
GISBERTUS. Does it strike you as a poetic fiction?
CORNELIUS. Not at all, it's a Delphic oracle.
GISBERTUS. Do you always make friends by deferring to them?
CORNELIUS. I've never made enemies by being respectful.
GISBERTUS. But complaisance is sometimes unwelcome.
CORNELIUS. What's unwelcome doesn't deserve to be called complaisance.
GISBERTUS. And yet those who are driven by complaisance to do damage are the worst of people, as Cicero says.
CORNELIUS. I'd call them animals, not humans.
GISBERTUS. I'd rate a wild animal more highly than them.
CORNELIUS. Why?
GISBERTUS. Because animals recognize kindness shown to them.
CORNELIUS. Dogs are especially grateful.
GISBERTUS. But it's sad to be deferential to a person to no avail.
CORNELIUS. It would be better to have done nothing at all.
GISBERTUS. But how does the truth produce hate?
CORNELIUS. When you say something very wounding to someone.
GISBERTUS. Are people really irked by the truth?

CORNELIVS. Multis uero sermone mouetur bilis et anagyris.

GISBERTVS. Illorum salus est desperanda (teste Cicerone) quorum aures sunt occlusae ueritati.

CORNELIVS. Per Herculem nocuit semper suo nutu, et non aliorum consilio singula gerere.

30–34 anagyris … gerere.] anagyris. A

123. CONVIVIVM BACCHANALE, SIVE VLTIMA CENA DIERVM LVPERCALIVM

Hospes, Vxor, Puer, Seruus, Conuiuae, Martinus et Arnoldus, Citharoedus

HOSPES. O vxor, meum corculum, in cenam quid parabis obsonii?

VXOR. Nihil, nisi huius prandii reliquias mensae imponam.

HOSPES. Id dedeceret nihil habere carnis recentis et uix elixae.

VXOR. Quid ob unicam [G7v] cenam obsonatum irem?

HOSPES. Conuiuas nonnullos uocaui, hos oportet lautis excipere lancibus.

VXOR. Quos?

HOSPES. Dominum Martinum et Magistrum Arnoldum, filii nostri instructorem, tum fortassis et umbrae aliqui accedent.

VXOR. Qui isti essent umbrae?

HOSPES. Personati qui amicos hoc uesperi inuisunt.

VXOR. Laruis opertis hac nocte limen nostrum non patebit.

HOSPES. Nunc meum deliciolum, focum instrue carne elixanda, et ueru gallinas duas in cenam nobis coque.

VXOR. Seruum iube ut a laniis armum ouillum ferat.

HOSPES. Heus tu serue, ubi latitas?

SERVVS. Adsum, here.

HOSPES. In macellum i celeri gressu, ac carnis ouinae fer talenta sex.

SERVVS. Ibo ac uelox.

VXOR. Ego enectum gallinas uado.

HOSPES. Id facito.

PVER. Noctescit, pater, feram uinum in tempore; non tutum erit in tenebris uicatim cursitare.

CORNELIUS. Being told the truth makes a lot of them angry.

GISBERTUS. 'We must despair of the safety of those whose ears are closed to truth,' as Cicero says.

CORNELIUS. Indeed, it's always been harmful to do everything exactly as you wish, and not to follow others' advice.

123. A BACCHANALIAN BANQUET, OR THE LAST DINNER OF SHROVETIDE.

Host, Wife, Boy, Servant, Guests, Martinus and Arnoldus, Lute-player.

HOST. My dear wife, what will you be making for dinner?

WIFE. Nothing. I'm just going to put out the left-overs from this lunch.

HOST. It wouldn't be right not to have any fresh meat, freshly boiled.

WIFE. Why should I go shopping for a single dinner?

HOST. I've invited a few guests. We have to give them some good things to eat.

WIFE. Who?

HOST. Martin, and Master Arnold, our son's teacher. Then a few uninvited guests may turn up, too.

WIFE. Who might those uninvited guests be?

HOST. Maskers visiting their friends this evening.

WIFE. Our door won't be open to maskers tonight.

HOST. Now, darling, stoke up the fire to boil the meat, and spit-roast two chickens for us for dinner.

WIFE. Order the servant to fetch a shoulder of lamb from the butcher's.

HOST. Hey, Servant, where are you?

SERVANT. Here I am, Master.

HOST. Go quickly to the market and get six pounds of lamb.

SERVANT. I'll go quickly.

WIFE. I'm going to kill the chickens.

HOST. Do.

BOY. Night's falling, Father. I'll get the wine before it gets too late; it won't be safe to walk the streets in the dark.

HOSPES. Hic pecuniae sume in manus quattuor mensurarum, quamlibet sedecim mercaberis obolis, dicas matri ut singula percoquat, ego mox a somno surgam

PVER. Efficiam quod fiat ut iubes.

VXOR. Expergiscere marite, statim aderunt conuiuae, quinta sonuit.

HOSPES. Nunc me erigam. Serue, uade uisum ubi morentur inuitati a me, an emanere uelint.

SERVVS. En alias testudineo ueniunt gradu.

HOSPES. Nunc tu mensam ocius singulis para et instrue.

SERVVS. Dicto citius instructam reddam.

HOSPES. Gratulor uestro aduentui, mei conuiuae.

CONVIVAE. Sit tibi gratia.

HOSPES. Vbi nam latet tempus Lupercale?

CONVIVAE. Ignoramus, abire nosque deserere parat.

HOSPES. Prius in ipso hilarem ducemus compotatiunculam.

CONVIVAE. Ideo huc detulimus pedes, et istud nostrum uilli precamur boni consulas.

HOSPES. Hui nimium est, suffecisset medium, quis epotabit?

CONVIVAE. Ebibemus sine su- [G8r] dore, prolixam adhuc agemus compotationem ante digressum.

HOSPES. Abluite singuli manus et discumbite, in tempore incipiamus quo hilaritati sat restet spatii.

CONVIVAE. Vt tibi fuerit uisum.

HOSPES. Heus puer, ades dum, consecra cenam.

PVER. Benedicite.

CONVIVAE. Dominus.

PVER. Quicquid appositum est et quicquid apponetur benedicat nobis ille qui sua largitate pascit uniuersa. In nomine Patris et Filii et Spiritus Sancti.

CONVIVAE. Amen.

HOSPES. Nunc in cibum manus iniicite, quoad lautiora afferentur.

CONVIVAE. Nostri muneris non erimus nescii.

HOST. Take this money for four measures, whatever you can get for About sixteen Hellers. Tell your mother to cook everything, I'll soon get up.
BOY. I'll do what has to be done as you instruct.
WIFE. Get up, Husband. The guests will soon be here, the clock's struck six.
HOST. I'll get up now. Servant, go and see where the people I invited are, or whether they intend to stay away.
SERVANT. Look, they're coming at a snail's pace.
HOST. Now lay the table quickly with everything.
SERVANT. I'll set it as quick as a wink.
HOST. I'm pleased you have arrived, my guests.
GUESTS. Thank you.
HOST. Where is Shrovetide now?
GUESTS. We don't know, it's getting ready to leave us and go.
HOST. First, we'll have a cheerful little drinking-party in its honour.
GUESTS. That's why we've come here. We hope you'll like this drop of wine of ours.
HOST. Hey, that's too much, half would have been enough. Who's going to drink it all?
GUESTS. We'll drink it, no problem. We're going to have a long drinking-party before we leave.
HOST. Everyone wash their hands and sit down. We'll make a prompt start so as to leave plenty of time to enjoy ourselves.
GUESTS. As you see fit.
HOST. Hey, Boy, come here. Bless the meal.
BOY. Benedicite.
GUESTS. Dominus.
BOY. Now may he who feeds all creatures through his bounty bless what has been served and what is about to be served. In the name of the Father, and of the Son, and of the Holy Spirit.
GUESTS. Amen.
HOST. Now help yourselves to the food, till finer dishes are served.
GUESTS. We won't be reluctant to do our duty.

HOSPES. Calices reple uino tu serue, ut stas tanquam Marpesia cautes?

MARTINVS. Bibere plus appeto quam edere, hunc ego exsorbebo calicem.

VXOR. Interbibendum est, ne in stomacho cibus putrescat, marite hoc te salutabo poculo.

HOSPES. Tibi non incommodet ipsius haustus.

ARNOLDVS. Et ego Martine hunc scyphum tibi propino.

MARTINVVS. Saluti sit tibi.

HOSPES. Vt ita Chrysippum agitis? Non delectat uos cibus?

CONVIVAE. Iuuat plurimum, sed esurimus modice.

HOSPES. Hoc uitrum uolo quisque ordine exsiccet, ego glaciem secabo, et classicum canam.

CONVIVAE. Et nos post te, ipsum elambemus.

HOSPES. Age, hunc tibi propono Martine, uide ut aequali mihi respondeas haustu.

MARTINVS. Non recuso.

HOSPES. Vbi scyphus sistit? Cur non obambulat? Puellulae istae siti pereunt.

ARNOLDVS. Epotauimus ipsum omnes, in uxore tua moratur.

VXOR. Ego ipsum exhauriam ubi hunc bolum peredero.

HOSPES. Serue, tolle haec ac alia affer edulia, muta quadras et mundas redde.

VXOR. Marite, excipe conuiuas, ut moris est, ad carnes tostas.

HOSPES. Aduentus uester me delectat, ad has gallinas [G8v] et buccellam carnis porcinae in ueru paratam uos uocaui, oro aequo accipite animo. Si parcus et modicus est cibus, largior erit potus.

CONVIVAE. O hospes, apparatum lautiorem quam opus fuisset fecisti, non debueras nostri causa diem festum instituisse.

HOSPES. Tempori inseruiendum est nonnihil, dierum licentia et patinarum exigit lautitiam. Arnolde, hunc calicem ad imum usque tibi praebibo.

ARNOLDVS. Prosit tibi.

HOST. Fill the cups with wine again, Servant – why are you standing there like a block of stone?
MARTINUS. I'm keener to drink than to eat; I'll empty this cup.
WIFE. You must drink whilst eating, so as the food doesn't rot in your stomach. Husband, I drink this cup to you.
HOST. May the draught not harm you.
ARNOLDUS. And Martin, I drink this goblet to your health.
MARTINUS. Your good health.
HOST. Why are you holding back like that? Don't you like the food?
GUESTS. We like it very much, but we're not very hungry.
HOST. I want everyone to drain this glass in turn. I'll break the ice and make a start.
GUESTS. And after you we'll drink it up.
HOST. I drink this to you, Martinus, make sure you drink the same amount to me.
MARTINUS. I won't refuse.
HOST. Where is the goblet? Why's it not passing around? Those girls are dying of thirst.
ARNOLDUS. We've all drunk from it, it's stopped at your wife.
WIFE. I'll finish it after I've eaten this mouthful.
HOST. Servant, take these dishes away and bring on others. Change the plates and bring back clean ones.
WIFE. Husband, serve our guests to roast meats, as is the custom.
HOST. I'm delighted that you've come. I invited you to eat these chickens and this piece of spit-roasted pork, and I beg you to accept them and be satisfied with them. Though the food may be sparing, the drink will be more plentiful.
GUESTS. You have provided finer fare than was necessary, our host. There was no need for you to have organized a party on our account.
HOST. We must observe the season to some extent. The lack of restraint of this time demands sumptuous dishes. Arnoldus, I drink this cup to the bottom as a toast to you.
ARNOLDVS. Your good health!

MARTINVS. Hoc poculum tibi praebibo, ut et tu deinde exsorbeas.

ARNOLDVS. Praebibitis nulli quam mihi uideo. Quid monstri alitis? Creditis me metam esse in quam dirigantur pocula, ut sagittae in scopum? Citharoede, hoc cyatho te adorior, ut nobis a cena dulcem exhibeas citharae pulsum.

CITHAROEDVS. Accipiam abs te libenter.

HOSPES. Serue, affer bellaria, uideo conuiuas anhelare choream.

MARTINVS. Nos uiri non, forte hae nymphae saliendi amore ardent.

HOSPES. Mox surgemus.

VXOR. Edant prius, ut ita maturare conaris?

ARNOLDVS. Quis usque ut uultur edere potest?

MARTINVS. Si uisum fuerit hospiti tollatur cibus.

HOSPES. Fiat. Puer, adsis, et hymnum postremum recense.

PVER. Gratias dicimus Deo trino in personis, uni in essentia, qui sua immensa potentia condidit omnia, gubernat uniuersa, qui nos indignos famulos hoc uesperi suo pauit munere, ipse nobis largiatur ut post hoc exilium secum in aeternum fruamur caelitum laetitia, suoque potiamur conspectu, per Iesum Christum.

CONVIVAE. Amen.

HOSPES. Habeo uobis conuiuae humanissimi gratiam, quod ad hoc conuiuiolum meum exiguum dignati sitis uenire, oro lubenti accipite animo quae praesto fuere, uice alia delicatiora exhibebo.

CONVIVAE. Grati erimus, et quandoque par pari referemus.

HOSPES. Ci- [H1r] tharoede, nunc fac resonare citharam.

CITHAROEDVS. Ludere nescio nisi cantus agrestes et rusticos, non regios.

HOSPES. Id refert nihil, nescis illud Bebelii, cuiuscumque fistulae cantus ualet amanti choreas?

CITHAROEDVS. Age, salite, ipse ludam.

MARTINVS. Ipse sat feci choreae, fessus sum.

MARTINUS. I drink this cup to you, so that you've got to drain it in turn.
ARNOLDUS. I see that you're not drinking to anyone other than me. What kind of a monster are you feeding? Do you think I'm the goal the cups are directed at, like arrows at a target? Lute-player, with this goblet I request you to let us hear the sweet throbbing of the lute after dinner.
LUTE-PLAYER. I'll accept it from you willingly.
HOST. Servant, bring on the desserts. I see the guests would like to dance.
MARTINUS. Not us men. Perhaps these girls are dying to dance.
HOST. We'll leave the table soon.
WIFE. Let them eat first. Why are you trying to hurry like that?
ARNOLDVS. Who can eat as much as a vulture?
MARTINVS. If the host sees fit, let the table be cleared.
HOST. Do so. Boy, come and say the final grace.
BOY. We give thanks to God, three in persons, one in essence, who in his immense power created all and governs all; who has fed us unworthy servants this evening by his kindness. May he grant that after this exile we may enjoy with him the bliss of those who dwell in Heaven, and that we may enjoy the sight of him. Through Jesus Christ.
GUESTS. Amen.
HOST. I thank you, my cultured guests, for being pleased to come to this poor little party of mine. I beg you to accept willingly what was available. Another time I'll offer you finer fare.
GUESTS. We'll be grateful, and some day we'll return the compliment.
HOST. Lute-player, now strike up the lute.
LUTE-PLAYER. All I can play are country songs, not royal ones.
HOST. That doesn't matter. Don't you know Bebel's proverb, 'the sound of anyone's flute is good enough for a lover to dance to'?
LUTE-PLAYER. Right then, dance, I'll play.
MARTINVS. I've danced enough, I'm tired.

HOSPES. Vxor, instrue rursus mensam scribiliginibus et aliis bellariis mellitis ac saccaro conditis.

VXOR. Omnia diu sunt parata.

HOSPES. Nunc uenite uos conuiuae ad has scribiligines, sumemus nocturnam commessationem, hora exigit. Si quem hoc halec delectat salsugine erutum, attingat.

CONVIVAE. Nunc praesto est ieiunium.

HOSPES. Cras in prandio rursus una auspicium sumemus temporis esurialis, in his meis aedibus, sicuti nunc inuicem peregimus dies Lupercales.

CONVIVAE. Tu uale in crastinum.

HOSPES. Valete et uos. Faxit Deus ut anno abhinc proximo rursus una simus, laetiores, et minus delictis contaminati, ac interim crebro.

CONVIVAE. Id dii superi nobis et tibi concedant.

FINIS.

24 i] ii A; 33 percoquat] percoquet A | 42 mei] mi A | 52–55 follows A; B and C omit l. 54. | 53 hilaritati] hilaritatis A | 72 scyphum] cyphum A B C | 82 scyphus] cyphus A B C | 95 est] et A | 134 scribiliginibus] stribiliginibus A B C | 137 scribiligines] stribiligines A B C | 143 peregimus] peregrimus A | 145 anno abhinc] anno ab hinc A C; anno hinc B

HOST. Wife, lay the table again with pastries and other desserts made with honey and sugar.

WIFE. Everything's been ready for ages.

HOST. Now come, you guests, and eat these pastries. We'll have a nighttime feast, the hour demands it. If anyone like this pickled herring, he should serve himself.

GUESTS. Now Lent is here.

HOST. Tomorrow at lunch we'll begin the time of fasting together, here in my house, just as we have now spent Shrovetide together.

GUESTS. Goodbye, till tomorrow.

HOST. And goodbye to you. May God grant that next year we may be together again, happier, and less stained by sins, and often in the meantime.

GUESTS. May the gods grant that to you and to us.

THE END.

Conuiuia

HERMANNVS SCHOTTENNIVS HESSVS

STVDIOSAE IVVENTVTI S. P. D.

QVAE renascuntur, nosti, tenera et studiosa iuuentus, immutantur paululum, nouique aliquid secunda natiuitate accipiunt. Sic homines per baptismum renati mundi ab originali peccato fiunt. Phoenix unica auis Arabiae igne seipsum comburens renascitur iunior et pulchrior. Vetuli serpentes pelliculam uetustam, per angustam arborem repentes, deponunt, tandemque a rugoso senio liberantur. Nihil usqueadeo est quod renascendo uel temporis progressu non immutetur, lepidiusque et candidius reddatur. Ideo et mihi nuper, quum hae confabulationes denuo a typographis essent excudendae, placuit ut prodirent elimatiores, locupletaeque triginta conuiuiis sequentibus. Conuiuia addidi, non collocutiones pueriles. Quicquid enim agitur inter homines, dum otiantur, poculis indulgetur, nam inde amicitia oritur, odium et maeror discutiuntur, hilaritas et beneuolentia mutua acquiruntur. Auxi his conuiuiis, grandibus dictis descriptis, ut et tu adolescas grandescasque sermone adultorum, non semper puerum sones loquendo.

Vale, Coloniae, Millesimo quingentesimo uigesimo sexto.

[H2r]

QVAE SEQVVNTVR CONVIVIA, accesserunt ab auctore anno. M. D. XXVI.

HERMANNUS SCHOTTENNIUS HESSUS

SENDS HIS FONDEST GREETINGS TO STUDIOUS YOUTH

Tender and studious youth, you know that all things that are reborn are changed slightly, and in their second birth take on something new. Thus human beings reborn through baptism are cleansed of original sin. The Phoenix, the only bird of Arabia, consumes itself in fire, and is reborn younger and more beautiful. Old snakes slough off their old skins by crawling through narrow gaps in trees, and are at last freed from wrinkled old age. There is nothing at all which rebirth or the advance of time does not alter and make fairer and more agreeable. In the same way recently, when these colloquies were due to be reprinted by the publisher, I decided they should come out more polished, and augmented by the thirty following *conuiuia*. I have added banquets, not dialogues of boys. For whatever goes on amongst men, when they take their leisure, when they enjoy a drink, this gives rise to friendship, hatred and sorrow are driven away; joy and mutual goodwill are achieved. I have added these banquets, written in grown-up language, so that you grow older and more mature using adult talk, and do not always sound like a boy when you speak.

Farewell, from Cologne, 1526.

THE *CONVIVIA* WHICH FOLLOW were added by the author in the year 1526.

1. CONVIVIVM TELESPHORIANVM SIVE ESVRIALE

Hospes, Vxor, Puer, Seruus, Conuiuae, Martinus, Arnoldus

HOSPES. Suntne obsonia mox percocta et matura esui?

VXOR. Ferme, iube sterni mensam.

HOSPES. Heus Puer, ubi latitas?

PVER. Adsum, here.

HOSPES. Mensam suo apparatu decorato. Statim conuiuae aderunt, nam prandendi hora imminet.

PVER. Expediam festinanter.

HOSPES. Tu Serue uinum prome hornum et bimum ac absinthio conditum.

SERVVS. Efficiam, Domine.

HOSPES. Cereuisiae quoque unum aut alterum poculum.

VXOR. Omnia edulia sat cocta sunt, accubitum iremus si adessent conuiuae.

HOSPES. Spero quod actutum aduenient. Ostium credo pulsant. I Puer, resera fores.

PVER. Ibo. En adestis, herus uos moratur.

CONVIVAE. Ipsi iam adsumus. Saluus sis, hospes noster, ut uales hoc esuriali tempore?

HOSPES. Valeo pugilice. Salui et uos sitis, uestrum aduentum desiderabam. Illico manus abluite et accumbite mensae.

CONVIVAE. Faciemus, primus tu accumbe.

HOSPES. Hic in sella mihi est locus. Puer, benedic prandium. [H2v]

PVER. Benedicite.

CONVIVAE. Dominus.

PVER. Quicquid appositum est apponeturque cibi et potus, benedicere et consecrare uelit dextera Christi, sumentibusque salubre reddere. In nomine Patris et Filii et Spiritus Sancti.

CONVIVAE. Amen.

PVER. Pater noster...

HOSPES. Orationem Dominicam et Salutationem Angelicam quisque secum oret. Nunc cibo fruimini, alius nunc est quam hesterno uesperi cibatus edendus.

CONVIVAE. Sic dierum conditio exigit.

HOSPES. Hoc iusculum pisarum exsorbete, conferet cerebro et stomacho non oberit.

1. A 'TELESPHORIAN' OR LENTEN BANQUET

Host, Wife, Boy, Servant, Guests, Martinus, Arnoldus

HOST. Are the dishes nearly cooked and ready to eat?

WIFE. Nearly. Order the table to be set.

HOST. Hey, Boy! Where are you?

BOY. Here I am, Master.

HOST. Lay the table with food. The guests will be here directly, it's nearly lunchtime.

BOY. I'll see to that very quickly.

HOST. And you, Servant, bring out the new wine and last year's, and wine flavoured with wormwood.

SERVANT. I will, sir.

HOST. And one or two glasses of beer.

WIFE. All the dishes are cooked, we could sit down if the guests were here.

HOST. I hope they'll arrive immediately. I think they're knocking at the door. Boy, go and open the door.

GUESTS. Here we are. Greetings to you, our host! How are you this Lenten season?

HOST. I'm fighting fit. Greetings to you, too, I was looking forward to your coming. Wash your hands straight away and sit down at the table.

GUESTS. We will, you sit down first.

HOST. My place is here in this chair. Boy, say grace.

BOY. Benedicite.

GUESTS. Dominus.

BOY. May Christ's hand be pleased to bless the food and drink that has been served and will be served, and make them beneficial to those who eat them. In the name of the Father, and of the Son, and of the Holy Spirit.

GUESTS. Amen.

BOY. Our Father ...

HOST. Let everyone say the Lord's Prayer and the Hail Mary privately. Now enjoy the food – we have to eat food of a different kind now than yesterday evening.

GUESTS. The nature of the season requires it.

HOST. Eat this pea soup, it's good for the brain, and it won't harm your stomach.

CONVIVAE. Proderit per Herculem, medebiturque dolori capitum nostrorum ex hesterna compotatione contracto.

HOSPES. Ideo imbibite ipsum dum calet et feruet. Nunc haleces has edite, elixas aut tostas.

CONVIVAE. Desidiosi non erimus.

HOSPES. Edite et bibite, uobis non ministrabo. Incommodabit uestro uentri, si a cibo quieueritis. Serue, aliud edulii affer, mundosque orbes redde. Nunc de hoc uino absinthio condito singuli primum facietis haustum, salubre est. Praebibo tibi, Martine, tu proximo tuo propines.

MARTINVS. Non obsit tibi bibenti. Hoc, Arnolde, tibi praebibo.

ARNOLDVS. Sit salutiferum.

HOSPES. Ordine quisque lambat de ipso. Vt sic abstemii estis? Neque potu neque cibo utimini alacriter. Forte hic cibus uos parum delectat?

CONVIVAE. Ab hesterna cena adhuc saturi sumus.

VXOR. Obsonia haec palato non adeo arrident, ut quae Lupercalibus diebus edimus.

MARTINVS. Tempori seruiendum est; cuticulam hactenus curauimus, nunc genium fraudare oportet.

HOSPES. Breue est tempus, homini sano curriculo abibit.

ARNOLDVS. Bene ualenti [H3r] et piscium copia abundanti, non his quibus panis nudus est rodendus.

VXOR. Diligenti Deum nihil est difficile.

MARTINVS. Verum est, nam ut Plautus inquit, 'Amor condimentum est, amara dulcia faciens.' Sed admiramur quis primus hoc esuriale tempus sanciuit.

HOSPES. Maiores nostri sanctique Patres Ecclesiae et Pontifices, in exemplum Prophetarum et Christi, qui se ieiunio macerarunt.

ARNOLDVS. Cur est uocatum tempus Telesphorianum?

HOSPES. Aiunt Telesphorum Papam Quadragesimam sic instituisse, ut ab Ecclesia peragitur.

ARNOLDVS. Quid prodest tamen?

GUESTS. It'll be good for us, indeed, and it'll help the headache we got from last night's drinking-party.

HOST. So sup it up while it's piping hot. Now eat these boiled or fried herrings.

GUESTS. We won't be slow to do that.

HOST. Eat and drink, I'm not going to serve you. It'll do your stomach harm if you don't keep eating food. Servant, bring on other food, and clean plates! Now each of you have a draught of this wine flavoured with wormwood, – it's healthy. I drink to you, Martinus; you drink to your neighbour.

MARTINUS. May the wine not harm you who drink it. Arnoldus, I drink this one to you.

ARNOLDUS. Your good health.

HOST. Everyone have a drink of it in turn. Why are you so restrained? You aren't eating or drinking up quickly. Does this food not please you much?

GUESTS. We're still full from last night's dinner.

WIFE. These dishes aren't as pleasing to the taste as what we eat during Shrovetide.

MARTINUS. We must observe the season. We've being doing ourselves well up till now, and now it's time to deny ourselves.

HOST. The time is short, it'll fly past for a healthy person.

ARNOLDUS. For someone healthy who has plenty of fish – not for those who are forced to nibble dry bread.

WIFE. To someone who loves God, nothing is hard.

MARTINUS. That's true, for as Plautus says, 'Love is a seasoning that makes bitter food sweet.' But we wonder who first ordained this time of fasting.

HOSTS. Our ancestors, and the holy Fathers of the Church and the Popes, after the example of the Prophets and Christ, who mortified themselves by fasting.

ARNOLDUS. Why's it called the 'Telesphorian' season?

HOST. They say that Pope Telesphorus established Lent in the form in which it's observed by the Church.

ARNOLDUS. But what good does it do?

HOSPES. Vitia corporis comprimit, animam saluat, uentri pestem, crumenae commodum et crapulae decoctionem affert.

MARTINVS. Cur non indictum est oleum, ut butyrum et lacteus cibus?

HOSPES. Lac et butyrum naturae sunt sanguineae, nam lac est sanguis uaccarum, colore tantum mutato, sed oleum nihil in se carni affine habet.

ARNOLDVS. Quare a cibis quibusdam arcemur, non autem ab aliquo potus genere?

HOSPES. Sic nostris placuit maioribus, et non tantum saginat potus ac cibus.

VXOR. Loquendo tempus teritis, et interim cibus frigore corrumpitur.

HOSPES. Quisque strenue edat et potitet, ipse nullius edulii sum cupidus, nam stomacho non admodum ualeo.

MARTINVS. Et nos parum bene ualemus.

HOSPES. Puer, tolle haec, et nuces, pira et ficus affer et libum mellis. Arnolde, hoc scypho te adorior.

ARNOLDVS. Bibe salubriter.

HOSPES. Puer, singula conde et hymnum postremum dicito.

PVER. Quicquid sumpsimus potus ac cibi, id nobis salutiferum reddat ille qui [H3v] unus est salus omnium.

CONVIVAE. Amen.

HOSPES. Vos conuiuae boni et aequi accipite quae praesto fuere, meliora obsonare non potuimus.

CONVIVAE. Tu gratiam habe.

HOSPES. Gratulor uestro aduentui.

CONVIVAE. Grati nostro nomine tibi sint superi.

HOSPES. Nunc uos amici, gratiarum actionum haustum bibite singuli.

CONVIVAE. Tu nunc uale, nos nostros repetemus penates; quandoque par referemus.

HOSPES. Diu relatum est.

---

2 Conuiuae] Conuiua B C | 53 saturi] saturati C | 69 Telesphorum] Telesphorianum B C | 89 scypho] cypho B C

HOST. It curbs the weaknesses of the body; it saves the soul; it's a nuisance to the stomach, beneficial to the purse, and it allows us to work off the effects of too much drink.

MARTINUS. Why isn't oil forbidden, like butter and milk products?

HOST. Milk and butter have the nature of blood, for milk is cows' blood, just changed in colour; but oil contains nothing related to meat.

ARNOLDUS. Why are we kept from certain foods, but not from any kind of drink?

HOST. That was what our ancestors agreed on; and drink doesn't nourish you as much as food does.

WIFE. You're wasting time talking, and meanwhile the food's going cold and spoiling.

HOST. Everyone eat and drink vigorously. I don't want any food, my stomach isn't feeling too well.

MARTINUS. We aren't terribly well either.

HOST. Boy, take these dishes away and bring on nuts, pears, figs and a honey-cake. Arnoldus, I salute you with this cup.

ARNOLDUS. Drink to your health.

HOST. Boy, put everything away and say the final grace.

BOY. May the food and drink we have eaten be made beneficial by him who alone is the salvation of all.

GUESTS. Amen.

HOSTS. You guests, be content with what has been served; we weren't able to buy anything better.

GUESTS. Thank you.

HOSTS. I am glad you came.

GUESTS. In our name may the Gods be good to you.

HOST. Now, friends, each of you drink this draught as a grace.

GUESTS. Goodbye, we're going back home. Some day we'll return the invitation.

HOST. It's been put off for a long time.

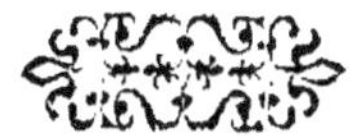

2. PYTHAGORICVM CONVIVIVM

Pythagoras hospes; Discipuli conuiuae

DISCIPVLI. Salute te impartimur plurima, uir sapientissime.

PYTHAGORAS. Eam et uobis opto.

DISCIPVLI. Esset nobis nonnihil tecum colloquendum, si audire uelles.

PYTHAGORAS. Audiam lubentissime, cur uenistis dicite.

DISCIPVLI. Adsumus cupidi litterarum, quas sub tua cupimus discere ferula, si in discipulos nos habere uelis.

PYTHAGORAS. In meam instructionem admitto nullum, nisi ipsius indolem et Mineruam sim exploratus.

DISCIPVLI. Quo tum ignotorum experimentum accipis ingenia qualia habeant?

PYTHAGORAS. Istud uestra refert nihil.

DISCIPVLI. Quibus infecunda contigit Minerua, eosne instruere laboras?

PYTHAGORAS. Illos colendos non suscipio, non minus ac agricola sterilem terram, quia laborem luderem.

DISCIPVLI. Non possent litteris imbui infeliciter nata ingenia?

PYTHAGORAS. Instruuntur opera magna, sed [H4r] profectu pusillo aut nullo. Agri enim non fertiles, etsi curantur, non tamen fruges proferunt.

DISCIPVLI. Precamur, colendissime philosophe, nos in tuorum discipulorum gregem suscipias.

PYTHAGORAS. De uestris ingeniis prius periculum sumam an apta sint litteris, tum instruendos assumam.

DISCIPVLI. Auscultabimus tuis dictis ad unguem libentissime.

PYTHAGORAS. Prandebo modo; meae assitis mensae, tum huius gymnasii mei ritus et leges cognoscetis.

DISCIPVLI. Parebimus tuo uerbo.

PYTHAGORAS. Puer, mensam cibo praepara, prandendi hora est. Adolescentes, uos mensae assidete, ego hic accumbam. Cibum consecremus. Omne quo uescemur modo cibum et potum nobis benedicere uelit Iuppiter caelitesque omnes, in nomine ipsius qui trinus est personis, sed unus in essentia.

DISCIPVLI. Amen.

2. A PYTHAGOREAN BANQUET

Pythagoras, host; Pupils, guests

PUPILS. Greeting to you, wisest of men.

PYTHAGORAS. And the same to you.

PUPILS. There's something we'd like to talk to you about, if you'd care to listen.

PYTHAGORAS. I'd be delighted to. Tell me why you've come.

PUPILS. We're here because we're keen to learn, which we'd like to do under your tuition.

PYTHAGORAS. I take no one on as a pupil unless I've examined his intellect and his character.

PUPILS. So how do you test what kind of intellect people unknown to you have?

PYTHAGORAS. That's none of your concern.

PUPILS. What happens to those who have dull wits? Do you attempt to teach them?

PYTHAGORAS. I don't take them on as students, any more than a farmer would take on infertile ground, for I'd be wasting my energy.

PUPILS. Could those born with poor intellects not be given instruction in letters?

PYTHAGORAS. They take an immense effort to teach, but they make little or no progress. For even if infertile fields are worked, they don't produce crops.

PUPILS. Esteemed philosopher, accept us into the company of your pupils, we beg you.

PYTHAGORAS. First I'll test your intellects, to see if they're suitable for learning; then I'll take you on as students.

PUPILS. We'll be delighted to listen to what you say carefully.

PYTHAGORAS. I'll have lunch first. Join me at table, then you'll learn the laws and usages of this school.

PUPILS. We'll do what you say.

PYTHAGORAS. Boy, set the table with food, it's lunchtime. You youths, sit at the table, I'll sit here. Let's bless the food. May Jupiter and all the celestial beings be pleased to bless everything we eat and drink, in the name of him who is three in persons, but one in essence.

PUPILS. Amen.

PYTHAGORAS. Iis obsoniis uulgaribus, pisis, piris, pomis, potuque uilissimo esurientes uos alite, non alium cibatum haec mensa habere solet.

DISCIPVLI. Nunquam carnes neque pisces?

PYTHAGORAS. Minime gentium. Essemus usqueadeo immanes et impii, ut uictitaremur carnibus animalium et piscibus?

DISCIPVLI. Esset illud impium et immane?

PYTHAGORAS. Detestabilissimum est humanae naturae.

DISCIPVLI. Passim tamen locorum his cibis aluntur homines.

PYTHAGORAS. Aliud philosophia nos docet, quae ab istis nos retrahit; brutorum uesci carnibus et piscibus maxime impium est.

DISCIPVLI. Quare? Doceas nos istud, humanissime praeceptor.

PYTHAGORAS. Nos philosophi dicimus animas esse immortales, et post mortem animalis in aliud transire corpus. Ideo si carnibus [H4v] beluinis uescerer, timerem mei patris animam ne deuorarem.

DISCIPVLI. Cur piscibus tum abstinere soles?

PYTHAGORAS. Piscis animal innocuum est nihil exitii hominibus inferens, ideo in ipsum nostris morsibus saeuire non decet.

DISCIPVLI. Vesceris aliis cibis omnibus?

PYTHAGORAS. Famem discipuli mei et ego sedamus alimento perquam exiguo et uili.

DISCIPVLI. Difficile nobis erit assuescere tam tenuiter uictitare. Lautis hactenus apud parentes aliti sumus.

PYTHAGORAS. Ferenda sunt uobis complura, si scientiae metam cupitis. Nam patientia philosophiae est radix et fulcimentum.

DISCIPVLI. Quibus legibus tui sunt addicti discipuli?

PYTHAGORAS. Variis, uni tamen praecipue.

DISCIPVLI. Quae illa est?

PYTHAGORAS. Vt per quinquennium taceant.

DISCIPVLI. Cur ipsis loqui prohibes?

PYTHAGORAS. Ideo ut tacendo audiant et discant ab aliis quid sit loquendum, antequam ipsi uerba proferant.

DISCIPVLI. Difficillima factu nobis ista uidentur.

PYTHAGORAS. If you're hungry, feed on these ordinary dishes: peas, pears, apples, and the basest of drink. This table never has any other kind of food.

PUPILS. Never meat or fish?

PYTHAGORAS. Good heavens, no. Would we be so brutal and impious as to feed on the flesh of animals and fish?

PUPILS. Would that be brutal and impious?

PYTHAGORAS. It's abominable to human nature.

PUPILS. Yet people eat those foods everywhere.

PYTHAGORAS. Philosophy teaches us differently, which is what keeps us from those foods: it's gravely wrong to eat the flesh of animals and fish.

PUPILS. Why? Teach us that, most civilized teacher.

PYTHAGORAS. We philosophers say that souls are immortal, and that after a living being's death they pass over into another body. And so if I were to eat the flesh of animals, I'd be afraid I might be eating my father's soul.

PUPILS. Why are you in the habit of abstaining from fish?

PYTHAGORAS. The fish is a harmless animal, presenting no danger to humans; and so it's not right for us to bite it violently.

PUPILS. Do you eat all other kinds of food?

PYTHAGORAS. My pupils and I assuage our hunger with very sparing and cheap food.

PUPILS. It'll be hard for us to get used to living so meagrely. Up to now we've been fed on fine food in our parents' houses.

PYTHAGORAS. You'll have to put up with a great many things if you want the totality of knowledge. For patience is the root and basis of all philosophy.

PUPILS. What laws do your pupils observe?

PYTHAGORAS. Several, but one in particular.

PUPILS. What is that?

PYTHAGORAS. To say nothing for five years.

PUPILS. Why do you forbid them to talk?

PYTHAGORAS. So that by being silent they will listen, and learn from others what they ought to say, before they make utterances themselves.

PUPILS. That strikes us as being very hard to do.

PYTHAGORAS. Viribus uestris si non conueniunt, alium praeceptorem quaerite.

DISCIPVLI. Experiemur quid uires nostri possint, et quid ferre recusent.

PYTHAGORAS. Sic facite, strenueque me docente litteras discite.

---

26 apta] apti B C | 49 istud] illud C | 71 discant] discant C; discunt B

3. PHILOSOPHICA MENSA

Plato hospes; Aristoteles, Cicero, Demosthenes conuiuae; Minister

PLATO. Mensam ac patinas accedite, litterarum feruidissimi adolescentes, iamdudum fortassis fame uobis crepuerunt intestina.

ARISTOTELES. Esuriei adhuc sentio nihil.

CICERO. Et ipse nondum famelicus sum.

DEMOSTHENES. Libros legendo esuriem prorsus non sensi.

PLATO. O nobiles litterarum cultores, qui chartis animos et corpora farcitis, mensae nunc accumbite, ciboque corporeo naturam [H5^r] fulciatis.

ARISTOTELES. Praesto sumus, uenerande praeceptor.

PLATO. Serue, edenda nobis tuis precibus consecra.

MINISTER. Quae iam sumemus edulia, ea et nos benedicat qui creauit uniuersa, terram, mare, caelum, omniaque in ipsis contenta, mortuorumque resurrectionem faciet, unus in essentia; licet cum populo sit dicendum multos esse deos, unus autem uerus est, qui dapem hanc nostram benedicat.

CONVIVAE. Amen.

Various ways of preparing fish, from an unidentified sixteenth-century German cook-book.

PYTHAGORAS. If it's beyond your powers, look for another teacher.

PUPILS. We'll test what our strength is capable of, and what it can't tolerate.

PYTHAGORAS. Do that, and study hard with me as your teacher.

3. A PHILOSPHICAL FEAST

Plato, host; Aristotle, Cicero, Demosthenes, guests; Servant

PLATO. Approach the table and the food, you eager young scholars, your insides have probably burst with hunger by now.

ARISTOTLE. I don't feel hungry at all yet.

CICERO. I'm not hungry either.

DEMOSTHENES. I've been reading, and haven't felt any hunger yet.

PLATO. O noble devotees of learning, who stuff your minds and bodies with books, sit down at table now and fortify the inner man with physical food.

ARISTOTLE. Here we are, revered teacher.

PLATO. Servant, bless our food with your prayers.

SERVANT. May we, and the food we are about to eat, be blessed by him who created all things: the earth, sea and sky and everything they contain, and who will make the dead to rise; one in essence. Though with the people we must say there are many gods, one alone is true; may he bless this our meal.

GUESTS. Amen.

PLATO. Esuriens nunc edat, famelicus edere non tentet, nam nociuus est omnis cibus qui praeter famem uel editur, uel ad edendum illectat.

ARISTOTELES. Palato cibum inferam, tum experiar an sibi sapiat.

PLATO. Potum praebe, tu Endymion, ut stas cogitabundus? Hac lance latrantem sedate stomachum eduliis, ultra nihil habebitis quam bellaria.

CICERO. Abunde satis erit, neque uultures uel lupi sumus.

PLATO. Potu hoc tenui et uili cibum subsidere facite.

DEMOSTHENES. Curabitur.

PLATO. Potus est non nectareus, sed philosophicus, rationem bibenti non adimens nec corpora debilitans.

ARISTOTELES. Conuenit litteris deditis, alias Minerua debilitata scientiae fulcimentum laberetur.

PLATO. Puer, patinam tolle et bellaria appone, butyrum, caseum, nuces et poma, mundasque quadras. De his edite epulis si prior patina minus uestris arrisit palatis.

CICERO. Oppido meis placuit faucibus.

PLATO. Edite perniciter, ne hic moremur diutissime.

DEMOSTHENES. Eruditissime praeceptor, exoptaremus unum a te, ut doceres quale debeat esse conuiuium philosophicum uel litteratorum?

PLATO. Quam lubentissime istud efficiam, uos quae dicam sitientibus auribus accipite.

ARISTOTELES. Aduertemus diligenter.

PLATO. Conuiuium philosophicum uel litterarium uel litteratorum tenue erit cibis et fru- [H5v] gale, sed prudentibus dictis et factis prouidis abundatissimum, operamque quilibet adhibebit ut doctior surgat a mensa quam ipsam accessit.

CICERO. Quid si nullus fiat sermo doctus, Latinus et prudens?

PLATO. Conuiuium philosophicum dicendum non erit.

CICERO. Compotandone certabunt poculis?

PLATO. Istud popularibus relinquant, ipsi litteraribus haustibus se inuicem exhilarent.

PLATO. Now let him who is hungry eat. But he should not eat as if he were starving, for any food eaten in excess of our hunger, or which tempts us so to eat, is harmful.

ARISTOTLE. I'll put the food in my mouth, then I'll find out whether I like it.

PLATO. Serve the drink, you dozy boy! Why are you standing lost in thought? Calm your clamouring stomachs with the food from this dish, you'll get anything else apart from desserts.

CICERO. It'll be quite enough; we aren't vultures or wolves.

PLATO. Wash the food down with this poor small beer.

DEMOSTHENES. We'll see to that.

PLATO. This drink isn't nectar; it's a philosophical drink that doesn't deprive the drinkers of their reason, or weaken their bodies.

ARISTOTLE. That's suitable for scholars, for otherwise when our intellect was weakened the basis for our knowledge would topple.

PLATO. Boy, take the plate away and serve the desserts: butter, cheese, nuts and apples, and clean plates. Eat these dishes if the first course didn't suit your taste.

CICERO. It pleased mine very much.

PLATO. Eat quickly, so as not to delay here too long.

DEMOSTHENES. Learned teacher, we would ask one thing of you: to teach us what a philosophical or literary banquet should be like.

PLATO. I'd be delighted to do that. You take in what I say eagerly.

ARISTOTLE. We'll pay careful attention.

PLATO. A philosophical or literary banquet will be sparse and frugal as regards food; but it will be abundant in wise words and prudent deeds, and everyone will make an effort to get up from the table more learned than when he sat down.

CICERO. What if no one says anything learned or wise in Latin?

PLATO. Then it can't be called a philosophical banquet.

CICERO. Will the guests compete in drinking?

PLATO. They should leave that to the common sort; they'll cheer one another with literary draughts.

ARISTOTELES. Obsoniis quibus uescentur?

PLATO. Stomachum quae non onerabunt, neque ingenii uires tollent.

DEMOSTHENES. Nunquam genio indulgebunt largius bibendo et edendo?

PLATO. Ad pocula indulgere genio quid aliud est quam ingenium, memoriam, thesaurum scientiae amittere et enecare?

CICERO. Nihil conuenit Baccho cum Pallade?

PLATO. Dissident odio maximo.

DEMOSTHENES. Tamen Bacchus excitare ingenium dicitur, cum quisque ad pocula discere conatur. Et Mantuanus dicit, 'Fluit melior post pocula sermo.'

PLATO. Eruditorum est longe a uulgo dissentire. Puer, hymnum a cibo profer.

PVER. Qui nos pauit sua gratia sit benedictus in saecula.

CONVIVAE. Amen.

---

49 abundatissimum] abundatissimum C; abundatissimam B | 66 dicit] dicat B C

4. DIOGENICVM CONVIVIVM

Diogenes hospes; Alexander, Aristippus, Chrysippus conuiuae

DIOGENES. Quid ita admirabundus me aspicis, tu rex Alexander?

ALEXANDER. Aspicio te quod ita dolio insides instar porci uel canis, quum ceteri homines in domibus suis sub tecto soleant agitare.

DIOGENES. Mores hi mihi arrident, placeant alii sui ritus, mea non refert.

ALEXANDER. Ecquid petis a me rege poten- [H6r] te totiusque orbis domino?

DIOGENES. Prorsus nihil, quam ut illud mihi non surripias, quod dare non potes.

ALEXANDER. Quid illud est?

DIOGENES. Stans ante dolium impedis solem, quia uas meum non ingreditur; ideo discede, meque solis splendore potiri concede.

ARISTOTLE. What food will they eat?
PLATO. Ones that don't weigh down the stomach, or take away the powers of the intellect.
DEMOSTHENES. Will they never indulge themselves by copious eating and drinking?
PLATO. What else is it to indulge yourself in drink than to lose and deprive yourself of your intellect, your memory and the treasury of your knowledge?
CICERO. Bacchus and Pallas don't get on?
PLATO. They disagree, and hate each other greatly.
DEMOSTHENES. Yet Bacchus is said to stimulate the mind, when someone is trying to learn things when drinking. And Mantuan says, 'Words flow better after a drink.'
PLATO. Scholars should disagree greatly with the common sort. Boy, say the grace after food.
BOY. May he who has fed us by his grace be blessed forever.
GUESTS. Amen.

4. A BANQUET OF DIOGENES

Diogenes, host; Alexander, Aristippus, Chrysippus, guests

DIOGENES. Why are you looking at me in such amazement, King Alexander?
ALEXANDER. I'm looking at you because you're sitting in a tub like a pig or a dog, whilst other people usually live in their houses under a roof.
DIOGENES. I like these habits. Let others be happy with their own practice, it's no concern of mine.
ALEXANDER. What is it that you ask of me, a mighty king and lord of all the world?
DIOGENES. Nothing at all, other than not to take away from me what you can't give me.
ALEXANDER. What is that?
DIOGENES. By standing in front of the tub you're blocking the sunlight, for it's not shining in. So go away, and allow me to enjoy the sunshine.

ALEXANDER. Discedam lubens, sed estne quid edulii quo hoc prandio stomachum satures?

DIOGENES. Tantum adhuc habeo, quo me pascam, sed tibi tuique similibus uentri deditis non famem expleret, sed ad edendum excitaret.

ALEXANDER. Dic cuius farinae sit cibus.

DIOGENES. Frustum panis aridi, duri et mucidi, parumque crudi et uiridis holeris.

ALEXANDER. Non ad ignem coquis holus ipsum?

DIOGENES. Natura mihi ollam dedit quo cruda coquo, digero et corpori apta facio.

ALEXANDER. Quae ista est olla?

DIOGENES. Stomachus in meo positus uentre nunquam quiescens, semper laborans et feruens, ad insumpti cibi decoctionem.

ALEXANDER. Frigidus cibatus et crudus non conuenit homini, ut medici dicunt.

DIOGENES. Natura medicorum est optima.

ALEXANDER. Conuiuas nunquam uocas in hoc dolium tuum?

DIOGENES. Non, quia quibus ego delector et contentus sum aliis hominibus displicent, et ab ipsis nauseant.

ALEXANDER. Prandebimus hodie tecum nos tres, ego, Aristippus et Chrysippus, si non aegre tuleris.

DIOGENES. Conuiuae mihi si esse uolueritis, esuriendum uobis erit, nam nihil hic est uestra delectans palata.

ALEXANDER. Tua erimus mensa contenti.

DIOGENES. Agite tum, in terram discumbite uel uestes substernite, neque lectos neque sellas habeo.

ARISTIPPVS. Esto, humi sedebimus stratis tunicis, tu mensam obsoniis para.

DIOGENES. [H6v] Mensa mihi est sinus, manus quadra, culter dentes.

CHRYSIPPVS. Porrige nunc nobis edenda.

DIOGENES. Deum prius salutate orationibus uestris.

ALEXANDER. Tu ut hospes hymnum praefare.

ALEXANDER. I'll gladly go away; but is there any kind of food we could fill our stomachs with this lunchtime?

DIOGENES. I've got enough to feed myself, but in the case of you and your ilk, who are devoted to your stomachs, it wouldn't satisfy your hunger, it would stimulate your appetite.

ALEXANDER. Tell me what kind of food that is.

DIOGENES. A crust of dry bread, hard and mouldy, and a little raw green cabbage.

ALEXANDER. Don't you cook the cabbage on the fire?

DIOGENES. Nature has given me a pot in which I cook raw things, digest them and make them suitable for my body.

ALEXANDER. What pot is that?

DIOGENES. The stomach inside me, never at rest, always working and bubbling so as to digest the food I take.

ALEXANDER. Cold and raw food isn't good for humans, so the doctors say.

DIOGENES. Nature is the best of doctors.

ALEXANDER. Don't you ever invite guests to this tub of yours?

DIOGENES. No, because the things that please me and satisfy me other people find unpleasing and disgusting.

ALEXANDER. Today the three of us will lunch with you, Aristippus, Chrysippus and I, if it won't annoy you.

DIOGENES. If you want to be my guests, you'll have to go hungry, because there's nothing here that would please your taste.

ALEXANDER. We'll be happy with your food.

DIOGENES. Well then, sit down on the ground or spread your clothes under you; I have neither couches nor seats.

ARISTIPPUS. Right, we'll spread out our tunics and sit on the ground. You set the food out on the table.

DIOGENES. My table is my lap, my plate is my hand, my teeth are my knife.

CHRYSIPPUS. Now let us have what we are to eat.

DIOGENES. First say your prayers to God.

ALEXANDER. As host, you say the prayer.

DIOGENES. Deus totius uniuersae creator, rector et gubernator, humani generis plasmator, pascens creata omnia, panem et holus ac aquam iam sumenda nobis benedicat.

CONVIVAE. Amen.

DIOGENES. Nunc acri morsu istos panis bolos edite et rodite.

ALEXANDER. Hui, durus est nimium, dentes ferme elido mordendo.

DIOGENES. Hic aquae intinge ut mollescat.

ARISTIPPVS. Nihil pani addemus obsonii?

DIOGENES. De hoc crudo hosculo aliquid addite, uel sine obsonio ipsum comedite.

ALEXANDER. Obsonium ubi deest, insipidus est panis.

DIOGENES. Hic in olla aliquid holeris elixi reconditum habeo, sed tepidum non est; illud edite.

CHRYSIPPVS. Immunda est olla; nauseo aspicere, nedum ex ipsa edere.

DIOGENES. Si nauseas, mihi sinas cui mel sapit.

ALEXANDER. Sitio, panis mihi labia exsiccat.

DIOGENES. Pura ista lympha sitim comprime, alius mihi potus non est.

ALEXANDER. O tu miserrime Diogenes, qui huiusmodi uictitas epuliis.

DIOGENES. Miser non sum, natura quantum expetit edo et habeo.

ALEXANDER. Malo me adhuc Alexandrum esse et regem quam Diogenem et philosophum pauperrimum.

DIOGENES. Et ego nollem e Diogene fieri Alexander.

ALEXANDER. Prorsus nihil aliud habes quod edamus?

DIOGENES. Pira et poma nonnulla mihi adhuc sunt, sed acerba et dura.

ARISTIPPVS. Illis non capimur, nam dentes hebetes faciunt. Tu uale, nos nostram reuisemus aulam regiam et dapsiles lances.

DIOGENES. May God, maker, ruler and governor of the whole universe, creator of the human race, who feeds all creatures, bless the bread, cabbage and water we are about to receive.

GUESTS. Amen.

DIOGENES. Now get your teeth firmly into those chunks of bread.

ALEXANDER. Oh, it's really hard. I'm nearly breaking my teeth biting it.

DIOGENES. Dip it in the water here to soften it up.

ARISTIPPUS. Won't we have anything else to eat with the bread?

DIOGENES. Add a bit of this raw cabbage, or else eat the bread on its own.

ALEXANDER. Bread is tasteless when there's nothing to eat with it.

DIOGENES. I have some boiled cabbage in the pot here, but it's not warm. Eat that.

CHRYSIPPUS. The pot's dirty. It disgusts me to look at it, let alone eat from it.

DIOGENES. If it disgusts you, leave it to me, I think it tastes delightful.

ALEXANDER. I'm thirsty, the bread's drying out my lips.

DIOGENES. Slake your thirst with this pure water, I have no other drink.

ALEXANDER. O, you wretched Diogenes, living on food like this!

DIOGENES. I'm not wretched; I eat and have as much as nature requires.

ALEXANDER. I still prefer to be Alexander and a king than Diogenes and the poorest of philosophers.

DIOGENES. And I wouldn't want to be changed from Diogenes into Alexander.

ALEXANDER. Have you absolutely nothing more we could eat?

DIOGENES. I've still got a few apples and pears, but they're hard and bitter.

ARISTIPPUS. We're not keen on those, because they blunt your teeth. Farewell, we'll go back to our royal palace and our luxurious food.

DIOGENES. Abite, ego hic in dolio naturae rimabor effectus.

---

7 canis] carnis C (corrected in erratum, sig. L8[r]).

5. ARISTIPPICVM CONVIVIVM SIVE AULICVM [H7[r]]

Aristippus hospes; Theophrastus, Crates, Anaxagoras, Diogenes, Minister

ARISTIPPVS. O Diogenes, e tuo proripe uase et nobiscum congredere in regis nostri palatium, pretiosioribus te excipiemus.

DIOGENES. Discedite ad uestram crapulam, ego mea delector inedia.

ARISTIPPVS. Famelice uiuas quoad placuerit, ipse aulice uictitare malo.

DIOGENES. Tu patinarius es philosophus, ipse contemplatione naturae plus capior quam opimis tuis patinis.

ARISTIPPVS. Alios conuiuas uocabo philosophos si tu aduenire recusas.

DIOGENES. Id facito.

ARISTIPPVS. Heus uos philosophiae cultores, Theophrastus, Crates et Anaxagoras, pluteos uestros seponite mecumque in regiam aulam pergite sumptum cibum.

PHILOSOPHI. Congrediemur lubentes.

ARISTIPPVS. Adsitis, ac studio maceratas uires mensa opipara reficite.

PHILOSOPHI. Comitabimur te, faciles sumus ubi conuiuae uocamur.

ARISTIPPVS. Ingrediemini igitur, prandendi tempus est, rex suique aulici mensae accumbunt.

PHILOSOPHI. In solum eamus locum, ubi aulicorum non est strepitus et praesentia.

ARISTIPPVS. Hanc cellulam intrabimus et nos includemus, quod non obruamur a pluribus.

PHILOSOPHI. Tum aperi et mensam obsoniis onera, esurimus acriter, nondum ientati sumus.

ARISTIPPVS. Mox culinae minister afferet edulia. En adest ut lupus in fabula.

MINISTER. Hunc cibum uobis Deus benedicat.

DIOGENES. Off you go. I'll reflect on the workings of Nature here in my tub.

5. A BANQUET OF ARISTIPPUS, OR A PALACE BANQUET

Aristippus, host; Theophrastus, Crates, Anaxagoras, Diogenes, Waiter

ARISTIPPUS. Diogenes, come out of your tub and come with us to our king's palace; we'll treat you to some excellent things.

DIOGENES. Go off to your carousing, I like my abstinence.

ARISTIPPUS. Live in hunger as long as you like; I prefer to live like a courtier.

DIOGENES. You're a philosopher of the dinner-plates. I'm fonder of contemplating Nature than of your rich dishes.

ARISTIPPUS. I'll invite other philosophers as guests if you refuse to come.

DIOGENES. Do.

ARISTIPPUS. Ho, Theophrastus, Crates and Anaxagoras, you exponents of philosophy! Forget your bookshelves and come with me to the royal palace to have some food.

PHILOSOPHERS. We'll be glad to come with you.

ARISTIPPUS. Do, and restore your forces, weakened by study, with some fine food.

PHILOSOPHERS. We'll come with you. We're accommodating when we're invited as guests.

ARISTIPPUS. Go in, then, it's time for lunch. The king and his courtiers are sitting down at table.

PHILOSOPHERS. We'll go to the only place where there aren't any courtiers, or the noise they make.

ARISTIPPUS. We'll go into this little room and close ourselves in, so we're not overrun by lots of people.

PHILOSOPHERS. Then open up and put food on the table. We're exceedingly hungry, we haven't had breakfast.

ARISTIPPUS. The waiter will bring food soon. Talk of the devil, here he is!

WAITER. May God bless this food.

PHILOSOPHI. Amen.

ARISTIPPVS. Benedictus qui est in aeuum, omnibusque uniuersis imperat, cuncta suo nutu gubernat, benedicere uelit quae nunc sumemus corporis stabilimenta.

PHILOSOPHI. Amen.

ARISTIPPVS. Nunc cultros stringite, uoragines uestras his primis epulis implete, quoad lautiora dabuntur. [H7v]

PHILOSOPHI. Impigre edemus, stomachos habemus fame crepitantes.

ARISTIPPVS. Tum ipsis medemini cibo et potu, de his aprinis clunibus uel leporinis sumite.

THEOPHRASTVS. Porcina carne prius uescemur.

ARISTIPPVS. Istam relinquite familiae, uos delicatiorem comedite. Ex hoc argenteo poculo omnibus uobis praebibo, et prius tibi Theophrasto.

THEOPHRASTVS. In Iouis bibas nomine.

ARISTIPPVS. Nunc bibe et tu, uinum est Lesbium.

THEOPHRASTVS. Illo teneor, nam meae est nationis.

CRATES. O Aristippe, tu hic argenteis edis patinis, aureisque bibis poculis, in nostris museis nos ligneis uasis bibimus et edimus.

ARISTIPPVS. Sapere uultis, sed plurimum desipitis, qui macra mauultis mensa in latebris uiuere, quam dapsilice apud principes.

ANAXAGORAS. Consulimus animae nostrae ipsam scientiae et uirtute decorantes.

ARISTIPPVS. At interim corpori obestis et mortem macie praeuenitis et anticipatis.

ANAXAGORAS. Philosophos id decet impallescere chartis, non usque genio indulgere.

ARISTIPPVS. Istud et ego quondam feci, optimumque credidi, tandem fame compulsus aulicus ut sum, fiebam.

THEOPHRASTVS. Philosophiam tu iam curas culinariam, sed nos litterariam.

PHILOSOPHERS. Amen.

ARISTIPPUS. May he who is blessed for eternity, who rules everything in the world, and governs all things according to his will, be pleased to bless the bodily sustenance we are now about to eat.

PHILOSOPHERS. Amen.

ARISTIPPUS. Now unsheathe your knives and fill the holes in your stomachs with these starters, until they bring finer food.

PHILOSOPHERS. We'll eat up smartly; our stomachs are rumbling with hunger.

ARISTIPPUS. Then comfort them with food and drink. Take some of these haunches of boar or hare.

THEOPHRASTUS. We'll have some pork first.

ARISTIPPUS. Leave that to the servants, you eat finer things. I drink to you all from this silver goblet, and first to you, Theophrastus.

THEOPHRASTUS. Drink in Jove's name.

ARISTIPPUS. Now you drink, too, it's Lesbian wine.

CRATES. Aristippus, here you eat off silver plates and drink from silver cups; in our scholars' dwellings we eat and drink from wooden vessels.

ARISTIPPUS. You claim to be wise, but really you're stupid, preferring to live off meagre food in your lairs rather than to feast with princes.

ANAXAGORAS. We look after our souls by equipping them with knowledge and virtue.

ARISTIPPUS. But while you do, you're harming your bodies and anticipating death by wasting away.

ANAXAGORAS. Philosophers ought to work hard at their books, not to live luxuriously.

ARISTIPPUS. I did that once too, and I thought it was excellent, but eventually hunger forced me to become the courtier I am.

THEOPHRASTUS. Now you do your philosophy in the kitchen, but we do ours from books.

ARISTIPPVS. Interdum etiam adhuc libris legendis incumbo, non totus ferior a litteris.

ANAXAGORAS. Male conuenit per Herculem philosophiae studio cum opiparis patinis.

ARISTIPPVS. Attamen dulce et corporis culturam gerere, simul et philosophiae utcunque studere.

THEOPHRASTVS. Nos malumus ad lucernam latere discentes et quieti, quam principum nutibus inseruire

ARISTIPPVS. Nescitis principibus uiris placuisse non ultimam et postremam esse laudem?

CRATES. Laus maior est uirtuti placuisse et adhaesisse.

ARISTIPPVS. [H8r] Abeant ista, quisque sua sorte uiuat, mihi haec fortuna arridet. Assas istas carnes ferinas decerpite, uinoque pretioso isto utimini.

THEOPHRASTVS. Saturi sumus, tollantur dapes, domum uersus regrediamur ad codices nostros.

ARISTIPPVS. Quando lubet, non uos morabor.

ANAXAGORAS. Hymnum igitur a cibo nobis ut hospes recense.

ARISTIPPVS. Laus, honor et gloria sit sempiterno Ioui caelo terraque imperanti, quia cibis nos pauit, famelici qui fuimus.

THEOPHRASTUS. I like that, because it comes from my country.

PHILOSOPHI. Amen.

ARISTIPPVS. Nunc litteraria uestra antra repetite, chartas uoluite et inuertite.

PHILOSOPHI. Tu uale, grati quandoque erimus quando licebit.

ARISTIPPVS. Non moror gratiam uestram, me alit rex et portat equus.

---

11 contemplatione] contemplationi B C | 44 medemini] medimini B C | 53 Aristippe] Aristippe C; Aristippi

ARISTIPPUS. I do still sometimes read books, I haven't abandoned literature completely.

ANAXAGORAS. By Hercules, the study of philosophy and rich food aren't compatible.

ARISTIPPUS. Yet it's pleasant to indulge your body, and apply yourself to philosophy at the same time.

THEOPHRASTUS. We prefer to sit learning by lamplight in tranquillity than to be at the beck and call of princes.

ARISTIPPUS. Don't you know that to please important people is by no means the least praiseworthy thing?

CRATES. It's more praiseworthy to serve truth and stand by it.

ARISTIPPUS. Enough of that! Let everyone live as his own class dictates. I love this station in life. Cut up that roast game, and drink that fine wine.

THEOPHRASTUS. We're full. Clear the plates, we're back off home to our books.

ARISTIPPUS. Whenever you like, I won't delay you.

ANAXAGORAS. Say the grace for us as host, then.

ARISTIPPUS. Praise, honour and glory be to the eternal Jove, ruler of heaven and earth, for feeding us, when we were hungry, with food.

PHILOSOPHERS. Amen.

ARISTIPPUS. Now back off to your literary dens, and thumb through your books forwards and backwards.

PHILOSOPHERS. Goodbye. We'll show our gratitude some time when we can.

ARISTIPPUS. A fig for your thanks; the king feeds me and my horse carries me.

6. REGIVM CONVIVIVM POST FERIAS EPIPHANIAE

Rex, Regina, Dux, Obsonator, Cancellarius, Secretarius, Cubicularius, Stultus, Seruus

REX. O mea Regina pulcherrima, quando conuiuium nostro regno et imperio debitum nostris aulicis exhibebimus et faciemus?

REGINA. Quando domino Regi meo generosissimo placuerit.

REX. Quid si ad hodiernam uesperam ipsius sumptus facerem?

REGINA. Non displicebit mihi.

REX. Habes quae cenam delicatam redderent?

REGINA. Sunt mihi gallinae tres, duo capi mediusque agnus.

REX. Sufficiet, gallinas cum carne agnina elixa, capos et agni medium ad ueru coquas.

REGINA. Executum reddam.

REX. Sic facito, ego interim aliis intentus ero.

OBSONATOR. O Rex noster, quando regale conuiuium tuis aulicis parabis?

REX. Ad uesperam. Tu obsonatum eas curaque ut singula in cenam sint parata, aut tuo defungeris magistratu.

OBSONATOR. Fidelis ero.

SERVVS. Magnifice domine Rex, sternam mensam? [H8v] Obsonia singula paene sunt percocta.

REX. Exequere tuum munus. Adsuntne ministri et satellites nostri?

SERVVS. Ad unum usque hic domi sunt.

6. A ROYAL BANQUET AFTER THE FEAST OF THE EPIPHANY

King, Queen, Duke, Caterer, Chancellor, Secretary, Chamberlain, Fool, Servant

KING. O my beautiful queen, when shall we give the banquet we owe our kingdom to our courtiers?

QUEEN. When it pleases my noble Lord the king.

KING. Suppose I were to pay for it this evening?

QUEEN. I would not object.

KING. Do you have food that would make for a fine dinner?

QUEEN. I have three chickens, two capons and half a lamb.

KING. That will be enough: cook the chickens with boiled lamb, capons, and spit-roast the half lamb.

QUEEN. I'll see to that.

KING. Do that, in the meantime I'll be occupied with other things.

CATERER. O our king, when will you hold the royal banquet with your courtiers?

KING. This evening. You go off to the market and see to it that everything is ready for the dinner, or you'll be failing in your office.

CATERER. I'll be reliable.

SERVANT. Your royal majesty, shall I lay the table? The various dishes are nearly cooked.

KING. See to your duty. Are our ministers and attendants here?

SERVANT. They're here in the house, every one.

REX. Age, tum auspicemur cenam. Potum habendum fac promas, uinique copiam affer, et intrent amici ceteri, nostraeque aulae domestici.

SERVVS. Iubebo. Iussit et uult generosus Rex meus ut intretis hibernaculum.

CONVIVAE. Intrabimus modo. Salue, Rex potentissime.

REX. Rex nomine, sed sine regno.

CONVIVAE. Denique egregium habere nomen nonnullos delectat, et praestat quam uocari ignominiosum.

REX. Mensam ordine accedite. Dux, Cancellarius, quisque ut gradu est superior, ita et accubitu sit.

CONVIVAE. Discumbat et Rex noster.

REX. Modo accumbam, et Regina mihi assidebit. Puer, benedictionis hymnum effare.

PVER. Benedicite.

CONVIVAE. Dominus.

PVER. Huius cenae regalis esculenta et potum benedicat ille qui rex regum est, nobisque faxit sint salutifera qui haec ipsa in sui facimus memoriam, quia ipse in mundum natus homo die decimotertio Reges et Magos suo aspectu exhilarauit. In nomine Patris et Filii et Spiritus Sancti.

CONVIVAE. Amen.

REX. Nunc hilares sitis potu et cibo, strenueque edite, sic ego iam Rex uester impero et uolo. Istam carnis buccellam domina Regina mea grato accipiat animo.

REGINA. Gratia sit domino Regi.

REX. Vos nostri aulici Chrysippi non sitis, sed cuticulam curate basilice.

CONVIVAE. Bibat Rex, tum et nos alii bibemus.

REX. Propino Reginae meae nobilissimae.

REGINA. Prosit domino Regi.

STVLTVS. Rex bibit, Rex bibit! Tandem cessa, noli exiccare, et mihi quippiam relinquas.

CONVIVAE. Quam minime facetus est morus ille.

STVLTVS. Clamando fatigabor.

REX. Ser- [I1^r] ue, assas affer carnes et haec aufer.

KING. Right, then we'll start the dinner. Bring out the drink that's to be drunk, bring on a supply of wine, and let our other friends, and the servants of our court, come in.

SERVANT. I'll give the command. My noble king desires and wishes you to come into the dining-room.

GUESTS. We will. Greetings, most mighty king.

KING. A king in name, but without a kingdom.

GUESTS. And yet some people are pleased to have an illustrious title, and it's better than to be called something disgraceful.

KING. Sit at table in order. Duke, chancellor, anyone whose rank is high should be seated accordingly.

GUESTS. And let our king sit down.

KING. I will, and my queen will sit by me. Boy, say the prayer of blessing.

BOY. Benedicite.

GUESTS. Dominus.

BOY. May he who is the King of Kings bless the food and drink of this royal dinner, and may he make them beneficial to us who do this in memory of him, for on the thirteenth day he gladdened the Kings and the Magi with his sight. In the name of the Father, and of the Son, and of the Holy Spirit.

GUESTS. Amen.

KING. Now be merry in food and drink, and eat heartily; so do I, who am now your king, wish and command. May the lady my queen graciously accept this morsel of meat.

QUEEN. I thank my lord king.

KING. And the rest of you, don't hold back, feed yourselves right royally.

GUESTS. Let the king drink, then the rest of us will drink.

KING. I drink to my noble queen.

QUEEN. Good health to the king.

FOOL. The king drinks, the king drinks! But hold, don't empty it, and leave me some.

GUESTS. That fool is so unfunny.

FOOL. I'll tire myself out shouting.

KING. Servant, bring on the roast meats and take these away.

SERVVS. Mox faciam. Hic est dominus Dux, Secretarius, Cancellarius, Cubicularius, quisque eorum dominum Regem et Reginam donant duabus uini mensuris.

REX. Gratiam habeant, certe minime decet regem uino donari a suis famulis.

CONVIVAE. Nonne et reges imperiorum a subiectis aluntur colonis?

REX. Fateor, capos illos tostos tu Secretari rumpe, frustaque assidentibus praepone, nosti quomodo sit ad mensam ministrandum.

SECRETARIVS. Lubens faciam ex Regis iussu.

REGINA. Regi hunc calicem medium praebibam.

REX. Sit commodo Reginae.

CONVIVAE. 'Regina bibit,' exclama tu fatue, ut deuoras cibum ac uultur!

STVLTVS. Regina bibit, Regina bibit, Regina bibit!

REX. Agninam illam carnem frustulatim disseca tu, Cancellari.

CANCELLARIVS. Perplacet. Hoc frustum Rex noster sibi retineat.

REX. Hilares agite sitis, post saeculum Gentiles hanc occupabunt terram, ut uulgo fertur. Omnibus hoc poculo praebibo.

CANCELLARIVS. Non obsit Regi. Stulte, clama, Rex bibet.

STVLTVS. Rex bibit, Rex bibit, Rex bibit !

REX. Tolle haec, Serue, nemo ipsis uescitur, bellaria affer.

SERVVS. Feci.

REX. Caseo hoc cibum subsidere facite, et butyro lenes facite animos.

SECRETARIVS. Ad iugulum usque saturi sumus, nequimus omnem penum stomacho recondere.

REX. Attamen buccellam minimam edite.

CONVIVAE. Non recusabimus istud.

STVLTVS. Regi domino meo praebibo.

REX. Prosit magnifico domino Stulto.

CONVIVAE. Stultus bibit, Stultus bibit, Stultus bipsit, bipsit, bipsit!

STVLTVS. Salua grammatica loquimini.

CONVIVAE. En et Stultus grammaticae peritus est.

SERVANT. I will, quickly. Here is the lord duke, the secretary, the chancellor, the chamberlain; each one of them offers two measures of wine to my lord the king and the queen.

KING. Thanks to them. Yet indeed it's not at all right for a king to be given wine by his servants.

GUESTS. Are not the sovereigns of kingdoms maintained by the inhabitants who are their subjects?

KING. Admittedly. Secretary, you divide up those roast capons, and serve pieces to the guests; you know how to serve at table.

SECRETARY. I will be delighted to do as the king commands.

QUEEN. I will drink this half cup to the king.

KING. Good health to the queen.

GUESTS. Fool, shout 'the queen drinks.' You're gobbling your food like a vulture!

FOOL. The queen drinks! The queen drinks! The queen drinks!

KING. Divide that lamb into pieces, chancellor.

CHANCELLOR. I will. Let our king keep this piece for himself.

KING. Be merry – 'après nous le déluge', as the saying goes. I drink this cup to you all.

CHANCELLOR. The king's good health.

FOOL. The king drinks, the king drinks, the king drinks!

KING. Take these away, servant, no one's eating them. Bring on the desserts.

SERVANT. Here we are.

KING. Make your food settle with this cheese, and soften your spirits with butter.

SECRETARY. We're full up, we can't fit all the food into our stomachs.

KING. But eat a little piece.

GUESTS. We won't refuse.

FOOL. I drink to my lord the king.

KING. To the good health of the excellent lord fool.

GUESTS. The fool drinks, the fool drank, the fool drunk, drunk, drunk!

FOOL. Get your grammar right when you talk!

GUESTS. Oh, the fool's an expert on grammar!

REX. Serue, tolle singula, omnes dormituriunt uideo.

CVBICVLARIVS. [I1v] Nox intempesta adest, cubitum eundi tempus est.

REX. Puer, gratiarum actionis hymnum loquere.

PVER. De hoc conuiuio Benedicamus Domino.

CONVIVAE. Deo sit gratia.

PVER. Ille qui est ab aeuo, manetque in aeternum unicus et solus Deus, et nos suis muneribus pascit, saluat et uiuificat, sit benedictus in saecula saeculorum.

CONVIVAE. Amen.

REX. Vos boni amici et aulici, gratis animis accipite quae affuere, meliora daturus sum, dum imperium meum locupletius factum fuerit.

CONVIVAE. Gratiam agimus, habemus et referemus domino Regi et Reginae de beneuolentia ostensa et impartita nobis.

---

22 obsonia] obsonia C; obsoniaque B | 112 referemus] referemus C; referremus B

7. CONVIVIVM AMICORVM

Socrates hospes; Iohannes, Petrus, Philippus conuiuae; Xanthippe uxor; Minister

SOCRATES. Hesterno die conuiuas uos uocaui per ministrum meum in hodiernum prandium, estisne uenturi?

CONVIVAE. Sumus utique.

SOCRATES. Tum me iam comitamini, meridies instat.

CONVIVAE. Perplacet.

SOCRATES. Hilares spero erimus, nisi uxor mea quippiam litis inceperit.

CONVIVAE. Est tum iam per te offensa?

SOCRATES. Veteri suo more ob asini prospectum iurgia parat.

CONVIVAE. Nos ipsam crateribus faciemus lepidam et placidam.

SOCRATES. Salue, mea Xanthippe, hic mecum ueniunt amiculi nostri in hodiernum prandium a me inuitati.

XANTHIPPE. Gaudeo, sint salui uestri aduentus amici intimi.

CONVIVAE. Gratiam habemus.

XANTHIPPE. Manibus ablotis, quando lubet ite accubitum.

KING. Servant, remove everything. I see that everyone's nodding off.

CHAMBERLAIN. It's the dead of night, it's bedtime.

KING. Boy, say grace.

BOY. For this festive board we thank the Lord.

GUESTS. Thanks be to God.

BOY. May he who is from all eternity, and who remains forever the one and only God, and feeds, saves and keeps us alive with his gifts, be blessed for ever and ever.

GUESTS. Amen.

KING. You, good friends and courtiers, be pleased to accept what was available. I will provide you with better fare when my kingdom grows wealthier.

GUESTS. We thank our lord the king and the queen for the kindness they have shown us, and we will repay it.

7. A BANQUET AMONGST FRIENDS

Socrates, host; Iohannes, Petrus, Philippus, guests; Xanthippe, wife; Servant

SOCRATES. Yesterday I had my servant invite you to lunch today – are you going to come?

GUESTS. We are indeed.

SOCRATES. Then come with me, it's nearly midday.

GUESTS. With pleasure.

SOCRATES. We'll be merry, I hope – unless my wife starts an argument of some kind.

GUESTS. Has she been annoyed by you, then?

SOCRATES. She has a long-standing habit of starting quarrels at the slightest provocation.

GUESTS. We'll make her agreeable and peaceful with a few drinks.

SOCRATES. Hallo, Xanthippe. I have our friends with me; they've come to lunch today at my invitation.

XANTHIPPE. I'm very glad. You're most welcome, my dearest friends.

GUESTS. We thank you.

XANTHIPPE. Wash your hands, and sit down whenever you please.

SOCRATES. Fiat, uos amici, uestes exuite, feruet hibernaculum calore, et ingrediemini.

CONVIVAE. [I2r] I tu prior.

SOCRATES. Sequimini, praecedam.

CONVIVAE. Hic commodior est aër quam foris, ubi mugit Boreas.

SOCRATES. Foris nasus muco concrescit ambulanti. Xanthippe, quando uisum tibi fuerit, edulia fac afferri.

XANTHIPPE. Iam adducentur.

SERVVS. Hic cibus edentibus sit salutaris.

SOCRATES. Edenda consecra.

SERVVS. Benedicite.

CONVIVAE. Dominus.

SERVVS. Quibus hoc in prandio uescemur alimenta et potus benedicta uelit esse ille qui omnibus benedicere solet, solus salutem affert, exitiaque tollit. In nomine sanctae et indiuiduae Trinitatis.

CONVIVAE. Amen.

SOCRATES. Cultellos mensae imponite et e patina comedenda accipite, amicissimi conuiuae.

IOHANNES. Non cures, ad mensam desides non erimus.

SOCRATES. Ab holusculo si abhorret quis uestrum, seponat et carnes edat.

PETRVS. Holeribus lubentes pascimur.

SOCRATES. Non admodum tinctum est.

PHILIPPVS. Istud nil refert, pinguedo nimia uocis affert raucedinem.

SOCRATES. Bibite et nunc, ne aridus in stomacho marcescat cibus. Cereuisiae haustum ad mensam semper primum sumere soleo.

PETRVS. Per Herculem opipari saporis est Cereris iste potus.

SOCRATES. Domesticus meus est potus, satis uilis, nam fruges perquam care ueneunt, ideo et magis exiguam oportet coquere cereuisiam non multum possidentem.

XANTHIPPE. Pernas illas aut caprinas carnes uel uitulinas rodite, quaecunque cuilibet sapuerint.

IOHANNES. Hospes, scypho hoc dimidio te impartiar.

SOCRATES. Bibes salutifere.

IOHANNES. Nunc et tu bibendo par pari referas.

SOCRATES. We will. Friends, take off your coats, the dining-room's really warm, and go in.

GUESTS. You go first.

SOCRATES. I'll go first, you follow me.

GUESTS. The air's more pleasant here than outside, where there's a north wind roaring.

SOCRATES. If you're walking outside the snot freezes in your nose. Xanthippe, when you decide, have the food served.

XANTHIPPE. It's being brought on now.

SERVANT. May this food bring health to those who eat it.

SOCRATES. Bless the food.

SERVANT. Benedicite.

GUESTS. Dominus.

SERVANT. May he who blesses all things, who alone brings salvation and wards off destruction, be pleased to bless the food and drink we enjoy at this lunch. In the name of the Holy and Undivided Trinity.

GUESTS. Amen.

SOCRATES. Put knives on the table, and serve yourselves to food from the dish, my dear guests.

IOHANNES. Don't worry, we won't be lazy at table.

SOCRATES. If anyone of you hates cabbage, put it to one side and eat the meat.

PETRUS. We like eating cabbage.

SOCRATES. It's not particularly moist.

PHILIPPUS. That doesn't matter; too much fat makes your voice hoarse.

SOCRATES. Drink now, so that the food doesn't rot in your stomachs. I always start my meals with a draught of beer.

PETRUS. My goodness, that beer has a splendid flavour.

SOCRATES. It's my own beer, rather poor quality, because grain is very dear, so someone who hasn't got a lot of money has to brew weaker beer.

XANTHIPPE. Eat those haunches of meat, or the goat or the veal, there'll be something to everyone's taste.

IOHANNES. Host, I drink this goblet to you.

SOCRATES. Your good health.

IOHANNES. Now you return the compliment by drinking.

SOCRATES. Inuitus maneo debitor ad pocula. Vxor, [I2v] haustum amicitiae tibi propino.

XANTHIPPE. Sit tibi bono. Petre, praebibo tibi.

PETRVS. Accipio lubens. Tibi non incommodet.

XANTHIPPE. Petre, aequali haustu et alteri praebibas.

PETRVS. Philippe, tantum tibi propinabo, quantum accepi ab hospita nunc nostra.

PHILIPPVS. Feliciter bibe, ut dignum est accipiam abs te lubentissime.

SOCRATES. Serue, carnes affer recentes (ut uocant), nitidosque orbes propone cuilibet.

SERVVS. Efficiam.

SOCRATES. De his agninis carnibus edite ad esuriei expulsionem. Assas carnes non expectetis, nam frustraremini.

PETRVS. Quantum sat est habemus, plura non exoptaremus.

SOCRATES. Licet parce instruxi focum, tamen ut amicos uos uocaui, credens uos boni consulturos mensae tenuitatem.

IOHANNES. Amici ad amicorum lances caseo et cerere redduntur contenti.

SOCRATES. Serue, affer bellaria, haecque conde, uel culinae affer ministrae.

SERVVS. Exequar.

SOCRATES. Hic nunc omnia habuistis obsonia. Si stomachos impleuistis, gaudeo; sin minus, boni tamen consulite.

IOHANNES. Satis superque praesto adfuit edulii.

SOCRATES. Serue, hymnum gratiarum rumina et lege.

SERVVS. Benedicamus Domino.

CONVIVAE. Deo gratias.

SERVVS. Dominus dominantium, omniumque quae in caelo et in terra sunt imperator et conseruator de his a nobis sumptis nutrimentis gratiam habeat in aeternum.

CONVIVAE. Amen.

SOCRATES. Aequis animis accipite quas obtuli escas, lautiores alia dabo uice.

SOCRATES. I don't like being a debtor in drinking. Wife, I drink this draught of friendship to you.

XANTHIPPE. Cheers. Petrus, I drink to you.

PETRUS. I accept gladly. Your good health.

XANTHIPPE. Petrus, drink the same amount to someone else.

PETRUS. Philippus, I drink the same amount to you as has just been drunk to me by our hostess.

PHILIPPUS. Your good health. I accept it from you gladly, as is fitting.

SOCRATES. Servant, bring on the new meats, as they call them, and give everyone clean plates.

SERVANT. I will.

SOCRATES. Eat enough of this lamb to drive away your hunger. Don't expect any roast meats, because you'll be disappointed.

PETRUS. What we have is enough, we wouldn't want any more.

SOCRATES. I may have stoked the fire rather sparingly, but I invited you as friends; thinking that you would be understanding about the meagreness of the food.

GUESTS. Friends at a dinner among friends are satisfied with bread and cheese.

SOCRATES. Servant, bring on the desserts, and put these away, or take them to the cook.

SERVANT. I will.

SOCRATES. Now you've had all the dishes. If you've filled your stomachs, I'm delighted; if not, take it in good part.

IOHANNES. There was enough food and more.

SOCRATES. Servant, think up a grace and read it.

SERVANT. Let us bless the Lord.

GUESTS. Thanks be to God.

SERVANT. May the Lord of Lords and governor and preserver of all that is in heaven and earth, be given everlasting thanks for the food which we have received.

GUESTS. Amen.

SOCRATES. Be content to accept the food I have served you; I'll give you finer fare another time.

IOHANNES. Lautissime fouisti nos, gratos aliquando nos exhibebimus.

---

5 estisne] estis ne C; estis ne ne B | 56 scypho] cypho B C | 72 frustraremini] frustraremini C; frustraremur B | 93 gratos] grati B C

8. FVNEBRE CONVIVIVM

Filius parentibus utrisque orbatus, hospes; Martinus, Conradus, Arnoldus et Mulieres aliquot [I3r]

FILIVS. O me infelicem adolescentem, me desolatissimum iuuenem, me miserrimum hominem, quo me nunc uertam? Quid uita mihi opus est? Mors praestaret. Cur uiuere exoptarem, cum mihi amicissimi parentes mei obierint, sola mea solatio et spes qui fuere? O tu crudelissima mors, quam acerbe me conturbasti.

ARNOLDVS. Vt ita agis? Vt sic eiulas et lamentaris, pudetne te?

FILIVS. Ah, quid me puderet, prae dolore et maestitia quid agam ignoro.

CONRADVS. Animum sume, precare Deum ut parentum animae quiete caelesti fruantur, lacrimis ipsos in uitam non reuocabis.

FILIVS. Ah, ah, uellem et mihi pestis uitam adimeret.

ARNOLDVS. Taceas illa, nondum Deo uisum est ut moriaris, mortem precari noli, adhuc citius quam placebit tibi aderit.

FILIVS. O Deus, miserere mei miserrimi, et ab hac luce tollas ut una sim cum manibus meorum dilectorum parentum.

MVLIERES. Lacrimas siste et precare requiem tuis defunctis parentibus. Nos huc uenimus uinum afferentes consolatum te, simulque et tecum exporrectum frontem.

FILIVS. Nunc non est mihi neque animus neque tempus laetitiae, frustra aduenistis, exhilarari re nulla possum.

MVLIERES. Animum laetum tibi reddemus fauente Deo, antequam hinc abibimus.

FILIVS. Istud si poteritis admirabor. Credo quod si natura mea a summo Ioue immutaretur, uix laetus fierem, adeo totum me luctus et dolor omnibus partibus corporis ut sagitta penetrauit.

IOHANNES. You've ministered to our needs splendidly. We'll show ourselves grateful on another occasion.

8. A FUNERAL BANQUET

Son, who has lost both parents, host; Martinus, Conradus, Arnoldus and some women

SON. O, I am an unhappy boy, a youth left all alone, the most miserable of men! Where am I to turn now? What use is life to me? Death would be better. Why would I want to live, when my dearest parents have died – they were my only hope and comfort. O cruel death, how bitterly you have perturbed me!

ARNOLDUS. Why are you behaving like that? Why are you weeping and wailing? Aren't you ashamed?

SON. Oh, why should I be ashamed? I don't know what to do for grief and sorrow.

CONRADUS. Pull yourself together, pray God that your parents' souls may enjoy the peace of heaven. You won't bring them back to life with those tears.

SON. Oh, oh, I wish the plague would take my life too.

ARNOLDUS. Don't say that. God hasn't seen fit for you to die yet. Don't beg for death, it'll be on you quicker than you'd like.

SON. O God, take pity on me in my misery, and take me from this life so that I may be together with the shades of my beloved parents.

WOMEN. Stop your tears and pray for the repose of your dead parents. We've come and brought some wine to console you, and to cheer you up at the same time.

SON. This isn't the time for gladness for me, and I'm not in the mood either. You've come in vain, I can't be cheered by anything.

WOMEN. We'll cheer you up before we leave, God willing.

SON. I'll be amazed if you can manage that. I believe that even if my nature was changed by Almighty God, I could still hardly be cheerful, so completely has grief and anguish pierced every part of my body, like an arrow.

MVLIERES. Vino te ab omni maerore illo liberabimus.

FILIVS. Tum potitabo uobiscum ut animum recipiam.

CONRADVS. Cibum et uinum [I3v] nos afferimus, quo te donabimus et ipso animum tuum aspergemus ut alacrior fiat, ut mente capti aqua perfunduntur.

FILIVS. Sedete, iubebo mensam sternere seruum.

MVLIERES. Nos ipsam linteo ipsae tegemus, sine famulum suum pensum persoluere.

FILIVS. Nunc edite et bibite, si quid opipari attulistis e uestris penatibus, hic omnes luctu sumus obruti et consternati quod ciborum penitus obliuiscimur, pane et potu contenti.

MARTINVS. Hac uice oculos a lacrimis terge et genio indulgeas.

FILIVS. Vix potuero.

CONRADVS. Vno aut altero calice epoto redibit mentis alacritas. Hoc poculo integro te consolabor ut post me ipsum et tu ebibas.

FILIVS. Timeo ut potuero, gemitus et cordis tormentum uix concedet.

ARNOLDVS. Conandum quippiam praeter opinionem, non demittendus animus. Constantia uel magnanimitas uiros et arguit et commendat; flere, lamentari, eiulare mulierum sunt, uiris inhonestissima.

CONRADVS. Poculum fac ebibas.

FILIVS. Propino tibi amicissime.

MARTINVS. Accipiam libenter. Bibas felici omine.

ARNOLDVS. Propino tibi, Iohannes dilecte, in honorem tuorum proborum parentum morte iam ablatorum tibi.

FILIVS. Illorum nomine per uices post te bibam. Vicina, hunc calicem ebibam, uis et tu deinde ipsum exiccare si tibi praebibero?

MVLIER. Volo, etiam si adhuc duplo esset maior.

FILIVS. Vt bibero, ita post me potabis et tu.

MVLIER. Faciam.

FILIVS. Viden, exorpsi, elambes et tu.

WOMEN. We'll use wine to free you completely from sadness.

SON. Then I'll drink with you, to cheer myself up.

CONRADUS. We've brought food and wine. We'll give them to you, and we'll sprinkle your spirits with them, so that they get livelier, the way insane people are drenched with water.

SON. Sit down, I'll order the servant to set the table.

WOMEN. We'll put the tablecloth on it ourselves; let your servant see to his own tasks.

SON. Now eat and drink, if you've brought any lavish food from your houses. Here we're all so overcome and unsettled by grief that we've completely forgotten about food; we're content with bread and water.

MARTINUS. Dry your eyes of tears this time, and enjoy yourself.

SON. I'll hardly manage it.

CONRADUS. Once you've drunk a glass or two your enthusiasm will come back. I'll console you with this full cup, so that you'll drain it after me.

SON. I doubt I'll be able to. My sorrow and mental torment will hardly allow it.

ARNOLDUS. You have to try something more than you think you can, you mustn't let your spirits droop. Steadfastness and bravery are the marks of men; weeping, grieving and wailing are for women, and disgraceful for men.

CONRADUS. Empty the cup.

SON. I drink to you most cordially.

MARTINUS. I'll accept it gladly. May you drink to your good health.

ARNOLDUS. I drink to you, my dear Iohannes, in honour of your fine parents who have now been taken from you by death.

SON. I'll drink after you in turn in their name. Good neighbour, I'll drink this cup; will you drain it afterwards if I drink it to you?

WOMAN. I will, even if it were twice as big.

SON. As I drink, you drink after me.

WOMAN. I will.

SON. There, I've emptied it; drink it dry yourself.

MVLIER. Non omittam. Tibi propino, Conrade.

CONRADVS. Bibas nomine superum.

ARNOLDVS. Vt nunc te habes, Iohannes dilectissime, nunquam maeror discutitur tibi in anima?

FILIVS. Labascit, nonnihil hilarior fio.

MARTINVS. Vinum solet ho- [I4r] minum curas utcumque magnas soluere.

FILIVS. Gaudeo uos me accessisse consolatum. Si unquam licebit per opes, rependam. Miror tamen unde mos sit ortus per uinum et conuiuium consolandi lugentes defunctos.

ARNOLDVS. A gentilibus Thracibus, qui hominum puerperia luctuosa, sed funera laetabunda habuerunt

---

7 obierint] obierint C; obierunt B | 8 qui] quae B C | 35 mente] menti B C | 38 ipsae] ipsae C; ipsi B | 55 tibi] tibi C; ibi B

9. CONVIVIVM NVPTIALE

Sponsus, Anna sponsa, Parentes amborum, Amici inuitati, Famuli, Citharoedi

SPONSVS. Vincti nunc sumus iugo matrimonii et capistro inextricabili.

ANNA. Laus superis, nostrum matrimonium fortunet Supremus.

SPONSVS. Id faciet spero si nos concorditer uixerimus.

PARENS. Salutem exopto tibi, fili mi.

SPONSVS. Gratiam habeo, mi pater.

PARENS. O filia mea, fac cum tuo marito uiuas tranquille.

ANNA. Discors ipsa nunquam ero, si ipse non litem seminauerit.

PARENTES. Ambobus sit felix fortunatum coniugium.

SPONSVS. Sic faciat Dei Filius ipsaque Virgo Deipara.

PARENTES. Sponsus mensae accumbat, tum et inuitati discumbent.

AMICI. Felicitatem initi matrimonii optamus sponso et sponsae.

SPONSVS. Gratia sit uobis omnibus.

WOMAN. I will indeed. I drink to you, Conrad.
CONRADUS. Drink in the gods' name.
ARNOLDUS. How are you feeling now, my dear Iohannes? Is the sadness in your soul not being dispelled at all?
SON. It's weakening, I'm getting a little cheerier.
MARTINUS. Wine usually lessens human cares, even great ones.
SON. I'm very glad that you've come to console me. If I ever have enough money, I'll repay you. But I wonder where the custom of using wine and feasting to console those who are mourning the dead originated.
ARNOLDUS. From the pagan Thracians, who considered that human births were sorrowful, but funerals were happy.

9. A WEDDING BANQUET

Bridegroom; Anna, the bride; both sets of Parents; invited Friends; Servants; Lute-players

BRIDEGROOM. Now we're joined by the marital bond, and a yoke that can't be undone.
ANNA. Thank heavens. May the Lord prosper our marriage.
BRIDEGROOM. He will, I hope, if we live in harmony together.
PARENT. I width you blessings, my son.
BRIDEGROOM. Thank you, Father.
PARENT. O my daughter, be sure to live at peace with your husband.
ANNA. I'll never be at odds with him, if he doesn't give rise to arguments.
PARENTS. May you both enjoy a happy and blessed marriage.
BRIDEGROOM. May God the Son and his Virgin Mother grant that.
PARENTS. Let the bridegroom be seated, then let the guests sit down.
FRIENDS. We wish the bride and groom happiness at the start of their marriage.
BRIDEGROOM. Thank you to all of you.

PARENS. Saluos uos aduenisse gaudeo nomine sponsi et sponsae.

AMICI. Vbi nam sponsum conueniemus?

PARENS. Iam aderit. En alias inter amicos nugatur, eum accedite.

AMICI. Salue, Sponse. Gratulamur tibi ob hunc diem genialem nouamque tuam nuptam et multum optamus felicitatis.

SPONSVS. Par uobis Deus referat, et quod dignati estis meas inuisere nuptias.

AMICI. Maiora tuorum parentum causa faceremus.

SPONSVS. Mutuum reddam si quandoque inseruire potuero uobis. Nunc discumbite, edendi tempus est. [I4v]

ANNA. Obsequemur.

SPONSVS. Vos famuli fercula afferte.

FAMVLI. Praesto sunt, tu conuiuis praeponito.

SPONSVS. Istud uos exequimini, ipse prandium consecrabo hymno. Benedicite.

ANNA. Dominus.

SPONSVS. Christus Dei Filius hoc prandium benedicere uelit, sua gratia donare, uelit nostro huic interesse conuiuio nuptiali, ut quondam in mundo humana carne, in Cana Galilaeae cum gloriosa sua matre Maria dignatus fuit adesse.

ANNA. Amen.

SPONSVS. Nunc amici omnes patinis et poculis uos consolamini et reficite.

ANNA. Facere istud esuries nos belle docebit.

SPONSVS. Fortiter edite, sat uini et cibi praeponetur.

AMICVS. Sponse, propino tibi in felicitatem tuarum nuptiarum.

SPONSVS. Sit saluti. Amici mei, cognati et agnati, praebete uos hilares rogo.

AMICI. Faciemus, ne cures. Quomodo pugni tibi placuerunt quos hodie in templo accepisti, fueruntne molesti?

SPONSVS. Mordebant me nonnihil, tamen in hoc me consolabar, quia uibices non intulerunt.

AMICI. Cur plagis ita nouos sponsos tundant, scisne?

PARENT. In the name of the bride and groom, I'm delighted you've come.

FRIENDS. Where will we meet the bridegroom?

PARENT. He'll be here soon. Look, he's over there joking amongst his friends, go up to him.

FRIENDS. Greetings, Bridegroom. Congratulations on this special day, and on your new bride. We wish you great happiness.

BRIDEGROOM. May God repay you, and the fact that you've been good enough to come to my wedding.

FRIENDS. We'd do more for your parents' sake.

BRIDEGROOM. I'll return the favour if ever I can be of service to you. Now sit down, it's time to eat.

ANNA. We'll do as you say.

BRIDEGROOM. Servants, serve the food.

SERVANTS. It's ready; you set it in front of the guests.

BRIDEGROOM. You see to that, I'll say grace over the meal. Benedicite.

ANNA. Dominus.

BRIDEGROOM. May Christ the Son of God be pleased to bless this meal, and to bestow his grace on it. May he be present at this wedding feast, as once in the world, in human flesh, he deigned to be present at Cana of Galilee with his glorious mother Mary.

ANNA. Amen.

BRIDEGROOM. Now, friends all, comfort and restore yourselves with the food and drink.

ANNA. Our hunger will show us how to do that very well.

BRIDEGROOM. Eat up, enough food and drink will be served.

FRIEND. Bridegroom, I drink to you and to the happiness of your wedding.

BRIDEGROOM. Cheers. My friends and relatives, behave merrily, I beg you.

FRIENDS. We will, don't worry. How did you like the blows you received in the church today? Did they bother you?

BRIDEGROOM. They hurt me a bit, but I consoled myself with the fact that they didn't raise any weals.

FRIENDS. Do you know why they give newly married men blows like that?

SPONSVS. Ignoro, nisi quod consuetudinis est.

AMICVS. Audi, tibi dicam sed ioco accipias.

SPONSVS. Non me offendet.

AMICVS. In aede sacra noui sponsi pugnis afficiuntur ut assuescant tum uerba, tum uerbera ab uxore noua sua sponsa ferre.

SPONSVS. Portendit illud?

AMICVS. Vtique, sed compertumne habes cur cereum lumen ardens sponsae praeferatur in templum?

SPONSVS. Non.

AMICVS. Ideo, qui uxorem ducit domum, flammam in aedes accipit et perpetuum tormentum.

SPONSVS. Spero talia me in sponsa mea non habiturum.

AMICI. Neque istud nos credimus.

PATER. O fili, circumeamus exceptum conuiuas, caro assa praeposita est.

SPONSVS. Congrediare tu pater meo lo- [15r] quere nomine.

PARENTES. Agimus, habemus et referemus uobis gratias, sponsus sponsa nosque ipsorum parentes agnati et cognati, par parique rependemus, ubi obsequio nostro indigueritis.

AMICI. Grati erimus, quod aduenimus sponte et lubentes fecimus.

SPONSVS. Vos ministri, tollite singula, tempus est ut munuscula dent amici et choreae ducantur.

FAMVLI. Faciemus uelociter.

SPONSVS. Gratiam dicamus Domino Deo qui nos pauit, suaque gratia has nuptias fortunare uelit.

AMICI. Amen. Hoc munusculo aureo sponsum et sponsam donamus, quoad nostri filii adoleuerint, tum repetemus.

PARENTES. Gratiam referimus, et recompensabimus.

---

6 ANNA.] An. C; AR. B | 14 SPONSVS.] SPONSVS. C; SpE. B | 21 AMICI] Ami. C; ANI. B | 31, 36 ANNA.] AN. B; Ami. C | 53 tundant] tundant C; tundantur B | 78 FAMVLI.] PA. B; Paren. C | 81 Amen. Hoc] Amen. AMI Hoc B C

BRIDEGROOM. I don't, I only know that it's the custom.

FRIEND. I've heard why. I'll tell you, as long as you accept it as a joke.

BRIDEGROOM. It won't offend me.

FRIEND. In the church, newly married men are given thumps so as they get used to suffering words, and blows, from their new wives.

BRIDEGROOM. Is that what it means?

FRIEND. Indeed it is. But are you aware why a burning candle is carried in front of the bride into the church?

BRIDEGROOM. No.

FRIEND. In the same way, someone who takes a wife is taking flames and eternal torment into his house.

BRIDEGROOM. I hope I don't have those in my wife.

FRIENDS. We don't think so either.

FATHER. Son, let's circulate and greet the guests, the roast meat has been served.

BRIDEGROOM. You come with me, Father, and speak in my name.

PARENTS. We, the bride and groom and their parents and relatives, thank you warmly; we'll repay your generosity when you have need of our services.

FRIENDS. We'll be grateful, for we came willingly and gladly.

BRIDEGROOM. Servants, take everything away, it's time for our friends to give us their presents, and for the dancing.

SERVANTS. We'll do that quickly.

BRIDEGROOM. We thank the Lord who has fed us, and who has been pleased to bless this wedding with his grace.

FRIENDS. Amen. We are giving this gift of money to the bride and groom until our own children grow up; then we'll ask for it back.

PARENTS. We thank you, and we'll return it to you.

10. CONVIVIVM EPICVREVM

Zeno hospes; Sardanapalus, Philoxenus et Aesopus conuiuae; Seruus

ZENO. O uos discipuli mei et conuiuae, quid in mundo felicissimum esse creditis, hominisque summum bonum?

SARDANAPALVS. Incerti sumus, tu nos ut praeceptor instrue.

ZENO. De summo hominis bono in mundo sententiae fuerunt uariae: aliqui in gloria, in diuitiis nonnulli, alii in uirtute, alii in sanitate corporis ponunt, omnibus autem illis nos uerius dicimus in uoluptate corporis, in cuticula scilicet curanda esse situm optimum hominis bonum.

PHILOXENVS. Qui hoc sciemus, colende praeceptor?

ZENO. Contemplamini animalia tam bruta quam rationalia, omnia uidebitis natura esse procliuia in uoluptatem, in gulam, in crapulam; et esuriem, famem aegre ferunt ferreque diu non possunt.

AESOPVS. Sentio et in meo corpore calcar esse incitans me ad curam palati, stomachi gulaeque saturitatem et expletionem. [I5v]

ZENO. Quod natura omnium rerum parens et alitrix ingenuit homini, quis hoc pessimum diceret?

SARDANAPALVS. Certe nullus sanae mentis.

ZENO. Optimum est quod conducit, prodest et iuuat, nonne?

PHILOXENVS. Inficias ire salua fronte nemo potest.

ZENO. Voluptas autem uel cura corporis ipsi homini confert plurimum: uitam conseruat, corpus alit, quo fulcito et uiuo, etiam anima, in homine pars nobilissima, ualet; corpus enim est animae stabilimentum et fulcimentum.

AESOPVS. Abeant igitur aerumnosi Solones, famelici illi philosophi, qui sua fraudant genia, se macerant, maluntque stomacho inani et uacuo philosophari quam saturi et pleno uentre.

ZENO. In meas uos iurate leges, mihi uos addicite, philosophiam uos docebo et animae et corporis culturam afferentem.

SARDANAPALVS. Tuae ferulae subdemus manus, praeceptor colendissime.

10. AN EPICUREAN BANQUET

Zeno, host; Sardanapalus, Philoxenus and Aesop, guests; Servant

ZENO. O my pupils and guests, what in the world do you think is the greatest felicity, and the supreme human good?

SARDANAPALUS. We aren't sure. You tell us, as our teacher.

ZENO. There have been various opinions on the supreme human good. Some identify it as reputation, some as wealth, others as virtue, some as bodily health. But to all of them we say that the greatest good of man is to be found in physical pleasure, in indulging oneself.

PHILOXENUS. How can we know this, esteemed teacher?

ZENO. Observe the animals, the brutes as well as the rational ones. You'll see that they're all inclined by nature to pleasure, to eating and drinking; they find it difficult to tolerate hunger, and they can't tolerate it for very long.

AESOPUS. In my body, too, I feel a stimulus urging me on to satisfy my hunger and fill my stomach.

ZENO. Who could describe as evil what nature, the mother and sustainer of all things, has implanted in man?

SARDANAPALUS. Certainly no one of sound mind.

ZENO. The highest good is what is helpful, useful and beneficial, is that not so?

PHILOXENUS. No one could honestly deny it.

ZENO. Yet pleasure, and care of the body, is highly beneficial to man: it preserves life, it feeds the body, and when that is strengthened, even the soul, the noblest part of man, is vigorous; for the body is the support and stay of the soul.

AESOPUS. So away with the carping Solons, those famished philosophers, who deprive and weaken themselves, and prefer to do philosophy on a gapingly empty stomach than on a full one.

ZENO. Swear obedience to my rules, attach yourselves to me; I will teach you a philosophy that involves taking care of both the soul and the body.

SARDANAPALUS. We'll submit ourselves to your tutelage, esteemed teacher.

ZENO. Non olim fecisse uos paenitebit, erudiam namque uos in philosophia lucernaria, quam ad lucernas domi egentes imbibunt Sophi ipsi. Deinde philosophiam Epicuream et uoluptariam, qua apud uulgares passim in tabernis, ubique apud principes et reges grata sit uestra et praesentia et conuictus.

PHILOXENVS. Quae ista erit philosophia uoluptatis?

ZENO. Vt aliis praescribere poteritis, quomodo studere crapulae, gulae et uentri debeant.

SARDANAPALVS. Istud si noscerem in loco uiatici magni aestimarem, nam nosco complures qui omnia metiuntur crapula.

ZENO. Xerxes rex Persarum repertori nouae uoluptatis constituit pretium.

PHILOXENVS. Ecquid aerumnosis aliis philosophis praemii pollicitus est, qui abstinentia uictitandum esse dicunt?

AESOPVS. Illis medium digitum ostentat.

ZENO. Permulti ubiuis gentium nostram [I6r] sententiam sequuntur, diu noctuque poculis et patinis addicti.

PHILOXENVS. Apud Milesios magno in pretio uoluptas habetur, fames spernitur, expellitur, extremumque malorum aestimatur.

ZENO. Sybaritae delicatissimi uictitantes in annum integrum unius conuiuii apparatum fecerunt. Conuiuas ante anni auspicium uocauerant, quo se ornandi restaret sat temporis.

SARDANAPALVS. O terque quaterque beatos et sapientes illos Sybaritas!

AESOPVS. Tarentini quoque molles et delicati sunt nuncupati, ob uoluptatis assiduum studium.

PHILOXENVS. Praecepta nobis praebe, quo illam uoluptatem felicissimum hominis bonum amplecti poterimus utrisque brachiis.

ZENO. You won't regret having done it, for I'll instruct you in the scholarly philosophy that the poverty-stricken scholars burn the midnight oil to absorb. Then I'll teach you the Epicurean philosophy of pleasure, which will make your presence and company welcome amongst the common people in all the taverns and amongst princes and kings everywhere.

PHILOXENUS. What will that philosophy of pleasure be?

ZENO. That you'll be able to tell others how they should cultivate eating, drinking and their stomachs.

SARDANAPALUS. If I knew that, I'd prize it as a great resource, for I know a lot of people whose yardstick is overindulgence.

ZENO. Xerxes the king of Persia offered a prize to someone who invented a new pleasure.

PHILOXENUS. And what prize did he promise to the other wretched philosophers who say that we should live in abstinence?

AESOPUS. He gave them the finger.

ZENO. Everywhere you look, there are lots of people following our opinion, dedicated to eating and drinking night and day.

PHILOXENUS. Amongst the Milesians they set great store by pleasure. Hunger is despised, rejected and regarded as the greatest of evils.

ZENO. The Sybarites, who lived most luxuriously, made food for a single banquet that lasted all year. They invited their guests before the beginning of the year, so that they'd have enough time to dress themselves.

SARDANAPALUS. Those Sybarites were three and four times happy and wise!

AESOPUS. The people of Tarentum, too, were called soft and self-indulgent, on account of their assiduous cultivation of pleasure.

PHILOXENUS. Provide us with some principles, so that we may embrace pleasure, the supreme human good, with open arms.

ZENO. Faciam, aduertite. Quoad uixeritis, edite, bibite, ludite, et cum uos mortales noritis, praesentibus uos explete, post mortem nulla uoluptas, post funera puluis eritis, ea habebitis quae libidine exsaturata in uita hausistis, ut quondam Sardanapalus ille noster rex Assyriorum in sepulchri sui epitaphio inscribi iussit.

SARDANAPALVS. Quam miseri hactenus desipuimus chartis addicti, inedia uitam egimus.

ZENO. Tandem resipite, non minus poculis et patinis quam lucernis philosophicis dediti sitis.

PHILOXENVS. Exequemur fidelissime.

ZENO. Edite, bibite, curate cuticulam, genio indulgete, sic et hominibus accepti eritis.

11. CONVIVIVM CANINVM VEL CEREALE

Salacon hospes; Codrus, Irus, Amyntas conuiuae

SALACON. Saluete, sodales mei pauperrimi, quid hic gradum sistitis, nihil uobis domi est negotii?

CODRVS. Nihil neque negotii, neque cibi, neque potus, sed esuriei plurimum. [I6v]

SALACON. Caretis et pane et aqua?

IRVS. Satis multum aquae in aedibus habemus, sed illa sitim, non famem comprimit.

SALACON. Si esuritis, uenite ad meos penates mecum commessatum.

AMYNTAS. Ah, quid tu nos aleres? Tibi frumenti est penuria et uictus.

SALACON. Domi meae mihi tantum adhuc suppetit commeatus quo uos saturabo uestrasque coniuges.

CODRVS. Credimus, uerbis nos pasceres abunde et nugis, at non mensae pabulo.

SALACON. Stomachis uos farciam, crepitantia intestina pacata efficiam. Saltem credite, et congrediemini.

IRVS. Fidem damus, sed uide ne nos ludos habeas.

ZENO. I will; pay attention. As long as you live, eat, drink, play, and since you realise that you are mortal, satisfy yourselves with what is to hand. After death there is no pleasure, once dead you will be dust; you will have the pleasurable experiences you enjoyed in life, as Sardanapalus, the king of the Assyrians, once ordered to be inscribed as an epitaph on his tomb.

SARDANAPALUS. We've lived so miserably and irrationally up to now, as slaves to books; we've been leading a life of starvation.

ZENO. But now repent, and devote yourselves to food and drink no less than to philosophical studies.

PHILOXENUS. We'll do that most faithfully.

ZENO. Eat, drink, live luxuriously, indulge yourselves, and this will also endear you to men.

11. A DINNER FIT FOR A DOG, CONSISTING OF BREAD

Salacon, host; Codrus, Irus, Amyntas, guests

SALACON. Greetings, my penurious friends! Why have your steps brought you here? Have you no business at home?

CODRUS. No business, and no food or drink either, just a lot of hunger.

SALACON. Have you no bread and water?

IRUS. We've got plenty of water at home, but that satisfies thirst, not hunger.

SALACON. If you're hungry, come to my house and eat with me.

AMYNTAS. Oh, how could you feed us? You lack grain and other food.

SALACON. At my house I still have enough for me to satisfy you and your wives.

CODRUS. We believe you – you'd feed us generously with words and jokes, but not with food.

SALACON. I'll stuff your stomachs, and I'll calm the rumblings of your insides. Just believe me, and come with me.

IRUS. We'll trust you, but make sure you're not kidding us.

SALACON. Ridere non soleo amicos, licet aerumnosus sim.

CODRVS. Quid nunc cibi habes quo uescemur?

SALACON. Aliquot mihi sunt frusta panis ostiatim collecta dura et forte mucida, uilisque cereuisia et iusculum emendicatum.

AMYNTAS. Victus est nobis genuinus, ad stipem namque rogandam nati credimur.

SALACON. Sedete et quiescite, in cibi sportula edenda quaeram.

CODRVS. Sed propera, acriter esurimus.

SALACON. Istos orbes panarios adipe linitos edite procenii loco quoad aliud attulero.

AMYNTAS. Precemur prius Deo nostro redemptori hymnum.

SALACON. Benedicite.

CONVIVAE. Dominus.

SALACON. Christus Dei filius Deus et homo, qui suo gratioso sanguine nos redemit, dignetur nobis exiguum et cereale prandium benedicere, qui sui sumus exemplar paupertate et mendicitate nostra. In nomine Patris et Filii et Spiritus Sancti.

CONVIVAE. Amen.

SALACON. Orbes nunc illos panarios carne unctos edite: caro discessit in aluum diuitum, nobis pauperibus in his orbibus reliquit pinguedinis uestigia.

CODRVS. O quam mellite sapiunt!

IRVS. Longe dulcius carnes, cuius iusculo madent, sapuerunt.

AMYNTAS. [I7r] Optimum condimentum fames est.

CODRVS. Verum, crudas fabas (ut uulgo fertur) sapere ac coctas efficit.

SALACON. Nunc eleemosynas has edite, durae sunt, attamen stomachum replebunt aeque ac mollissime forent.

IRVS. Sitio. Quid in lignea hac lagena est potus ?

SALACON. Cereuisia est e solo furfure cocta, quam uulgo tenuem potum dicunt.

CODRVS. Pytissabo eam.

SALACON. Facito, forte palato non displicebit.

CODRVS. Vtcumque ualet, uerum non satis igne est elixa.

SALACON. I may be a cause of distress, but I'm not in the habit of making fun of my friends.

CODRUS. So what food have you that we can eat?

SALACON. I have a few crusts of bread I collected round the doors; they're hard and probably mouldy, some inferior beer and some soup I begged.

AMYNTAS. That's proper food to us,

SALACON. Sit down and rest, I'll find something to eat in the food-basket.

CODRUS. But hurry, we're dying of hunger.

SALACON. Eat these bread trenchers spread with lard as a starter till I bring something else.

AMYNTAS. First let's say a prayer to God our Redeemer.

SALACON. Benedicite.

GUESTS. Dominus.

SALACON. May Christ, a man and the Son of God, who has graciously redeemed us with his blood, be pleased to bless our poor lunch of bread; for we imitate him in our poverty and destitution. In the name of the Father, and of the Son, and of the Holy Spirit.

GUESTS. Amen.

SALACON. Now eat those trenchers smeared with meat. The meat has passed into rich people's stomachs, leaving traces of fat in the trenchers for us poor men.

CODRUS. They taste delightful!

IRUS. The meat whose juices they're soaked in tasted much nicer.

AMYNTAS. Hunger is the best sauce.

CODRUS. Indeed. It makes raw beans taste like cooked ones, as the saying goes.

SALACON. Now eat these alms. They're hard, but they'll fill up your stomach just as much as if they were really soft.

IRUS. I'm thirsty. What drink's in this wooden pot?

SALACON. It's beer made only from husks of grain, what's commonly called small beer.

CODRUS. I'll have a taste.

SALACON. Do, it may not displease you.

CODRUS. It's reasonably strong, but it hasn't been boiled over a hot enough fire.

SALACON. Stomachus consumet quod ignis calore non praestitit.

AMYNTAS. Praeter hoc nihil quod edamus habes?

SALACON. Nonnihil iusculi mihi est, sed frigidum. Lignis careo, alias calidum facerem.

AMYNTAS. O te miserrimum Salaconem, cares lignis, tamen foris ambulas laute uestitus ac opulentissimus esses.

SALACON. Interdum conducticiis me orno uestibus.

CODRVS. Mortalium omnium nos miserrimi sumus, qui ad crepidinem et fores diuitum cogimur commeatum conquirere.

SALACON. Miseriae nostrae meminit Plautus dicens, 'Miser homo est, qui ipse sibi quod edit, quaerit et id aegre inuenit, sed ille miserior qui et aegre quaerit, et nihil inuenit, ille miserrimus qui cum esse cupit quod edat non habet.'

AMYNTAS. Sperandum, quod aliquando nostra fortuna immutabitur, nam omnium rerum (ut Comicus dixit) est uicissitudo.

IRVS. Salus unica nobis est, ut Capnion scripsit, quod nihil possumus perdere, cum nihil habeamus.

SALACON. Diuitum uita semper est sollicita et curarum plena.

CODRVS. Hinc soluemus anchoram. Emendicandi iam hora instat, nam apud diuites modo mensae tollentur.

AMYNTAS. Hymnum gratiarum actionis dicas.

SALACON. Deus pauperum consolator omniumque alumnus de habitis hic bolis gratiam habeat nobisque sit auxilio, ut alias dapes precarias nanciscamur. [I7v]

CONVIVAE. Amen.

SALACON. Nunc quisque diuitum aulas adeat stipem precatum in cenam.

CONVIVAE. Fiet, tu uale.

---

5 esuriei] esuriei C; esurei B | 83 nanciscamur] nanciscemur B C

SALACON. Your stomach will consume what the heat of the fire didn't manage.

AMYNTAS. Apart from this, have you nothing we can eat?

SALACON. I have a little broth left, but it's cold. I've no wood, or I'd heat it up.

AMYNTAS. O you poor Salacon, no wood, yet you walk about well dressed, as if you ate really well.

SALACON. At times I dress in hired clothes.

CODRUS. We're the most wretched of all mortals, having to collect our food on the doorsteps of the rich.

SALACON. Plautus mentions our plight when he says, 'It's a wretched man who looks for something to eat and can barely find it; even more wretched the man who can hardly manage to look for it, and finds nothing; but most wretched is he who, when he wants to eat something, hasn't got it.'

AMYNTAS. We must hope that our fortune will change some time, for as Terence says, 'everything has its ups and downs.'

IRUS. Our only saving grace, as Reuchlin put it, is that we can't lose anything, because we haven't got anything.

SALACON. Rich people's lives are always full of cares and worries.

CODRUS. We're leaving now. The hour for begging is nearly here, for at rich people's houses the tables are being cleared now.

AMYNTAS. You say grace.

SALACON. May God, the consoler of the poor and protector of all, be thanked for these morsels, and may he help us succeed in begging food elsewhere.

GUESTS. Amen.

SALACON. Now everyone go to rich people's houses and ask for an offering for dinner.

GUESTS. Right. Goodbye.

12. CONVIVIVM PLEBEIVM VEL VVLGARE

Henno hospes; Greta uxor; Dromo, Parmeno et Simo uicini et conuiuae

DROMO. Vbi est noster uicinus Henno?

GRETA. Non procul abest, quid ipsum quaeritis?

DROMO. Conuiuae sibi esse uolumus, si integrum fuerit.

GRETA. In horreo est dans pabulum equis, aduocabo ipsum. Heus, heus, Henno, adsis.

HENNO. Quid me uis?

GRETA. Hic nonnulli te conuentum expetunt.

HENNO. Adero celerrime. O mei uicini, quid uestri aduentus portendunt, quidue aduenistis?

SIMO. Venimus tecum pransuri; domi nostrae culinae algent, uxores in agris sunt et hortis.

HENNO. Per Herculem infelici auspicio aduenistis, ignoro an noster focus splendeat. Greta, ecquid in prandium nobis parasti eduliorum?

GRETA. Holusculum cum duobus frustellis carnis porcinae.

HENNO. Sufficiet, tum et butyro ac caseo uescemur, sed est ad edendum maturum?

GRETA. Paene. Quando uolueritis, linteo mensam tegam et prandium parabo.

HENNO. Quamprimum potueris facito, hi uicini forte esuriunt.

PARMENO. Non usqueadeo.

HENNO. Ex aquali lauetis manus et mensae adsidete.

DROMO. Fiet. Nunc quisque apud se orationem dicat, hic nullus est qui Latine cibum benedicat.

HENNO. Ipse dicam 'Benedicite, in nomine Patris et Filii et Spiritus Sancti, Amen.'

PARMENO. Est benedictio admodum succincta.

HENNO. Eam paroecianus quondam docuit me. Holere et carne illa porcina famem pelli- [I8^{r}] te, uenistis subiti hospites, ideo et praesentia boni consulite; si aduentus uestros praesciuissemus, splendidius parauissemus cibum.

12. A BANQUET OF COMMON PEOPLE

Henno, host; Greta, wife; Dromo, Parmeno and Simo, neighbours and guests

DROMO. Where's our neighbour Henno?

GRETA. He's not far away. Why are you looking for him?

DROMO. We're going to be his guests, if it's convenient.

GRETA. He's in the barn giving the horses their fodder, I'll call him. Hey, hey, Henno, come here!

HENNO. Why do you want me?

GRETA. There are some people here asking to see you.

HENNO. I'll be there in a tick. Neighbours, what does your arrival mean? Why have you come?

SIMO. We've come to have lunch with you. In our houses there's no fire in the kitchens, our wives are in the fields and gardens.

HENNO. Well indeed you've come at a bad time, I'm not sure whether our fire's lit. Greta, have you made us anything for lunch?

GRETA. A cabbage with two chunks of pork.

HENNO. That'll be enough. Afterwards we'll have butter and cheese – but is it ripe to eat?

GRETA. Almost. Whenever you like, I'll put the cloth on the table and get the lunch ready.

HENNO. Do it as soon as you can, these neighbours are probably starving.

PARMENO. Not particularly.

HENNO. Wash your hands with water from the jug and sit down at the table.

DROMO. Right. Now everyone say grace privately, there's no one here who can bless the food in Latin.

HENNO. I'll say, 'Benedicite, in nomine Patris et Filii et Spiritus Sancti, Amen.'

PARMENO. That's a pretty concise grace.

HENNO. The parish priest once taught me it. Satisfy your hunger with this cabbage and pork; you've arrived as unexpected guests, so be content with what there is. If we'd known you were coming we'd have made much better food.

PARMENO. Sileas, illa domestica patina et in aedibus nostris uiuimus, quidni et tum apud te ipsa essemus contenti?

SIMO. Multi patinas alienas spernunt, et in suis tuguriis uix nudo pascuntur pane.

DROMO. Ipse reiicio et contemno nihil praeter pugnos.

GRETA. Edite de holere illo, hodie in hortulo nostro recens est decerptum.

PARMENO. Belli saporis est, nam adipe madet.

SIMO. Porcina caro illa pinguet admodum.

HENNO. Sus erat nostra cura alitus et educatus. Simo, tibi praebibo de hoc potu nostro domestico.

SIMO. Tibi non incommodet.

DROMO. Tu mihi propines, nam sitio acerbe.

SIMO. Postquam bibero tibi lagenam porrigam.

DROMO. Bibe raptim, morari nequeo.

HENNO. Tu uxor mea dilecta, lactis coagulatae aliquid prome, si quempiam delectaret.

GRETA. Afferam, sed forte dulce non erit.

HENNO. Salubrius est sine dulcedine.

GRETA. Qui capitur lacte edat.

DROMO. Plurimum meo arridet palato.

PARMENO. Tempore aestus stomacho conuenit admodum, quia frigore suo ipsum perfundit.

HENNO. Si lubet, cibo non parcite; aut carne aut lacte uescimini.

PARMENO. Adulti sumus, edendum esse scimus ad dapes et patinas.

HENNO. Caseum, si quem habes pinguedine conditum, non e uitiato lacte paratum, eum deprome et butyri recentis nonnihil.

GRETA. Butyri illud Maio mense contusum a me, eo panem linite.

HENNO. De hoc caseo sumite aut butyro, ut lenes animis efficiamini. [I8v]

SIMO. Vicine noster Henno, tibi propino.

HENNO. Salutem opto imbibas.

DROMO. Fac tolli mensam, nobis in rus ad uxores eundum est.

PARMENO. Oh, be quiet. We live on ordinary food like that in our houses, too, so why wouldn't we be happy with it at yours?

SIMO. A lot of people turn their noses up at other people's food, and hardly even have dry bread to eat in their own cottages.

DROMO. The only thing I reject and avoid is being thumped.

GRETA. Eat the cabbage, it was cut freshly today in our garden.

PARMENO. It has a fine flavour, for it's dripping in fat.

SIMO. The pork makes it really fat.

HENNO. The sow was fed and reared by us. Simo, I drink this draught of our own beer to you.

SIMO. Your good health.

DROMO. You drink to me, for I'm really thirsty.

SIMO. As soon as I've drunk I'll pass you the pot.

DROMO. Drink quickly, I can't wait.

HENNO. Darling wife, serve some curds, if anyone would like them.

GRETA. I will, but they may not be sweet.

HENNO. They're healthier if they're not sweet.

GRETA. Anyone who likes curds, eat them.

DROMO. I really love them.

PARMENO.

HENNO. Don't spare the food, if you feel like it; eat the meat or the curds.

PARMENO. We're grown-ups, we know that dishes are there to be eaten.

HENNO. If you have any full-fat cheese, not made with sour milk, bring it out, and a bit of fresh butter.

GRETA. That butter was churned by me in May, spread it on your bread.

HENNO. Take some of this cheese or butter, to make your spirits gentle.

SIMO. Henno, our neighbour, I drink to you.

HENNO. Your good health.

DROMO. Clear the table. We have to go to our wives in the country.

HENNO. Vxor, conde singula. Gratia sit cunctipotenti Deo, qui nos alit sua clementia, crescereque e terra facit, quo nos indigni uescimur. Per Christum Dominum nostrum.

CONVIVAE. Amen.

HENNO. Vicini mei, parcum hoc prandiolum gratis accipite animis. Vile fuit, ut uillicorum solet esse mensa, uino caruimus, nam care uenit, bibentibusque obesse solet.

CONVIVAE. Tibi nunc agimus gratias. Si aliquando tibi libuerit, rursum et ad nostras edes patinas.

---

31 paroecianus] Parretianus B C

13. CONVIVIVM DIVITVM SIVE OPVLENTORVM

Croesus hospes; Crassus, Alcmaeon, Tantalus, Seruus, Vxor

CROESVS. Serue, i uocatum ad me Crassum, Alcmaeonem et Tantalum, ut mihi in prandio sint conuiuae, alioqui soli cenaturo.

SERVVS. Ibo facessum mandatum.

CROESVS. Dic me nolle ut emaneant.

SERVVS. Eloquar. Salue, Crasse.

CRASSVS. Et tu.

SERVVS. Rogat herus meus ut sibi conuiua esse digneris.

CRASSVS. Certe minus mihi iam est integrum.

SERVVS. Iussit ut dicerem se nolle recusari; etiam Alcmaeonem et Tantalum uocabo.

CRASSVS. Age, tum ueniam.

SERVVS. Facias. Abeo quaesitum et alios duos. Sis saluus, mi Alcmaeon.

ALCMAEON. Tu quoque.

SERVVS. Herum meum conuenire debes iam in prandium.

ALCMAEON. Prandebit solus?

SERVVS. Non, sed Crassus ipse aderit, et Tantalum iam ibo uocatum.

ALCMAEON. Tum lubens adueniam.

SERVVS. Praeter uos tres penitus neminem ad mensam inuitauit.

ALCMAEON. Abi Tantalum quaesitum, ego me accingam.

SERVVS. Ibo. Salue, Tantale honestissime. [K1r]

HENNO. Put everything away, wife. Thanks be to God Almighty, who feeds us in his mercy, and makes the food we unworthy people live on grow from the earth. Through Christ our Lord.

GUESTS. Amen.

HENNO. Neighbours, be content to accept this frugal lunch. It was humble, as peasants' food is. We had no wine, because it's dear, and it tends to be bad for those who drink it.

GUESTS. We thank you now. If ever you'd like to, eat at our tables another time.

13. A BANQUET OF WEALTHY PEOPLE

Croesus, host; Crassus, Alcmaeon, Tantalus, Servant, Wife

CROESUS. Servant, go and invite Crassus, Alcmaeon and Tantalus to be my guests at lunch, otherwise I'll have to eat alone.

SERVANT. I'll go and carry out your order.

CROESUS. Tell them I don't want them to stay away.

SERVANT. I will. Good day, Crassus.

CRASSUS. Good day.

SERVANT. My master asks you to deign to be his guest.

CRASSUS. It's not very convenient for me just now.

SERVANT. He told me to say that he doesn't want you to refuse; I'm going to invite Alcmaeon and Tantalus as well.

CRASSUS. Right, then I'll come.

SERVANT. Do. I'm off to ask the other two. Good day, Alcmaeon.

ALCMAEON. Good day.

SERVANT. You're to join my master now at lunch.

ALCMAEON. Will he be eating alone?

SERVANT. No, Crassus will be there, and I'm just going to invite Tantalus.

ALCMAEON. Then I'd love to go.

SERVANT. He's invited no one at all to eat apart from you three.

ALCMAEON. Go and ask Tantalus. I'll get myself ready.

SERVANT. I will. Good day, most honourable Tantalus.

TANTALVS. Et tu saluus sis.

SERVVS. Vult dominus meus ut secum prandeas, est quod te conuentum cupit.

TANTALVS. Iam uolebam auspicari prandium.

SERVVS. Parcas isti impendio in uesperam et aedes nostras inuise.

TANTALVS. Auscultabo et comitabor te.

SERVVS. Sic facies, et hero meo rem gratam facies.

CROESVS. Aduenire uestrum est gratum, mei amici. Vocaui uos, alioqui solus prandissem, quo nihil magis aduersum mihi est.

CONVIVAE. Et nobis acceptius nihil est quam aliena uiuere quadra.

CROESVS. Manibus aquam praebe tu, Serue. Lauetis, deinde accumbite. Tu Crasse istuc sedeas, tum tu Alcmaeon, deinde Tantale accubitum eas.

CRASSVS. Tu hospes superne et prior accumbas.

CROESVS. Hic mihi et meae uxori est sedendi locus. Benedicite.

CONVIVAE. Dominus.

CROESVS. Christus saluator omnium, redemptor et credentium, nobis huius prandii alimenta benedicta facere uelit, ut ipsa in salutem animarum sumamus.

CONVIVAE. Amen.

CROESVS. Has gallinas dirumpite, et iusculo exotico bolos panis madefacite.

CONVIVAE. Non negligemus.

CROESVS. Serue, uinum cyathis infunde uetus et nouum.

SERVVS. Effectum reddam.

CROESVS. Bibite hilariter, hospites mei, sat uobis largiar.

ALCMAEON. Impigri ad epulas esse solemus.

CROESVS. Poculum hoc uobis praebibam ut grati uestri sint aduentus.

TANTALVS. Salutifere sumas haustum istum.

CROESVS. Serue, tolle haec et assas carnes praebe et puras quadras.

CRASSVS. Alcmaeon, calicem medium tibi praebibo.

ALCMAEON. Sit commodo.

CRASSVS. Nunc et tu bibe.

TANTALUS. Good day to you.

SERVANT. My master would like you to eat with him; there's a reason he wants to meet you.

TANTALUS. I was just about to start lunch.

SERVANT. Save the expense till the evening, and come to our house.

TANTALUS. I will; I'll come with you.

SERVANT. Do, and you'll oblige my master.

CROESUS. I'm pleased you've come, my friends. I invited you because otherwise I'd have lunched alone, and there's nothing I dislike more.

GUESTS. And we like nothing more than living off someone else's food.

CROESUS. Servant, provide water for people's hands. Wash, then sit down. Crassus, you sit there, then you, Alcmaeon, then you sit there, Tantalus.

CRASSUS. You're the host; sit down first, in the highest place.

CROESUS. This is the place where my wife and I sit. Benedicite.

GUESTS. Dominus.

CROESUS. May Christ the saviour of all and redeemer of the faithful, be pleased to bless the food of this lunch, so that we may eat it to the salvation of our souls.

GUESTS. Amen.

CROESUS. Divide these chickens, and dip chunks of bread in their exotic gravy.

GUESTS. We will indeed.

CROESUS. Servant, pour old and new wine into the cups.

SERVANT. I'll see to that.

CROESUS. Drink merrily, my guests. I'll give you plenty.

ALCMAEON. We're not usually lazy when it comes to banquets.

CROESUS. I'll drink this cup to you in honour of your coming.

TANTALUS. May what you drink be to your good health.

CROESUS. Servant, take these away, and bring on roast meats and clean plates.

CRASSUS. Alcmaeon, I drink half a cup to you.

ALCMAEON. Cheers.

CRASSUS. Now you drink too.

VXOR. De his perdicibus, uel lepore aut capis illaridatis edite. Quisque suo palato iucundum accipiat.

CRASSVS. Croese hospes, propinabo tibi, si alteri praebibere uolueris.

CROESVS. Bibe, mei mune- [K1v] ris ad pocula immemor esse non soleo.

ALCMAEON. O quam delicatos et uoluptuarios dies agimus nos opulenti, cum interim pauperes esuriant.

TANTALVS. Panis uix sat habent nonnulli inopum.

CROESVS. Opum mihi tantum est quo exercitum alere uellem copiosum.

CRASSVS. Et ego et frugibus et aere abundo non parum.

TANTALVS. Argenti et bonorum aceruum et ego possideo.

CROESVS. Viuamus igitur genialiter.

CRASSVS. Posteris meis non multum relinquam.

TANTALVS. Opibus ego quoad uixero potiar, nepotes mei si egebunt, quaerant, ut ipse quondam feci.

VXOR. Sed interim cibi estis immemores.

CROESVS. Serue, bellaria affer.

CRASSVS. Illa non expectabimus, alio nos uocant negotia. Fac hymnum legi, nobis abeundum est.

CROESVS. Benedictus qui est in saecula saeculorum, nostro nomine habeat laudem et honorem, nostrique misereatur.

CONVIVAE. Amen.

WIFE. Eat these partridges, or hare, or these larded capons. Everyone take something that pleases his taste.

CRASSUS. Croesus, our host, I'll drink to you if you're prepared to drink to someone else.

CROESUS. Drink, I'm not usually neglectful of my duty in drinking.

ALCMAEON. What pampered lives of pleasure we rich people live, whilst the poor are starving.

TANTALUS. Some of the poor hardly have enough bread.

CROESUS. I have enough wealth to feed a large army.

CRASSUS. And I have a great deal of grain and money.

TANTALUS. And I own a huge quantity of silver and possessions.

CROESUS. So let's live with good cheer.

CRASSUS. I'm not going to leave much to my descendants.

TANTALUS. I'm going to do what I want with my wealth in my lifetime. If my children are short, they can earn it, as I once did myself.

WIFE. But in the meantime you're forgetting the food.

CROESUS. Servant, bring on the desserts.

CRASSUS. We'll not wait for them, we have other business that calls us. Have grace said, we must be off.

CROESUS. May he who is blessed for ever and ever have praise and honour in our name, and may he have mercy on us.

GUESTS. Amen.

14. CONVIVIVM PASCHALE

Paterfamilias; Iohannes, Marcus, Benedictus, Iasperus, Gotfridus, Tilmannus; Famuli domus

PATERFAMILIAS. Vt se habent uestri stomachi et uentres, suntne uacui?

FAMVLI. Crepitant instar ueteris membranae librorum et nouarum solearum.

MARCVS. Ecastor ilia mihi crepant, fauces lippiunt fame, crura ferre me nolunt, brachia uix tollere possum, ita uiribus ieiunio sum exhaustus, instar lucernae oleo exiccato.

PATERFAMILIAS. Aqua manus abluite, paschalibus et nouis cibis amissas corporeas uires resarciemus.

BENEDICTVS. Impigre nos accingemus patinis istis.

PATERFAMILIAS. Benedicite.

FAMVLI. Dominus.

PATERFAMILIAS. Haec est dies quam fecit Dominus, exultemus et laetemur in ea. Pascha nostrum immolatus est Christus, itaque epulemur in azymis sinceritatis et ueritatis, Alleluia. Pater noster... Ouum quisque accipiat, deinde de perna et aliis carnibus.

TILMANNVS. Esuries et fames mihi fuit uehemens.

PATERFAMILIAS. Eam mutes iam saturitate.

IASPERVS. Laus superis quod ad hunc diem superstites mansimus.

GOTFRIDVS. Gaudeo plurimum huiusmodi pisces in patinas rediisse.

MARCVS. Hi pisces robur praebent maius quam esurialis cibus.

BENEDICTVS. Istud hodie experiar an uires accipiam ualidiores.

PATERFAMILIAS. Alterum edite ouum si lubet.

MARCVS. Vnum adhuc edam.

TILMANNVS. Pernam ego petam cultro, experiarque ut sapiat.

BENEDICTVS. Marce, quot oua una uice posses ingurgitare?

MARCVS. Octo sine opera et labore.

IOHANNES. Dura an mollia?

MARCVS. Adhuc fluida, non indurata.

IOHANNES. At cuius generis uel farinae?

14. AN EASTER BANQUET

Father of the family; Iohannes, Marcus, Benedictus, Iasperus, Gotfridus, Tilmannus; Servants of the house

FATHER. What state are your stomachs in? Are they empty?

SERVANTS. They're crackling like the pages of old books or new sandals.

MARCUS. My insides are rumbling, I swear, my throat's burning with hunger, my legs can't carry me, I can hardly raise my arms, so worn out has my strength been by fasting, like a lamp that's run out of oil.

FATHER. Wash your hands in water, we'll restore the physical strength we've lost with new Easter food.

BENEDICTUS. We'll get ready for those dishes pretty smartly.

FATHER. Benedicite.

FATHER. Dominus.

FATHER. This is the day that the Lord has made, let us rejoice and be glad in it. Christ our Passover has been sacrificed; therefore let us feast on the unleavened bread of sincerity and truth, Alleluia. Our Father …

Everyone take an egg, then some ham and other meats.

TILMANNUS. I was overpowered by hunger and starvation.

FATHER. Exchange it now for a full stomach.

IASPERUS. Thank heavens that we've survived to this day.

GOTFRIDUS. I'm particularly pleased that fish like this are back on our plates again.

MARCUS. These fish give us more strength than Lenten food.

BENEDICTUS. Today I'll see if I get more strength back.

FATHER. Eat another egg if you like.

MARCUS. I'll eat another one.

TILMANNUS. I'm taking my knife to the ham, to see if it tastes good.

BENEDICTUS. Marcus, how many eggs can you eat at one go?

MARCUS. Eight, without any trouble.

IOHANNES. Hard- or soft-boiled?

MARCUS. Pretty runny, not too hard.

IOHANNES. And what kind?

MARCVS. Gallinis parta.

IOHANNES. Aestimabam ea quae ad saepes iam sole torrentur.

MARCVS. Illa tibi uulturi essent apta.

TILMANNVS. Tu in ouis edendis octo aliorum munere posses fungi.

IASPERVS. Edendo ipsa pensum meum belle persoluere uellem, si certatim comederemus.

PATERFAMILIAS. Carnes iusculo elixas affer tu Puer. Praebibo uobis hoc sacro Paschatis die.

FAMVLI. Conferat tibi bibenti.

PATERFAMILIAS. Inuicem uobis praebibite, laetosque animos poculis uobis facite.

GOTFRIDVS. Iohannes, amicitiae et caritatis haustu te adoriar.

IOHANNES. Accipiam abs te lubenter.

BENEDICTVS. Hero nostro propino.

PATERFAMILIAS. Bibe feliciter. Puer, assas carnes prome, his saturi sumus.

IOHANNES. Benedicte, uitrum hoc tibi medium propino, uerum tu bibe quantum uolueris. [K2v]

BENEDICTVS. Auspicato bibes, tum et ipse potabo.

IASPERVS. Thylmanne, a prandio tuas aedes inuisemus omnes, uis nos ouis excipere?

TILMANNVS. Ne gru quidem largiar. Tabernae hospes non sum, si conuiuari uultis, diuersoria accedite.

GOTFRIDVS. Marcus nos medio agno, frustoque uitulinae carnis exciperet, si suum domicilium adiremus.

MARCVS. Ad Kalendas Graecas.

BENEDICTVS. Nihil immune nobis dares his sacris feriis?

MARCVS. Nil nisi sellas et scamna uobis impartiar.

BENEDICTVS. Istis tu stomachum ieiunum pascas.

PATERFAMILIAS. Cibo utimini ut tollatur, appetit hora contionem sacram audiendi. Qui assa carne delectatur Chrysippum non agat. Puer, bellaria fac adsint, et haec ut tollantur.

TILMANNVS. Marce, haustum Paschalem tibi propino.

MARCUS. Hen's eggs.
BENEDICTUS. I thought you meant the kind of eggs that are drying in the sun by the hedges.
MARCUS. They'd do well for a vulture like you.
TILMANNUS. You can do the work of eight other people when it comes to eating eggs.
IASPERUS. I hope I'd acquit myself well in an egg-eating contest.
FATHER. Boy, bring on the meats boiled in stock. I'll drink to you this holy Easter Day.
SERVANTS. Good health to you who drink!
FATHER. Drink to one another, and be merry in your drink.
GOTFRIDUS. Iohannes, I honour you with this draught of friendship and love.
IOHANNES. I'll accept it from you gladly.
BENEDICTUS. I drink to our master.
FATHER. Your good health. Boy, serve the roast meats, we've had enough of these ones.
IOHANNES. Benedictus, I drink this half glass to you; but you drink as much as you want.
BENEDICTUS. Your good health! You drink first, then I will.
IASPERUS. Tilmannus, after lunch we'll go to your house. Are you prepared to give us eggs?
TILMANNUS. I won't give you a sausage. I'm not an innkeeper; if you want to party, go to the alehouses.
GOTFRIDUS. Marcus would give us half a lamb and a piece of veal if we went to his house.
MARCUS. When Hell freezes over!
BENEDICTUS. Wouldn't you give us anything free on this holy day?
MARCUS. I'll let you have nothing other than chairs and stools.
BENEDICTUS. That's what you fill your stomach with when it's empty.
FATHER. Eat the food up so as it can be taken away, it's nearly time to hear the sermon. Anyone who likes roast meat, don't hold back. Boy, have the desserts served, and these dishes taken away.
TILMANNUS. Marcus, I drink an Easter draught to you.

MARCVS. Quid Paschalem? Vini haustum malo, eo corculum meum iuuo.

PATERFAMILIAS. A cibo templa adite auditum sacram contionem precesque uespertinas, et ad cenam in tempore adsitis denuo, sacratissimae hodie sunt feriae.

GOTFRIDVS. Nusquam ibimus nisi fortassis ad Marcum, degustatum de ouis suae mensae.

MARCVS. Si ueneritis, ante fores uobis manendum erit.

PATERFAMILIAS. De his nouis et Paschalibus obsoniis benedicimus Domino.

FAMVLI. Deo gratias.

PATERFAMILIAS. Benedictus et gloriosus sit Dei Filius, qui hodierna die a morte resurgens ab aeterna nos liberauit morte.

FAMVLI. Amen.

---

68 ieiunum] ieiunum C; ieiunium B

15. CONVIVIVM NVNDINARIVM SIVE DEDICATIONIS TEMPLI

Villicus, Vxor; Pistor, Textor, Calcearius ex urbe ciues; [K3r] **Seruus**

VILLICVS. Cura, uxor mea Elsa, ut sacrificio missae peracto piper ceteraque obsonia sat cocta sint; forte ex urbe nos amiculi nonnulli inuisent.

VXOR. Enitar pro uiribus. Tu seruum iube scopis uerrere pauimentum horrei uel cubiculi, in quo conuiuae sedebunt prandentes.

VILLICVS. Serue, cubiculum istud a pulueribus redde purissimum, parietibusque adhaerentes aranearum telas depone, ne quid sit quod conuiuiis nauseam inferat.

SERVVS. Curabo.

VILLICVS. Piperis habeas praecipuam curam, ne uel aduratur neue insipidum fiat, nam ipsum imprimis nundinarum tempore palatis aduenarum placere solet.

VXOR. Quae culinae sunt munia sine te exequar bellissime, me coquere permitte et tu cocta edas. Satis adulta sum, non egeo in coquendo te instructore.

MARCUS. An Easter draught? I prefer a draught of wine, that's what delights my heart.

FATHER. After the meal, go to the churches to hear the sermon and Vespers, then be back again in time for dinner: this is a high holiday.

GOTFRIDUS. We aren't going anywhere, except perhaps to Marcus's house, to taste the eggs from his table.

MARCUS. If you do, you'll have to stay outside the door.

FATHER. For these new Easter dishes, we bless the Lord.

SERVANTS. Thanks be to God.

FATHER. May the Son of God be blessed and glorious, who, rising this day from death, freed us from everlasting death.

SERVANTS. Amen.

15. A FAIR BANQUET

Farmer, Wife; Baker, Weaver, Shoemaker, who live in the city; Servant

FARMER. Elsa, my wife, see that after Mass the pepper and the other dishes are cooked; some of our friends from the city may visit us.

WIFE. I'll do what I can. Servant, order the floor of the barn or the room where the guests will sit and eat lunch to be swept with a broom.

FARMER. Servant, make that room completely free from dust, and take down the spiders' webs on the walls, so that there's nothing to disgust the guests.

SERVANT. I'll see to it.

FARMER. Take particular care with the pepper, so that it doesn't get burnt or lose its flavour, for it's the thing that particularly pleases the taste of visitors at fair time.

WIFE. I'll see to what has to be done in the kitchen perfectly well without you – let me do the cooking and you eat the food. I'm quite grown up, I don't need you to tell me what to do when I'm cooking.

VILLICVS. Hic adueniunt tres amiculi ex urbe.

VXOR. Qui sunt?

VILLICVS. Pistor noster socer, Calcearius affinis et Textor cognatus nobis.

VXOR. Veniunt inuicem?

VILLICVS. Etiam et manibus consertis se ut amicissimi ducunt.

VXOR. Subito nunc tu Serue mensam sterne, singulaque quibus opus erit impone.

SERVVS. In illo moram non faciam.

VXOR. Ipsa cum obsoniis properabo ocissime.

PISTOR. Sis saluus, o Villice, quid geris?

VILLICVS. Salui sitis et uos, gratulor uestro aduentui.

PISTOR. Vbi nundinae sunt, uel nundinarum gaudium in templone uel ad focum?

VILLICVS. Spero quod utrobique.

TEXTOR. Praestat in coquina quam in templo nundinas esse, nam stomachis prodest magis.

VILLICVS. At plebeiarius noster mauult in aede sacra nundi- [K3v] nas celebrari.

CALCEARIVS. Vnus ille homo est, cuius inexplebilis est loculus.

VILLICVS. Adsitis, limen transcendite, mox prandium instruetur.

PISTOR. Vbi uxor latet?

VILLICVS. In culina ad focum. Ad posticum si opus est mictum ite, iam piper percoctum erit.

TEXTOR. Vrina non premimur. Salue Elsa, ut uales? Tu sollicita Martha es.

VXOR. Grati aduenistis, ualeo bellissime, sed sine pecunia. Cubiculum intretis, iam obsonia mittam a foco.

VILLICVS. Ex aquali hoc manus mundate, tum mensae adsidete. Loco ‘Benedicite’ quisque orationem apud se dicat, hic doctus non est.

PISTOR. Cruce signemus consecrabimusque cibum nosipsi ubi eruditus defuerit.

VILLICVS. Piper hoc degustate, spero palatis placebit.

TEXTOR. Sapidum est oppido.

CALCEARIVS. Adueniat uxor tua.

FARMER. Here come three friends from the city.
WIFE. Who are they?
FARMER. The baker and the shoemaker our in-laws, and our relative the weaver.
WIFE. Are they coming together?
FARMER. Yes, they're accompanying each other like the best of friends, arm in arm.
WIFE. Servant, set the table quickly, and put everything necessary on it.
SERVANT. I won't delay.
WIFE. I'll hurry with the food as fast as I can.
BAKER. Greetings, Farmer, how are you doing?
FARMER. Greetings to you too. I'm pleased you've come.
BAKER. Where is the fair, or the joys of the fair? In the church or at home?
FARMER. Both, I hope.
WEAVER. It's better for the fair to be in the kitchen than in the church, because it does the stomach more good.
FARMER. But our parish priest prefers the fair to be celebrated in the church.
SHOEMAKER. That's one man whose cash-box can't be filled!
FARMER. Come in, come over the threshold, lunch will soon be ready.
BAKER. Where's your wife got to?
FARMER. In the kitchen at the fire. If you need to, go to the back door for a pee, the pepper will be cooked any time now.
WEAVER. We don't need to relieve ourselves. Hello, Elsa, how are you doing? You're a busy Martha.
WIFE. Welcome. I'm fine, but I've no money. Come into the sitting-room, I'll send the food from the fire now.
FARMER. Wash your hands with water from this jug, then sit down at the table. In place of the 'Benedicite' everyone say a private prayer, there's nobody learned here.
BAKER. We'll bless the food with the sign of the Cross ourselves if there's no scholar present.
FARMER. Taste this pepper, I hope it'll please you.
WEAVER. It's really tasty.
SHOEMAKER. Your wife should join us.

VILLICVS. Illa culinae penso executo adueniet. Edite alacriter, caro in pipere cocta lepusculus heri est a me uenatus.

PISTOR. Licet tibi per nobiles uenari lepores?

VILLICVS. Nundinarum hoc tempore concedunt.

CALCEARIVS. O Elsa, coquere nosti dapsilice.

VXOR. Coquo more uillico et agresti, ut rustici edunt.

PISTOR. Sat opimus est apparatus et delicatus.

VILLICVS. Bibite de hac uillana nostra cereuisia, in urbe pretiosiorem haberetis.

TEXTOR. Satis iucunda est sapore.

VXOR. Piper hoc lambite, tum intus denigrabimini.

PISTOR. Multum ipsius edimus.

VILLICVS. Vxor, tolle piper et tostas affer carnes. Tu Serue uinum cyathis infunde. Vinum hoc hic in nostro oenopolio uenditur sedecim obolis.

PISTOR. Vili aere uenit, dignum ut carius uenderetur.

TEXTOR. Praebibo tibi, Villice.

VILLICVS. Prosit tibi. Agninam carnem ad ueru paratam attin- [K4r] gite, delicatiorem non habebitis. Omnibus praebibo ut accepta sit uestra praesentia.

CALCEARIVS. Bibe Dei nomine.

PISTOR. Audio utricularium, choreas ludit; pergemus illuc et nos.

VXOR. Prius oremus.

VILLICVS. Agimus gratias uero Christianorum Deo ob omnia nobis praestita beneficia.

PISTOR. Amen.

VILLICVS. Nunc abite ductum choreas.

---

33 gaudium in] gaudium in C; gaudium in in B | 59 Adueniet. Edite] adueniet. Edite C; adueniet. VIL. Edite B

FARMER. She'll come when she's finished her work in the kitchen. Eat quickly, the meat cooked in the pepper is a small hare I hunted yesterday.
BAKER. Do the nobles allow you to hunt hares?
FARMER. They allow it at this fair-time.
SHOEMAKER. Elsa, you can cook splendidly.
WIFE. I cook in the rustic, peasant style, the way country people eat.
BAKER. The food's really rich and sumptuous.
FARMER. Drink some of this country beer of ours; in the city you'd have finer stuff.
WEAVER. It has a really delicious flavour.
WIFE. Eat up the pepper, then you'll be black inside.
BAKER. We've eaten a lot of it.
FARMER. Take away the pepper, Wife, and serve the roast meats. You, Servant, pour wine into the cups. This wine's sold here in our wine-shop for sixteen Hellers.
BAKER. That's cheap, it's worth a higher price.
WEAVER. I drink to you, Farmer.
FARMER. Cheers. Take some spit-roasted lamb, you won't get anything finer. I drink to you all to welcome your coming.
WEAVER. Drink in the name of God.
BAKER. I hear the bagpiper playing dances. Let's go there too.
WIFE. Let's pray first.
FARMER. We give thanks to the true God of Christians for all the favours he has rendered us.
BAKER. Amen.
FARMER. Now off you go to dance.

Anonymous artist, *Piper and Lute Player* (Geisberg, G 1588)

16. CONVIVIVM CAMPESTRE

Campum uiridem animi recreandi gratia accedunt Horatius hospes, Henricus, Volfgangus, Maximilianus conuiuae, et matronae nonnullae

HORATIVS. Quam dulciter et iucunde nunc aura blanditur. Undique locorum floridum est, herbis et frondibus nascentibus.

HENRICVS. Omnia nunc uirent, nunc formosissimus annus.

VOLFGANGVS. Germinant nunc omnia, prata, agri, horti, et siluae.

MAXIMILIANVS. Auiculae aërem nunc perstrepunt dulci cantu e nidis quibus hieme tota delituerunt, erumpunt.

HORATIVS. Egrediuntur et nunc homines agminatim in campum uel pomerium, cibo et potu in uiridibus locis se oblectantes.

HENRICVS. Exeamus et nos ad horas aliquot, quid usque insidemus fumosis et obscuris tectis? In apertum campum cum auibus repetemus.

VOLFGANGVS. Rusticari nunc conueniret, si commeatum haberemus quo nos ut alii solent homines exhilaremus.

HORATIVS. Ipse nobis impartiar pernam suillam et duas uini mensuras.

MAXIMILIANVS. Tum deinde reliquum sumptum faciemus nos.

HENRICVS. Pari asse deponemus nos alii.

VOLFGANGVS. Nymphas bellulas oportet et congredi, alias hilaritatis haberemus nihil.

HORATIVS. [K4v] Vxorculae nostrae et famulae comites erunt nobis, quae sub palliis cibatum ferent.

MAXIMILIANVS. Non diu moremus, si quo ire uolumus, properemus antequam uespera appetat.

HORATIVS. Audi tu, uxor mea, sportulam obsonatoriam para ac reple perna hodie elixa, et uini aliquot prome mensuras. In pomerium expatiatum ibimus.

VXOR. Dicto citius expediam.

HORATIVS. Nos praecedemus, tu cum culinae ministra sequere, ad portam nos inuenietis.

16. A PICNIC

Horatius the host, Henricus, Volfgangus and Maximilianus the guests, and several women, go to a green field to cheer their spirits

HORATIUS. How sweet and pleasant and soothing the air is now. Everywhere is covered in flowers, as the grass and the foliage start to grow.

HENRICUS. Now everything's green, the year's at its most beautiful.

VOLFGANGUS. Everything's budding now, the meadows, the fields, the gardens and the woods.

MAXIMILIANUS. Now the birds are making the air ring with their sweet song, and they're coming out from the nests they've been sheltering in all winter.

HORATIUS. And now people are going off in their droves to the countryside, enjoying food and drink in green places.

HENRICUS. Let's go out for a few hours as well, why should we stay any longer in dark, smoky houses? We'll go back to the open fields with the birds.

VOLFGANGUS. Now would be a good time to go to the country, if we had food we could cheer ourselves with, as other people do.

HORATIUS. I'll provide us with a haunch of ham and two measures of wine.

MAXIMILIANUS. And then we'll pay for the rest.

HENRICUS. The rest of us will contribute an equal amount.

VOLFGANGUS. Some pretty girls need to come along, or else we'd have no fun.

HORATIUS. Our wives and serving-maids will accompany us, and they'll carry the food under their cloaks.

MAXIMILIANUS. Let's not delay if we want to go somewhere. Let's hurry before evening draws near.

HORATIUS. Listen, Wife, prepare a picnic basket and put the ham that was boiled today in it, and bring out a few measures of wine. We're going for a walk in the fields.

WIFE. I'll do that as quick as a wink.

HORATIUS. We'll go on ahead. You follow us with the cook, you'll find us at the city gate.

VXOR. Sat est, uos pedetemptim praecedite.

HORATIVS. Eamus, pone subibit coniunx.

HENRICVS. Quam delectabile est iam deambulare et repere, sub frondibus et in uiridi gramine.

VOLFGANGVS. Est per Herculem.

MAXIMILIANVS. At quod pomerium accedemus?

HENRICVS. Vbi minus hominum erit.

HORATIVS. Ibi conueniet, ne multos nostrorum gestium habeamus spectatores.

VOLFGANGVS. Possent et multi suspicari matronas quae aderunt inhonestas esse, nobisque amicas meretriceas.

MAXIMILIANVS. Videbimus ubi maior erit solitudo.

HENRICVS. Hic in oenopolio aliquid uini et nostro nomine emamus.

VOLFGANGVS. Vbi lagena est in qua feremus?

MAXIMILIANVS. Ad fidem dabunt uinum qui uendunt, mox redditurum et relaturum te dicas.

VOLFGANGVS. Quantum portam?

HENRICVS. Quattuor mensuras mercare, tum inter nos exsoluemus.

VOLFGANGVS. Vbi nos reperiam?

MAXIMILIANVS. Ad portam te manebimus.

HORATIVS. En alias a longe subsequitur uxor mea, famula comitante.

HENRICVS. Moremur eas tum et uinum a nobis emptum afferetur.

HORATIVS. Sistemus gradus, perplacet mihi.

VXOR. Vt ita praecurritis, uix potuimus assequi.

HORATIVS. Lento tamen gradu iuimus.

MAXIMILIANVS. Adest et nostri aeris uinum.

HORATIVS. In [K5r] gramen nunc decumbamus. Vxor, deprome quod attulisti dapis, tu famula uinum cyathis infunde.

VOLFGANGVS. Aegre in oenopolio lagenam mutuo dabant mihi, quia ipsis ignotus eram.

HORATIVS. Edamus nunc et poculis nos oblectemus.

WIFE. Right you are. You go on ahead slowly.
HORATIUS. Let's go. My wife will follow on behind us.
HENRICUS. How delightful it is to walk and creep under the trees and in the green grass.
VOLFGANGUS. It is indeed.
MAXIMILIANUS. But which part of the fields will we go to?
HENRICUS. Where there are the fewest people.
HORATIUS. That'll be the right place, so that we won't have a lot of people looking at what we do.
VOLFGANGUS. A lot of people could suspect that the women with us aren't respectable, that they're girlfriends of ours who are prostitutes.
MAXIMILIANUS. We'll see where there's the most solitude.
HENRICUS. Here in the wine-shop we'll buy some wine in our name, too.
VOLFGANGUS. Where's a flask to carry it in?
MAXIMILIANUS. The people who sell the wine will let us have one on trust, tell them you'll bring it back and return it to them soon.
VOLFGANGUS. How much will I bring?
HENRICUS. Buy four measures, then we'll pay for it amongst ourselves.
VOLFGANGUS. Where will I find you again?
MAXIMILIANUS. We'll wait for you at the gate.
HORATIUS. Look, my wife's following a long way off, with the servant-girl beside her.
HENRICUS. Let's wait for them, then the wine we bought will be brought up.
HORATIUS. I approve. We'll stop.
WIFE. Why are you running ahead? We could hardly catch you up.
HORATIUS. But we went at a slow pace.
MAXIMILIANUS. And the wine we bought is here too.
HORATIUS. Let's lie down on the grass. Wife, take out the food you brought, and you, Servant-girl, pour the wine into the cups.
VOLFGANGUS. They weren't keen to lend me the flask in the wine-shop, because they didn't know me.
HORATIUS. Now let's eat and enjoy the drink.

MAXIMILIANVS. O quam lepidum est et iucundum hoc in loco.
HORATIVS. Propino tibi, uxor.
VXOR. Bibe bonis auibus.
HENRICVS. Praebibo tibi.
MAXIMILIANVS. Sit commodo.
HORATIVS. Pernam degustate, tum bibere delectabit uos.
VOLFGANGVS. Adhuc a prandii cibo saturi sumus.
HORATIVS. Edere si non libet, alacrius bibite.
MAXIMILIANVS. Sitienti propino.
HENRICVS. Ille ego ipse sum, tibi pari haustu respondebo.
VOLFGANGVS. Puella illa et potu et cibo abstinet.
VXOR. Puellarum non est bibere, sed summis labris data pocula lambere et pytissare.
HORATIVS. Hesperus instat, redeundum est domum.
MAXIMILIANVS. Quando lubet, in nobis mora non erit.
HORATIVS. Exsurgite, hinc abeamus.
HENRICVS. Celeres congrediemur.

---

3 Volfgangus] Vuolffgangus B | 25 asse] asse C; esse B | 60 Horatius] Henricus B C (but cf. ll. 36–39).

17. CONVIVIVM SATYRICVM SIVE INVECTIVVM

Iuuenalis hospes, Bartoldus, Georgius, Antonius, Martinus conuiuae, Seruus

IVVENALIS. Salui sitis, litterarum cultores feruidi.
BARTOLDVS. Talis sis et tu, poeta eloquentissime.
IVVENALIS. Quid inuicem negotii geritis?
GEORGIVS. Equidem otium, non negotium agimus.
IVVENALIS. Nihil litterarii tractatis?
BARTOLDVS. Commentamur mutuo nescio quae.
IVVENALIS. Non uos premit aestus? Vmbras petite aut tecta, non parum incommodat rabies illa canicularis stellae quam nunc sol incolit.
ANTONIVS. [K5v] Domibus sat per hiemem morati sumus.
IVVENALIS. Has meas aedes et tecta subite, potu uos excipiam.

MAXIMILIANUS. It's so charming and delightful in this place.
HORATIUS. I drink to you, Wife.
WIFE. Your good health.
HENRICUS. I drink to you.
MAXIMILIANUS. Cheers.
HORATIUS. Eat the ham, then drinking will really please you.
VOLFGANGUS. We're still full from what we ate at lunch.
HORATIUS. If you don't care to eat, drink all the more keenly.
MAXIMILIANUS. I drink to whoever's thirsty.
HENRICUS. That's me. I answer you by drinking the same amount.
VOLFGANGUS. That girl isn't eating or drinking anything.
WIFE. Girls shouldn't drink, they should just take little sips and tastes from the cups they've been given.
HORATIUS. The evening's coming, it's time to go back home.
MAXIMILIANUS. Whenever you like, we won't delay.
HORATIUS. Get up, let's leave.
HENRICUS. We'll all go quickly.

17. A SATIRICAL BANQUET, OR A BANQUET OF INVECTIVE

Iuvenalis, host; Bartoldus, Georgius, Antonius, Martinus, guests; Servant

IUVENALIS. Greetings, you passionate literary scholars.
BARTOLDUS. And the same to you, most eloquent poet.
IUVENALIS. What business have you together?
GEORGIUS. It's pleasure, not business
IUVENALIS. Aren't you engaged in a literary task?
BARTOLDUS. We're commenting on something or other together.
IUVENALIS. Don't you find the heat oppressive? Go into the shade, or indoors. The savage heat of the dog-star, the constellation the sun's in now, is very uncomfortable.
ANTONIUS. We've stayed indoors enough during the winter.
IUVENALIS. Come into my house, I'll give you something to drink.

MARTINVS. Sumptui isti parcas, non sitimus oppido.

IVVENALIS. Obsequimini subitoque adsitis, nugabimur mutuo. Ipse canus, adolescentibus litteris deditis delector, ut nihil supra.

GEORGIVS. Frontem perfricabimus et tua subibimus tecta.

IVVENALIS. Accedite audentibus animis, meumque non fugite senium, ipse et olim adolescens fui.

BARTOLDVS. Canos tuos non fugimus, sed formidamus ignoti et pueri, tibi in litteris emerito militi conuiuere.

IVVENALIS. Serue, i promptum cereuisiae pocula aliquot et uini.

SERVVS. Celerrime curabo.

IVVENALIS. Potus aestus tempore in pretio est, magnique aestimatur, ubi calore arent labella.

SERVVS. Hic potus prosit bibentibus.

IVVENALIS. Adolescentibus uobis litterarum cupidis praebibo.

CONVIVAE. Salutem precamur ut potes.

IVVENALIS. Quisque uestrum labia potu madida faciat, deinde edite, nunc potus acceptior est cibo, sed utro plus delectamini, eo utimini.

CONVIVAE. Vtroque iuxta gaudemus.

IVVENALIS. Sitim postquam sedaueritis, litterarii aliquid nugabimur inuicem.

CONVIVAE. De litteris loqui nostras ingeniorum excedit uires, ipsas primoribus labiis uix degustauimus.

IVVENALIS. Intelligo non usqueadeo ipsarum rudes uos esse, ut dissimulatis.

GEORGIVS. Per Apollinem et Palladem expertes sumus ipsarum.

IVVENALIS. Ideo me capulari sene nunc ut duce utimini, respondeteque quae quaeram.

BARTOLDVS. Respondebimus nota, ad ignota obticebimus.

IVVENALIS. Festis diebus quid gentilibus olim erat negotii a meridie sacris deorum peractis?

MARTINUS. Save the expense, we aren't particularly thirsty.

IUVENALIS. Do what I say and come quickly, we'll chat together. I'm an old man, and I like youths committed to scholarship more than anything else.

GEORGIUS. We'll be bold and come into your house.

IUVENALIS. Come in, be bold, and don't be repelled by my old age, I was a youth once myself.

BARTOLDUS. We aren't repelled by your old age. We're ignorant boys, and we're afraid to be in your company; you're a past master of letters.

IUVENALIS. Servant, go and fetch some glasses of beer and wine.

SERVANT. I'll see to that very quickly.

IUVENALIS. In hot weather drink is prized, and it's much appreciated when your lips are parched by heat.

SERVANT. May this drink be to the good health of those who drink it.

IUVENALIS. I drink to you boys who are eager to be scholars.

GUESTS. We wish you as much health as possible.

IUVENALIS. Each of you wet his lips, then eat. Drink is more welcome than food now, but whichever pleases you more, take that.

GUESTS. We love both equally.

IUVENALIS. When you've quenched your thirst, we'll chat about some literary topic together.

GUESTS. Talking about literature goes beyond the power of our intellects; we've hardly begun to study it.

IUVENALIS. I know that you aren't quite as ignorant of literature as you pretend to be.

GEORGIUS. By Apollo and Pallas Athene, we know nothing about it.

IUVENALIS. So take me, an old man with one foot in the grave, as a guide: answer what I ask.

BARTOLDUS. We'll answer when we know something; when we don't, we'll say nothing.

IUVENALIS. What did the pagans do long ago on holidays in the afternoon, after the rites of the gods were over?

GEORGIVS. Per tenebras scio et andabatorum more. [K6r] A praeceptore quondam me audiuisse recordor, quod in agris, in uiarum compitis conueniebant, ibidemque mutuis uerbis in se per uices inuehebant, in curribus stantes.

IVVENALIS. Vere dicis, quisque alteri sua, si quae habuit, scelera obiecit et aperuit.

ANTONIVS. Non aegre ferebat qui conuitiabatur?

IVVENALIS. Vitiatus rursus in suum conuitiatorem dicebat, ut carnis morsu petitus remordere solet.

GEORGIVS. Spectaculum mehercule iucundum fuit uisu et auditu.

IVVENALIS. Sic et uos adolescentuli exercere ingenia deberetis, ut unus alium nunc laudaret, nunc uero increpando laederet.

BARTOLDVS. Amicitia mox tum rumperetur.

IVVENALIS. Praedicendum esset ut quisque alterius boni consuleret uerba.

GEORGIVS. Quid si experiremur, an unus alterum suis posset coloribus depingere.

IVVENALIS. Istud efflagito sedulo, unus auspicium sumat.

GEORGIVS. Cuculi progeniei te esse credo per Herculem, pusillus namque corpore es, sed uoce magna et uirili, canis instar bouis, itaque miror quomodo in tam paruo corpusculo tuo tanta uis spiritus resideat.

BARTOLDVS. Tu unus eorum qui manticam a tergo non uident, aliena non sua cernunt uitia, sic tu me pusillum corpore arguis, cum tu quolibet pygmaeo minor sis, gressu tamen superbo, rubea tunica, tiara pretiosa incedens alium et Herculem te putans, ac nuper Hannibalem te esse asserebas, cum ne musculum fugare posses.

ANTONIVS. En tu Martine ades? Vocaris tu Martinus, ubi equus tuus, cui nuper insidebas? Quis tu es? Ambulas nunc pedibus, ab equo non ad asinum, sed terram transcendisti. [K6v]

GEORGIUS. I can make a tentative guess at that. I remember I once heard from my teacher that they came together in the fields and at crossroads, and there they stood in their chariots and attacked one another verbally.

IUVENALIS. You're right. Everyone revealed and reproached another person's misdeeds, if he had any.

ANTONIUS. Didn't the people who were reproached take it badly?

IUVENALIS. The injured party said something back at the person who had reproached him, just as someone who's been bitten will bite back.

GEORGIUS. I say, the sight was amusing to see and hear!

IUVENALIS. You boys should exercise your wits in the same way, and one should now praise another, and now castigate him with reproaches.

BARTOLDUS. Then friendship would soon be broken.

IUVENALIS. You would have to say at the start that everyone should take what the other says in good part.

GEORGIUS. Why not try and see if one can paint another in his true colours?

IUVENALIS. That I earnestly ask. Someone make a start.

GEORGIUS. By Hercules, I believe you're born of a cuckoo, for you're tiny in body, but your voice is big and manly, like a bulldog's. And so I wonder how there can be such strength of soul in your tiny little body.

BARTOLDUS. You're one of the people who can't see the beam in your own eye, who can see others' faults but not his own; and so you accuse me of being small in body, when you're smaller than any pygmy. And yet you walk proudly, in your red tunic and your expensive hat, thinking yourself a second Hercules, and recently you were saying you were Hannibal, though you couldn't frighten a mouse away.

ANTONIUS. Oh, is that you, Martinus? Call yourself Martinus, where's your horse that you used to ride on? Who are you? Now you're walking on foot; you've really come down in the world: not just 'from a horse to a donkey', but from a horse right down to the ground.

MARTINVS. Tu nasute ridere sine, tu trium terunciorum homo, tu pumilio, tu Lerna malorum, tu morionum hospes stultitiaeque domicilium.

IVVENALIS. Abunde ingenia ostendistis, nunc bibite, tum demum regrediemini domum.

MARTINVS. Abibimus, tu gratiam habe.

18. CONVIVIVM LAVDATORIVM

Demosthenes hospes; Gerardus, Theodericus, Kilianus, Vilhelmus conuiuae

DEMOSTHENES. Conuiuas uos uolo a meridie.

THEODERICVS. A meridie? Cur non prandii hora?

DEMOSTHENES. Lauta mihi non est culina, sed macra, plenaque aranearum telis, non pinguibus suum pernis.

GERARDVS. Per superos, bellus homo es, uocare uis conuiuas saturos, non famelicos, facillimum tum est sine impendio conuiuatorem esse.

DEMOSTHENES. Conuiuium apparabo merendinarium, quod a meridie loco cibi merendinarii agitur inter homines.

KILIANVS. Ecquid nobis immune dabis?

DEMOSTHENES. Satis cereuisiae et edulii nonnihil, quo bibendi excitetur cupiditas.

VILHELMVS. Ad quam ueniemus horam?

DEMOSTHENES. Circiter primam, neque diutius moramini.

THEODERICVS. Aderimus in ipso sono primae horae.

DEMOSTHENES. Rogo in tempore huc pedes ferre, agemus palaestram quandam litterariam.

KILIANVS. Post sublatum prandium huc feremus pedes.

DEMOSTHENES. Postremum occupabit scabies.

GERARDVS. Ratum sit quod loqueris. Postremus qui uenerit, malo afficietur; domum iam pransuri ibimus.

DEMOSTHENES. Discedite, propediem huc remigrate.

VILHELMVS. Salue Demosthenes orator eloquentissime, hic aduenimus omnes, quid nunc nostra tibi conferet praesentia?

MARTINUS. Stop laughing, you smartypants, you threepenny man, you midget, you sink of evils, you welcomer of fools and dwelling of folly!
IUVENALIS. You've shown your wits amply. Now drink, and then go back home.
MARTINUS. We're off. We thank you.

18. A LAUDATORY BANQUET

Demosthenes, host; Gerardus, Theodericus, Kilianus, Vilhelmus, guests

DEMOSTHENES. I would like you as guests this afternoon.
THEODERICUS. Afternoon? Why not at lunchtime?
DEMOSTHENES. My food isn't luxurious, it's meagre; my kitchen's full of cobwebs, not fat hams.
GERARDUS. By the gods, you're the fine fellow! You want to invite guests who are full, not hungry – that makes it very easy to give a banquet without expense.
DEMOSTHENES. I'll furnish an afternoon banquet, of the kind that's held amongst men in the afternoon, in lieu of an afternoon meal.
KILIANUS. And what will you give us?
DEMOSTHENES. Plenty of beer and some food to stimulate the desire to drink.
VILHELMUS. What time will we come?
DEMOSTHENES. Around one, don't delay any longer.
THEODERICUS. We'll be there on the very stroke of one.
DEMOSTHENES. Come here in good time, I ask you, we're going to have a literary contest.
KILIANUS. We'll come here after eating lunch.
DEMOSTHENES. A pox on the last one here.
GERARDUS. Agreed. Devil take the hindmost. We're off home to have lunch.
DEMOSTHENES. Off you go; come back here before long.
VILHELMUS. Hello, Demosthenes, most eloquent of orators. We've all come here; how will our presence benefit you?

DEMOSTHENES. In amoenissimo horto meo apud domus posticum situm sub arboribus com- [K7r] potabimus et una nugabimur.

KILIANVS. In nobis mora non erit.

DEMOSTHENES. Serue, ad hortum fer potum, cereuisiam scilicet pretiosiorem et bolum aut alterum carnis.

SERVVS. Praestabo effectum.

DEMOSTHENES. Me comitamini in horti amoenitatem.

GERARDVS. Paribus sequemur passibus.

DEMOSTHENES. Hortulum hunc in deliciis meis habeo, estque unicum delectamentum meum.

VILHELMVS. Est iucundissimus locus.

DEMOSTHENES. Sub hanc arborem sedebimus quiescentes et de hoc potu exigui ualoris sitim curabimus; praebibo cuilibet uestrum calicem hunc.

KILIANVS. Salutem tibi ferat bibenti.

DEMOSTHENES. Congarriemus, postquam quisque calicem istum ebiberit.

GERARDVS. Bibimus nunc ordine omnes, quid iam tibi placet?

DEMOSTHENES. Exercitiine aliquid indies habetis quo studium uestrum corroboretur, magisque grandescat in uobis profectus scientiae?

VILHELMVS. Nil nisi epistolas scribimus.

DEMOSTHENES. Exercitatio quaedam est, qua nihil est iuueni utilius.

GERARDVS. Quae illa est?

DEMOSTHENES. Quod aetate sibi parem uel peritia puerum modo uituperet, modo laudet.

KILIANVS. Eam artem uituperandi uel laudandi ubi disceremus?

DEMOSTHENES. In rhetorica, quam uestra indoles non sufficit capere, uel uti ipsa. Sed alium laudare uel uituperare ingenii exercendi gratia, ante artem cognitam etiam et laudis et honoris est.

VILHELMVS. Laudaturus alium auspicium unde sumat?

DEMOSTHENES. In my very pleasant garden that lies near the back door of the house we'll drink together under the trees and chat with one another.

KILIANUS. We won't delay.

DEMOSTHENES. Servant, take some drink to the garden – good quality beer, and a mouthful or two of meat.

SERVANT. I'll see to that.

DEMOSTHENES. Come with me to the pleasant garden.

GERARDUS. We'll follow at your speed.

DEMOSTHENES. This little garden is my favourite spot; it's my only source of amusement.

VILHELMUS. It's a delightful place.

DEMOSTHENES. We'll sit down and take our rest under this tree, and we'll slake our thirst with this poor drink. I drink this cup to each one of you.

KILIANUS. May it bring you good health!

DEMOSTHENES. We'll chat together, and afterwards everyone will drink off this cup.

GERARDUS. We've all drunk in order. What's your pleasure now?

DEMOSTHENES. Have you any kind of daily exercise to reinforce your study, and to help you make greater progress in knowledge?

VILHELMUS. We write nothing but letters.

DEMOSTHENES. Nothing is more useful to a youth than one particular exercise.

GERARDUS. Which is?

DEMOSTHENES. To take a boy equal to him in age or learning, and now to criticize him, now to praise him.

KILIANUS. Where would we learn that art of praising or criticizing?

DEMOSTHENES. In rhetoric, which your capacities aren't sufficient to grasp or employ. But it's laudable and honourable to praise or criticize someone else as an intellectual exercise even before you know that art.

VILHELMUS. Where does someone who wants to praise someone else begin?

DEMOSTHENES. A corpore, a genere uel progenie, a fortunae dotibus et scientia, probitate uel moribus. Edite buccellas aliquot et bibite, tum uicissim uos laudabitis.

GERARDVS. Ipse glaciem secabo. Bellus tu homo es, Theoderice, candidis capillis, modesto uultu, gressu testudineo, facie alba, ingenio fecundo, parentibusque opulentis.

THEODERICVS. Te me fricantem refricabo. Quod [K7ᵛ] mihi das laudis omne id tibi competit: pulcher es adolescens, flaua coma, honesto aspectu, gradu egregio, Minerua fertili, et maioribus diuitibus prognatus.

KILIANVS. O Vilhelme, audi a me tui praeconium. Parentibus percepi te ortum praeclaris scioque non sterili esse indole, statura non deformi, scientia non contemnenda, assiduusque es librorum lector.

VILHELMVS. Et tu albae gallinae es filius, neque infelici ingenio, corporis habitu decoro, ut nihil supra.

DEMOSTHENES. In laudando alium, semper illud Plinii in mente habete, hoc ipsum esse amantis, non nimium laudare.

---

67 GERARDVS.] Bar. B C | 74 KILIANVS.] An. B C

19. CONVIVIVM DECLAMATORIVM

Paedagogus hospes; Iohannes, Hermannus, Albertus, Iacobus conuiuae; Seruus.

PAEDAGOGVS. Hodie dies est, quo a lectionibus feriari est receptum.

IOHANNES. Noscimus, quid deinde?

PAEDAGOGVS. Scitis etiam quid sit otiari a lectionibus gymnasii? Vel quid sit agendum dum a scholae negotiis est libertas?

HERMANNVS. Tum ludendum est in campo, pila, uel globo per annulum ferreum, uel cursu, uel palaestra dimicatoria, aut colluctando.

PAEDAGOGVS. Scopum nondum tetigisti, toto aberras caelo.

DEMOSTHENES. With his body, his family or descent, with his gifts of fortune and his knowledge, his goodness or his morals. Eat a few mouthfuls and drink, then you'll take turns at praising one another.

GERARDUS. I'll make a start. You're a handsome man, Theodericus, with your fair hair, your modest expression, your slow walk, your pale face, your fertile intellect, and your wealthy parents.

THEODERICUS. You stroke me, so I'll stroke you back. The praise you give me all applies to you. You're a good-looking boy, with yellow hair, an honest look, an admirable walk, a keen intelligence; and you're born of rich parents.

KILIANUS. Vilhelmus, hear your laudation from me. I see that you are the child of distinguished parents, and I know that your character is not lacking in qualities, your body not misshapen and your knowledge not to be despised.

VILHELMUS. You're a blue-eyed boy, too; your intellect is not wretched, your physical appearance is unbeatably handsome.

DEMOSTHENES. When praising someone, always bear in mind Pliny's words, that a lover should not praise excessively.

19. A DECLAMATORY BANQUET

Teacher, host; Iohannes, Hermannus, Albertus, Iacobus, guests; Servant

TEACHER. Today's the established day for being free from lessons.

IOHANNES. We know. And so?

TEACHER. Do you know what it means to be off school? Or what you ought to do when you have free time away from schoolwork?

HERMANNUS. Then you should play in the fields: ball, or knocking the ball through the iron ring, or running, or fencing, or wrestling.

TEACHER. You haven't got it right yet, you're completely wrong.

IOHANNES. Eo modo tamen feriae litterariae a nobis hactenus nostrisque maioribus dum litteras didicerunt peractae sunt.

PAEDAGOGVS. Istud nihil aliud est quam uacatione a gymnasio abuti. A prandio huc me accedite, erudiam uos ad horulam unam quid sit uacare a librorum lectionibus, et quomodo ferias scholasticas commode collocare poteritis.

ALBERTVS. Adueniemus prandii peracta fabula.

PAEDAGOGVS. Hic uos opperiar, in tempore facite adsitis.[K8r]

IOHANNES. Certe reuertemur propediem.

PAEDAGOGVS. Magnae fidei adolescentes uos nunc uideo, quod promissos aduentus re exequimini. Assidete, nonnihil potus afferri faciam quo linguas irrigemus, promptius ut loquamur.

HERMANNVS. Nostri gratia ne assis impendium facias.

PAEDAGOGVS. Serue, aliquid uini prome et affer.

SERVVS. Expediam quam rectissime.

PAEDAGOGVS. Cupitis nunc audire quid sit otiari a lectionibus gymnasii?

IOHANNES. Anhelamus cupide.

PAEDAGOGVS. Post haustum hunc factum eloquar. Hoc poculo uestros aduentus excipio.

HERMANNVS. Gratiam habemus.

PAEDAGOGVS. Bibat et quisque uestrum. Nunc quae pollicitus sum praestabo. A schola quotiescunque feriabimini hoc exercitii habeatis.

IACOBVS. Quod genus?

PAEDAGOGVS. Audita ruminetis, et breuiusculam oratiunculam quandam concinnate, in rei uel personae cuiuspiam laudem uel uituperium, quod declamitare olim uocitabant.

IACOBVS. Nescimus qua arte declamationes conficiemus.

IOHANNES. Yet that's the way school holidays have been spent by us up to now, and by our parents when they were at school.

TEACHER. That's nothing but an abuse of the holiday. Come to me here after lunch, and for an hour or so I'll teach you what it means to be free of lessons, and how you can make profitable use of the days off school.

ALBERTUS. We'll come when lunch is over.

TEACHER. I'll wait for you here, make sure you're here quickly.

IOHANNES. We'll definitely come back very soon.

TEACHER. I see now that you're boys of your word, since you keep the promise you made to come. Sit down, I'll have some drink brought to lubricate our tongues, so that we can speak more fluently.

HERMANNUS. Don't spend money on us.

TEACHER. Servant, fetch some wine and bring it here.

SERVANT. I'll do it as best I can.

TEACHER. Now, do you want to hear what it means to be off school lessons?

IOHANNES. We're absolutely aching to know.

TEACHER. After this draught I'll explain how it is. I toast your coming with this cup.

HERMANNUS. Thank you.

TEACHER. Each of you must drink, too. Now I'll do what I promised. Every time you're off school, do this exercise.

IACOBUS. What kind of exercise?

TEACHER. Think over what you've heard, and put together a short speech praising or criticizing something or someone. That's what was called 'declamation' in olden times.

IACOBUS. We don't know the method for composing declamations.

PAEDAGOGVS. Rudem et impolitam orationem connectite quoad artem didiceritis. Vnicam a me accipite declamationem in litterarum laudem. Litterae, id est scientiae, nobilissimae sunt, neque unquam satis laudatae, neque laudari ut dignae sunt a quoquam possunt, multum namque boni et frugis afferunt, per ipsas posteritati gesta indicantur temporum peractorum, per ipsas uirtutes, felicitas, magistratus, honores, laudes dantur et accumulantur, facilius quam per opes, ipsae semel adeptae nunquam, neque in uita, neque post funera decorare aut ornare cessant habentem. Dixi. [K8v]

IOHANNES. Periculum et ipse faciam, commendaturus uirtutes.

PAEDAGOGVS. Age facito, ingenio utere tuo felicissimo.

IOHANNES. Virtus res est ardua maxime, difficilisque acquisitu, tandem adepta felicissimum reddit, omnibus quibus egemus praestat, nam illi nihil deesse dixerunt scriptores, quem penes esset uirtus; uirtus omnia in se habet. Virtus ad sidera uehit, uitium ad ima Tartara mittit. Dixi.

PAEDAGOGVS. Bibite nunc omnes, ordine quisque calicem exsiccet.

HERMANNVS. In harenam et ego descendam prudentiae praeconium dicturus. Prudentia uirtutum omnium nobilissima. In cognitione rerum consistit, qua cognitione nihil est homini honestius. Scire laudabile, nescire uitiosissimum est. Vir prudens, rerum peritus, uno minor est Ioue, inquit poeta; ignorans a caudice differt nihil. Dixi.

PAEDAGOGVS. Calicem quem meritus es bibe, ceterisque praebibe.

ALBERTVS. Palaestram ineam et ego liberalitatis encomium prolaturus. Liberalitas ea uirtus est quae humanum, pium et benignum docet esse hominem, datque ubi dandum est, seruat ubi retinendum est, docet sua non prodigere, neque tenax esse Euclio Plautinus. Dixi.

PAEDAGOGVS. Bibe poculum quod meritus es, et aliis propina. Sic uestra otia transigite, tum in eruditos euadetis uiros.

---

43 declamationes] declamitationes B C | 52 ipsae] ipsae C; ipse B | 57 Iohannes] Iohannes C; B continues this as part of Paedagogus's speech; 75 est, docet sua] est, sua B C | 75–76 tenax esse] tenax ex esse B C (but C corrects to 'tenax esse' in erratum, sig. L8r

TEACHER. String together a rough-and-ready speech, until you learn the art. Listen to a single declamation from me in praise of literature. Literature, that is, knowledge, is noble; it has never been praised enough, and cannot be praised as it deserves by anyone; for it brings a great deal of good and profit. Through it the happenings of past times are shown to posterity; through it virtues, happiness, offices, honours and praise are given and accumulated, more easily than by wealth. Once acquired it never ceases to distinguish him who has it, neither in life nor after death. I have spoken.

IOHANNES. I'll have a go, too, at praising virtues.

TEACHER. Go on, employ your fine intelligence.

IOHANNES. Virtue is very hard to realize, and difficult to acquire; yet once acquired it brings great felicity. It provides everything we lack, for writers have said that he who possesses virtue lacks nothing; virtue contains all things in itself. Virtue takes us to the stars; vice sends us down to the depths of Tartarus. I have spoken.

TEACHER. Now drink, everyone; each one drain the cup in order.

HERMANNUS. I'll enter the contest too; I'll deliver the praise of practical understanding. It is the noblest of all virtues. It consists in the knowledge of affairs, and nothing is more honourable for man than that knowledge. Knowledge is praiseworthy, ignorance is a grave flaw. The man skilled in practical affairs is one step below Jove, says the poet; the ignorant man is no different from a block. I have spoken.

TEACHER. Drink the cup you've deserved, and drink to the others.

ALBERTUS. I'll enter the fray too, and deliver an encomium of generosity. Generosity is the virtue that teaches man to be humane, dutiful and kind. It gives where it is right to give, and saves where it is right to keep back. It teaches us not to squander our possessions, and not to be close-fisted like Plautus's Euclio. I have spoken.

TEACHER. Drink the cup you've deserved, and toast the others. Spend your free time like this, then you'll become learned men.

20. CONVIVIVM RECONCILIATORIVM

Hospes; Arnoldus, Henricus inimici inuicem; Iasperus, Crato reconciliatores

HOSPES. Vt sic rixamini inuicem canum more, nihil uos pudet?

HENRICVS. Iste malorum Lerna suis semper uerbis me insectatur malis, nequeo ipsi obuius fieri, uel [L1r] quin aliqua iniuria me prosequatur.

ARNOLDVS. Tu me tuis dictis semper laceras, rodisque ac ossa caniculi, praedico tibi ut mordere et differre apud alios me cesses, aut clauum clauo trudam, quod senties cum magno tuo malo.

HENRICVS. Ah tu Pygmaeo minor, quid narras? Ientaculi uice quod est esurienti, id tu mihi esses si ad pugnos uentum fuerit.

ARNOLDVS. Sim pumilio quantumuis pusillus, tamen a te ut inter simias asinus tractari nolo, neque pessundari.

CRATO. Huiusmodi silere uerba, istas lites componite, longe praestat pax et concordia quam simultas et discordia.

HENRICVS. Tranquillus et quietus esse uellem, nihilque secum aut conuictus aut commercii habere, sed liber ab ipso fieri nequeo, insequitur me passim ut umbra corpus, succulique scrofam.

ARNOLDVS. Tuo consortio carebo facillime.

HOSPES. Taceat uterque, scio quid faciemus quo uos reconciliatos reddemus.

HENRICVS. Quid? Exprime.

HOSPES. Compotatiunculam ad cereuisiae pocula agemus, tum inter potandum uestris animis discutiemus rancorem illum mutuum.

HENRICVS. Lubet mihi, diuersorium istud cereuisiarium intremus. Sequimini, uos belli helluones poculorum.

HOSPES. Domi nostrae in umbra sedebis tranquillius, securius et iucundius.

CRATO. Praestat suis interesse penatibus quam alienis.

HENRICVS. Potus feratur abunde, tum calculum et rationem impendii faciemus.

20. A BANQUET OF RECONCILIATION

Host; Arnoldus and Henricus, mutual enemies; Iasperus, Crato, conciliators

HOST. Why are you fighting amongst yourselves like dogs? Aren't you ashamed of it at all?

HENRICUS. That sink of vices is always harassing me with his insults; I can't meet him without being sent on my way with some affront.

ARNOLDUS. You're always tormenting me with your words, gnawing at me like dogs at bones. I'm warning you to stop criticizing and defaming me to others, or I'll give you a taste of your own medicine, and you'll feel it really hurting you.

HENRICUS. You're smaller than a pygmy, what are you saying? I'd eat you for breakfast if it came to blows.

ARNOLDUS. I may be a really small person, but I refuse to be treated like a fool, or to be done down, by you.

CRATO. Don't say words like that; make up your quarrels, peace and harmony are far better than feuding and discord.

HENRICUS. I'd like to be quiet and peaceful, and to have no contact or communication with him, but I can't get free of him; he follows me everywhere like a shadow following a body, or piglets following a sow.

ARNOLDUS. I can easily do without your company.

HOST. Shut up, both of you. I know what we'll do to reconcile you.

HENRICUS. What? Tell us.

HOST. We'll have a little beer-drinking session, and as we drink we'll dispel the rancour you feel for each other from your minds.

HENRICUS. I like the idea. Let's go into that alehouse. Follow me, you brave topers!

HOST. At our house you can sit in the shade, and it'll be quieter, safer and more agreeable.

CRATO. It's better to be in your own house than someone else's.

HENRICUS. Bring plenty to drink, then we'll calculate the expenses.

IASPERVS. Adsint et potoria pocula.

HOSPES. Afferentur modo.

IASPERVS. Prospera sit cereuisia bibentibus.

HOSPES. Et tibi afferenti.

CRATO. Vos duo hactenus inuidiosi inuicem et mutuo poculum exhaurite in felicem uestrae concordiae euentum.

HENRICVS. Bibam, ubi siti laborauero.

CRATO. Arnolde, tibi propino.

ARNOLDVS. Commode et fortunate bibas.

IASPERVS. Vinum biberemus, id conuenit reconcilia- [L1v] tioni.

HENRICVS. Duae mensurae uini ferantur, alteram ipse exsoluam.

ARNOLDVS. Alterius sumptum ipse dabo.

HOSPES. I latum uinum, ego calices uitreos eluam.

IASPERVS. Hic uinum affero, sit felix fortunatumque de ipso potitantibus.

CRATO. Nunc animi prius mutua inuidia turgescentes immutabuntur.

HOSPES. Heus tu Henrice, ut ita obstipo sedes capite? Hanc uini pateram propino tibi integram.

HENRICVS. Accipiam lubens postquam ad fundum fuerit exhausta.

HOSPES. Viden? Exsorpsi.

HENRICVS. Video, et mihi nunc repleas ipsum.

HOSPES. Faciam, en tibi, ipsam funditus imbibas.

HENRICVS. Istud leuissimum mihi factum erit.

IASPERVS. Arnolde, ut siles? Fac a te haustum propinatum accipiam.

ARNOLDVS. Hoc poculum uini tibi praebibo.

IASPERVS. Faustum sit tibi opto.

ARNOLDVS. Bibendo fac respondeas.

IASPERVS. Faciam actutum.

HOSPES. Feruent adhuc animi uestri odio mutuo?

HENRICVS. Nequaquam.

HOSPES. Vtrique calicem uini praebibam quo discordiam in concordiam mutetis.

HENRICVS. Fiet, tu bibe.

IASPERUS. And make sure there are drinking cups.

HOST. They'll be brought directly.

IASPERUS. Good health to those who drink this beer.

HOST. And to you who bring it.

CRATO. You two, so far you've been hostile to each other. Drink a glass together to successfully reaching harmony.

HENRICUS. I'll drink when I'm thirsty.

CRATO. Arnoldus, I drink to you.

ARNOLDUS. May the drink bring you benefit and fortune.

IASPERUS. We would drink some wine, it's good for reconciliation.

HENRICUS. Bring two measures of wine, I'll pay for one myself.

ARNOLDUS. And I'll pay for the other.

HOST. Go and fetch the wine, I'll wash out the glasses.

IASPERUS. I've got the wine. May it bring happiness and good fortune to those who drink it.

CRATO. Now your minds, which were previously bursting with mutual hostility, will be changed.

HOST. Hey, Henricus, why are you sitting with your head down like that? I drink this whole cup of wine to you.

HENRICUS. I'll be glad to accept it after it's been drained to the bottom.

HOST. You see? I've drained it.

HENRICUS. I do. Now fill it up for me.

HOST. Right. Over to you. Drink it completely dry.

HENRICUS. That'll be easy for me to do.

IASPERUS. Arnoldus, why are you quiet? Make me accept a drink from you.

ARNOLDUS. I drink this cup of wine to you.

IASPERUS. May it bring you good fortune.

ARNOLDUS. Make sure you drink back to me.

IASPERUS. I will, straight away.

HOST. Are your minds still bubbling with hate for each other?

HENRICUS. Not at all.

HOST. I'll drink a cup of wine to both of you, so that you turn your discord into harmony.

HENRICUS. Right, drink.

HOSPES. Euacuaui, nunc partite inter uos calicem illum, medium quisque epotet.

HENRICVS. Arnolde, medium tibi propino.

ARNOLDVS. Sit felix faustumque.

HENRICVS. Medium bibi, nunc tu ad fundum epota.

ARNOLDVS. Faciam, uiden?

CRATO. Consertis manibus nunc discordiam deuouete, concordesque uos uicturos promittite. Placet istud utrique?

HENRICVS. Arridet mihi.

ARNOLDVS. Et mihi displicet minime.

CRATO. Ista sancita est reconciliatio.

HENRICVS. Miror qui fiat quod ad uini calices homines in mutuam redire gratiam solent.

CRATO. Deus uini habetur Bacchus ipse, qui aliquando dicitur Lyaeus, a 'luo', id est, 'soluo', quia uinum tristitiam et inuidiam soluit.

---

89 Lyaeus, a 'luo'] Lyeus, a Lyeo B; Lieus a lieo C

21. CONVIVIVM HISTRIONVM SIVE PARASITICVM

Nero hospes; Buttubatta, Gnatho, Curculio [L2r]

NERO. Vnde proditis, uos rudes, tremuli, panosi alacresque animis histriones?

BVTTVBATTA. E foro.

NERO. Quid ibi quaestus estis adepti?

BVTTVBATTA. Lucri prorsus nihil, homines nunc sapiunt Solones, tertiumque Catonem prae se ferunt.

NERO. Non plus uestris capiuntur gesticulationibus?

GNATHO. Asserunt mimorum se sat domi habere, se ipsos utcunque histrionice gestus exhibere.

NERO. Vertuntur nunc omnia, ut quae prius in deliciis sunt habita, nunc iacent et nihili ducantur.

CVRCVLIO. Timemus quod esuriendo ad restim nobis res ueniet, quum uictum solitum denegabunt homines.

NERO. Animos non despondete, ipse solus uos tres integri anni curriculo adhuc pascam, ab aliis destituti si fueritis.

BVTTVBATTA. Grati erimus domino regi nostro unico praesidio.

HOST. I've emptied it. Now you share this cup between you; each of you drink half.

HENRICUS. Arnoldus, I drink half to you.

ARNOLDUS. May it bring you good fortune.

HENRICUS. I've drunk half, now you drain it to the bottom.

ARNOLDUS. I will – do you see?

CRATO. Now join hands and renounce your enmity, and promise you'll live in harmony. Do you both agree?

HENRICUS. That pleases me.

ARNOLDUS. And it doesn't displease me.

CRATO. This reconciliation is confirmed.

HENRICUS. I wonder how it comes about that people are often reconciled when they drink wine.

CRATO. Bacchus is considered the god of wine; sometimes he's called Lyaeus, from the Greek 'lueo', meaning 'set free', because wine sets you free from sadness and ill-will.

21. A MIMES' OR PARASITES' BANQUET

Nero, host; Buttubatta, Gnatho, Curculio

NERO. Where have you come from, you clumsy, shaking, ragged, keen-spirited mimes?

BUTTUBATTA. From the forum.

NERO. What wealth did you acquire there?

BUTTUBATTA. No loot at all; people are now as wise as Solon, or as a third Cato.

NERO. Do your mimings no longer appeal to them?

GNATHO. They say they've got enough mimes at home, and that they put on shows for them as best they can.

NERO. Everything's changing now, so that what used to be in favour is now neglected and regarded as worthless,

CURCULIO. We're afraid there'll be nothing for it but to die of hunger, because people will refuse us the living we're used to.

NERO. Don't be downhearted; I'll feed the three of you myself for a whole year if you're abandoned by others.

BUTTUBATTA. We'll be grateful to our lord the king, our only protection.

NERO. Estis famelici? Libetne cibum ingurgitare?

GNATHO. Per Herculem perque omnes deos patellarios esurimus acerbissime.

NERO. Pingue hic sumen, pinguiaque exta edite, deuorate, igne et uino calidos facite.

BVTTVBATTA. O nostrum praesidium et unicum asylum, tu ille nobis es Iupiter, id est, iuuans pater, ille nobis est deus tutelaris; tutaris nos a saeua stomachi tyrannide, scilicet fame.

NERO. Deus uester ero, adiutor et alumnus, si ea quae interrogerauero mihi responderitis.

GNATHO. Ad uerba quaecumque uolueris, dicemus nobis comperta.

NERO. Quae populi de me est sermo? Verum audire delector, uerum mihi dicite de me, quae fertur uulgo sententia.

BVTTVBATTA. Passim ad astra te ferunt, pium, benignum, aequum, prudentem, diuitem, potentem, omniumque horarum hominem te esse dicunt, et qui possit aequa discernere lance, quid distent aera lupinis.

NERO. O lepidi histriones, ob istud nuntium tri- [L2v] tis uos donabo lacernis, calidoque sumine.

GNATHO. Quae diximus ex oraculo sumus locuti, ita nos patellarii iuuent dii nostri.

NERO. Vos semper iure feci plurimi, uestrum genus semper credidi mundo utilissimum, hominibusque diuinitus datum esse.

BVTTVBATTA. Non facile quis dixerit laudem et encomium nostri albi. Nos hominum sumus solamina, nos solacia, maestorum consolatores, ueri assertatores. Sine nobis uino et mulieribus hilares esse nequeunt mortales. Immo nos etiam nostris solis facetiis alacres facimus. Natura nobis est semper laeta, semper aeque serena, non nubila mens ut ceteris hominibus serus maerorem saepe aduehens.

NERO. Sed agite, quem uos me facitis?

GNATHO. Immo longe maiorem nos te ad astra ferimus, te deum facimus, et si quid est deo maius, multus est nobis in ore rex Nero, rex liberalissimus.

NERO. Are you hungry? Would you like to take on some food?

GNATHO. By Hercules and all the gods of dishes, we are most grievously hungry.

NERO. Eat fat sow's udder and fat offal here, devour them, and warm yourselves with the fire and wine.

BUTTUBATTA. O our protection and only refuge, you are our Jupiter, our 'juvans pater', our 'helping father'; for he is our tutelary god. You protect us from the cruel tyranny of the stomach, hunger.

NERO. I'll be your god, helper and guardian, if you'll answer me the questions I put to you.

GNATHO. Whatever you ask us, we'll tell you what we know.

NERO. What do the people say about me? I love to hear the truth, tell me the truth about me, in public opinion.

BUTTUBATTA. Everywhere they laud you to the skies; they call you a faithful, kindly, just, provident, wealthy, powerful man, a 'man for all seasons', one who can impartially discern the true from the false.

NERO. O you charming mimes, for that news I'll give you some worn cloaks and some hot udder.

GNATHO. What we've said we spoke in absolute truth, so help us all our gods of the dishes.

NERO. I've always thought highly of you, and rightly so. I've always believed that your sort are useful to the world, and a gift of the gods to man.

BUTTUBATTA. It's not easy to pronounce the praise and encomium of our trade. We are people's solace and relief, the consolers of the sad, the declarers of truth. Without us, wine and women, mortals cannot be merry. We even cheer ourselves up with our own jokes. Our nature's always happy, always equally cheerful. We don't have a troubled mind like the rest of men, which often brings on sadness at length.

NERO. But what's your view of me?

GNATHO. Oh, we laud you to the skies as being far greater than us; we make you a god, or greater than a god if that's possible. Of the generous king Nero we speak a great deal.

NERO. Verbis istis semper apud me commeatum, dapsilesque lances, tritasque lacernas, in promptu reperietis.

BVTTVBATTA. Gratia sit domino regi de praesentibus patinis, futura dum accipiemus, etiam pares gratias habebimus.

NERO. At quales in plebeiorum penatibus uos geritis?

BVTTVBATTA. In aedes admissi culinas patinasque lautas petimus, illas exedimus, lingimus, lambimus, rodimus. Damnosi sumus patinis et culinis, nudamus homines argento, dapibus et esca.

NERO. Pocula non efflagitatis?

GNATHO. Hirudines sumus poculorum, bibere non desinimus, quoad guttula restat. Nos Vulcani sumus filii, quicquid tangimus comburimus et consumimus.

NERO. Approbatne uulgus album uestrum?

CVRCVLIO. Nobis calculum adiicit album, dicens oportere uersutum esse, ac rota est figularis, nullumque hominem esse frugi quin bene et male facere sciat ut nos.

NERO. Nunquam ad uerbera uobis res ue- [L3r] nit?

BVTTVBATTA. Creberrime ulmeis pigmentis nobis pellis pingitur, uerum ad pugnos induratam cutem habemus.

NERO. Pelles uestras istis meis poculis iam farcite et patinis, tum minus ferire ipsum dolebit uobis.

---

58 reperietis.] reperietis semper. B C | 67 Hirudines] Hirundines C | 75 pingitur] pungitur B C

22. CONVIVIVM NVGATORIVM

Salibus et nugis recensendis certant Hospes; Poeta, Somniator conuiuae; Seruus, Nugo

HOSPES. Bouem mactaui domi, ad intestina comedenda rogo sitis mihi conuiuae uos quinque.

NVGO. Plures nostrum sunt, gratiam habe in aliam uicem.

HOSPES. Plus carnis et intestinorum mihi est quam uos deuorare poteritis.

POETA. Attamen incommodum est, tantus conuiuarum coetus.

HOSPES. Minime gentium, rancida mihi fient boum intestina sine conuiuis. Solus sum cum solo famulo, omnia nequimus deuorare, nam uultures non sumus.

NERO. For words like those you'll always find provisions, fine dishes and cast-off cloaks waiting for you at my house.

BUTTUBATTA. We give thanks to our lord the king for the dishes we have been given. When we receive any in the future we'll be equally grateful.

NERO. But how do you behave in ordinary people's houses?

BUTTUBATTA. When we're let into the house we make for the kitchens and the sumptuous dishes: we devour them, we lick them, we lap them up, we gnaw them. We do damage to dishes and kitchens, we strip people of their money and their food.

NERO. Don't you demand wine?

GNATHO. We're the leeches of the wine-cups; we never stop drinking as long as there's a drop left. We're the sons of Vulcan, whatever we touch we burn and consume.

NERO. Do the common people approve of your clan?

CURCULIO. We've got their vote! They say you have to be as crafty as you can, and that no one's good for anything if he can't do good and bad like we can.

NERO. Don't you ever end up getting beaten?

BUTTUBATTA. Our skins are often 'painted with elm pigment', but we have hides that are hardened to blows.

NERO. Stuff those skins of yours with my food and drink, then beatings like that won't hurt you so much.

22. A BANQUET OF TRIFLES

A contest in retailing jokes and nonsense between: Host; Poet, Dreamer, guests; Servant, Joker

HOST. I've slaughtered an ox at home, and I'm inviting you five to be my guests in eating up the offal.

JOKER. There are rather a lot of us; thanks, but another time.

HOST. I have more meat and offal than you can eat.

POET. Yet such a big group of guests is inconvenient.

HOST. Not at all, without guests the offal will go off. I'm alone with a single servant, we can't eat up everything, we aren't vultures.

SOMNIATOR. Tum fac pateant aedes, intrabimus tecum uisuri quo nos excipere uelis.

HOSPES. Felicibus auibus limen transcendite. Gratulor uobis felices aduentus in domicilio meo.

NVGO. Felix sit et tibi ac commoda haec habitatio.

HOSPES. Serue, promptuarium resera, carnesque totas deprome, cereuisiam praebe et calices, quaeque conuiuio apta conueniunt ministra.

SERVVS. Claues promptuarii praebe, occlusum est.

HOSPES. Velox redi.

NVGO. Festinare tantopere haud opus est, expectabimus facillime, fame non premimur.

HOSPES. Quid tum? Aliquem tamen in stomacho habebitis locum bolis aliquot. Tu Serue unum aut alterum intestinorum ueru ad prunas torreas.

SERVVS. Exequar.

HOSPES. Vos interim de his carnibus sumite.

NVGO. Fiet.

HOSPES. Ipse exemplo uobis ero prius in quadram buccellam decerpendo.

POETA. Age, tum [L3v] fenestram edendi et nobis aperies, ut hospitis est munus.

HOSPES. Vinum hoc pytissate, palatis sapiet.

SOMNIATOR. Propino tibi.

HOSPES. Bibas prospere.

SOMNIATOR. Certe nobile est, et cum quolibet alio sapore certaret.

HOSPES. Tale est ut ad egenorum mensam bibitur.

SOMNIATOR. Et acre et suaue est.

HOSPES. Exta illa calida, dum feruent, edite, frigida insipida fiunt.

POETA. Ipsis non parce utemur.

HOSPES. Vt ita silentes et taciti estis? Quod in corde uoluitis, an curam prolium educandarum?

NVGO. Non, istarum sollicitudinem matribus et uxoribus relinquimus.

DREAMER. Then throw open your house, we'll come in with you and see what you're going to give us.
HOST. A hearty welcome to my house. I'm very glad you've come.
JOKER. And may this dwelling be fortunate and agreeable for you.
HOST. Servant, open up the larder and bring out all the meats. Serve beer and glasses, and provide anything needed for a banquet.
SERVANT. Let me have the keys of the larder, it's locked.
HOST. Be back soon.
JOKER. There's no need to hurry so much; we're quite prepared to wait, we aren't dying of hunger.
HOST. Come, come, you'll have some room in your stomachs for a bite or two. Servant, barbecue one or two pieces of offal.
SERVANT. I will.
HOST. In the meantime, take some of this meat.
JOKER. Right.
HOST. I'll set you an example and be first to take a piece for my plate.
POET. Right, then you'll give us the encouragement to eat too, as is a host's duty.
HOST. Try this wine, it'll please your taste.
DREAMER. I drink to you.
HOST. Your good health.
DREAMER. It's excellent indeed, its taste could compete with any other wine.
HOST. It's the kind that's drunk at poor people's meals.
DREAMER. It's both tart and sweet.
HOST. Eat that cooked offal while it's hot; when it's cold it loses its flavour.
POET. We'll not hold back.
HOST. Why are you eating so quietly and saying nothing? What are you thinking about – the worry of bringing up your children?
JOKER. No, we leave that worry to mothers and wives.

HOSPES. Sumite animos hilares bibendo. Quis nobis scomma aliquod recensebit, quo ridebimus? Tu istud facito, Nugo uocaris, fac et nugeris nobis nonnihil.

NVGO. Scommatum uel facetiarum expers sum, attamen quod scio dicam. Mulieres uetulae in templo orantes clunibus attrahunt pedes, scitis qua gratia?

HOSPES. Ignoramus, tu dicito.

NVGO. Ideo, ut si quid per posticum uenti emiserint non perdant sine fruge, sed ipso pedes calefaciant, ut Plautinus ille Euclio nocte follem ori astringebat, in quem anhelitum mitteret et mane ignem cum ipso excitaret.

SOMNIATOR. Audite et me. Somnium hac nocte habui multum me inuenisse auri et argenti, lepidaeque nymphae adiacere me amplexanti, at expergiscens sensi felem mihi adesse lingens maxillas meas, nam madebant ex hesterna crapula.

HOSPES. Tu Poeta poeticas facetias nobis narra, tum omne impendium huius conuiuii immune habebitis.

POETA. Aures arrigite, uersus audietis lepidos in hara poetica natos, undecim scilicet hos:

Dum uina bibo,   tristari non bene quibo.
In haustu primo   laetor sub pectoris imo.
In cordis fundo   laetor dum bibo secundo.
Post ternum potum   uinum mox fit mihi notum.
Et potus quar- [L4r] tus laetum   reddit atque facetum.
Et potus quintus   laetam mentem facit intus.
Dum bibo bis ter,   sum qualibet arte magister.
Potu septeno   frons efficitur sine freno.
Potus bis quartus   mihi sensus tollit et artus.
Sed si plus bibam,   *kannen*, *pott*, omnia frangam.
Vt corpus redimam,   *rock*, *hemmet*, omnia uendam.

HOSPES. Ridiculi per Herculem sunt et poculis apti uersus.

POETA. Ipsos boni consulite, qualis sum poeta, tales et dico uersus.

HOSPES. Immunes uos omnes iam hic a symbolo fecisti.

POETA. Gratiam referemus olim.

---

68 uina bibo] uina bibo C; bibo uina B

HOST. Cheer yourselves up by drinking. Who's going to tell us a funny story to make us laugh? you do that, you're called a joker, so tell us some jokes.

JOKER. I don't know many jokes or anecdotes, but what I know I'll tell you. When old women pray in church their feet stick into their backsides; do you know why?

HOST. No, tell us.

JOKER. So that if they let any wind out through their bums they won't lose the benefit of it – they'll warm their feet with it, just like Euclio in Plautus tied a bag to his mouth when he was asleep to catch his breath so as he could fan the fire with it in the morning.

DREAMER. Listen to me, too. Last night I had a dream that I'd found lots of gold and silver, and that charming girls were lying with me and I was kissing them, and when I woke up I realised the cat was beside me and was licking my jaws, because they were wet from the previous night's carousing.

HOST. Poet, tell us some poetic jokes, then you'll all be let off paying for this party.

POET. Listen up, you're about to hear some elegant verses produced in the poetic hatchery, eleven of them, as follows:
When I drink wine, I just can't feel sad.
At the first draught, I'm happy in the bottom of my heart,
I feel joy in the depths of my soul when I drink the second.
After the third drink, the wine makes itself felt.
The fourth draught makes me happy and jokey,
And the fifth drink makes me joyful inside.
The sixth drink gives me a degree in any subject.
At the seventh I lose all inhibitions.
The eighth takes away all my senses and strength.
But if I drink more, I'll break the jug, the pot, everything.
To redeem my body, I'll sell my coat, my shirt, everything.

HOST. Ridiculous verses indeed, just right for drinking.

POET. Don't be too harsh on them. The kind of verses I speak reflects the kind of poet I am.

HOST. Now you've all exempted yourselves from paying a share of the expenses.

POET. We'll express our thanks to you some time.

23. CONVIVIVM TABERNARIVM, VBI CERTO ASSE ET NVMMIS PRAESENTIBVS CONVIVATVR ET SOLVITVR

Tabernarius; Iasperus, Henricus, Maximilianus, Volfgangus, Georgius, Arnoldus uiatores

IASPERVS. Ho ho, nemon huc prodit? Vacant hae aedes?

TABERNARIVS. Quis fores pulsat clamandoque domum personat?

IASPERVS. Salue, hospes Tabernarie.

TABERNARIVS. Et tu.

IASPERVS. Ecquid lauti habes obsonii? Dapsilicene instruxisti focum? Nostri hic sex peregre profecti adsunt, ex itinere fessi et esurientes, cibique et potus cupidissimi.

TABERNARIVS. Satis reconditum cibi habeo, si uobis aes exsoluendi suppetit.

HENRICVS. Bonorum Daton habemus pecuniasque Croesi et Crassi aequamus opulenta.

TABERNARIVS. Isti assidete mensae, fercula iam afferri faciam, quiescite interim.

MAXIMILIANVS. Faciemus, at tu festina. Acerrima nobis fames est, qualem ab incunabulis habuimus nunquam.

TABERNARIVS. Morbo isti medebor pulcherrime. De ista perna uoragines uentris farcite, mox lautiores patinas afferam, sed cibum consecrate prius.

VOLFGANGVS. Benedicite.

HENRICVS. Dominus.

VOLFGANGVS. Christus Dei filius, salutis humanae auctor [L4v] et conseruator, tabernarium hoc prandium nobis benedictum reddat.

HENRICVS. Amen.

VOLFGANGVS. Nunc edemus, ipse morari nequeo.

IASPERVS. Ede, non morabimus quin et nos cibum sumemus.

ARNOLDVS. Durum est et admodum salsa caro ista.

MAXIMILIANVS. Potu salsedinem pelle.

ARNOLDVS. Cantharum medium ebibam.

VOLFGANGVS. Tum ad fundum ipse exsiccabo.

23. A BANQUET IN THE TAVERN, WHERE THE PARTY IS PAID FOR IN READY CASH

Innkeeper; Iasperus, Henricus, Maximilianus, Volfgangus, Georgius, Arnoldus, travellers

IASPERUS. Hello! Hello! Is no one coming? Is this house empty?

INNKEEPER. Who's knocking on the door and making the house ring with shouting?

IASPERUS. Good day, landlord.

INNKEEPER. Good day to you.

IASPERUS. What fine food have you got? Have you stoked up the fire lavishly? The six of us have come from abroad; we're tired and hungry from our journey, and we're dying for food and drink.

INNKEEPER. I've got plenty of food in store, if you've got the money to pay for it.

HENRICUS. We have the wealth of Datos, the riches of Croesus, and our affluence is on a par with Crassus.

INNKEEPER. Sit down at that table. I'll have the food served soon; rest yourselves in the meantime.

MAXIMILIANUS. We will, but you hurry up. We have a violent hunger, such as we haven't felt since we were babies.

INNKEEPER. I'll cure that problem very well. Stuff the gaps in your stomachs with that ham. I'll bring some finer dishes soon, but first say grace.

VOLFGANGUS. Benedicite.

HENRICUS. Dominus.

VOLFGANGUS. May Christ the Son of God, the author and preserver of human salvation, bless this our meal in this tavern.

HENRICUS. Amen.

VOLFGANGUS. Now we'll eat; I can't wait.

IASPERUS.

ARNOLDUS. That meat's tough and pretty salty.

MAXIMILIANUS. Take away the saltiness with a drink.

ARNOLDUS. I'll drink half a pot.

VOLFGANGUS. Then I'll empty it completely.

GEORGIVS. Heus, heus, Hospes, cereuisiae plus prome, haec epota est.

TABERNARIVS. Abunde cereuisiam afferam, placetne et uinum?

MAXIMILIANVS. Vtique, quanto pretiosius fuerit, tanto ipso plus delectabimur.

TABERNARIVS. Hic uinum affero nectareum, nectari caelestium deorum ne latum unguem cedens, eo hilares uos reddite.

IASPERVS. Faciemus, alia obsonia praebe assi si quid habes; elixis non oblectamur.

TABERNARIVS. Sunt mihi capi duo illaridati et anser in ueru adhuc calidi, de ipsis quid afferam? Dicite utrum ansere an capis palata plus gaudeant uestra.

IASPERVS. Anserem feras, capos tibi serues.

TABERNARIVS. Accipite eum, pinguem, et adipe multa ac si tener uitulus esset.

HENRICVS. Ho ho, sodales optimi, lassitudinem itinere longo adeptam nunc curate, incidimus in caelum.

MAXIMILIANVS. Praebibo tibi, guttur mihi constringit anserina ista caro.

IASPERVS. Ex postico anseris edas.

VOLFGANGVS. Oleto ipsius iam capior magis quam si uiueret.

TABERNARIVS. O uos conuiuae, ut nunc stomachis ualetis? Estne factum melius?

MAXIMILIANVS. Longe praestantius intestina nunc uigent, quam dum adueniebamus.

IASPERVS. Hospes, propino tibi.

TABERNARIVS. Prosit, bibere nondum cupio, inpransus sum. Bibite uos basilice, ipse impendiorum immemor non ero.

GEORGIVS. Et nos tuorum obsoniorum non obliuiscemur.

TABERNARIVS. Istud decet ad mensam. Hic caseum accipite, qui aduenarum hic solet esse terror.

MAXIMILIANVS. Nos perterrescet minime, sat aeris habe-[M1r]mus, unde symbolum pendemus.

GEORGIUS. Hey, hey, landlord, fetch some more beer, this stuff's all been drunk.

INNKEEPER. I'll bring plenty of beer; would you like some wine, too?

MAXIMILIANUS. We would indeed. The dearer it is the more we'll like it.

INNKEEPER. Here I've brought some wine like nectar, not a whit worse than nectar of the gods; make yourselves merry with that.

IASPERUS. We will. Serve other food, if you have any roast meat; we're not keen on boiled meat.

INNKEEPER. I have two larded capons, and a spit-roasted goose; they're still hot. Tell me whether the goose or the capons are more to your taste.

IASPERUS. Bring us the goose and keep the capons for yourself.

INNKEEPER. Here it is, fat and with plenty of grease, as though it was a tender calf.

HENRICUS. Ho ho, my good companions, now remedy the tiredness the long journey caused us, we've landed in Heaven.

MAXIMILIANUS. I'll drink to you, that goose-meat's tightening my throat.

IASPERUS. You're eating from the parson's nose.

VOLFGANGUS. I like what's in the goose's backside better now than I would if it was alive!

INNKEEPER. How are your stomachs doing now, guests? Better?

MAXIMILIANUS. Our insides are in much better shape now than they were when we arrived.

IASPERUS. Landlord, I drink to you.

INNKEEPER. Cheers! I don't want to drink yet, I haven't eaten. You drink up right royally, I'll remember what you've spent.

GEORGIUS. And we won't forget your food.

INNKEEPER. That's the right way at table. Have this cheese, it usually puts strangers here off.

MAXIMILIANUS. It won't put us off, we've enough money to pay the bill.

TABERNARIVS. Edite de ipso uel butyro quantum lubet.

IASPERVS. Tolle mensam, Hospes, sat edimus, hinc abeundum est.

TABERNARIVS. Non abeundum, sed soluendum, quisque uestrum tribus albis symbolum soluet.

VOLFGANGVS. Hui, tantum? Vix cibus ualuit tantum.

TABERNARIVS. Vini bibistis multum.

MAXIMILIANVS. O uos sodales optimi, hinc quomodo euademus, quo pendemus symbolum?

IASPERVS. Hospes, aes in numerato non habemus, nostra chirographa tibi dabimus, mox exsoluturi, et e patria tibi aes missuri.

TABERNARIVS. Chirographa non accipio, nam litterarum expers sum, sed uel pecuniam uel exuuias.

HENRICVS. Nunc uersuum quorundam recordor:

Est bona uox 'holl wyn', melior 'schenk yn',
optima 'drynck aus'.
Est mala uox 'rechen', peior 'bezalen',
pessima 'den rock aus'.

TABERNARIVS. Sit pessimum uel optimum, aut soluite, aut uestes exuite.

IASPERVS. Accipe has uestes; ad uesperam, uel summum cras repignorabimus et redimemus.

---

18 assidete] assedete B C | 26 Dominus.] Amen B C | 60 ualetis] ualete B ualeits C | 68 mensam. Hic] mensam, Hic C; mensam. TA. Hic B | 93 uel summum] uel summum C; uel ad summum B

24. CONVIVIVM NATALE

Macrinus, natalem diem celebrans; Persius, Castor, Pollux conuiuae; Coquus, Seruus

MACRINVS. Io, io, o festiuissimum diem, o candidissimum solem hodiernem, feliciorem integer annus habet nullum.

PERSIVS. Vnde tantum hodierni die encomium profers?

MACRINVS. Ignorabas hodie mihi esse diem natalem?

PERSIVS. Per Herculem non cogitabam, non tum natalitio tuo die nos tuos amicos epulis et mensa excipis?

INNKEEPER. Have some of it, or some butter, as much as you like.

IASPERUS. Clear the table, landlord. We've eaten enough, we must be going.

INNKEEPER. Paying, not going. Each of you owes three Albus for your share.

VOLFGANGUS. What, as much as that? The food was hardly worth that much.

INNKEEPER. You've drunk a lot of wine.

MAXIMILIANUS. My fine friends, how are we going to get out of this? How will we pay the bill?

IASPERUS. Landlord, we haven't got any cash on us. We'll give you our IOUs, promising to pay you soon, and to send you the money from where we live.

INNKEEPER. I don't accept IOUs, I can't read. I just accept money or your clothes.

HENRICUS. Now I remember a few verses:

A good word is 'bring wine';
a better one's 'pour it out',
the best is 'drink up';
A bad word is 'the bill',
a worse one's 'pay up',
the worst is 'off with your coat'.

INNKEEPER. Best or worst, either pay or take off your coats.

IASPERUS. Take these coats. By the evening, or at latest tomorrow, we'll repay you and redeem them.

24. A BIRTHDAY PARTY

Macrinus, celebrating his birthday; Persius, Castor, Pollux, guests; Cook, Servant

MACRINUS. Hurrah, hurrah, for the most joyous of days! The sun shines brightly today, there isn't a happier day in all the year!

PERSIUS. Why are you singing such a hymn of praise to today?

MACRINUS. Didn't you know it was my birthday today?

PERSIUS. It wasn't in my mind, I swear. So aren't you going to treat us, your friends, to a luxurious meal?

MACRINVS. Vtique, adsitis meo prandio omnes quattuor, meum diem genialem mecum celebretis.

CASTOR. At quantum impendii faciet quisque?

MACRINVS. Sumptus nihil impendetis, ipse feram omnia mea crumena.

POLLVX. Age, perplacet, condicimus, non opus est nobis scindere paenulam.

CASTOR. Vbi conuiuae uocamur [M1v] sumus facillimi, ubi ad erogandam pecuniam, surdi et auribus mortui.

MACRINVS. At natalitiis muneribus me ut donetis oportet.

PERSIVS. Ipsa mittemus lubentissime.

MACRINVS. Coque, suntne edulia percocta?

COQVVS. Quando lubet accubitum ite.

MACRINVS. Seruue, estne mensa decorata quibus solet ornari?

SERVVS. Est, et diutissime.

MACRINVS. Lauetis, mi conuiuae, et discumbite.

CASTOR. Prior discumbere tuum est ut hospitis.

MACRINVS. Benedicite.

PERSIVS. Dominus.

MACRINVS. Cunctipotens Deus, caeli et terrae Dominus, bonorum omnium auctor, creator, saluator humanae creaturae, hoc natali conuiuio cibum et potum nobis pransuris salubria facere uelit.

PERSIVS. Amen.

MACRINVS. Nunc epulis negotium sumite et poculis.

POLLVX. Otium non agemus.

MACRINVS. Salsuginosam illam carnem uel porcinam gustate.

CASTOR. Fiet.

MACRINVS. Serue, ad cyathos sta, uideque ne siccitate hient.

SERVVS. Curabo.

MACRINVS. Iurulentas fer carnes, his siccis non est delicium magnum; quadras alias porrige.

SERVVS. Exequi uolo.

MACRINVS. Carnibus istis iurulentis fruimini quoad assae afferentur.

MACRINUS. I certainly am. Come to my party, all four of you, and celebrate my birthday with me.
CASTOR. But how much is each of us going to spend?
MACRINUS. You won't spend anything, I'll pay for it all with my money.
POLLUX. Well, that's great. We'll come, you won't have to keep us from leaving.
CASTOR. When we're invited as guests we're very accommodating; when it's a question of spending money we're deaf, our ears are dead.
MACRINUS. But you have to give me birthday presents.
PERSIUS. We'll give you them gladly.
MACRINUS. Cook, is the food ready?
COOK. Sit down to eat whenever you like.
MACRINUS. Servant, is the table set with everything that's usually on it?
SERVANT. It is, and has been for a long time.
MACRINUS. Wash your hands, my guests, and sit down.
CASTOR. You must sit down first, as the host.
MACRINUS. Benedicite.
PERSIUS. Dominus.
MACRINUS. May Almighty God, the lord of heaven and earth, the author of all good things, the creator and saviour of the human creation, be pleased to make the food and drink at this birthday meal beneficial to us who are about to eat it.
PERSIUS. Amen.
MACRINUS. Now to the task of eating and drinking.
POLLUX. We won't be lazy about it.
MACRINUS. Taste that corned meat, or the pork.
CASTOR. Right.
MACRINUS. Servant, see to the drinking-cups, and make sure they don't run dry.
SERVANT. I will.
MACRINUS. Bring on the meat in gravy, the dry meats aren't particularly delightful. Give us other plates.
SERVANT. I'll see to that.
MACRINUS. Enjoy those meats in gravy until the roasts are brought on.

PERSIVS. Facile est contentum esse patina tali poculisque lepidis.

MACRINVS. Genio indulgete, Epicurique uiuite.

PERSIVS. Propino tibi in felix auspicium sequentis anni.

MACRINVS. Hodie alium auspicor annum meae aetatis.

PERSIVS. Tibi nunc est exordium anni, ut omnibus mortalibus, ipso Circumcisionis die.

MACRINVS. Assas carnes fac adsint, famule.

SERVVS. Efficiam celerrime.

MACRINVS. Orbes tolle, aliosque praepone.

CASTOR. Omen felix tibi hoc poculo opto, o Macrine.

MACRINVS. Et tibi ipsum non sit infelix.

POLLVX. Age, bibendo mihi par referas.

MACRINVS. Non differam, omnibus uobis ad has tostas carnes praebibo, in gratiam, quod hoc natali meo die me inuisistis.

CASTOR. Lubentes fecimus, maiora uelimus, si inseruire tibi poterimus.

MACRINVS. Decerpite assum, ipsum propositum est ut edatur, non ut rursum in culinam deferatur.

POLLVX. Strenue nostrum agimus [M2r] munus.

PERSIVS. O Macrine, hilarem hunc sumas diem, genio affatim indulge, diisque gratias habe, qui hoc die uitae munere te fungi fecerunt et concesserunt.

MACRINVS. Istud hodie feci, facio et quoad hic dies durauerit faciam.

CASTOR. Macrine, scisne cur munera mittantur ab amicis illi cuius est dies natale?

MACRINVS. Puto quod signum sit amicitiae, eo munere gaudeant natum in mundum esse eum cui mittant.

CASTOR. Vt die Circumcisionis donantur xenia, ob noui auspicium anni, ita ipso die natali nato homini.

MACRINVS. Verisimile est.

CASTOR. Sic res est.

MACRINVS. Serue, bellaria appone, et cyathos aspice an sitiant.

PERSIUS. It's easy to be contented with food like this and pleasant drinks.

MACRINUS. Spoil yourselves, and live like Epicurus.

PERSIUS. I drink to a happy start to your next year.

MACRINUS. Today I'm starting another year of my life.

PERSIUS. This is the start of your year, as the feast of the Circumcision is for all mortals.

MACRINUS. Have the roast meats brought, Servant.

SERVANT. I'll see to that immediately.

MACRINUS. Take away the plates and set out others.

CASTOR. I dedicate this cup to you, Macrinus – good luck!

MACRINUS. And may it not be unfortunate for you.

POLLUX. I drink to you: you do the same to me.

MACRINUS. I won't refuse. I drink to all of you to accompany these roast meats as a thanks for visiting me on my birthday.

CASTOR. We were glad to. We'd be pleased to do more if we could be of service to you.

MACRINUS. Help yourselves to the roast, it's been served to be eaten, not to be taken back to the kitchen.

POLLUX. We'll do our duty assiduously.

PERSIUS. Enjoy today, Macrinus, give yourself a thorough treat, and be thankful to the gods who have graciously allowed you to enjoy the gift of life today.

MACRINUS. I've done that today, and I'll continue as long as the day lasts.

CASTOR. Macrinus, do you know why presents are sent by friends to the person whose birthday it is?

MACRINUS. I think it's a sign of friendship; the gift expresses their joy that the person they send them to was born into the world.

CASTOR. In the same way as New Year presents are given on the Circumcision, they're given to people on their own birthdays.

MACRINUS. That sounds likely.

CASTOR. It's the truth.

MACRINUS. Serve the desserts, Servant, and check the cups to make sure the wine hasn't run out.

PERSIVS. Nunquam uidi calices sitire.

MACRINVS. Intelligenti pauca satisfaciunt. Caseo hoc ora exiccate, butyroque animos si maerent lenite.

POLLVX. Macrine, praebibo, optoque felix sit tibi dies natalis posteraque aetas.

MACRINVS. Commode bibas.

CASTOR. Fac deponi dapes, expatiabimur aliquantulum.

MACRINVS. Serue, mensam tolle.

CASTOR. Legamus hymnum.

MACRINVS. Deus misericors et iustus, qui in hanc lucem nos creauit, creatosque pascit sua gratia, benedictus sit in aeternum et ultra.

PERSIVS. Amen.

MACRINVS. Boni consulite habita obsonia.

PERSIVS. Tu pro liberalitate ista gratiam habe.

2–3 Pollux Conuiuae; Coquus,] Pollux, Coquus, Conuiuae, B C | 53 SERVVS.] Seru. C; FA. B | 67 fecerunt] fecit B C | 67 concesserunt] concessit B C

25. CONVIVIVM DELICATORVM PALATORVM

Coloniensis, Vestualus, Thuringius, Saxo, Sueuus, Hessus, Franco, Phrysius, Obsonator

COLONIENSIS. Heus, heus, contubernales optimi, quid agemus? Tempore hoc licentioso conuiuabimurne inuicem? Viuemus semper Stoicos? Nunquam cum Horatio spargemus nuces? Patiamurque uel inconsulti haberi?

VESTVALVS. Iucundum esset conuiuari, si opulentae nobis essent crumenae.

COLONIENSIS. Ego omnium nostrorum nomine nummos exponam et sumptum si post factum calculum quisque sua parte mihi reddere promittit.

VESTVALVS. Pollicemur ad [M2v] sacramentum.

COLONIENSIS. Audin tu obsonator, in conuiuium delicatum obsonia mercatum uade, sed cura ut lautissima quaeque emas.

PERSIUS. I've never seen wine running!

MACRINUS. A few words are enough, if you understand them. Dry your mouths with this cheese, and if your minds are sad, soothe them with butter.

POLLUX. I drink to you, Macrinus, and wish that your birthday and the rest of your life may be happy.

MACRINUS. Your good health.

CASTOR. Have the food cleared, we'll go for a little walk.

MACRINUS. Servant, clear the table.

CASTOR. Let's say grace.

MACRINUS. May the merciful and just God, who created us and placed us in this world, and who feeds us in his mercy, be blessed in eternity and beyond.

PERSIUS. Amen.

MACRINUS. Don't be too critical about the food we've had.

PERSIUS. Thanks to you for your generosity.

25. A GOURMETS' BANQUET

A man from Cologne, a Westphalian, a Thuringian, a Saxon, a Swabian, a Hessian, a Franconian, a Frisian, Caterer

MAN FROM COLOGNE. Ho there, my fine companions, what shall we do? Shall we party together at this time of freedom? Will we always live like Stoics? Will we never become mature along with Horace? Or will we allow ourselves to be seen as thoughtless?

WESTPHALIAN. It would be lovely to carouse together, if we had fat purses.

MAN FROM COLOGNE. I'll lay out the money on behalf of us all, if each one of you promises for his part to repay me after we've worked out the expenses.

WESTPHALIAN. We solemnly swear we will.

MAN FROM COLOGNE. Listen, Caterer, go and buy dishes for a gourmet banquet; but make sure you buy really luxurious ones.

OBSONATOR. Aeris satis si habuero, obsonando acinctissimus ero.

COLONIENSIS. Accipe aureum istum, et quantum opus fuerit, obsoniis splendidis impende.

OBSONATOR. Pollucibiliter obsonabo.

COLONIENSIS. Redeas Pegaseo gradu, et uorans uiam. Obsonatum misi qui mercabitur nobis edulia ampliter.

THVRINGIVS. Aderit etiam mox?

COLONIENSIS. Apud propolas cibum coctum emet, tum coquendi labore non egemus.

SAXO. At quod obsonii afferet?

COLONIENSIS. Iussi ut delicatissima quaeque quaereret et mercaretur.

SVEVVS. Cuius palato? Forte tuo obsonabit.

COLONIENSIS. Quicquid culinaria taberna habuerit opipari et cocti, istud nobis compararet.

HESSVS. Aduenietne oppido?

COLONIENSIS Dicto citius aderit, nos interim mensam sternemus.

FRANCO. En alias redit obsonator, sub pallio ferens nescioquid.

COLONIENSIS. Saluus aduenisti, obsonator noster. Quid splendidi mercatus es nobis?

OBSONATOR. Admodum calida, nescio an pinguia.

HESSVS. Proh, carnes affert suillas et uitulinas, quis illis delectatur? Porcina est immunda, lepram gignens. Vitulina insaluberrima febrem pariens morbumque et moros gestire facit.

OBSONATOR. Mercatus sum quae potui consequi, delectus mihi non erat, alias haec non attulissem.

COLONIENSIS. Edamus haec dum desunt splendidiora.

FRANCO. Vere dicis, boni consulenda sunt uilia, ubi pretiosis laboratur.

HESSVS. Edat igitur quisque esuriens, fames ipsi condimentum dabit quo sapient, etiam dulcissime.

CATERER. If I have enough money, I'll be very ready to buy the food.

MAN FROM COLOGNE. Take this Gulden and spend as much as you need on sumptuous foods.

CATERER. I'll buy food fit for a banquet.

MAN FROM COLOGNE. Come back as fast as ever you can. I've sent someone off to the shops to buy us an ample supply of food.

THURINGIAN. Will he be back soon?

MAN FROM COLOGNE. He's going to buy cooked food at the shops, then we don't need to trouble ourselves cooking it.

SAXON. But what sort of food will he bring?

MAN FROM COLOGNE. I told him to look for the most delicious things and buy them.

SWABIAN. Whose taste is he going to shop for? Yours, no doubt.

MAN FROM COLOGNE. Whatever fine cooked food the cookshop has, he was to buy it.

HESSIAN. Will he arrive soon?

MAN FROM COLOGNE. He'll be here quicker than a wink, in the meantime we'll lay the table.

FRANCONIAN. Look, there's the caterer coming back, carrying something or other under his cloak.

MAN FROM COLOGNE. Welcome, caterer. What superb food have you bought for us?

CATERER. Very hot stuff, I'm not sure how fat it is.

HESSIAN. Yuk, he's brought pork and veal, who likes them? Pork is unclean, and it causes diseases. Veal is really unhealthy; it gives you fever and sickness, and makes you go crazy.

CATERER. I bought what I was able to get. I had no choice, or I wouldn't have brought these.

MAN FROM COLOGNE. Let's eat these, since there's nothing more splendid.

FRANCONIAN. You're right. You have to make do with poor things when there's a lack of fine ones.

HESSIAN. So everyone who's hungry, eat up. Hunger will provide the spice that'll make the food taste good, delicious even.

OBSONATOR. Aut manus admouete aut solus exedam.

SVEVVS. Quod mercatus es, ede, nos esurire malumus.

OBSONATOR. Nunc in portu nauigabo, resque mea in uado erit, cum solus haec deuorare debeo.

THVRINGIVS. Nihil aliud tibi erat apud propolas?

OBSONATOR. Ne mu quidem.

COLONIENSIS. Bibamus copiosius, et quo in cibo egemus in potu recompensemus. Mox domum ibo quaesitum [M3r] piperis aliquid zinzibere conditi.

VESTVALVS. Ipse si in patria essem, haberem quo latrantem stomachum replerem.

HESSVS. Quid?

VESTVALVS. Patinam fabarum, deinde lentium, deinde pisarum, tum lactis, tum pultis, tum holerum, tum raparum. Haec fercula quibus desunt, potiuntur crassissima carne porcina.

THVRINGIVS. In laribus meis paternis dulce iusculum de halece ederem, tabernam potoriam accedens in sinum sumerem halec salsugine erutum, de quo lamberem inter potandum, ut sitim acciperem.

FRANCO. O nobilem meam Franconiam, in qua uini suauis bibuntur calices. Ibidem si essem, uiuerem indulgentius.

SAXO. In Saxonia mea et nobilis ac satis crassa cereuisia potatur.

HESSVS. Hassia mea caprinis carnibus abundatissima est, in ipsaque obsonia pinguia et multo iusculo eduntur.

SVEVVS. Sueui mei uino et nucum copia superbiunt.

PHRYSIVS. Phrysii nostri butyro fertilibusque caseis nobiles sunt et laudabiles.

FRANCO. Quid tu Coloniensis ais? In quo tuam Coloniam effers?

COLONIENSIS. Opus non est praeconio, satis se ipsam commendat.

FRANCO. Dapes opiparae uobis Coloniensibus nullae sunt aliae quam piper rugosum.

COLONIENSIS. Ah, uos inopes Germaniae orientalis uel superioris, uos aquae bibuli!

CATERER. Get a move on, or I'll eat it all myself.
SWABIAN. Eat what you've bought; we'd rather go hungry.
CATERER. I'm really in clover now – I have to eat this myself.
THURINGIAN. Couldn't you get anything else at the shops?
CATERER. Not a sausage.
MAN FROM COLOGNE. Let's drink all the more abundantly, and make up in drink what we lack in food. I'll go home soon and get some pepper cooked with ginger.
WESTPHALIAN. If I was in my own parts, I'd have something to fill my gaping stomach.
HESSIAN. What?
WESTPHALIAN. A dish of beans, then lentils, then peas, then milk, then pottage, then cabbage, then turnips. People who are without those dishes think they beat the fattest pork.
THURINGIAN. In my own region I'd have the sweet juice of the herring. When I went to the alehouse I'd take a pickled herring in my pocket, and I'd nibble it as I drank, to work up a thirst.
FRANCONIAN. O my noble Franconia, where we drink cups of sweet wine. If I were there, I'd be living the good life.
SAXON. In my native Saxony we drink noble, rather thick beer.
HESSIAN. My Hessia abounds in goat meat. There we eat fat foods with lots of gravy.
SWABIAN. My Swabians pride themselves on having lots of wine and walnuts.
FRISIAN. Our Frisians are famed and distinguished for their butter and their rich cheeses.
FRANCONIAN. And what do you say? How do you extol
your city of Cologne?
MAN FROM COLOGNE. It has no need of a laudation, it commends itself sufficiently.
FRANCONIAN. For you people in Cologne, fine food means nothing but wrinkled peppers.
MAN FROM COLOGNE. You poor folks from Upper Germany, you water-drinkers!

FRANCO. Si nostrates aquam non biberent, diu Rhenus uos occidentales Germanos submersisset.

OBSONATOR. Quisque suam repetet domum, nequeo uestris palatis arridentia obsonare, nam nimium dissident.

---

12 mihi] mihi C; mi B | 22–23 uiam. Obsonatum] uiam. Co. Obsonatum B C | 63 lentium] lendium B C

26. CONVIVIVM HELLVONVM POCVLIS SESE VRGENTIVM

Hermannus, Arnoldus fratres; Iasperus, Georgius

HERMANNVS. Sitio affatim, quid consilii praebes, mi frater?

ARNOLDVS. Remedium non est aliud magis praesentaneum siti quam epotatio crebra poculorum.

HERMANNVS. Pocula quid iuuant uacua?

ARNOLDVS. Pocula puto non inania, sed potu referta, ua- [M3v] cua uasa pocula non merentur dici.

HERMANNVS. Qui hoc?

ARNOLDVS. Pocula (ni fallor) dicuntur calices, quasi potum continentes uel continentia.

HERMANNVS. Potatum quo nos conferemus?

ARNOLDVS. In eas aedes ubi conuenire soliti sumus.

HERMANNVS. Iniucundum est duobus solis compotare, si quos haberemus congerrones siue compotores.

ARNOLDVS. Forte in ipso domicilio cereuisiario quosdam inueniemus nostri consortii.

HERMANNVS. Accedamus Iasperum, ueterem nostrum commilitonem.

ARNOLDVS. Perplacet, confestim eamus.

HERMANNVS. Heus, heus, Iaspere, esne domi?

IASPERVS. Non sum.

HERMANNVS. Nonne te loquentem audimus?

IASPERVS. Non Iasperum, sed forte Theologum auditis.

FRANCONIAN. If our folks didn't drink water, the Rhine would have drowned you Lower Germans long ago.

CATERER. Everyone go back to his own house. I can't supply food that pleases you all, your tastes are too different.

26. A BANQUET WHERE BIG EATERS EGG ONE ANOTHER ON TO DRINK

Hermannus and Arnoldus, brothers; Iasperus, Georgius

HERMANNUS. I'm really thirsty. What advice do you give me, my brother?

ARNOLDUS. There's no quicker remedy for thirst than frequently emptying cups.

HERMANNUS. What good are empty cups?

ARNOLDUS. I'm not thinking about empty cups, I'm thinking about ones filled with drink. Empty vessels don't deserve to be called cups.

HERMANNUS. Why's that?

ARNOLDUS. Unless I'm mistaken, 'cups' is the name given to vessels that have drink in them.

HERMANNUS. Where will we go to drink?

ARNOLDUS. We'll go to the house where we've been in the habit of meeting up.

HERMANNUS. It's no fun for two people to drink together; I wish we had some boon-companions to drink with us.

ARNOLDUS. Perhaps we'll find some of our company in that alehouse.

HERMANNUS. Let's go to Iasperus, our old schoolmate.

ARNOLDUS. Great, let's go straight away.

HERMANNUS. Hey, Iasperus, are you at home?

IASPERUS. No.

HERMANNUS. Can't we hear you talking?

IASPERUS. Not Iasperus. Perhaps you hear 'the Theologian'.

HERMANNVS. Ecce, obliti per Herculem fuimus istius tui cognominis. Quid agis? Latitas semper et adsides theologicis tuis libris?

IASPERVS. In grammaticis regulis sudaui et legi. Quid uenitis? Quid expetitis?

HERMANNVS. Venimus curatum cuticulam tecum ad pocula.

IASPERVS. Haec domus ad algidam dicitur culinam, nihil neque cibi, potus, neque ignis est.

HERMANNVS. Adest cantharus quo potus feratur?

IASPERVS. Fideliam habemus, non stanneum cantharum.

ARNOLDVS. Dulcior est potus ex fictili poculo quam stanneo.

HERMANNVS. Istud est quod dixit Agathocles rex filius figuli, qui rex maluit ex fictilibus uasis quam aureis bibere.

IASPERVS. Hic e regione in taberna coquinaria cereuisiam feram, interim expectetis.

HERMANNVS. At redi uelox, sitimus fortiter et acerbissime.

IASPERVS. Hic redeo, felix sit cereuisia bibentibus.

ARNOLDVS. Et tibi afferenti non sit infelix.

IASPERVS. Hoc poculo ebibendo, aut totum, aut medium combibemus.

HERMANNVS. Arridet, sit ratum quod loqueris.

IASPERVS. Hermanne, praebibo tibi integrum poculum.

HERMANNVS. Esto, accipio libenter.

ARNOLDVS. En Georgi, unde tu proripis?

GEORGIVS. E laribus meis adsum, uisum uenio quid hic geratur.

HERMANNVS. Hic potatur, genioque indulgetur.

GEORGIVS. Istud uideo.

IASPERVS. Assideas, sisque nobis compotor.

GEORGIVS. Aere careo.

HERMANNVS. [M4r] Praediuitem habemus conuiuii principem, Iasperum nostrum tertium Catonem et octauum sapientem.

IASPERVS. Nasum uestrum nosco, nasuti estis, praeter hoc nihil.

HERMANNUS. By heavens, we'd forgotten that nickname of yours. What are you up to? Are you always hidden away, sitting over your theological books?

IASPERUS. I've sweated away reading the rules of grammar. Why have you come? What do you want?

HERMANNUS. We've come to indulge ourselves drinking with you.

IASPERUS. This house is called 'Cold Kitchen House'; there's no food, or drink, or fire.

HERMANNUS. Is there a pot we could fetch drink in?

IASPERUS. We've got a pot, but not a pewter one.

ARNOLDUS. Drink tastes better from a clay pot than it does from a pewter one.

HERMANNUS. That's what King Agathocles, the son of a potter, said. When he was a king he preferred to drink from clay cups than golden ones.

IASPERUS. I'll fetch beer from a cookhouse in the neighbourhood; you wait for me.

HERMANNUS. But come back quickly, we've got a fierce, raging thirst.

IASPERUS. I'm back. May the beer be fortunate for those who drink it.

ARNOLDUS. And may it be fortunate for you who bring it.

IASPERUS. We'll drink together and drain either the whole of this pot, or the half of it.

HERMANNUS. A good idea; what you say's agreed.

IASPERUS. Hermann, I drink a whole cup to you.

HERMANNUS. Right, I'm glad to accept.

ARNOLDUS. Hello, Georgius, where have you come from?

GEORGIUS. From my own house. I've come to see what's going on here.

HERMANNUS. Drinking, and having a good time.

GEORGIUS. I see that.

IASPERUS. Sit down and join us in drinking.

GEORGIUS. I've no money.

HERMANNUS. We have someone very wealthy to preside over the party: Iasperus, a third Cato and an eighth Sage.

IASPERUS. I know your wit: you're jokey, nothing more.

ARNOLDVS. Hui, bibite plenis poculis, commilitones optimi, exemplum uobis dabo, calcarque addam calicem hunc ingurgitando.

IASPERVS. Ho ho, instar uaccae bibis.

ARNOLDVS. Vsque adeo sapuit, desinere et cessare non possum.

HERMANNVS. Georgi, tibi propino.

GEORGIVS. Accipio lubens.

HERMANNVS. Vt desidetis tam siccis palatis? Calices osculamini ipsisque linguas madefacite.

ARNOLDVS. Non feriabimur.

HERMANNVS. Cereuisiae plus feras, haec epota est.

IASPERVS. Asses tres porrigite.

ARNOLDVS. Ad calculum feras, in digressu soluemus.

IASPERVS. Sin minus feceritis, uestibus uos nudabo.

HERMANNVS. Nunc eas ocius.

IASPERVS. Felix faustaque sit quam fero cereuisia bibenti et soluere uolenti.

ARNOLDVS. Quid? Non esset salubris satisfacere recusanti?

IASPERVS. Iste non bibat.

ARNOLDVS. Nunc tanto cupidius bibemus. Hui, bibite plenis buccis, sodales optimi, bibite ad iugulum usque.

GEORGIVS. Quid illud conferret?

ARNOLDVS. Multum sane, quantum quis plus potu madet, tanto peritior est, iucundior et hilarior.

IASPERVS. Hermanne, hoc te saluto calice.

HERMANNVS. Non obsit, ebibe, aut non suscipiam a te.

ARNOLDVS. Abeundi tempus est, uespera imminet.

IASPERVS. Exsoluite prius impendium.

HERMANNVS. Ad Graecorum Kalendas.

IASPERVS. Memor ero, ubi locus fuerit.

---

36 poculo] poculo C; potu B | 37 HERMANNVS.] A. B; Ar. C

ARNOLDUS. Oh, drink deeply, my fine companions! I'll set an example and spur you on by pouring this cup down me.
IASPERUS. Ho, ho, you're drinking like a cow.
ARNOLDUS. It was really delicious, I just can't stop.
HERMANNUS. Georgius, I drink to you.
GEORGIUS. I accept gladly.
HERMANNUS. Why are you sitting around with dry throats? Let's kiss the cups and wet our lips with them.
ARNOLDUS. We won't be lazy about that.
HERMANNUS. Bring more beer, this stuff's all been drunk.
IASPERUS. Let me have some money.
ARNOLDUS. Put it on the slate, we'll pay when we leave.
IASPERUS. If you fail to, I'll take your clothes off you.
HERMANNUS. Now go quickly.
IASPERUS. May the beer I bring be fortunate and favourable to those who drink it and are prepared to pay for it.
ARNOLDUS. What? Would it not do any good to a person who refused to pay?
IASPERUS. He won't get to drink it.
ARNOLDUS. Now we'll drink all the more eagerly. Oh, drink big mouthfuls, my good companions, drink up to your necks.
GEORGIUS. What good would that do?
ARNOLDUS. A lot. The more someone drinks, the more knowledgeable, agreeable and cheerful he is.
IASPERUS. Hermannus, I toast you with this cup.
HERMANNUS. Your good health. Drink it all, or I won't accept it from you.
ARNOLDUS. It's time to go, it's nearly evening.
IASPERUS. Pay what you owe first.
HERMANNUS. On the first of Never!
IASPERUS. I'll remember that, when the right time comes.

27. CONVIVIVM COMMILITONVM LITTERARIORVM ASSES SVOS CONGERENTIVM

Henricus, Iacobus, Arnoldus, Petrus, Cornelius

HENRICVS. A meridie quid operis faciemus?

IACOBVS. Inscius sum.

HENRICVS. Si me audire uelitis, scirem quid facere conferetur.

IACOBVS. Exprime audacius.

HENRICVS. Vt asse cuiuslibet apposito conuiuiolum instauraremus, diu non compotauimus.

ARNOLDVS. Facile dictu est, sed difficile factu.

HENRICVS. Qui hoc?

ARNOLDVS. [M4v] Aere laboramus.

PETRVS. Neque cingulus neque marsupium neque assis minimus mihi est.

CORNELIVS. Et mihi assis non est, quo restim emerem.

HENRICVS. Consilium dabo, ut nonnihil aeris acquiratis. Parentibus uel cognatis dicite libellum aliquem albo nummo uos empturos, et illum deinde potatiunculae insumemus; quisque nonnisi unius albi nummi (ut uulgo dicitur) sumptum faciet.

IACOBVS. Optimum consilium et acceptandum.

HENRICVS. Quisque illico domum eat, et tantum aeris a parentibus uel amicis petat.

IACOBVS. Curabimus.

HENRICVS. Ac praepeti gradu redite.

PETRVS. Ibimus uiam uorantes.

ARNOLDVS. Redeo et uoti compos factus pecuniam affero.

IACOBVS. Praesto et ego sum, a matre hoc nummo donatus.

PETRVS. Venio ipse quoque licet serus, quia diu pater nolebat annuere et marsupium laxare.

HENRICVS. Vbi tu tam serus moratus es? Quid te detinuit?

27. A BANQUET OF SCHOOLMATES WHO POOL THEIR MONEY

Henricus, Iacobus, Arnoldus, Petrus, Cornelius

HENRICUS. What are we going to do in the afternoon?

IACOBUS. I don't know.

HENRICUS. If you're prepared to listen to me, I know what it would be good to do.

IACOBUS. Tell us boldly.

HENRICUS. For each of us to put down some money and organize another little drinking-party. We haven't drunk together for a long time.

ARNOLDUS. Easy to say, but hard to do.

HENRICUS. Why?

ARNOLDUS. We're strapped for cash.

PETRUS. I haven't got a belt or a pouch, or the least amount of money.

CORNELIUS. And I haven't got enough money to buy a rope to hang myself.

HENRICUS. I'll advise you how to make some money. Tell your parents or relatives that you're going to buy some book or other for an Albus, then we'll spend the money on a little drinking-party. Each of us will only spend an Albus, as they call it.

IACOBUS. An excellent idea; we should accept it.

HENRICUS. Everyone go straight home and ask their parents or friends for that amount of money.

IACOBUS. We'll see to that.

HENRICUS. But come back quickly.

PETRUS. We'll go like the wind.

ARNOLDUS. I'm back; I got what I asked for and I've brought the money.

IACOBUS. I'm here too; my mother gave me this coin.

PETRUS. I'm here too, though I'm late, because for a long time my father refused to approve and loosen his purse-strings.

HENRICUS. Where have you been for so long? What held you up?

CORNELIVS. Dura ceruix meae nutricis, quae decies assem in manu uertit et reuertit, antequam exponit.

HENRICVS. Rennuebat tibi tantillum nummorum?

CORNELIVS. Aegre extorsi, et ferme lacrimantibus oculis.

HENRICVS. Velocissime nunc potatum eamus, uiuamusque cereuisiarii potatores, dum nequimus Bacchanalia.

IACOBVS. Quo concedemus?

HENRICVS. Ad aedes meas, ibi solitudine fruemur, potitabimus et 'Io, io, io' cantabimus, nemine percipiente. Intretis, pulcherrimi combibones et commilitones litterarii.

ARNOLDVS. Aequum est, ut qui totis diebus sudantes et laboriosi consedemus in gymnasio litterario, animis tristibus, trementibusque corporibus ob praeceptoris saeuitiam et ferulae metum, sic et nos ad pocula exhilaremus aliquando.

PETRVS. Decet ut qui miseriarum fuerunt, etiam laetitiae sint participes.

HENRICVS. Quisque uestrum nummos mihi det, ego princeps conuiuii ero.

CORNELIVS. Muneris istud habeas, sed fideliter exequere, non aliquid pecuniae recondas in loculum.

HENRICVS. Potum et triticeum panem mercabor, quoad teruncium habuero, ibo iam latum cereuisiam.

IACOBVS. Vade et celer redi. [M5r]

HENRICVS. Tardus non ibo. En redeo. Potus hic cerere coctus saluti sit omnibus bibentibus ipsum, sed praebibere est meum, tibi propino, Arnolde.

ARNOLDVS. Accipio libenti animo.

PETRVS. Iacobe, libetne bibere?

IACOBVS. Liberet si haberem.

PETRVS. Hunc calicem tibi praebibam medium.

IACOBVS. Id facito, cupio.

PETRVS. Bibe nunc et tu.

IACOBVS. Aliquid panis triticei da, edere oportet me dum bibo.

CORNELIUS. My nurse's stubbornness. She turned the coin over and over in her hand before she handed it over.

HENRICUS. Did she refuse you as small a sum as that?

CORNELIUS. I had difficulty in wringing it out of her; I almost had tears in my eyes.

HENRICUS. Now let's go and drink really quickly, and let's live as beer-swillers, since we can't celebrate the Bacchanalia.

IACOBUS. Where will we go?

HENRICUS. To my house. We'll be alone there, we'll carouse and sing happy songs, and no one will hear us. Come in, my fine classmates and drinking-mates.

ARNOLDUS. We've been sitting together for days in school, sweating and toiling, feeling depressed and trembling on account of our teacher's violence and the fear of the cane. It's only fair that we should cheer ourselves up by drinking from time it time.

PETRUS. It's right that people who've had a share in misery should have a share in happiness too.

HENRICUS. Everyone give me their money, I'll preside over the party.

CORNELIUS. You can have that office, but carry it out honestly, don't hide some money in your money-box.

HENRICUS. I'll buy as much drink and wheaten bread as the money will stretch to. I'm off to fetch the beer.

IACOBUS. Go, and come back quickly.

HENRICUS. I won't delay. Here I am back. May this beer be to the health of all who drink it, but it's my place to drink to someone. I drink to you, Arnoldus.

ARNOLDUS. I'm delighted to accept.

PETRUS. Iacobus, would you care to drink?

IACOBUS. I would, if I had any drink.

PETRUS. I'll drink half this cup to you.

IACOBUS. Do, I accept.

PETRUS. And now you drink.

IACOBUS. Give me some wheaten bread, I have to eat when I drink.

HENRICVS. Cuius est bibere? In quo sistit amphora? Potitet, quo et nos alii potu fruamur.

ARNOLDVS. Vide ne deficiat cereuisia, alioqui pugnos edes, aut uersus caput tibi cantharum mittemus.

HENRICVS. Non cupio istam fortunam et commoditatem, satis superque adhuc restat, uos saltem inuicem praebibite.

IACOBVS. Corneli, tu sitim potu non comprimis, propino tibi huius calicis medium.

CORNELIVS. Salutiferum tibi sit.

PETRVS. Hoc ebibam, tum non sine fruge sumptum feci.

HENRICVS. Pecuniae suae quem paenitet potu se consoletur.

IACOBVS. Ipse ad summum iugulum me implebo, cogitaboque nummos quos e domo paterna attuli stomacho et uentri me imisisse.

ARNOLDVS. Non falsus erit cogitatus, nam bibuli domum in uentre referunt, quod mane extulerunt aedibus in crumena.

CORNELIVS. At abeamus hinc, tempestiuum est.

IACOBVS. Fiat.

---

9 compotauimus] compotauimus C; computauimus B | 25 praepeti] praepeti C; perpeti B | 65–70: C copies B, which attributes ll. 65–68 to Henricus, then specifies Henricus as speaker at l. 69.

28. CONVIVIVM LVCRI LVSORII

Albertus, Christianus, Vesselus, Matthias, Dionysius; Staphyla mulier

ALBERTVS. Attendite, attendite sodales et collusores carissimi, uestes induite in tempore hinc ut discedamus, morabimur etiam adhuc horulam in potatorio domo.

CHRISTIANVS. Agemus compotatiunculam? Repetenda mihi est domus paterna, alioqui si serus uenero pugnos edam.

ALBERTVS. Non annum peragemus bibendo, pedibus insistendo lucrum ludi consu- [M5v] memus.

VESSELVS. Quantum aeris dedit uictoria?

ALBERTVS. Albos nummos tres.

MATTHIAS. Nullos nigros nummos?

ALBERTVS. Nugas agere incipis.

HENRICUS. Whose turn is it to drink? Where's the jug stopped? Let him drink, so as the rest of us can enjoy the drink.

ARNOLDUS. Make sure the beer doesn't run out, or you'll get thumped, or we'll throw the jug at your head.

HENRICUS. I don't want that distinction, and there's still enough left and more, so you drink to one another.

IACOBUS. Cornelius, you're not slaking your thirst with drink. I drink the half of this cup to you.

CORNELIUS. Your good health.

PETRUS. I'll drink this dry, then I won't have spent my money without having anything to see for it.

HENRICUS. Anyone who regrets his money can console himself with drink.

IACOBUS. I'm going to fill myself right up, and I'll think that I've put the money I brought from my father's house into my stomach.

ARNOLDUS. The thought isn't wrong, because drinkers bring back home in their bellies what they took away from their house in their purses in the morning.

CORNELIUS. But let's leave, it's high time.

IACOBUS. Right.

28. BANQUET WITH MONEY WON AT GAMING

Albertus, Christianus, Vesselus, Matthias, Dionysius; Staphyla, a woman

ALBERTUS. Listen, my dear friends and gaming-companions, get your clothes on quickly so that we can leave here, we're going to stay for an hour or so in the alehouse.

CHRISTIANUS. Are we going to have a drinking-party? I've got to go back to my parents' house, or else if I arrive late I'll get a thumping.

ALBERTUS. We're not going to spend a year drinking, we'll drink our winnings standing up.

VESSELUS. How much did our win give us?

ALBERTUS. Three White-pennies.

MATTHIAS. No Black-pennies?

ALBERTUS. You're starting to talk rubbish.

DIONYSIVS. Eamus, non diu sistemus pedes in proximum hic ad portam, ubi baculus stramine obsitus extensus est.

MATTHIAS. Ibidem uenit cereuisia pretio suo respondens.

CHRISTIANVS. Es notus mulieri uendenti?

MATTHIAS. Sum, comitamini, ego praecedam.

ALBERTVS. I prae, nos in pedes sequemur. Heus, heus, nemon huc prodit? Staphyla, ubi lates? Promes nobis cereuisiae mensuram.

STAPHYLA. Lubentissime. Subite tectum, non foris ac mendici pedes figite et stetis. Accipite et bibite prospere.

MATTHIAS. Tu prius bibas ut dignum est.

STAPHYLA. Faciam, ne incantasse me potum suspicemini.

MATTHIAS. Minime illud timemus.

STAPHYLA. Ite accubitum mensam, quid pedibus insistendo biberetis?

ALBERTVS. Aeque stantes ac sedentes tempus prodigitis. Libet e poculo bibere?

CHRISTIANVS. Placet, porrige fictile aliquod.

STAPHYLA. Nunc infundite.

VESSELVS. Aegre effunditur, ubi nullus restat potus.

STAPHYLA. Detis, plus promam.

MATTHIAS. Duas nunc porrexisti mensuras.

STAPHYLA. Verum est, cupitis buccellam panis, quo bibere plus delectet?

ALBERTVS. Non, non, ad parentes eundum et properandum nobis est, ibi cenitabimus.

STAPHYLA. Si placuerit, sponte impartiar uobis.

CHRISTIANVS. Iuxta gratiam habe, ac si dedisses.

VESSELVS. Propere abeamus, moramur nimium.

MATTHIAS. Staphyla, denuo i eductum potum, deinde discedemus.

DIONYSIVS. Conueniet tertia mensura consumpta calculum facere, nam omne trinum perfectum est.

STAPHYLA. Haec tertia sit uobis salutifera.

ALBERTVS. Praebibas mihi, dulcior est potus post haustum a muliere e cantharo factum.

DIONYSIUS. Off we go, we won't stand long near the door that has a stick covered with straw sticking out over it.

MATTHIAS. They sell beer there that's worth its price.

CHRISTIANUS. Does the barmaid know you?

MATTHIAS. Yes, come with me, I'll go in first.

ALBERTUS. On you go, we'll follow in your footsteps. Hey, ho, is there no one here? Staphyla, where are you? Fetch us a measure of beer.

STAPHYLA. I will, gladly. Come on in, don't stand outside like beggars. Take this and drink it; your good health.

MATTHIAS. You drink first, as is right.

STAPHYLA. I will, so as you don't think I've put a spell on the drink.

MATTHIAS. We aren't worried about that at all.

STAPHYLA. Go and sit at the table. Why would you drink standing up?

ALBERTUS. You're wasting time whether you stand or sit. Do we want to drink from a cup?

CHRISTIANUS. Yes, give us a pottery cup of some kind.

STAPHYLA. Now pour the drink.

VESSELUS. It's hard to pour when there's no drink left.

STAPHYLA. Pour it, I'll fetch some more.

MATTHIAS. Now you've given us two measures.

STAPHYLA. That's right. Do you want a bit of bread, to make drinking more pleasant?

ALBERTUS. No, no, we have to hurry off to our parents', we'll be dining there.

STAPHYLA. If you'd like, I'll let you have some free.

CHRISTIANUS. Thanks, just as much as if you'd given it to us.

VESSELUS. Let's be off quickly, we're delaying too long.

MATTHIAS. Staphyla, go and draw another drink, then we'll go.

DIONYSIUS. It's a good time to work out the expenses after having the third drink, for all groups of three are perfect.

STAPHYLA. May this third one bring you good health.

ALBERTUS. Drink to me; drink tastes better after a woman has taken a draught from the cup.

STAPHYLA. Leporis in me cadauerosa muliere nihil est; si triginta annis iunior essem! [M6r]

DIONYSIVS. Nondum usqueadeo annis confecta es, adhuc butyrum (ut uulgo prouerbium est) tuis in labiis liquefieret.

STAPHYLA. Minime per Pollucem, ex senio edentula facta sum, conuenio ad libidinis prurientis titillationem expellendam.

ALBERTVS. Tu totum diem transigeres nugamentis. Bibe, ut hinc soluamus anchoram.

MATTHIAS. Propino tibi.

ALBERTVS. Felicitatem bibas.

DIONYSIVS. Ceteris propines, ipse exsoluam potum. Audin Staphyla, tres cantharos cereuisiae habuimus, nonne?

STAPHYLA. Verum est.

MATTHIAS. Nummos tene, nos discessum faciemus.

STAPHYLA. Ite bonis auibus.

ALBERTVS. Sit tibi nox felix et fausta.

STAPHYLA. Vobis quoque sit fortunata et fecunda. Quandocumque fores praeteritis meas, huc potatum concedite. Si praesentes non habueritis nummos, ad fidem cereuisiam dabo.

MATTHIAS. Faciemus.

CHRISTIANVS. Quam callida in suum quaestum est anus illa, reuocare nos et allicere conatur, quo saepe potui insumamus nummos apud se.

VESSELVS. Superstites semitres albos in quid conferamus?

ALBERTVS. In compotatiunculam proximi nostri congressus.

MATTHIAS. Aedes suas quisque adeat, hic digrediendum est nobis, prosperam precor uobis noctem.

DIONYSIVS. Et nos tibi quoque.

---

7 Agemus] Ageremus C | 26 suspicemini] suspicemini C suspicimini B

29. CONVIVIVM VLTIMI DIGRESSVS, DVM DISCESSVS MONVMENTVM COMPOTATVR

Crato, Nicolaus, Fridericus; Laurentius pater discessuri; Puer

CRATO. In cenam uos tres uolo conuiuas, si integrum, uobisque cordi fuerit.

STAPHYLA. I'm an emaciated woman, there's no attractiveness in me. If I was thirty years younger …

DIONYSIUS. You're not completely worn out by age yet. Butter would still melt on your lips, as the saying goes.

STAPHYLA. Not at all! I've become toothless with age; I'm good for turning people off.

ALBERTUS. You'd spend the whole day talking nonsense. Drink, so as we can up sticks here.

MATTHIAS. I drink to you.

ALBERTUS. May you drink happiness.

DIONYSIUS. Drink to the others, I'll pay for the drink. Tell me, Staphyla, we've had three jugs of beer, right?

STAPHYLA. Right.

MATTHIAS. Here's the money; we'll be on our way.

STAPHYLA. Go, with my best wishes.

ALBERTUS. May you have an untroubled, favourable night.

STAPHYLA. And may it be fortunate and fruitful for you too. Any time you're passing my door, come in and drink. If you haven't got any cash on you, I'll give you the beer on tick.

MATTHIAS. We will.

CHRISTIANUS. That old woman's really clever about making money. She calls us back and tries to lure us into spending money on drink at her place often.

VESSELUS. What'll we spend the one and a half Albus we've got left on?

ALBERTUS. On drinks the next time we meet up.

MATTHIAS. Each of you go home to his own house, we've got to leave here. I wish you a prosperous night.

DIONYSIUS. And we wish the same to you.

29. A FAREWELL BANQUET, WHERE PEOPLE DRINK TO SOMEONE'S DEPARTURE

Crato, Nicolaus, Friedricus; Laurentius, the father of the boy who is about to leave; Boy

CRATO. I'd like you three as guests, if it's convenient and if it would please you.

NICOLAVS. Vnde tanta tibi liberalitas, quod conuiuas nos uocas [M6v] cum soleas esse Plautino Euclione tenacior?

CRATO. Cum ipso tenacitatem commutaui liberalitate.

NICOLAVS. Qui tam subito?

CRATO. Cras hinc abibo exulatum peregre.

NICOLAVS. Forte in litterarum emporium proficisceris?

CRATO. Istud faciam.

LAVRENTIVS. Tum monumento digressus nos donabis ad hodiernum cenam.

CRATO. Sic fiet, uos adsitis, exporrigemus frontem genialiter.

NICOLAVS. Adueniemus, at qua hora?

CRATO. Sexta postquam sonuerit facite ut domi nostri sitis.

FRIDERICVS. Curabimus. Tu abi, nos in tempore sequemur.

CRATO. Vos fumi uenditores dicam, si me non inuiseretis.

NICOLAVS. Viri sumus, promissa facto exequemur.

FRIDERICVS. Donabimusne ipsum uino, si commessatum ipsum adierimus?

LAVRENTIVS. Minime gentium, sui muneris est nos tingere poculis et uino in discessus monumentum, nostrum uero pensum erit si quandoque remigrauerit huc saluus, uino excipere ipsum.

NICOLAVS. Ibimus tum ad cenam ipsum conuentum?

FRIDERICVS. Quidni? Id dedeceret, addixisse ipsi et emanere.

LAVRENTIVS. Quotam sonuit horam?

NICOLAVS. Quintam, et sexta instat.

LAVRENTIVS. Eamus igitur, si accincti estis, ne in nobis sit mora.

FRIDERICVS. Properare opus non est, licet nos post cenae auspicium uenire.

NICOLAVS. Fores pulsa aut tintinnabulo sonum facito.

CRATO. En mei commilitones, gratum mihi est quod uenistis, desperabam de aduentu uestro.

FRIDERICVS. Tales non sumus qui factis dissonant a uerbis. Sed ubi pater est? Anne hic domi?

CRATO. Intus insidet, hibernaculo ingrediemini.

NICOLAVS. Praeeas tu.

CRATO. Sequimini.

NICOLAUS. Why so much generosity, inviting us as guests, when you're usually tighter than Plautus's Euclio?

CRATO. Like him, I've exchanged generosity for miserliness.

NICOLAUS. Why so suddenly?

CRATO. Tomorrow I'll be leaving here, to go into exile in foreign parts.

NICOLAUS. Are you going off to a school, by any chance?

CRATO. I am indeed.

LAURENTIUS. Then you'll give us a celebration of your departure at dinner today.

CRATO. That's right. You be there, and we'll enjoy ourselves and have good cheer.

NICOLAUS. We'll come, but what time?

CRATO. Be at our house after it's struck six.

FRIDERICUS. We'll see to that. Off you go, we'll follow you in good time.

CRATO. If you don't visit me I'll say you make empty promises.

NICOLAUS. We're men; we'll do what we've promised.

FRIDERICUS. Shall we give him some wine, if we're going to his party?

LAURENTIUS. Not at all. His duty is to treat us to wine and a farewell celebration; ours will be to treat him to wine if he ever comes back here safe and sound.

NICOLAUS. So will we go to the dinner to be with him?

FRIDERICUS. Of course. It'd be disgraceful to have promised him and then to stay away.

LAURENTIUS. What time has it struck?

NICOLAUS. Five, and six is coming soon.

LAURENTIUS. Right, let's go if you're ready, let's not delay.

FRIDERICUS. There's no need to hurry, it's all right if we arrive after dinner has begun.

NICOLAUS. Knock on the door or ring the bell.

CRATO. Hallo, my guests! I'm pleased you've come, I was despairing of your arrival.

FRIDERICUS. We're not the sort whose deeds don't match their promises. But where's your father? Is he at home?

CRATO. He's sitting inside, go into the sitting-room.

NICOLAUS. You go first.

CRATO. We'll follow.

PATER. Qui adsunt?

CRATO. Commilitones mei aliquot.

LAVRENTIVS. Bonus uesper sit tibi, heros.

PATER. Et uobis; grati sint uestri aduentus.

NICOLAVS. Gratiam habe. Aduenimus huc exporrectum frontem cum Cratone ueteri nostro sodale, qui cras se hinc peregrinaturum alio dixit.

PATER. Digne fecistis, est mihi acceptum uestrum aduenire. Manibus [M7^r] aquam accipite, iamiam mensae accumbemus. Puer, consecra cenam.

PVER. Benedicite.

PATER. Dominus.

PVER. Huius nostrae cenae fercula et potus benedicat et consecret Deus, qui sua suauitate nutrit omne uiuens, pascit creaturas omnes, nullumque sibi fidentem et iustum deserit. Velit et nos hoc uesperi alere cibo et potu in animae nostrae salutem et suum honorem. In nomine Patris et Filii et Spiritus Sancti.

PATER. Amen. Nunc discumbite, hilarem sumemus hanc cenam.

NICOLAVS. Tu discumbe, nos assidebimus.

PATER. Hic mihi solet esse sedes. Puer, obsonia affer.

PVER. Adsunt.

PATER. Vino reple vitreos calices.

PVER. Curabo.

PATER. Has carnes iusculo elixas edite, mox delicatiora dabuntur.

LAVRENTIVS. Munus noster exequemur belle.

PATER. Praebibo uobis tribus, qui dignati estis huc uenire cenatum ad monumentum discessus filii mei.

NICOLAVS. Bibas feliciter.

LAVRENTIVS. Crato, hoc poculo te adoriar.

CRATO. Suscipiam ex corde.

FRIDERICVS. Nicolae, propino tibi.

NICOLAVS. Sit commodo.

PATER. Puer, tolle hanc patinam et alia edulia affer.

PVER. Porrige.

FATHER. Who's here?

CRATO. Some schoolmates of mine.

LAURENTIUS. A good evening to you, sir.

FATHER. And to you; you're most welcome.

NICOLAUS. Thank you. We've come to enjoy ourselves with Crato our old companion, who told us that he's leaving here for somewhere else tomorrow.

FATHER. You've done the right thing, and your arrival is welcome to me. Take water for your hands, we're just about to sit down at the table. Boy, say grace.

BOY. Benedicite.

FATHER. Dominus.

BOY. May God, who feeds every living thing so pleasingly, who feeds all creatures, and who does not desert anyone who is righteous and who trusts in him, bless and consecrate the food and drink of this our meal. May he be pleased to feed us this with food and drink this evening, to the salvation of our souls and to his own honour. In the name of the Father, and of the Son, and of the Holy Spirit.

FATHER. Amen. Now sit down, and we'll eat this joyful dinner.

NICOLAUS. You sit down and we'll sit beside you.

FATHER. This is my usual seat. Boy, bring on the food.

BOY. Here they are.

FATHER. Fill the glasses with wine.

BOY. I will.

FATHER. Eat these boiled meats, there'll be finer food served soon.

LAURENTIUS. We'll do our duty well.

FATHER. I drink to the three of you who have been kind enough to come to my son's farewell dinner.

NICOLAUS. Your good health.

LAURENTIUS. Crato, I dedicate this cup to you.

CRATO. I'll accept wholeheartedly.

FRIDERICUS. Nicolaus, I drink to you.

NICOLAUS. Good health.

FATHER. Boy, take away this plate and bring on the other dishes.

BOY. Here you are.

PATER. Assas has frigidas carnes comedite; quisque ad suam decerpat quadram.

NICOLAVS. Crato, ut saluus discedas feliciorque redeas, hoc uitrum tibi propino.

CRATO. Commode bibas.

PATER. Crato, quocumque ueneris, uide ut probus, fidelis, diligens litterarum, fugiens ludi, amans Dei et probitatis sis; nulli quam tibi olim proderit.

CRATO. Honestissime agam. Ne cures, mi pater.

PATER. Cura, tibi luditur si non feceris. Puer, tolle mensam et hymnum gratiarum actionis dicas.

PVER. De sumpta cena benedicamus Domino.

PATER. Deo gratias.

PVER. Cuius benignitate pasti sumus, conseruamur uiui et salui, sit benedictus, gratiamque sempiternam habeat.

CRATO. Amen.

PATER. Vos adolescentes gratiam habete de aduentu.

NICOLAVS. Et tu de cena tua.

PATER. Praebibo uobis potum gratiarum.

NICOLAVS. Prosit, nunc abeundi tem- [M7v] pus est. Crato, cras in digressu te alloquemur.

CRATO. Sic fiet; iam ualete.

30. CONVIVIVM DISCEPTATORIVM ET LITTERARIVM

Iasperus, Iohannes, Henricus, Marcus, Maximilianus

IASPERVS. Vos opulenti, uos locupletissimi, quando e uestris loculis conuiuium aliquod nobis instruetis?

IOHANNES. Conuiuari tu semper expetis, si piscis esses, uiuarium omne exsorberes, in quo reconditus esses.

IASPERVS. Ille potus non iuuaret me, sitire mallem.

HENRICVS. Ad conuiuium impendiosum sex albos immunes dabo.

MAXIMILIANVS. Et tantum ipse addam.

MARCVS. Io, io, nunc bibemus et ad Epicureorum morem cuticulam curabimus.

HENRICVS. Hic pecuniam meam expendam.

FATHER. Eat these cold roast meats. Each of you cut off a piece for his own plate.
NICOLAUS. Crato, I drink this glass to you: may you be safe when you leave, and even happier when you return!
CRATO. Your good health.
FATHER. Crato, wherever you go, be sure to be virtuous, trustworthy and devoted to your studies, to avoid gambling, and to love God and virtue. That will be very much to your benefit one day.
CRATO. I'll behave very honourably. Don't worry, Father.
FATHER. Be sure you do. You're deceiving yourself if you don't. Boy, clear the table and say grace.
BOY. For the dinner we have eaten, let us bless the Lord.
FATHER. Thanks be to God.
BOY. May he by whose grace we have been fed and preserved safe and well, be blessed and thanked forever.
CRATO. Amen.
FATHER. You boys, thank you for coming.
NICOLAUS. And thank you for the dinner.
FATHER. I'll drink a drink of thanks to you all.
NICOLAUS. Your good health! Now it's time to go. Crato, tomorrow we'll console you as you leave.
CRATO. Right. Goodbye for now.

30. A LITERARY DEBATING BANQUET

Iasperus, Iohannes, Henricus, Marcus, Maximilianus

IASPERUS. You really rich people, when are you going to open your money-boxes and arrange some kind of party for us?
IOHANNES. You're always asking for a party. If you were a fish you'd drink all the water in the pond you were kept in.
IASPERUS. That kind of drink wouldn't please me, I'd prefer to go thirsty.
HENRICUS. I'll contribute six Albus to an extravagant party.
MAXIMILIANUS. And I'll add the same amount.
MARCUS. Hurrah, now we'll drink and do ourselves well like Epicureans.
HENRICUS. I'll pay out my money here.

IASPERVS. Redde et tuam.

MARCVS. Accipe.

IASPERVS. Ibo latum uinum Creticum uel uulgare.

MAXIMILIANVS. Quod uulgo uenditur illius multo plus ista mercabimur pecunia.

IASPERVS. Ferendo uinum ab impendio liber ero.

MAXIMILIANVS. Triticeos panes aliquot emas, unde rodemus et uino perfundemus.

IASPERVS. Nosco, securi sitis, expediam quam rectissime.

HENRICVS. I celeri gressu.

IASPERVS. Hic affero uini mensuras quattuor, quamlibet uiginti teruncciis.

MAXIMILIANVS. Tu cyathis infunde.

IASPERVS. Sed hunc calicem latori debitum primus ebibamus.

HENRICVS. Bibe et praeliba, sitne ueneno infectum, tum nos securius et audentius bibemus.

IASPERVS. Propino tibi.

HENRICVS. Sit tibi bono. Omnibus bibulis uobis praebibo.

MAXIMILIANVS. Sit saluti tibi poculorum baratro.

HENRICVS. Istud conuitiari nihili pendo.

MAXIMILIANVS. Iaspere, hoc cyatho te aggrediar.

IASPERVS. Accipiam grato animo. Agite uos combibones optimi, hic inter pocula litterarii aliquid tractemus, ne tempus (ut Plautus inquit) comburamus sine fruge.

MARCVS. Conueniet, nam ut Persius ait, 'Ecce, inter pocula quaerunt Romulidae saturi, quid dia poemata narrent'.

IASPERVS. Ego [M8r] disserenda praeponam, uos respondete.

MAXIMILIANVS. Faciemus.

IASPERVS. Vtrum melius esse creditis, doctum esse et uirtute praeditum, uel indoctum et uitiis inquinatum?

MAXIMILIANVS. Lippi et tonsores istud diiudicarent, uirtutem et scientiam toto caelo praestare uitiis et inscitiae.

IASPERVS. Causam dicite.

IASPERUS. And hand over yours, too.

MARCUS. Here it is.

IASPERUS. I'll go and get some Cretan wine, or ordinary wine.

MAXIMILIANUS. You'll get much more ordinary wine with that amount of money.

IASPERUS. Because I fetch the wine I'll be exempt from making a contribution.

MAXIMILIANUS. Buy a few wheaten loaves for us to nibble and dip in the wine.

IASPERUS. I know, don't worry, I'll see to it as correctly as I can.

HENRICUS. Go quickly.

IASPERUS. I've brought four measures of wine, as much as I could get for twenty Heller.

MAXIMILIANUS. Pour it into the cups.

IASPERUS. But first let's drink this cup that's owed to the person who fetches the wine.

HENRICUS. Drink it first to check if it's poisoned, then we'll drink it more boldly and confidently.

IASPERUS. Cheers.

HENRICUS. Your good health. I drink to all you topers.

MAXIMILIANUS. Your good health, you boozer!

HENRICUS. I don't dive a damn about mockery like that.

MAXIMILIANUS. Iasperus, I'll challenge you with this cup.

IASPERUS. I accept gladly. Right, fellow-drinkers, let's talk about some literary topic as we drink, so as not to 'burn up' the time unprofitably, as Plautus puts it.

MARCUS. A good idea, for as Persius says, 'Lo, as they drink, the sons of Romulus enquire what new things divine poetry is relating.'

IASPERUS. I'll suggest things to discuss, and you reply.

MAXIMILIANUS. Right.

IASPERUS. Do you think it's better to be learned and endowed with virtue, or unlearned and tainted with vices?

MAXIMILIANUS. Everyone could tell you that virtue and knowledge are vastly superior to vice and ignorance.

IASPERUS. Tell me the reason.

MAXIMILIANVS. Virtus ad aethera uehit, uitia ad manes praecipitant. Scientia decorat hic in mundo, et post uitam hanc lucere facit homines quasi splendor firmamenti. Indocti digitis extensis exsibilantur, nihilque a caudice differunt.

IASPERVS. Vtrum praeualet pax et concordia, uel lis et discordia?

HENRICVS. Pax, nam nutrit omnia, conseruat singula et res paruas auget, diuinitus mortalibus data. Discordia omnia dissipat, conseruat nihil, diabolica est, ab imis inferis in mundum missa.

IASPERVS. Vtrum litteratum et inopem esse, uel indoctum et opulentum praestat?

IOHANNES. Litteras scire et inopem esse.

MAXIMILIANVS. Inopes tamen nequeunt emergere et passim pessundantur.

IOHANNES. Pauperes et docti ubique in uiros euadunt, nam artem quaeuis alit terra.

IASPERVS. Ideo, sodales dilectissimi, quicquid agimus, curemus semper ut operam litteris nauemus, chartis impallescamus, ut et olim pedes caeno extrahamus, pennas nido extendamus, nostris maioribus aut pares fiamus, aut praeluceamus uirtute.

HENRICVS. Hactenus illa, bibite ordine omnes, discedendum est.

MAXIMILIANVS. Propino tibi.

HENRICVS. Libenti animo suscipiam.

IASPERVS. Gratiam agimus uobis heris et heroibus nostris de hoc impendioso conuiuio nobis largito.

HENRICVS. Quod fecimus sodalitatis causa accipite et gratis.

IASPERVS. Vbi nostrae creuerint opes, uices pares reddemus.

FINIS.

Coloniae in officina honesti ciuis Petri Quentell.
Anno M. D. XXVI

---

32 Sit] Sit C; Si B | 32 bono. Omnibus] bono, Omnibus C; bono HE. Omnibus B | 38 comburamus] comburemus B C | 68 extrahamus] extrahemus B C | 68 extendemus] extendamus B C

MAXIMILIANUS. Virtue raises you to the heavens, vice hurls you into Hell. Knowledge does one credit here in the world, and after this life it makes men shine like the light of the heavens. The unlearned are pointed at and jeered; they're no different from blocks of wood.

IASPERUS. Which is better: peace and harmony, or strife and discord?

HENRICUS. Peace, for it supports and preserves everything, and makes small things greater; it was sent to mortals by the gods. Discord destroys everything and preserves nothing; it is diabolical, sent into the world from the depths of Hell.

IASPERUS. Is it better to be learned and poor, or ignorant and wealthy?

IOHANNES. To have learning and be poor.

MAXIMILIANUS. Yet poor people can't get on in life, and everywhere they're at the bottom of the heap.

IOHANNES. Poor people who are learned end up as important men everywhere, for any ground will provide a living for skilled work.

IASPERUS. And so, my dear companions, whatever we do, let's always take care to devote our energies to learning, to labour hard at our books, so that eventually we may pull our feet out of the mud, and stretch our wings beyond the nest, and either equal, or excel, our parents in virtue.

HENRICUS. That's enough. Drink up in order, we have to go.

MAXIMILIANUS. I drink to you.

HENRICUS. I accept it willingly.

IASPERUS. We thank you, our lords and masters, for the extravagant feast you have offered us.

HENRICUS. Accept what we've done for the sake of companionship and asking no reward but thanks.

IASPERUS. When our wealth has increased, we'll return the compliment.

THE END

Cologne, at the press of the honest citizen Peter Quentel.

1526

Georg Pencz, *Family at Table* (Geisberg, G. 1011)

Notes to the *Confabulationes*

Confabulationes tironum litterariorum

confabulatio: LL, 'conversation, discussion' (*TLL*, IV, col. 169, ll. 38–66; *MLWb*, II, col. 1288, l. 39–col. 1289, l. 16; *DMLBS*; *MLLM*). Used by Erasmus and other NL authors: 'Confabulatio pia' (Erasmus, *Colloquia*, p. 171, l. 1501); 'Materia confabulationis frugiferae' (ibid., p. 241, l. 318; cf. p. 316, l. 66).

tironum: CL 'tiro', a raw military recruit; by extension a novice of any kind (*OLD*).

Hermannus Schottennius Hessus candido lectori

13–14 **ut inquit Cicero:** ll. 14–18, 'quod [...] restinxit', are almost verbatim from Cicero, *Orator*, 1.4–5; ll. 19–21, 'Demosthenes [...] defecerunt', closely imitate ibid., 2.6.

21 **semipaganus:** Coined by Persius (*Satires*, Prologue, 6), to mean an unworthy member of the community of poets.

22 **camelus saltans:** Erasmus, *Adagia*, 1666, 'Camelus saltat': 'Ubi quis indecore quippiam facere conatur, et invita, ut ajunt, Minerva' (*LB*, II, 630A).

26 **quorum ingenia humi repunt:** Cf. 'Sermones [...] repentes per humum' (Horace, *Epistulae*, 2.1.250–51, quoted Erasmus, *Adagia*, 1988, 'Humi serpere', *LB*, II, 704C).

26–27 **nondum a limine salutarunt:** Erasmus, *Adagia*, 891, 'A limine salutare': 'Qui [...] rudimenta modo [degustarunt]' (*LB*, II, 362F–363A).

27 **primoribus labiis:** CL, 'Superficially' (Erasmus, *Adagia*, 892, 'Primoribus labiis degustare'; Otto, 892).

Et genere et moribus adolescenti ingenuo Gisberto Sterckenberg

4–8 **Platonem [...] consecutionem:** This anecdote is not recorded. It perhaps reflects the fact that Plato saw his spoken lectures as the authentic expression of his philosophy, and produced his written works only afterwards, as a popularizing measure (*OCCL*[1], p. 331; *OCCL*[2], p. 442).

12 **Mineruam:** A metaphorical equivalent for 'ingenium' (Otto, 1118–22, 'Minerua'). See note to colloquy 45, l. 12.

24 **Suis [...] expectationibus:** Schotten's frequent use of 'suus' where CL would require 'eius', and of 'se' in place of 'is', especially 'sibi' and 'secum' for 'ei' and 'cum eo', is a ML feature (Stotz, IX, 38). Cf. note to colloquy 53, l. 27, and Macardle, *Confabulations*, pp. 138–39.

33 **19. Kalendas Martias:** See the discussion of the date of the dedication in Section Ic.

1) Difficile esse Latinum discere sermonem, et unde dicatur sermo Latinus

14 **schola sermonis Latini uel Germanici:** German schools, teaching the '3 Rs' to the sons of merchants and craftsmen, had been multiplying since the late fourteenth century, as the civic and mercantile importance of German grew (Isenmann, pp. 182–83). Both the son and the nephew of the Cologne chronicler Hermann von Weinsberg went to a 'Deusche schoil' after failing at Latin schools (*BW*, II, pp. 115, 263).

30 **poetae scribunt [...]:** Cf. Isidore of Seville, *Etymologiae*, 15.1.50. A fanciful explanation; the name probably derives from the adj. 'latus', 'broad', referring to the broad plain of Latium (Pauly, VI, col. 1165).

2) De salutatione matutina

The formulations of this colloquy reflect those of Erasmus's *Colloquia*, e.g. 'Auspicanti quippiam' (*Colloquia*, pp. 128–29). The colloquy, specifically ll. 12–15, 32–33, shows considerable similarities with Heyden's much shorter 'Salutatio matutina' (*Formulae*, I, sig. G4[v]). On Heyden's use of Schotten, see Macardle, *Confabulations*, pp. 124–27.

3–4 **Bonum mane; Semper sane:** Typically ML rhyming greeting. Cf. 'Bona dies, semper quies' (Walther, 35221).

16 **Felix sit [...] exordium:** Cf. 'Felix sit exortus huius diei' (Erasmus, *Colloquia*, p. 128, l. 108); 'Haud inauspicatum diei exordium' (ibid., p. 173, l. 1559).

28 **Faxit [...] illuxerit:** Cf. 'Precor vt hic dies tibi candidus illuxerit' (Erasmus, *Colloquia*, p. 128, l. 106).

3) De salutatione pomeridiana

The formulations of this colloquy reflect those of Erasmus's *Colloquia*. The colloquy shows considerable similarities with Heyden's much shorter 'Salutatio meridiana' (*Formulae*, II, sig. G4^{v}).

6 **Saluus sis tu quoque:** 'Saluus sis tu quoque' (Erasmus, *Colloquia*, p. 32, l. 31).

13 **Salus sit tibi:** 'Salus tibi' (Erasmus, *Colloquia*, p. 32, l. 30).

19 **Iubeo te saluere:** 'Saluere te iubeo' (Erasmus, *Colloquia*, p. 127, l. 53).

40–41 **ex sententia:** Cf. 'Res omnis cecidit ex sententia' (Erasmus, *Colloquia*, p. 145, l. 664). Erasmus, *Adagia*, 2794, 'Omnia ex sententia cedunt'.

4) De salutatione uespertina

Many formulations in ll. 19–34 seem inspired by those in Erasmus, *Colloquia*, p. 129, ll. 109–12, though none is identical. The colloquy shows considerable similarities with Heyden's much shorter 'Salutatio Vespertina' and 'Sub primam facem noctis' (*Formulae*, III and IV, sig. G5^{r}).

5–9 **Bonum serum [...]:** CL 'serus' only as adj. 'Serum' as noun is ML, also frequent in NL (e.g. Dasypodius (1536); Serranus; Estienne). 'Bonum serum, non sero' (Heyden, *Formulae*, sig. G5^{r}); 'Ad serum' (Vives, *Exercitatio*, XI, p. 84).

10 **Capnion:** 'Vxor, bonum sero' (Reuchlin, *Henno* (1498), l. 45).

12 **uillanus:** Adj., ML, 'rustic, boorish' (Stotz, V, 68.3; DuC, VIII, p. 331; *MLLM*, s.v., 2, 3; *LLMA*; *NWL*).

14 **'Bonum uesper':** Cf. 'Bonus uesper' (Heyden, *Formulae*, III, sig. G5^{r}).

25 **Faustam habeas noctem:** Cf. 'Sit tibi fausta nox' (Erasmus, *Colloquia*, p. 129, l. 112).

5) De uerbis dum itur cubitum

This colloquy shows considerable similarities with Heyden's shorter 'Dum itur cubitum' (*Formulae*, V, sig. G5^{r-v}).

Specifically, Schotten's ll. 3–4 and 11–16 closely parallel Heyden, ll. 1–10 (sig. G5^{r-v}).

3 **Quota est hora?:** The first of the many references in the *Confabulationes* to mechanical clocks as the standard of time measurement. See Macardle, *Confabulations*, pp. 86–90.

16 **Endymion:** A youth who slept for ever on Mount Latmos, proverbial for a lazy person (Otto, 600; Erasmus, *Adagia*, 863, 'Endymionis somnum dormis'). 'Facesse hinc Endimion' (Heyden, *Formulae*, V, sig. G5^{r-v}).

20 **Epimenides:** A Cretan prophet, said to have slept for fifty-seven years (Otto, 601; Erasmus, *Adagia*, 864, 'Ultra Epimenidem dormis'). 'Epimenides, somniatorum princeps' (Erasmus, *Colloquia*, p. 38, l. 201 (cf. ll. 199–210) and p. 187, ll. 2018–27).

26 **solidum 28–29 qualem praeceptor noster praebet ferula:** CL 'solidus' denotes a coin; in ML it translates German 'Schilling', which also means a beating, probably of twelve strokes (Grimm, 'Schilling', 5; Wander, IV, 182). Frequent in Luther; e.g. 'so geb man jm ein schilling'; 'einen guten schilling leiden' (cited Grimm, IX, col. 153).

6) De cubitu resurgendo

This colloquy shows considerable similarities with Heyden's shorter 'Dum reditur cubitu' (*Formulae*, VI, sig. G5^{v}–G6^{r}). Specifically, Schotten's ll. 3–9 are closely similar to Heyden's ll. 1–5.

19 **Lyncei [...] oculi:** CL adj. from the Argonaut Lynceus, famous for his keen sight (Otto, 1003). Erasmus, *Adagia*, 1054, 'Lynceo perspicacior' (cf. Walther, 37984, 36623). 'quod te uel Lynceum reddet' (Erasmus, *Colloquia*, p. 233, l. 74; cf. p. 284, l. 261; p. 284, l. 261).

22–23 **calidum deserere nidum:** 'Nidus' for 'bed', much used by Schotten, is Erasmian: 'Mature me confero ad nidum' (*Colloquia*, p. 175, l. 1622; cf. p. 338, l. 168; p. 359, l. 498). This meaning seems otherwise unknown in CL, LL and ML; the normal figurative sense is one's home, e.g. 'Tu nidum seruas' (Horace, *Epistulae*, 1.10.6; cf. Forcellini, 'nidus', 4).

7) De ientaculo sumendo

This colloquy shows broad similarities with Heyden's two colloquies, XII, 'De Ientaculo' and XIII, 'De reditu à ientaculo' (*Formulae*, sig. G8[v]–H1[r], H1[r–v]).

6 **Domum uersus:** A breakfast break during morning school, often between 7 am and 8 am, was common in the early sixteenth century (Heyden, *Formulae*, XII, sig. G8[v], and XIII, sig. H1[r]; Casey, *Paul Rebhun*, pp. 47–49).

18 **ientaris:** CL 'ientare'. Schotten regularly has the deponent form 'ientor', a ML usage (*DMLBS*, 'jentare'; cf. *TLL*, VII,1, col. 247, ll. 33–49). Cf. colloquies 8, ll. 7, 8; 13, l. 5; 78, l. 19.

19 **cui pro obsonio addo caseum:** CL 'obsonium', 'food other than bread and wine'. Cheese was a byword for the simplest of food: 'Si caseum haberem, non desiderarem opsonium' (Erasmus, *Adagia*, 2389, quoting Apostolios, *Proverbia*, 7.81; cf. Walther, 28308a).

21 **panis iurulentus:** NL, chunks of bread served in meat broth: 'Panem iurulentum; eyn brot inn eyner suppen' (Heyden, *Formulae*, sig. H1[r]); cf. 'Offas panis madefactas iure carnium' (Erasmus, *Colloquia*, p. 337, l. 126).

23 **fruendum esse fortuna dum praesto est:** Cf. 'Praesentem fortunam boni consule. Man můß die zeit nemen wie sie kompt' (Franck, II, fol. 114[r]; Wander, I, 1758; parallels 1737–67). Cf. 'When Fortune smiles, embrace her' (*ODEP*, F 615).

24–25 **delicata iuuentus omni aetati nocet:** Cf. 'Delicata uita uite maxime aducrsaria est' (Walther, 36172h2).

8) De prandio

6 **fortiter esurio:** The use of 'fortiter' for 'very much, greatly' begins in LL (*TLL*, VI, col. 1165, l. 80–col. 1166, l. 9). It is characteristic of ML (DuC, III, p. 74; *MLLM*; *DMLBS*, s.v., 2b).

13 **horam undecimam:** 10 am was a more usual time for lunch (cf. colloquies 14, l. 23 and 67, l. 8; Kluppel, *Chronik*, ed. by Jürges, p. 154) but 11 am was by no means unknown (*BW*, V. p. 119); cf. colloquy 13, l. 21.

19 **halec:** Also 'alec', etc. CL, a fish sauce or a small fish; ML and NL, usually 'herring' (*MLLM*, 'alec', 2, 3; *LLMA*, 'allec'; *DMLBS*, 'allec', 1, 2; Dasypodius, 'Halec'; Grimm,

'Hering', 4). This fish was particularly popular in Cologne, since the fourteenth century the most important distribution centre for North Sea herring (Brill, 'Der Heringshandel', esp. pp. 45–49; cf. Kuske, 'Der Kölner Fischhandel').

26 **halec erutum salsugine:** Cf. colloquy 123, l. 139. Here probably pickled herring from the barrel. Cf. recipes for fish preserved or boiled in vinegar or wine in the MS cookbook HAStK, 7004, 27, fols 1^{r}–2^{r}.

9) De uictu pomeridiano

1 **uict[us] pomeridian[us]:** Synonymous with CL 'merenda' (l. 29), a light afternoon meal, and 'cibum merendinarium' (l. 15). Many sixteenth-century school regulations prescribe a break between about 2 pm and 3 pm when food might be eaten (Casey, *Paul Rebhun*, pp. 47–49).

6 **rem acu tetigisti:** Plautus, *Rudens*, 1306; Otto, 16; Walther, 40688; Erasmus, *Adagia*, 1393, 'Rem acu tetigisti'. A favourite phrase of Erasmus: (*Colloquia*, p. 155, l. 980 and n.; cf. p. 427, l. 111; p. 609, l. 211; p. 664, l. 412, etc.).

15 **merendinarium:** Not recorded in CL, LL, ML or NL dictionaries; but cf. LL 'merendinare' (*DMLBS*; DuC, V, p. 353) and ML 'merendina' (= 'merenda') (DuC, V, p. 353; *LLMA*).

33 **esuriei:** 'Esuries', LL (*TLL*, V,2, col. 865, ll. 28–81; *GLL*; *DLFAC*; *MLWb*, III, col. 1392, l. 67–col. 1393, l. 6; *DMLBS*; *MLLM*).

10) De cena

17 **mensam sternere; 18 ad cyathos stare:** Regular tasks of the boys of the medieval and early modern household. Cf. colloquies 65 and 67.

20 **popina:** CL 'cook-shop, restaurant'. The sense 'kitchen', intended here, is ML (*RMLWL*).

28–29 **noctem nihil boni [...] afferre?:** Perhaps some proverbial echoes: cf. 'Nox nemini amica' (Walther, 39038a1). But the line (cf. colloquy 123, ll. 29–30) seems to refer to the objective dangers of early modern Cologne: See Macardle, *Confabulations*, pp. 68–70.

11) De postcenio

1 **postcenio:** 'Postcenium', NL, a light evening collation or dessert after dinner ('Pocoenium [sic], schlafftrunck', Golius, 334; *LPLR*, 'postcoenium', 'dessert': e.g. Erasmus, *Epistolae*, 2711, l. 35). English 'after-supper', 'rere-supper', 'rere-banquet' (all *OED*).

8 **amabo:** Colloquial ellipsis, common in Roman comedy (e.g. Terence, *Eunuchus*, 130, 150, 534, etc.). Often regarded as fawning or effeminate (Dasypodius (1536a); *TLL*, I, col. 1956, l. 62). 'Dissere, amabo' (Erasmus, *Colloquia*, p. 193, l. 2210).

10 **gestio [...] audire:** 'Audire gestio' (Erasmus, *Colloquia*, p. 417, l. 13).

13 **dubiam cenam:** Terence facetiously describes a 'cena dubia', a 'doubtful' dinner, as one with so many dishes that 'you're doubtful which dish to sample first' (*Phormio*, 342). The term became established for 'sumptuous meal, banquet'; cf. Erasmus, *Adagia*, 1323; Golius, 334).

18 **Lucernam feram istuc:** A practical measure; and citizens of Cologne carrying lights on the street at night were exempt from the curfew (Kemp, 'Die Wohlfahrtspflege', pp. 17, 18); cf. note to colloquy 10, l. 28.

24 **Mensam [...] cui parentes accumbunt:** The anachronistic 'accumbere', 'recline', probably imitates Erasmus (*Colloquia*, e.g. p. 241, l. 296, p. 336, ll. 106, 111). In CL the verb takes the accusative ('accumbere mensam'); other cases, esp. the dative, are a LL tendency (*TLL*, I, col. 340, ll. 26–33).

25 **bolum opiparum:** Schotten's characteristic use of 'bolus' for 'morsel', 'mouthful', is ML (DuC, I, p. 693; *DMLBS*, s.v., 1; *LLMA*; criticized by Massebieau, *Les colloques scolaires*, p. 128). The word is Erasmian (*Adagia*, 2650, 'Tribus bolis', *ASD*, II–6, p. 451, ll. 472–73; cf. Dasypodius (1536), 'Bolus. Ein stuck odder brock'), but it is avoided by some humanists (e.g. Vives, *Exercitatio*).

12) De potu postremo a cena

11 **Ventris anhelitu:** A fart; the phrase is not recorded in this sense, for which standard CL is '[uentris] crepitus'

(*OLD*, 'crepitus', c): 'Emisit clarum ventris crepitum' (Erasmus, *Colloquia*, p. 448, l. 365).

12 **rapas:** Medieval and early modern medicine knew root vegetables were powerful causes of flatulence (Albala, *Eating Right*, pp. 61, 94).

13 **I prae, [...] sequar:** Extended version of the formulaic exit line 'I prae, sequar' of Roman comedy (e.g. Terence, *Eunuchus*, 908; Plautus, *Cistellaria*, 773, etc.).

13) De inuitatione ad ientaculum

12 **Serio loquor:** 'Serio loquor' (Erasmus, *Colloquia*, p. 35, l. 124).

14) Inuitandi alium ad prandium

7 **Bouem mactauimus, ad intestina hospites tractabimus:** The offal of slaughtered animals had to be eaten up quickly or given away. Since the obvious guests or recipients were friends and neighbours, offal, e.g. blood sausage, was often a token of friendship (Albala, *Eating Right*, p. 73). German cookbooks have numerous suitable recipes (Ehlert, 'Les manuscrits culinaires', p. 127): e.g. the MS cookbook HAStK, 7004, 27 (*ca.* 1500), fols 15^{r}–16^{r}: 'Ein lebersultz', also using lungs; 'lungen kuchen' of chopped lung, spleen and heart; 'Ein Gebacks von kelber lungen'; 'Ein lebersultz Gele'.

10 **Vmbra:** CL, 'uninvited guest'. Erasmus, *Adagia*, 9, 'Vmbrae'; cf. Erasmus, *Colloquia*, p. 191, l. 2139; p. 222, l. 35; p. 232, l. 36).

12 **umbris non est parata sedes:** 'Umbris non est locus'; 'Inuocatus nullus est locus'; 'Ungeladenen Gästen ist nicht gestuhlet' (Wander, I, 1353; parallels 1347–53).

13–14 **conuiuam subitum [...] esse acceptiorem:** Cf. 'Sponte qui uenit, gratior hospes erit' (Walther, 30258). 'Ein ungebetener Gast ist der liebste fast' (Wander, I, 1349; parallels 1348, 1349, 1353).

19 **Ego [...] recessus:** Cf. 'sanctos recessus mentis' (Persius, *Satires*, 2.73); 'imos animi [...] recessus' (Statius, *Siluae*, 4.6.4).

15) Vocandi alium ad cibum pomeridianum

14 **uulturem:** 'Tu vide vulturem expleueris' (Erasmus, *Colloquia*, p. 41, l. 288).

16) Vocandi alium ad cenam

25 **postremum me amicum habuisti:** Cf. 'Si id facis, hodie postremum me uides' (Terence, *Andria*, 322).

30 **frontem perfrico:** The forehead was seen as the seat of modesty (Forcellini, 'frons', 3, 4; *TLL*, VI, col. 1355, l. 83–col. 1359, l. 3). Hence 'frontem perfricare', 'put away one's modesty or inhibitions'. Erasmus, *Adagia*, 747, 'Faciem perfricare, frontis perfrictae'; cf. *Colloquia*, p. 163, l. 1235; p. 390, l. 24; p. 616, l. 164..

33–34 **'Vinum modice sumptum acuere ingenium':** Medieval and early modern commonplace: 'Vinum modice sumptum acuit ingenium' (Walther, 44296c; cf. 33493). 'Vinum et ingenium excitat et facundiam ministrat' (Erasmus, *Colloquia*, p. 201, l. 2455).

17) De modo studendi

13 **me macero litteris:** Cf. 'Immodico studio te maceras' (Erasmus, *Colloquia*, p. 35, l. 115).

18 **Nunc naso me suspendis:** 'Naso me suspendis adunco' (Erasmus, *Colloquia*, p. 143, l. 609, based on Horace, *Sermones*, 1.6.5.). Erasmus, *Adagia*, 722, 'Naso suspendere'; Otto, 1198.

19 **ex animo loquor:** 'Emoriar, ni loquor ex animo [...] Ex animo loquor' (Erasmus, *Colloquia*, p. 144, ll. 614–15; cf. p. 154, l. 926). Erasmus, *Adagia*, 946, 'Audi, quae ex animo dicuntur'.

18) De epistola conficienda

3 **labia mordens:** Erasmus, *Adagia*, 2669, 'Mordere labrum': 'qui stomachatur, animoque ringitur, sumtum ab indignantium gestu' (*LB*, II, 900A).

11 **adhibet limam:** CL frequently uses 'lima', 'file', figuratively for the polishing of a literary work (*TLL*, VII,2, col. 1400, ll. 55–82); e.g. 'Defuit et scriptis ultima lima meis' (Ovid, *Tristia*, 1.7.30).

20 **Cudis tu epistolam:** 'Cudo' for 'compose' is LL (*TLL*, IV, col. 1285, ll. 41–54; *DLFAC*, s.v., 2).

21 **pro uiribus:** Frequent in Erasmus's *Colloquia*: 'Adnitimur pro viribus' (p. 164, l. 1253; cf. p. 172, l. 1539; p. 191, l. 2135).

23 **in magnis [...] uoluisse sat est:** Otto, 1853, citing Propertius, 2.10.6; Walther, 11820, 37423k; cf. 7730, 26037, etc.). A favourite humanist tag: Erasmus, *Adagia*, 1755, 'In magnis et uoluisse sat est' (*ASD*, II–4, p. 184, l. 752, citing other examples).

28 **prouinciam** in the original sense of 'task, duty' (*OLD*, s.v., 1). Cf. Erasmus, *Adagia*, 1341, 'Capere prouinciam, tradere prouinciam'.

29 **glaciem secabo:** NL image, probably coined by Filelfo: 'Posteaquam ipse glaciem fregi (ut aiunt)' (*Epistolae*, fol. CLVIII^{r}). Popularized by Erasmus, *Adagia*, 2495, 'Scindere glaciem'. 'Scindere glaciem [...] Einen weg oder einbruch machen' (Franck, II, fol. 90^{v}; cf. Wander, I, 800).

19) De repetenda lectione

6 **Arrige aures:** Otto, 215; Erasmus, *Adagia*, 2156, 'Auribus arrectis'; cf. *Colloquia*, p. 205, ll. 2595, 2599; p. 321, l. 57); 'Arrige auris, Pamphile' (Terence, *Andria*, 933).

24 **Theseum:** Theseus is a by-word for the helpful companion (Zenobius, *Paroimiai*, 5.33; Otto, 1779; Erasmus, *Adagia*, 427, 'Non absque Theseo').

32 **manibus et pedibus:** Erasmus, *Adagia*, 315, 'Manibus pedibusque': 'Extremum conatum significantes' (*ASD*, II–1, p. 422, l. 376, citing Terence, *Andria*, 676). Otto, 1034.

20) De Corycaei metu auscultantis eos qui non Romano utuntur sermone

This colloquy is probably inspired by Mosellanus, *Paedologia*, 16 (pp. 22–23). There are considerable verbal similarities with Heyden's shorter 'De cauendis in scholis Coricæis' (*Formulae*, X, sig. G8^{r}). See Macardle, *Confabulations*, p. 111.

1 **Corycaei:** The inhabitants of Mt Korykos in Ionia passed on overheard information about shipping to pirates (Strabo, *Geography*, 14.1.32; Pauly^{1}, XI, col. 1451); hence 'Corycaeus' for 'spy' (Otto, 449; *LPLR*, 'rapporteur, délateur'; Dasypodius, '[ein] außspäher/ was man handle'). Erasmus, *Adagia*, 144, 'Corycaeus auscultauit'. 'Corycaeus' was one name given in German schools to boys secretly instructed to report pupils not speaking

Latin (Erasmus, *Colloquia*, p. 150, l. 800; Mosellanus, *Paedologia*, 16, p. 23, l. 19; Hegendorff, *Dialogi*, 2, sig. C8^{v}; Heyden, *Formulae*, X, sig. G8^{r}. More common was 'lupus' (Mosellanus, *Paedologia*, 16, p. 23, ll. 23–25; Crecelius, 'Crailsheimer Schulordnung', p. 247).

1 **auscultantis eos:** The B reading 'auscultantis in eos' is wrong: 'auscultare' in this sense takes a simple accusative (*TLL*, II, col. 1534, ll. 47–57).

21 **manum non uertero:** An expression of indifference (Otto, 1041). Erasmus, *Adagia*, 221, 'Manum non uerterim. Digitum non porrexerim': 'It does not trouble me, it is no concern of mine' (*ASD*, II–1, p. 334, ll. 783–84; *CWE*, XXXI, p. 253).

26 **quando corrigor:** 'Quando' as conj. rather than 'cum' in CL is colloquial, esp. frequent in Plautus. It is widespread in LL, ML and NL: see Macardle, *Confabulations*, pp. 140–41.

29 **diploidi:** 'Diplois': CL, a kind of cloak; but ML, as here, a doublet (DuC, III, p. 122; *DMLBS*, s.v., a; Diefenbach; Stanbridge, *Vulgaria*, p. 28). '[Thoracem (jerkin)] simplum, an diploidum?' (Vives, *Exercitatio*, I, p. 2).

32 **saepiuscule:** CL 'saepicule'. 'Saepiuscule' originates in Priscian's sixth-century gloss on Plautus, *Casina*, 703: 'Saepi[us]cule, peccas.' (Plautus, *Comoediae*, ed. by Lindsay, I, *Casina*, l. 703; Lodge, *Lexicon Plautinum*, II, p. 569). The word is frequent in NL, esp. from the later sixteenth century on (cf. *RMLWL*, 'sepe'; Dasypodius, 'saepe'): 'Saepiuscule [...] sudorem detergere' (Della Casa, *Galateo*, trans. by Chytraeus (1588), p. 13); 'Spes [...] saepiuscule frustratur' (Abel, *Carmina* (1590), sig. I4^{r}).

34 **saeuior Orbilio:** Lucius Orbilius Pupillus, Horace's famously severe teacher: 'Plagosum [...] Orbilium' (Horace, *Epistulae*, 2.1.71). 'Is vel Orbilio plagiosior est' (Erasmus, *Colloquia*, p. 183, l. 1896).

21) De somno plus aequo extenso

There are similarities with Mosellanus, *Paedologia*, 14, p. 21. See Macardle, *Confabulations*, p. 111.

28 **Iacias aleam:** 'Iacienda est alea' (Erasmus, *Colloquia*, p. 283, l. 227). 'Iacta alea est' (Suetonius, *Iulius*, 32). Otto, 55. Erasmus, *Adagia*, 332, 'Omnem iacere aleam'.

22) De morbo socordiae quem scholasticis ascribunt

Cf. colloquy 74. There are also parallels with the discussion of 'scholasticus morbus' in Mosellanus, *Paedologia*, 27, pp. 34–35: see Macardle, *Confabulations*, p. 113.

7 **Cuius farinae?:** Of what kind or class (Otto, 643; Erasmus, *Adagia*, 2444, 'Nostrae farinae').

13 **Diuino; 14 diuinare:** Edition A has the deponent forms 'diuinor', 'diuinari', characteristic of ML (*MLWb*, III, col. 883,ll. 47, 57).

17 **toto caelo aberras:** Otto, 283; Erasmus, *Adagia*, 49, 'Toto coelo errare'; cf. ibid., 48, 'Tota erras uia'.

18 **iueris:** For the perfect of 'eo' Schotten regularly uses 'iui', rarer than the form 'ii' (*TLL*, V, 2, col. 626, l. 78–col. 627, l. 26).

23 **intus et in cute:** 'In every respect', 'inside out' (Otto, 492, citing Persius, *Satires*, 3.30; Erasmus, *Adagia*, 889, 'Intus et in cute').

24 **a uertice ad pedes:** Otto, 1822; 'A uertice [...] ad imos' (Horace, *Epistulae*, 2.2.4).

30 **ouorumque sorbitiuncula:** LL 'sorbitiuncula', dim. of CL 'sorbitio', 'food in liquid or semi-liquid form' (Forcellini; DuC, VII, p. 529; *DLFAC*; cf. *LLMA*, 'sorbicium'). LL, ML and NL 'sorbitiuncula' can refer to hot, sweetened drinks, often medicinal (Erasmus, *Epistolae*, 867 (III, p. 398), ll. 132–33, 137); to thicker soups and porridges (cf. Serranus, s.v. 'sorbeo'; Estienne, 'Sorbitio alicae, [...] De la froumentee'); or even to cakes or pancakes (Köbler, *Lateinisch-althochdeutsches Wörterbuch*, p. 742); '[Thamar ...] coxit sorbitiunculas' (Vulgate, 2 Regum 13.8; cf. 13.6, 10). 'Ouorum sorbitiuncula' probably means an easily digested custard-like dish like those described in a MS cookbook of *ca.* 1500 (HAStK, 7004, 27, fols 24^{r}–25^{r}), e.g. 'Ein gemeyn eier muß' (milk, flour, eggs) and one specifically for invalids: 'Ein lÿnds essen kyntbettern &c. Vnd Swachen luden.'

38 **In promptu causa est:** 'Close at hand', i.e. 'obvious': Erasmus, *Colloquia*, p. 153, l. 906; cf. Ovid, *Remedia Amoris*, 162.

38 **a labore feriantur:** 'Ferior', 'take a holiday from, refrain from', LL (*TLL*, VI, col. 517, l. 9–col. 519, l. 2; *GLL*; *DMLBS*, s.v., 2; *MLLM*).

23) De metu ferulae

22 **captionis:** 'Captio', CL, 'trickery, sophistry'. The sense 'catching' intended here is LL and ML (*TLL*, III, col. 365, ll. 23–57; *MLWb*, II, col. 249, ll. 6–15; *DLFAC*, s.v., 1; *DMLBS*, s.v., 5).

24 **consulis:** 'Consulere' in CL means 'seek counsel, consult' (*TLL*, IV, cols 576–84). The ML sense 'give counsel, advise' is frequent in NL (*MLWb*, II, col. 1661, ll. 4–22; *DMLBS*, s.v., 4, 6; Serranus; Tournoy and Tunberg, 'On the Margins of Latinity?', p. 153). Cf. colloquies 47, l. 8, 80, l. 23; *conuiuium* 5, l. 59.

33–34 **pituitae [...] non esse obnoxium:** Translates German 'den Schnupfen haben', 'have the cold', figuratively 'be stupid, obtuse' (Grimm, 'Schnupfen', 2; Wander, IV, 308–09). 'Er hat den schnuppen' (Luther, *WA*, LI, p. 648, no. 96).

35 **Corneae fibrae homo:** 'Fibra': the viscera as the seat of the feelings (*OLD*, s.v., 5a). Otto, 437, citing Persius, *Satires*, 1.47; Erasmus, *Adagia*, 645, 'Cornea fibra', 'heart-strings of horn' (*CWE*, XXXII, p. 95).

24) De excusatione absentiae a ludo litterario

33 **qui tesseram fregerit:** 'Tessera hospitalis', a token divided between two friends who can recognize each other by joining the pieces; hence figuratively, 'friendship'. Thus 'tesseram frangere', 'violate a friendship': 'Hic apud nos, iam, Alesimarche, confregisti tesseram' (Plautus, *Cistellaria*, 503). Otto, 1769; Erasmus, *Adagia*, 950, 'Confringere tesseram'.

25) Quare schola dicatur ludus

14 **pistrinum:** The treadmill, a punishment for criminals; figuratively, a place of drudgery (Otto, 1432). 'Pistrinum [...] Metaph. Ein harte dienstbarkeit/ oder ein schwer/ überlestig geschäfft' (Dasypodius, 1536, 'Pinso'). 'Non

minus quam si in pistrinum aliquod mihi sit redeundum' (Mosellanus, *Paedologia*, 11, p. 19, ll. 5–6).

26 **Nosco cute expertus:** Cf. Apostolios, *Proverbia*, 20.87, 'Χρὸϊ δεῖλα, Ex cute manifestum'. Similar to 'intus et in cute'; cf. note to colloquy 22, l. 20.

43 **ut Terentius inquit:** 'Nam deteriores omnes sumus licentia' (Terence, *Heautontimorumenos*, 483).

26) De die qua otiatur a lectione.

12 **peracta fabula:** A theatrical image, literally 'when the play is over'. Cf. Erasmus, *Adagia*, 1852, 'Sic est ad pugnae partes re peracta ueniendum'.

15 **in pomerio:** 'Pomerium', CL, a bare strip of land surrounding the city walls.

20 **facultas diuagandi:** 'Diuagor', 'wander, wander about', LL (Forcellini, 'devagor'; *TLL*, V,1, col. 1568, ll. 31–49; *DMLBS*).

30 **Platea Ouium:** The Schaafenstraße in the quiet St Aposteln district of Cologne (cf. colloquy 97, l. 32). See Macardle, *Confabulations*, pp. 58–59.

28 **symbolo:** CL, properly 'symbola' or 'symbole', the individual's contribution towards the cost of a common meal (e.g. Terence, *Andria*, 88). 'Symbolum' is used by Erasmus (*Colloquia*, e.g. p. 55, l. 752; p. 56, l. 774; p. 60, l. 895) and is common in NL (Golius, 333, 413).

34–35 **non teruncium dabis:** The Roman 3-oz copper teruncius was a by-word for an insignificant amount of money: cf. Erasmus, *Adagia*, 709, 'Ne teruncium quidem insumpsit', citing Cicero, *Epistulae ad Atticum*, 5.17.2). 'Ne teruncium quidem misit' (Erasmus, *Colloquia*, p. 135, l. 332).

27) De aestate

There are a few general similarities with Hegendorff, *Dialogi*, 2, 'De aestate' (sig. C8^{r}–D1^{r}).

7 **hibernaculum:** CL, winter quarters or accommodation. Here corresponding to German 'Stube', a living-room heated by a stove (Golius, 312; Moser, 'Zum Aufkommen der Stube'). Erasmus prefers 'hypocaustum' (*Colloquia*, p. 334, ll. 42, 51, etc.; cf. Golius, 312).

17–18 **latum frondes redolentes:** Leafy branches, 'Maien', were fixed to doors and windows both to celebrate spring and to ward off witches, magic and lightning (Wrede, *Rheinischer Volksbrauch*, p. 46; Klersch, I, p. 201; *HDA*, V, cols 1515–24, esp. 1515–17). They were also sent as presents from men to women (*BW*, I, p. 133; V, p. 143).

22 **clamando [...] 'Hic frondes redolentes':** Clearly translates a vendor's street-cry; but no sources of it have been found. A similar cry, 'Hi breng'k ink den ersten Mai in't Hûs', was sung by children in the Grafschaft Mark, approximately 60 km north-east of Cologne (*HDA*, V, col. 1516).

44 **cochleae agendo uitam:** Erasmus, *Adagia*, 3357, 'Cochleae uita': 'De iis qui parce paruoque uiuunt aut contracti a negociis luceque forensi semoti' (*LB*, II, 1038D). 'Sed tu mihi videre cochleae vitam agere' (Erasmus, *Colloquia*, p. 139, l. 457).

28) De autumno

There are a few general similarities with Hegendorff, *Dialogi*, 3, 'De autumni tempore' (sig. D1^{r}–D2^{r}).

3 **tempus istud pestiferum:** cf. ll. 5–9. Cf. 'Mox et autumnus sexcenta morborum genera effundet' (Mosellanus, *Paedologia*, 35, p. 42, ll. 23–24); 'Constat Autumnum magnum malorum agmen hominibus adferre' (Hegendorff, *Dialogi*, 3, sig. D1^{r}).

6–7 **Autumnale [...] festum Sancti Bartholomaei:** The apostle's feast (24 August) marked the beginning of autumn. The feast is mentioned in Hegendorff, *Dialogi*, 3 (sig. D1^{r}).

29 **pediculi:** Fleas are constantly mentioned as a curse by schoolboys (Erasmus, *Colloquia*, p. 130, l. 167 and n.; Mosellanus, *Paedologia*, p. 42, ll. 20–21).

33 **adimunt uocis sinceritatem:** Common medical opinion: 'Nuces vulgares grauant linguam, & sermonem impediunt' (Gratarolus, *De conseruanda valetudine*, p. 175).

35 **a cibo abhorreo qui me aquam potare cogit:** Medieval and early modern dietetics generally disapprove of water as a drink, probably reflecting concerns about tainted sources of water (Albala, *Eating Right*, pp. 120–22).

29) De hieme

There are a few parallels with Mosellanus, *Paedologia*, 20, pp. 26–27.

8 **crepidae:** CL, sandals of a particular design. ML, as here, 'shoe, boot' (*MLWb*, II, col. 2006, ll. 1–4; *DMLBS*). Cf. Vives, *Exercitatio*, XI, p. 81.

8 **crepidae me calere faciunt:** The causative use of 'facere' is LL and ML (Macardle, *Confabulations*, p. 137).

10 **chirothecae:** ML (Stotz, IV, 29.3; DuC, II, pp. 310–11; *MLWb*, II, cols 537–38; *LLMA*; *MLLM*; *DMLBS*; *LPLR*, Dasypodius, 'Cheirotheca'; Golius, 201).

17 **in caelo essem:** Cf. Otto, 288; Erasmus, *Adagia*, 500, 'In coelo esse': 'Supra modum fortunatum esse ac gloriosum' (*ASD*, II–1, p. 568, ll. 157–58).

21 **post fornacem latui:** 'Post' is used spatially in CL (*TLL*, X,2, col. 162, l. 25–col. 163, l. 20), but more usual would be 'ad' or 'iuxta': cf. 'ad caminum [...] adsidere' (Mosellanus, *Paedologia*, p. 26, l. 32); 'iuxta hypocaustum' (Erasmus, *Colloquia*, p. 334, l. 56). However, cf. 'recubans post vaporarium' (Erasmus, *Colloquia*, p. 392, l. 93). 'Post fornacem' may reflect German 'hinter dem Ofen (sitzen)'; cf. 'post fornacem delitescere' (Bebel, *Facetien*, p. 11; cf. p. 49).

22 **torrebasne poma? 23 et pira:** See notes to colloquy 37, ll. 35, 36.

32 **Sed serius fortassis quam uelles:** Cf. 'Fortasse citius quam velles' (Erasmus, *Colloquia*, p. 437, l. 150).

33 **Et haec olim [...]:** 'Reuocate animos, maestumque timorem | mittite; forsan et haec olim meminisse iuuabit' (Vergil, *Aeneid*, 1.202–03).

34–35 **dulcius nihil [...] quos superauimus:** 'Iucundum est meminisse laborum actorum' (Erasmus, *Colloquia*, p. 148, l. 733). Erasmus, *Adagia*, 3827, 'Iucundum malorum praeteritorum memoria', based on Cicero, *De finibus*, 2.105.

36–37 **ut [...] scribit Vergilius:** In *Aeneid*, Book 2, the distressed Aeneas narrates the sack of Troy. As he says, 'Quis talia fando [...] Temperet a lacrimis!' (2.6–8).

30) De uere

There are some distant similarities with Hegendorff, *Dialogi*, 1, 'De ueris temperie' (sig. C6v–C7v).

17 **Putabam uiolas a rusticis egestas:** Reference to the medieval comic story of Neidhart and the violet: the courtier Neidhart finds the first violet of spring, covers it with his hat and goes to fetch the Duchess, planning to present it to her. In his absence a peasant steals the flower and defecates in its place, and the hat is removed in the presence of the entire court to reveal the stool. The story is frequently treated in late-medieval vernacular literature, notably in plays (*Neidhartspiele*, ed. by Margetts, passim; *Neithart Fuchs*, pp. 153–62; *VL*, VI, cols 893–98). References to this coarse tale are uncommon in humanist literature.

19 **Bona uerba quaeso:** Terence, *Andria*, 204. 'Bona verba' (Erasmus, *Colloquia*, p. 141, l. 544).

21 **meo ipsius gladio cado:** Otto, 759; Erasmus, *Adagia*, 51, 'Suo sibi hunc iugulo gladio, suo telo' (cf. Terence, *Andria*, 957). 'Suo gladio [...] iugulari dicitur, qui suis ipsius dictis reuincitur aut qui suopte inuento doloue capitur' (*ASD*, II–1, p. 166, ll. 528–29).

22 **Incidisti in foueam [...]:** Erasmus, *Adagia*, 52, 'Incidit in foueam, quam fecit' (cf. Vulgate, Psalm 7.16). Schotten's placing of this expression immediately after the synonymous 'meo ipsius gladio cado' (l. 21) probably reflects Erasmus's juxtaposition of the two formulae.

32 **Facile amicos tibi parabis:** Cf. note to colloquy 122, ll. 1–2.

35 **ut alius inquit comicus:** 'Homo homini deus est, si suam officium sciat', from the playwright Caecilius Statius (*Comicorum Romanorum Fragmenta*, ed. by Ribbeck, l. 264).

35–36 **ut [homo] homini alteri deus sit:** Otto, 517; Erasmus, *Adagia*, 69, 'Homo homini Deus', said of someone 'who has conferred sudden and unlooked-for salvation, or who has brought help by some great benefaction' (*CWE*, XXXI, p. 112).

31) De festo Sancti Galli

3 **dies Sancti Galli:** St Gall, sixth- to seventh-century Irish missionary monk, active in France and the Allemannic regions. He was the patron, *inter alia*, of hens and geese. Feast 16 October (*Legenda aurea*, CXCII (190), pp. 879–81; Grotefend; *ÖH*).

14 **prosternationi galli:** The sport of shooting at a cock or goose buried in the ground with only its head showing: popular at fairs in the Cologne region. See Macardle, *Confabulations*, pp. 62–63. 'Prosternatio' is ML, and rare (*LLMA*; *RML WL*, 'prostratio'); CL is 'prostratio'.

18 **Sis animi praesentis:** 'Fac praesenti sis animo' (Erasmus, *Colloquia*, p. 183, l. 1903). Erasmus, *Adagia*, 2905, 'Animus praesens'. 'Fac animo haec praesenti dicas' (Terence, *Eunuchus*, 769).

23 **(ut aiunt) rex:** In the Rhineland, the boy who 'killed' the bird was called 'Hahnenkönig' or 'Ganskonink': See Macardle, *Confabulations*, p. 63.

27 **Omne mouebo saxum:** cf. Erasmus, *Adagia*, 330, 'Omnem mouere lapidem', 'leave no stone unturned', 'try everything, leave nothing unattempted' (*CWE*, XXXI, p. 340).

32) De festo Sancti Lamberti

St Lambert, bishop of Maastricht (b. 633–38; martyred 698–701). His feast, 17 September (*Legenda aurea*, CXXXIII (134), pp. 596–97; Grotefend), traditionally began the season when the working day had to be prolonged by artifical light (Klersch, I, pp. 245–46).

11 **Ludimagistro ut manus farciam:** CL figurative uses of 'farcire' do not include 'stuffing' with money (*TLL*, VI, cols 279, l. 23–281, l. 28). This sense seems ML: e.g. 'farcire marsupia' (*DMLBS*, 'farcire', a). Perhaps also some influence from German: 'Eim die hend schmieren (or salben)' (Pauli, *Postilla*, XXIII^{r}; Wander, II, 318). On this custom see Macardle, *Confabulations*, p. 75.

33 **Nummum [...] quem indocti album uocant:** The 'indoctus' word 'albus' is ML (*LLMA*, s.v., 2). It translates 'Wyspennynge' a coin whose high silver content made it almost white (Schwerhoff, 'Köln rüstet sich zur Gottestracht' p. 133).

34 **obolum:** CL 'obolus' can signify any small amount of money: e.g. 'ne obolum quidem' (Mosellanus, *Paedologia*, 2, p. 5, l. 10); but often used by humanists for 'Heller', e.g. by Schotten as Arts Faculty Receptor: 'xi fl 4 alb. & 3 obulos' (HAStK, 150, A 516, 84[v]). Cf. 'Obulum habeo; ich hab eynen heller' (Heyden, *Formulae*, XVII, sig. H4[r]). Golius, 427; Grimm, 'Heller', 'obolus'.

33) De eligendo episcopo.

A church or school community electing a Boy Bishop, or 'Schulbischof', often for the feast of St Nicholas (6 December) was one of the ubiquitous medieval ceremonies of 'misrule'. The chosen boy presided, episcopally vested, over the services of a defined period, often preaching a mock sermon (Dürr, *Commentatio*, passim; Falk, 'Die Schul- und Kinderfeste', pp. 229–48; Bömer, *Die lateinischen Schülergespräche*, I, p. 102; Meisen, *Nikolauskult und Nikolausbrauch*, pp. 307–33; Klersch, I, p. 65; Herborn, 'Fast-, Fest- und Feiertage', pp. 34–36; Shahar, 'The Boy Bishop's Feast', citing further literature). Cf. Mosellanus, *Paedologia*, 21, 'De feriis divi Nicolai deque creando episcopo' (pp. 27–28); but the only close similarity between Mosellanus and Schotten is that in both one of the boys is reluctant to be made a 'bishop'.

Schotten's colloquy is important evidence for the custom in early-sixteenth-century Cologne; otherwise, it is mentioned only twice by Weinsberg in 1566 and 1570 (*BW*, II, pp. 157, 210). The seventeenth-century diocesan prohibition of the custom shows that the 'bishop' held office for over three weeks, from St Nicholas till the Holy Innocents, 28 December (Macardle, *Confabulations*, p. 82, ns 108, 111). It also shows that in the seventeenth century the 'Bishop' rode around, episcopally vested and with a band of 'retainers', to show himself and to collect money. This custom, known all over Europe (Shahar, 'The Boy Bishop's Feast', pp. 245–46) will presumably have been the case in the previous century.

The extant sources give no idea of how many schools in Cologne elected their own 'Bishop'. Weinsberg mentions St Aposteln and possibly St Jakob (*BW*, II, pp. 157, 210).

3 **die Lunae:** The dates fit 1524: see Macardle, *Confabulations*, pp. 81–83.

5 **Cui tuam dabis uocem? 8 Inconcinna est locutio:** 'Vox' meaning 'vote', and 'uocem dare', are ML (*MLLM*, 'vox', 6; DuC, 'vox', 3, VIII, p. 381; *LLMA*, 'vox', 2).

26 **gentilium:** 'Gentilis' (noun and adj.) is CL, but the sense 'heathen, pagan' is Christian LL (Stotz, V, 34.8; *TLL*, VI, col. 1869, l. 35–1872, l. 50; *DLFAC*, s.v., 3; *DMLBS*, s.v., 5; Dasypodius, 'gens'). 'In gentilium libris' (Mosellanus, *Paedologia*, p. 16, ll. 3–4).

34–36 **Platoni in cunis dormienti:** A well-known legend (e.g. Valerius Maximus, *Facta et dicta*, 1.6, ext. 3; Pliny, *Naturalis Historia*, 11.55).

34) De eligendo rege

Drawing lots to choose a 'king' ('Hauskonink') and his 'court' on Epiphany Eve, 5 January, was a Cologne family custom frequently described by Weinsberg: see Macardle, *Confabulations*, pp. 63–64. Schotten's description is valuable because it predates Weinsberg's first mention of the custom in 1552, suggesting that the usage had taken root in at least some circles in Cologne by the start of the sixteenth century. The colloquy shows similarities with Mosellanus, *Paedologia*, 25 (pp. 31–33); but Mosellanus moves into a learned discussion of the identity and nature of the original kings.

12 **hanc uesperam solemnem:** Presumably Epiphany Eve, even though colloquy 35 refers to Christmas.

15 **frontem [...] exporrigunt:** 'Smooth the wrinkled brow', i.e. 'be cheerful'. Erasmus, *Adagia*, 748, 'Frontem exporrigere, frontem contrahere'; 'Exporrigamus frontem' (Erasmus, *Colloquia*, p. 45, l. 407; p. 196, l. 2296).

16 **Ecquid uoluptatis domi habetis?:** Schotten often has 'ecquid', usually 'is there anything that …?' (*TLL*, V,2, col. 54, l. 80–col. 55, l. 31), instead of simple 'quid?', a usage common in Plautus (*Aulularia*, 270; *Epidicus*, 688) and Terence (*Andria*, 871; *Phormio*, 474). Cf. colloquies 102, l. 15; 118, l. 5, etc.).

21 **Chartulis pilleo impositis:** Weinsberg's family drew 'breiffgin', slips marked with the titles of *Rex*, *Cantzlar*, *Hoffmeister*, *Schenk*, *Narr* and consorts, as well as mottos from a hat in order of age (*BW*, V, pp. 220–21).

25 **uel matri uel ancillis uenditatur:** Weinsberg's servants were present at the meal; sometimes the maid became

Queen (*BW*, V, pp. 220–21). Schotten's spelling 'uendicatur' is common in ML and early NL.

29 **Potu omni nos alii regem donamus:** Weinsberg says that each guest gave the 'king' a 'firdel weins' (*BW*, V, pp. 350–51).

29–30 **alio tempore suo aere:** The 'Koninksessen', typically held in Shrovetide; depicted in *conuiuium* 6. See Macardle, *Confabulations*, pp. 63–64.

35) De festo natali Christi

The colloquy is clearly indebted to Mosellanus, *Paedologia*, 24, 'De feriis nataliciis Christi' and Hegendorff, *Dialogi*, 4, which mention the time taken up practising Christmas liturgical chants (Mosellanus, p. 30; Hegendorff, sig. D3^r). Mosellanus elsewhere refers to boys finding singing at Mass onerous: 'Nostrae cantiones supra modum prolixae' (*Paedologia*, p. 17, l. 28).

15–16 **A pridiano Thomae [...] ad alteram Circumcisionis diem:** From the eve of St Thomas the Apostle (20 December) till the day after the Circumcision (2 January), the standard school holiday in Cologne (cf. *BW*, V, p. 349).

20 **in templo:** The use of CL 'templum' for Christian churches is LL (Stotz, I, 15.3; Forcellini; *DLFAC*, s.v., 2; *GLL*). Not unknown in ML (DuC, VIII, pp. 52–53; *MLLM*; *RMLWL*); but very frequent in humanist NL (*LPLR*; Erasmus, *Colloquia*, p. 258, l. 835; Mosellanus, *Paedologia*, p. 17, l. 10).

33–34 **frigore perirem:** Mosellanus also mentions the extreme winter cold in churches (*Paedologia*, 24, p. 30, l. 25).

36) De tempore Bacchanali

There was a long Shrovetide entertaining season in Cologne, from Epiphany till mid-Lent (Herborn, 'Fast-, Fest- und Feiertage', p. 38; Hofmann, 'Weinsberg und die kölnische Fastnacht', p. 88). However, little is known of the late-medieval and early modern celebrations (Klersch, I, pp. 93–151; id., *Die Kölnische Fastnacht*, pp. 37–39; Herborn, 'Fast-, Fest- und Feiertage', pp. 37–42). See Macardle, *Confabulations*, pp. 75–76. This colloquy shows some some parallels with Mosellanus, *Paedologia*, 27, 'De Bacchanalibus Christianorum' (pp. 34–35), and slight similarities with Hegendorff, *Dialogi*, 6, 'De festis Bacchanalibus' (sig. D4^{r-v}).

1 **De tempore Bacchanali:** 'Tempus Bacchanale' is a Humanist alternative to 'Carnispriuium' (l. 10): (*LPLR*, 'Bacchanalia', 'Bacchanalis'). 'De Bacchanalibus Christianorum' (Mosellanus, *Paedologia*, 27, pp. 34–35).

4 **Quadragesimam:** For 'Lent', Christian LL (Forcellini, 'quadragesimus', 4; *DLFAC*, s.v., 1; *GLL*; DuC, VI, pp. 582–83; *MLLM*).

5 **Opinor nouem:** This long period between Christmas and Lent would fit the years 1522 and 1525: see Macardle, *Confabulations*, pp. 85–86.

10 **Carnispriuium:** ML (Stotz, VI, 60.2; DuC, II, p. 179: 'Tempus, quo carnibus *privari* [...] incipiunt Fideles, ante jejunia Quadragesimae'; *LLMA*). Though Vilhelmus (l. 13), and so presumably Schotten, disapproves, the word was widely used by NL authors: (*LPLR*); 'Diebus stultificiis carnisprivii' (Bebel, *Facetien*, p. 19; cf. pp. 36, 125). Massebieau, *Les colloques scolaires*, p. 128, regards the word as acceptable. Cf. *LPLR*, 'carnispriuialis': 'de ludo carnispriuiali' (Johann Botzheim, in Erasmus, *Epistolae*, 2117, l. 5); 'dies carnispriuiales' (Diel, p. 53; cf. Planitz and Buyken, *Schreinsbücher*, glossary, p. 819).

23 **Lupercale:** Lupercalia, Roman fertility and purification festival (15 February), when the 'Luperci', men naked but for wolf-masks and goatskin loincloths, ran through the streets, striking passers-by with strips of goathide; a blow was supposed to ensure conception in women (Pauly, VII, cols 509–10; *OCY*, p. 80).

28 **A Valerio Maximo:** Valerius Maximus, *Facta et dicta*, 2.2.9. Cf. Livy, *Ab Urbe Condita*, 1.5.1; Ovid, *Fasti*, 2.267–452, etc.).

33 **in honorem Panos:** As explained by Ovid (*Fasti*, 2.283–88). Pan protected sheep from wolves.

37) De Quadragesima

8 **De Fortuna [...] quod rotae insistat:** the common image of the Goddess Fortuna on her wheel, expressing the fickleness of fortune. 'Fortunae rotam' (Cicero, *In Pisonem*, 10.22, quoted Otto, 695). Cf. the Georg Pencz woodcut 'Wheel of Fortune' (1534) (Geisberg, G. 1010).

12 **curauimus cutem:** Literally 'cultivate a sleek skin'. As Erasmus, *Adagia*, 1375, 'Curare cuticulam', explains, this demanded fine food, baths, cosmetics and sleep (LB, II, 546E); hence figuratively, 'lead a self-indulgent life' (Otto, 494; Horace, *Epistulae*, 1.2.29). Cf. Erasmus, *Colloquia*, p. 45, ll. 407–08, p. 129, l. 122, etc.); Dasypodius, 'Cuticula': 'Curare cuticulam, Wollust pflegen / des leybs wol warten'.

18 **carnes prohibentur:** In the 1520s Lenten fare was restricted to fish, fruit and vegetables, 'fischwirk, felt- und boumgewechs' (*BW*, V, p. 297). Meat, eggs and milk products were still forbidden.

18–19 **quae solae pascunt corpus:** Meat was the early modern food of choice for health and strength (Albala, *Eating Right*, pp. 61, 67, 70, etc.); sometimes even seen as necessary for health (Castellanus, *Kreophagia*, cit. Albala, *Eating Right*, p. 45). However, cf. note to l. 27.

20 **Etiam pisces multos saginant; 21 Neruos adeo non roborant, ut caro:** Cf. 'Augustinus: Sunt et pisces, qui multum addant alimenti [...]. Christianus: Sed in genere plus alunt carnes' (Erasmus, *Colloquia*, p. 228, l. 59–229, l. 61). But Galen and many medieval and Renaissance dietaries saw fish as a cold, watery, phlegmatic food (Albala, *Eating Right*, pp. 44, 95–96, 102–03). However, cf. note to l. 27.

25 **Monachi:** 'Monachus', LL (Stotz, IV, 11.15; *TLL*, VIII, col. 1396, l. 81–1399, l. 70; DuC, V, pp. 451–53; Forcellini; *GLL*; *MLLM*; *LLMA*; *DLFAC*; Blaise, § 375; *DMLBS*, s.v., 1–3). Frequent in Erasmus (e.g. *Colloquia*, p. 298, l. 20).

25 **coenobiis:** 'Coenobium' is LL (*TLL*, III, col. 1414, ll. 29–62). It was more widely used in ML (Stotz, IV, 11.9; *MLWb*, II, col. 774, l. 71–col. 777, l. 23; *DLFAC*; *DMLBS*; *MLLM*; Dasypodius, 'coenobium').

25 **Pythagorice:** Pythagoras and the Pythagoreans were proverbially abstemious (Aristotle, *Fragmenta*, 195; Diogenes Laertius, *Lives*, 8.19). Cf. 'Pythagoricum conuiuium' (no. 2).

27 **Crassa [...] capita:** As well as referring to fatness, this may reflect the dietetic theory that 'crass' foods produce 'crass' (dulled) intelligence (Albala, *Eating Right*, p. 127). Erasmus's Folly sees monks as vulnerable to this, and

fatty food – esp. fish – as one cause (*Moriae Encomium*, *ASD*, IV–3, p. 162, l. 568, Listrius's note).

29 **monasteriorum:** 'Monasterium', LL (Stotz, IV, 11.8; *TLL*, VIII, col. 1402, l. 58–1404, l. 74; *DLFAC*; Blaise, §§ 375, 380; *GLL*; DuC, V, pp. 454–58; Forcellini; *MLLM*; Dasypodius, 'monos').

33 **In [...] hebdomadibus esurialibus:** 'Esurialis' is CL (*TLL*, V,2, col. 865, ll. 24–27; *OLD*) but extremely rare and ironically humorous: 'Ita uenter gutturque resident esurialis ferias' (Plautus, *Captivi* 468). It is not used in ML. Schotten frequently uses it, without comic intent, to mean 'Lenten'.

35 **Pisis et piris in fornace tostis:** Common Lenten food: 'Solent enim agrestes homines silvestria pira torrere et reservare ad ieiunium quadragesimale' (Bebel, *Facetien*, p. 7); cf. Erasmus, *Ecclesiastes*, *ASD*, V–4, p. 158, ll. 494–95; id., *Epistolae*, 1452, ll. 28–29. Recipes in MS cookbook of *ca.* 1500 (HAStK, 7004, 27, fols 22^{v}–23^{v}).

36 **Ficubus:** 'Ficus' in transferred sense for 'sweetmeat' is not attested; but the sweetness of figs was almost proverbial in antiquity (*TLL*, VI, col. 652, l. 49).

36 **qui rusticis mel sapiunt:** Cf. Bebel's anecdote of the rural preacher who, thinking of peasants' fondness for the sweetness of dried pears, spoke of '[Amor] dei, qui adeo dulcis est sicut iusculum torridorum pirorum' (Bebel, *Facetien*, p. 7).

38) De festo Paschatis

The motif of a battle or war between sausages and herrings, or similar symbols of Shrovetide or Easter and Lent, is widespread. A play on the subject was performed in Zittau on Ash Wednesday 1504; other treatments include Peter Jordan, *New Zeytung* (1540); *Das Volksbuch vom Finkenritter* (Zwickau, 1913), sig. A2^{v}; Fischart, *Flöh Hatz* (1573), epilogue; *Ambraser Liederbuch*, ed. by Bergmann, 1845, no. 142 (all in Bolte, 'Eine kölnische Fastnachtsdichtung').

1 **Paschatis:** 'Pascha', LL (DuC; *DLFAC*, s.v., 4; Blaise, §§ 190, 199; *LLMA*; *DMLBS*, s.v., 3).

12 **Nosti Thuringiam [...]:** This may refer to the Thuringian villages of Heringen and Kalbsrieth.

21 **Paschales:** 'Paschalis', LL (DuC; *DLFAC*; Blaise, § 199; *LLMA*; *DMLBS*).

39) De festo Pentecostes

8 **ieiunium:** Regulations for the Pentecost vigil fast were not of the strictest, nor absolutely standardized: e.g. milk products were allowed at one meal (Amberg, *Ceremoniale Coloniense*, pp. 202, 203 (MS 65v)); eggs were not forbidden, but adults were encouraged to abstain (Diel, p. 60).

18 **sacram Synaxin:** 'Σύναξις': originally the service, based on synagogue worship, celebrated before the Eucharist. By patristic times it had come to mean the Eucharist itself (*Patristic Greek Lexicon*, ed. by Lampe, 'σύναξις', B, 1, 10, 11; *LThK*², IX, col. 1225). LL 'synaxis' (Stotz, IV, 11.10; Forcellini; *DLFAC*; *LLMA*; *RMLWL*) is frequently used by humanists for Mass or Holy Communion: e.g. Erasmus, *Colloquia*, p. 177, l. 1715–16; 'Muniendus es | Sacra synaxi' (Macropedius, *Hecastus*, ll. 1263–64). Cf. colloquy 59, l. 11. In the early sixteenth century most laypeople made only an annual Easter communion; but since the late fifteenth century communion on some major feasts, such as Pentecost, had become relatively common for those who were trying to deepen their spiritual lives (*GEK*, II,2, pp. 105–06). 'Certi etiam devoti se tunc praeparare consueuerunt ad sacram communionem pro quaerendo augmento gratiae Spiritus Sancti, quod ualde laudibile est.' (Diel, p. 60).

24 **confiteor:** CL word; but the sense 'confess one's sins' is Christian LL (Stotz, V, 34.9; *TLL*, IV, col. 227, ll. 35–44; *DLFAC*, s.v., 5).

40) De festo Sancti Martini

In Cologne as elsewhere in north-west Germany and the Netherlands, 10 November, the eve of the feast of St Martin of Tours, was a night when children went round the houses singing songs for gifts in cash or kind. The colloquy shows clear parallels with Mosellanus, *Paedologia*, 18, 'De canticis deque feriis divi Martini': see Macardle, *Confabulations*, pp. 64–65, 112.

7 **In macra die, scilicet Veneris:** Friday was a day of abstinence from meat. St Martin's Day fell on a Friday in 1524.

28 **integrum erit:** Schotten seems to understand 'integrum' as 'suitable, convenient' (cf. *conuiuium* 12, l. 6, etc.), whereas the closest CL sense is 'undecided' (*OLD*, 'integer', 2). Cf. 'integrum est', 'it is in a person's power, open to them' (*DMLBS*, 'integer', 6g); 'Res est mihi integra, res est in mea potestate' (Forcellini, 'integer', 15).

33 **quo octo uictitabam dies:** Cf. 'Quandoquidem corrasurum me spero, quo hiemem commodius transigere valeam' (Mosellanus, *Paedologia*, p. 25, ll. 22–24).

39–40 **ad Graecorum Kalendas:** The Greek calendar, unlike the Roman, did not use a 'Kalends'; hence the saying, meaning 'never' (*OCY*, p. 316). More often 'ad kalendas Graecas' (Erasmus, *Colloquia*, p. 160, l. 1124; p. 497, l. 149; Erasmus, *Adagia*, 484; Otto, 301).

41) De xeniis mittendis

The colloquy shows distinct similarities with Mosellanus, *Paedologia*, 25, 'De novi anni ingressu [...] deque missitandis strenulis' (pp. 31–33), and with Hegendorff, *Dialogi*, 5, 'De Epiphanias feriis' (sig. D3^{r}–D4^{r} (sig. D3^{r})). See Macardle, *Confabulations*, pp. 112–13.

1 **xeniis:** CL 'xenium', 'present', often from host to guests. 'Non dimittam uos absque xeniis' (Erasmus, *Colloquia*, p. 262, ll. 958–59; cf. p. 263, l. 1004).

6 **Hui, tam cito?:** 'Hui, tam cito?' (Erasmus, *Colloquia*, p. 343, l. 139; Hegendorff, *Dialogi*, sig. D1^{r}).

6 **noui anni dies:** In early modern Cologne the calendar year began on Christmas Day, as the traditionalist Weinsberg tirelessly stresses (e.g. *BW*, V, p. 349); but even he celebrated 1 January too, reflecting the gradual infiltration of this date in the Holy Roman Empire in the sixteenth century (e.g. *BW*, V. p. 186 (1580); p. 193 (1582); Grotefend, p. 12). Friends exchanged a present, 'newjar' or 'fruntschaft' (*BW*, V. p. 193; cf. Herborn, 'Fast-, Fest- und Feiertage', pp. 32–34).

12 **strenam farinaceam:** CL 'strena', a Roman New Year gift. Cakes or pretzels were a common New Year present in the Rhineland (*KL*, IV, col. 1397).

21 **panniculum emunctorium:** 'Panniculus' is CL. 'Emunctorius' as adj. meaning 'used for wiping', as here,

seems unattested in CL, LL, ML or NL (cf. Massebieau, p. 129). As adj. it appears very rarely, meaning 'that cleanses by draining' (*DMLBS*). As noun, 'emunctorium' is attested once meaning 'handkerchief' (*DMLBS*, s.v., 1a); it usually means 'wick-snuffer' or 'anatomical drainage channel' (Forcellini, s.v., 1, 2; *TLL*, V, 2, col. 539, ll. 76–540, l. 2; *DMLBS*, s.v., 2, 3; *MLLM*). Schotten's collocation 'panniculus emunctorius' seems unattested in texts or dictionaries.

25 **interula:** CL, abbrev. of 'tunica interula', an undergarment (*TLL*, VII, 1, col. 2304, ll. 27–38). Frequent in ML for 'shirt, vest' (DuC, IV, p. 398; *DMLBS*, s.v., 1; *DLFAC*; Dasypodius). Used by Erasmus (*Colloquia*, p. 399, l. 356) and Vives (*Exercitatio*, XI, p. 79, XXI, p. 194).

25 **ulna:** 'Forearm', in CL already used as a linear measure. ML as equivalent to 'ell' (DuC, VIII, p. 363; *LLMA*, s.v., 1; *RMLWL*; Dasypodius, 'Ein klaffter'; Golius, 437). 'Quindecim [...] ulnas' (Reuchlin, *Henno*, ll. 259–60).

31–32 **cultros amicitiam rumpere:** The superstition that knives given as presents will 'cut' friendship was, and still is, widespread (*HDA*, VI, col. 206).

39 **me ipsum non nosco:** Erasmus, *Adagia*, 595, 'Nosce teipsum'. 'Γνῶθι σεαυτόν' was one of the 'oracles' inscribed at the Temple of Apollo at Delphi (Apostolios, *Proverbia*, 6.64; Otto, 1236).

42) De pecunia danda in nouae scholae ingressu.

27 **artifices mechanicos:** 'Mechanicus', adj., is late CL (*TLL*, VIII, col. 515, l. 61–col. 516, l. 25), but the sense 'manual, artisanal' is ML (DuC, V, p. 318; *DMLBS*, s.v., 2, 4; *LLMA*). Cf. colloquy 112, l. 1.

30 **sibi uindicant:** Schotten's spelling 'uendicant' is common in ML (Stotz, VII, 28.8). Cf. colloquy 68, l. 21.

31 **in ipsorum album referuntur:** CL 'album', 'official list, register'. Often figuratively for 'group or class of person': e.g. 'In album tuorum amicorum [...] me numera' (Schotten, *Vita honesta*, sig. Av[r]; cf. Dasypodius, 'Album').

43) Non semper esse studendum

3 **Paucis te uolo:** 'Sosia, | adesdum: paucis te uolo' (Terence, *Andria* 29; cf. Plautus, *Aulularia*, 199; *Miles gloriosus*, 375).

28 **Ad tenuem lancem litteras melius imbibi:** Dietary commonplace (Albala, *Eating Right*, p. 67). Cf. 'Plenus uenter non studet libenter' (Walther, 21595; Wander, I, 248); 'Ein voller Bauch studirt nicht gern' (Franck, I, fol. 19^{r}). Erasmus, *Adagia*, 2518, 'Pinguis uenter non gignit sensum tenuem' (i.e. 'mentem subtilem'). Cf. colloquy 83, l. 9.

33 **suum fraudare genium:** To deny one's nature what it needs: 'Egomet me defrudaui animumque meum geniumque meum' (Plautus, *Aulularia*, 725; cf. Terence, *Phormio*, 44). Cf. note to colloquy 86, l. 3.

37–38 **quum corpus sit animae promptuarium:** 'Promp-t(u)arium' for 'storeroom' is late CL; the general sense 'room, chamber', is LL (*TLL*, X,1, col. 1899, ll. 16–64; col. 1899, l. 65–col. 1900, l. 7; *DLFAC*, s.v., 2; *GLL*). This image may derive from Plato's view of the body-soul relationship (*Phaedo*, 78d, 79c, 81b). Cf. the body as 'animi domicilium' (Erasmus, *De conscribendis epistolis*, *ASD*, I–2, p. 452, ll. 9–10).

44) Quem ludum debeant iuuenes exercere

The sequence of colloquies 44, 46–50, devoted to children's games, is to some extent inspired by the five which Erasmus added to the 1522 edition of the *Colloquia*, and which from the edition of September 1524 on he grouped into a continuous sequence of 'Lusus pueriles': 'De lusu', 'Pila', 'Ludus globorum missilium', 'Ludus sphaerae per anulum ferreum', 'Saltus' (*Colloquia*, pp. 163–71). It is uncertain whether Schotten's tight grouping is independent, or inspired by Erasmus's editorial change. Erasmus felt that a boy's character emerged most plainly in games; hence civilized games and sportsmanlike behaviour were a necessary part of education (*De civilitate morum*, *LB*, I, 1042 E–F). In this he was typical of Renaissance educational writers. Mosellanus only briefly refers to ball and marbles (*Paedologia*, 15, 'De ludendi ratione', pp. 21–22).

5 **Ludus iste non scholasticorum est:** Games like dicing are routinely deprecated from classical to early modern

times: ‘Vetita legibus alea’ (Horace, *Carmina*, 3.24.57); ‘Trocho lude. Aleam fuge’ (*Disticha Catonis*, 36, 37); ‘Alea damnosa’ (Erasmus, *De pueris instituendis*, *ASD*, I-2, p. 41, l. 19). In medieval times the concern seems to have been the associated betting and cheating (Isenmann, p. 158). Hence Schotten (*Colloquia philosophica*, sig. AA3^{r}–4^{r}) deplores the ‘cupiditas’ caused by betting on dice; the Crailsheim school rules forbid dice and cards ‘nisi rector sit presens’ (Crecelius, ‘Crailsheimer Schulordnung’, p. 260).

13 **tertius Cato:** Someone who imitated the two exemplars of rectitude, M. Porcius Cato ‘the Censor’ and his great-grandson M. Cato Uticensis, was a ‘third Cato’. ‘Tertius e caelo cecidit Cato’ (Juvenal, *Satires*, 2.40; Otto, 358; Walther, 31383); Erasmus, *Adagia*, 783, ‘Tertius Cato’.

23 **Natare, dimicare et certare luctando:** Camerarius’s approved sports, also based on classical models, are similar: ‘pila, cursus, saltatio, pugna, lucta’ (*Praecepta*, sig. b3^{r}); ‘Luctationes [...] aggredimur, et digladiationes, et pilam iacimus, et spatia decurrimus’ (‘De gymnasiis’, ibid., sig. d5^{r}).

26 **charta lusoria:** Both words are CL, but ‘charta’ for ‘playing-card’ is ML and NL (*DMLBS*, s.v., 5; *LPLR*, s.v., A), as is the combination ‘charta lusoria’ (DuC, II, p. 296; Dasypodius, ‘Chartae lusoriae, Charten spyl’). This reflects the fact that playing cards reached Europe only in the later fourteenth century (Hoffmann, *The Playing Card*, p. 12). Cf. ‘Ludus chartarum’ (Vives, *Exercitatio*, XXI, pp. 190–202) and ‘folia lusoria’ (ibid., VI, p. 21).

26 **talis:** Dice made of bones which could rest on only four faces; the cubic *tessera* or *alea* had six sides (Erasmus, *Colloquia*, p. 623, ll. 83–87). Weinsberg lists *tali*, ‘koiten’, amongst his boyhood games (*BW*, I, p. 57; cf. Wrede, *Neuer Kölnischer Sprachschatz*, II, p. 253). Erasmus added ‘’Αστραγαλισμός siue talorum lusus’ to the 1529 edition of the *Colloquia* (pp. 620–28).

45) De eleemosynis colligendis.

1 **eleemosynis:** LL ‘ele[e]mosyna’ or ‘ele[e]mosina’, ‘alms’ (Stotz, IV, 9.7; *TLL*, V,2, col. 350, l. 64–351, l. 77; *DLFAC*, ‘eleemosyna’, 2; Blaise, § 482; DuC, III, pp. 246, 248; *DMLBS*, ‘elemosina’; *LLMA*, ‘ele(e)mosyna’, 2;

Dasypodius, 'eleemosyna'). This (German 'Almosen') was the proper term for the money and food given to begging schoolboys and students. Many early modern towns licensed or otherwise regulated scholars' begging (Essen: Reichart, *Alltagsleben*, p. 26; Nuremberg, Osnabrück: Lassotta, *Formen der Armut*, I, p. 349, n. 1996).

5 **decimas nostras:** ML 'decima', often pl. 'decimae', 'tithe(s)' (Stotz, III, 36.6; *DLFAC*, 'decima', 4; DuC, III, pp. 23–26; *DMLBS*, 'decimus', 4; *LLMA*, 'decima', 1; *MLLM*, 'decima'; Dasypodius (1536a), 'decem'). 'Decimis [...] quae sufficiunt sacerdotibus' (Erasmus, *Colloquia*, p. 332, ll. 254–255). By contrast with 'eleemosyna', this is a humorously improper use of the word.

11 **Mihi non fit uerisimile:** 'Mihi verisimile non fit' (Erasmus, *Colloquia*, p. 205, l. 2611; cf. p. 38, l. 213).

12 **Pinguis Mineruae homo:** Otto, 1118–22, 'Minerua', esp. 1120, 'Pingui Minerua'; 1119, 'Crassa Minerua'; Erasmus, *Adagia*, 37, 'Crassa Minerua. Pingui Minerua. Crassiore musa'. 'Satis tu quidem pingui Minerua philosopharis' (Erasmus, *Colloquia*, p. 466, l. 476).

17 **paroecianis:** 'Paroecianus', 'parochianus', LL. As adj. 'connected with a diocese or parish' (*LLMA*, 'parochianus', I); as noun usually 'parishioner' (DuC, VI, p 179; *DMLBS*, s.v., 3b; *LLMA*, 'parochianus', II, 2). The sense 'parish priest', as here, is rare (DuC, VI, p 179; *DMLBS*, s.v., 2a; *LLMA*, 'parochianus', II, 1).

37 **momentanea:** LL and ML (*TLL*, VIII, col. 1390, l. 39–col. 1391, l. 15; DuC, V, p. 450; *MLLM*, 'momentaneus'; *DMLBS*, 'momentaneus'; Serranus, s.v. 'momentum').

46) De ludo pilae

Many colloquy collections describe ball games, which were popular and seen by contemporary dietetics as particularly health-giving because they exercise all parts of the body (Gratarolus, *De conseruanda valetudine*, p. 133; cf. Albala, *Eating Right*, p. 131). Schotten similarly commends ball-playing in the *Colloquia philosophica* (sig. AA3r–4r). Whereas Erasmus's 'pila palmaria' (*Colloquia*, pp. 165–67) is a cross between handball and 'real' tennis, Schotten's game is identical with that played in Paulus Niavis, *Dialogus*, no. 5 (Bömer, *Die lateinischen Schülergespräche*, I, p. 25) and with 'Stocklegrüebligs' or 'Löchliballen' (Rochholz, *Alemannisches Kinderlied*, no. 15).

Each player has a hole in the ground (ll. 18–21). The player into whose hole the ball is thrown has to try to hit the other players with it; they attempt to avoid him (cf. ll. 22–24, 32). Anyone hit nine times is pelted by the others. A similar game used boys' caps in lieu of a hole (Klersch, II, p. 137).

25–26 **neminem tetigisti, notula tibi appingatur creta:** Presumably a variant of the game described above: failure to hit another player means a 'minus point' like that for being hit; the chalk marks record the misses.

47) De ludo globorum missilium, quos 'omnia' uocant Colonienses tirunculi litterarii

1 **Lud[us] globorum missilium:** The formula imitates Erasmus, 'Ludus globorum missilium' (*Colloquia*, pp. 167–68); but Erasmus's game is played with a large ball. Schotten describes the game of marbles (*Specken*, *Spickern*, *Schussern*, *Klicker*, *Schnellkügelchen*, etc.), one of the commonest spring children's games all over Europe, widely recorded in fifteenth- and sixteenth-century German sources (Zingerle, *Das deutsche Kinderspiel*, pp. 27–28; Klersch, II, pp. 138–40). The game of marbles is described in several colloquy collections, e.g. Heyden, *Formulae*, no. XIX, sig. H5$^{\mathrm{r-v}}$; Paulus Niavis, *Dialogus*, no. 5; Camerarius, 'De gymnasiis dialogus', in *Praecepta*, sig. d6^{r}; Comenius, *Orbis Pictus*, no. 136, pp. 276–77).

1 **'omnia':** Latinized form of the Ripuarian *Ommer*, local Cologne word for marbles (*Rheinisches Wörterbuch*, VI, p. 400, 4–20; also 'Ummer', 'Ümmer', 'Ümmes', etc.: ibid., IX, p. 45, 35–37). Cf. Beemelmans, 'Bilder aus dem Kölner Volksleben', p. 139, Wrede, *Neuer Kölnischer Sprachschatz*, II, pp. 253–54. See Macardle, *Confabulations*, p. 60.

9 **Globularem:** Cf. 'ludum [...] globularem' (Mosellanus, *Paedologia*, 15, p. 22, l. 7).

10 **globulis:** CL, but the sense 'marbles' is ML and NL: 'Ludemus globulis; wir wöllen klückern' (Heyden, *Formulae*, sig. H5^{r}); 'Globulus', [...] Ein schusser' (Serranus, s.v. 'globus'); 'Globulis ludere, mit kuglen spilen' (Golius, 230).

15 **Fiat fossiculus:** A common version of the game involved pitching the marbles into a small hole in the ground. Those which missed were won by another player if he hit them with one of his marbles (Paulus Niavis, *Dialogus*, no. 5, described by Bömer, *Die lateinischen Schülergespräche*, I, p. 25; Camerarius, 'De gymnasiis dialogus', in *Praecepta*, sig. d6^{r}). Fischart's Gargantua plays at 'grüblein' (*Geschichtklitterung*, p. 263; quoted Zingerle, *Das deutsche Kinderspiel*, p. 28). In Cologne this was known as 'Külche', meaning a small depression (Wrede, *Neuer Kölnischer Sprachschatz*, II, pp. 253–54; cf. III, p. 157; description in Klersch, II, p. 140).

17 **carceres:** The 'traps' from which racing chariots were released in the circus (*TLL*, III, col. 434, ll. 29–76). Erasmus uses 'carcer' for the starting point of games (*Colloquia*, p. 170, l. 1474). Here, the line from which the marbles were pitched, in German the 'Aan' (Wrede, *Neuer Kölnischer Sprachschatz*, II, pp. 253–54).

18 **ligneolo:** CL knows 'ligneolus' only as adj., 'wooden' (*TLL*, VII,2, col. 1383, ll. 37–43). The noun 'ligneolum', 'small piece of wood', is ML (*DMLBS*, 'ligneolus', b, c). Cf. note to colloquy 70, ll. 9, 11.

19–25: The conversation here is obviously inspired by the exchanges in Erasmus, 'Ludus sphaerae per annulum ferreum' (*Colloquia*, p. 169, esp. ll. 1430–36).

28 **Quibus fortuna prius aspirat, tandem aduersatur:** Not a proverb, but similar to several, e.g. 'Quem diu Fortuna fouit, de repente deserit' (Walther, 39840p1; cf. 9867, 23727, 35868k); 'Wen das Glück hebt auss der nider, den stürtzt es plötzlich wider' (Petri, *Der Teutschen Weissheit*, II, p. 626; Wander, I, 1761, parallels 1761, 1762).

48) De ludo globorum qui torquentur per annulum.

This game is described, as 'Ludus sphaerae per anulum ferreum', in Erasmus's colloquies (*ASD*, I–3, pp. 168–70). Similar to croquet, pall-mall and the modern Belgian *Beugelbaan* or *Jeu de passe*, it was played on beaten earth, using wooden implements to propel wooden balls through a hoop, and to knock opponents' balls out of play (Erasmus, *Colloquies*, trans. by Thompson, p. 22; Hoyoux, 'Un "jeu" d'Erasme', passim; Comenius, *Orbis Pictus*, no. 136, p. 276, with ill.).

1 **globorum:** 'Globus' for 'ball' is ML and NL (*DMLBS*, s.v., 2a).

17 **Flagellum:** 'Whip, lash', ML also 'flail'. Not recorded as the term for the implement with which this game is played in ML or NL dictionaries and texts. 'Claua, bandy' (Comenius, *Orbis Pictus*, p. 276) or 'vola' ('bat, racquet') (Erasmus, *Colloquia*, p. 169, l. 1422) seem more suitable.

25 **eris mihi magnus Apollo:** Refers to the riddle 'Dic, quibus in terris – et eris mihi magnus Apollo – | tris pateat caeli spatium non amplius ulnas' (Vergil, *Eclogues*, 3.104–05; Otto, 130).

28 **uerbum Vergilii:** The source is in fact the line 'Nullus ubique potest felici ludere dextra', from the *Carmina duodecim sapientium*, a collection of late-CL verse frequently reproduced in medieval MSS (*Anthologia Latina*, I, 2, p. 61, no. 503, line attributed to Vomanius; *Carmina Burana*, I,3, p. 62, no. 213, l. 9). Used verbatim in Vives, *Exercitatio*, VI, p. 21).

32 **promptitudo:** LL, usually 'mental quickness', 'presence of mind' (Forcellini; *TLL*, X,2, col. 1900, ll. 25–28; DuC, VI, p. 529; *DLFAC*; *RMLWL*; *LPLR*; *NWL*). 'Dicendi legendique promptitudinem' (Erasmus, *De recta [...] pronuntiatione*, *ASD*, I–4, p. 102, l. 994).

49) De ludo saltus

Jumping is another exercise particularly recommended by early modern dietetics (Albala, *Eating Right*, p. 131). This colloquy shows similarities with Heyden, XIX, 'De missione à literis' (*Formulae*, sig. H5^{r-v}).

3 **ciconiarum proles 5 quia longissima habetis crura:** The allusion is vernacular, not classical. Antiquity knew the stork as 'long' on account of its neck, not its legs (Pauly, II, col. 1020); but all over Germany rhymes and songs address the stork as 'Langbein'. Well known is 'Klapperstorch' in *Des Knaben Wunderhorn*: 'Storch, Storch, Langbein [...] (Brentano, *Sämtliche Werke*, VIII, p. 319; cf. 'An den Storchschnabel', ibid., p. 318). Others in *HDA*, VIII, cols 498–507 (esp. cols 500, 501, 506).

7 **unumquemuis:** The correct CL order is 'quemuis unum' (*OLD*).

8 **prouoco:** 'Ad hoc certamen te prouoco' (Erasmus, *Colloquia*, p. 41, l. 290).

9 **in harenam [...] descendam:** Erasmus, *Adagia*, 883, 'In harenam descendere' 'certamen inire' (*LB*, II, 361E).

23 **palmam dabo:** Cf. 'palmam tribuere', 'award the palm', in Erasmus, *Adagia*, 204, 'Palmam ferre.'

34–35 **Quod paene fit [...] uotum:** Proverbial phrase: cf. 'Beinahe ist nicht ganz' (Wander, I, 303; parallels 303, 935; V, 949). 'Aristotle saith, Quod fere fit, non fit, sed quod vix fit, fit' (Edgeworth, *Sermons*, p. 336).

50) De certamine cursus

21 **tecum palaestram ineo:** CL 'palaestra', literally 'wrestling-place'. The figurative use of 'palaestram ineo' to mean the same as 'in harenam descendo' (cf. p. 42, l. 12; colloquy 49, l. 9) seems unattested in CL.

51) An ille sit doctus semper (ut putant rustici) qui magnos potest legere libros

In Schotten's *Colloquia philosophica*, no. 20, Desiderius warns Cyriacus that too many books can confuse the student: 'Profecto si librorum copia doctos faceret, aut bonos, doctissimi omnium atque optimi esse possent, qui ditissimi, cum contrarium constet.' (sig. BB2^{v}).

6 **Ecclesiae:** 'Ecclesia', LL and ML (Stotz, IV, 9.2; *TLL*, V,2, col. 32, l. 59–40, l. 26; *DLFAC*; Blaise, § 346; *GLL*; *MLWb*, III, col. 1081, l. 62–1084, l. 25; *DMLBS*; *MLLM*).

6–7 **quem uulgus pastorem appellitat:** 'Pastor' for 'parish priest' is ML (*DMLBS*, s.v., 4b; *MLLM*, s.v., 3; *LLMA*, s.v., 1; *LPLR*), and the word had made its way into the vernacular: e.g. 'bei dem pastor parscheier geessen' (*BW*, V, p. 61). Schotten clearly sees it as substandard, but it is used by Erasmus: e.g. 'Atqui pastorem decet hospitalitas' (*Colloquia*, p. 389, l. 3).

33 **ut inquit Erasmus:** Cf. 'Noli committere vt codices eruditos habeas, ipse ineruditus' (Erasmus, *De ratione studii*, *ASD*, I–3, p. 69, l. 45).

37 **Vbique extant bibliothecae litterariae:** There were indeed numerous private libraries in Cologne in the early sixteenth century (*Alte Un.*, pp. 309–10); notable were those of Tilman Gravius, the Cathedral Chapter

secretary (Chaix, 'Humanisme et élites urbaines', p. 205; Erasmus, *Epistolae*, III, p. 25, note to 610, l. 47); Peter Rinck (Werhahn, 'Die Bücher des Dr. Peter Rinck'; Schmid, *Stifter*, pp. 85–89; Quarg, 'Ganz Köln', pp. 105–08); Johann (II) Rinck (Schmid, *Stifter*, p. 183 and n. 171; Schotten, *Vita honesta*, sig. Aiii^{v}). Books identified in modern collections show that some *bursa* libraries were extensive (Röhrig, *Reste alter Bibliotheken*, pp. 90–96 and Anlage 21, pp. XXIX–XXXI; Quarg, 'Ganz Köln', p. 72).

52) De praeceptore eligendo

The colloquy develops Erasmus's advice on choosing a teacher in *De ratione studii* (*ASD*, I–3, p. 68, ll. 11–18 and passim). Cf. colloquy 53.

16–17 **utrisque (ut aiunt) brachiis amplexandus:** Not a CL set phrase, or the direct translation of a vernacular one. But cf. Erasmus, *Adagia*, 1854, 'Obuiis ulnis', 'With open arms' (*CWE*, XXXIV, p. 111), which Erasmus glosses as 'ambabus manibus' (*ASD*, II–4, p. 250, l. 727).

19 **Si [...] reddit:** Cf. 'Neque enim fieri potest, vt is recte quemquam erudiat, qui sit ipse ineruditus' (Erasmus, *De ratione studii*, *ASD*, I–3, p. 68, ll. 11–12).

25 **qui uir sit:** 'Libet experiri, qui vir sies' (Erasmus, *Colloquia*, p. 167, ll. 1347–48).

31–32 **qualis praeceptor, tales [...] discipulos:** Cf. 'Wie der Lehrer, so der Schüler' (Wander, III, 2).

53) An praeceptor litterarius sit colendus tamquam parentes

The colloquy develops Erasmus's comparison of the teacher with the parent in *De ratione studii*: 'Fac omnibus modis efficias, vt ille [praeceptor] patris in te, tu filii in illum vicissim induas affectum. [...] non minus deb[emus] iis a quibus recte vivendi rationem, quam a quibus vivendi initia sumpsimus' (*ASD*, I–3, p. 68, ll. 13–16). Cf. colloquy 52.

11 **par pari referre:** Otto, 1337. Frequent in Roman comedy (e.g. Plautus, *Mercator*, 629; Terence, *Phormio*, 212) and in Erasmus (e.g. *Adagia*, 35; *Colloquia*, p. 165, l. 1305; p. 201, l. 2476; p. 279, l. 79).

20 **uerbis [...] uerbera:** A common pun in CL (e.g. Terence, *Heautontimorumenos*, 356). 'Hi mihi non verbis, sed

verberibus coercendi videntur' (Mosellanus, *Paedologia*, 9, p. 16, ll. 23–24). 'Si non obtemperaret verbis [...] verberibus eam emendaret' (Erasmus, *Colloquia*, p. 307, ll. 200–01).

27 **sibi:** CL 'se' is almost exclusively reflexive: CL would demand 'ei' or 'eius' here. Schotten's frequent use of 'se' in place of 'is', esp. 'sibi' and 'secum' for 'ei' and 'cum eo', and of the adj. 'suus' for 'eius', is a ML feature (Stotz, IX, 38).

40 **uita nihil est nobilius:** 'Nihil quicquam est homini uita pretiosius' (Seybold, *Viridarium* (1677), p. 356; Wander, II, 1836; parallels, ibid.).

42 **Aristoteli:** Aristotle said the learned were superior to the unlearned 'as the living are to the dead' (Diogenes Laertius, *Lives*, 5.11). Cf. 'Sine doctrina vita est quasi mortis imago' (*Disticha Catonis*, III, 1).

54) De nundinis et munerum nundinariorum emptione

This colloquy shows some similarities with Mosellanus, *Paedologia*, 1, 'De nundinis' (p. 4). The permanent market activity in Cologne and the influence of the great Frankfurt fairs meant that fairs in Cologne declined as early as the thirteenth century, leaving only the week-long 'Jahrmarkt' at the *Gottestracht*, in the second week after Easter (see Macardle, *Confabulations*, pp. 109–10). However, this colloquy does not seem specific to Cologne, but rather designed as a generic description of a fair.

13 **Qui spe uiuit, miseram agit uitam:** Cf. 'Qui spe aluntur, pendent, non viuunt' (Erasmus, *Colloquia*, p. 135, l. 334); 'Wer von Hoffnung lebt, stirbt am Hunger' (Wander, II, 726).

55) De nundinis Francfordiensibus

The twice-yearly Frankfurt fairs were of crucial significance for the Cologne economy (Irsigler, 'Köln, die Frankfurter Messen [...]', passim). See Macardle, *Confabulations*, pp. 59–60.

7 **in foribus:** The figurative sense 'near at hand' seems to be LL (*TLL*, VI, col. 1064, ll. 15–19): 'Statim in foribus peccatum aderit' (Vulgate, Genesis 4.7). Cf. 'Mariae natalis in foribus est' (Hegendorff, *Dialogi*, sig. D1r). There is perhaps influence from German 'vor der Tür', 'close at hand'.

27–28 **Dicunt [...] tractare ut asinum inter simias:** Erasmus, *Adagia*, 441, 'Asinus inter simias' (based on ''όνος 'εν πιθήκοις', Aulus Gellius, *Noctes Atticae*, 2.23.9): 'When a person finds himself among satirical and insolent people, himself being a dull fellow whom they mock with impunity' (*CWE*, XXXI, p. 421). The allegations that travellers to Frankfurt are cheated and robbed are not supported by contemporary evidence, such as Arnold Buchelius's record of his boat-trip from Cologne to the Frankfurt fair in September 1587 (Keussen, 'Die drei Reisen', I, pp. 93–94).

32 **aureum:** 'Aureus' for 'aureus nummus', 'Gulden', is frequent in ML and NL (DuC, I, p. 485; *MLWb*, I, col. 1248, ll. 4–29; Dasypodius, 1536, 'Aurum': 'Aureus absolutè, ein güldin'). 'Centum aureos' (Bebel, *Facetiae* (1570), sig. B6^{r}; cf. C2^{v}, etc.; *NWL*).

56) De uitando mendacio

2 **Euergislus:** St Evergis[i]lus, successor of St Severinus as bishop of Cologne; martyred *ca.* 593. Patron of glaziers and stained-glass artists; feast 24 October (*SEECO*, V, 1, pp. 8–9).

7 **Anguem minus odi quam mendacium:** 'Minus anguem odi, quam pisces' (Erasmus, *Colloquia*, p. 207, l. 2662); cf. 'Odisse aeque atque angues' (Plautus, *Mercator*, 761).

19 **Solones:** Solon, Athenian legislator of the sixth century BC, a byword for severe rectitude (e.g. 'Aerumnosi [...] Solones', Persius, *Satires*, 3.79). He famously deplored a fictional tragedy of Thespis, remarking that 'lying', if tolerated on stage, would soon take root in public life (Plutarch, *Solon*, 29.4).

28 **Credat hoc Iudaeus Apella:** Phrase expressing utter disbelief: 'Credat Iudaeus Apella, | non ego' (Horace, *Sermones*, 1.5.100–01). **Apella**, variant of 'Apelles', a common name for freedmen; almost certainly not 'a'+'pellis', 'without a [fore]skin' ((Horace, *Opera*, ed. by Wickham, II, p. 70; id, *Satires*, I, ed. by Brown, p. 149).

32 **Vulgo fertur, 'Furarium mendacium comitatur':** Walther, 14643a, 'Mendax est furax'. Cf. 'Et hoc uitium [theft] esse tuo [lying] cognatum testatur etiam populare prouerbium' (Erasmus, *Colloquia*, p. 320, ll. 11–12);

'Mendaces aiunt furibus esse pares' (Camerarius, *Praecepta*, sig. c6^{r}).

57) De confessione

This colloquy shows clear similarities with Mosellanus, *Paedologia*, 28, 'De ieiunio deque confessione, quam vocant' (pp. 35–36). On confession in sixteenth-century Cologne see *GEK*, II,2, pp. 113–30; Vollmer, *Agenda Coloniensis*, pp. 258–71. See the discussion in Macardle, *Confabulations*, pp. 115–17.

1 **confessione; cf. 22 a confessore; 34 confessor; 28–29 confessionem audientes:** Here as elsewhere, Schotten is content with the standard Latin terminology for confession, and does not attempt to use more humanist terms. See Macardle, *Confabulations*, Chapter 4, esp. p. 135.

6 **Adhuc sat restat temporis:** The placing of this colloquy immediately before no. 58, set just before Easter, suggests that Iodocus is referring to the obligation on all Catholics of 'years of discretion' to make a yearly confession, and to receive the Eucharist at Easter. This obligation had been laid by 'Omnis utriusque sexus', Canon 21 of the Fourth Lateran Council (1215) (Denzinger, 812). Parishioners were reminded every Lent, and advised not to postpone confession without good reason (e.g. Diel, pp. 19–23, 49, 41). The boys' dialogue, ll. 3–12, rehearses a pious commonplace.

13 **plebeiario:** 'Plebeiarius' for 'parish priest' is not found in dictionaries. The commonest ML term is 'plebanus' (see note to colloquy 90, l. 36). 'Plebeiarius' may be a humanist alternative to 'plebanus', or calqued on ML 'plebeium', 'parish' (*LLMA*), 'plebeius', 'parochial' (Stotz, V, 4.8; *LLMA*), and 'plebeianus', 'parish priest' (*LPLR*, *LLMA*).

14 **cuipiam monachorum:** The canonical principle of confessing only to one's own parish priest had been diluted during the Middle Ages: from 1312 the mendicant orders were allowed to confess people not under their pastoral care (Tentler, *Sin and Confession*, p. 64; Vollmer, *Agenda Coloniensis*, pp. 263–64). Sixteenth-century German penitential manuals list various juridical and conscientious reasons for choosing another

confessor (*Peycht Spigel*, sig. B8v–C1r; cf. *Manuale Parrochialium sacerdotum*, sig. A4v).

16 **deuotionis:** CL 'Deuotio' means 'consecration' or 'curse'; the sense 'devotion, piety' is LL and ML (*TLL*, V,1, col. 879, l. 19–880, l. 35; *DLFAC*, s.v., 2; Blaise, §§ 1, 21, 46, 434; DuC, 'devotus', 1, III, p. 91; *DMLBS*, s.v., 2; *LLMA*, s.v., 2; *MLLM*, s.v., 3).

17 **pecuniae nihil expetunt; 18 tamen acciperent, si daretur:** The *Beichtgeld*, theoretically a voluntary offering (*Manuale Parrochialium sacerdotum*, sig. A4v) was often in practice a customary fee (Tentler, *Sin and Confession*, p. 71; cf. Lea, *A History of Auricular Confession*, I, pp. 404–11; *GEK*, II, 2, p. 126). The *Peycht Spigel* describes it ambivalently as not compulsory but fitting, 'zimlich' (sig. C5r). The specific prohibition, in texts like Campeggio, *Constitutio ad remouendos abusus* (sig. A4r), of demanding money for sacramental actions shows that such demands were made. In 1588 Weinsberg refused an Augustinian's demand for a *Beichtgeld*, but afterwards freely offered him 6 Albus (*BW*, V, pp. 302–03).

20 **Metuebam olim puer:** In the fifteenth and sixteenth centuries the minimum age for confession varied considerably, but was generally lower than that for the reception of the Eucharist (usually between ten and twelve: Lea, *A History of Auricular Confession*, I, pp. 400–04; *Agenda S. Coloniensis Ecclesiæ*, 1637, p. 70). Weinsberg made his first confession in 1525 at the age of seven, but first received Communion in 1527 at nine (*BW*, I, pp. 40, 51). Like Iodocus here, Weinsberg was afraid of confession at first ('ich wolt lieber durch ein fur sin gangen, dan gebicht haben'), but quickly got used to it (*BW*, I, p. 40).

22–23 **Dicebatur [...] clauus infigeretur:** This sounds like a motif from vernacular comic literature, but no source has been identified. However, Weinsberg regarded the confessional as a place of bizarre goings-on: 'Ich hab wol seltzam dingen dar von gehoirt und gelesen, sult emans davon vil sagen, der mogt vor uncatholischs gehalten werden' (*BW*, V, p. 303). Might this have been an 'urban legend' current in Schotten's Cologne?

25–28 **Confiteris tu ex chartula? [...] Prohibent [...] nonnulli:** Some penitential manuals actually suggest writing lists of sins (*Manipulus curatorum*, 1509, sig. J5^{r}; Tentler, *Sin and Confession*, p. 86). The practice was never officially prohibited, but often discouraged (Lea, *A History of Auricular Confession*, II, p. 283).

37 **Certe parum doctus fuit:** Tentler, *Sin and Confession*, (p. 128) wonders whether penitents ever actually doubted their confessor's intellectual competence, a possibility envisaged in some penitential manuals. Iodocus's remark suggests that some did.

58) De cena suprema Christi cum discipulis et die Parasceues

In the Maundy Thursday *mandatum* ceremony, the superior of a monastery washed the monks' feet in memory of Christ's washing his disciples' feet after the Last Supper. In medieval monasteries this was often followed by a *mandatum pauperum*, where the poor received a token washing and a small meal (Schäfer, 'Fußwaschung'). The colloquy points to Schotten's relationship with the Cologne Antonite monastery: see Macardle, *Confabulations*, pp. 174–84.

2 **die Parasceues:** 'Parasceue', LL: senses include 'Good Friday' as here (*GLL*; *DMLBS*, s.v., 3; *DLFAC*; Blaise, § 190).

4 **post triduum:** The Sacred Triduum, beginning on Maundy Thursday and lasting till Holy Saturday (Blaise, § 190).

8 **magis […] esuriendum est:** the Triduum fast was even stricter than that of Lent: 'Arctius ieiunium eius diei Parasceues' (Diel, p. 52).

14 **ouis Paschalibus:** In Cologne, 'pooscheier' (Parscheier), a standard Easter treat (Wrede, *Rheinischer Volksbrauch*, pp. 40–41; Klersch, I, p. 172). 'Bei dem pastor parscheier geessen' (*BW*, V, p. 61). Cf. colloquy 120, 'De ouis colligendis circa Paschatis ferias' and 'Conuiuium Paschale' (no. 14), esp. ll. 19–45.

16 **spes […] leuat aduersa:** Cf. 'Hoffnung in Not ist Leidens Trost' (Petri *Der Teutschen Weissheit*, II, p. 383; Wander, II, 724; parallels 723, 724; V, 1446).

25 **Antonio diuo:** 'Diuus' as adj. is LL (*TLL*, V,1, col. 1658, l. 62–1659, l. 12; *GLL*). In the sense 'saint', as here, the word is infrequent, sometimes expressly avoided, in ML (DuC, III, p. 152; *MLWb*, III, col. 899, l. 67–900, l. 63;

MLLM; *DMLBS*, s.v., 3c: most examples from the sixteenth century), but it is frequent in humanist NL (*LPLR*). Common in Erasmus, *Colloquia*: 'Christo, ac diuis aliquot' (p. 172, l. 1514; cf. p. 173, l. 1564; p. 174, l. 1584; p. 175, l. 1626); cf. Mosellanus, *Paedologia*, p. 3, l. 24; p. 25, ll. 2, 15, 28, etc.).

27 **Placentas duas triticeas; 29 calix uini:** A small meal of wheaten cakes and wine typically followed the *mandatum*: 'fiat coena in pane et vino ficis et rasinis et oblatis' (Amberg, *Ceremoniale Colniense*, p. 132); wine and 'Mendelbrot' at St Ursula, *ca.* 1500 (Klersch, I, pp. 165–66).

34 **Quidni?:** Retort frequent in Erasmus, *Colloquia* (p. 180, l. 1821; p. 367, l. 112; p. 369, l. 206; p. 370, l. 237; p. 401, l. 443). Cf. Mosellanus, *Paedologia*, p. 20, l. 22.

38 **aduenis dextera manus:** Washing hands instead of feet was customary in some Cologne churches: e.g. at the Cathedral in the fourteenth century (Amberg, *Ceremoniale Coloniense*, pp. 132, 133) and at St Aposteln, *ca.* 1400, where laypeople were included (Odenthal, *Das älteste Liber Ordinarius*, pp. 123–24).

40 **Praeceptorem:** 'Praeceptor' was the standard term for Antonite superiors (Macardle, *Confabulations*, p. 174).

59) De sumptionis Eucharistiae praeparatione

6 **Edere mihi non licet:** Michael then decides to eat something to keep his strength up (l. 10): in the early sixteenth century the Eucharistic fast was not standardized or particularly rigorous. Dicl, who allows a 'refectio modica' before bedtime (p. 46), is typical (cf. *GEK*, II,2, pp. 99–112, esp. p. 108).

13 **Vesperi os colluo aqua [...]:** Mainly to avoid food being washed out from between the teeth into the mouth, breaking the Eucharistic fast (*Missale Diocesis Coloniensis*, 1525, sig. aij^{r}). But fifteenth- and sixteenth-century instructions often stress cleanliness as part of the preparation for the Eucharist (*GEK*, II,2, p. 107).

21 **opitulamen:** ML (Stotz, VI, 63.2; *LLMA*; *DMLBS*). Used by humanists (*LPLR*, examples from de Bovelles and Bucer).

25 **hostia:** CL, 'sacrificial victim'. The sense 'host, Eucharistic wafer' is ML (DuC, IV, p. 244; *MLLM*, s.v., 1; *LLMA*, s.v., 1; *DMLBS*, s.v., 2).

25 **Nosti quid facies [...] ; 27 potu depono, non digito detraho:** Communicants were instructed to avoid the irreverence of touching the host with teeth or fingers. The drink mentioned here is probably unconsecrated wine, regularly offered to communicants in Cologne and other dioceses in the sixteenth century (Klersch, III, p. 59; Vollmer, *Agenda Coloniensis*, pp. 280–84; *GEK*, II,2, p. 104). Similar is Diel's advice: 'subtiliter cum lingua sua dissoluat iterumque ad calicem uini uadat, modicum quid accipiendo in adiutorium sibi, donec inumserit plenarie, ne Sacramento irreuerentia fiat' (Diel, p. 46).

30 **Quousque [...] fuerit decocta:** Catholic theology assumes that the Presence of Christ in the Eucharist ceases when the Eucharistic species is corrupted, e.g. by digestion (*CE*, 'Presence, Real', IV). 'Decoquo' for 'digest' is LL and ML (*TLL*, V,1, col. 204, ll. 20–31; *DMLBS*, s.v., 3a; cf. *MLWb*, III, col. 114, ll. 41–50; *GLL*; Serranus, s.v. 'coquo'). Standard CL for 'digest' is 'concoquo' (*TLL*, IV, col. 82, l. 3–col. 83, l. 11). CL 'decoquo' is usually 'boil, stew' (*TLL*, V,1, col. 201, l. 55–col. 203, l. 62).

31 **Estne expuendum [...] in terram?; 34–35 satius tamen esset [...] in parietem sputum emittere:** More standard advice to communicants. 'Non statim exspuendum est in terram [...] ad spatium uidelicet ad minus unius horae' (Diel, p. 46); '[...] Alioquin in tali loco expuendum est: qui sit mundus et honestus: ubi sputum nequeat conculcari' (*Manuale Parrochialium sacerdotum*, sig. A3^{v}).

60) De more post gymnasia triuialia accedendi scholas praecelsas, quas bursas appellant

The negative depiction of university *bursae* here may reflect Schotten's humanist disapproval of their curriculum and teaching methods: see Macardle, *Confabulations*, pp. 29–41, 152–58.

1 **triuialia:** The application of CL 'triuium' and 'triuialis' to the 'trivium' of grammar, rhetoric and dialectic is late

ML (Stotz, I, 7.4; III, 38.1; DuC, VIII, pp. 189–90; *MLLM*; *LLMA*; *RMLWL*; *LPLR*).

2 **bursas:** The halls or hostels providing accommodation and tuition for students in the Cologne Arts Faculty. The animus of this colloquy may reflect Schotten's views on, and perhaps personal involvement in, the attempts in the 1520s to reform the curriculum of the Cologne *bursae*: see Macardle, *Confabulations*, pp. 29–41. CL 'bursa' (orig. 'byrsa') is a leather hide (*TLL*, II, col. 2266, ll. 5–13). From the ML sense 'purse, moneybag' (*MLWb*, I, col. 1626, l. 36–1627, l. 39; *MLLM*, 'byrsa', 4; *DMLBS*, s.v., 2) develop various senses including 'allowance, scholarship, student grant' (*DMLBS*, s.v., 5; *LPLR*, s.v., B). In late-medieval university parlance 'bursa' refers originally to the student's contribution to a common fund; then to the community of those who contribute (the 'bursales'); then to the institution to which the payment is made (Schwinges, 'Sozialgeschichtliche Aspekte', pp. 530–31 and note 10; *LPLR*, s.v., C, 'collège universitaire'; cf. Stotz, III, 37.5).

18 **Loquenturne ei [...] lapides:** Otto, 913. 'Quia mi misero cerebrum excutiunt | tua dicta, soror: lapides loqueris' (Plautus, *Aulularia*, 151–52).

22–23 **nudis capitibus:** On admission to the MA at 'inception', Cologne students were presented with a red cap, 'birretum'; indeed, 'birettare' was a synonym for 'incept' (Tewes, *Bursen*, p. 16). At inception in 1537, Weinsberg wore 'ein kogel [hood] [...] und ein sanguinen bonet' as the 'insignia magistrorum artium.' (*BW*, I, p. 115). In 1499 the cap was explicitly forbidden to students below MA status (HAStK, 150, A 480, fol. 279[v]; *Alte Un.*, p. 297). There were similar prohibitions in other universities (Fletcher, 'Wealth and Poverty', pp. 412–13; Cobban, 'Medieval Student Power', p. 371; *HUE*, II, p. 348).

34 **Noli mihi tutor esse:** 'Tutor', 'guardian', for someone overly officious is a largely Plautine usage: e.g. 'Quid tu curas [...] nisi tu mi es tutor?' (*Aulularia*, 430; cf. *Vidularia*, 23); 'Ne sis mihi tutor' (Persius, *Satires*, 3.96). Otto, 1807.

35 **gymnasia [...] philosophica:** Humanists often regard 'bursa' as substandard: e.g. 'bursa (ut nominant)' (Zasius,

in *Amerbachkorrespondenz*, II, no. 985, 38). Some use CL synonyms, most frequently 'gymnasium' (Meuthen, 'Artesfakultät', p. 382).

41 **gradus inanium nominum: gradus** for 'university degree' is ML (Stotz, III, 37.3; *MLLM*, s.v., 10; *LLMA*, s.v., 3; *DMLBS*, s.v., 15; *LPLR*; cf. DuC, IV, p. 92). **inanium nominum:** Humanists often see medieval academic terminology as substandard or obscure: e.g. 'Baccalaureatus (ut uocant)' (Bebel, *Facetien*, p. 23). Erasmus, *De recta [...] pronunciatone*, *ASD*, I–4, pp. 25–26, discusses the etymology of the names of degrees.

41–42 **magno [...] ueneunt:** High fees for matriculation, lodging, tuition, examinations and degrees were a much resented source of Arts Faculty funds (von den Brincken, 'Die Stadt Köln', pp. 37–38; *Alte Un.*, p. 295). Weinsberg, whose BA, LicA, MA and JCivB had cost 58 Gulden, was deterred by the expense from attempting the Doctorate in Law (*BW*, I, pp. 114–15, 137).

61) De deponendis (ut aiunt) cornibus beanitatis

The *depositio beanii* was the university initiation ceremony, where freshmen were ritually insulted and 'operated' on to remove the horns which they supposedly had (*Manuale Scholarium*, sig. A2v–A5r; cf. Thorbecke, *Geschichte der Universität Heidelberg*, I, Abt. 1, pp. 54–57; Dinkelius, *De origine [...]*; Fabricius, *Die Akademische Deposition*; Löhr, 'Rede bei einer depositio beanismi'; Bauer, *Sittengeschichte*, pp. 74–82, with seventeenth-century illustrations; *HUE*, II, pp. 349–51).

Details of the *depositio* in Cologne are few (*Alte Un.*, pp. 168–174). Weinsberg records his own in 1534, and that of his nephew Hermann at the Bursa Laurentiana in 1578, when each student paid a steep 1½ Gulden, spent on a party afterwards (*BW*, I, p. 103; III, p. 21).

Erasmus disapproved of the *depositio* as barbarous, humiliating and potentially violent (*De pueris instituendis*, *ASD*, I–2, p. 61, ll. 1–12). In 1503 the Cologne Arts Faculty threatened punishments for violent depositions, but was still complaining about abuses in 1523 (*Alte Un.*, p. 169; Bianco, I,2, p. 313).

2 **beanitatis:** 'Beanitas', abstract noun from ML 'beanus', 'freshman', from French 'bec jaune', 'greenhorn' (*MLLM* and *LPLR*, 'beanus'; *LLMA*, 'beanus', 1; Stotz, V, 79.6). 'Beanum exuere' (Erasmus, *De pueris instituendis*, *ASD*, I–2, p. 61, l. 2). 'Beanitas' is not otherwise attested: cf. 'beanismus' (*LLMA*).

4–5 **'Odit figulus figulum':** Otto, 660; Erasmus, *Adagia*, 125, 'Figulus figulo inuidet, faber fabro.'

13 **cornua [...] gerere; 17 Hircum olere:** The proverbial flaws of the *beanus*: see the description of the ceremony above. **Hircum olere:** Erasmus, *Adagia*, 1848, 'Pastillos Rufillus olet, Gorgonius hircum' (based on Horace, *Sermones*, 1.2.27); Erasmus, *Adagia*, 2366, 'Anus hircum olet.'

20 **frustis panis delinitis:** Almost certainly 'chunks of bread spread with fat or butter', with CL 'delenio' or 'delinio', 'soften', used for 'linio', 'smear': cf. 'orbes panarios adipe linitos' (*conuiuium* 11, l. 31).

28 **sordities:** LL (Forcellini; DuC, VII, p. 530; *GLL*).

34 **non tamen de capite agitur:** 'Sed tamen non agitur de capite' (Erasmus, *Colloquia*, p. 183, l. 1906).

62) Quod difficile et amarum sit a tepefacto surgere lecto

25 **indusio indormiui:** 'Indusium', CL, 'outer tunic'. Here 'shirt'; whether as outer or undergarment is unclear (cf. *DMLBS*,; Dasypodius, 'hembd'; Golius, 199). 'Muta mihi lineum indusium' (Erasmus, *Colloquia*, p. 158, ll. 1070–71). Early modern people habitually slept naked (cf. l. 23): on 13 January 1587 the cold forced Weinsberg to sleep in his shirt for the first time in thirty or forty years (*BW*, V, pp. 282–83).

28 **uermes gigni:** Early modern medicine believed that heating the surface of the body drew the natural heat away from the innards; this meant imperfect digestion, 'et haec potissima causa est vermium' (*De conservanda bona valetudine*, fol. 4^{r}; cf. Durante, *Il tesoro della sanità*, p. 16; Albala, *Eating Right*, p. 61). Cf. note to colloquy 69, l. 17.

63) De profectione in peregrinae urbis gymnasium litterarium

Leaving Cologne for an education at one of the celebrated humanist *gymnasia* of the Lower Rhine or the Netherlands, such as Düsseldorf, Emmerich, 'sHertogenbosch, etc., was a familiar scenario (cf. colloquy 92). See Macardle, *Confabulations*, pp. 37–41.

15 **More andabatarum:** CL 'andabata', a gladiator who fought blindfold. Hence 'more andabatarum', 'blindly', 'indiscriminately' (Hieronymus, *Adversus Heluidium*, 5 (*PL*, 23, 168c); Otto, 105; Dasypodius, 'Andabatarum more, On vnderscheyd, vnfürsichtig'). Erasmus, *Adagia*, 1333, 'Andabatae.'

32 **anchoram soluam:** '[Get ready to] leave' (Otto, 104). Cf. Erasmus, *Adagia*, 24, 'Sacram anchoram soluere'; ibid., 1517, 'Ancoras tollere'. 'Perfauste soluas ancoram; ich wünsch das du mit glück hinfarest' (Heyden, *Formulae*, sig. I2^{r}).

34 **bellos homunculos agemus:** Favourite phrase of Erasmus: 'Bellos homunculos agemus' (*Colloquia*, p. 196, l. 2296; p. 447, ll. 319–20; cf. p. 126, l. 41). Based on Varro, *Saturarum Menippearum fragmenta*, 335.

64) Quando quis satis scientiae habeat, uel sciat

4 **ueterane miles:** 'Veteranus miles immodicis excubiis sese macerauit' (Erasmus, *Colloquia*, p. 206, ll. 2624–25).

10 **prioribus labiis:** Usually 'primoribus labiis': cf. note to p. 42, l. 27.

11 **encomium:** LL (*TLL*, V,2, col. 560, ll. 3–7, examples fifth to sixth century; *LPLR*). 'Haud suaue encomium' (Erasmus, *Colloquia*, p. 155, l. 983).

14 **amusos:** CL 'amusos' (adj., usually Greek declension) means 'ignorant of music' (*TLL*, I, col. 2027, ll. 55–59). The general sense 'ignorant, uncultured' which Schotten obviously intends (cf. colloquy 103, l. 12) is NL: 'Qui ne scait rien, Qui n'est point propre aux lettres' (Estienne, 1561, p. 91); 'Etranger aux Muses, non instruit' (*LPLR*). Cf. 'Crassulis [...] et amusis theologis' (Erasmus, *Epistolae*, 535, ll. 28–29); 'Amusos inter [...] quid agis?' (Euricius Cordus, *Epigrammata*, fol. 273^{r}).

27 **artes [...] manuarias:** ML and NL phrase, more often 'artificia manuaria' (*DMLBS*, 'manuarius'; Dasypodius, 'Artificium manuarium, alias Mechanicum, Ein handtwerck'). 'Manuarium aliquod artificium' (Mosellanus, *Paedologia*, 7, p. 13, ll. 24–25).

31 **Nestoris:** Nestor, the aged king of Pylos who advised the Greeks during the Trojan War (Homer, *Iliad*, 1.247–84; 2.554–55; 11.511–20, 655–803, etc.), an exemplar of longevity, eloquence and wisdom (Otto, 1223, 1224; Erasmus, *Adagia*, 566, 'Nestoris senecta'; 156, 'Nestoris eloquentia').

33–34 **Retulit se [...] discere:** This anecdote is not found in Homer's passages on Nestor, *Iliad* 1, 2 or 11 or *Odyssey* 3 or 10.

35 **Quem Plato litteratum censuit?:** An unidentified reference.

65) De more standi ad cyathos

1 **standi ad cyathos:** See note to colloquy 10, l. 18. Serving drink at table was a standard responsibility of boys in the early modern burgher family: cf. colloquies 10 and 67.

13 **Valerio Maximo** (cf. ll. 10–18): The 'caristia' (22 February), a 'conuiuium sollemne', where family quarrels could be settled in a congenial atmosphere (Valerius Maximus, *Facta et dicta*, 2.1.8).

20 **Facile credidero:** 'Facile credo' (Erasmus, *Colloquia*, p. 185, l. 1980).

32–33 **alteri tradere [...] lampadem:** Otto, 909; cf. Varro, *Res rusticae*, 3.16.9. Erasmus, *Adagia*, 138, 'Cursu lampada trado'. 'Lampadem hanc trado Theophilo' (Erasmus, *Colloquia*, p. 233, l. 77).

66) Quibus utendum uerbis, dum uinum foris emptum mensae affertur

Formulae for 'blessing' wine are found in Hegendorff, *Dialogi*, 7, 'De rerum salutatione' (sig. D4[v]) and Heyden, *Formulae*, XXVII (sig. I1[v]). Schotten also uses them in the *Conuiuia*, passim.

6 **haud difficilis ero:** Cf. 'Quod ni esset, haud me tibi difficilem praeberem' (Erasmus, *Colloquia*, p. 189, l. 2095).

67) De modo sternendi mensam

Setting the table and serving at meals are typically the province of the boys of the late medieval and early modern family: cf. colloquy 10. The rules of the Crailsheim school in 1480 state: 'Decorum enim est in quocumque scolari ut sciat omnia necessaria proponere mense [...] et postea dicere gracias cum devotione.' (Crecelius, 'Crailsheimer Schulordnung', p. 247; cf. p. 259). Several colloquy collections describe a comparable situation, e.g. Erasmus, 'Pietas puerilis': 'Adornata parentibus mensa, recito consecrationem, deinde prandentibus ministro' (*Colloquia*, p. 174, ll. 1613–14). Cf. Heyden, *Formulae*, sig. H2^{r-v}, H2^{v}–3^{r}.

22 **Panis nondum est decorticatus:** 'Decortico': CL, but meaning 'remove bark, rind or hide' (*TLL*, V, 1, col. 213, ll. 54–66; *MLWb*, III, col. 122, ll. 8–35; *DMLBS*; *MLLM*); the sense 'remove the crust' is not recorded. Erasmus thought removing crusts over-refined (*De ciuilitate morum*, *LB*, I, 1038E), but they were often avoided by the better-off, not least because some dietaries saw them as a dangerously drying food (Albala, *Eating Right*, p. 95). Preparing the bread was another task for the boys: 'panes prescidere senioribus' (Crecelius, 'Crailsheimer Schulordnung', pp. 247, 259).

25 **uorans uiam:** 'Si sapiet uiam uorabit' (Catullus, 35.7).

27 **Quadras:** 'quadra': CL, a quadrant section of a round cake or loaf, or a slice of bread; ML and NL, as here, a plate or trencher (*LPLR*; Dasypodius, Serranus, 'Ein viereckiger teller'; Estienne, 'Un trenchoir, ou tailloir, et assiette'). This sense may derive from the use of slices of bread as trenchers: cf. *conuiuium* 11, ll. 31, 42.

28 **Aereas uel ligneas?:** Wooden plates were common well into the seventeenth century (cf. inventory of 1652 in Reichart, *Alltagsleben*, p. 297).

30 **Circinum:** CL 'circinus', 'compasses, dividers', is not recorded as a name for a table implement. However, it is also a synonym for 'circulus' (*TLL*, III, col. 1098, ll. 39–54), which is common ML and NL for a ring to set a dish on: 'Circulus, schüsselring' (Golius, 317). 'Circulus mensarius, Ein disch ring' (Dasypodius; Serranus); 'Apta circulum. stell den schüsselring' (Heyden, *Formulae*, sig. H3^{r}); 'Deinde impono circulum cum salino. Then I set on

the wreath with the salt-seller' (Hoole, *Childrens Talke*, p. 66). Note that Hoole, like Schotten, associates the *circulus* with the salt-cellar. The fact that only one ring is mentioned reflects the early modern practice of guests serving themselves from a single large dish in the middle of the table: cf. the Georg Pencz woodcut 'Ein Tischzucht' (1534) (Geisberg, G. 1011).

33 **poculum adde cereuisiae; 35 Calices uini elue:** Some early modern dietaries warn against combining beer and wine (Menapius, *De ratione victus salubris*, p. 565; Albala, *Eating Right*, p. 111); yet Weinsberg specifically mentions drinking both at his meals (*BW*, II, p. 266; Herborn, 'Straßen wie diese', pp. 23–24).

68) Miserum esse in prandio uenire peracta fabula

5 **Fleres [...] siccis oculis:** Not a CL set phrase. Possibly inspired by 'Pessimi parentium, qui liberos suos sepeliunt flere contenti, ut obiter ab rogo siccis oculis revertantur!' (*Declamationes maiores*, 10.16, second century AD, attrib. to Quintilian). It may reflect vernacular proverbs like 'Wer weinen will, muss zuvor nasse Augen haben' and 'Se wênt dröge as de Swîne' (Wander, V, 121).

28 **'plaudite':** The exhortation to clap at the end of a play: e.g. 'Spectatores, [...] plaudite atque exsurgite' (Plautus, *Truculentus*, 968). Hence figuratively the end of anything: e.g. 'Neque sapientibus usque ad "plaudite" ueniendum est' (Cicero, *De Senectute*, 70). Schotten may have taken this theatrical image, and that of 'peracta fabula' (l. 26; cf. colloquy 26, l. 12) directly from *De Senectute*, where both are used within the space of a few lines.

69) De uuis carpendis

In the 1520s wine was still the dominant alcoholic drink in Cologne, and small vineyards covered much of the outlying suburbs (*Topogr.*, I, p. 114*; *KiM*, p. 124). There are some similarities with Mosellanus, *Paedologia*, 8, 'De vindemia et aucupio' (pp. 14–15); see Macardle, *Confabulations*, pp. 59, 110.

12 **Multi nocte lectum concacant:** Medical theory saw ripe wine-grapes as dangerously laxative because they accelerated the digestion of other food: 'Ventrem laxant

[...] ventositatem, inflationes & ventris dolorem generant [...] alium cibum in corruptionem trahunt' (*De conservanda bona valetudine*, sig. D2[r–v]; cf. Gratarolus, *De conservanda valetudine*, p. 169).

17 **At in nocte primum fit digestio:** Early modern medicine believed that the 'concoction' of food in the stomach, an important part of the process of 'digestio', was most efficient at night, when the body's heat was drawn inwards (Albala, *Eating Right*, p. 61). Cf. note to colloquy 62, l. 28.

27 **Omnium rerum est satietas:** Common proverb: 'Omnium rerum satietas est.' (Walther, 39294; cf. 39279). Used by Hegendorff, *Dialogi*, sig. C8[v]; Camerarius, *Praecepta* (1536), sig. b4[v]; Vives, *Exercitatio*, XXI, p. 201.

35 **Harpocratem:** Harpocrates, Greek form of one manifestation of the Egyptian god Horus, depicted as a youth pressing his finger to his lips as an example of silence and secrecy (Pauly, V, cols 742–43; Pauly[1], VII, col. 2410; VIII, cols 2435–36). Cf. Erasmus, *Adagia*, 3052, 'Reddidit Harpocratem', meaning 'he imposed silence on him', citing Catullus, 74.4 (*LB*, II, 981E). Otto, 791.

70) De cerasis

9 **ligneolo circumligata; 11 Ligneolum [...] continens cerasa:** ML 'ligneolum', 'small piece of wood' (cf. note to colloquy 47, l. 18). Here either a sliver of flexible wood used to tie the bunch of cherries, or erroneously for 'ligamen', 'ligamentum', 'ligatura' or 'ligaculum'.

22 **Metuis ne caelum ruat:** Proverbial for the over-cautious (Terence, *Heautontimorumenos*, 719; Otto, 286); cf. Erasmus, *Adagia*, 464, 'Quid si coelum ruat?'.

31 **par uel impar:** A popular Roman children's game. One player clasped a number of small objects (nuts, beans, etc.) in his hand, then quickly opened and closed the hand, giving a brief glimpse to the other player, who guessed whether they were even or uneven in number: if right he won the objects, if wrong he lost an equal number (Pauly[1], XVIII, cols 1483–84; Vives, *Exercitatio*, VI, p. 19). The game was seen as quintessentially childish: 'Ludere par impar, equitare in arundine longa' (Horace, *Sermones*, 2.3.248).

33 **ut ipsos dem praeceptori:** No known sources record schoolmasters being given cherry-stones, but the stones were used in brewing and their juice or infusion was reputed to break up kidney or bladder stone (*De conservanda bona valetudine*, sig. I4^{r}); so the sale of the stones may have been a perk of some schoolmasters.

71) De fabis, et cur sit prouerbium 'Fabis uirentibus furunt mori'

Beans have long been regarded as causing nightmares and even madness: '[Faba] poterit somnia ferre mala [...] Hanc fuge, si placidae somnia noctis amas' (Eobanus Hessus, *Bonae valetudinis praecepta*, sig. diii^{v}; cf. Gratarolus, *De conseruanda valetudine*, p. 164; Albala, *Eating Right*, pp. 119–20, 137).

1–2 **'Fabis uirentibus furunt mori':** Widespread proverb. 'Cum faba florescit, stultorum copia crescit' (Walther, 4136; cf. 6511, 7176a). 'Die bonen blüst gibt vil gecken' (Fischart, *Binenkorb*, quoted Grimm, 'Bohnenblüst'; cf. Wander, I, 425).

23 **Pythagoras:** Numerous cults, including the Pythagoreans, abstained from beans (Aristotle, *Fragmenta*, 195; Diogenes Laertius, *Lives*, 8.19). The reasons may have included the allegedly befuddling 'vapours', the belief that beans contained the souls of the dead, and the sense that they were sacred (Burkert, *Lore and Science*, pp. 183–85; *The Pythagorean Golden Verses*, ed. by Thom, pp. 218–21). Cf. Erasmus, *Adagia*, 2, viii, 'A fabis abstineto'.

39 **Saepe nauigo Anticyras:** Anticyra was a place of healing using the hellebore which grew there (Pliny, *Naturalis Historia*, 22.133; cf. Otto, 596). Thus 'Nauiget Anticyras' was said of someone mentally unbalanced (Otto, 117; Erasmus, *Adagia*, 752, 'Nauiget Anticyras'; cf. Franck, II, fol. 53^{r}). 'Solis aestus [...] capita Anticyris digna [facit]' (Hegendorff, *Dialogi*, 2, sig. C8^{v}). Dasypodius, 'Antycira' [sic]: 'Nauiget Antyciras, Er ist nit bey sinnen.'

39 **edo nasturtium:** Watercress, a purgative and general panacea (*De conservanda bona valetudine*, fols 90^{r}, 98^{r-v}). 'Ede nasturtium!' was a proverbial exhortation to sleepy or dull people (Otto, 1197; Erasmus, *Adagia*, 754, 'Ede nasturtium'). Schotten's close juxtaposition of 'nauigo

Anticyras' and 'edo nasturtium' probably reflects their proximity in Erasmus's *Adagia*.

72) De missa indies audienda

This colloquy contrasts with Erasmus's 'Pietas puerilis', which rejects the 'superstition' that a day not begun with Mass will be unlucky (*Colloquia*, pp. 171–81, esp. p. 176, ll. 1661–68). See Macardle, *Confabulations*, p. 101.

Schotten uses an interesting mixture of terminology for liturgical times and offices. Some are LL and ML: **1 missa** (Stotz, V, 4.4); cf. 'missam, vt appellant' (Erasmus, *Colloquia*, p. 176, l. 1662); **11–12 praecipuis sanctorum festis et summis**; **18 sacrificio missae**; **19 audis missam**; **21 die festo uel Dominico** (Stotz, V, 4.10). Others are NL, humanist: **10 matutinis sacrificiis** (= Mass; cf. 'matutina sacra', Mosellanus, *Paedologia*, p. 30, l. 26); **16, 17 templum** (see note to colloquy 35, l. 20); **29 aedes sacra**.

6 **Hisce diebus quos sacros habemus:** This colloquy is not clearly located in time; and the time-sequence of those preceding it is not consistent: 69: autumn; 70: summer; 71: early summer.

16 **templum accedo:** Gaspar in Erasmus's 'Pietas puerilis' stops in a church on the way to school every morning, though only to pray, not to hear Mass (*Colloquia*, p. 173, ll. 1561–65).

26–27 **si primum quaesierimus regnum Dei [...]:** 'Quaerite autem primum regnum et iustitiam eius et haec omnia adiicientur uobis' (Vulgate, Matthew 6.33). Perhaps inspired by Erasmus's discussion of this verse in the *Colloquia* (p. 260, ll. 902–04).

73) Quomodo iuuenis in litteris profecturus se gerere debeat

24–25 **'Cum diis manum admoue':** Cf. Erasmus, *Adagia*, 518, 'Cum Minerua manum quoque moue'. 'The adage warns us not to relax our efforts in reliance on divine assistance' (*CWE*, XXXII, p. 15).

28–29 **chartis impallescam:** 'At te nocturnis iuuat impallescere chartis' (Persius, *Satires*, 5.62).

74) Cur scholastici tam desides sint ad laborem

Cf. colloquy 22, and the discussion of the 'scholasticus morbus' in Mosellanus, *Paedologia*, 27, pp. 34–35. See Macardle, *Confabulations*, p. 113.

4 **manibus insinuatis:** Literally with hands inserted in a fold, 'sinus', of one's toga (*TLL*, VII,1, col. 1918, ll. 40–44). A sign of idleness: 'Vacuus et otiosus insinuatis manibus' (Apuleius, *Metamorphoses*, 9.5.5).

23–24 **in die diui Gregorii:** 12 March, the feast of St Gregory, pope, confessor and doctor of the Church, when, in early modern Germany, new boys, sometimes costumed as angels, priests, apostles, etc., were ceremonially led to school and were given fruit, nuts and biscuits (Bebel, *Facetien*, p. 49; Hospinianus, *Festa Christianorum*, fol. 50^{v}; Kaemmel, *Geschichte des deutschen Schulwesens*, pp. 202–03; Falk, 'Die Schul- und Kinderfeste', pp. 237–40). Weinsberg describes the schoolboys of St Jakob and St Georg going round the houses 'versoikende, off auch kinder vurhenden weren, die man uff die scholl wolt doin' (*BW*, I, pp. 37–38). The custom continued into the eighteenth century, particularly in Protestant schools (Schauer, 'Das sogenannte Gregorius-Fest', passim).

35 **Assuefactio:** ML (*MLWb*, I, col. 1086, ll. 63–72; *DMLBS*; *RMLWL*; *LPLR*, 'adsuefactio'). Common in scholastics (e.g. Aquinas, *Super Sententiis*, lib. 3, d. 33, q. 1 a 2 qc. 1 s.c. 2), but also found in NL authors: e.g. 'Assuefactio mutabit, quod naturale esse ducis' (Vives, *Exercitatio*, X, p. 63); 'Tantum valet assuefactio' (Erasmus, *De contemptu mundi*, *ASD*, V–1, p. 63, ll. 657–58); 'Fideli ad omnem uirtutem adsuefactione' (Bucer, *Opera Latina*, XV, p. 239, l. 6).

35–36 **altera ferme natura:** 'Consuetudine quasi alteram quandam naturam effici' (Cicero, *De finibus*, 5.25.74); cf. Erasmus, *Adagia*, 3825, 'Vsus est altera natura.'

75) Quod promissa stultos exhilarant

3 **in portu nauigabo:** Otto, 1455; Erasmus, *Adagia*, 46, 'In portu nauigare'. '"To navigate in harbour", by which we mean that we are now out of danger' (*CWE*, XXXI, p. 97). 'Nunc huius periculo fit: ego in portu nauigo' (Terence, *Andria*, 480).

6 **lupus hians:** Some CL references are to the fish 'lupus', the bass (e.g. Horace, *Sermones*, 2.2.31). However Erasmus, *Adagia*, 1258, 'Lupus hiat', quotes only texts describing the wolf, which was said to pursue its prey with mouth wide open, and to wander on with jaws gaping if it failed to catch it (*LB*, II, 508B). 'Lupus hians' (Erasmus, *Colloquia*, p. 152, l. 876). **deludaris:** Cf. 'Scriba [...] coruum deludet hiantem' (Horace, *Sermones*, 2.5.56).

7 **aurei montes:** Cf. 'Non montis auri pollicens' (Terence, *Phormio*, 68). Erasmus, *Adagia*, 815, 'Aureos montes polliceri'. '"To promise mountains of gold" [...] Make immense promises and offer most extensive expectations' (*CWE*, XXXII, p. 188). 'Anglus [...] promittebat montes aureos Virgini Vualsamgamicae' (Erasmus, *Colloquia*, p. 327, l. 87). Walther, 35038.

19–20 **'Promisisse sat est, praestare opus non est':** This saying seems unattested; indeed what are recorded are phrases asserting the opposite: e.g. 'Quicquid promiseris facito' (*Dicta Septem Sapientum*, p. 2); 'Was du nicht halten willst, sollst du nicht versprechen' (Schmidt-Wiegand, *Deutsche Rechtsregeln*, 'versprechen'; cf. Walther, 39764a8c, 39764a8e, etc.; Wander, IV, 1589–96). Perhaps Schotten is developing a proverb like 'Versprechen ist eins und halten ein anderes' (Wander, IV, 1591; parallels 1592, 1593, 1595).

24–25 **'Bona nomina [...]':** 'Nomen' in the sense of 'debt, loan' (*OLD*, s.v., 22, 23). 'Bona nomina fiunt mala, si numquam interpelles' (Walther, 35226a; Wander, IV, 366); cf. 'Gute Schuld verdirbt, wer's nicht bald erwirbt' (Wander, IV, 366).

76) De omasis deportandis post bouem mactatum

See the notes on colloquy 14, 'Inuitandi alium ad prandium'.

77) De conuiuio opiparo et lauto

A brief foretaste of the thirty 'conuiuia' which Schotten added to the 1526 second edition of the *Confabulationes*, probably imitating the numerous 'conuiuia' in Erasmus's *Colloquia*. The number of borrowings from the 'Conuiuium profanum' in particular is notable: see notes below.

1 **conuiuio opiparo et lauto:** 'Hoc conuiuium opiparum [...] ac lautum iudicarim' (Erasmus, 'Conuiuium profanum', *Colloquia*, p. 208, ll. 2714–15).

13 **Ipse nequeo ferre 14 Insalubre etiam est:** Erasmus's aversion to the fumes and heat of German stoves was well known (e.g. Erasmus, *Epistolae*, 1248, ll. 9–11 and note to l. 10). Schotten's exchange resembles a passage in Erasmus's colloquy 'Diversoria': Bertulphus complains that German innkeepers always overheat their rooms; Gulielmus finds this unhealthy (*Colloquia*, p. 335, l. 82–p. 336, l. 95).

19 **procenium:** Not recorded in CL, LL, ML or NL dictionaries. Used by some humanists: 'Hospes meus subinde procaenium peragere solet' (Hegendorff, *Dialogi*, 4, sig. D2^{v}); 'Ut [...] aptiores simus ad procoenium' (Schoepper, *Ectrachelistis* (1544), sig. F5^{v}). Here clearly '*hors-d'œuvre*, starter', and probably distinct from CL 'antecenium', a meal eaten earlier in the day than the main meal.

23 **Domi meae sum, stabo uel assidebo mensae:** Cf. 'Ego domi sum, vel stans coenabo, si lubeat, vel obambulans' (Erasmus, 'Conuiuium profanum', *Colloquia*, p. 197, l. 2349).

26–30: Saying grace was another duty of the early modern schoolboy (e.g. Crecelius, 'Crailsheimer Schulordnung', p. 247). This grace, the first of several in the *Confabulationes*, resembles one in the 'Convivium profanum' (Erasmus, *Colloquia*, p. 198, ll. 2365–66). But Schotten follows late-medieval models in his 'antiphonal' form and rhyme ('apponetur – sanctificetur', ll. 28–29): cf. *The Babees Book*, ed. by Furnivall, pp. 382–96 (p. 392). Erasmus's graces generally follow patristic models: e.g. 'Convivium profanum' (*Colloquia*, p. 198, ll. 2365–66; cf. *Precationes aliquot [...]*, *LB*, V, 1210B; p. 214, ll. 2916–26); 'Convivium religiosum' (ibid., p. 240, ll. 291–94; p. 261, ll. 935–38).

78) De conuiuio tenui et frugali

11 **gratulor uestro aduentui:** 'Gratulor aduentui tuo' (Erasmus, *Colloquia*, p. 46, ll. 427–28).

26–27 **non uulturis aut lupi stomachum habemus:** Vultur: see note to colloquy 15, l. 14. **lupi:** 'Quorsum tot epulae?

Num me lupum existimas?' (Erasmus, 'Conuiuium profanum', *Colloquia*, p. 197, l. 2323; cf. p. 41, l. 289).

32 **hymnum:** CGk ''ὕμνος', adopted by LL, predominantly in Christian usage (Stotz, IV, 9.16; *TLL*, VI, col. 3143, l. 55–col. 3145, l. 45; *DLFAC*; Blaise, § 11). Schotten's usual term for grace at meals, possibly imitating usage in Erasmus, *Colloquia* (e.g. p. 261, l. 932).

79) De auibus, columbis et piscibus capiendis

13–14 **Per auium [...] studia multa interiisse ingenia:** Cf. 'Per pisces et aues multi periere scholares' (Gartner (1574), p. 180; Wander, I, 1031); 'Fische fangen und Vogelstellen verderben manchen jungen (guten) Gesellen' (Wander, I, 1032; variants 1031, 1032).

27 **non opto Catonis prudentiam:** Not a set phrase, but Cato is an exemplar of *prudentia*, as of most virtues. Cf. note to colloquy 44, l. 12.

80) De balneis ingrediendis

In the early sixteenth century the public began to lose confidence in baths, which had been so popular in Germany in the fifteenth century; the advent of syphilis was a major factor. Cf. Erasmus's 'Diversoria' (1523) (*Colloquia*, p. 336, ll. 100–02). Note how Schotten juxtaposes this colloquy with nos 81–83, on plague, war and famine. See Macardle, *Confabulations*, p. 74.

8 **ut Sirenes fugio:** Not a set phrase; but Sirens are a byword for danger particularly common in the Renaissance (Vredeveld, '"Deaf as Ulysses to the Siren's Song"', passim). Cf. Homer, *Odyssey*, 12.167; Otto, 1657; Erasmus, *Adagia*, 3207, 'Ceram auribus obdis'; Erasmus, *Colloquia*, p. 180, ll. 1800–01.

10 **Scabie infectus sum:** 'Scabies Gallica' is the commonest name for syphilis (*LPLR*, 'scabies'). 'Abominanda lepra quam [...] scabiem gallicam vocant' (Erasmus, *De pueris instituendis*, *ASD*, I–2, p. 34, l. 19; cf. p. 54, l. 19). Here, however, 'scabies' presumably means a simple skin disease.

21 **sententia Terentii:** This quotation is not found in Terence.

36 **Pegaseo gradu:** 'Actas Pegaseo corripiet gradu' (Seneca, *Troades*, 385). Otto, 1374; cf. Erasmus, *Adagia*, 3146, 'Pegaso uelocior'.

81) De pestis saeuitia

Colloquies 81, 82 and 83 deal with plague, war and famine, the conventional Unholy Trinity of ills of late-medieval and early modern society. Though Cologne, like most European cities, was visited by the plague on numerous occasions in Schotten's time, this colloquy does not appear to describe an actual outbreak in Cologne; it may be inspired by the discussion of the plague in Leipzig in Hegendorff, *Dialogi*, 2, sig. C8^{r}. See Macardle, *Confabulations*, pp. 60–62.

4 **Patriam iam fugio:** The only effective prophylactic was to leave the area of the epidemic (Isenmann, p. 34). Cf. 'Fleuch pald, fleuch verr, kum wider spôt: | Das sind drey kreuter in der nôt | für all apptecken und doctor.' (Hans Volz, quoted in Keil, 'Seuchenzüge', p. 115).

4 **ut aues Auernum:** Lake Avernus near Puteoli was thought to be the entrance to the underworld. Legend said that its fatal sulphurous exhalations prevented birds from flying over it (Lucretius, *De rerum natura*, 6.744; Isidore, *Etymologiae*, 13.19.8; Pauly^{1}, II, col. 2286).

14 **Menalca:** Vocative of Menalcas, a shepherd in Vergil, *Eclogues*, 2, 5, 7 and 10.

22 **genu cruri propius est:** Used by Schotten, *Colloquia moralia*, sig. p7^{r}. Otto, 1324. Cf. Erasmus, *Adagia*, 290, 'Genu sura propius'; 'The knee is closer than the calf' (*CWE*, XXXI, p. 309).

27 **ordinis Sancti Alexii:** The Alexian order, which made the nursing of plague victims a speciality. In Cologne they had a general responsibility for funerals: see Macardle, *Confabulations*, pp. 61–62.

30 **Mulieribus adsunt moniales:** 'Monialis', LL (*TLL*, VIII, col. 1416, l. 70; DuC, V, p. 506; *MLLM*; *LLMA*; *DMLBS*, s.v., 1b–4; *LPLR*). Originally a shortened form of LL 'sanctimonialis' (Stotz, VI, 168.4; DuC, VII, pp. 298–99; *DLFAC*; Blaise, § 375; Forcellini, s.v., 3; *MLLM*; *RMLWL*). In Cologne, Beguines were particularly associated with tending the dying, including plague victims: see Macardle, *Confabulations*, p. 62.

37–38 **tot sepelire eodem tempore:** Certain churches (e.g. St Alban and St Kolumba) had supplementary graveyards for times of plague and other epidemics (*Topogr.*, I, p. 146*).

49 **Vergilius:** 'O terque quaterque beati, | quis ante ora patrum Troiae sub moenibus altis | contigit oppetere!' (Vergil, *Aeneid*, 1.94–96).

51 **ex oraculo Apollinis:** Otto, 130. 'Haec ex oraculo Apollinis [...] puta' (Cicero, *Brutus*, 1.2.6).

82) De bellorum incommodo

This colloquy is probably based on literary models such as Erasmus's lament over the war between Francis I and Charles V (1521–1525), and his deploration of machines of war, esp. cannon (*De conscribendis epistolis*, *ASD*, I–2, p. 207, l. 7–p. 208, l. 1; p. 419, ll. 16–17; *CWE*, XXV, pp. 10–11, 138).

21 **Aiunt in Germania:** From the fifteenth century on the invention of gunpowder and the cannon was regularly attributed to a German monk, 'Master Berthold Schwarz', possibly a Konstanz cleric active in the 1330s (*NDB*, II, p. 162). Conrad Celtis, *Odes*, 3.8, 'Exsecrat Germanum inuentorem Bombardae'.

83) De annonae caritate

Sixteenth-century climate change caused a disastrous harvest and steeply rising grain prices in 1523 in many areas of Germany, including Cologne: see the detailed discussion in Macardle, *Confabulations*, pp. 83–85.

3 **Quid sibi uult macies ista tua?:** Cf. 'Quid sibi vult hic pallor? quid macies?' (Erasmus, *Colloquia*, p. 136, l. 368).

9 **Libris incumbenti non conuenit saturitas:** Cf. note to colloquy 43, l. 28.

20 **aureo nummo:** 'Aureus nummus', the Cologne Gulden or Goldgulden: see Macardle, *Confabulations*, pp. 56–57.

28 **Per filium cuiusdam senatoris:** A reminder of the far-flung contacts of Cologne merchants.

84) Quam delicate in oppidis, et quam misere ac tenuiter victitent in agris

12 **pulmentis hordaceis:** 'Pulmentum', in CL any savoury dish; the sense 'porridge, pottage' intended here is LL and ML (DuC, VI, pp. 563–64; *RMLWL*, 'pulmentum', 'pulmentarium'; *LLMA*, 'pulmentum', 2; 'pulmentarium', 1). 'Coxit autem Iacob pulmentum' (Vulgate, Genesis

25.29); 'avenario pulmentario nutritum' (Bebel, *Facetien*, p. 40).

18 **Vestes [...] oppignorant:** In *conuiuium* 23, ll. 91–94, drinkers with no money leave the innkeeper their clothes as a pledge.

24 **uorsuram soluunt:** CL, literally 'pay one creditor with money borrowed from another'; often used figuratively for 'exchange one difficulty for another' (Erasmus, *Adagia*, 923, 'Vorsuram soluere', quoting Terence, *Phormio*, 780; cf. Estienne, 1561, p. 1371).

34 **super choenice non sedent:** The sense intended here, 'they don't worry about where where the next meal will come from', may derive from a mistaken reading of Erasmus, *Adagia*, 2, iii, 'Choenici ne insideas': see Macardle, *Confabulations*, pp. 99–100.

85) Facile emergi eos, qui opulenti sunt

1 **emergi:** The standard infinitive is 'emergere' (as in. l. 9); here Schotten probably imitates Terence's 'middle passive' use: 'unde emergi non potest' (*Adelphoe*, 302; cf. *TLL*, V,2 , col. 473, ll. 28–39).

12 **Iacent et pessundantur ubique:** 'Dat census honores, | census amicitias; pauper ubique iacet' (Ovid, *Fasti*, 1.217–18).

18–19 **Eruditorum turbam [...] fuere:** Perhaps reflects Mosellanus's 'Constat multos humili natos loco [...] ad eruditionis fastigium ascendisse' (*Paedologia*, 7, p. 13, ll. 14–16). Detailed studies, however, prove that poor students were in fact considerably disadvantaged in the late-medieval university; those who managed to take higher degrees were often marginalized in their subsequent careers (Schwinges, *Deutsche Universitätsbesucher*, pp. 441–65, esp. p. 446).

23 **Phoenice rariorem:** Erasmus, *Adagia*, 1610, 'Phoenice rarior'; Walther, 35235; cf. Otto, 1408.

29 **ruditatem:** 'Ruditas', late CL or LL (Forcellini; *RMLWL*). The more precise sense 'ignorance' is LL and ML (Forcellini; DuC; *LLMA*, s.v., 1).

86) De nuptiis

This colloquy reflects many details of wedding receptions in Cologne. See Macardle, *Confabulations*, pp. 66–67.

3 **indulgebo genio:** Favourite phrase of Erasmus: e.g. *Adagia*, 1374. 'Exporrigemus frontem [...] Indulgebimus genio' (*Colloquia*, p. 45, ll. 407–08; cf. p. 196, ll. 2296–97). The opposite of 'suum defraudare genium': cf. note to colloquy 43, l. 33.

13 **sum exploratus:** Deponent forms of 'exploro' are unrecorded in CL, LL, ML and NL (cf. *TLL*, V,2 , col. 1744, l. 43–col. 1750, l. 17).

15 **duo millia aureorum; 18 Quantum ipsa afferet?; 20 Duces tu sponsam?; 26 A prandio habebitisne choreas?; 27 Saliemus mire ad tybiam et tympanum:** all standard details of Cologne weddings: see Macardle, *Confabulations*, pp. 66–67.

29–32 **quippiam lauti e sponsa:** The slightly risqué joke is probably a nod to the sexual innuendo associated with marriage festivities; cf. the fifteenth-century 'Laienregel' of Dietrich Engelhus (*Quellen und Forschungen*, ed. by Langenberg p. 102).

33 **Nasum tuum nosco:** 'Age, noui nasum tuum' (Erasmus, *Colloquia*, p. 153, l. 918).

87) De uino dando in illius Sancti die, cuius nos nomen gerimus

20 **tingere te uino:** Cf. 'Egone te meis immunem tingam poculis?' (Erasmus, *Colloquia*, p. 210, ll. 2772–73, based on Horace, *Carmina*, 4.12.22–23).

33 **ethnicorum:** 'Ethnicus' (adj. and noun), 'gentile, pagan', is Christian LL (Stotz, V, 3.10; *TLL*, V,2 , col. 923, l. 53–col. 924, l. 23; *DLFAC*; Dasypodius). 'Exemplum [...] philosophorum ethnicorum' (Erasmus, *Colloquia*, p. 316, ll. 57–58; cf. p. 396, l. 253); 'Ex ethnicorum saturnalibus' (Mosellanus, *Paedologia*, p. 32, ll. 13–14; cf. p. 39, l. 2, etc.).

88) De primo sacerdotis sacrificio

6 **annum uigesimum quartum:** Twenty-four is the modern canonical age for priestly ordination; sixteenth-century norms were less precise (*KL*, X, col. 351).

9 **Addisce [...] spargere nuces:** This conflates two ideas: (a) Walnuts were children's playthings, and 'nuces relinquere' means 'put away childish things' (e.g. Persius, *Satires*, 1.10). (b) At the Roman wedding

ceremony the bridegroom scattered walnuts. Primarily a fertility ritual, this may have had overtones of relinquishing childhood: 'Sparge, marite, nuces' (Vergil, *Eclogues*, ed. by Coleman, note to 8.30). At any rate, this meaning was supposed by numerous Renaissance commentators, including Erasmus, *Adagia*, 435, 'Nuces relinquere': 'Sponsus [...] nuces spargebat utpote iam pueritiae renuncans (*ASD*, II–1, p. 508, l. 780). Schotten presumably follows Erasmus in using 'nuces spargere' as a synonym of 'nuces relinquere'.

89) De exequiis defunctorum peragendis

This colloquy and the next describe funeral customs peculiar to Cologne, and criticize the venality of priests, showing attitudes widespread in the city in the early sixteenth century. See Macardle, *Confabulations*, pp. 70–74.

12–13 **Oblatam pecuniam; 20 Tres, in tribus altaribus; 24 Conducimus [candelas]:** See Macardle, *Confabulations*, pp. 70–74.

22 **sacellanis:** 'Sacellanus', 'chaplain, curate', ML (*RMLWL*; *LPLR*, citing Bucer, Erasmus and Beatus Rhenanus).

90) De sepultura

3 **Candelae per fenestras extensae:** A usage long prescribed in Cologne. See Macardle, *Confabulations*, p. 71.

22 **Terra coemiterii emenda est:** 'Coemeterium' is Christian LL (*TLL*, III, col. 1411, ll. 23–57; *DLFAC*; Blaise, p. 35; Dasypodius). Schotten's spelling 'cimiterium' is typically ML (Stotz, VII, 73.2). On the selling of cemetery space see Macardle, *Confabulations*, pp. 73–74.

24 **aedituo:** CL 'aedituus', 'one in charge of a temple', in LL applied to keepers of Christian churches (*TLL*, I, col. 934, ll. 64–74; *DLFAC*, s.v., 2;). ML and NL, 'verger, sexton, parish clerk' (*MLWb*, I, col. 290, ll. 33–56; *LLMA*; *DMLBS*, s.v., b, c; *LPLR*; Dasypodius). More acceptable to humanists than the ML terms 'campanator', 'ianitor', etc. 'Aedituus [...] respondet sacrifico' (Erasmus, *De conscribendis epistolis*, *ASD*, I–2, p. 269, ll. 6–7).

30 **'Domini est terra [...]':** 'Domini est terra et plenitudo eius; orbis terrarum et uniuersi qui habitant in eo' (Vulgate, Psalm 23.1).

36 **plebani:** 'Plebanus', 'parish priest', ML (Stotz, V, 4.8; DuC, VI, p. 364; *LLMA*, s.v., II, 1; *MLLM*; *RMLWL*; *LPLR*). Cf. ML 'plebeianus' (*LLMA*, *LPLR*).

91) De Anno Iubilaeo

1 **Anno Iubilaeo:** 'Iubilaeus', LL (Stotz, IV, 35.8; *TLL*, VII,2, col. 574, l. 28–col. 575, l. 24; *DLFAC*; *DMLBS*). The custom of the 'annus Iubilaeus', the Holy Year, with a plenary indulgence conditional on pilgrimage to Rome, began in 1300; from 1475 it was held every twenty-five years (*LThK*, IV, col. 1325; *NCE*, VII, pp. 56–57; *KL*, VI, cols 1906–11). The boys are clearly discussing the coming Holy Year of 1525, held under Pope Clement VII, beginning at Christmas 1524. 1500 was probably the apogee of the Holy Year, with 1525 already showing signs of a waning popularity as spiritual life became more internalized and criticism of pilgrimage intensified (*KL*, VI, col. 1909; Champ, *The English Pilgrimage to Rome*, pp. 51–55). Well known is Erasmus's critique of pilgrimage; e.g. *Moriae Encomium* (*ASD*, IV–3, pp. 136–38) and 'De votis temere susceptis' and 'Peregrinatio religionis ergo' (*Colloquia*, pp. 147–50; 470–94).

7 **sacerdotium:** CL, 'priesthood', 'office or dignity of a priest'. The sense 'benefice', as here, is ML (DuC, s.v., 1; *LLMA*, s.v., 2; *LPLR*; cf. *MLLM*, s.v., 8). It is frequent in Erasmus (*Epistolae*, II, no. 413, l. 24; and cf. note to colloquy 111, l. 7).

14 **in litteris Pontificis Romani:** Holy Years are announced by papal bulls (e.g. *CIC*, Extravagantes communium, lib. V, 'De poenitentiis et remissionibus', cap. IV, cols 355–57, for 1475). (*LThK*, IV, col. 1325; *NCE*, VII, pp. 56–57; *KL*, VI, col. 1910).

16–17 **Cuilibet uere paenitenti et Romam hoc anno accedenti:** Reflects the language of the papal bulls: cf. 'Omnibus [...] ad basilicas ipsas accedentibus reuerenter uere poenitentibus' (*CIC*, Extravagantes communium, lib. V, 'De poenitentiis et remissionibus', cap. I, III, col. 344, ll. 45–54).

17 **condonari scelera et poenam:** Pilgrims to Rome enjoyed a plenary indulgence: remission also of the 'poena' or temporal punishment for sins confessed (*CIC*, Extravagantes communium, lib. V, 'De poenitentiis et

remissionibus', cap. I, III, col. 344, ll. 40–56; col. 349, ll. 8–12; also ibid., cap. IV, III, col. 356, ll. 34–37).

18 **et his in terris:** Though this is not Alexius's point, Cologne had since 1394 had its own internal 'pilgrimage', the *Römerfahrt*, an indulgenced visit to nine major churches, on the model of the Roman basilicas (Gelenius, pp. 94–97; *REK*, X, p. 642).

25–26 **Audiui exortum [...] a ueteribus Iudaeis:** In pre-Exilic Judaism every fiftieth year was a Jubilee Year, when debts were pardoned and slaves freed (Leviticus 25.25–54; *CIC*, Extravagantes communium, lib. V, 'De poenitentiis et remissionibus', cap. I, gloss: III, col. 346, ll. 57–61; *NCE*, VII, pp. 56–57).

92) De tempore quo librorum lectiones auspicantur

4–5 **cor [...] est comedendum:** Erasmus, *Adagia*, 2, vii, 'Cor ne edito', one of the 'Pythagorica symbola': 'Hoc est, ne curis tuum ipsius animum excrucies' (*ASD*, II–1, p. 96, ll. 898–99). Cf. Plutarch, *Moralia*, 12E; Diogenes Laertius, *Lives*, 8.17; Apostolios, *Proverbia*, 12.86). 'Er frißt oder nagt sein Hertz ab' (Franck, II, fol. 86^{r}).

28 **Haec [...] meminisse**: Cf. note to colloquy 29, ll. 34–35.

93) De tempore quo lectionibus librorum colophon imponitur

2 **colophon:** CL, an end or finish. The erroneous derivation from the navy and cavalry of the city of Colophon, who could put a decisive end to any battle (Strabo, *Geography*, 14.1.28), is repeated by Erasmus, *Adagia*, 1245, 'Colophonem addidit' (*LB*, II, 498F–499D (498F); cf. Dasypodius, 'Colophon'). Otto, 410.

4 **In articulis [...] computas:** 'Articulus', 'joint', may be synonymous with 'digitus', 'finger' as frequently in CL (*TLL*, II, col. 693, ll. 23–77); but people also counted using the individual joints. At Worms, Luther counted off thirteen points made by an opponent: 'in articulos digitorum numeravi' (*WATr*, V, no. 5342a, p. 67, l. 1).

9 **Ad umbilicum [...] ducentur:** CL 'umbilicus', in the sense of the ornamented end of the cylinder on which a papyrus roll was wound (*OLD*, s.v., 2e); hence 'librum ad umbilicum reuoluere' (Seneca, *Suasoriae*, 6.27; Otto,

1816). Figuratively, to draw anything to a close: Erasmus, *Adagia*, 132, 'Ad umbilicum ducere'.

31 **allisionem:** LL (*TLL*, I, col. 1697, ll. 5–12; *MLWb*, I, col. 480, ll. 24–36; *DMLBS*). 'Sed inter haec [...] frequentes incursiones, lapsus, allisiones' (Camerarius, *Praecepta*, sig. d6^{r}).

94) De ebrietate uitanda

19 **uerbum [...] Thaletis:** Thales, Greek philosopher, early sixth century BC (Pauly, XII/1, cols 236–38). The source is actually Apuleius, *Florida*, 20, where it is attributed to an unnamed sage.

29–30 **scelestos non audere potu madere:** The source of this saying has not been found.

95) De cereis gerendis in festo Purificationis Mariae

The pious practice of buying expensive wax candles for the feast of the Purification of the Blessed Virgin ('Candlemas', 2 February) was an obvious target for reformers (e.g. Luther, *Vermahnung an die Geistlichen*, *WA*, XXX,2, p. 253; Hospinianus, *Festa Christianorum*, fols 41^{r}–43^{r}) and for humanists (Mosellanus, *Paedologia*, 26, 'De cereis in feriis beatae virginis gestandis', which clearly inspired Schotten's colloquy). See Macardle, *Confabulations*, pp. 101–03.

12–13 **Adulterorum [...] lapidibus additis:** Carrying candles and stones hung on chains was originally an ecclesiastical, later a civil punishment for adulterers and other notorious sinners (*HRG*, II, cols 703–06 (705); IV, col. 1950–51). The punishment was frequent in Cologne in the 1520s (*BRStK*, e.g. III, p. 142, no. 666; p. 211, no. 281; p. 213, nos 291, 294). One Cologne *Turmbuch* contains a picture of candles and stones on chains (HAStK, 30 (V+V), G 213, fol. 180^{r}, repr. in Irsigler and Lassotta, *Bettler und Gaukler*, ill. 67, p. 280).

15 **Vnius talenti:** The CL 'talentum' was about 26 kg (*OLD*, s.v., 1); the sense 'pound', intended here, is ML (DuC, VIII, p. 16, s.v., 1; *MLLM*, s.v., 1; *LLMA*, s.v., 1; Dasypodius).

16 **Sufficeret semilibrae:** The standard weight for congregational candles: 'Faculae mediae librae [...] pro populo' (Hospinianus, *Festa Christianorum*, 41^{r}).

22–23 Plus placet [...] quam celebris pompa: Cf. 'Sacrificium Deo spiritus contribulatus; cor contritum et humiliatum Deus non despicies' (Vulgate, Psalm 50.17).

27–28 prouerbium est, 'Pauperes et uilia offerunt': No source of such a saying has been identified.

31 consuetudini non satages: CL 'satagere' means 'busy oneself', etc. The sense 'try, endeavour' is ML (*MLLM*; *RMLWL*). Schotten's intended sense, 'satisfy' (cf. colloquy 103, l. 14), is given in *DEL*, but no examples are known.

33 Platonis [...] uerbum: Actually the first aphorism of the 'Seven Sages of Greece': 'Omnibus placeto', attributed to Periander of Corinth (*Dicta Septem Sapientum*, p. 2).

35 Diui Pauli uerbum: 'Modo enim hominibus suadeo aut Deo aut quaero hominibus placere, si adhuc hominibus placerem, Christi servus non essem' (Vulgate, Galatians 1.10).

96) De sertis in die celebri ferendis

The colloquy looks to be based on Mosellanus, *Paedologia*, 33, 'De coronis gestandis', pp. 40–41, which describes the custom of wearing crowns of roses or other flowers, though not on any particular occasion. Wreaths were regularly worn on special occasions in medieval and early modern times, even by men (Grimm, 'Kranz', 4a, b). Kilianus's name-day would be 8 July.

24 in foro mercabor; 25 Solido; 26 Tribus nummis: Mosellanus also mentions the cheapness of crowns, or the flowers to make them (*Paedologia*, p. 40, ll. 18–19).

97) De conuiuio inter cereuisiae baratra celebrando

See the discussion of this colloquy in Macardle, *Confabulations*, pp. 58–59.

1 cereuisiae baratr[um]: Here someone who gulps down large quantities of beer: CL 'barat(h)rum', 'pit, gaping abyss', sometimes jokingly for 'stomach' (e.g. Plautus, *Curculio*, 121). Cf. 'Sit saluti tibi poculorum baratro' (*conuiuium* 30, l. 33). There may be confusion with CL 'balatro', 'buffoon', in ML and NL often written 'baratro' (*TLL*, II, col. 1691, ll. 54–75); 'Baratro, Ein fraß verschlemmer' (Dasypodius).

8 **instar testudinis:** Cf. 'Testudinem, ubi collecta in suum tegumen est, tutam ad omnes ictus uideo esse' (Livy, *Ab urbe condita*, 36.32, quoted by Erasmus, *Adagia*, 2238, 'Domus amica, domus optima', *LB*, II, 791D).

12 **Licuit mihi nunquam per occupationes:** 'Non licuit per occupationes' (Erasmus, *Colloquia*, p. 36, l. 131; p. 144, l. 623).

32 **Platea [...] Ouium:** The Schaafenstraße in Cologne: see note to colloquy 26, l. 30.

98) De conuiuio uicissitudinario, quod sacerdotes inter se agunt

Meals of the kind described here were organized by individual parishes, such as St Jakob (*BW*, IV, p. 75; V, pp. 90, 94, 395) and by the 'Fraternitas Pastorum Coloniensium', the association of the city's nineteen parish priests (Dorn, 'Der Ursprung der Pfarreien', pp. 144–50; Macardle, *Confabulations*, pp. 68, 72).

1 **vicissitudinario:** 'Vicissitudinarius', adj., ML, 'happening by turns' (DuC, VIII, p. 321). Cf. *MLLM*; *LLMA*, 'vicissitudo', 1, 'le fait de rendre à son tour'; *LLMA*, 'vicissitudinalis', 'qui arrive à tour de rôle').

9–10 **quod a serto capitis uocitant:** German 'Kränzlein' or 'Kränzchen' (diminutive of 'Kranz', 'wreath'), frequently used for such communal meals: the guest who received the wreath had to host the next meal (Grimm, 'Kränzlein', 4; 'Kränzchen', 3a, c; *BW*, V, p. 82; II, pp. 221, 222;). Weinsberg records numerous 'Kränzchen' (e.g. *BW*, I, pp. 348, 356; II, pp. 21, 90, 221–24; V, pp. 82), esp. those of the churchwardens of St Jakob (*BW*, IV, p. 75; V, pp. 90, 94, 395).

21 **decem aureos nummos:** This figure, almost two months' earnings for many skilled workers in the 1520s (Lassotta, *Formen der Armut*, I, p. 415), seems high. But it is probably realistic: an elaborate 'banneressen' for twenty-one guests in 1571 cost Weinsberg 64 Gulden, about 22 Gulden at 1520s prices (*BW*, V, p. 223; Macardle, *Confa-ulations*, p. 68).

25 **basilice:** Cf. 'Valeo [...] basilice' (Erasmus, *Colloquia*, p. 132, l. 214). 'Graeci βασιλικῶς pro magnifice [...] dicunt' (Erasmus, *Adagia*, 1786, *LB*, II, 660B). A largely Plautine word (*Persa*, 29, 462, 806).

28–29 **Vinum hornum et bimum:** Corresponding to the German 'newer und firner wein', frequently used by Weinsberg (e.g. *BW*, V, pp. 120, 241, etc.)

99) Cur conuiuium istud instituerunt sacerdotes uel alii

4 **'Nihil sine causa':** Common proverb, probably based on 'Nihil in terra sine causa fit' (Vulgate, Job 5.6). 'Nicht on ursach' (Franck, I, fol. 145^{r}).

23 **Horatius; 24 Horatii uerbum:** Actually Ovid, *Epistulae ex Ponto*, 2.3.8.

100) Exemplo sacerdotum etiam conuiuiorum ineunt circulum Gerardus et Henricus

3–4 **Seniorum uita [...] est iuniorum instructio:** Not recorded as a Latin proverb; perhaps translates vernacular proverbs such as 'Wie die Alten sungen, so lernten es die Jungen' (Petri, *Der Teutschen Weissheit*, II, p. 788); 'Was die alten thun, das lernen die jungen' (Luther, *WA*, LI, p. 649, no. 106).

101) De moribus mensae

3 **'Iuuenem nihil tam exornat quam ingenui mores':** Cf. 'Puerum ingenuum decent ingenui mores' (Erasmus, *Colloquia*, p. 161, l. 1170).

5 **E tripode locutus:** The Pythian priestess at Delphi sat on a three-legged stool to pronounce oracles of Apollo; hence what is spoken 'ex tripode' is reliable, definitive: Erasmus, *Adagia*, 690, 'Ex tripode', citing Apostolios, *Proverbia*, 17.86, 'Τάδ' 'εκ τρίποδος'; Otto, 130).

10 **sine moribus probis scientia nihil habet laudis:** A scholastic principle also dear to Erasmian Christian humanists: Rabelais's famous 'Science sans conscience n'est que ruine de l'âme' repeats a motif of the school of St Bernard (Rabelais, *Œuvres*, I, p. 262 and n. 1).

20–21 **ad mensam uerecundari decere neminem:** 'Verecundari neminem apud mensam decet, | nam ibi de divinis atque humanis cernitur' (Plautus, *Trinummus*, 478–79). Erasmus, *Adagia*, 4007, 'Apud mensam uerecundari neminem decet', notes the irony that the line is spoken by the gluttonous slave Stasimus; the table does in fact demand 'uerecundia', restrained and decent behaviour (*LB*, II, 1183B).

24 **Neminem a cibis debere abstinere:** Erasmus encourages boys to pass on a portion of particularly choice food served to them to another guest (*Colloquia*, p. 162, ll. 1206–08). But he disapproves of the exaggerated politeness of guests who will not serve themselves, and even put back what they are given (*Adagia*, 4007, *LB*, II, 1183B). Camerarius similarly criticizes German women and children who give choice food which they have been served to others (*Praecepta*, sig. b1^{r-v}).

30–31 **si uel indecore biberis, comederis, uel cibum attigeris:** Examples of such gaffes in Reimerus Allemannicus, *Phagifacetus*, transl. by Sebastian Brant: gulping drink down, or not wiping the mouth before drinking; eating everything on one's plate; eating straight from the serving dish, or keeping one's hands in the dish too long (Umbach, pp. 59–60, 69, 47 (sigs. c4^{v}–c5^{r}, b5^{r-v}, a6^{v})). A similar list in Erasmus, *De civilitate morum puerilium* (LB, II, 1038B–41C, esp. 1038E–40D).

102) De feriis diui Blasii

St Blasius's Day (3 February) was an important Cologne holiday, with a children's 'Heischegang': see detailed treatment in Macardle, *Confabulations*, pp. 65–66.

3 **cuspidem illam:** A pointed stick, presumably to spear the gifts of bread and pork on: see Macardle, *Confabulations*, p. 66.

22–25 **Blasii simulachrum [...] habens caput porcinum baculo infixum:** The pig, or pig's head, is frequent in the iconography of St Blasius; it derives from his legend; (*LCI*, V, cols 416–19; Macardle, *Confabulations*, p. 66).

103) De eloquentia et barbarie

9 **inter coruum et cygnum:** Cf. 'Tam subito coruus, qui modo cygnus eras' (Martial, *Epigrams*, 3.43.2, referring to an old man dyeing his hair). Cf. notes to colloquy 113, ll. 16–17, 23–24.

21–22 **in aliqua coquorum officina effictum:** Humanists commonly dub barbaric or medieval Latin 'kitchen' Latin: e.g. 'Culinaria est elegantia' (Erasmus, *Colloquia*, p. 33, l. 70); 'Oratio [...] culinaria' (ibid., p. 36, ll. 139–40).

24 **mihi cerebrum excutis:** 'Mihi misero cerebrum excutiunt | tua dicta' (Plautus, *Aulularia*, 151–52).

29 **compositionem:** 'Compositio' is the harmonious arrangement of words in prose (Quintilian, *Institutio oratoria*, 9.4.116; cf. Erasmus, *De conscribendis epistolis*, *ASD*, I–2, p. 222, ll. 1–10).

104) An omne perdatur tempus quod studio non impartitur, ut dixit Plinius

1–2 **An [...] impartitur:** 'Nam perire omne tempus arbitrabatur, quod studiis non impenderetur' (Pliny the Younger, *Epistulae*, 3.5.16). Schotten probably quotes not directly from Pliny but from Erasmus, *De ratione studii*: 'Plinianum illud semper animo insideat tuo: Omne perire tempus, quod studio non impertias' (*ASD*, I–3, p. 70, ll. 58–59). Schotten's 'impartitur' reflects Erasmus's 'impertias', not Pliny's 'impenderetur'. The sentiment is described as **Plinii iunioris uerbum** (l. 8), whereas Pliny the Younger is reporting the view of his uncle Pliny the Elder; similar confusion in **Plinius Secundus in epistolis dicit de Plinio Iuniori** (ll. 27–28).

28 **tempus balneo:** 'In secessu solum balinei tempus studiis eximebatur' (Pliny the Younger, *Epistulae*, 3.5.14).

30 **etsi libros non tractabat:** Pliny the Elder in fact dictated and was read to whilst being rubbed down and dried, stopping only when actually in the water (Pliny the Younger, *Epistulae*, 3.5.14).

105) Cum aetate esse sapiendum

9 **dulce esse [...] desipere in loco:** 'Dulce est desipere in loco' (Horace, *Carmina*, 4.12.28, quoted by Erasmus, *Moriae Encomium*, *ASD*, IV–3, p. 178, l. 897).

17 **Primum est posse tacere:** Cf. 'Virtutem primam esse puto compescere linguam. | Proximus ille deo est, qui scit ratione tacere' (*Disticha Catonis*, I, 3); 'Audito multa, loquere pauca' (*Dicta Septem Sapientum*, p. 3).

31 **Nescis Amyclas tacendo periisse?:** The story went that a law in Amyklai strictly forbade spreading rumours of siege: when the Spartans did attack, the inhabitants dared not mention the fact, and the town was quickly taken (Servius, commentary on Vergil, *Aeneid*, 10.564; cf. Erasmus, *Adagia*, 801, 'Amyclas perdidit silentium'). The story was probably invented to explain the proverbial phrase 'tacitae Amyclae', which, however,

refers to Amunclae in Campania (Vergil, *Aeneid*, 10.564; cf. Otto, 103; Pauly[1], I, cols 1996–97).

36 **praeceptum Periandri Corinthii:** 'Meditatio totum est' (Walther, 38168, attributed to Periander).

106) De nouis indumentis

4 **Mutaberis in aliud animal?:** 'Quum [...] velut in aliud animal transformareris' (Erasmus, *Colloquia*, p. 386, ll. 397–98).

19 **omni conatu:** Cf. Erasmus, *Adagia*, 2729, 'Omni conatu invadere'.

29 **Horatii [...] sententia:** 'Ut pueris olim dant crustula blandi | doctores, elementa uelint ut discere prima' (Horace, *Sermones*, 1.1.25–26).

107) Tractare dicunt fabrilia fabros Eberhardus et Fabritius

1 **Tractare [...] fabrilia fabros:** 'Quod medicorum est | Promittunt medici; tractant fabrilia fabri' (Horace, *Epistulae*, 2.1.115–16). 'Fabri fabrilia tractant' (Walther, 36798; cf. 39764a9a); 'Tractent fabrilia fabri' (Erasmus, *Colloquia*, p. 520, ll. 916–17).

27 **praesentionarios:** 'Praesentionarius' is not recorded in CL, LL, ML or NL dictionaries or authors; clearly formed from ML 'praesentia', a payment to clergy present at a service (DuC, VI, pp. 468–69; *LLMA*, 'praesentia', 3). Cf. Grimm, 'Präsenzer', 'qui sacris adsistentes honorariis nummis donat.'

108) Ad mensam laeta et non tristia debere esse colloquia

9 **scomma:** LL, from CGk 'σκῶμμα', joke or jibe, often improper (Forcellini; *NLW*). 'Non me fallit tuum scomma' (Erasmus, *Colloquia*, p. 143, ll. 609–10; cf. p. 196, l. 2294; p. 49, l. 528).

19 **Tenebimus ora intenti omnes:** 'Conticuere omnes, intentique ora tenebant' (Vergil, *Aeneid*, 2.1).

20–21 **ad mensam sedendo iuuenescere homines:** The source is not found; it may be a variant of the sentiment that wine is rejuvenating (see note to l. 30).

29 **et Phyllida solus habebis:** 'Dic, quibus in terris inscripti nomina regum | Nascantur flores, et Phyllida solus habeto' (Vergil, *Eclogues*, 3.106–07); cf. note to colloquy 48, l. 25.

30 **Sententia Horatii:** Cf. '[Vinum] quod me Lucanae iuuenem commendet amicae' (Horace, *Epistulae*, 1.15.18–21), quoted by Erasmus: Bacchus is depicted as a youth because 'Vinum [...] senibus quoque ipsis iuuentam quandam reddere videtur' (*Colloquia*, p. 200, l. 2447; cf. ll. 2444–58). Cf. Erasmus, *Adagia*, 1219, 'Vinum senem etiam vel nolentem, saltare compellit'; Walther, 44296c3, 44296b7).

109) Ante et post cibum hymnum esse dicendum

10 **Porcorum:** Cf. 'Ad mensam residens et panem non benedicens | Ille surget sicut sus et sedet sicut asellus' (Walther, 397).

110) De capite aperiendo

30 **Lex erat apud eos:** Not a law but a custom: cf. Pliny, *Naturalis Historia*, 28.17.60: 'maiores [...] capita [...] aperiri aspectu magistratuum [...] iussere'; discussed by Plutarch, *Moralia*, 4.10. Standard Renaissance etiquette (e.g. Erasmus, *Colloquia*, p. 162, ll. 1201–03).

111) De fertili sacerdotio

The colloquy is influenced by Erasmus's colloquy 'De captandis sacerdotiis' (*Colloquia*, pp. 150–54), where Pamphagus has been to Rome to look for a benefice.

7 **Opimum [...] sacerdotium:** Despite the reading 'optimum', what is intended is probably 'opimum sacerdotium', a typically Erasmian collocation: 'cui contigit opimum sacerdotium [...]' (*Colloquia*, p. 152, l. 883); 'Sacerdotiis opimis onustus' (*De conscribendis epistolis*, *ASD*, I–2, p. 227, l. 18).

10 **Aureo hamo:** 'Aureo hamo piscari' means to fish risking the loss of tackle worth more than the catch (Otto 783; cf. Erasmus, *Adagia*, 1160). Schotten seems to have taken the sense 'use bribery' from the use in Erasmus's 'De captandis sacerdotiis' (*Colloquia*, p. 152, ll. 866–67): see Macardle, *Confabulations*, pp. 97–98.

11 **Argenteum [...] hamum:** Cf. 'Aureamne an argenteam [escam]?' (Erasmus, 'De captandis sacerdotiis', *Colloquia*, p. 153, l. 894).

15 **centum aureos nummos:** A considerable sum, well above the bare sixty Gulden a year earned by master masons, carpenters or roofers in the 1520s (Lassotta, *Formen der Armut*, I, p. 415).

16 **nymphae:** 'Nympha' for 'girl' in Erasmus, *Colloquia*, e.g. p. 201, l. 2457; p. 205, l. 2616. **et tibi et nymphae quam ales:** Cf. 'Non deerit Eua, cui sit opulentum sacerdotium' (Erasmus, *Colloquia*, p. 152, l. 887).

18 **Sapies in rem tuam:** Cf. 'Blitea et luteast meretrix nisi quae sapit in vino ad rem suam' (Plautus, *Truculentus*, 854).

31 **audaces Fortuna iuuat:** 'Audentis Fortuna iuuat' (Vergil, *Aeneid*, 10.284). Cf. 'Fortes Fortuna adiuuat' (Terence, *Phormio*, 203; Cicero, *Tusculanae disputationes*, 2.4.11; Erasmus, *Adagia*, 145).

31–32 **desidenti [...] assa non aduolat columba:** Common proverb: 'Non volat in buccas assa columba tuas' (Walther, 18719, 39017a5; cf. 18591, 18936a; *DAPR*, 534).

112) De officio mechanico addiscendo

A trade apprenticeship, perhaps in conjunction with study at a German school, was the classic route for the boy unequal to the demands of the Latin school ('[puer] dury ingeny vel ebetis et stolidi': Crecelius, 'Crailsheimer Schulordnung', p. 247). Though this colloquy presents leaving the study of 'litterae' as near-tragic, the influential middle classes in Cologne were often engaged in trade and craft. Social boundaries between merchants and artisans were fluid (Kellenbenz, 'Wirtschaftsgeschichte Kölns', pp. 334–35; Jütte, 'Household and Family', pp. 168–70).

1 **officio mechanico:** 'Officium' for 'craft, trade', is ML (Stotz, III, 29.13; DuC, VI, p. 38; *MLLM*, s.v., 9; *LLMA*, s.v., 7; *DMLBS*, s.v., 5a). 'Mechanicus': see note to colloquy 42, l. 27.

6 **susceptant:** 'Suscepto' is a LL variant of CL 'suscipio' (Forcellini; *DLFAC*; *GLL*; *RMLWL*).

9 **lapidi loquebar:** 'Lapis' denotes a dull person: 'Quid stas, lapis?' (Terence, *Heautontimorumenos*, 831). Erasmus, *Adagia*, 389, 'Lapidi loqueris'. Walther, 37810a2, 'Lapidi loqueris'. Otto, 911; cf. 1610.

10 **mortuo uerba feci:** Otto, 1146. Erasmus, *Adagia*, 386, 'Mortuo uerba facit', citing Plautus, *Poenulus*, 840).

11 **Sapient nimis sero:** Cf. Erasmus, *Adagia,* 28, 'Sero sapiunt Phryges', based on a line from the *Equus Trojanus* of Naevius or Livius Andronicus (*Tragicorum veterum fragmenta*, p. 234, quoted by Cicero, *Epistulae ad familiares*, 7.16). Also Erasmus, *Colloquia*, p. 727.

17 **ciconia [...] depingi:** 'Ciconia', a mocking gesture (exact details uncertain) of hand and fingers behind the victim's back, imitating the stork's neck and beak: 'O Iane, a tergo quem nulla ciconia pinsit' (Persius, *Satires*, 1.58; Persius, transl. by Lee, p. 75, note to l. 58; Harvey, *Commentary on Persius*, p. 33; Persius, *Satiren*, ed. by Kißel, pp. 186–87). **depingi:** Schotten seems to have read or remembered Persius's 'pinsit' as 'pinxit', a reading actually found in some Persius MSS (*A. Persi [...] Saturarum Liber [...]*, ed. by Clausen, p. 6, l. 58, apparatus).

20 **Bellorum satellites fient:** Erasmus similarly equates mercenaries with thieves and assassins in *De pueris instituendis* (1529): 'latronem aut sicarium [assassin] aut, quod his simillimum est, mercenarium militem' (*ASD*, I-2, p. 60, ll. 15–16).

26–27 **'Optat [...] caballus':** Erasmus, *Adagia*, 571, based on Horace, *Epistulae*, 1.14.43; Walther, 20289a, 39316p2.

113) Eos raro probos fieri, quibus in teneris parentes nimium indulgent

3 **Telesphorus:** (a) Greek general, fourth century BC (Diogenes Laertius, *Lives*, 5.79; Pauly, XII/1, col. 97); (b) The second-century Pope St Telesphorus: see note to 'Conuiuium Telesphorianum siue esuriale' (no. 1), l. 69.

16–17 **Principem probum nigro cygno inuenis rariorem:** Walther, 36060c, 'Cygno nigro pius tyrannus rarior'.

23–24 **albo coruo est rarior:** 'Coruo quoque rarior albo' (Juvenal, *Satires*, 7.202; Walther, 3587; cf. 35797b). 'Talium maritum non minus rara est copia, quam alborum coruorum' (Erasmus, *Colloquia*, p. 307, ll. 228–29). Cf. Erasmus, *Adagia*, 3635, 'Coruus albus'.

28–29 **Virtute [...] qui in purpura repserit:** 'Quid non adultus concupiscet, qui in purpuris repit' (Quintilian, *Institutio Oratoria*, 1.2.6). 'Quomodo modestus erit vir [...] qui repsit in purpura?' (Erasmus, *De pueris instituendis*, *ASD*, I–2, p. 35, ll. 18–19).

114) Qui parentes suos diligant filios

26 **tanquam Dauo Terentiano:** In Terence, *Andria*, 190–195, the slave Dauus, pretending not to understand his master, asks him to speak plainly, 'aperte loqui' (194).

31 **Quintilianus inquit:** 'Mollis illa educatio, quam indulgentiam uocamus, neruos omnes mentis et corporis frangit' (Quintilian, *Institutio Oratoria*, 1.2.6).

115) Quis noster sit amicus

11 **Homerum quandoque dormitare:** 'Quandoque bonus dormitat Homerus' (Horace, *Ars poetica*, 359).

30 **crocodili:** Crocodiles were reputed to shed tears on seeing a human being, whom they would then eat (Erasmus, *Adagia*, 1360, 'Crocodili lacrimae', *LB*, II, 543A–B; Dasypodius, 'Crocodilus': 'Crocodili lachrimae, Erdicht weynen'; cf. Walther, 37795a1). Hence crocodiles are an image of the hypocrite: 'Hypocrita germanus crocodili' (Walther, 34309).

32 **Momus:** Greek god of mockery and criticism. He complained that the man made by Hephaestus had no windows in his breast to allow his secret thoughts to be seen (Lucian, *Hermotimus*, 20; Pauly, VIII, col. 351). Erasmus, *Adagia*, 474, 'Momo satisfacere'.

116) Quis nobis sit inimicus

3 **tu hominis somnium:** Erasmian phrase: 'Somnium hominis' (*Colloquia*, p. 158, l. 1060; p. 303, l. 69). Erasmus *Adagia*, 1062, uses 'Somnium' for 'Rem futilem, inanem et nihili', 'something baseless, empty and of no account' (*LB*, II, 430C; *CWE*, XXXIII, p. 51); he cites 'Tu [...] sapientia es, | ille somnium' (Terence, *Adelphoe*, 394–95).

20 **Argus:** The many-eyed watchman Argos was proverbially all-seeing (Otto, 162; Pauly, I, cols 1069–70). 'Hic vel Argum fallat' (Erasmus, *Adagia*, 474, *LB*, II, 211B).

24 **Nocumenti:** 'Nocumentum', 'harm, damage', is LL and ML (Forcellini; DuC, V, p. 600; *DLFAC*; *MLLM*; *LLMA*;

DEL; Dasypodius, 'noceo'). Used by NL authors: 'damnum et nocumenta' (Locher, *Stultifera navis*, p. 104); 'Tot laedunt [...] nocumenta' (Eobanus Hessus, *Operum farragines duo*, fol. 208^{v}).

30 **te deplumandi:** 'Deplumare' is ML (Stotz, VI, 116.2; DuC, III, p. 69; *MLWb*, III, col. 350, l. 65–col. 351, l. 20; *DMLBS*; *LLMA*; Dasypodius, 'pluma'). 'Captos | deplumare leui tactu' (Mantuanus, *Eclogae*, VI, sig. r viii^{v}).

117) De monasterio et religionis ingressu

3 **praefixum:** CL 'praefigo' means 'impale, affix, obstruct'. Schotten's sense 'decide [in advance]' is LL (*TLL*, X,2, col. 634, ll. 43–55; col. 635, l. 18–col. 636, l. 28; *DLFAC*; *GLL*; *LLMA*, s.v., 1; *MLLM*, s.v., 1; *RMLWL*, 'prefigo'). This sense is used by humanist writers (*LPLR*): e.g. '[tempus quod tibi] natura seu fortuna praefixerat' (Petrarca, *Opera omnia*, I, p. 240, ll. 45–46).

32 **Erinys:** CL, a Fury, or in transferred sense 'frenzy'. Cf. Erasmus, *Adagia*, 3195, 'Erinnys ex tragoedia'.

118) Non omnes doctos esse, qui capite redimiti sunt rubeo tegmine

This colloquy may be partly inspired by Erasmus's illustrations of his adage 'Multi thyrsigeri, pauci Bacchi.' (*Adagia*, 606; cf. note to ll. 30–31 below): 'Non omnes vere Theologi, qui pileum Theologicum gerunt [...] Non omnes Monachi, qui cucullo onerantur [...] Non omnes Reges, qui diademate insigniuntur. Non omnes Episcopi, qui mitram gerunt bicornem' (*LB*, II, 263E–F).

2 **rubeo tegmine:** The mark of the degree of MA: see note to colloquy 60, ll. 22–23.

9 **diademate 28 tiara 36 pilleolo:** CL terms for different kinds of headgear, presumably more acceptable to humanists than ML 'birettum' (see note to colloquy 60, ll. 22–23). Cf. 'Septenarum artium diademate seu pileolo condecoraui infra scriptos licentiatos' (HAStK, 150, A 481, fol. s165^{r} (1526)). 'Hodie magisterii diademate, at thiara sum redimitus' (Schotten, *Colloquia philosophica*, sig. BB4^{r}). But all are ML for ecclesiastical headgear: **diadema** for 'mitre' (LLMA, s.v., 2); so too **tiara** (DuC, s.v., 1, VIII, p. 105; *LLMA*; *RMLWL*; *MLLM*); **tiara** is

also used for clergymen's headgear generally (DuC, s.v. 2, VIII, p. 105); **pilleolus** is frequent for 'biretta' (DuC, VI, p. 323; *LLMA*; *RML WL*).

23 **spe uana me lactatum uideo:** 'Nolim te lactare vana spe' (Erasmus, *Colloquia*, p. 145, l. 657).

30–31 **'Narthecophori multi, Bacchi uero pauci':** Proverb originating in Plato, *Phaedrus*, 69C (Otto, 391). 'Narthecophoros' means the bearer of the thyrsus, the rod carried by devotees at the rites of Bacchus (Pauly, VIII, cols 718–19; XII/1, col. 526). Erasmus, *Adagia*, 606, 'Multi thyrsigeri, pauci Bacchi.' (cf. Franck, II, fol. 88v–89r). 'At caue, ne cum Nartecophorus es Bacchus non sis.' (Schotten, *Vita honesta*, sig. Eiiiv).

37 **Hedera uiridis uinum nihil commendat:** Erasmus, *Adagia*, 1520, 'Vino vendibili suspensa hedera nihil opus' (Walther, 44296a8). A bush had been the sign of a tavern since Roman times, probably because of the Bacchic associations of the ivy bush (Pauly, III, cols 886–87). Cf. 'a tauerners bush' (More, *Workes*, 642/1, quoted *OED*2, 'bush', 5a); *BW*, I, p. 312; III, p. 88.

119) Quibus sit utendum uerbis dum aliquid a praeceptore flagitatur

9–10 **mihi [...] animus in pedes labitur:** Not a CL phrase, or one attested in LL, ML or NL sources.

120) De ouis colligendis circa Paschatis ferias

3 **Buttubatta:** Used as a common noun in a comedy by Naevius, seemingly to mean 'trivia' (*Livi Andronici et Cn. Naevi fabularum reliquiae*, ed. by Müller, 36.24). Schotten is probably thinking of the swindler Buttubatta in Reuchlin's play *Sergius* (1496), who passes off a skull as a relic.

7 **suppactori calceario:** Not recorded in dictionaries or texts. Standard CL for 'shoemaker' is 'sutor', 'calcearius', or 'calceolarius', which Schotten uses in 'Conuiuium nundinarium' (no. 15), passim.

22–23 **Multitudinem ouorum, an apud saepes olentium?: Oua** here seems to be a comic term for 'animal dropping' (usage otherwise unrecorded). **Saepes olentium** is seemingly 'dung-heap': 'Saepes' in ML denotes many kinds of enclosure (*RMLWL*). Cf. the same joke in 'Conuiuium Paschale' (no. 14), l. 40.

29 **'Christe qui lux':** The Lent and Passiontide compline hymn 'Christe, qui lux es et dies' (*Analecta Hymnica*, LI, pp. 21–23). The hymn, believed to banish the Devil and nightmares, was extremely popular in Germany: there are numerous vernacular translations, from the fourteenth century to Catholic and Lutheran hymnbooks of the earlier sixteenth century (*VL*, 1, cols 1211–13; Wackernagel, II, nos. 478, 566, 567, 1037, 1096; III, nos 161, 384, 645; Lyon, '"Christe qui lux es et dies"', passim).

121) Nusquam nunc tutam esse fidem

4 **Sanguinem paene flerem:** 'Cur non [...] sanguinem, ut dicitur, flerem?' (Hegendorff, *Dialogi*, 4, sig. D2[r]). Erasmus, *Adagia*, 1365, 'Sanguine flere', based on Zenobius, *Paroimiai*, 1.34, etc.). 'Sanguinem flere. Es möcht ein steinen hertz erbarmen' (Franck, II, fol. 74[r]).

9 **compatiens:** LL, like 'compatior' and its derivatives (*TLL*, III, col. 2025, ll. 75–84; *MLWb*, II, col. 1042, ll. 15–19; *MLLM*).

27–28 **semper nocuit differre paratis:** Based on 'Tolle moras: semper nocuit differre paratis' (Lucan, *Pharsalia*, 1.281; Walther, 17080b, 31438, 43856);

28 **mora sua cuilibet est nociua:** Legal maxim, 'Regula iuris' XXV, *CIC*, lib. VI (*CIC*, ed. by Friedberg, II, col. 1122).

122) Quod obsequium amicos, ueritas odium pariat

The colloquy reflects the discussion in Cicero, *De amicitia*, 89–100, esp. 89–93; see notes to ll. 1–2, 18 and 31–32 below.

1–2 **obsequium [...] pariat:** 'Hoc tempore obsequium amicos, ueritas odium parit' (Terence, *Andria*, 68); cited by Cicero (*De amicitia*, 89). Frequent in Erasmus: (*Adagia*, 1853, 'Obsequium amicos, veritas odium parit'; *De ratione studii*, *ASD*, I–2, p. 128, ll. 6–7; *De copia*, *ASD*, I–6, p. 250, l. 309). Cf. colloquy 30, ll. 32–33.

7 **raptitius [...] liber:** Not recorded in CL, LL, ML or NL dictionaries or authors. Clearly formed from CL 'raptito', alternative form of 'rapto', 'carry off, plunder'.

18 **ut inquit Cicero:** Cf. 'maxima autem culpa in eo, qui et ueritatem aspernatur et in fraudem obsequio impellitur' (Cicero, *De amicitia*, 89).

28 **aceto perfundit:** 'Aliquem aceto perfundere', 'pour vinegar over someone', submit someone to acerbic or scornful remarks. 'Italo perfusus aceto' (Horace, *Sermones*, 1.7.32); 'Mordaci lotus aceto' (Persius, *Satires*, 5.86).

29 **Tangitur** [...] **ulcus:** 'hoc ulcus tangere' (Terence, *Phormio*, 690).

30 **mouetur bilis et anagyris:** 'Anagyris' (-os) is the stinkweed; the proverb 'Μὴ κινεῖν τὴν 'ανάγυριν', 'do not touch the stink-weed', means 'let sleeping dogs lie' (cf. Zenobius, 2.55; Erasmus, *Adagia*, 65, 'Anagyrim commoves'). Schotten's mistaken use of 'anagyrim mouere' as a synonym for 'bilem mouere', 'stir up anger', may misinterpret an allusion to the proverb by Erasmus: 'Porro theologos silentio transire fortasse praestiterit [...] nec hanc anagyrim tangere, vtpote genus hominum mire superciliosum atque irritabile' (*Moriae Encomium*, *ASD*, IV–3, p. 144, ll. 381–83). The reference to the theologians' irritability may have misled Schotten into understanding 'anagyrim tangere' as similar to 'ulcus tangere' or 'bilem mouere'.

31–32 **Illorum salus** [...] **ueritati:** 'Cuius autem aures clausae ueritati sunt, [...] huius salus desperanda est' (Cicero, *De amicitia*, 90).

123) Conuiuium Bacchanale, siue ultima cena dierum Lupercalium

This colloquy contains several borrowings from Erasmus's 'Conuiuium profanum' (*Colloquia*, pp. 196–215), for example the Shrove Tuesday setting and various textual details: see notes below.

18 **Laruis opertis** [...] **limen nostrum non patebit:** See Macardle, *Confabulations*, p. 76.

47 **istud nostrum uilli:** 'Quid te hoc villi delectat?' (Erasmus, 'Conuiuium profanum', *Colloquia*, p. 198, l. 2386; cf. Terence, *Adelphoe*, 786).

58 **Quicquid appositum est** [...]: Imitated from the grace in Erasmus's 'Convivium profanum': 'Quicquid appositum

est et quicquid apponetur, felix et sacrum esse iubeat, qui sua benignitate pascit vniuersa. Amen' (*Colloquia*, p. 198, ll. 2365–66). Cf. note to colloquy 77, ll. 26–30.

65–66 **ut stas tanquam Marpesia cautes?:** Mount Marpessa on Paros was a source of white statuary marble (Pauly, VII, col. 944). Vergil describes Dido in the underworld, reacting to Aeneas as coldly 'quam si dura silex, aut stet Marpesia cautes' (Vergil, *Aeneid*, 6.471; quoted by Erasmus, *Encomium Moriae*, *ASD*, IV–3, p. 106, l. 640; cf. Otto, 1689).

72 **scyphum:** CL 'scyphus', 'large goblet'. Schotten's spelling 'cyphus' (cf. l. 82, *conuiuia* 1, l. 89; 7, l. 56) is ML (Stotz, VII, 273.3), but also used by Erasmus (*Colloquia*, p. 49, l. 532; p. 55, l. 743; p. 56, l. 771; p. 60, l. 901).

74 **Chrysippum agitis:** 'Tu nunc Chrysippum agis' (Erasmus, 'Conuiuium profanum', *Colloquia*, p. 199, l. 2415). Erasmus (ibid., ll. 2417–19) applies to the Stoic philosopher Chrysippus the story told by Valerius Maximus of Chrysippus's contemporary Carneades: that he was so preoccupied by logical problems that he would have eaten nothing at dinners had a slave not fed him (*Facta et dicta*, 8.7.ext.5). Diogenes Laertius says that Chrysippus was sometimes tipsy at drinking parties (*Lives*, 7.183). See Macardle, *Confabulations*, p. 98.

77 **classicum canam:** 'Sound the trumpet as the signal for battle'; by extension, signal the beginning of anything: 'Theologi [...] ad hos tumultus classicum canant' (Erasmus, *Colloquia*, p. 135, ll. 312–13).

115–120 **Gratias [...] Christum:** Imitated from the final grace in Erasmus's 'Conuiuium profanum': 'Gratias agimus tibi, Pater coelestis, qui tua ineffabili potentia condidisti omnia, tua inscrutabili sapientia gubernas vniuersa, tua inexhausta bonitate cuncta pascis ac vegetas [...]' (*Colloquia*, p. 214, ll. 2916–20).

116 **condidit:** 'Condo' for 'create' is Christian LL (*TLL*, IV, col. 154, ll. 30–55; Blaise, § 136; *DMLBS*, s.v., 2b; Dasypodius, 'do'): 'Deum [...] qui condiderit coelum ac terram' (Erasmus, *Colloquia*, p. 365, ll. 59–60).

130 **illud Bebelii:** 'Cuiuscunque fistulae cantus valet choreas amanti' (Bebel, *Adagia*, sig. kiii[v]).

134 **scribiliginibus:** Schotten wrongly has 'stribiliginibus' (CL 'stribiligo', 'linguistic solecism'). There is confusion with 'scrib(i)ligo', 'striblita' and 'strebligo', ML variants of CL 'scrib(i)lita', 'cheese tart' (Plautus, Poenula, 43; Diefenbach, 'scriblita'). ML 'scriblita', etc. often denotes a pretzel (Diefenbach, 'scriblita, bretsel ader ring'; Dasypodius; Golius, 340; Bebel, *Facetien*, p. 16; cf. Vives, *Exercitatio*, XVII, p. 152).

Notes to the *Conuiuia*

Hermannus Schottennius Hessus studiosae iuuentuti s.p.d.

7 **Phoenix unica auis Arabiae:** Perhaps from Lactantius, *Carmen de aue Phoenice*, where the Phoenix lives in the Near East (p. 584), and is the only bird in the region: 'Hoc nemus [...] auis incolit unica Phoenix, | Vnica' (p. 585).

1) Conuiuium Telesphorianum siue esuriale

The meal is set on Ash Wednesday, the day after the dinner in colloquy 123: see ll. 33–35, 38–39 53, etc.

10–11 **uinum [...] absinthio conditum:** Roman recipe (e.g. Columella, *De re rustica*, 12.35). A medieval and early modern medicine and beverage (Fuchs, *De historia stirpium*, p. 5; Zedler, *Universallexikon*, I, cols 191–93). 'Vinum absinthites, wermůtwein' (Golius, 348).

69 **Aiunt Telesphorum Papam [...]:** A seven-week Lenten fast was (reputedly) introduced by the second-century Pope St Telesphorus (*Liber Pontificalis*, I, pp. 56–57; *NCE*, XIII, p. 792).

76 **Lac et butyrum naturae sunt sanguineae:** Milk was believed to be 'twice-concocted blood' (Albala, *Eating Right*, p. 75).

2) Pythagoricum conuiuium

The frugality of Pythagoras and his school was proverbial: 'Ego te Pythagorica coena excipiam, aut fortasse frugaliore' (Erasmus, *Colloquia*, p. 195, ll. 2277–78). Cf. 'Sint mihi Pythagorae mensae' (Mantuanus, *Eclogae*, sig. r iii^{r}).

50 **animas esse immortales:** The dietary restrictions of the Pythagorean school reflected belief in the transmigration of souls (Pauly, X, cols 651, 656–57).

55 **piscis animal innocuum est:** Plutarch, *Moralia*, 729D–E; Diogenes Laertius, *Lives*, 8.19. Erasmus, *Adagia*, 2, xxxvi, 'A piscibus abstineto'.

69 **Vt per quinquennium taceant:** Diogenes Laertius, *Lives*, 8.10.

3) Philosophica mensa

30 **potu [...] tenui:** ML 'potus tenuis', 'small beer', weak beer for everyday consumption. 'Potus tenuis, cerevisia quotidiana, domi cocta, secundaria' (Grimm, 'Haustrunk'). 'Dünne-bier' (Lexer, *Mittelhochdeutsches Handwörterbuch*, III, col. 128). Cf. 'cerevisia tenuis (Vives, *Exercitatio*, VII, p. 24).

66 **Mantuanus:** 'Pocula prehende, fluet melius post pocula sermo' (Mantuanus, *Eclogae*, 9.22, sig. s viii^{r}).

4) Diogenicum conuiuium

Named after Diogenes of Sinope (412/403–324/321 BC), founder of the Cynical school of philosophy (Diogenes Laertius, *Lives*, 6.20–81; Pauly, III, cols 598–600). Known for his ascetic lifestyle: 'Diogenem [...] qui crudis oleribus ac simplici aqua victitabat' (Erasmus, *Colloquia*, p. 202, ll. 2492–93); 'Diogenica [coena]' (ibid., p. 195, ll. 2277–79).

2, etc. **Alexander:** Alexander the Great, king of Macedonia (356–323 BC), the object of several quips and ripostes of Diogenes (Pauly, I, cols 468–74; Diogenes Laertius, *Lives*, 6.38, 44, 45, 60, 63, 68). **Aristippus:** Probably Aristippus the pupil of Socrates (Pauly, I, cols 1103–04). **Chrysippus:** Stoic philosopher, third century BC (Diogenes Laertius, *Lives*, 7.179–89; Pauly, II, cols 1177–83).

11–18: Based on an anecdote in Diogenes Laertius, *Lives*, 6.38.

34 **Frigidus cibatus et crudis non conuenit homini:** Early modern dietetics thought that cold foods slowed down the system and that raw ones like salad were harmful (Albala, *Eating Right*, pp. 12, 102, 110, 165–66, 254).

55 **plasmator:** Christian LL (Forcellini; DuC, VI, p. 357; *GLL*; *DLFAC*; *RMLWL*; *MLLM*; *NLW*). Used by NL authors: 'Saluator, omniumque plasmator' (Ravisius Textor, *De claris mulieribus*, sig. di^{v}, diii^{r}); 'Plasmator hominis Deus' (Bebel, *Liber hymnorum*, fol. XXX^{r}).

65 **insipidus:** LL (*TLL*, VII,1, col. 1919, ll. 5–27; *GLL*; *DLFAC*; *DMLBS*, s.v., 1; *MLLM*).

5) Aristippicum conuiuium siue aulicum

1 **Aristippicum**: After Aristippus of Cyrene, fifth–fourth century BC, hedonist philosopher (Pauly, I, cols 1103–04).

2, etc. **Theophrastus:** Peripatetic philosopher, fourth–third century BC; pupil and successor of Aristotle (Pauly, XII/1, cols 385–93). **Crates:** Krates, the name of several dramatists and philosophers, fifth–second century BC (Pauly, VI, cols 809–14). **Anaxagoras:** Philosopher, fifth century BC (Pauly, I, cols 667–68).

17 **pluteos:** CL 'pluteus', usually 'screen, partition', is used for 'bookshelf' in classical literature only in Juvenal, *Satires*, 2.7 and Persius, *Satires*, 1.106.

57 **dapsilice:** Unattested in CL, LL, ML and NL: the recorded forms are 'dapsile' and 'dapsiliter' (*TLL*, V,1, col. 38, ll. 70–73; *MLWb*, III, col. 25, ll. 11–15; *DMLBS*, I, pp. 558–59). Cf. *conuiuia* 15, l. 63 and 23, l. 11.

6) Regium conuiuium post ferias Epiphaniae

This depicts the 'Koninckseessen' given by the man chosen as 'king' on Epiphany Eve (cf. colloquy 34, ll. 29–30): see Macardle, *Confabulations*, pp. 63–64.

3 **Cubicularius:** CL noun; but the sense 'chamberlain' as here is ML (DuC, II, p. 641; *MLWb*, II, col. 2058, ll. 39–72; *DLFAC*, s.v., II, 1; *DMLBS*; *MLLM*, s.v., 1; *LPLR*).

28 **nostraeque aulae domestici:** Servants were present at the 'Koninckseessen' in the Weinsberg household (*BW*, V, pp. 220–21).

81–82 **post saeculum Gentiles hanc occupabunt terram:** The origin of this proverbial-sounding phrase has not been found.

87 **Caseo hoc cibum subsidere facite:** Cheese was regarded as the ideal food to seal the stomach and promote digestion (Fridaevallis, *De tuenda sanitate*, p. 151; Albala, *Eating Right*, p. 60).

87–88 **butyro lenes facite animos:** 'Mitem nec mirum dat sensum dulce butirum' (Walther, 14946); cf. 'Botter makt 'nen sachten Sinn' (Wander, I, 521). Butter is mentioned as having the same effect in *conuiuia* 12, ll. 67–68, and 24, l. 81.

106 **uiuificat:** 'Viuifico', Christian LL (Forcellini; *GLL*; *DLFAC*; Blaise, §§ 232, 398). 'In Christo omnes uiuificabuntur' (Vulgate, 1 Corinthians 15.22).

7) Conuiuium amicorum

12 **ob asini prospectum:** I.e., 'at the slightest provocation': a potter went to law after a donkey looked into his shop, breaking some items (Otto, 187). Erasmus, *Adagia*, 264, 'De asini prospectu'.

45–46 **pinguedo nimia uocis affert raucedinem:** Cf. note to colloquy 28, l. 33.

47–48 **ne aridus in stomacho marcescat cibus:** A dry stomach was thought to 'concoct' food too fast, reducing the nutritional benefit (Albala, *Eating Right*, p. 57).

8) Funebre conuiuium

76 **A gentilibus Thracibus:** The Trausians, a Thracian tribe, grieved at births and rejoiced at funerals (Herodotus, *Histories*, 5.4).

9) Conuiuium nuptiale

49–50 **pugni [...] quos hodie in templo accepisti; 61–62 cur cereum lumen [...] praeferatur:** Neither of these customs or interpretations is otherwise documented. See notes to colloquy 86, and Macardle, *Confabulations*, p. 75.

10) Conuiuium Epicureum

Named after Epicurus (*ca.* 342–*ca.* 270 BC), whose philosophy was often misrepresented as merely hedonistic (Pauly, III, cols 1130–40); 'Epicureum prandium video, ne dicam Sybariticum' (Erasmus, *Colloquia*, p. 248, l. 517).

2, etc. **Zeno:** Here presumably the Epicurean philosopher Zeno of Sidon, second–first century BC (Pauly, XII/2, cols 752–53). **Sardanapalus:** Legendary Assyrian king, renowned for his luxurious life (Pauly, XI, col. 54). Erasmus, *Adagia*, 2627, 'Sardanapalus'. However, Schotten's figure is not the original Sardanapalus (see ll. 73–75). **Philoxenus:** Here probably Philoxenos of Leukas, gastronomic poet, fourth century BC (Pauly, IX, col. 897).

20 **alitrix:** LL spelling of CL 'altrix' (*TLL*, I, col. 1770, ll. 65–66).

39 **lucernaria:** Schotten imitates Erasmus's use of the LL adj. 'lucernarius', 'connected with lamps' (*TLL*, VII, 2, col. 1701, l. 82–col. 1702, l 53) to mean 'scholarly': 'philosophis lucernariis' (*Encomium Moriae*, *ASD*, IV–3, p. 96, l. 477; cf. note). Cf Erasmus, *Adagia*, 671, 'Olet lucernam': 'De re meditata, multoque studio elucubrata' (*LB*, II, 290D).

54 **medium digitum ostentat:** In antiquity as today, an offensive gesture. Erasmus, *Adagia*, 1368, 'Medium ostendere digitum'.

57 **Apud Milesios:** The city of Miletus enjoyed a high standard of living (Erasmus, *Adagia*, 308, 'Domi Milesia'; 849, 'Fuere quondam strenui Milesii').

60 **Sybaritae:** Sybaris was a notoriously wealthy and luxurious city (Pauly, XI, cols 1124–25). 'Epicureum prandium video, ne dicam Sybariticum' (Erasmus, *Colloquia*, p. 248, l. 517). Erasmus, *Adagia*, 1165, 'Sybaritica mensa'.

65 **Tarentini:** Tarentum in southern Italy was devoted to leisure and pleasure: 'molle Tarentum' (Horace, *Sermones*, 2.4.34; Otto, 1743; Pauly, XII/1, cols 20–33).

11) Conuiuium caninum uel cereale

1 **caninum:** 'Caninus' in the sense of 'fit for a dog': 'prandium caninum' (Varro, *Saturarum Menippearum fragmenta*, 575).

2, etc. **Salacon:** A common noun meaning 'braggart, posturer' (Cicero, *Ad Familiares*, 7.24.2); but previously thought to be the name of a pauper who pretended to be rich (Forcellini, 'Salaco'). **Codrus:** Here presumably the proverbially poor poet (Juvenal, *Satires*, 3.203–08); cf. 'Sint mihi Pythagorae mensae, Codrique supellex' (Mantuanus, *Eclogae*, sig. riii^{r}). **Irus:** A beggar (Homer, *Odyssey*, 18). **Amyntas:** Here presumably the shepherd in Vergil, *Eclogues*, 2, 3, 5, 10.

47 **Optimum condimentum fames est:** Erasmus, *Adagia*, 1669, 'Optimum condimentum fames' (based on Cicero, *De finibus*, 2.28.90). 'Fames optimum condimentum' (Walther, 36858a2).

48–49 **crudas fabas [...] ut coctas efficit:** Cf. 'Fame[s] effic[it], ut crudae etiam fabae saccarum sapiant' (Erasmus, *Adagia*, *ASD*, II–4, p. 130, l. 17–p. 131, l. 18). 'Fabas mellifluas facit esuries tibi crudas' (Walther, 8621; cf. Bebel, *Adagia*, sig. Lvi^{v}); 'Hunger macht rohe bonen süss' (Franck, II, fol. 75^{v}; Wander, II, 914; parallels 910, 914).

55 **Pytissabo eam:** CL 'pytisso', from CGk 'πυτίζω' (*OLD*): literally 'spit out wine after tasting it', i.e. 'taste or sip wine' (only in Terence, *Heautontimorumenos*, 457–58). 'At pitissas, non coenas' (Erasmus, *Colloquia*, p. 47, l. 481). Cf. *conuiuium* 22, l. 35.

58–59 **Stomachus consumet quod ignis calore non praestitit:** The Hippocratic view of digestion as a 'concoction' of food by heat in the stomach dominated medical thinking till the seventeenth century (Albala, *Eating Right*, pp. 17, 56–57).

68–71 **Plautus:** Cf. Plautus, *Captiui*, 461–63.

73 **ut Comicus dixit:** 'Omnium rerum, heus, uicissitudost' (Terence, *Eunuchus*, 276). Erasmus, *Adagia*, 663, 'Omnium rerum uicissitudo est'.

75 **ut Capnion scripsit:** 'Qui pauper est nihil timet, nihil potest perdere' (Reuchlin, *Henno*, l. 150).

81 **alumnus:** CL 'nursling, ward, protégé'. Schotten's meaning 'guardian, protector' (cf *conuiuium* 21, l. 29) is LL and ML (*TLL*, I, col. 1795, ll. 38–83; *DLFAC*, s.v., 4; *MLWb*, I, col. 529, ll. 44–59; *DMLBS*, s.v., 3; *LLMA*, s.v., 2; *MLLM*, s.v., 2).

12) Conuiuium plebeium vel uulgare

2, etc. **Henno; Greta; Dromo:** characters from Reuchlin's play *Henno*. **Dromo; Parmeno; Simo:** characters from various plays by Terence.

13) Conuiuium diuitum siue opulentorum

2, etc. **Croesus:** Proverbially wealthy king of Lydia (Otto, 468). **Crassus:** The proverbially wealthy Marcus Licinius Crassus (115–53 BC) (Otto, 457; Pauly, VII, cols 161–62). **Alcmaeon:** Name of several historical and mythological figures (*OCCL*). **Tantalus:** Greek mythological figure, punished in Tartarus by 'tantalizing' deprivation of food and drink (*OCCL*).

38–39 **aliena uiuere quadra:** Juvenal, *Satires*, 5.2.

65 **illaridatis:** 'Illar(i)dare' is unattested in CL, LL ML and NL texts and dictionaries, except DuC (IV, p. 292), in the sense 'spit roast', mistakenly citing Apicius. Here

probably synonymous with ML 'lardare', either in the sense 'fatten' (*DMLBS*, 'lardare', 1b), or 'lard', i.e. pierce meat and insert strips of bacon or other fat meat (*DMLBS*, 'lardare', 1a).

14) Conuiuium Paschale

8 **fauces lippiunt fame:** Cf. Plautus, *Curculio*, 318.

16–19 **Haec est dies [...] in ea:** Vulgate, Psalm 117.24; also (without 'est') the gradual at Mass, and an antiphon at Lauds, of Easter Sunday (*The Missal [...]*, p. 440; *Breviarium Romanum*, Pars Verna, p. 228). **Pascha nostrum [...] Alleluia:** the Alleluia verse at Easter Sunday Mass, adapted from Vulgate, 1 Corinthians 5.7b–8 (*The Missal [...]*, p. 441).

61 **Ne gru quidem:** CGk 'γρῦ', literally 'dirt under the fingernails', by extension 'morsel, bit'. Erasmus, *Adagia*, 703, 'Ne gry quidem'.

15) Conuiuium nundinarium siue dedicationis templi

As repeated references in the text make clear, the fair here is a village fair held on the day of the dedication of the parish church (German *Kirchweihfest* or *Kirmes*).

16) Conuiuium campestre

26–27 **Nymphas bellulas oportet et congredi, alias hilaritatis haberemus nihil:** Cf. 'Ducamus nobiscum virgines, nam eo minus molesta erit deambulatio' (Erasmus, *Colloquia*, p. 214, ll. 2931–32).

17) Conuiuium satyricum siue inuectiuum

1 **inuectiuum:** 'Inuectiuus', adj., LL (Forcellini; *TLL*, VII,2, col. 125, ll. 11–62; *GLL*; *DMLBS*, s.v., 2; *LLMA*; *MLLM*).

70–71 **canis [...] bouis:** 'Canis bouis', otherwise unrecorded, presumably ML term for 'bulldog'.

73 **manticam a tergo non uident:** 'Not seeing the knapsack on one's own back' means being unaware of one's own faults. Erasmus, *Adagia*, 590, 'Non uidemus manticae quod in tergo est' (cf. Otto, 1032).

79–80 **ubi equus tuus [...]?:** St Martin (see colloquy 40) is very frequently depicted on a horse (*LCI*, VII, cols 573–79).

83 **tu Lerna malorum:** All kinds of refuse were disposed of in Lake Lernē (Erasmus, *Adagia*, 227, 'Lerna malorum', citing Strabo, *Geographica*, 8.6.8).

18) Conuiuium laudatorium

22 **Postremum occupabit scabies:** Roman children's game: 'Occupet extremum scabies' (Horace, *Ars Poetica*, ed. by Brink, l. 417 and note; Otto, 1598). Erasmus, *Adagia*, 3303, 'Extremum occupet scabies'. 'Den letzsten kommen die rauden an' (Franck, I, fol. 52^{v}; Wander, III, 45).

78 **albae gallinae [...] filius:** 'A white hen's son', a person favoured by fortune (Otto, 749). Erasmus, *Adagia*, 78, 'Albae gallinae filius' (based on Juvenal, *Satires*, 13.141).

80 **istud Plinii:** 'Sed hoc ipsum amantis est, non onerare eum laudibus' (Pliny the Younger, *Epistulae*, 1.14.10).

19) Conuiuium declamatorium

68–69 **inquit poeta:** The source has not been found.

69 **a caudice:** 'Caudex, stipes, asinus, plumbeus' (Terence, *Heautontimorumenos*, 877).

76 **Euclio:** Miser in Plautus, *Aulularia*.

20) Conuiuium reconciliatorium

10 **clauum clauo trudam:** Otto, 396. Erasmus, *Adagia*, 104, 'Clauum clauo pellere'.

12–13 **Ientaculi uice quod est esurienti:** No source has been found for this phrase, similar to the modern 'I eat people like you for breakfast'.

21 **succuli:** LL 'Suc(c)ulus', 'piglet' (Forcellini; *GLL*).

30 **diuersorium [...] cereuisiarium:** 'Alehouse', an otherwise unrecorded combination of CL 'diuersorium', 'inn', and 'cer[e]uis[i]arius', LL, 'connected with beer' (*GLL*, *DMLBS*; *MLWb*, II, col. 499, ll. 64–72).

89 **Lyaeus:** 'He who sets free', cult title of Bacchus (Pauly, III, col. 657); from CGk 'λύω', 'loosen, liberate'.

21) Conuiuium histrionum siue parasiticum

2, etc. **Nero:** Lucius Domitius Ahenobarbus, Roman emperor AD 54–68 (Pauly, VIII, cols 851–55). **Gnatho:** parasite in Terence, *Eunuchus*. **Curculio:** parasite in Plautus, *Curculio*.

14–15 **ad restim nobis res ueniet:** Erasmus, *Adagia*, 421, 'Ad restim res rediit' (based on Terence, *Phormio*, 686; cf. Otto, 1528).

21 **Per [...] deos patellarios:** Based on 'di [...] omnes, magni minutique et etiam patellarii' (Plautus, *Cistellaria*, 522).

36–37 **omniumque horarum homo:** Otto, 830 (Suetonius, *Tiberius*, 42; Quintilian, *Institutio*, 6.3.110). Erasmus, *Adagia*, 286, 'Omnium horarum homo'; 'The man [...] whose company is always delightful' (*CWE*, XXXI, p. 304). 'Ego futurus sum omnium horarum homo' (Erasmus, *Colloquia*, p. 182, l. 1873). Thus Erasmus described Thomas More (*Moriae Encomium*, *ASD*, IV–3, p. 68, l. 19); cf. the famous translation 'a man for all seasons' (Whittinton, *Vulgaria*, pp. 64–65).

38 **quid distent aera lupinis:** I.e., the difference between real money and lupin seeds, which represented coins in Roman games and plays. Erasmus, *Adagia*, 279, 'Quid distent aera lupinis' (based on Horace, *Epistulae*, 1.7.23); Otto, 978.

67 **Hirudines [...] poculorum:** Cf. 'Me conuortam in hirudinem et eorum exsugebo sanguinem' (Plautus, *Epidicus*, 188; cf. Otto, 814).

71–72 **uersutum [...] ac rota est figularis:** 'Vorsutior es quam rota figularis' (Plautus, *Epidicus*, 371; Otto, 1556).

75–76 **ulmeis pigmentis [...] pingitur:** Switches of elm were used in corporal punishment: cf. 'Quem [...] pingent pigmentis ulmeis' (Plautus, *Epidicus*, 626). Schotten's reading 'pungitur' is surely a mistake.

22) Conuiuium nugatorium

57–59 **ut Plautinus ille Euclio [...]:** Plautus's miser Euclio is said to tie a bag over his mouth while sleeping so as not to lose any breath (*Aulularia*, 302–03).

68–78 **Dum uina bibo [...] omnia uendam:** A poem in Leonine metre found in several variants in fifteenth- and sixteenth-century MSS (Walther, 6427; cf. 33488, etc.; *Initia*, 5003).

23) Conuiuium tabernarium, ubi certo asse et nummis praesentibus conuiuatur et soluitur

16 **Bonorum Daton:** The city of Daton or Datos in Thrace was proverbially wealthy (Pauly, III, col. 333; Pauly[1], IV, cols 2229–30).

18 **assidete:** Schotten's spelling 'assedete' (cf. *conuiuium* 23, l. 18) is typical of ML (*MLWb*, I, col. 1067, ll. 50–51; *DMLBS*, 'assidere', 1').

34 **salsedinem:** 'Salsedo', LL (Forcellini; *GLL*).

87–90 **Est bona uox [...] 'den rock aus':** Couplet found in several variants in several fifteenth- and sixteenth-century MSS (Walther, 7316; cf. 7315, 7318; *Initia*, 5616).

24) Conuiuium natale

16 **scindere paenulam:** 'Tear the cloak' in one's eagerness to drag a guest into the house, or to stop him from leaving (Otto, 1321). Erasmus, *Adagia*, 99, 'Scindere penulam'.

30–31 **creaturae:** 'Creatura', 'creation' (as here) or 'creature', LL (*TLL*, IV, col. 1116, l. 44–col. 1117, l. 50; *MLWb*, II, col. 1989, l. 48–col. 1990, l. 24; *DMLBS*, s.v., 2).

74–75 **die Circumcisionis [...] ob noui auspicium anni:** See note to colloquy 41, l. 6.

25) Conuiuium delicatorum palatorum

6 **Stoicos:** Probably intended to represent the CGk adverb 'Στωϊκῶς', 'Stoically'.

21 **Pollucibiliter obsonabo:** 'Parasitos, obsonate pollucibiliter' (Plautus, *Mostellaria*, 24).

41 **Porcina [...] lepram gignens:** A surprising sentiment: medieval and early modern dietetics generally regarded pork as an ideal food (Albala, *Eating Right*, p. 49).

41–43 **Vitulina [...] moros gestire facit:** Early modern dieticians had concerns about veal, but not this one (Castellanus, *Kreophagia*, p. 115; Moffett, *Healths Improvement*, pp. 57, 61; Albala, *Eating Right*, pp. 96, 272).

53–54 **resque mea in uado erit:** In shallow water, i.e. out of danger (Otto, 1843; Plautus, *Aulularia*, 803; Terence, *Andria*, 845). Erasmus, *Adagia*, 45, 'In uado'.

56 **Ne mu quidem:** A misunderstanding on Schotten's part. CGk 'μῦ', 'muttering sound', is used in the phrase 'Ne

my quidem facere audet', 'He does not even dare say *mu*', i.e. 'he is too scared to make any protest' (Erasmus, *Adagia*, 702; *CWE*, XXXII, p. 129; Otto, 1149). The correct expression here would be 'ne gru quidem': see note to *conuiuium* 14, l. 61.

26) Conuiuium helluonum poculis sese urgentium

17 **domicilio cereuisiario:** 'Domicilium cereuisiarium', 'alehouse': an otherwise unrecorded combination of LL 'cer[e]uis[i]arius' (see note to *conuiuium* 20, l. 30) and 'domicilium' in a ML sense of 'inn' (*ML Wb*, III, col. 944, ll. 58–68).

37 **Agathocles:** Tyrant of Syracuse, fourth–third century BC. The son of a pottery manufacturer, as ruler he cultivated the common touch (Diodorus Siculus, *Bibliotheca Historica*, 19.5–21.17, esp. 19.2.7, 19.9.6–7; Pauly, I, cols 237–39).

57–58 **tertium Catonem et octauum sapientem:** Cf. two consecutive *Adagia* of Erasmus: 789, 'Tertius Cato' (see note to colloquy 44, l. 13); and 790, 'Sapientum octauus' (based on Horace, *Sermones*, 2.3.296; Otto, 1581). The 'Seven Sages of Greece' were first listed by Plato (*Protagoras*, 343A).

27) Conuiuium commilitonum litterariorum asses suos congerentium

15 **quo restim emerem:** Erasmus, *Adagia*, 248, 'Nec obolum habet, unde restim emat'; Hegendorff, *Dialogi*, sig. C7r; cf. Otto, 1528.

79–80 **bibuli [...] in crumena:** Though this sounds proverbial, no such saying has been identified.

28) Conuiuium lucri lusorii

3, etc. **Staphyla:** An old woman in Plautus, *Aulularia*.

13 **Nullos nigros nummos?:** A pun on 'albi nummi' (see note to colloquy 32, l. 33). It may allude to the *Möhrchen* ('little Moor'), a coin worth one Heller, so called because of its dark colour (Schwerhoff, 'Köln rüstet sich zur Gottestracht', p. 134).

16 **baculus stramine obsitus extensus:** A stylized bush, the sign of an alehouse. Cf. note to colloquy 118, l. 37.

28 **Ite accubitum mensam:** See note to colloquy 11, l. 24.

53–54 **adhuc butyrum [...] liquefieret:** Cf. 'Die Butter schmilzt ihm noch im Munde', said of young or inexperienced people (Wander, I, 524).

29) Conuiuium ultimi digressus, dum discessus monumentum compotatur

19 **fumi uenditores:** 'Smoke-sellers', CL, 'makers of baseless and misleading promises' (Otto, 730; cf. Martial, *Epigrams*, 4.5.7). Erasmus, *Adagia*, 241, 'Fumos vendere'. 'Fumos huiusmodi magno uendo' (Erasmus, *Colloquia*, p. 323, ll. 124–25).

45 **heros:** Hyperbolic. CL 'heros' can mean a man of outstanding bravery, wisdom, etc. (*TLL*, VI, col. 2663, l. 49–col. 2664, l. 29); in ML 'lord, baron, nobleman' (DuC, 'heroicus', IV, p. 203; *MLLM*; *DMLBS*, s.v., 3; *LLMA*); 'Heros, ein herrlicher Rittermäßiger mann' (Golius, 109).

57 **creaturas:** See note to *conuiuium* 24, ll. 30–31.

30) Conuiuium disceptatorium et litterarium

1 **disceptatorium:** The adj. 'disceptatorius', from CL 'disceptatio', 'debate, dispute', is recorded only in *LPLR*, as used by Budé, *Opera omnia*, IIIB, p. 30, l. 43.

33 **tibi poculorum baratro:** Cf. note to colloquy 97, l. 1.

37–38 **ne tempus [...] comburamus:** Cf. 'Ubi [...] hunc comburamus diem' (Plautus, *Menaechmi*, 152).

39–40 **'Ecce [...] narrent':** Persius, *Satires*, 1.30–31.

45 **Lippi et tonsores:** 'Bleary-eyed men and barbers', proverbial purveyors of gossip (Otto, 1794). Erasmus, *Adagia*, 570, 'Notum lippis ac tonsoribus' (based on Horace, *Sermones*, 1.7.3).

50 **firmamenti:** 'Firmamentum' (CL 'support, stay') in the sense of 'sky, firmament' is LL (*TLL*, VI, col. 805, l. 76–col. 806, l. 35; *GLL*; *DLFAC*, s.v., 4; Blaise, § 289; *DMLBS*, s.v., 3; *MLLM*, s.v., 3).

68 **pedes caeno extrahamus:** Cf. 'Caeno cupiens euellere plantam' (Horace, *Sermones*, 2.7.27).

68–69 **pennas nido extendamus:** Erasmus, *Adagia*, 593, 'Pennas nido maiores extendere', 'enhance one's estate and position in society', based on Horace, *Epistulae*, 1.20.21. Otto, 1423.

IIIc. Index of Schotten's Non-Classical Latin

This index lists: words which are not CL (i.e. LL, ML, NL); CL words not used in their CL sense; and words and phrases which appear to be mistakenly used. Most entries are discussed in the notes.

deuotio (*devotion, piety*) 57, 16.
diadema (*cap, biretta*) 118, 9.
dies Dominicus (*Sunday*) 72, 21.
dies festus (*religious holiday*) 72, 21.
dies macra (*fast day*) 40, 7.
diplois (*doublet*) 20, 29.
disceptatorius, adj. (*pertaining to debate*) *conuiuium* 30, 1.
diuagor (*wander off*) 26, 20.
diuersorium cereuisiarium (*alehouse*) *conuiuium* 20, 30.
diuinor (for diuino) 22, 13 (Edition A only).
diuus (*saint*) 58, 25.
domicilium cereuisiarium (*alehouse*) *conuiuium* 26, 17.
Dominicus: see dies Dominicus.

ecclesia (*church*) 51, 6.
eleemosyna (*alms*) 45, 1.
emunctorius, adj. (*for blowing the nose*) 41, 21.
encomium (*laudatory speech*) 64, 11.
Epiphania (*Epiphany*) *conuiuium* 6, 1
esurialis (*fasting, fast-, Lenten*) 37, 33.
esuries (*hunger*) 9, 33.
ethnicus (*pagan, heathen*) 87, 33.
eucharistia (*eucharist*) 59, 1.
exploror (for exploro) 86, 13; *conuiuium* 2, 11.

facio (causative use) 29, 8.
farcio: see manus farcio
feriae natales Christianae (*Christmas*) 36, 3–4.
ferior (*take a holiday, refrain from*) 22, 38.
festum natale Christi (*Christmas*) 35, 1.
festum sancti (*saint's day*) 72, 11.
flagellum (*stick used in the game of hitting the ball through the hoop*) 48, 17.
(in) foribus (*close at hand*) 55, 7.
fortiter (*greatly*) 8, 6.

gentilis (*pagan, heathen*) 33, 26.
glaciem seco (*make a beginning, pioneer*) 18, 29.
(ludus) globorum missilium (*the game of marbles*) 47, 1.
(ludus) globularis (*the game of marbles*) 47, 9.

globulus (*marble*) 47, 10.
globus missilis (*marble*) 47, 1.
globulus missilis per pollicem (*marble*) 47, 13.
globus (*ball*) 48, 1.
globus per annulum ferreum (*croquet-like game*) *conuiuium* 19, 10–11; cf. colloquy 48, 1.
gradus (*university degree*) 60, 41.
gymnasium triuiale (*grammar school*) 60, 1.

halec (*herring*) 8, 19.
halec erutum salsugine (*pickled herring*) 8, 26.
heros (*gentleman, nobleman*) *conuiuium* 29, 45.
hibernaculum (*heated living-room*) 27, 7.
hostia (*host, Eucharistic wafer*) 59, 21.
hymnus (*hymn*) 78, 32.

ientor (for iento) 7, 18.
illarido (*lard*; perhaps *spit-roast*) *conuiuium* 13, 65.
indusium (*shirt*) 62, 25.
insipidus (*tasteless*) *conuiuium* 4, 65.
integrum est (*it is convenient*) 40, 28.
interula (*shirt*) 41, 25.
inuectiuus, adj. (*relating to invective*) *conuiuium* 17, 1.
iubilaeus, adj.: see Annus Iubilaeus.

ligneolum (*small piece or sliver of wood*) 47, 18; cf. 70, 9.
(pedum) lotio (*Mandatum, washing of feet on Maundy Thursday*) 58, 17.
lucernarius, adj. (*scholarly*) *conuiuium* 10, 39.
ludus globorum missilium (*the game of marbles*) 47, 1.
ludus globorum qui torquentur per annulum (*croquet-like game*) 48, 1; cf. *conuiuium* 19, 10–11.
ludus globularis (*the game of marbles*) 47, 9.
lusorius, adj.: see charta lusoria.

macra dies (*fast day*) 40, 7.
manuariae (artes) (*crafts, skilled trades*) 64, 27.
manus farcio (alicui) (*line someone's palm with money*) 32, 11.
mechanicus (*artisanal*) 42, 27.
merendinarius, adj. (*pertaining to the middle of the day*) 9, 15.

potus tenuis (*small beer*) *conuiuium* 3, 30.
praeceptor (*superior of a hospitaller monastic order*) 58, 40.
praefigo (*arrange*) 117, 3.
praesentionarius (*priest paid for celebrating services*) 107, 27.
procenium (*hors-d'œuvres, starter*) 77, 19.
promptitudo (*alertness, dexterity*) 48, 32.
promptuarium (*chamber, storeroom*) 43, 38.
prosternatio (*knocking down*) 31, 14.
prosternatio galli (*the sport of shooting at a cock*) 31, 14.
pulmentum (*porridge, pottage*) 84, 12.

quadra (*plate, trencher*) 67, 27.
Quadragesima (*Lent*) 36, 4.
quando (for cum) 20, 26.

raptitius liber (*notebook, commonplace book*) 122, 7.
ruditas (*ignorance*) 85, 29.

sacellanus (*chaplain, curate*) 89, 22.
sacerdotium (*benefice*) 91, 7.
sacra Synaxis (*Eucharist, Mass*) 39, 18.
sacrificia (*Mass*) 72, 10.
sacrificium (*Mass*) 88, 1.
sacrificium missae (*Mass*) 72, 18.
saepiuscule (*rather often*) 20, 32.
salsedo (*saltiness*) *conuiuium* 23, 34.
sancti festum (*saint's day*) 72, 11.
satago (*satisfy*) 95, 31.
scomma (*joke, witty remark*) 108, 9.
scribiligo (*pastry, pretzel*) 123, 134.
se (for is) 53, 27; 123, 118, and frequently.
serum (*evening*) 4, 5.
solidus (*Schilling*) 5, 26.
(hominis) somnium (*worthless man*) 116, 3.
sorbitiuncula: see ouorum sorbitiuncula.
sordities (*dirt, filth*) 61, 28.
stribiligo (spelling of scribiligo) 123, 134.
succulus (*piglet*) *conuiuium* 20, 21.
suppactor calcearius (*shoemaker, cobbler*) 120, 7.
suscepto (*take on*) 112, 6.

suus (for eius) p. 44, 24; 40, 37, and frequently.
symbolum (for symbola) 26, 33.
Synaxis (*eucharist, mass*) 39, 18.

talentum (*pound*) 95, 15.
templum (*church building*) 35, 20.
tempus Bacchanale (*Shrovetide*) 36, 1.
tenuis: see potus tenuis.
tiara (*hat, biretta*) 54, 21; cf. 118, 9.
(gymnasium) triuiale (*grammar school*) 60, 1.
triuialis (*pertaining to the academic 'trivium'*) 60, 1.

uendico (spelling of uindico) 42, 30.
uentris anhelitus (*fart*) 12, 11.
uicissitudinarius (*happening by turns*) 98, 1.
uillanus, adj. (*rustic, boorish*) 4, 12.
uiuifico (*give life*) *conuiuium* 6, 106.
ulna (*ell*) 41, 25.
uocem do (*vote*) 33, 5.
utrisque brachiis (*with open arms*) 52, 16–17.

Hans Weiditz, *Cheesemaker and his Wife* (Geisberg, G. 1517).

Select Bibliography

Items are listed either under abbreviated titles, or in the main list of secondary literature.

Abbreviations:

Periodicals, series, and frequently cited works referred to by abbreviated titles.

ADB:	*Allgemeine Deutsche Biographie*, ed. by Historische Commission bei der königlichen Akademie der Wissenschaften (Bayern), 66 vols (Leipzig: Duncker und Humblot, 1875–1912).
AHVN:	*Annalen des Historischen Vereins für den Niederrhein, insbesondere die alte Diözese Köln.*
Alte Un.:	Keussen, Hermann, *Die alte Universität Köln: Grundzüge ihrer Verfassung und Geschichte*, VKG, 10 (Cologne: Creutzer, 1934).
AMKG:	*Archiv für mittelrheinische Kirchengeschichte.*
ASD:	Erasmus, Desiderius, of Rotterdam, *Opera omnia Desiderii Erasmi Roterodami*, ed. by Jan Hendrik Waszink and others (Amsterdam: North Holland, 1969–).
Bianco, I:	Bianco, Franz Joseph von, *Die alte Universität Köln und die späteren Gelehrten-Schulen dieser Stadt, nach archivarischen und anderen zuverlässigen Quellen.* I. Theil. Erste Abtheilung: *Die alte Universität Köln* (Cologne: Gehly, 1855).

Bianco, I, 2: Bianco, Franz Joseph von, *Die ehemalige Universität und die Gymnasien zu Köln, so wie die an diese Lehr-Anstalten geknüpften Studien-Stiftungen von ihrem Ursprunge bis auf unsere Zeiten.* II. Theil, 2nd edn (Cologne: Gehly, 1850).

Blaise: Blaise, Albert, *Le vocabulaire latin des principaux thèmes liturgiques*, rev. edn, ed. by Antoine Dumas, OSB (Turnhout: Brepols, [1966]).

BRStK: *Beschlüsse des Rates der Stadt Köln 1320–1550*, ed. by Manfred Huiskes and Manfred Groten, PGRG, 65, 5 vols (Düsseldorf: Droste, 1988–1990).

BW: *Das Buch Weinsberg. Kölner Denkwürdigkeiten aus dem 16. Jahrhundert*, ed. by Konstantin Höhlbaum and others, PGRG, 3, 4, 16, 5 vols (Leipzig: Dürr, and Bonn: Hanstein, 1886–1926; repr. Düsseldorf: Droste, 2000).

CCFr: *Catalogue Collectif de France* (Paris, Bibliothèque Nationale de France), online at: <http://ccfr.bnf.fr/portailccfr/servlet/LoginServlet>.

CE: *The Catholic Encyclopedia*, ed. by C.G. Herbermann and others, 17 vols (New York: The Encyclopedia Press, 1913–1922).

CIC: *Corpus Iuris Canonici In Tres Partes Distinctum; Glossis Diversorum illustratum [...]*, 3 vols (Lyon: J.A. Huguetan and G. Barbier, 1671).

CIC, ed. by Friedberg: *Corpus Iuris Canonici*, ed. by Emil Friedberg, 2 vols (Leipzig: Tauchnitz, 1879, 1881).

CoE: *Contemporaries of Erasmus. A Biographical Register of the Renaissance and Reformation*, ed. by Peter G. Bietenholz and Thomas B. Deutscher, 3 vols (Toronto: University of Toronto Press, 1985–1987).

CWE: *Collected Works of Erasmus*, ed. by Alexander Dalzell and others (Toronto, University of Toronto Press, 1974–).

DBE: *Deutsche Biographische Enzyklopädie*, ed. by Walter Killy and others, 13 vols in 15 (Munich: Saur, 1995–2000).

DBI: *Deutscher Biographischer Index*, ed. by Willi Gorzny and others, 4 vols (Munich–London–New York–Oxford–Paris: Saur, 1986).

Dasypodius: Dasypodius, Petrus, *Dictionarium Latino-Germanicum* (Strasbourg: W. Rihel, 1536; repr., ed. by Gilbert de Smet, Hildesheim: Olms, 1974).

DEL: Stelten, Leo F., *Dictionary of Ecclesiastical Latin* (Peabody, Mass.: Hendrickson, 1995).

Denzinger: *Enchiridion symbolorum, definitionum et declarationum de rebus fidei et morum*, ed. by Henricus Denzinger; 34th edn, rev. by Adolfus Schönmetzer, SJ (Barcelona–Freiburg im Breisgau–Rome–New York: Herder, 1967).

Diefenbach: Diefenbach, Lorenz, *Novum glossarium Latino-Germanicum mediae et infimae aetatis [...]* (Frankfurt am Main: Sauerländer, 1867).

Diel: *Die pfarramtlichen Aufzeichnungen (Liber consuetudinum) des Florentius Diel zu St. Christoph in Mainz (1491–1518)*, ed. by Franz Falk, Erläuterungen und Ergänzungen zu Janssens Geschichte des deutschen Volkes, 4:3 (Freiburg: Herder, 1904).

Disticha Catonis: Cato, Marcus Porcius the Censor (attrib.), *Disticha Catonis*, ed. by M. Boas (Amsterdam: North Holland, 1962).

DLFAC: Blaise, Albert, *Dictionnaire latin-français des auteurs chrétiens* (Strasbourg: Le latin chrétien, 1954; repr. Turnhout: Brepols, 1975).

DMLBS: *Dictionary of Medieval Latin from British Sources*, ed. by R.E. Latham and D.R. Howlett (Oxford: Oxford University Press for the British Academy, 1975–).

DuC: Du Cange, Charles, *Glossarium mediae et infimae Latinitatis*, rev. edn, ed. by Léopold Favre, 10 vols (Niort: Favre, 1883–1887).

EETS: Early English Text Society, Publications.

Erasmus, *Epistolae*: *Opus Epistolarum Desiderii Erasmi Roterodami*, ed. by P.S. Allen and others, 11 vols (Oxford: Clarendon, 1907–1945).

Estienne: Estienne, Robert, *Dictionarium Latinogallicum, postrema hac aeditione valde locupletatum* (Paris: C. Estienne, 1552).

Estienne, 1561: Estienne, Robert, *Dictionarium Latinogallicum [...] plurimum adauctum* ([Paris]: [C. Estienne], [1561]).

Festschr. Köln: *Festschrift zur Erinnerung an die Gründung der alten Universität Köln im Jahre 1388*, ed. by Hubert Graven (Cologne: Schroeder, 1938).

Forcellini: Forcellini, Egidio, *Totius Latinitatis Lexicon [...]*, rev. edn, ed. by Vicenzo De Vit, 10 vols (Brescia: Typis Aldinianis, 1860–1887).

Franck: *Sprichwörter/ Schöne/ Weise/ Herzliche Clugreden/ vnnd Hoff sprüch [...] Beschriben vnnd außgeleget/ Durch Sebastian Francken*, 2 vols (Frankfurt am Main: C. Egenolff, 1541).

Geisberg : Geisberg, Max, *The German Single-Leaf Woodcut. 1500–1550*, rev. and ed. by Walter L. Strauss, 4 vols (New York: Hacker Art Books, 1974).

GEK: *Geschichte des Erzbistums Köln*, ed. by Norbert Trippen and others (Cologne: Bachem, 1972–).

Gelenius: Gelenius, Aegidius, *De admiranda, sacra et civili magnitudine Coloniae Claudiae Agrippinensis Augustae Ubiorum urbis libri IV* (Cologne: J. Kalkhoff, 1645).

GiK: *Geschichte in Köln.*

Glasner: Glasner, Peter, *Die Lesbarkeit der Stadt*, 2 vols. [I]. *Kulturgeschichte der mittelalterlichen Straßennamen Kölns.* [II]. *Lexikon der mittelalterlichen Straßennamen Kölns* (Cologne: DuMont, 2002).

GLL: Souter, Alexander, *A Glossary of Later Latin to 600 A.D.* (Oxford: Clarendon Press, 1949).

Golius Golius, Theophilus, *Onomasticon Latinogermanicum, in usum scholae Argentoratensis collectum [...] Cum praefatione Ioannis Sturmii* (Strasbourg: J. Rihel, 1579; repr., with intro. by Gilbert de Smet, Documenta Linguistica, Reihe II, Hildesheim: Olms, 1972). *VD 16*, G 2635.

Grimm: Grimm, Jakob and Wilhelm Grimm, *Deutsches Wörterbuch*, 16 vols and index (Leipzig: Hirzel, 1854–1971).

GW: *Gesamtkatalog der Wiegendrucke*, ed. by Kommission für den Gesamtkatalog der Wiegendrucke (Leipzig: Hiersemann, then Stuttgart: Hiersemann and Berlin: Akademie, then Stuttgart: Hiersemann, 1925–).

HDA: *Handwörterbuch des deutschen Aberglaubens*, ed. by Hanns Bächtold-Stäubli and others (Berlin: de Gruyter, 1927–1942).

HL: *Humanistica Lovaniensia.*

HRG: *Handwörterbuch zur deutschen Rechtsgeschichte*, ed. by Adalbert Erler and Ekkehard Kaufmann, 5 vols (Berlin: Schmidt, 1971–1998).

HUE: *A History of the University in Europe*, ed. by Walter Rüegg, 4 vols (Cambridge: Cambridge

University Press). I. *Universities in the Middle Ages*, ed. by Hilde de Ridder-Symoens (1992). II. *Universities in Early Modern Europe (1500–1800)*, ed. by Hilde de Ridder-Symoens (1996).

Initia: *Carmina medii aevi posterioris latina.* I. *Initia carminum ac versuum medii aevi posterioris latinorum: alphabetisches Verzeichnis der Versanfänge mittellateinischer Dichtungen*, ed. by A. Hilka and H. Walther (Göttingen: Vandenhoeck & Ruprecht, 1959–1969).

Isenmann: Isenmann, Eberhard, *Die deutsche Stadt im Spätmittelalter 1250–1500. Stadtgestalt, Recht, Stadtregiment, Kirche, Gesellschaft, Wirtschaft*, UTB Große Reihe (Stuttgart: Ulmer, 1988).

JKGV: *Jahrbuch des Kölnischen Geschichtsvereins.*

Jöcher: Jöcher, Christian Gottlieb, *Allgemeines Gelehrten-Lexicon [...]*, 11 vols (Leipzig: n.pr., 1750–1897; repr. Hildesheim: Olms, 1960–1961).

KL: *Kirchenlexikon oder Encyclopädie der katholischen Theologie und ihrer Hilfswissenschaften*, ed. by Heinrich Joseph Wetzer and Benedikt Welte, 2nd edn, rev. by Joseph Cardinal Hergenröther and Franz Kaulen, 12 vols (Freiburg im Breisgau: Herder, 1886–1901).

KiM: Keussen, Hermann, *Köln im Mittelalter: Topographie und Verfassung* (Bonn: Hanstein, 1918).

Klersch: Klersch, Joseph, *Volkstum und Volksleben in Köln. Ein Beitrag zur historischen Soziologie der Stadt*, 3 vols (Cologne: Bachem, 1965–1969).

Kuske, *Quellen*: *Quellen zur Geschichte des Kölner Handels und Verkehrs im Mittelalter*, ed. by Bruno Kuske, PGRG, 33, 4 vols (Bonn: Hanstein, 1917–1934; repr. Düsseldorf: Droste, 1978).

KVK: *Karlsruher Virtueller Katalog* (Universität Karlsruhe, Universitätsbibliothek), online at:

<http://www.ubka.uni-karlsruhe.de/kvk.html>.

LB: Erasmus, Desiderius, of Rotterdam, *Opera omnia emendatiora et auctiora [...]*, ed. by Jean Le Clerc, 10 vols (Leiden: P. Vander Aa, 1703–1706).

LCI: *Lexikon der christlichen Ikonographie*, ed. by Engelbert Kirschbaum, SJ and Wolfgang Braunfels, 8 vols (Rome–Freiburg–Basel–Vienna: Herder, 1968–1976).

Legenda aurea: Voragine, Jacobus de, *Legenda aurea: vulgo Historia Lombardica dicta*, ed. by Theodor Graesse (Dresden–Leipzig: Arnold, 1846).

LLMA: Blaise, Albert, *Lexicon Latinitatis Medii Aevi praesertim ad res ecclesiasticas investigandas pertinens. Dictionnaire latin-français des auteurs du Moyen-Age*, Corpus Christianorum Continuatio Medievalis (Turnhout: Brepols, 1975).

LPLR: Hoven, René, *Lexique de la prose latine de la Renaissance* (Leiden: Brill, 1994).

LThK: *Lexikon für Theologie und Kirche*, 2nd edition, ed. by Josef Höfer and Karl Rahner, 10 vols and index (Freiburg: Herder, 1957–1967).

LThK^3: *Lexikon für Theologie und Kirche*, 3rd edition, ed. by Walter Kasper and others (Freiburg: Herder, 1993–).

Matrikel: *Die Matrikel der Universität Köln*, ed. by Hermann Keussen and others, 7 vols, PGRG, 8 (Bonn: Hanstein). I. *1389–1475* (^{2}1928); II. *1476–1559* (1919); III. *Nachträge 1389–1559 und Register zu Bd. I und II* (1931); IV. 1559–1675, bearb. Ulrike Nyassi and Mechthild Wilkes (1981); V. 1675–1797, bearb. Ulrike Nyassi and Mechthild Wilkes (1981); VI. Register, 1559–1797, A–H, bearb. Manfred Groten and Manfred Huiskes (1981); VII. Register, 1559–1797, I–Z, bearb. Manfred Groten and Manfred Huiskes (1981).

Meuthen, *Universität*: *Kölner Universitätsgeschichte. Herausgegeben von der Senatskommission für die Geschichte der Universität zu Köln*, 3 vols (Cologne–Vienna: Böhlau, 1988), I: Meuthen, Erich, *Die alte Universität*.

MLLM: Niermeyer, J.F., and C. Van de Kieft, *Mediae Latinitatis Lexicon Minus*, revised edn, ed. by J.W.J. Burgers, 2 vols (Leiden–Boston: Brill, 2002).

ML Wb: *Mittellateinisches Wörterbuch bis zum ausgehenden 13. Jahrhundert*, ed. by Bayerische Akademie der Wissenschaften and Deutsche Akademie der Wissenschaften in Berlin (Munich: Beck, 1967–).

MStAK: Mitteilungen aus dem Stadtarchiv von Köln.

NCE *The New Catholic Encyclopedia*, 2nd edn, ed. by Bernard L. Marthaler, OFMConv and others, 15 vols (Detroit: Thomson Gale, 2003).

NDB: *Neue Deutsche Biographie*, ed. by Historische Kommission bei der Bayerischen Akademie der Wissenschaften (Berlin: Duncker & Humblot, 1952–).

N&K: Nijhoff, Wouter, and M.E. Kronenberg, *Nederlandsche Bibliographie van 1500 tot 1540*, 3 vols (The Hague: Martinus Nijhoff, 1923–1971).

NLW: Ramminger, Johann, *Neulateinische Wortliste. Ein Wörterbuch des Lateinischen von Petrarca bis 1700*, on-line at <http://www.neulatein.de>.

NUC: *The National Union Catalog. Pre-1956 Imprints*, ed. by the American Library Association, 754 vols (London–Chicago: Mansell, 1968–1981).

OCCL[1]: *The Oxford Companion to Classical Literature*,

ed. by Sir Paul Harvey (Oxford: Oxford University Press, 1937).

OCCL[2]: *The Oxford Companion to Classical Literature*, ed. by M.C. Howatson (Oxford: Oxford University Press, 1989).

OCY: Blackburn, Bonnie J., and Leofranc Holford-Strevens, *The Oxford Companion to the Year* (New York: Oxford University Press, 1999).

ODEP: *The Oxford Dictionary of English Proverbs*, 3rd edn, rev. by F.D. Wilson (Oxford: Clarendon Press, 1970).

OED: *The Oxford English Dictionary*, 2nd edn, prep. by J.A. Simpson and E.S.C. Weiner, 20 vols (Oxford: Clarendon Press, 1991).

ÖH: *Ökumenisches Heiligenlexikon*, online at <http://www.heiligenlexikon.de>.

OLD: *Oxford Latin Dictionary*, ed. by P.J.W. Glare, corrected edn (Oxford: Clarendon Press, 1996).

Otto: Otto, August, *Die Sprichwörter und sprichwörtlichen Redensarten der Römer* (Leipzig: Teubner, 1890).

Pauly[1]: Pauly, August Friedrich von, *Real-Encyclopädie der classischen Altertumswissenschaft*, rev. edn, ed. by G. Wissowa and others, 49 vols (Stuttgart–Weimar: Metzler, 1894–1978).

Pauly: *Der neue Pauly: Enzyklopädie der Antike*, ed. by Hubert Cancik and Helmuth Schneider (Stuttgart: Metzler, 1996–).

PGRG: Publikationen der Gesellschaft für Rheinische Geschichtskunde.

PL: *Patrologiae cursus completus [. . .] Series Latina*, ed. by Jacques-Paul Migne, 221 vols (Paris: Migne; last vol. Garnier, 1844–1890).

QGSK — *Quellen zur Geschichte der Stadt Köln*, ed. by Joachim Deeters and others, 2 vols (Cologne: Bachem, 1996).

REK: — *Die Regesten der Erzbischöfe von Köln im Mittelalter*, ed. by Richard Knipping and others, PGRG, 21 (Düsseldorf: Droste, 1901–).

RMLWL: — Latham, Ronald Edward, *Revised Medieval Latin Word-list from British and Irish Sources* (London: The British Academy, 1965).

SEECO, V,1: — *Series episcoporum ecclesiae catholicae occidentalis ab initio usque ad annum 1198*, ed. by Odilo Engels and Stefan Weinfurter (Stuttgart: Hiersemann, 1982–). Series V. *Germania*, Tomus I. *Archiepiscopatus Coloniensis*, ed. by Stefan Weinfurter and others (1982).

Serranus: — Serranus, Joannes, *Dictionarium latino-germanicum, quo singulae uoces latinae, germanice simpliciter interpretantur pro literarum tyronibus ex aliquot nostri temporis autoribus comportatum, & in ordinem alphabeticum congestum* (Nuremberg: J. Petreius, 153; repr., ed. by Gilbert de Smet, Documenta Linguistica, Reihe 1, Wörterbücher des 15. und 16. Jahrhunderts, Hildesheim: Olms, 1974).

Stein: — *Akten zur Geschichte der Verfassung und Verwaltung der Stadt Köln im 14. und 15. Jahrhundert*, ed. by Walther Stein, 2 vols, PGRG, 10 and 10.2 (Bonn: Behrendt, 1893–1895; repr. Düsseldorf: Droste, 1993).

Stotz: — Stotz, Peter, *Handbuch zur lateinischen Sprache des Mittelalters*, 5 vols (Munich: Beck, 1996–2004). (Citations refer not to the volumes but to the seven books into which the work is divided.)

TLL: — *Thesaurus Linguae Latinae, ed. auctoritate et consilio academiarum quinque Germanicarum:*

Berolinensis, Gottingensis, Lipsiensis, Monacensis, Vindobonensis (Leipzig, then Stuttgart: Teubner, 1900–).

Topogr.: Keussen, Hermann, *Topographie der Stadt Köln im Mittelalter*, 2 vols (Bonn: Hanstein, 1910; repr. Düsseldorf: Droste, 1986).

VD 16: *Verzeichnis der im deutschen Sprachbereich erschienenen Drucke des XVI. Jahrhunderts*, hrsg. von der Bayerischen Staatsbibliothek in München in Verbindung mit der Herzog August Bibliothek in Wolfenbüttel (Stuttgart: Hiersemann, 1983–).

VD 16 online Online at <http://bvba2.bib-bvb.de/V/8UNFJN7GXVRLP1K8C4Q1UIA2FYRJX7Y25FCKMFNHJ9DQD6VH52-67766?func=file&file_name=search_vd16>.

VKGV: Veröffentlichungen des Kölnischen Geschichtsvereins, e.V.

VL: *Die deutsche Literatur des Mittelalters. Verfasserlexikon.* 2nd edn, ed. by Kurt Ruh and others (Berlin–New York: de Gruyter, 1978–).

Vulgate: *Biblia Sacra Vulgatae Editionis [...]*, ed. by Michael Hetzenhauer, OFMCap (Regensburg–Rome: Pustet, 1922).

WA: Luther, Martin, *Werke. Kritische Gesamtausgabe (Weimarer Ausgabe)* (Weimar: Böhlau, 1883–).

WATr. Luther, Martin, *Werke. Kritische Gesamtausgabe (Weimarer Ausgabe)*, *Tischreden*, 6 vols (Weimar: Böhlau, 1912–1921).

Walther: *Proverbia sententiaeque Latinitatis medii aevi. Lateinische Sprichwörter und Sentenzen des Mittelalters in alphabetischer Anordnung, gesammelt und hrsg. von Hans Walther*, 6 vols, Carmina Medii Aevi Posterioris Latina, II/1–6

(Göttingen: Vandenhoeck & Ruprecht, 1963–1967).
and

Proverbia sententiaeque Latinitatis medii ac recentioris aevi. Nova series. Lateinische Sprichwörter und Sentenzen des Mittelalters und der frühen Neuzeit in alphabetischer Anordnung, aus dem Nachlaß von Hans Walther hrsg. von Paul Gerhard Schmidt, 3 vols, Carmina Medii Aevi Posterioris Latina, II/7–9 (Göttingen: Vandenhoeck & Ruprecht, 1982–1986).

The numbering of the items in the two series is continuous.

Wander: Wander, Karl Friedrich Wilhelm, *Deutsches Sprichwörter-Lexikon. Ein Hausschatz für das deutsche Volk*, 5 vols (Leipzig: Brockhaus, 1867–1880; repr. Darmstadt, Wissenschaftliche Buchgesellschaft, 1964).

ZVV: *Zeitschrift des Vereins für Volkskunde.*

Zwei Jahrtausende: *Zwei Jahrtausende Kölner Wirtschaft. Herausgegeben im Auftrag des Rheinisch-Westfälischen Wirtschaftsarchivs zu Köln von Hermann Kellenbenz, unter Mitarbeit von Klara von Eyll*, 2 vols (Cologne: Greven, 1975).

Archival sources:

Cologne, Historisches Archiv der Stadt Köln (HAStK). (See Kuphal, 'Die Archive der Universität Köln', and Deeters, *Die Bestände des Stadtarchivs Köln bis 1814*.)

Bestand 30 (Verfassung und Verwaltung) (V+V):

N 230: Collection of printed broadsheet funeral regulations from the years 1578–1795. Relevant items are listed separately in the bibliography below.

N 807: Two funeral regulations, 1578, 1592.

V 108: (fols 17r–19r): Reply of the City Council to the 1525 citizens' articles (see Bestand 56, 385).

Bestand 150 (Universität) (Un):

A 36–42: University of Cologne, Matricula, 7 vols. 36: I (1389–1425). 37: II (1425–1466). 38: III (1466–1502). 39: IV (1502–1559). 40: V (1559–1627). 41: VI (1627–1709). 42: VII (1754–1788) and University chronicle.

A 230 (previously 114a): 19th–20th-c. copy of extracts made by Nikolaus Brewer from the *Dekanatsbuch* of the Theology Faculty. I: 1398–1658. (Not Brewer, *Collectio statutorum, decretorum et responsorum facultatis theologicae* as stated in *Matrikel*, II, p. 793)).

A 478–482: University of Cologne, *Dekanatsbuch* of the Arts Faculty, 5 vols. 478: I (1406–1440). 479: II (1440–1457). 480: III (1458–1499). 481: IV (1500–1565). 482: V (1565–1612).

A 516: Receptor's (Treasurer's) Book of the Arts Faculty, 1518–1564.

A 760 (previously 390a): *Historia ACADEMIAE ARTIVM AGRIPPINENSIS. praecipuè Gymnasii Laurentiani, et Artium aliorum omnium*, a short history of the *Bursa Laurentiana*, to 1530, with continuations up to 1788. Paper MS, 14 fols.

Bestand 7004:

27: Cookbook, Rheinfranken or Mainfranken, 15th c., second half. Paper, 66 fols (Previously Hs. G.B. 4° 27).

Bestand 7030 (Chroniken und Darstellungen) (C+D):

49–52: *Das Buch Weinsberg*, the chronicle of Hermann von Weinsberg. 49: 'Liber iuventutis', 1518–1577; 50: 'Liber senectutis', 1578–1587; 51: 'Liber decrepitudinis', 1588–1597; 52: 'Claickboich'.

53–60: Various documents, accounts, wills and codicils pertaining to Hermann von Weinsberg's chronicle.

Schotten's works:

Ludus grammaticus latinae Linguae tramitem ostendens (Cologne: S. Kruffter, 1525). Sole known copy: Augsburg, Staats- und Stadtbibliothek, shelfmark Phil. 1226.

Meta Studii literarii [e]t quomodo in eam sint ducenda omnium scientiarum genera, necnon cur sit inuentus labor literarius: Et quantum toto coelo, nunc aberrent hij, qui a literis se abdicant/ Autore Hermanno Scottennio Heßo (Cologne: S. Kruffter, [1525]). *VD 16*, S 4029.

Confabulationes tyronum literariorum, ad amussim Colloquiorum Erasmi Roterodami, authore Hermanno Schotten. Heso [sic] (Augsburg: S. Ruff, July 1525). *VD 16*, S 4005.

Ludus martius sive bellicus, co[n]tinens simulachrum, originem, fabulam, & finem dissidij, habiti inter Rusticos & Principes Germaniae Orie[n]talis. Anno. 1525 Autore Hermanno Schotte[n]nio Hesso. [...] (Cologne: P. Quentel, 1526). *VD 16 online*, ZV 24274.

Ludus Martius sive bellicus: Mars- oder Kriegsspiel, ed. and trans. by H.-G. Roloff, Bibliotheca Neolatina, 1 (Bern–Frankfurt–New York–Paris: Lang, 1990).

Ludus imperatorius sive caesareus, continens umbraticam imaginem, horum temporum, regnante Diuo Carolo quinto, illiusque Caesaris diuinas uictorias, imperij felicem exitum, & laudem, autore Hermanno Schottennio Hesso. Cui accedit, & Ludus Martius, de discordia principum & rusticorum Germaniae, anni M. D. XXV (Cologne: P. Quentel, 1527). *VD 16*, S 4027.

Instructio prima puerorum [...] per colloquia mutua (Cologne: [P. Quentel], 1527). *VD 16*, S 4026.

Vita honesta sive virtutis [...] (Cologne: P. Quentel, 1527). *VD 16*, S 4030 (much reprinted). Quoted from the edition of Antwerp: A. Goinus, 1540.

Elementale Dialectices Eivsdem quoq[ue] artis origo, utilitas & fructus pingui minerua a Grammatica ad Dialecticam pro-

gressuris prelibandum & frugiferum, Autore Hermanno Schottennio Hesso (Cologne: [P. Quentel], 1528). *VD 16 online*, ZV 25766.

Centuria epistolarum proverbialium quibus in providentia humanarum rerum. instructio. eruditio. & calliditas per adagia docentur & traduntur (Cologne: [P. Quentel], 1529). *VD 16*, S 4002.

Colloquia philosophica, & consolatoria, ac exhortatoria, vtriusque fortunæ ferendæ modum docentia, iuxta Senecæ & Francisci Petrarche consilia, ne inexperta rerum adolescentia temere sapiat, neve in prosperis plus æquo gestiat, atque in aduersis animam non despondeat. Authore Hermanno Schottennio Hesso (Cologne: P. Quentel, 1535). *VD 16*, S 4004.

Colloquia moralia ex variis philosophorum dictis condita [...] (Cologne: P. Quentel, 1535). *VD 16*, S 4003.

Other Sources:

References to classical literature, unless otherwise stated, are not to specific editions; any convenient edition may be used.

Abel, Michael, *Carminum [...] libri IIII [...]* (n.p., n. pr., 1590). *VD 16*, A 20.

Agenda S. Coloniensis Ecclesiæ. Hoc est: Liber Pastoralis, in quo continentur, quae in sacramentis administrandis, aliisque ritibus Sacris peragendis, ad Parochorum, ac Sacerdotum animarum curam habentium, officium spectant, [...] (Cologne: P. Cholinus and the heirs of B. Gualtherus, 1637).

Albala, Ken, *Eating Right in the Renaissance*, California Studies in Food and Culture, 2 (Berkeley: University of California Press, 2002).

Amberg, Gottfried, *Ceremoniale Coloniense. Die Feier des Gottesdienstes durch das Stiftskapitel an der hohen Domkirche zu Köln bis zum Ende der reichsstädtischen Zeit*, Studien zur Kölner Kirchengeschichte, 17 (Siegburg: F. Schmitt, 1982).

Die Amerbachkorrespondenz, im Auftrag der Kommission für die Öffentliche Bibliothek der Universität Basel bearb. und hrsg. von Alfred Hartmann (Basel: Universitätsbibliothek, 1942–).

Analecta Hymnica medii aevi, ed. by Clemens Blume and Guido M. Dreves, 55 vols (Leipzig: Fues, 1886–1922; repr. Frankfurt: Minerva, 1961); *Register*, ed. by M. Lütolf, 2 vols in 3 (Berne–Munich: Francke, 1978).

Andronicus, Livius, *Livi Andronici et Cn. Naevi fabularum reliquiae*, ed. by Lucian Müller (Berlin: Calvari, 1885).

Anthologia Latina, sive Poesis latinae supplementum, ed. by Franz Buecheler and Alexander Riese, 5 vols (Leipzig: Teubner, 1894–1926; repr. Amsterdam: Hakkert, 1964).

Apicius, *L'Art culinaire. De re coquinaria*, ed. and trans. by Jacques André, Collection des Universités de France (Paris: Les Belles Lettres, 1974).

Apostolios, Michael, of Byzantium, *Proverbia*, quoted from *Michaelis Apostolii Paroemiae [...]* (Leiden: Elzevier, 1619).

The babees book [...]. Manners and Meals in Olden Time, ed. by Frederick J. Furnivall, EETS, o.s., 32 (London: EETS, 1868). Subsequently published under the title *Early English Meals and Manners*.

Bahlmann, P., 'Die Lambertus-Feier zu Münster i. W.', *ZVV*, 5 (1895), 174–80.

Barlandus, Hadrianus, *Dialogi XLII ad profligandam e scholis barbariem utilissimi* (Louvain: P. Martin Alost, 1524); cited from the edition of Antwerp: J. van der Loe, 1550.

Barth, Susanne, 'Petrus Mosellanus: *Paedologia*', in *Handbuch zur Kinder- und Jugendliteratur 1570 bis 1750*, ed. by Theodor Brüggemann and Otto Brunken, 2 vols (Stuttgart: Metzler, 1987–1991), I, cols 414–29.

Bauer, Max, *Sittengeschichte des deutschen Studententums* (Dresden: Aretz, [1928]; repr. Schernfeld: SH, 1991).

Bebel, Heinrich, *Adagia Germanica*, in [*Bebeliana opuscula nova*] (Strasbourg: J. Grüninger, 1508), sig. Ii^{r}–Miii^{r}.

——, *Facetien: drei Bücher. Historisch-kritische Ausgabe*, ed. by Gustav Bebermeyer, Bibliothek des Literarischen Vereins in Stuttgart, 276 (Leipzig: Hiersemann, 1931; repr. Hildesheim: Olms, 1967).

——, *Facetiarum [...] libri tres, a mendis repurgati [...]* (Tübingen: [Widow of U. Morhard], 1570).

——, *Liber hymnorum in metra noviter redactorum [...]* ([Tübingen]: [J. Otmar], [1501]). *VD 16*, H 6513.

Beemelmans, Wilhelm, 'Bilder aus dem Kölner Volksleben im XVI. Jahrhundert', *JKGV*, 15 (1933), 135–52.

Benzing, Josef, *Die Buchdrucker des 16. und 17. Jahrhunderts im deutschen Sprachgebiet*, 2nd edn (Wiesbaden: Harrassowitz, 1982).

Bömer, Alois, *Die lateinischen Schülergespräche der Humanisten. Auszüge mit Einleitungen, Anmerkungen und Namen- und Sachregister. Quellen für die Schul- und Universitätsgeschichte des 15. und 16. Jahrhunderts*, Texte und Forschungen zur Geschichte der Erziehung und des Unterrichts in den Ländern deutscher Zunge, 1 (Berlin: Harrwitz, 1897; repr. Amsterdam: Schippers, 1966).

Bolte, Johannes, 'Eine kölnische Fastnachtsdichtung Peter Jordans (um 1540)', *JKGV*, 16 (1934), 108–19.

Brant, Sebastian, *De moribus et facetijs mense. Thesmophagia* (Basel: M. Furter, 1490).

Brentano, Clemens, *Sämtliche Werke und Briefe. Historisch-kritische Ausgabe*, ed. by Jürgen Behrens, Anne Bohnenkamp, and others (Stuttgart: Kohlhammer, 1975–).

Breuer, Wimmar, *Burgbann und Burgmeile von Köln* (Cologne: Jacobi, 1921).

Breviarium Romanum ex decreto Sacrosancti Concilii Tridentini restitutum [...] (Florence: Birindelli, 1857).

Brill, Franz, 'Der Heringshandel in der Reichsstadt Köln und seine museale Darbietung', in *Im Schatten von St. Gereon. Erich Kuphal zum 1. Juli 1960*, VKGV, 25 (Cologne: der Löwe, 1960), pp. 45–52.

Brincken, Anna-Dorothee von den, 'Die Stadt Köln und ihre hohen Schulen', in *Stadt und Universität im Mittelalter und in der früheren Neuzeit*, ed. by Erich Maschke and Jürgen Sydow, Stadt in der Geschichte. Veröffentlichungen des Südwestdeutschen Arbeitskreises für Stadtgeschichtsforschung, 3 (Sigmaringen: Thorbecke, 1977), pp. 27–52.

Bucer, Martin, *Martini Buceri Opera Latina*, ed. by F. Wendel and others (Paris: Presses universitaires de France, then Leiden: Brill, 1954–).

Budé, Guillaume, *Opera omnia [...]*, 4 vols (Basel: N. Episcopius, 1557; repr. Farnborough: Gregg, 1966–1969).

Burkert, Walter, *Lore and Science in Ancient Pythagoreanism*, trans. by Edwin L. Minat, Jr (Cambridge: Harvard University Press, 1972).

Camerarius, Joachim, *Praecepta vitae puerilis [...]. Vitae morumque [...] praecepta exposita versibus. De gymnasiis dialogus* (Basel: J. Herwagen, 1536). *VD 16*, C 430.

Campeggio, Lorenzo, *Constitutio ad remouendos abusus et ordinatio ad cleri uitam reformandam per [...] D. Laurentium tituli sanctae Anastasiae [...]* (Cologne: P. Quentel, 1525). *VD 16*, C 619.

Canones concilii prouincialis Coloniensis [...] celebrati. Anno 1536 [...] (Cologne: P. Quentel, 1538).

Carmina Burana, ed. by Alfons Hilka and Otto Schumann, 2 vols (Heidelberg: Winter, 1930–1970).

Casey, Paul, *Paul Rebhun* (Stuttgart: Steiner, 1986).

Castellanus, Petrus, *Kreophagia siue de esu carnium libri IV* (Antwerp: Verdussius, 1626).

Celtis, Conrad, *Libri odarum quatuor [...]* (Strasbourg: J. Schurer, 1513).

Chaix, Gérald, 'Humanisme et élites urbaines à Cologne au XVIe siècle', in *Humanismus und höfisch-städtische Eliten im 16. Jahrhundert*, ed. by Klaus Malettke and Jürgen Voss (Bonn: Bouvier, 1989), pp. 195–210.

Champ, Judith, *The English Pilgrimage to Rome. A Dwelling for the Soul* (Leominster: Gracewing, 2000).

Chaumartin, H., 'Le compagnon de Saint-Antoine', *Aesculape*, 20 (1930), 233–56.

Clemen, Carl, 'Der Ursprung des Martinsfestes', *ZVV*, 28 (1918), 1–14.

Cobban, Alan B., 'Medieval Student Power', *Past and Present*, 53 (1971), 28–66.

Comenius, Jan Amos, *Orbis sensualium pictus*, trans. by Charles Hoole, 3rd edn (London: T.R. for S. Mearne, 1672; facs. repr. Sydney: Sydney University Press, 1967).

Comicorum Romanorum [...] fragmenta, ed. by Otto Ribbeck, 3rd edn (Leipzig: Teubner, 1898).

Cordus, Euricius, *Euricii Cordi Epigrammatum Libri III* (Erfurt: M. Maler, 1520). *VD 16*, C 5080.

Corsten, Severin, 'Universität und Buchdruck in Köln. Versuch eines Überblicks für das 15. Jahrhundert', in Severin Corsten, *Studien zum Kölner Frühdruck. Gesammelte Beiträge 1955–1985*, Kölner Arbeiten zum Bibliotheks- und Dokumentationswesen, 7 (Cologne: Greven, 1985), pp. 123–37.

Crecelius, Wilhelm, 'Crailsheimer Schulordnung von 1480 mit deutschen geistlichen Liedern', *Alemannia*, 3 (1875), 247–62.

Creutz, Rudolf, 'Pest und Pestabwehr im alten Köln', *JKGV*, 15 (1933), 79–119.

De conservanda bona valetudine Opusculum Scholae Salernitanae, [...] cum Arnoldi Nouicomensis [...] Enarrationibus [...] (Frankfurt am Main: C. Egenolff, [after 1551]). *VD 16*, R 558, R 559, R 560.

Decreta et Statuta dioecesanae synodi Coloniensis ([Cologne: J. Busaeus, 1661?]).

Decreta et Statuta dioecesanae synodi Coloniensis (Cologne: J. Busaeus, 1667).

Deeters, Joachim, *Die Bestände des Stadtarchivs Köln bis 1814. Eine Übersicht*, MStAK, 76 (Cologne–Weimar–Vienna: Böhlau, 1994).

Della Casa, Giovanni, *Galateus, seu de Morum Honestate [...] Interprete Nathane Chytraeo [...]* (Frankfurt: Heirs of A. Wechel, 1588). *VD 16*, C 1225.

Dicta Septem Sapientum e Graecis, in *Prima Morum et Pietatis Praecepta [...]* (Edinburgh: T. Ruddiman, 1739).

Dinkelius, Johannes, *De origine, causis, typo, et ceremoniis illius ritus, qui vulgo in scholis depositio appellatur, oratio M. Johannis Dinckelii. Additum est Judicium [...] Martini Lutheri de hoc ritu [...]* (Erfurt: J. Mechler, 1578). *VD 16*, D 1745.

Dorn, Johannes, 'Der Ursprung der Pfarreien und die Anfänge des Pfarrwahlrechts im mittelalterlichen Köln', *Zeitschrift der Savigny-Stiftung für Rechtsgeschichte, Kanonistische Abteilung*, 5 (1915), 122–64.

Dürr, Franciscus Antonius, *Commentatio historica de episcopo puerorum, vulgo vom Schul-Bischoff*, in *Thesaurus iuris ecclesiastici potissimum Germanici sive dissertationes selectae in ius ecclesiasticum*, ed. by Antonius Schmidt, 7 vols (Heidelberg: Göbhardt, 1772–1778), III, pp. 58–83.

Durandus, Gulielmus, *Rationale divinorum officiorum*, ed. by Anselme Davril, OSB and Timothy M. Thibodeau, 3 vols, Corpus Christianorum Continuatio Mediaevalis, 140–40B (Turnhout: Brepols, 1995–2000).

Durante, Castore, *Il tesoro della sanità* (Venice: Muschio, 1586) quoted from the edn (Venice: D. Imberti, 1643).

Edgeworth, Roger, *Sermons very fruitfull, godly and learned. Preaching in the Reformation c. 1535–c. 1553*, ed. by Janet Wilson (Cambridge: D.S. Brewer, 1993).

Erasmus, Desiderius, of Rotterdam, *Adagia*, ed. by M.L. van Poll-van de Lisdonk and others, *ASD*, II–1 (1993); II–4 (1987); II–5 (1981); II–6 (1981).

——, *Colloquia*, ed. by L.-E. Halkin and others, *ASD*, I–3 (1972).

——, *Ecclesiastes*, ed. by Jacques Chomarat, 2 vols, *ASD*, V–4 (1991); V–5 (1994).

——, *The Colloquies*, trans. by Craig R. Thompson (Chicago–London: Chicago University Press, 1965).

——, *Moriae Encomium id est Stultitiae Laus*, ed. by Clarence H. Miller, *ASD*, IV–3 (1979).

——, *De pueris statim et liberaliter instituendis*, ed. by Jean-Claude Margolin, *ASD*, I–2 (1971), pp. 1–78.

——, *De recta Latini Graecique sermonis pronuntiatione*, ed. by M. Cytowska, *ASD*, I–4 (1973), pp. 1–103.

——, *De ratione studii*, ed. by Jean-Claude Margolin, *ASD*, I–2 (1971), pp. 79–151.

——, *De civilitate morum puerilium*, *LB*, I, cols 1033–44.

Eulenburg, Franz, *Die Frequenz der deutschen Universitäten von ihrer Gründung bis zur Gegenwart*, Abhandlungen der sächsischen Gesellschaft der Wissenschaften, philologisch-historische Klasse, 24,2 (Leipzig: Teubner, 1904; repr. Berlin: Akademie, 1994).

Fabricius, Wilhelm, *Die Akademische Deposition (Depositio cornuum.) Beiträge zur Deutschen Litteratur- und Kulturgeschichte, speciell zur Sittengeschichte der Universitäten* (Frankfurt am Main: Völcker, 1895).

Falk, Franz, 'Die Schul- und Kinderfeste im Mittelalter', *Frankfurter zeitgemäße Broschüren*, N.F., 1 (1880), 229–48.

Filelfo, Francesco, *Elegantes et familiares epistolae* (Louvain: T. Martens, [1515]).

Fischart, Johann, *Geschichtklitterung (Gargantua)*, ed. by A. Alsleben (Halle: Niemeyer, 1891).

——, *Binenkorb des heyl. römischen imenschwarms, seiner hummelszellen (oder himmelszellen) hurrnaußnäster, brämengeschwürm vnd wäspengetöß* (Christlingen [= Strasbourg: B. Jobin], 1579). *VD 16*, M 1046.

Fletcher, John M., 'Wealth and Poverty in the Medieval German Universities with Particular Reference to the University of Heidelberg', in *Europe in the Late Middle Ages*, ed. by J.R. Hale and others (London: Faber and Faber, 1965), pp. 410–36.

Fridaevallis, Hugo, *De tuenda sanitate* (Antwerp: C. Plantijn, 1568).

Fuchs, Leonhart, *De historia stirpium commentarii insignes [...]* (Basel: M. Isengrin, 1542), cited from the repr. *The Great Herbal of Leonhart Fuchs. De historia stirpium commentarii insignes, 1542*, ed. by Frederick G. Meyer and others, 2 vols (Stanford, CA: Stanford University Press, 1999).

[*Funeral directive, Cologne, 1578*] Printed single sheet. No title. Begins: 'VNsere HErn vom Radte kommen in gewiße erfarung [...]' Ends: 'Sic actum et conclusum VIII. Augusti Anno LXXVIII.' (n.p., n.pr., 1578).

[*Funeral directive, Cologne, 1592*] Printed single sheet. No title. Begins: 'WJr Bürgermeister vnd Rathe des heiligen Reichs Freyer Statt Cölln/ [...]' Ends: 'Geben Mitwoch am 9. tag *Septembris. Anno M.D.LXXXXJJ*. (n.p., n.pr., 1592).

[*Funeral directive, Cologne, 1597*] Booklet. No title. Begins: 'WJr Bürgermeistere vnd Rhat des Heyligen Reichs freyer

Statt Cölln/ [...]' Ends: '[...] am *11. Junij. Anno M.D.XCVII*' (n.p., n.pr., 1597). Large 4°, A1–4.

Gartner, Andreas, *Proverbialia dicteria, ethicam et moralem Doctrinam complectentia [...]*, 3rd edn ([Frankfurt am Main]: [C. Egenolff], 1574). *VD 16*, G 25.

Gerard, John, *The Herbal or General History of Plants. The Complete 1633 Edition as Revised and Enlarged by Thomas Johnson*, facsimile repr. (New York: Dover, 1975).

Gescher, Franz, *Der Kölner Stadtdechant und die Vereinigung der stadtkölnischen Pfarrer: Urkunden und Akten bis zum Ausgang des 14. Jahrhunderts*, MStAK, 40 (Cologne: Böhlau, 1929), pp. 164–243.

Götze, Alfred, *Die hochdeutschen Drucker der Reformationszeit* (Berlin: de Gruyter, 1963).

Gratarolus, Gulielmus, *De Literatorum et eorum qui magistratibus funguntur conservanda præservandaque valetudine [...] Compendium [...]* ([Basel: Petri], 1555); cited from the edition of Frankfurt: Z. Palthenius for widow of P. Fischer, 1596. *VD 16*, G 2888.

Grotefend, Hermann, *Taschenbuch der Zeitrechnung des deutschen Mittelalters und der Neuzeit*, 12th edn, rev. by Jürgen Asch (Hanover: Hahnsche Buchhandlung, 1982).

Grotefend online, ed. by H. Ruth: <http://www.manuscripta-mediaevalia.de/gaeste/grotefend/ grotefend.htm>.

Harvey, Reginald Alfred, *A Commentary on Persius*, *Mnemosyne*, Supplementum, 64 (Leiden: Brill, 1981).

Haselberg, Johann, *Eyn lobspruch der Keyserlichen freygstath* [sic] *Coellen [...]* (Cologne: M. von Neuß, 1531). *VD 16*, H 700.

Hegendorff, Christoph, *Dialogi pueriles,* in Mosellanus, P., *Paedologia Petri Mosellani Protegensis in puerorum usum conscripta & aucta. Dialogi XXXVII. Dialogi pueriles Christophori Hegendorphini XII. lepidi æque, ac docti* (Strasbourg: J. Knobloch, 1 July 1523), sig. C5v–D7v.

Herborn, Wolfgang, 'Fast-, Fest- und Feiertage im Köln des 16. Jahrhunderts', *Rheinisches Jahrbuch für Volkskunde*, 25 (1983/1984), 27–61.

——, '"Straßen wie diese". Zum Alltagsleben einer Kölner Straße im 16. Jahrhundert', *GiK*, 15 (1984), 6–36.

Hessus, Helius Eobanus, *Bonae valetudinis conservandae praecepta ad magnificum D. Georgium Strutiaden, authore Eobano Hesso [...]* (Paris: S. Colin, 1533).

——, *Operum farragines duo* (Schwäbisch Hall: [P. Braubach], 1539). *VD 16*, E 1437.

Heyden, Sebaldus, *Formulae puerilium colloquiorum*, in Sebaldus Heyden, *Nomenclatura rerum domesticarum* (Mainz: I. Schöffer, 1534; repr., ed. by Peter O. Müller and Gaston van der Elst, Documenta linguistica, Reihe I, Hildesheim: Olms, 1998).

Hoffmann, Detlef, *The Playing Card. An Illustrated History*, 3rd edition (Leipzig: Edition Leipzig, 1973).

Hofmann, Winfried, 'Hermann von Weinsberg und die kölnische Fastnacht im 16. Jahrhundert', *Rheinisch-westfälische Zeitschrift für Volkskunde*, 10 (1963), 82–98.

Hoole, Charles, *Childrens Talke, English & Latine, divided into several Clauses [...] Pueriles Confabulatiunculae, Anglo-Latinae, in varias clausulas distributae [...]* (London: For the Company of Stationers, 1659).

Horace (Quintus Horatius Flaccus), *Opera*, ed. by Edward C. Wickham, 2nd edn (Oxford: Clarendon Press, 1912).

——, *Ars poetica*, ed. by C.O. Brink, vol. II of C.O. Brink, *Horace on Poetry*, 2 vols (Cambridge: Cambridge University Press, 1963–1971).

——, *Satires*, I, ed. and trans. by P. Michael Brown (Warminster: Aris & Phillips, 1993).

Hospinianus, Rodolphus, *De festis Iudaeorum et ethnicorum: Hoc est, de origine, progressu, ceremoniis et ritibus festorum dierum Iudaeorum, Graecorum, Romanorum, Turcarum et Indianorum, libri III [...]*, 2nd edn (Zürich: R. Wolf, 1611).

——, *Festa Christianorum. Hoc est, de origine, progressu, ceremoniis et ritibus festorum dierum Christianorum liber unus [...]*, 2nd edn (Zürich: R. Wolf, 1612).

Hoyoux, Jean, 'Un "jeu" d'Erasme', *Bibliothèque d'Humanisme et Renaissance*, 4 (1937), 78–80.

Huyskens, Albert, 'Junggraf Wilhelm von Waldeck an der Universität Köln 1509/10', *AHVN*, 97 (1915), 78–110.

Irsigler, Franz, 'Köln, die Frankfurter Messen und die Handelsbeziehungen mit Oberdeutschland im 15. Jahrhundert', in *Köln, das Reich und Europa. Abhandlungen über weiträumige Verflechtungen der Stadt Köln in Politik, Recht und Wirtschaft im Mittelalter*, ed. by Hugo Stehkämper, MStAK, 60 (Cologne: Neubner, 1971), pp. 341–429.

——, 'Kölner Wirtschaft im Spätmittelalter', in *Zwei Jahrtausende*, I, pp. 217–319.

——, and Arnold Lassotta, *Bettler und Gaukler, Dirnen und Henker. Außenseiter in einer mittelalterlichen Stadt: Köln 1300–1600*, dtv 30075 (Munich: Deutscher Taschenbuch Verlag, 1989).

Jütte, Robert, 'Household and Family in Late Sixteenth-Century Cologne: The Weinsberg Family', *The Sixteenth Century Journal*, 17 (1986), 165–82.

Kaemmel, Heinrich Julius, *Geschichte des deutschen Schulwesens im Übergange vom Mittelalter zur Neuzeit. Aus seinem Nachlasse hrsg. von O. Kaemmel* (Leipzig: Duncker & Humblot, 1882; repr. Hildesheim: Olms, 1986).

Keil, Gundolf, 'Seuchenzüge des Mittelalters', in *Mensch und Umwelt im Mittelalter*, ed. by Bernd Herrmann (Stuttgart: Deutsche Verlagsanstalt, 1986), pp. 108–28.

Kellenbenz, Hermann, 'Wirtschaftsgeschichte Kölns im 16. und beginnenden 17. Jahrhundert', in *Zwei Jahrtausende*, I, pp. 321–427.

Kemp, Jacob, 'Die Wohlfahrtspflege des Kölner Rates in dem Jahrhundert nach der großen Zunftrevolution' (unpubl. doctoral thesis, University of Bonn, 1904).

Keussen, Hermann, 'Die drei Reisen des Utrechters Arnoldus Buchelius nach Deutschland, insbesondere sein Kölner Aufenthalt', I, *AHVN*, 84 (1907), 1–102; II, *AHVN*, 85 (1908), 43–114.

Klersch, Joseph, *Die Kölnische Fastnacht von ihren Anfängen bis zur Gegenwart*, Schriften des Bundes Deutscher Karveval, 1 (Cologne: Bachem, 1961).

Kluppel, Konrad, *Konrad Kluppels Chronik und Briefbuch*, in *Waldecker Chroniken*, ed. by Paul Jürges and others, Veröffentlichungen der historischen Kommission für

Hessen und Waldeck, VII,2 (Marburg: Elwert, 1914), pp. I–XXXVII, 1–179.

Köbler, Gerhard, *Lateinisch-althochdeutsches Wörterbuch*, Arbeiten zur Rechts- und Sozialwissenschaft, 43 (Gießen: Arbeiten zur Rechts- und Sozialwissenschaft-Verlag, 1996).

Künast, Hans-Jörg, *'Getruckt zu Augspurg'. Buchdruck und Buchhandel in Augsburg zwischen 1468 und 1555* (Tübingen: Niemeyer, 1997).

Kulturströmungen und Kulturprovinzen in den Rheinlanden: Geschichte – Sprache – Volkskunde, ed. by Hermann Aubin, Theodor Frings, and Josef Müller (Bonn: Röhrscheid, 1926; repr. Darmstadt: Wissenschaftliche Buchgesellschaft, 1966).

Kuphal, Erich, 'Die Archive der Universität Köln', in *Festschr. Köln*, pp. 548–637.

Kuske, Bruno, 'Der Kölner Fischhandel vom 14.–17. Jahrhundert', *Westdeutsche Zeitschrift für Geschichte und Kunst*, 24 (1905), 227–313.

Lactantius, L. Coelius Firmianus, *Carmen de aue Phoenice*, in *L. Coelii Lactantii Firmiani Diuinarum Institutionum Libri VII [...]* (Antwerp: J. Gymnich, 1555), pp. 584–89.

Lassotta, Friedrich-Arnold, *Formen der Armut im späten Mittelalter und zu Beginn der Neuzeit. Untersuchungen vornehmlich an Kölner Quellen des 14. bis 17. Jahrhunderts*, 2 vols (Cologne: Hundt, 1993).

Lea, Henry Charles, *A History of Auricular Confession and Indulgences in the Latin Church*, 3 vols (Philadelphia: Lea Brothers, 1896).

Das Leben in der Stadt des Spätmittelalters. Internationaler Kongreß Krems an der Donau 20. bis 23. September 1976, Österreichische Akademie der Wissenschaften, Philosophisch-historische Klasse, Sitzungsberichte, 325; also Veröffentlichungen des Instituts für mittelalterliche Realienkunde Österreichs, 2 (Vienna: Österreichische Akademie der Wissenschaften, 1977).

Lexer, Matthias, *Mittelhochdeutsches Handwörterbuch*, 3 vols (Leipzig: Hirzel, 1872–1878).

Le Liber pontificalis, ed. by Louis Duchesne and Cyrille Vogel, 3 vols (Paris: Boccard, 1886–1957).

Locher, Jacobus, *Stultifera navis* (Basel: J. Bergmann de Olpe, 1498). Cited from the edition of Basel: S. Henricpetri, 1572). *VD 16*, B 7081.

Lodge, Gonzalez, *Lexicon Plautinum*, 2 vols (Leipzig: Teubner, 1924–1933; repr. Hildesheim: Olms, 1962).

Löhr, Gabriel M., 'Rede bei einer depositio beanismi (Fuchsentaufe) von 1465 im Kölner Dominikanerkloster', *AHVN*, 111 (1927), 186–91.

Looz-Corswaren, Clemens von, 'Die Kölner Artikelserie von 1525', in *Kirche und gesellschaftlicher Wandel in deutschen und niederländischen Städten der werdenden Neuzeit*, Städteforschung, A 10 (Cologne–Vienna: Böhlau, 1980), pp. 65–153.

Lurz, W., 'Heiliges Jahr', *LThK*², V, cols 125–26.

Lyon, Dorothy Wilberforce, '"Christe qui lux es et dies" and its German, Dutch, and English Translations', *American Journal of Philology*, 19 (1898), 152–92.

Macardle, P.G., 'Our Reading of an Early "Documentary Drama": Schottennius's *Ludus Martius* (1526)', *Daphnis*, 18 (1989), 391–420.

——, 'Cologne Life and Cologne University Humanism. The *Confabulationes tyronum literariorum* (1525) and their Author Hermannus Schottennius Hessus', *HL*, 42 (1993), 126–59.

——, 'Matthias Wagener and Traces of Antonite Humanism in Cologne', *Journal of the Warburg and Courtauld Institutes*, 57 (1994), 254–63.

——, *Confabulations. Cologne Life and Humanism in Hermann Schotten's* Confabulationes tironum litterariorum *(Cologne, 1525)*, Durham Modern Languages Series, GM10 (Durham: DMLS, 2007).

Macropedius, Georgius, *Hecastus*, in *Drei Spiele vom sterbenden Menschen*, ed. by Johannes Bolte (Leipzig: Hiersemann, 1927).

Manipulus curato[rum] officia sacerdotu[m] s[ecundu]m ordine[m] septe[m] sacramento[rum] perbreuiter complectens (Hagenau: H. Gran for J. Knobloch, 1508) *VD 16*, G 4054. Also (Basel: N. Lamparter, 1517) *VD 16*, G 4055; and (Lyon: G. Rouillié, 1569).

Mantuanus, Johannes Baptista, *Eclogae*, in *Eclogae. Vergilii. Calphurnii. Nemesiani. Francisci Pe[trarchi]. Ioannis Boc[acii]. Ioan[nis] bap[tistae] Ma[ntuani]* (Florence: F. Giunta, 1504), sig. p iiii^r – t vii^r.

Manuale curatoru[m] predicandi prebens modu[m]: tam latino q[uam] vulgari sermone practice illuminatu[m] [...] ([Basel: M. Furter], January 1506). *VD 16*, S 10229.

Manuale Parrochialium sacerdotum (Landshut: J. Weißenburger, 22 December 1513). *VD 16*, M 674; others: M 672, 673, 675–677.

Manuale scholariu[m] qui stude[n]tiu[m] vniversitates aggredi ac postea p[ro]ficere in eis intendunt ([Deventer: J. de Breda, *ca.* 1500]).

Manuale scholarium, ed. by Friedrich Zarncke, in *Die deutschen Universitäten im Mittelalter: Beiträge zur Geschichte und Charakteristik derselben*, Erster Beitrag (Leipzig: Weigel, 1857), pp. 1–48, 221–32.

Margetts, John, 'Das Bauerntum in der Literatur und in der Wirklichkeit bei Neidhart und in den Neidhartspielen', in *Deutsche Literatur des späten Mittelalters,* Hamburger Kolloquium 1973, Publications of the Institute of Germanic Studies, University of London, 22 (Berlin: Schmidt, 1975), pp. 153–63.

Massebieau, Louis, *Les colloques scolaires du seizième siècle et leurs auteurs (1480–1570)* (Paris: Bonhoure, 1878; repr. Geneva: Slatkine, 1968).

Mering, Friedrich Everhart Freiherr von, and Ludwig Reischert, *Die Bischöfe und Erzbischöfe von Köln nach ihrer Reihenfolge, nebst Geschichte des Ursprunges, des Fortganges und des Verfalles der Kirchen und Klöster der Stadt Köln, mit besonderer Bezugnahme auf die Kirchen und Klöster der Erzdiözese* (Cologne: Lengfeld, 1844).

Meisen, Karl, *Nikolauskult und Nikolausbrauch im Abendlande. Eine kultgeographisch-volkskündliche Untersuchung*, Forschungen zur Volkskunde, 9–12 (Düsseldorf: Schwann, 1931).

Menapius, Gulielmus, *De ratione victus salubris* (Basel: B. Westheimer, 1541). *VD 16*, G 3289.

Meuthen, Erich, 'Die Artesfakultät der alten Kölner Universität', Gesellschaft für Rheinische Geschichtskunde, Vorträge, 25 (Düsseldorf: Droste, 1989), 367–93.

Mezger, Werner, 'Rückwärts in die Zukunft. Metamorphosen der schwäbisch-allemannischen Fastnacht', in *Fastnacht/ Karneval in europäischen Vergleich*, ed. by Michael Matheus, Mainzer Vorträge, 3 (Stuttgart: Steiner, 1999), pp. 121–73.

Die Mirakelbücher des Klosters Eberhardsklausen, ed. by Paul Hoffmann and Peter Dohms, *PGRG*, 64 (Düsseldorf: Droste, 1988).

The Missal in Latin and English, ed. by J. O'Connell and H.P.R. Finberg (London: Burns Oates and Washbourne, 1958).

Missale Diocesis Colonie[n]sis: ia[m] vltimo recognitu[m]: adauctum quoq[ue]: & in meliore[m] redactu[m] ordine[m]: lo[n]geq[ue] castigati[us] imp[re]ssum q[uam] vnq[uam] pri[us]. [...] (Paris: N. Prévost for Arnold Byrckman, 8 November 1525).

Moffett, Thomas, *Healths Improvement [...]*, rev. edn, corr. by Christopher Bennet (London: J. Kingston, 1565).

Mosellanus, Petrus (= Schade, Peter), *Paedologia Petri Mosellani Protegensis in puerorum usum conscripta & aucta. Dialogi XXXVII. Dialogi pueriles Christophori Hegendorphini XII. lepidi æque, ac docti* (Strasbourg: J. Knobloch, 21 June 1523).

——, *Paedologia*, ed. by Hermann Michel, Lateinische Litteraturdenkmäler des XV. und XVI. Jahrhunderts, 18 (Berlin: Weidmann, 1906).

Moser, Oskar, 'Zum Aufkommen der "Stube" im Bürgerhaus des Spätmittelalters', in *Das Leben in der Stadt des Spätmittelalters*, pp. 207–28.

Neithart Fuchs, in *Narrenbuch: Kalenberger. Peter Leu. Neithart Fuchs. Markolf. Bruder Rausch*, ed. by Felix Bobertag, *Deutsche National-Literatur*, 11 (Berlin–Stuttgart: Spemann, [1884]), pp. 141–292.

Neidhartspiele, ed. by John Margetts, Wiener Neudrücke, 7 (Graz: Akademische Druck- und Verlagsanstalt, 1982).

Niavis, Paulus, *Latinum ydeoma pro novellis studentibus* (Leipzig: K. Kachelofen, [*ca* 1488]).

——, *Dyalogus Magistri Pauli Niavis in quo litterarum studiosus [...] cum beano [...] loquitur* ([Leipzig]: [W. Stöckel], [*ca* 1501]).

Odenthal, A., *Der älteste Liber Ordinarius der Stiftskirche St. Aposteln in Köln. Untersuchungen zur Liturgie eines mittelalterlichen kölnischen Stifts*, Studien zur Kölner Kirchengeschichte, 28 (Siegburg: Schmitt, 1994).

Orme, Nicholas, *Medieval Children* (New Haven–London: Yale University Press, 2001).

Paas, Theodor, *Das Alexianerkloster in Köln-Lindenthal in seiner geschichtlichen Entwicklung*, ed. by Bernhard Giergen (Köln-Lindenthal: Kloster der Alexianerbrüder, 1934).

A Patristic Greek Lexicon, ed. by G.W.H. Lampe (Oxford: Clarendon Press, 1961).

Pauli, Simon, *Postilla, Das ist Außlegung der Episteln und Evangelien, an Sontagen und fürnemesten Festen [...]*, 3 vols (Magdeburg: W. Kirchner, 1572).

Persius Flaccus, Aulus, *Satiren*, ed. and trans. by Walter Kißel (Heidelberg: Winter, 1990).

——, *A. Persi Flacci et D. Juni Juvenalis Saturae*, ed. by Wendell Vernon Clausen (Oxford: Clarendon Press, 1959; rev. edn 1992).

——, *The Satires of Persius. The Latin Text with a Verse Translation* by Guy Lee (Liverpool: Cairns, 1987).

Peters, J., 'Zur Geschichte der Römerfahrt', *Katholische Kirchenzeitung (Köln)*, 14 (1 April 1923), pp. 1–6.

Petrarca, Francesco, *Francisci Petrarchae [...] Opera quae extant omnia [...]*, 4 vols (Basel: H. Petri, 1554). *VD 16*, P 1708.

Petri, Friedrich, *Der Teutschen Weissheit [...]* (Hamburg: von Ohr, 1605; facs. repr. ed. by Wolfgang Mieder, Bern: Lang, 1983).

Peycht Spigel der sünder (Nuremberg: H. Stuchs, 1510). *VD 16*, B 1511.

Planitz, Hans, and Thea Buyken, *Die Kölner Schreinsbücher des 13. und 14. Jahrhunderts*, PGRG, 46 (Weimar: Böhlau, 1937).

The Pythagorean Golden Verses, ed. by J.C. Thom (Leiden: Brill, 1995).

Quarg, Gunter, *'Ganz Köln steckt voller Bücherschätze'. Von der Ratsbibliothek zur Universitäts- und Stadtbibliothek 1602–2002* (Cologne: Universitäts- und Stadtbibliothek Köln, 2002).

Quellen und Forschungen zur Geschichte der deutschen Mystik, ed. by Rudolf Langenberg (Bonn: Hanstein: 1902).

Rabelais, François, *Œuvres complètes*, ed. by Pierre Jourda, 2 vols (Paris: Garnier, 1962).

Ranke, Ermentrude von, 'Die wirtschaftlichen Beziehungen Kölns zu Frankfurt am Main, Süddeutschland und Italien im 16. und 17. Jahrhundert', *Vierteljahrsschrift für Sozial- und Wirtschaftsgeschichte*, 17 (1923), 54–94.

Rautenberg, Ursula, *Überlieferung und Druck. Heiligenlegenden aus frühen Kölner Offizinen*, Frühe Neuzeit, 30 (Tübingen: Niemeyer, 1996).

Ravisius Textor, Johannes, *De memorabilibus et claris mulieribus* (Paris: S. Colines, 1521).

Reichart, Andrea, *Alltagsleben im späten Mittelalter. Der Übergang zur frühen Neuzeit am Beispiel der Stadt Essen (1400–1700)*, Essener kulturhistorische Studien, 1 (Essen: Item, 1992).

Reuchlin, Johannes, *Sergius uel capitis caput cum commentario Georgij Simler Vuimpinenensis* (Pforzheim: T. Anshelmus, 1508). *VD 16*, R 1287.

——, *Henno. Komödie. Lateinisch und deutsch*, ed. and trans. by Harry C. Schnur, Reclams Universalbibliothek, 7923 (Stuttgart: Reclam: 1970).

Rheinisches Wörterbuch, ed. by Josef Müller and others, 9 vols (Bonn: Bouvier, 1928–71).

Rochholz, Ernst Ludwig, *Alemannisches Kinderlied und Kinderspiel aus der Schweiz. Gesammelt und sitten- und sprachgeschichtlich erklärt [...]* (Leipzig: Weber, 1857; repr. Geneva: Slatkine, 1979).

Röhrig, Hans-Hermann, 'Reste alter Bibliotheken in der theologischen Abteilung der Kölner Gymnasialbibliothek' (unpubl. dissertation, Bibliothekar-Lehrinstitut des Landes Nordrhein-Westfalen, Cologne, 1957).

Schaefer, Heinrich, 'Inventare und Regesten aus den Kölner Pfarrarchiven', I. *AHVN*, 71 (1901), 1–215; II. ibid., 76 (1903), 1–263; III. ibid., 83 (1907), 1–219.

Schäfer, Thomas, 'Fußwaschung', in *LThK*², IV, cols 476–78.

Schauer, H, 'Das sogenannte Gregorius-Fest; mit besonderer Beziehung auf das alt-weimarische Land', *Zeitschrift für die historische Theologie*, 22 (1852), 147–62.

Schmid, Wolfgang, *Stifter und Auftraggeber in spätmittelalterlichen Köln*, Veröffentlichungen des Kölnischen Stadtmuseums, 11 (Cologne: Kölnisches Stadtmuseum, 1994).

Schmidt-Wiegand, Ruth, *Deutsche Rechtsregeln und Rechtssprichwörter. Ein Lexikon* (Munich: Beck, 1996).

Schoepper, Jacob, *Ectrachelistis siue decollatus Johannes*, in *Iacobi Schoepperi [...] Comoediae et tragoediae sacrae et novae, accuratissime recognitae* (Cologne: M. Cholinus, 1562), sig. a6ᵛ–F8ᵛ.

Schwerhoff, Gerd, 'Köln rüstet sich zur Gottestracht: Eine Morgensprache vom 23. März 1478', *QGSK*, II, pp. 129–35.

Schwinges, Rainer Christoph, 'Sozialgeschichtliche Aspekte spätmittelalterlicher Studentenbursen in Deutschland', in *Schulen und Studium im sozialen Wandel des hohen und späten Mittelalters*, ed. by Johannes Fried, Vorträge und Forschungen, herausgegeben vom Konstanzer Arbeitskreis für mittelalterliche Geschichte, 30 (Sigmaringen: Thorbecke, 1986), pp. 527–64.

——, *Deutsche Universitätsbesucher im 14. und 15. Jahrhundert. Studien zur Sozialgeschichte des Alten Reiches*, Veröffentlichungen des Instituts für Europäische Geschichte Mainz: Beiträge zur Sozial- und Verfassungsgeschichte des Alten Reiches, 6 (Stuttgart: Steiner, 1986).

Seybold, Johann Georg, *Viridarium Selectissimis Paroemiarum et Sententiarum Latino-Germanicarum flosculis amoenissimum [...]* (Nuremberg: W.M. Endter, 1677).

Shahar, Shulamith, 'The Boy Bishop's Feast: A Case-Study in Church Attitudes towards Children in the High and Late Middle Ages', in *The Church and Childhood*, ed. by Diana

Wood, Studies in Church History, 31 (Oxford: Blackwell, 1994), pp. 243–60.

Siuts, Hinrich, *Die Ansingelieder zu den Kalenderfesten. Ein Beitrag zur Geschichte, Biologie und Funktion des Volksliedes* (Göttingen: Schwartz, 1968).

Stanbridge, John, *Vulgaria*, in *The Vulgaria of John Stanbridge and the Vulgaria of Robert Whittinton*, ed. by Beatrice White, EETS, o.s., 187 (London: EETS, 1932), pp. 1–30.

Tentler, Thomas N., *Sin and Confession on the Eve of the Reformation* (Princeton: Princeton University Press, 1977).

Tewes, Götz-Rüdiger, *Die Bursen der Kölner Artisten-Fakultät bis zur Mitte des 16. Jahrhunderts*, Studien zur Geschichte der Universität zu Köln, 13 (Cologne–Vienna: Böhlau, 1993).

——, 'Die Universität Köln im Umbruch: Aus Protokollen des Dekans der Artisten-Fakultät, 1522–1526', in *QGSK*, II, pp. 161–67.

Thorbecke, August, *Geschichte der Universität Heidelberg.* I. *Die älteste Zeit. 1386–1449* (Heidelberg: Koester, 1886). No further parts appeared.

Tournoy, Gilbert, and Terence Tunberg, 'On the Margins of Latinity? Neo-Latin and the Vernacular Languages', *HL*, 45 (1996), 134–75.

Tragicorum Romanorum fragmenta, ed. by Otto Ribbeck, 3rd edn (Leipzig: Teubner, 1897).

Tunberg, Terence O., 'De Erasmi declamationibus deque declamatiuncula, quae *Oratio Episcopi* inscribitur', *HL*, 55 (2006), 9–24.

Umbach, Silke, *Sebastian Brants Tischzucht (Thesmophagia 1490)*, Gratia. Bamberger Schriften zur Renaissanceforschung, 27 (Wiesbaden: Harrassowitz, 1995).

Varro, Marcus Terentius, *M. Terentii Varronis Saturarum Menippearum fragmenta*, ed. by Raymond Astbury (Leipzig: Teubner, 1985).

Vergil (P. Vergilius Maro), *Eclogues*, ed. by Robert Coleman (Cambridge: Cambridge University Press, 1977).

Vives, Johannes Ludovicus, *Exercitatio Linguae Latinae* (Antwerp : C. Plantijn, 1538), cited from Vives, *Colloquia sive*

Exercitatio Latinae linguae [...] notis illustrata (Gouda: F. Hoola, 1662).

Vollmer, Thomas, *Agenda Coloniensis. Geschichte und sakramentliche Feiern der gedruckten Kölner Ritualien*, Studien zur Pastoraltheologie, 10 (Regensburg: Pustet, 1994).

Vredeveld, Harry, '"Deaf as Ulysses to the Siren's Song": The Story of a Forgotten Topos', *Renaissance Quarterly*, 54 (2001), 846–82.

Wackernagel, Karl Eduard Philipp, *Das deutsche Kirchenlied von der ältesten Zeit bis zu Anfang des XVII. Jahrhunderts [...]*, 5 vols (Leipzig: Teubner, 1864–1877; repr. Hildesheim: Olms, 1964).

Werhahn, Heinz Martin, 'Die Bücher des Dr. Peter Rinck', in *Kölner Schule. Festgabe zum 60. Geburtstag von Rudolf Juchoff*, ed. by Hermann Corsten, Arbeiten aus dem Bibliothekar-Lehrinstitut des Landes Nordrhein-Westfalen, 7 (Cologne: Greven, 1955), pp. 179–88.

Whittinton, Robert, *Vulgaria*, in *The Vulgaria of John Stanbridge and the Vulgaria of Robert Whittinton*, ed. by Beatrice White, EETS, o.s., 187 (London: EETS, 1932), pp. 31–128.

Wrede, Adam, *Altkölnischer Sprachschatz. Auf Grund archivalischer Quellenstoffe der Reichsstadt Köln vom 12. Jahrhundert bis 1815 als Wörterbuch bearbeitet [...], Lieferung 1. a–amandel* (Bonn: Klopp, 1928). No further fascicles appeared.

——, *Neuer Kölnischer Sprachschatz*, 3 vols (Cologne: Greven, 1956–1958).

——, *Rheinischer Volksbrauch im Kreislauf des Jahres*, Rheinisches Volkstum, 4 (Düsseldorf: Schwann, [1935]).

Zedler, Johann Heinrich, *Großes vollständiges Universal-Lexicon aller Wissenschaften und Künste [...]*, 68 vols (Halle–Leipzig: J.H. Zedler, 1732–1754; repr. Graz: Akademische Druck- und Verlagsanstalt, 1961–1964).

Zenobius, *Paroimiai*, in *Paroimiai hellēnikai. Adagia siue prouerbia graecorum ex Zenobio [...] Diogeniano & Suidae collectaneis [...]*, ed. by Andreas Schottus (Antwerp Plantijn-Moretus, 1612).

Zingerle, Ignaz Vincenz, *Das deutsche Kinderspiel im Mittelalter*, 2nd edn (Innsbruck: Wagner, 1873).

EU authorised representative for GPSR:
Easy Access System Europe, Mustamäe tee 50,
10621 Tallinn, Estonia
gpsr.requests@easproject.com

www.ingramcontent.com/pod-product-compliance
Lightning Source LLC
Chambersburg PA
CBHW070924100726
47908CB00001B/89

* 9 7 8 0 7 1 9 0 8 1 8 5 9 *